# Butler's Past Comes Alive

## Ralph Goldinger

**Butler's Past Comes Alive**

Published by
New Horizons Publishing Company
New Wilmington, PA 16142

Library of Congress Catalog No.: 99-067889

ISBN 1-884687-24-5

Printed in the Unites States of America

# Contents

# PROLOGUE

I often reflect upon the experiences generated by my two, earlier books, *Historic Saxonburg and Its Neighbors*, and *Butler County, the Second Hundred Years* which I co-authored with Audrey Fetters. As a result of our humble efforts at documenting some of the county's history, it has been our good fortune to meet many wonderful people. Recently, I was showing slides and discussing local history in a Butler County, church hall when a very-gracious, elderly lady asked me, "You've been studying the local area for years. If you had to summarize Butler County's history in one short paragraph, what would it be? I'd like to hear your answer." Well, the more I thought about it I realized that this lady had dealt me a very profound question and I must admit that I was unable to answer it extemporaneously, especially with the kind of answer that the question deserved. But since that evening I have often pondered her query, have formulated an answer and would like to offer it now. I hope she reads this.

To put it as concisely as I can—Butler County's progress has been a result of many things; none of which were more important than these three: (1) petroleum, (2) railroads, and (3) visionary people who were driven by the desire for success. That is my answer in one sentence, now please allow me to elaborate.

It began with petroleum. Butler County was just a backwater community before oil was discovered, but the black gold changed everything. By the 1880's many local people had prosperity dripping from every pore. Thousands of dollars changed hands in the most unlikely places. The Argyle Savings Bank opened on August 22, 1872 in Petrolia, and operated until April 22, 1891. It was listed in the Standard Oil Company codebook along with seven Cleveland banks, six New York City banks, and an Oil City bank. For some years, the money turnover in Petrolia was greater than in all other Butler County banks combined. But that story has been well documented in *Butler County, the Second Hundred Years*, Lenn McCorry's *Beautiful, Bountiful, Butler County*, and several of the older Butler County histories.

Let us just note in passing that most of Butler County's oil-boom towns of the late 1800's were exciting places where fortunes were made and lost overnight. Today most of those towns are just memories, but the children and grandchildren of those oil pioneers have more than memories. Many of Butler's prominent families would not be here today had it not been for the attraction of the oil of yesterday. The mansions of the oil rich are with us yet, and many of the businesses created with oil money continue to provide jobs for Butlerites.

The second part of my answer deals with railroads, a topic which is covered in chapter six of this book. We will not elaborate on the impact of railroads upon our county until we reach that chapter other that to declare--railroads attracted industry and industry attracted workers. It was as simple as that.

That brings us to the third part of my answer. As I researched old, history books and newspapers, and interviewed people in preparation for this book, I repeatedly encountered or was told of amazing individuals--I call them success-driven visionaries. Many geographical areas, of course, have highly motivated individuals, but I really believe that due to some inexplicit variable, Butler has been blessed with more than its share of such folks--men and women who had visions and were not afraid to take chances--were not fearful of spending their money in hopes of starting something great and profitable. Some are not that old; they are still working today; others have been taken by the grim reaper but they accomplished much and left a legacy before they departed. I decided that these people, more than any other single factor, made Butler County what it is and that their stories should be told--thereby hangs a tale.

It is certainly true that a "get rich quick" motive drives many entrepreneurs. Would you not agree that the kinds of people attracted by Butler County's oil boom would be of the same mentality and ilk as those who trekked to California in 1849—adventurous and hopeful of riches? Perhaps the draw of the petroleum industry is the quirk of fate which accounted for Butler's dynamic; for at the end of the nineteenth century Butler was innundated with individuals who came here to make a fortune in the oil fields. Each and every one endured a great deal of difficulty and hard work and some struck it rich; they were rewarded for their determination. It's what we call self-discipline today--work hard now; receive reward later. These folks were of the mentality that whenever they were faced with adversity, they dealt with it. They would allow nothing to get in their way. How could Butler County experience failure when it possessed such people?

Consider if you will, a few examples from my first two books: Johnny Muder of Saxonburg was an entrepreneur whose attitude typified that of many Butlerites. When Saxonburg's economy was facing dire straits, Muder took the situation under consideration and came up with what he thought would be the solution. Silk was at that time a very important fabric, so Muder said, "Why not make Saxonburg the silk center of western Pennsylvania?" In order to achieve his goals, the entrepreneur even went so far as to procure a number of silkworms, and plant some mulberry trees; the silkworm flourishes on mulberry leaves. A silk industry for Saxonburg however, was a dream that never came to fruition. The silk business unraveled largely because of the great amount of labor involved, but an observant person might yet find a mulberry tree growing in the Saxonburg area as a reminder of Muder's efforts. [This summer, as I was walking in the forest near Saxonburg I came upon a mulberry tree. "It was probably one of Johnny Muder's," I thought, "which had been transplanted deep in the woods by birds or animals."]

We are not yet finished with Johnny Muder because he wasn't finished--he didn't accept defeat with the failure of the silk industry. Muder launched his second attempt to revive Saxonburg's economy. He would bring canary raising to Saxonburg—if not silk, then why not canaries? As you probably know, canaries were used in early mines; they were detectors of dangerous gasses, which sometimes settled in sections of the mine shafts. Today the canaries have been replaced by exhaust fans and electronic detection devices but back in the nineteenth century there was a market for the little, yellow birds. You guessed it—the canary idea never flew, but Johnny Muder was anything but a failure; you see, he was still Saxonburg's funeral director, postmaster, tavern owner and a respectable artist. He tried, and according to his way of thinking, "To try and to fail is better than to have never tried at all."

Another Butler County resident, John Roebling, the famous-bridge builder, showed a determined spirit when he accepted the contract to build a section of the Pennsylvania Canal across the Allegheny River near Freeport. [This project surely ranks a close second to the Brooklyn Bridge.] For the first time in history, large cables for suspending a great-wooden trough were strung in place, wire by wire. Six months went by; in cold and sleet, in wind and snow Roebling was up on the towers, out on the catwalk, swinging aloft in the boatswain's chair directing every step of the operation. The aqueduct was a sturdy-timber flume, sixteen and one-half feet wide at the top, ten feet wide at the bottom, and eight and one-half feet deep—wide enough and deep enough, when filled with water, to carry the boats of the Pennsylvania Canal. Bracketed out from each side of the flume were planked towpaths eight feet wide for the mules which pulled the canal boats. The total weight of the water supported on the spans was over two thousand tons. Roebling received much of the same criticism as did an earlier builder named Noah. Scoffers predicted that the trough's downfall was imminent, but when the aqueduct was opened on May 22, 1845, water poured in and to the hecklers' dismay, all held. On top of the spans floated the canal boats, high and safe above the currents of the Allegheny River. There are those who dream and there are those who go out and do it.

Much of Butler's prosperity was due to two, freethinking entrepreneurs. John Hansen and Diamond Jim Brady had a dream. They quit their respective jobs, borrowed three million dollars from Andrew Mellon and founded the Standard Steel Car Company in a newly constructed building in Lyndora. Employment at the plant eventually peaked at around 4000 and Standard's payroll bolstered Butler's economy for more than seventy-five years. At a time when the demand for railroad cars was insatiable, Butler was the home of the largest, freight-car manufacturer in the world thanks to the courage of these two impresarios.

Dr. Frank W. Preston was a man of many interests; he was fascinated by the topography and landforms around the Muddy Creek area. Preston was certain that the area had been greatly influenced by the Wisconsin glaciation of 14,000 years ago. In 1950 the State of Pennsylvania was examining several sites within the state for potential state parks. To show his seriousness in convincing the state to consider Muddy Creek, Preston donated three hundred acres of his own land toward the creation of such a park. Preston and other local benefactors however, came to the realization that the project they envisioned would be too expensive for local magnanimity. But, as we have already seen, Butlerites have never been shrinking violets when a worthwhile community project needs action. Four hometown men took the bull by the horns and made a trip to Harrisburg to negotiate for the park. Attorney George Kiester, John Eisler of Eisler Nurseries, Gustav Benz, president of the Butler Chamber of Commerce, and Chandler Huselton, a manager at Armco, met with state senators and Dr. Maurice K. Goddard, forests and waters secretary for the state of Pennsylvania. The trip was not in vain; a commitment was made and the park opened in 1970.

Sir Herbert Austin, the manufacturer of the English vehicle which bore his name, was looking for a United States location where he could build his popular automobile. When it looked as if Sir Herbert would select a location in Grand Rapids, Michigan, Butlerites quickly responded. At a meeting of the Butler Board of Commerce, in just thirty minutes time, 175 local merchants and professional people pledged $250,000 in 1928 dollars toward the cause of bringing the Austin to Butler! An additional $200,000 was pledged within the next few days! Sir Herbert was contacted and convinced of the merits of a Butler location; $450,000 was quite an enticement. On May 21, 1930 the American Austin Car Company began production at its new Butler plant. People who procrastinate often miss out—local visionaries put up their cash and it returned to them.

During World War II the United States Army found that it was in dire need of a light-weight, general-purpose vehicle. The government, in an effort to solve the problem, invited thirty-five firms to bid on the project and submit a prototype vehicle which would be tested before a contract was awarded. Only three companies rose to the challenge—Ford, Willys-Overland and the Bantam Company of Butler.

The Butler Bantam crew worked seven days a week and well into the nights. Their test vehicle rolled off the assembly line on September 22, 1940, and Butler resident Ralph Turner drove it to Holabird, Maryland, arriving just thirty minutes before the deadline. Two other Butlerites who had helped build it, Chester Hempfling and Harold Crist, followed the Jeep in another vehicle. The Bantam passed the tests with flying colors and won the contract. The army ordered 1500 Jeeps from the burgeoning Butler company.

The above represents just a few of the examples of motivated individuals who came to Butler County and caused our area to flourish. You will meet many more in the chapters you are about to read. But this compendium is not exclusively about such individuals--this book also contains a number of disparate topics, from a recipe for "sticky buns" to Buffalo Bill's farewell visit to the county. A large part of the information was discovered in old newspapers. Dave Craig found most of these references as he was researching the history of the Diehl Baking Company. He kept finding gems of local history in those old dailys and weeklys, which although weren't related to his topic, were yet fascinating. Almost daily he would stop at May's Music Shoppe and show Dick May and me his latest "discovery." Our interest in these old stories and news items and the ensuing discussions began to whet our appetites for more local history. We did not realize how much is out there. Personally, I thought that all of the best topics had been investigated--I was wrong. Dave gradually gave me a stack of nearly one hundred, newspaper articles and most of them are included in this book. I think that there is something here for everybody--as Dave Malarkey would say, "a smattering of topics."

Before you turn to chapter one, I would like to offer the following disclaimer. Dozens of people were interviewed in preparation for this book. To check the validity of all the information given by those interviewed would be impossible. Naturally, being concerned as to historical validity, I did what I could. For example: I directed many of the same questions to several of those interviewed and compared the responses as an accuracy check. I also examined city directories and old newspapers if available, to see if the stories and the time frames given were accurate. Some of the more personal and bizarre information gathered in the interviews was left out either because I could not verify it, I believed that it fell into the realm of myth and/or folklore, or I felt that it might cast aspersions upon present-day descendants of those involved. Examples of topics left in the file cabinet are references to humpbacks, mental defectives, ghosts, flying saucers, cheating spouses, illigitimate children, suicides, KKK and Blackhand membership. It really surprised me to find that a large number of people believe in ghosts and love ghost stories. For those folks I have included a couple of very brief and innocuous episodes.

## IN MEMORIAM

Most of the newspaper articles in this compendium were diligently transcribed by Audrey Craig. She spent countless hours reading these old, faded, sometimes-illegible articles and transferring them to computer disks. Audrey also spent many moments of her days waiting in the car while her husband, Dave, checked some reference in the library or got sidetracked into a long conversation with some history buff. She never complained because she knew how important this bicentennial history is to Dave, besides; Audrey had also developed a love for the "old happenings." On August 13, 1999, before she could see the final results of her work, Audrey passed away unexpectedly. We are dedicating this book to Audrey Craig. She is gone but not forgotten as her memory lives on in this book and in our hearts.

# 𝕱𝖗𝖎𝖊𝖓𝖉𝖘 𝖆𝖓𝖉 𝕭𝖊𝖓𝖊𝖋𝖆𝖈𝖙𝖔𝖗𝖘 𝖔𝖋 𝕷𝖔𝖈𝖆𝖑 𝕳𝖎𝖘𝖙𝖔𝖗𝖞

═══════

I would like to thank the following individuals and businesses for helping finance the publication of this book:

═══════

JOHN W. THROWER, INC.

BUTLER COUNTY FORD

GERALDINE FREEHLING

DU-CO CERAMICS COMPANY

MAY'S MUSIC SHOPPE

MARMON/KEYSTONE CORPORATION

DON PAUL'S JEWELRY AND REPAIR

AGR INTERNATIONAL INC.

PENN UNITED TECHNOLOGY INC.

THE BUTLER MALL

FRIEDMAN'S SUPERMARKETS

HAYS & HARTZELL REALTY

THROM & SONS AUCTION COMPANY

HOME REALTY COMPANY

O. H. NICHOLAS TRANSFER & STORAGE CO.

WHEATON WORLD WIDE MOVERS

ED SHIELDS REALTOR

# Questions and Answers

**Things You Always Wanted to Know About Butler**

(Author's note: These questions and answers are a continuation of the 200 questions and answers in chapter 7 of *Butler County, the Second Hundred Years.*)

201. What Butler County woman, accused of witchcraft, was shot and killed by a Butler County man who was never prosecuted for her murder? Ann Girty

202. What Butler County town once had ten distilleries operating within a three-mile radius? Forestville

203. What famous person could have been seen hanging by his feet, around 1929, in front of the Capitol Theater on South Main Street? Harry Houdini

204. What early, Butler County man observed his workers from a stone chair? Father Rapp sat on a carved stone chair on Vinyard Hill on the outskirts of Harmony. It was his place of meditation and it was also a good vantage point from which to watch his workers. If Father Rapp noticed any irregularities he alerted the foremen by blowing a bugle.

205. Who climbed the outside wall to the roof, of the Butler Savings & Trust Company bank at the corner of Main and Jefferson Streets? People associated with the carnivals who called themselves "human flies."

206. What Butler attorney lived to be 105 and is now buried between his first and second wives? W. D. Brandon

207. What two Butler churches display inverted crosses? St. Peter's Roman Catholic and St. Peter's Episcopal churches each display an inverted cross because St. Peter was crucified in an upside-down position.

208. How was one of Butler's Chinese laundry operators murdered in 1931? Ye Wing Lee was found brutally murdered in his laundry. He had been stabbed in the stomach with a butcher knife and a screwdriver had been thrust into his brain.

209. What Butler attorney had a photographic memory and became the librarian at Western Penitentiary while he was serving time there? Porter Lowry

210. What Butler boy was broadcasting radio from his Main Street house as early as the 1920's? Norman Matlack

211. What Butler Doctor operated a tonsil and adenoid hospital at 422 North Main Street? Dr. Clarence E. Imbre

212. What Butler bakery had an oven capable of baking 12,000 loaves of bread in a twenty-four hour period? Diehl's Bakery

213. What building on Cliff Street had a cork-lined room? Limberg's Ice Cream Company

214. Who led Sam Mohawk to the Lord before the Indian was executed? Lutheran minister, Gotlieb Bassler

215. What is the oldest, tower clock in the Western Hemisphere? The Bentel House Museum in Harmony, has a clock which was made in 1650.

216. Who sold two, beautiful Duisenberg cars for thirty-five dollars each and why? Jack and Gertrude Campbell sold the Duisenbergs because they thought the cars were "gas hogs."

217. What boy ran away from home at age fourteen, came to Butler, and eventually became one of this city's most prominent businessmen? Jacob Ziegler

218. What Main Street building had a park of sorts on the roof where tenants could hang out their wash and gardeners could cultivate a few plants? The Duffy Flats was just one of several such roof tops.

219. What part of the old Standard Motor Company building at the corner of Main and Brady Streets continues to exist and is in use today? The basement

220. Why were many of Butler's oldest houses painted a unique, yellow color? The yellow paint was made from a clay deposit which was found along the Connoquenessing Creek and was free for the taking.

221. What Butler congregation originally met under the trees at the southern margin of the old North Cemetery? St. Andrew's United Presbyterian Church

222. Who was the first female chiropractor in Butler County? Her office was closed by the authorities. Blanche Porterfield

223. What Butler Barber was accused of being a German spy during World War II? Julius Yoos

224. What village near the city of Butler was expected to become a very busy industrial center of 6000 or more people but it never grew to more than fourteen houses? Queen Junction

225. What materials did the early pioneers use as filler between the logs in their homes? If the log structure were to be covered with clapboards, then a mixture of clay and straw would suffice. Otherwise the pioneers mixed sand, lime, cow hair, and dung, which all dried to a hard plaster.

226. Who stood on Main Street and passed out free samples of cider and why? Billy Eisler, owner and operator of Treesdale Farms, about 1930, passed out free samples of cider in front of Mardorf's store as a promotional gimmick.

227. What was the most popular drink in Butler County until about 1850? Whiskey

228. What famous racecar driver was killed at the Butler Fair track when it was at the present high-school location? Frank Kelly of Ebensburg, PA, in a 1933 race, was thrown from his car during a four car pileup and was run over by another car. This happened right in front of the grandstands.

229. What Butler bridge was paved with wooden bricks to keep the weight down? The Wayne Street Viaduct was paved with wooden bricks. This was not an unusual practice during the early years of this century.

230. Builders of country-federal houses included on the second floor, a "captive room." What was its purpose? The room was a small bedroom which could be accessed only by going through the master bedroom. Young, female servants, often relatives, slept there where their presence and the coming and going of visitors could be monitored and controlled.

231. What Butler dentist was battered to death when his long raincoat was caught in his oil well flywheel? Dr. Aver

232. What are Belgian blocks and where might they be seen in Butler? Belgian blocks were very effective as ballast to steady empty steamships. As ships were loaded with freight the inexpensive blocks were thrown off onto the riverbanks or dock areas. Paving companies acquired the blocks free for the hauling or for a very reasonable fee, and many city streets are paved with the blocks. The area around the old Pennsylvania Railroad Station near the corner of Monroe and Jefferson Streets sports a sizable number of these Belgian blocks. Most are under the asphalt parking lot at Snack-N-Pack.

233. Was there ever a jewelry factory in Butler? According to John Autenreith there was a jewelry factory on Pillow Street in the 1920's.

234. What Butler car dealer had, as a promotional attraction, a marathon pianist who played nonstop for five days? Lindsay Pontiac Sales at 218 South Main Street.

235. Are there any stories regarding buried treasure in the Butler area? Yes—when the Franklin Glass Company of the Southside was being prepared for razing, a large envelope marked "very important" was found in the office. The contents of the envelope revealed that before the glass company was built a sizable quantity of fake, silver dollars was buried in a swamp at the site. The swamp was later filled with silicon waste which was a by-product of the glass-making process. Those piles of waste are still called the "sow belly." The counterfeit, silver dollars had been produced in the Stone House area by a man named Holiday and his henchmen. The "silver dollars" buried in the Franklin glass area were never recovered. Holiday and his entire gang of counterfeiters went to prison. The dies were discovered around 1950 hidden in a cave near Camp Bucoco.

236. Why was Butler called the "glad-hand city?" Butler was a friendly place; people always extended their hands in warm greetings.

237. Why does Butler have a Pepper Street and a Dr. Pepper Street? Pepper Street joins Center Avenue five blocks up the hill. It was named for Mayor Harry Pepper. Dr. Pepper Street meets West Pearl Street near its western extremity. The Dr. Pepper bottling plant was located there.

238. Who operated a bus service along what is now Route 38 between North Washington and Butler? Sam Muscatello

239. What did pioneer mothers use to pacify the crying baby? A crust of bread which had been soaked in whiskey

240. Where in Butler County could underground, coal miners hear vehicle traffic passing overhead? Mine

shafts which had their entrances in Cosco extended all the way to the present Clearview Mall area. Miners underneath Route 8 could hear traffic passing overhead.

241. Why were the annual races called "orange crate derbies" in Butler but "soapbox derbies" everywhere else? Butler was not affiliated with the official "soapbox derby" organization in Akron and was therefore not allowed to use the "soapbox derby" name.

242. Where in the city of Butler did the Ku Klux Klan hold rallies during the 1920's and 30's? In the cemeteries on North Main Street Hill and in the old silk mill on Institute Hill.

243. Why did piano players for the silent movies have to be very good at playing by ear? It was too dark in the theaters to read music.

244. Where did the name of Butler's new, turn-of-the-century park, Alameda, originate? A contest was held to name the new park and the winner chose "Alameda" after the waterfront promenade in Santiago, Cuba.

245. Why did John F. Kennedy eat at the Williard Hotel rather than the Nixon when he visited Butler in 1960? The owner of the Nixon Hotel had recently changed its name to the Nixon Lodge. If you remember, Henry Cabot Lodge was Nixon's running mate and the name change was a play on words--enough said.

246. What Latin American emperor, when he was in Butler, was mobbed to the point that the local newspaper had to plea for curious Butlerites to give the dignitary some space? Don Pedro, the Emperor of Brazil

247. Why was there nearly a brawl in front of Butler's Arlington Hotel between a visiting minstrel band and the consolidated bands of Butler? Hi Henry's Minstrels had made it a point to play in Butler each year during fair week. Fifty Butler band members were meeting in front of the courthouse in anticipation of a parade down Main Street. Hi Henry's Minstrels had already begun a performance half a block away, in front of the Arlington Hotel. The Butler bands began to march and swept through causing Hi Henry's Minstrels to disperse.

248. What caused the explosion at the Butler Brewery which killed three men in 1903? The paint used inside the beer vats was highly combustible. While painters were at work, a light bulb broke creating a spark which caused the explosion.

249. What Butler gasoline station had an indoor, horseshoe court on the second floor? Central Parking & Supply Company at 125 East Jefferson Street, where the city parking lot is today.

250. What Butler attorney slept during the day and did business only at night? John R. Pillow

251. What Butler industry had more accidents than any other? According to Bob Brandberg, son of Dr. Brandberg, the answer is the Standard Plate Glass Company. Bob remembers his father's stitching of wounds sans novocain.

252. What Butler state trooper traveled to South Dakota and brought back murderer Irene Schroeder? Billy Boettner

253. What apartment building on Main Street was the location of many high-school dances during the 1930's? The Sterling Apartments at 415 North Main Street.

254. What evangelist visited Butler in 1911 and was so popular that many of the babies born at that time were named after him? French E. Oliver.

255. Where was court held while a new courthouse was being built in 1853 and 1854? In the basement of the Presbyterian Church.

256. Who was the first Butler resident to own an airplane? Robert Headland

257. Who was Butler's first aviator to be killed in an airplane accident? Leo McElligott

258. Why did Zachery Taylor Hockenberry shoot Nancy Ann McCandless's nose off, accidentally killing her in the process? He wanted her for himself and he thought that no other man would be attracted to her if she had no nose.

259. What Butler company sold large lollipops all over the U.S.? The Morrison Candy Company

260. How many people lived in Butler County in 1800, shortly after the Cunningham Brothers arrived and founded the borough of Butler? Approximately four thousand

261. What company on North Bluff Street manufactured approximately 115 dozen pair of gloves every day? Butler Glove and Mitten Company in 1910.

262. The Butler County jail was only attacked by a mob once. What was the occasion? Jerry Bennett was being held in the jail for an alleged assault on a young girl. The event took place in September 1902.

263. Who has a photograph of a drawing of Sam Mohawk?  John Autenreith

264. One of the most ruthless, terror-inspiring, murderous gangs the U.S. ever experienced came out of Butler County.  Who were they?  The Gibson Brothers

265. Where can one see a grindstone from the mill which succeeded the Cunningham Mill?  The stone may be seen at the Fuelgraf Electric Company which is on the site of the old Cunningham Mill.

266. Who were the only two men hanged at the Butler County Jail?  Sam Mohawk and Zachary Taylor Hockenberry.

267. What Butler man had the fifth Kentucky Fried Chicken franchise in the United States?  William A. Morgan Jr.

268. Were cigars ever manufactured in Butler?  In addition to Joe Feldblum's cigar-manufacturing business which was discussed in *Butler County, the Second Hundred Years*, pg. 39, a man named Morris had a cigar factory on the south side of Amy Avenue in the house nearest to Bluff Street.  It operated from approximately 1930 until 1950.

269. What Butler County village once printed its own money?  Harmony

270. What Butler man gave away an entire newspaper business.  John Negley gave the *Democratic Herald* newspaper to John and Samuel Coll in 1855.

271. What famous American songwriter spent a summer vacation in Harmony?  Stephen Foster

272. In what way was the Spanish-American War good therapy for Americans?  Americans had not yet gotten over the Civil War; we were still a divided nation in many ways.  The Spanish American War, especially our superior performance and the short time it took to defeat Spain, drew Americans together and made our citizens proud.

273. What Butler philosopher was often compared to Plato of ancient Greece?  David Dougal

274. How did Cosco get its name?  It was named for the Consolidated Coal Company which operated there.

275. What was Johnny Zavacky's claim to fame?  Around 1930 at the age of sixteen Zavacky built a small airplane of his own design and flew it about the length of a city block.  He lived on Butler's West End near Pillow Street and Sixth Avenue.  His plane was later hung from the roof of the Butler Theater to advertise a World War I movie.

276. What Butler County town was the scene of a prize fight with over 1,500 fans in attendance and more than $50,000 wagered?  In May 1847 a prizefight was staged in Shakley Grove, Petrolia.  The fight featured Big Red Mullen, a driller, versus Stop Cock Jim, a pipeline gauger also known as Lightning Jim.  Bare-knuckle national champion Ben Hogan refereed the match.   Lightning Jim was the victor in the fourth round.

277. What unusual business was being carried on at Center Avenue around 1910?  The manufacture of thousands of corncob pipes

278. Where in Butler County was found very beautiful samples of marble—brown, white, striped and black?  The marble deposit, very unusual for this area, was found near Rough Run in West Winfield—about one hundred years ago experts said it was worth $1200 per ton.  The owners were keeping secret the location and all information pertaining to the marble.

279. What Butler County town had a plant which manufactured and sold nearly 3000 beds each day?  East Butler was the location of the Pittsburgh Hickson Company in 1912.

280. What is the oldest bank building yet standing in Butler?  The John Berg and Company Bank conducted business in the building located at 318 East Jefferson Street.

281. What were the most important holidays celebrated by the early settlers?  The most popular holidays were Washington's Birthday and Independence Day.  Christmas, Easter and New Year's Day were not celebrated much.  People of German descent did celebrate Christmas.  Thanksgiving was celebrated infrequently in late August.  President Lincoln established Thanksgiving as an official holiday in 1863.

282. What Butler factory had the capacity to produce 2500 gross of buttons every day?  The Butler Button Company was doing business at 331 Negley Avenue Company in 1911.

283. Where was the first electric-eye, door opener in Butler?  Kroger's, at their Pillow Street location, had an electric eye mounted on two posts between which their customers passed.  It was quite a novelty.

284. Where was Butler's municipal  building in the 1920's and 30's?  The building was located on North

Main Street between the English Lutheran Church and the T. W. Phillips building. It was a two-story, brick building which had been the Schreiber House hotel when it was built in 1860.

285. What was the first three-story hotel in Butler? H. J. Klinger erected a three-story hotel at the northeast corner of Main and Jefferson Streets in 1852. It later became the Hotel Lowry, then in 1921 it was razed for the construction of the Guaranty Trust Company.

286. Why was every bar in Butler closed for a short time in 1894? There was a strong temperance movement in Butler County which dated all the way back to 1829 when a temperance society was formed. In 1831-32, William Campbell and Matthew Lowrie visited every house in Butler and succeeded in procuring from most of the women and children, a signed pledge to refrain from alcohol. The efforts of Butler's temperance society caused the temporary closing of the bars in 1894.

287. Where was the Spaide Shirt Factory? The shirt factory was located at 165 Brugh Avenue and is now the remodeled Morgan Management Building.

288. Why is there a "French Kate Hill" just south of Petrolia on Route 268? The story of Ben Hogan may be found in *Butler County, the Second Hundred Years*, chapter 20. Hogan teamed up with "French Kate" and fifteen "ladies of questionable morals," and followed the oil business around western Pennsylvania. Hogan and his stable of pulchritudinous tarts followed the oil excitement to Petrolia in 1870. Hogan eventually became a Christian, moved to Chicago and spent the rest of his life trying to atone for his wicked ways. French Kate lived out her days in a house just south of Petrolia near the present Witco Corporation main gate.

289. What is a "selenfenster?" Pioneers of German descent constructed a small window in their homes. It was opened after somebody died in the belief that it enabled the soul of the deceased to depart for heaven. The belief yet persists among some of Pennsylvania's Amish.

290. The Pilgrims arrived in North America in 1620. By 1700 the number of English settlers had risen to 70,000. How many log cabins had they constructed? None

291. What Butler priest published a newspaper? The Thought and Action print shop in 1936 was located on South Monroe Street near the fire station. The shop did custom printing and published a newspaper which was edited by Father Marinaro of St. Michael's Church.

292. What Butler merchant opened a toy store even though his father and grandfather were successful tailors and were also in the retail-clothing business? Joseph Aland Jr.

293. Why didn't the pioneers have trees near their houses? It was a common belief among the early settlers that trees kept air from circulating and stagnant air could cause diseases. The word malaria literally means "bad air."

294. What common fruit was avoided by the pioneers because they believed it to be poisonous? Tomatoes were called Jerusalem apples and/or love plants. Their only use was ornamental.

295. Why was pork rather than beef, the choice of most early families? Pork was much easier to preserve by pickling, salting, and smoking. Beef did not lend itself as well to these processes and was therefore more scarce than pork products.

296. What was a business slogan used by the G. & Y. Clothing Store? "We may be Green and Young but we know the business."

297. Who were the attorneys who defended Sam Mohawk? George W. Smith and Lewis Z. Mitchell

298. Who was Putt Mossmann? Mossmann was a champion, horseshoe pitcher who traveled from town to town around 1930. He demonstrated his skills at Butler's Roessing Field, the present site of Emily Brittain School, where he stacked the peg full from bottom to top. His accurately tossed horseshoes could light matches which were tied to the horseshoe pegs. Eyewitnesses say he never made an error. Mossmann made a living conducting these performances and selling a type of horseshoe he had invented and patented.

299. What were some vegetables and fruits which were raised by the Indians but had been unknown in Europe? Corn, squash, beans, pumpkins, peaches, pears, cherries, quince and certain kinds of apples were all being raised and used by the Indians before Europeans arrived on our shores.

300. What Butler County man achieved more fame and rose to a higher distinction than any other? William Perry of Butler was appointed and served as Secretary of Defense during the Clinton administration. Until that time, U.S. Senator, Walter Lowrie had attained the highest political office of anyone from Butler.

# FRIEDMAN'S SUPERMARKETS...
## 99 Years And Good As Ever

One of Butler's oldest and most enduringly successful businesses is the Friedman Supermarket enterprise. From its humble beginning in Lyndora the supermarket chain now has stores in Saxonburg; Chicora; Morgantown, West Virginia; and their four Butler supermarkets at Brady Street, Greater Butler Mart, Mercer Road, and the BiLo at Point Plaza.

Jacob Friedman immigrated to the United States from Austria-Hungary in or around 1899. He first located in McKeesport where he worked as an apprentice blacksmith, but a hand injury forced him to seek other means of earning a livelihood. When the Standard Steel Car Company was launching its business in 1902 and thousands of immigrants were surging into Lyndora seeking jobs, Jacob Friedman saw an opportunity in Butler County. He and his wife, Helen Kohn Friedman, moved into an apartment in Lyndora above what is now Kosar's Bar and commenced what turned out to be a long career in the mercantile business. He started on a "shoestring" by borrowing $25, purchasing a pushcart, and becoming a street vendor. He sold notions and produce from his cart, and his trading area consisted mainly of Lyndora and the Pillow Street area of Butler.

Business was good and he soon graduated to his first store on Lyndora's Main Street near the old post office. Polk's *City Directory* for 1912 shows a general store on Kohler Avenue near Chesapeake Street and the third store was on Fairground (Hansen) Avenue near Armco's Wheel Works. The Fairground Avenue store was operated by Jacob Friedman, Joseph Pollock and Anthony Morris. That same directory also lists Jacob and his wife Helen as being the proprietors of a furniture store in Lyndora. Jacob Friedman's business enterprises had become diversified and were growing. Satellite Friedman's stores were opened in small Butler County towns such as Mars. Friedman's was the first western Pennsylvania grocery to divide its stores into departments such as meat, fruit and bread. A horse cart delivery service covered outlying areas such as Chicora, Bruin and Petrolia.

On June 25, 1918 Mr. Friedman opened one of the largest grocery stores in the Butler area. The new store was located at 120 West Jefferson Street where the Outdoor Army Store stands today, and was the finest grocery store in Butler. The store was intended to satisfy all of the shopper's grocery needs; it contained a complete selection of meats, fruits, vegetables, and fish. It was operated on a strictly cash basis and a delivery system was implemented for special deliveries at certain hours to each district in the town. It was the first grocery store to sell produce directly from area farms. At that time it was common practice for many of the farm families to help one another with the harvesting and threshing of grain. The farmer on whose farm the cooperative venture was taking place then hosted a feast to show his appreciation and feed the hungry harvesters. One of Friedman's many specialties was supplying meats for these threshing dinners. The supermarket also provided meats and groceries to the many and varied stands at the busy annual Butler fair. He guaranteed two deliveries a day to the fairgrounds.

On June 4, 1922, Friedman's Jefferson Street store was severely damaged by a fire of unknown origin. The fire was discovered at 2:00 a.m. by Butler barber, John Beneigh, who happened to be walking home and noticed flames inside the store. Mr. Beneigh ran to the Central fire station and notified the men on duty there. The firemen responded quickly using the city's new Pope Hartford truck and the newly acquired, state-of-the-art chemical apparatus to extinguish the fire. Had it not been for Beneigh's early detection of the fire, it may well have spread over

**"The Model Market" - 1945 - Main Street between the present Burger Hut and Pinkerton Goodyear Tire Center - Carole Friedman Bitter (in stroller) and mother Alyce Friedman**

**Friedman's Saxonburg Supermarket - Grand Opening - July 27, 1960**

Left to right: Milton Friedman, Jacob Friedman, unidentified, Harold Friedman, Reldon Cooper, unidentified, Ronald Safier

an entire block or more. Even with the early detection, losses were estimated at $8,000 in 1922 dollars. Damaged goods were removed from the shelves and Friedman's was open for business the day following the fire. In 1948 Friedman's West Jefferson Street store became a self-service unit, the first self-service supermarket in Butler. When Donahue's opened grocery stores in Pittsburgh they patterned their stores after Friedman's.

On November 16, 1949, Friedman's opened their second store. Continuing what now had become a family tradition, the new store was the most modern food market in Butler's history. This new store was a new two-story building constructed specifically for Friedman's located at the northeastern corner of Monroe and Maple Streets. The building was three times as large as the West Jefferson Street store and adjacent to it was a resurfaced parking lot with spaces for 125 automobiles. The state-of-the-art building featured tile construction, concrete floors, modern fluorescent lights, and was "completely fire and vermin proof." The eight-foot-long meat slicer was one of only two of its kind in western Pennsylvania. The new store also boasted a 75-foot self-serve refrigerator. Friedman's was the first store in this part of the state to feature magic-carpet mats. When a customer stepped on one of the mats, the door automatically opened. Friedman's anticipated eliminating long lines by opening two express and four regular check-out lanes. The store also employed young men to carry groceries to the cars of customers desiring this courtesy. Friedman's new store represented a $140,000 investment and employed fifty people. The new store opened at 9:00 a.m. and closed at 9:00 p.m. six days a week.

As part of the grand opening celebration, the first 2,500 women who entered the store received flowers. Samples of the store's products were given to customers, and 200 lucky customers won food baskets of Golden Dawn products valued at $5 each (Over the years Friedman's has been affiliated with Clover Farm, Golden Dawn and until 1984, Foodland). An orchestra entertained opening day shoppers. According to the *Butler Eagle*, Friedman's was the first local business to place a paid advertisement in the newspaper congratulating the firms who had built their new building and/or made the installations.

Milton X. Friedman, eldest son of Jacob, was the supervisor of the new store on Monroe Street and the West Jefferson Street Friedman's supermarket. Milton's younger brother Harold was the grocery manager. Lester Grenberger was in charge of meats, and Ralph Grillo operated the produce department (Ralph later became the proprietor of the City Market on West Jefferson Street). At sixty-seven years of age, Jacob Friedman continued to be active in the business in an advisory capacity. A cousin, Milton Friedman, was involved for years in the meat end of the business and later, purchased the store on West Jefferson Street and ran it as a single proprietorship.

Jacob Friedman died on October 20, 1960, at the age of 78. He left his wife Helen; two sons, Milton and Harold; and three daughters, Mrs. Albert (Hilda) Golanty of Pittsburgh and Florida, Mrs. Allen (Alice) Safier of McKeesport; and Mrs. Edward (Margaret) Friedman of Harrisburg, nine grandchildren, fourteen great-grandchildren and four great-great-grandchildren. All five of the Friedman children were born in the apartment above Kosar's Bar where Mr. Friedman originally settled when he arrived in Lyndora.

Friedman's is perhaps the only business in town which is now into the fourth generation. Frederick Harold Bitter, at eleven years of age, presently helps with Sample Fests and Kid's Weeks.

The history of success for Friedman's Supermarkets has resulted from steady growth and a commitment to

**Grand Opening - Greater Butler Mart Friedman's - November 1974**

people and to constantly remodeling and installing state-of-the-art innovations and departments.

A third generation grocer, Dr. Carole F. Bitter became president of the family-owned company in May 1976. She has donated her time to the community through her work with Butler Memorial Hospital, the Butler County Chamber of Commerce, the United Way of Butler County, the

Left to right: Frank Stanko, Bob Northeime, Corky Donaldson, Pete Pintell, Jayne Friedman, Harold Friedman, Carole Friedman Bitter, unidentified, unidentified, Ron Eichenlaub (rear), Dale Eichenlaub

Downtown Butler Renaissance Commission, the Irene Stacy Mental Health Center, and many other organizations over the years. Carole's sister Nancy Friedman Crerar is also a shareholder and board member of Friedman's Supermarkets.

The company which is celebrating its 99th anniversary, has a slogan "We Believe in Butler," and its employees and associates are active in community work. Since 1988 Friedman's has sponsored an annual "Grocers fight Cancer Day," which donates funds to the Butler Unit of the American Cancer Society. More than $30,000 has been collected at Friedman's locations since the event began.

Friedman's has been one of the guarantors of the Butler 10K Race since it began in 1976 and food banks and

countless other organizations have been the recipients of food and donations from Friedman's. The firm has donated over 15 tons of food to the Butler Area Merchants Association auction since 1982 and had worked closely with Armco on its food bank orders in the 1980's as well as the Coalition for the Unemployed, the Human Relations Association, the Salvation Army, and the Rotary Club's Turkey Roundup in more recent years.

**West Jefferson Street Friedman's - 1940's**

Front row, left to right: Jacob Friedman, Helen Friedman, Janice Golanty
Standing, left to right: Milton Friedman, Alan Safier, Alice Friedman Safier, Margaret Friedman, Harold Friedman, Al Golanty, Hilda Friedman Golanty, Sam Miller (Miller's Meat Market)

John Negley was one of Butler's earliest settlers. Upon his arrival to the area in 1800 he secured employment at the Cunningham brothers' grist mill. Just six years later he purchased the mill from Samuel Cunningham, who had decided to return to eastern Pennsylvania after the death of his brother John. Over the ensuing years, Mr. Negley became a very prominent Butlerite, serving as the county's first treasurer, an early prothonotary, and also one of Butler's earliest county commissioners. In 1809 Mr. Negley was elected to the state legislature. In addition to his political interests, Negley founded various businesses and acquired a considerable amount of real estate.

A son, John Henry Negley, was born in 1823. He followed in his father's footsteps. He was admitted to the bar in 1845 and became Butler County's first district attorney. He became the proprietor and editor of the *Democratic Herald* newspaper in 1855. In 1869 he purchased the *Butler Citizen* newspaper which he published until 1888. J. H. Negley certainly knew Butler as well as anyone of his era. In 1891 he published his recollections of Butler in a twelve part series in the *Butler Citizen*.

Audrey Fetters discovered the Negley articles and painstakingly transcribed them in their entirety. She has long had a desire to publish the recollections for the enjoyment of the people of Butler but has been unable to fulfill this ambition. So this one's for you Audrey, and the people of Butler County.

# RECOLLECTIONS OF BUTLER

ED. CITIZEN— Recently on meeting a friend, now one of our elder citizens, our conversation turned upon the wonderful changes in Butler within our time and he suggested they should be written, and that I should give what he termed my reminiscences of the town. In turn I suggested that he should perform the task. However, he urged it on me and after due consideration I have concluded to do so. But at the outset we wish it understood that these "recollections" which name we prefer to call them, are but our recollections, as we write only of what "hangs on memory's walls," without consulting a book, paper or document and therefore they are not given or not to be taken as absolute history. The great change that has taken place in our town, in men, families, persons and things during the past fifty years has suggested the thought, and if these recollections of half a century will be the means of preserving a record of any of these, or prove of interest to any of our citizens, we will have accomplished our object. At present, Butler is like unto a strange city to our older citizens and they feel and realize the fact that they are almost strangers in a new and strange place.

## ORIGINAL BUTLER

To begin properly it is first of importance that the original limits or boundaries of the town should be stated, for its enlargement from time to time has made it four-fold of what it was fifty years ago. All of the first ward and much of the second, third, fourth and fifth wards of the present town, have been added to the original. The following is about the first or old boundary. On the south and to what was known as "the commons," building lots were laid out to the alley along and south of the present residences of William Campbell and R.C. McAboy, the alley running east and west to near the Connoquenessing creek at either end: on the west to near the creek and about twenty rods below the present George Walter mill, as southwest corner, and on the east reaching the creek near to and below the present opera house. From there it followed up and near the creek to a large tree that stood on the bank near where the present bridge known as the Boyd bridge now is, south and not far from the West Penn Railroad depot. Thence due north along what is now called Monroe Street to where the same will meet what is now East Penn Street, but which originally was but an alley. This was the northeast corner. Thence it went due west along said now Penn Street crossing Main Street between the properties of the heirs of the late General Purviance and Isaac Colbert, Esq. and on to a point where present West Penn would intersect an alley, northwest corner running thence due south crossing Cunningham St. near the residence of Mr. C. Otto and on to the creek again near the present Jail Street bridge and from there up the creek some thirty rods to the place of beginning. So it will be seen Butler was not as large in territory fifty years ago as it is at present. By the additions, north, south, east and west, it is now more than a square mile in extent. Its population in 1840 was less than one thousand.

## THE COMMONS

It should be stated that what was known as "the commons" some five or six acres composed a part of the original plan of Butler laying on the south end, and running from creek to creek east and west and bounded on the south by the property of the late John Negley, who owned all the balance of land in that bend of the creek below the commons and then in Butler Township. These commons were reserved and set apart as such by the original donors of our county seat, John and Samuel Cunningham, for the general use and benefit of its people. One and perhaps the principal use then derived from them was that enjoyed by the cows of its citizens which, on being relieved of their milk in an evening hastened to or were driven to "the commons" there to repose in comfort and safety for the night. How different from now, when if your cow should happen to be out late at night, she is mercilessly seized by order of town council impounded and imprisoned in some small and uncomfortable pen until you redeem her. The Cunningham donors were good and merciful men, in that they were merciful to the beasts in providing for them. The commons abounded in every variety of tree, great and small among them plentifully being the crabapple tree the fragrance of whose blossoms in the spring was most enchanting to the sense of smell and the beauty of whose flowers most pleasant to the eye. Hickory nuts, chestnuts, hazel nuts, wild cherries and berries were also gathered there by the small boys of fifty years ago. Good building stone also covered the commons and from which the stone for the foundations of the first houses and barns were taken. Large rocks were these, upon which the children climbed and the goats delighted to sport. The celebrated "federal spring" named so in honor of the politics of the days of General Washington is close upon the south borders of the old commons. It is now the property of Mr. John M. Smith who has neatly enclosed it and is no longer accessible to the general public, who often sought its pure and refreshing waters. The Indians passing through Butler in those days made it a point to reach that spring to quench their thirst and lay in the sun and rest there. But the commons were finally sold—by virtue of an act of legislature—and the proceeds of sales of lots laid out thereon were devoted to educational purposes, the present large school house on Jefferson St. being principally built from the sales about fifteen years ago. Upon some of these lots are now the fine residences of John N. Patterson, L. J. McCandless, Mr. Bole, John Kopp, John M. Smith, Mrs. Dunn, Al. Walter, Kafer, Moorehead, Haffner, the new and very elegant house of Mr. D. B. Campbell, Mr. Eisler, Mr. Joseph Balph and others some of which it is said will have to be removed if the contemplated widening is made of the street leading from McKean to the bridge passing over to Springdale.

Butler, Dec. 29, 1890

ED. CITIZEN—We closed last week with what was known as "the commons" in the south end of town and propose in this to continue on along Main Street from the south to the north and with our recollections of the older families and principal citizens of fifty years ago, where they lived and what became of some of them and in this way stating the squares or lots they then owned or lived upon, and who are the present owners with the changes in buildings on the same, etc.

## OLD CITIZENS—AYRES SQUARE

We begin with the square consisting of three lots, owned and resided upon by General William Ayres, one of the earliest settlers in Butler. This square is now owned in equal parts by Ex-Judge E. McJunkin and Mr. William Campbell, Sr. General Ayres lived in a part of the house. Mr. McJunkin is now living in the brick part. The other part—log framed—was used by him for his law office and was torn down by Mr. McJunkin when he purchased same, some 35 years ago, and who built the brick instead, now occupied as his law office. Mr. William John Ayres, son of the General, occupied this frame part for some years as a jewelry and watch repairing shop. He was the father of Captain H. A. Ayres--yet among us. Mr. Campbell built his brick dwelling on his part of the square where he now resides, about 40 years ago.

General Ayres in person was a large man and very dignified in appearance and manner, very particular in his ways and punctilious in his habits. He always dressed well in great neatness and always in the same cut and color of cloth. In some respects he might have been called "a gentleman of the old school." He had a large law practice and was careful in business, one result of which was that on his death in 1843, more judgments were found of record in his favor than of any other man in the county. He left an estate of about $150,000. He was the first prothonotary of the county and was a member of the Constitutional Convention of 1838, to reform the Constitution of Pennsylvania. These are the only offices we believe he ever held.

## BRINKER-CAMPBELL SQUARE

The square across the street from the Ayres one was known, fifty years ago as the Brinker and Campbell one. William Campbell, Esq. lived in a house about where the present residence of Robert C. McAboy stands. He was quite a large, portly man, of great physical strength, the greatest, perhaps except one, of any then about the town. Acting as a justice of the peace for many years, he was familiarly known as "Squire Campbell." He was also a prothonotary of the county and held many other positions of trust. Our present William Campbell, Sr. is his only living son and his son William, whom we may term William the third, is a grandson as is Mr. John S. Campbell.

Col. Jacob Brinker occupied the balance of this square and built the hotel now known as the Willard House and now being so much enlarged and improved by Mr. William Reihing, the present owner. A frame attached at the south

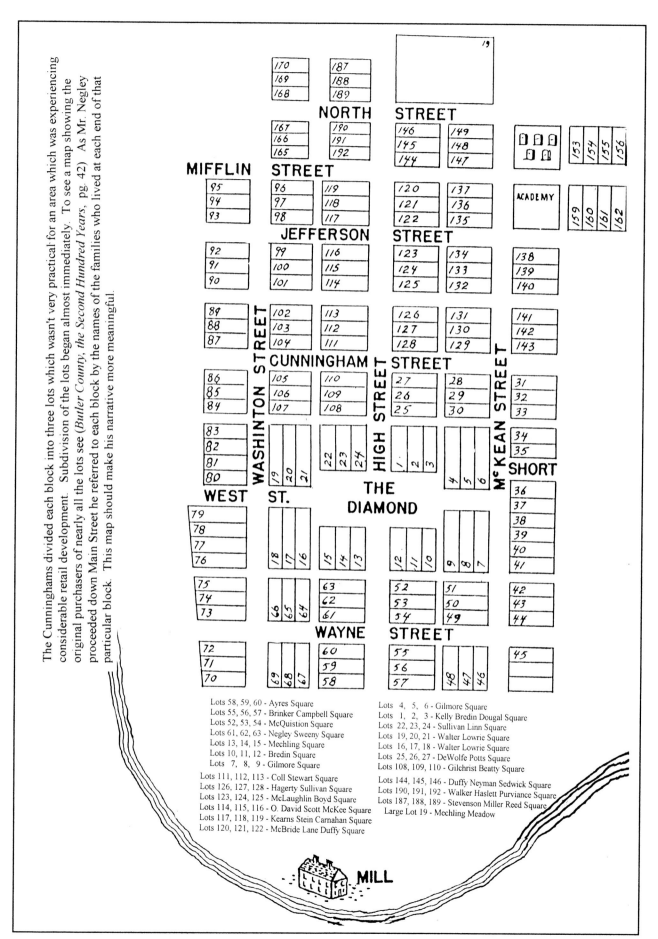

The Cunninghams divided each block into three lots which wasn't very practical for an area which was experiencing considerable retail development. Subdivision of the lots began almost immediately. To see a map showing the original purchasers of nearly all the lots see (*Butler County, the Second Hundred Years*, pg. 42) As Mr. Negley proceeded down Main Street he referred to each block by the names of the families who lived at each end of that particular block. This map should make his narrative more meaningful.

**NORTH STREET**

**MIFFLIN STREET**

**JEFFERSON STREET**

**WASHINTON STREET**

**CUNNINGHAM STREET**

**HIGH STREET**

**McKEAN STREET**

**SHORT**

**WEST ST.**

**THE DIAMOND**

**ACADEMY**

**WAYNE STREET**

Lots 58, 59, 60 - Ayres Square
Lots 55, 56, 57 - Brinker Campbell Square
Lots 52, 53, 54 - McQuistion Square
Lots 61, 62, 63 - Negley Sweeny Square
Lots 13, 14, 15 - Mechling Square
Lots 10, 11, 12 - Bredin Square
Lots 7, 8, 9 - Gilmore Square

Lots 111, 112, 113 - Coll Stewart Square
Lots 126, 127, 128 - Hagerty Sullivan Square
Lots 123, 124, 125 - McLaughlin Boyd Square
Lots 114, 115, 116 - O. David Scott McKee Square
Lots 117, 118, 119 - Kearns Stein Carnahan Square
Lots 120, 121, 122 - McBride Lane Duffy Square

Lots 4, 5, 6 - Gilmore Square
Lots 1, 2, 3 - Kelly Bredin Dougal Square
Lots 22, 23, 24 - Sullivan Linn Square
Lots 19, 20, 21 - Walter Lowrie Square
Lots 16, 17, 18 - Walter Lowrie Square
Lots 25, 26, 27 - DeWolfe Potts Square
Lots 108, 109, 110 - Gilchrist Beatty Square

Lots 144, 145, 146 - Duffy Neyman Sedwick Square
Lots 190, 191, 192 - Walker Haslett Purviance Square
Lots 187, 188, 189 - Stevenson Miller Reed Square
Large Lot 19 - Mechling Meadow

**MILL**

end was where the late Hon. William Hazlett first established and published The *Butler County Whig* newspaper, 45 years ago. This frame was removed by the late Michael Zimmerman, Esq. who became owner of the property about 45 years ago and who built a brick addition to the hotel instead. Before that the late former Sheriff John Pollock and his son-in-law, Mr. George Cooper, yet living at Glade Mills, kept hotel there and subsequently it was kept by the late Mr. Benjamin Jack, Mr. Geo. W. Campbell and perhaps others. Col. Brinker was a large, heavy set man, very active in military affairs and otherwise enterprising. He had been sheriff of the county, between 1830 and 1840. Our present, Mrs. Thomas S. McNair is the only child of his we believe now living here. When Mr. Reihing completes his improvements to the old Brinker House, the Willard with its three stories will be the largest hotel in the town.

## McQUISTION SQUARE

Passing over Wayne Street the next square north, same side, was known as the Joseph McQuistion one. Mr. McQuistion lived in the house now lived in by his son, Harper , in part and in part by Mr. John Stein, the baker, and present owner. This house is said to be one of the very oldest of the log-framed houses of the town, perhaps the oldest yet standing. Mr. Stein has recently erected a fine brick on the lower corner, now occupied by Greb and Vogely for their new shoe store. Mr. Casmir Wise is above in a new brick building. There is the present store-room of Mr. J. M. Arthurs. Then above is the new meat market shop of Mr. Adam Kummer. Then the part and houses belonging to Mrs. Christian Harley. On her part, the alley corner, the late Samuel A. and John N. Purviance built and had their first law office, afterwards the office of George Walter Ziegler and other attorneys. This corner was afterwards for a long time occupied as a meat market by the late Lewis and Nicholas Miller, the father of Mrs. Harley, and by Mr. Kummer and others and is now used as a confectionery store, in the name of A. A. Marshall. A barber shop is also at present on Mrs. Harley's part. Mr. Joseph McQuistion was a shoe-maker

by trade. He had his shop on this corner. Fifty years ago his shop was the place to get your best boots and shoes. He died about 1856. He has many nephews and nieces living in or near the town, but his son Harper is the only child now hereabouts.

## NEGLEY-STEWART SQUARE

The square across the street from the McQuistion one was known fifty years ago as the Negley and Sweeney one. John Sweeney, Esq. owned the upper lot where now stands the Eitenmiller Hotel, and built the original house there, which has recently been enlarged by Mr. Henry Eitenmiller, the present owner. Like all the first hotels and houses, it was but a two-story one. Now it has been made three, like others of the old ones and most of the new ones being built. Nothing perhaps indicates the progress of improvement now going on so strikingly as this raising of old two storied houses to three and the building of nearly all the new ones to the same number. John Sweeney, Esq. was a justice of the peace in Butler for a number of years. He has been dead for near fifty years and not a single child or descendant of his remains or exists hereabout that we know of. Anthony Wise deceased, first owned and lived in this house after him.

The late John Negley, Esq. owned the balance of the square down to Wayne Street. Part of this, fifty years ago was purchased from him by the late Mr. Thomas Stehle, whose daughter Mrs. Aland, now owns same and resides in part of the buildings thereon. Other parts owned by her are the house in which Mr. Lorry Roessing now lives, and the house in which is the store of Mr. O. M. Phillips. Mr. Stehle was an ingenious man, a mechanic, a worker in fine brass, iron and tinware. In connection with these he carried on gun and other repairing, in a shop where Mr. Phillips' store now is. Subsequently he kept a restaurant and refreshment room there, which was fitted up in a novel and well arranged manner for supplying of his many customers with their wants.

His entertainment rooms were much frequented and he was courteous and obliging to his patrons. He died but a few years ago. Adjoining Mrs. Aland's property is the present residence and lot of Miss Sarah McQuistion. The house in which she lives is part of one of the oldest buildings of Butler. It with a front part that was to it, composed one of the first hotels of the town for many of its first years. Samuel Marquis kept a public house there for some years. Mr. Bennett Dobbs followed with a temperance house. We forget much but the sign in front of his house, we will never forget. It was a snake with many heads, red, blood-shot eyes and darting tongues, intended to illustrate and forewarn all as to the poisonous and evil tendencies of intoxicating drinks. The front part of this stand was torn away about 40 years ago by Mr. James A. Negley for the erection of other buildings. The *Democratic Herald* paper was removed to and published in the part upper story, of that yet standing, and owned by Miss McQuistion, by the late Col. Joseph P. Patterson, father of John N. This was done in March 1855. On the illness of Col. Patterson, November of the same year, the writer of this, very unexpected to himself, became the owner of the paper and published the same there until July 1858 when he sold or rather gave it away to John and Samuel Coll who removed it elsewhere. Col. Patterson died March 4, 1856. The writer had previously about 1850 built his first law office there standing in front of Miss McQuistion's present home and which was removed to the rear end of same when her mother purchased all that part of the lot, about 1864. Mr. Felix C. Negley, now of Pittsburg and his brother James A., now of Philadelphia built and established the first store house, frame, on the corner where the store of Jacob Boos now is. This in about 1848. Shortly after Mr. James A, Negley removed it and erected the then large brick store and kept store there for some years, part of the time in connection with the late J. G. Muntz, Esq. Mr. Adam Troutman, our present successful merchant, had his first schooling , in store life there, part of the time in connection with Mr. Muntz. Mr. Boos, present owner, has just recently much enlarged and improved it and it is now one of the largest and finest in town. The late Mr. John Pollock McQuistion kept store there for a number of years after 1864 when he sold it to Mr. John Berg who sold to Mr. Boos last summer.

## MECHLING SQUARE

North of last described square and up the street, same side to Diamond was the older Jacob Mechling, Esq. square. This is now compactly built up, both on Main Street and Diamond front. The front on the Main Street side of this square was purchased about 20 years ago [1871] by Walter L. Graham, Esq. from Mrs. Judge Buffington of Kittanning, Pa., a daughter of Mr. Mechling, who inherited it by will of her father. Mr. Graham soon after his purchase erected the large building on the corner until recently known as the Brady House, Mr. Owen Brady having become owner, and now owned, much improved, and occupied by the Butler County National Bank. Mr. Graham sold lots from there down to Moses Sullivan, Esq. and others, where now stand the law offices of Levi McQuistion, Esq., A. T. Black, Esq., (built by the late Harrison Black, Esq., his brother), and the building now owned by Mrs. Sloan, built by Mr. Sullivan and now used in part as a billiard room.

Next to that was the lot and law office built by the late General John N. Purviance, which has recently changed owners several times and is now, or but recently occupied as a drug-store by Mr. W. W. Dunlap. Then down and adjoining was a lot sold to Mr. James Vogeley, now the property of the heirs of the late Mr. Wuller. From there to the corner is the present property of Mr. Chris Stock, with his tin shop and store on corner this corner building however was erected by the late Leonard Wise, Jr., to whom Mr. Graham sold that lot, and who had a tin shop there until deceased recently. James Vogeley kept a bakery and grocery in his part, where the present Mr. R. A. White keeps the same and helps to supply our people with fresh bread, cakes and pies, besides having a neat confectionery store there. When Mr. Graham bought this front lot where was not a single building on it, except what became and is now the *Butler Citizen* office. The writer of this bought of him the balance of the lot fronting on the Diamond and adjoining the Brady or present bank building to which the *Citizen* office was removed in the spring of 1872, from the Ritter & Ralston store building opposite the Lowry House, where in an upper story, he had published it during the three years previous. Next to *Citizen* office on Diamond is the law office of Col. John Thompson & Son; and next to it is that of R.P. Scott, Esq., and next to it that of Hon. Charles McCandless in whose building Newton Black, Esq., and Frank Kohler, Esq., also have their law offices. On the ground upon which these three offices now stand was the old Mechling Hotel, celebrated as a hostelry for many of the early years of Butler. The house in which Col. Thompson & Son have their office was a part of the old hotel.

Where the offices of Messrs. Scott and McCandless stand was the principal part of the old hotel, log framed and which was torn away years ago to give place to the present buildings. Mr. Mechling, Sr. himself lived in a small neat frame house which stood where the fine residence of John Q. A. Kennedy, Esq. now stands. He was much of the old fashioned gentleman in his manner, was always neatly dressed, very honest and careful in business, was an early member of the legislature from this county and one of its first prothonotaries. His son late, Jacob Mechling Jr. followed him in keeping the old hotel and during his time added to it the present *Citizen* office building. He was also a prothonotary of the county elected in 1842. Our present Mr. Thomas Mechling is the youngest son of the elder and is we believe, his only child now living. Mrs. Mechling was a favorite with the small boys of more than 50 years ago, from a kind habit she had of giving them taffy on Christmas days — real taffy, which she made on every Christmas morning for their especial enjoyment.

(9 January 1891)                                    J. H. N.

## BREDIN SQUARE

Across Main Street from the Mechling is the square of the late Hon. John Bredin, which retains the same name as fifty years ago, and is, we believe, the only square in the town that does so, or that remains in the possession of children or descendants of the original owner. Two of its lots are now owned by two of the daughters of the late Judge Bredin, Mrs. Nancy Cummings and Mrs. Elvira Lyon, and the other one by a grand-daughter, Mrs. Clarence Walker. A small part of Mrs. Lyon's lot being the front one on Main Street was however owned until but recently by her brother, Joseph B. Bredin, Esq., who sold same to Mr. H. W. Koonce of Mercer County, who is about to erect there a fine store house. She has also recently sold some parts of the lot. Mrs. Cummings and Mrs. Lyon live in the house on the corner of this lot, erected by their father and lived in by him during his lifetime. Parts of it since his death, May 1851, have also been occupied for law and other offices.

The first bank of any kind in Butler was located in the room now used as an office by James F. Brittain, Esq. and perhaps others. This bank was established about 1858, by former Judge James Bredin, oldest son of the late Judge John Bredin, and with whom was connected perhaps in its origin, the late James Campbell. Mr. Isaac Cummings, deceased, was its cashier. The house used as an office by the late Judge Bredin was a frame one, attached on south end of his dwelling, in which he had his library and law books, and in which the writer studied when reading law with him. This building has long since disappeared. On the middle lot of Mrs. Cummings, facing on Diamond Park, now vacant is where once stood one of the very early public houses of the town known as the Funk Hotel being kept by a Mr. Adam Funk. In this hotel or house it is said some of the early courts of the county were held. It was a large log building and was torn away near fifty years ago. A low frame store house also stood on this lot, on the west side of Funk House which was also used as a dwelling, among those living there, remembered by the writer was a widow Miller, mother of the present Hon. George W. Miller of Washington, Pa., who but recently was United States Marshal for the western district of Pennsylvania. On the remaining east lot is the fine residence and office of Clarence Walker Esq., the main house of which was built by Hon. E. McJunkin in the fall of 1851. He sold same shortly after to Hon. James Bredin, who lived there until he sold to Mr. William Stoughton, who lived there until again purchased by Mr. McJunkin, and now owned and resided in by Mr. Walker.

The late John Bredin became judge of our courts in 1831, appointed, as the judges then were, by the governor of the state. He remained judge until his death, which happened, as we state, in May 1851, suddenly and during a week in which he was holding a court here. His district was Beaver, Mercer and Butler Counties. When Lawrence County was erected out of Mercer and Beaver Counties, 1850, it was attached to or rather remained in his district. The writer accompanied him in a sleigh and with a deep snow on the ground to the first court he held at New Castle. All the incidents to the opening of that first court were very plain in style and are remembered with much pleasure. Judge Bredin, however, if not good sleighing, always traveled his circuit on horse back. This was his favorite mode of traveling. The lawyers of that day also generally went to the courts of neighboring counties on horse back. Buggies were but little in use then.

Judge Bredin used a large pair of saddle bags on his journeys, in which he carried all the legal papers, decisions, etc., necessary for him to take. He was an able lawyer and laborious judge performing an immense amount of work while acting as such. Although but self-educated, he was a man of much literary taste and culture. His library contained books upon most all subjects of science and literature. He was also very fond of agricultural pursuits and when not holding courts he engaged in various improvements on his lands. One of his many enterprises was the successful turning of the channel of the creek below town, cutting off and shortening its course near half a mile, and forming now, as can be yet seen, what is called the Vogeley island. He also was a prominent member with the late Mr. Henry Muntz of Zelienople, the late Mr. George Miller of this place, and others in the formation of a Bible society, for the spread of the Bible among the then poor of this county. In political affairs he was at all times quite active, attending among other things the national conventions of his party, then generally held at Baltimore for the nomination of its candidates for president.

Personally, he was affable, easy of access, generous, a true friend and a charitable man. He had more of the elements of a really great man than any of the public men of Butler of his day. The Judges had just been made elective before his death and had he lived a month or so longer his friends expected to see him nominated as one of the first judges of the supreme court of the state, for which, he was a candidate and for which they were urging him. He was followed as judge here by Judge Agnew, yet living, and he in turn by Judge McGuffin, deceased, and he by Judge McJunkin and James Bredin, and now by our present ones, Judges Hazen and McMichael.

## THE GILMORE SQUARES

Continuing around the Diamond from the Bredin square brings us to one of the old time Gilmore squares, so called from the late Hon. John Gilmore, who, fifty years ago, owned both of the squares on the east end of the Diamond. The brick house now owned by Mrs. Catharine Graham and now resided in by her and her sister, Mrs. Elizabeth Porterfield, was erected by Mr. Gilmore near 50 years ago. Mrs. Graham is the widow of the late John Graham, Esq., a good man and a very distinguished member of the Butler Bar, whose early death was a cause of great sorrow and regret to all our then citizens, as well as a great loss to our bar. He had purchased and lived in this house and died in same in 1860. Mrs. Porterfield's first husband was Mr. Cornelius Coll, a man highly respected and esteemed by all who knew his many noble traits of character. Few men of the town were more accurate scholars than was Neal Coll, as he was familiarly called, and his good judgment of men and things was often sought for. He was a most excellent printer, and was a clerk in the prothonotary's office for several years. He died Nov. 13, 1853, much lamented by many personal friends.

Where the above Mrs. Graham house stands formerly stood a popular blacksmith's shop carried on by the late Colonel Manasseas Gillespie and the late Mr. Sam'l Paulhemas of Centre Twp. Mr. Paulhemas became known as "Vulcan" from a notable political event that occurred in the town in 1838. It was during the election for a governor that year. One party, the Whigs, had run-up a flag at the Mechling, now bank corner on the street, in honor of their cause and candidate, Joseph Ritner for governor. This displeased the Democrats, whose candidate was David R. Porter, to such an extent that they determined to tear down the flag. In this movement Mr. Paulhemas, who was a very ardent Democrat , took a leading part, appearing upon the ground, hammer in hand and apron on, to assist in the great work of bringing down the Whig flag. There was much party spirit and excitement in town at the time and the late Parker C. Purviance, Esq., a noted humorist of those days, wrote and published a comedy on the subject, entitled "The Flag; A Comedy in 5 Acts." In this comedy he represented Mr. Paulhemas in the character of "Vulcan" which name adhered to him for a long time. Other characters in the comedy were an ex-sheriff of the county, Mr. John Welsh, who was described as "Johnny Trot." The late James G. Campbell, Esq. was called "Trip" and a Mr. David Wilson who was a rather talkative man, was characterized as "Davy Blatherskite." Other leading citizens of the town were characters in this comedy of Mr. Purviance and it had a great sale and was in great demand at the time. Col. Gillespie removed to Donegal Twp., where he died some years ago.

### Market Houses

The revival of activities of the curb market on the lot at the rear of the municipal building calls to mind the spasmodic efforts made in decades past to establish a market house in the city. For forty years at least there has been talk about a market house, curb markets and the like.

Several times proposals have been before the city council and the boards of commerce and boards of trade to organize a company for the purpose of building a market house, but the matter mever got any farther than resolutions on paper and some fine speeches by promoters.

Butler really had a market in use at one time. How it was started, where the building was located and what eventually became of it is shrouded in mystery and beyond the recollections of the oldest inhabitants.

Just the same, Butler had a market house. There are documentary records to prove it. In April 1818, soon after the organization of the borough, the town council ordered "repairs on the market house, such as boarding in below the benches."

How long the market house had existed before this date does not appear on the records. The same year the borough council passed an ordinance establishing certain market days and rules for preventing sheep and swine from running on the streets and alleys, and persons from galloping horses on the streets.

The following year, 1819, the borough council included the market house in its budget and made a tax levy of four mills on the dollar, enough to meet the expenses of erecting a pound or pen for pigs on William Beatty's lot, back of the present Troutman & Sons store, and a place for sheep in Eli Skeer's stable. A place for the drunk and disorderly human element of the town isn't mentioned.

In 1821 the borough council at its meeting in September, issued orders to sell the market house. An attempt to rescind this order was made at the October meeting but failed.

The probability is that the market house stood somewhere about the public square. It was used for years and finally abandoned. *Butler Eagle*, June 24, 1925, James A. McKee

Across the street, on Diamond, east end, was the other John Gilmore square upon which now is the Riddle offices, owned by W.H.H. Riddle, Esq. This building was erected by the late Hon. Samuel A. Gilmore, son of John, who lived there, and with his brother, late Hon. Alfred Gilmore, occupied the old office there as their law office. The old gentleman himself lived, before he removed to the Mrs. Graham house, in a log-framed house that stood where the

present house of the late Capt. Jacob Ziegler now stands. Capt. Ziegler, "Uncle Jake" bought and built there, tearing away the old one. Hon. John Gilmore for many years was one of the prominent men of Butler. He was a member of the state legislature, a state treasurer and a member of congress, about 1830. He was a large, very fine looking man, and much respected as a gentleman in every way. He died between the fifties and sixties. His son Alfred also became a member of congress. elected in 1848 and again in 1850. Samuel A. Gilmore was a leading member of the bar, with a large practice for many years. In 1846 he was appointed president judge for the district of Fayette, Washington, and Greene Counties and removed to Uniontown, Fayette Co., Pa., where he lived until his decease, about ten years ago. Alfred died in Scranton, Pa., last summer. (16 January 1891)
J. H. N.

ED. CITIZEN.— The next square, around the Diamond from the last described Gilmore one, may be termed the Kelley-Bredin-Dougal one of fifty years ago. The late Patrick Kelley, Sr., lived upon the lot

**Diamond Hay Scales**

Who among the old residents of the town can recall when the public hay scales adorned the public square in front of the court house? Sam Sykes was the master of the scales and weighed the hay, coal, cattle and anything else heavy that farmers wanted weighed for more than a score of years. The scales stood where the soldiers monument now stands.

Then there was a time when the county commissioners spent real money building an iron fence around the park to keep the cows, goats, and pigs owned by the villagers from overrunning the place. The fence was abandoned after the city council passed an ordinance banishing pig pens from the back alleys and forbidding cows to run at large on the streets.

It is within the memory of the present generation that the park was rescued from its jungle-like appearance, cleared of rubbish and the soldier's monument erected. The Butler County Monument Association was organized in 1902 for the purpose of erecting a monument to the memory of the soldiers and sailors of the Civil War. G. D. Swain of Harmony was chairman, T. J. McCandless of Butler, secretary, and Charles Duffy of Butler, treasurer. Committees were organized in every district in the county to raise funds.

The board of directors had its own troubles. A controversy arose over the location of the monument. Some suggested the old public cemetery on the site of the present Junior high school building. Others wanted it on the east end of the park. A majority favored the present location.

The monument was completed and dedicated July 4, at a cost of $3,500. The address turning it over to the county was made by G. D. Swain and the acceptance address was made by Capt. George W. Feeger. *Butler Eagle*, 6-3-1925, James A. McKee

next to Gilmore, an alley dividing. He kept there perhaps the most frequented and popular hotel of the town, 50 years ago. His large patronage came mainly from the fact that his hotel was where it was said pure Irish whiskey could be got. The sign in front of his house, on Diamond, could be plainly seen from all around. It had on it the picture of a large buck deer with spreading antlers. Hence "The Sign of the Buck" became the common name of his hotel, and invitations to go down to " The Sign of the Buck" were very frequent in those days.

Many were the meetings held there of various kinds, some of them democratic in object, and one of which in particular, in the beginning of 1844 was a very lively one in its nature. A regular row took place, during which the chairman of the meeting made his escape through a back window of the room in which the meeting was being held. And strange to say too the dispute among them was on the tariff question. The militia companies when on review-- "muster days"—were very partial to the Buck Hotel. One company, on a certain occasion, breaking ranks when drilling on the Diamond and making for "The Buck" pell-mell, and despite all the efforts of its officers to restrain them. Part of the old Buck yet stands in which George R. White, Esq. has his present law office. The other part was torn down a few years ago and a fine brick erected where it stood by the late Mrs. Margaret Mitchell. In this Williams & Mitchell, attorneys, have their law office. This frame on the alley corner, we believe was erected by the late George W. Smith, Esq. and Lewis Z. Mitchell, Esq., in which they had their law office, 40 years ago. It was subsequently the *Eagle* printing office, and is now the law office of Thomas Robinson Esq.

The elder Patrick Kelley, keeper of "The Buck" was a fine old Irish gentleman, one of the olden kind. He was very polite and attentive to his customers, was always neatly dressed and always a gentleman. He was father to Patrick Kelley, Jr., late deceased, who lived and kept hotel for many years on the corner where now stands the large new Reiber building, and who also was much of a gentleman and an active and useful citizen of the town in his day serving as a justice of the peace for some years. His personal friends called him "Alderman Kelley." He was father to our present John K. Kelley. His widow is still living there.

The late Maurice Bredin, Esq. owned and lived upon the middle lot of this square. The large brick he lived in is now "The Diamond Hotel" at present owned and kept as a public house by Mr. James Sellers, who recently enlarged and improved it. Squire Bredin as he was called kept a store in this house 50 years and more ago. He was one of the earliest merchants of the place, and it is said brought his goods over the mountains on horse back and pack saddle. Like other of the first comers Maurice Bredin was a large man in person, very sociable, and very fond of the discussion of public questions. He was an especial favorite with the young men of the town, who frequently invited him to their debating societies in which he always took part. The young men of that day were not only encouraged by his presence with them but also by the frequent declaration to them, to-wit: that Butler had more home talent within it than most any other place. He had a remarkable power over figures, or the faculty to quickly and accurately cast up almost any sum or numbers. He was elected a commissioner of the county about 1842 and held other positions of trust in his day. He died in 1852. The late James M. Bredin, Esq. of Franklin, Venango County, was his oldest son and is well and favorably remembered by many of our citizens. Benjamin W. Bredin, Esq., his youngest son is now also living in Franklin, Pa., and is one of its most enterprising and successful business men, being engaged there in the banking and other business.

The other lot of this square is one of the two celebrated Dougal ones which, as they extend down Main Street, we will skip over for the present and continue on around the Diamond.

## SULLIVAN-LINN LOTS

The lot on the northwest side of Diamond and next to that of Mr. Dougal's west lot, we will call the Linn lot, as Dr. George Linn was the first person we recollect of living there. The house upon it was recently the residence of the late Mrs. Elanor Cunningham, and is now in the entire possession of Dr. Samuel Graham and family for residence and office. Dr. George Linn erected the main part of this house. Dr. Graham, we believe, erected the present office part. Dr. George Linn was one of the best and most highly esteemed physicians Butler ever had. He had a good practice, was a good man, and his death in 1833, was greatly regretted. He was the uncle to our present Dr. H. C. Linn and therefore grand uncle to our present Gib. Linn Esq.

The next lot, now owned and resided upon by our fellow citizen, Lewis Z. Mitchell, Esq., is what was known as the Sullivan lot. The late John Sullivan, Esq. erected the house in which Mr. Mitchell now resides and has his office. It is said to be the first brick house built in Butler and the best one at the time. Mr. Sullivan sold the property to the late John Welsh, an ex-sheriff of the county and he to the late George W. Smith, Esq., and he to Mr. Mitchell when Mr. Smith and family removed to Kansas in 1855. Mr. Sullivan owned other lots and erected other buildings in the town in his day and was one of the active promoters of its early prosperity. He was public spirited in all that concerned its welfare and as a man was open in the expression of his opinion and pronounced in all his views. He served a term as prothonotary of the county from 1836 to 1839, and held various other posts of trust; Mr. Sullivan died in 1854. He was the father of our present Col. John M. Sullivan, who is his only son. Mr. Welsh was a tailor by trade and a very active man in the affairs of the town. Mr. Smith was a prominent lawyer, particularly in criminal cases, generally defending criminals among them the Mohawk case with Mr. Mitchell, his partner.

## THE WALTER LOWRIE SQUARES

The two squares in the rear of the court house, west end of Diamond, were known as the Walter Lowrie squares. The lot where the jail now stands was owned by him but is now, with the one adjoining west, the property of the county. Upon this, where jail now is on corner, was a frame house built by Mr. Lowrie and painted a yellowish color and from a paint said to have been made from some clay or earth obtained in those days along the creek. Several of the first frame houses of the town received their first ornamental coloring from a paint made from this material found along the Connoquenessing. In this house the late Mr. W. W. Brandon, uncle to our present W.D. Brandon, Esq., had a store 50 years or more ago. The late Mr. Clark McPherrin also had his first store there, probably for a time with a Mr. Jonathan Plummer. Mr. McPherrin afterwards removed his store to the east Dougal lot. Both he and Mr. Brandon were men of much moral worth and highly respected as citizens. Both are long since deceased and are now remembered but by few living. Henry Krug, Sr., and the late Mr. Samuel S. Wilson, father of present County Treasurer James S. Wilson, also once lived in this house.

The late Col. Francis McBride lived there at one time, and he and our present L.Z. Mitchell, Esq. had their law office there, as McBride & Mitchell, attorneys. Col. McBride had been sheriff of the county, about 1830, and afterwards studied law and was admitted to the bar. He was a portly man, gentlemanly in his manners and generous in his nature, and a particular friend and favorite with the young men of the town in his day. Many others lived or had their offices in this old house among them the writer of this, who in the summer of 1850 had his law office in corner room of same.

The old jail stood in the rear or west of the present one. It was a stone building perhaps 45 by 27 feet and two storied. In some of its windows were great iron bars, crossed from and through which prisoners in those days could often be seen looking out upon the street. Men were imprisoned for debt in those days and up to the year 1842 when the law abolishing imprisonment for debt in this state was passed. We well recollect seeing men standing behind these bars who were put in jail because they could not pay their debts, under a law that we now look back upon in wonder, and which if now in existence, no jail could possibly be made large enough to hold all that would be liable to be put there for that cause.

But the most notable event in connection with the old jail was that growing out of an attempt to rescue the Indian Mohawk from its walls and to deal summary punishment upon him. This was in the summer of 1843, and shortly after Mohawk had been imprisoned. A fear prevailed in the upper part of the county among the friends and neighbors of Mr. Wigton, whose wife and family had been most cruelly murdered by Mohawk, that the jail was insecure and that in some way he might escape punishment. This fear was increased by various reports to that effect, and resulted in a combined and determined effort to prevent any such escape. The people up there assembled , duly armed and organized, and were marching to Butler, under the command of the late Col. Samuel London, of now Clay Twp. The sheriff, the late James G. Campbell, had of course his duty to perform under the law and to prevent such a rescue of a prisoner. He summoned every man to his aid, called out the posse comitatus, the people, to assist him in defense of the jail, appointed a press body, consisting of the late John Graham, Esq., Lewis Z. Mitchell, Esq., and others, whose duty it was to impress and force all into service. One very funny incident occurred in this duty. A young Irishman, lately arrived, was in the crowd in front of the jail, looking on the scene in wonder. He was ordered to take up arms for service, but he objected and instead of doing so broke away and ran. Nearly the whole crowd ran to catch him, around the courthouse and down South Main Street to what is now the Eitenmiller Hotel, where a priest was then staying and to whom he rushed in and claimed the protection of. He made good his escape, by safely reaching the garret of the house, but frightened almost to death. The two military companies of the town had been ordered out by the sheriff for duty, one, the German Guards under Capt. Doerr, promptly responded for service, the other, the late DeKalb Grays, under Capt. Ziegler, did not respond with the same alacrity. The whole town was in great excitement. At every door and window of the jail, and all around on its walls and at every approach to it men were stationed, with guns in hand, and ordered to defend the jail at any extremity. But this extremity fortunately, did not come. The rescuing party, however, had reached as near town as the then Sleppy Hotel, now the Berg farm, a mile up the Mercer road. Here they were met by some of the then principal citizens of the town. Judge Bredin, Mr. Beatty, Samuel A. Gilmore and others, speeches were made to them and assurances given that Mohawk should be more safely secured, and be tried and punished, by due process of law. Mohawk had been confined in a basement room of the jail, a very dungeon looking place called the murderers cell, in the middle of the floor of which was a huge iron ring, to which by strong chains attached to his feet. He was secured until tried and executed in the early part of 1844. Where he was buried, then in the woods, is now fast becoming a part of our growing town, lots being recently laid out and sold and houses built in that vicinity.

## OTHER LOWRIE SQUARE

Across from jail square is the other one belonging to the late Hon. Walter Lowrie, now owned and lived upon by Mrs. S. C. Sullivan, widow of the late Hon. Charles C. Sullivan. Mr. Lowrie erected about 1828, the large dwelling now resided in by Mrs. Sullivan. He was one of Butler's principal old time citizens and if not its greatest man he certainly achieved more fame and rose to a higher distinction than any of her other former public men. He came here, a poor young man from what is now Allegheny Twp., and became a merchant clerk in stores and clerk to the county commissioners. He was finally elected to the state senate from this then district, and before the close of his term there he was chosen by the legislature a United States Senator to represent this state in congress. It is recorded that when the balloting began he received but four votes from fellow members who knew his worth and who continued to vote for him, day after day and ballot after ballot, until finally he was elected, the only United States Senator Butler County ever had. How different was that way of choosing a U.S. Senator from the present caucus system, into which members now go and thereby smother the choice of their constituency, their own choice as well as their own convictions of right and duty to their constituents. After serving his term in the U.S. Senate Mr. Lowrie was chosen its clerk, and after serving as such for some years he was chosen chief secretary of the board of foreign missions of the Presbyterian Church of America, when he removed to New York City and which post he held to the time of his death in 1868. He is succeeded to that office by one of his sons, Rev. John C. Lowrie. Another son, Walter, a minister and missionary, was killed by pirates in the China sea. Another, Reuben, also a missionary, perished in India. Another Matthew B. Lowrie, Esq., was a member of our bar and died in Cuba, where he had gone for his health. Another, Jonathan Roberts Lowrie, Esq., died recently in Huntingdon County, Pa.

The religious character of Mr. Lowrie may be seen from the calling of three of his above sons. He was a deeply religious man, and one of our very few public men who ever carried into his public life the morals and principles of his private home life. He was in a word a Christian statesman. At all times he was modest and unassuming in all the relations of both his public and private life. In person be was a rather tall man, being over six feet in height and in complexion he was quite dark.

The late Charles C. Sullivan, Esq., father of present Charles A. and Moses Sullivan, Esquires, became the owner of the square and mansion, about 1840 and died there in the early part of 1860. The law office attached, built by Mr. Sullivan, is now occupied in part by Walter L. Graham, Esq., so named after Mr. Lowrie.

Jan'y 20, 1891                    J. H. N.

## DOUGAL LOTS

ED. CITIZEN;—The two lots of the late Mr. David Dougal are so well known to even our present citizens as to be easily located. The rapid change that has come over them within the past few years is a subject of general remark. When Mr. Dougal died but a little over nine years ago they were covered with small frame buildings, generally called "shanties." Now they are covered with some of the largest and finest brick buildings in our town. Mr. Dougal bought them at the original sale of lots in Butler, 1803 and held on to them until his death on Nov. 8, 1881. No change of ownership in them took place in all this time, which, perhaps cannot be said of any other of the original lots of Butler. Mr. Dougal in this respect may be said to have been the nearest—or latest— connecting link between the present and the original town. Certainly no one survives him in this respect. He was the last of the very early and first citizens.

The new brick Schenk block stands upon the Diamond end of one of one of these lots. This was lot No. 1 in the original plan of lots and is said to have been bid in by Mr. Dougal at the sum of $100. Now it is probable that $20,000 could be got for it without a building on it, and with its present half-dozen or more new large brick's, its aggregate value now would exceed $50,000. The first building we recollect of seeing where the Schenck one now stands was a low frame, on the corner, and is thought to have been erected by the late John and Peter Duffy as their first store-house in Butler. And here we might remark that the homes upon Mr. Dougal's lots were generally built by others and not by him as is very generally supposed. They were built by persons to whom he gave ground leases and who no doubt at the time were glad to get the privilege to build under a lease. Mr. Dougal built but little himself. This small frame on the corner in time gave way to a larger log-frame, erected for a public house and used as such for a number of years and by different parties, among them Michael Spohn and a man named Robison. Our present Mr. William Richey kept a restaurant and lived there for some years. It was also often used by attorneys for law offices. The late Edward M. Bredin,Esq. had his office there at one time; also the late John Graham, Esq. and others. Mr. Pringle was there for a while, and the last store there we believe was that of Mr. Elias Kirk. Before one of its tenants of about 40 years ago had left it he had papered one of its rough-boarded rooms with common wall paper and to illustrate Mr. Dougal's idea of improvements, he refused to let it be used for a postoffice saying, with some indignation, to a newly appointed postmaster, who applied to him to rent it, "Sir, do you think I am a fool to let that fine room be destroyed by a postoffice." That settled it, and the new postmaster, the late Mr. Daniel Coll, had to look elsewhere for an office.

Next to this last was a small frame and next to that and where our present postoffice now stands, Dr. Byers building was another small frame, erected by the late Mr. Clark McPherrin already referred to for his store room, more than 50 years ago. Mr. McPherrin had lost both of his legs, at the knees, and notwithstanding this made him very short in stature. He moved about without crutches of any kind and with much rapidity. He was an active business man and prominent in all good works. Several followed him in this house he built, among the first being the late Jacob Ziegler and James McGlaughlin with the *Democratic Herald*, where that paper, in 1842, was first established and published. Mr. McGlaughlin having been elected prothonotary of the county in 1845, the *Herald* was continued there by a company for two or three years, headed by the late Samuel G. Purvis, Esq., father of the present Purvis men. After this Mr. McGlaughlin again, in connection with the late Mr. Cornelius Coll, published the *Herald* there for a time. This Clark McPherrin building was also used as the postoffice at one time, and had for its tenants various other persons for various other purposes, until Dr. Byers became owner of the ground and erected his fine building there. Where Mr. Brandon's law office now is, was the lower part of Dr. Byers' building, stood a queerly constructed house, lived among others, for some years by the late Thaddeus Niggle, father of the present Niggle men, who carried on there a bakery and candy store. This house, like some others on Mr. Dougal's lots, had but one chimney in it, built in the center of the house, with a fire place on every side to accommodate all its rooms.

Where the *Eagle* printing office now stands a frame once stood, used often as a dwelling, tailor shop, and other purposes. Where William A. Forquer, Esq., has now his new brick residence and office stood a frame, in which Mr. Dougal stayed and had his office for many years previous to his going across the street to the one he afterwards occupied. In this house Mr. Dougal would often receive his Pittsburg friends, the late Judges William McCandless and William B. McClure, son-in-law of Mrs. Collins, for whose land in this county Mr. Dougal was the agent. They came nearly ever summer, notifying Mr. Dougal in advance of their coming and who on these occasions would spruce up a little in his dress in order to properly receive them. They had unlimited confidence in and admiration for Mr. Dougal and liked to enjoy his company at all times possible.

## OTHER LOT

Across the street was the other Dougal lot, on which perhaps were more of the so-called shanties than the other, until a disastrous fire, in 1864, burned down all the lower end and to the Vogely alley. This lot was No. 24 in the plan of original lots. On its Diamond end where now stands the new and fine brick block of the Messrs. Huselton and Anderson, was the frame store erected about 1834 by the late William S. and Henry N. Boyd. This was Mr. William S. Boyd's first venture in Butler. With his brother Henry until the latter died, he kept there a grocery and restaurant. He prospered rapidly in business and finally bought and removed his store down to corner of Main and Jefferson Streets, building there about 1850, the brick now a part of the George Reiber building. Mr. Boyd was a very enterprising man and did much for Butler. He spent his latter years in laying out, 1872, and improving present Springdale, a part of his then farm, and all who knew him will feel regret that he did not live to witness the great growth and present proportions of that part of our present town that he took so much interest in advancing. He died in 1884. Numerous persons occupied afterwards, the house he built on the Dougal corner for a store and other purposes, the late Mr. Samuel Sykes and family being among the last there. On the Diamond and where now is the rear end of the Huselton building stood a small tailor shop that we think nearly every tailor in or about town had as his shop at one time. The late Andrew Carnes, ex-sheriff, elected in 1848, had his tailor shop there. Before this Sheriff Carnes was also engaged in the mercantile business in the Boyd store, and probably in connection with Mr. Boyd for a time. The late James Glenn, Esq. also had his tailor shop there, about 1852, which he carried on in connection with the office of justice of the peace which he then held. Mr. Glenn was the father of the present Glenn citizens.

On Main Street and where now is the fine and just new brick of Mr. J. F. Shaffer, stood the celebrated little shanty used so long as a "squires office." Within our recollection the late Samuel G. Purvis, Esq. had his justice's office there, commencing with his first election, 1845 and re-elected in 1850, 1855, 1860, and 1865. He must have had his office here about 20 years, doing a great deal of business. He resigned the office some years before he died in 1879. The late J. G. Muntz, Esq. also had his justice's ofice there, being first elected in 1871 and then again 1876. He also did a large business as justice in his office

Copyright 1905 by the Rotograph Co.
A 5883 Main Street, Butler, Pa.

and was regarded by all as a very correct and efficient magistrate. Previous to this, however, the present William S. Ziegler, Esq., and others may have had their offices there. Mr. Muntz died April 12, 1880. He was followed by the present Lewis F. Walker, Esq. had his justice's office there until he removed it to the Brady building and from there to present Forquer one.

Next to this and where present I. J. McCandless' fine brick now stands was the small, narrow frame in which Mr. Dougal lived from the time he crossed over the street, already spoken of. Here Mr. Dougal had his office and lodged for about 30 years, and until he went out to his farm in Summit Twp., 1879 or 1880, and where he died Nov. 8, 1881. Much that has been said and written about this office of Mr. Dougal and his habits there, we think does him great injustice. It was not the most cleanly place and might have been called somewhat dirty, or dusty rather, at times, but to say that anything like bad odors came from it, we think, is not correct. And Mr. Dougal while careless and indifferent as to his dress, was by no means a dirty man in his habits. His furniture in his room was very scant, and his books, maps and papers, although very valuable were in his late days often laying around rather loose and dusty. But his bed was the only real novelty. For some reason he discarded the common bedstead and in place thereof made one for himself. This consisted, at head and foot of some old chairs or boxes, stretching from which were poles or what looked like common fence rails. Upon these he had two large feather beds, between which he slept. If not the most cleanly looking at all times, they doubtless were very comfortable. Why he used such a bed is a question, but, we think, the real solution of it is that he wanted a solid, unyielding bottom to his bed. It is well known that the old bed cords—ropes—would sink in time, or often get loose, and Mr. Dougal, may be, did not fancy being put in a hole, in that way. Of modern springs and mattresses he probably had not heard. His manner of sleeping may also have been acquired from early habits of life and as a surveyor among the early settlers, in the log cabins of that day. Mr. Dougal always took his meals or boarded out among his many tenants, many of them in that way paying their rent.

The next, and where the New York Bazaar building now stands, was a queerly constructed low brick, in which Mr. James A. Shanor had his shoe and candy shop for quite a time. It was shed-like in shape and built by Mr. Dougal from the brick gathered up and remaining from the great fire, 1864, that burnt down all his buildings from there down to Vogley alley. The buildings burned by that fire stood where the Bazaar, Mrs. Gilkey and the present Ketterer fine buildings now stand. They were frame and occupied for offices, shops, etc. One, the lower one, was where the *Repository* newspaper was last published by the late David Shannon, John Little and Joseph McMurtrie. The *Repository* ceased its existence there and with them about 1840. The late William B. Lemmon, Esq. had the postoffice there when he was postmaster, 1848. The late Mr. George Miller, father of Harvey and brothers, had his cabinet making salesroom there about the time it was burnt down. No buildings were erected on this burnt district, except the James Shanor one, until the present ones recently erected by Mr. Ketterer and the late Mrs. Gilkey.

## DAVID DOUGAL

In speaking of Mr. Dougal's lots and the former buildings upon them we occasionally referred to some of his particular traits of character, but as to his general character, his extensive learning and his personal appearance, but little has yet been said. That he was a very eccentric man, a very odd man, all who ever saw him or were in his company well know. But that he was an impure man in mind or body is certainly not correct. True he ignored all modern ways and modes of life and was remarkably independent in thought and action. His style of dress was not of the latest cut or fashion and in this he was peculiar. For instance, he never wore but one suspender to uphold his pantaloons, but this one was so thrown over one shoulder and crossed in such a way as to answer the purpose of a pair. He never wore the common linen shirt, with ironed bosom and so forth, but instead a plain coarse muslin one, opened in front and at collar generally. He never used a necktie of any kind. His shoes were generally untied. His coat and vest were off in the summer. In this condition he would sit before his office in pleasant weather and passers-by who knew him would be sure to stop and converse with him, or to hear him talk. For Mr. Dougal was a philosopher, bearing the same relation to Butler it might be said that Plato bore to Athens in his day. And had Mr. Dougal opened a school as Plato did, in some pleasant garden or academy, he might have gathered around him as many students as did the Athenian philosopher. But Mr. Dougal taught upon the street, always to attentive listeners. His conversational powers were good, his manner of speech deliberate and dignified. His subjects were history, general and local, geography, geology, the winds, the storms, astronomy in general and the North Star in particular. Mr. Dougal was considerable of a star gazer, and often at night might be seen studying the stars. His knowledge of astronomy was extensive and his discourse upon that as well as upon most all sciences was entertaining.

Mr. Dougal was also of an inventive turn of mind. For a long time he endeavored to invent or perfect the so-called "perpetual motion machine," and for this purpose had collected in his office a number of small pieces of pine wood and other material from which he sought to construct a machine with a pendulum, which he tried to make vibrate, after the manner of a clock. But after repeated efforts and long and patient work he had to abandon his ambition to discover a perpetual motion.

Mr. Dougal was also fond of music. He kept a violin, or so-called fiddle, upon which he often amused himself, generally at night. About 1870, he attempted to set to the music of his fiddle any pleasant piece of poetry that came under his eye, and for that purpose on one occasion he brought to the writer of this, some poetry he was practicing upon and desired to have it published.

Mr. Dougal had a great fear of fire. Whether this fear arose from the fire that swept away some of his houses we do not know, but after that he had a great dread of the man or boy who came about his premises lighting matches or cigars. It is told of him that upon one of his visits to Pittsburgh, he heard by night the fire bells of the city ringing and this so alarmed him that he arose from his bed, hastily dressed himself and started for his home here on foot in the darkness of the night. While Mr. Dougal had other peculiar traits, yet he was in its early days a very useful citizen to Butler, doing most of the early surveying, buying and selling many of its lots, and always selling on easy terms to all.

In person Mr. Dougal was tall and erect, taller perhaps than any of the large men coming here with him, but not so heavy or strong as some of them. He walked erect and straight and when he moved about he moved like a monarch, always grave and serious and dignified in bearing. His complexion was rather fair, and in his youth the color of his hair must also have been light or brown. His eyes were hazel. His teeth remained with him and good to the end, a remarkable thing for a man of so great an age. As stated, he died November 8, 1881. Upon a photograph before us of him taken August 26, 1873, is written, from information derived from himself, that he was born September 23, 1778. This would make his age at death 103 years, 1 month and 15 days. This photograph of him was made through Judge Wilson McCandless on his last visit to this place, and in it Mr. Dougal is represented in a sitting position and Judge McCandless standing by his side, looking down upon him with great regard. As stated, about a year before his death he went out to a farm he had east of Butler 2 or 3 miles, and lived with his German tenants upon it until he died. In his will he gave this farm to the people who last cared for him. He was buried in the German Lutheran Church grave yard there [*Gruenwald Cemetery*], and a monument marks the place where he was laid. Christian ministers visited him in his last days and we are told he died in the full faith of the Christian religion.

## DEWOLFE-POTTS SQUARE

In taking up this square next after last Dougal lot spoken of, we are following the original plan of lots of Butler, which crossed the street at No. 24 and made the old DeWolfe lot, now Doctor Balph and others, No.25. The late Dr. H. C. DeWolfe we suppose was known to but few of our present citizens. While among the early yet he was not one of the first comers. He was one of the early physicians and came as we understood, from the Yankee State of Rhode Island. He built and owned the brick house of which a part was torn away only last summer, by Dr. J. F. Balph, and upon the site of which Mr. Balph has now his fine new brick drug store and residence. The other part, owned by Dr. Waldron, and in front room of which is now a meat market yet stands and the two parts composed the old DeWolfe residence. The first office of present Savings Bank was in the room now used as a meat market. At the lower end and attached to Dr. DeWolfe's residence was a small brick used as his office. In it were his medicines, and the jars he had there, filled with medicinal liquids of bright colors, exceeded in number any doctor's office in the town then or at the present day. They were nicely arranged in rows around the room and attracted the attention of all passers by. The doctor also had a huge mortar and pestle in which he ground and compounded his medicines, making a noise sometimes that could be heard at some distance on the street. Where this office stood now stands the barber shop of our present prosperous and fashionable barber, Mr. Richard Hughes, Jr.

### Early Butler

One of the men who helped advertise Butler in the days of the town's infancy was Henry M. Brackenridge, son of Judge J. H. Brackenridge of Pittsburgh, who was appointed clerk to William Ayers, the first prothonotary of the Butler County courts in February 1804. The town site had been surveyed and the first sale of lots was held in August, the previous year.

In later years Henry M. Brackenridge became a distinguished lawyer and historian. In his "Recollections of the West," a historical work much quoted, considerable space is given to his first winter spent in the town of Butler and his story of the opening of the first court has been quoted in practically every history of Pennsylvania. He notes his coming from Pittsburgh to Butler in these words:

"On my arrival at Butler there were a few log houses just raised, but not sufficiently completed to be occupied. It was not long until there were two taverns, a store and a blacksmith shop. It was . then a town. The country around was a howling wilderness with the exception of a few scattered settlements as far removed from each other as the kraals in the neighborhood of the Cape of Goodhope.

That was in February 1804. Twenty years later, according to the late Thomas Mechling, a son of Jacob Mechling, born in the town in 1810, deer came down from the hills at night and looked into windows at the back of the old hotel at the corner of Main and Jefferson Streets. Wolves could be heard howling at night in the forests and bears were plentiful.

The early attorneys who came here from Pittsburgh to attend court took delight in telling stories about Butler County and its people, calculated to amuse Pittsburgh audiences, but to have the opposite effect on residents of Butler. Steele Semple and his brother, Cunningham S. Semple, were counted the leaders in this class. Both were good story tellers. Before the advent of the stage coach the judges and attorneys rode on horseback from town to town in the western part of the state attending court.

The Semples enlarged on the leanness of Butler County. They asserted that when a whipoorwill left Allegheny County to fly across Butler County it would provide rations for the trip, and that on account of the shortness of the clover, the bees were obliged to get down on their knees to gather even a scant supply of honey. Later on when Butler's hotels began to serve buckwheat cakes, sausages and honey in unlimited quantities to their guests, these same merrymakers conferred on Butler, the title of "The Buckwheat County," a name continued to the present time.
*Butler Eagle*, 6-5-1925, James A. McKee

Dr. Henry Champion DeWolfe was a prominent man as well as a physician, taking an active part in the affairs of the town, 50 years ago. He was at all times an exceedingly well dressed man, wearing ruffles on his shirt bosom and ruffled cuffs on his wrists. These bosom ruffles were large, showy and waving, when added to white pants and vest, which he usually wore in summer, made him perhaps the most fashionably dressed man in the town. He always rode a fleet horse on which to visit his patients, and took pride in telling of the feats of his horse, on one occasion in particular in which it kept in advance or beat a rain storm to town when he was returning home from a visit to a country-patient. He had a large practice and was much of a gentleman in all respects. He died about 1854. One of his sons, Dr. Tensard R. DeWolfe is also deceased 1858. The other, Mr. Champion DeWolfe, Jr. is yet living. The late William Timblin, Esq., a prominent and able lawyer in his time, was a son-in-law. Mr. Timblin, we believe, lived and had his office in the old DeWolfe house for a time before his death, which happened in 1856. Dr. DeWolfe owned but this one lot of this square, the other two being known as the Potts lots, 50 years ago.

## POTTS LOTS

The lots where now stand the Renno, Frank, Krug and Heineman buildings owned by the late John Potts, Sr., who was one of the early comers to and enterprising citizens of Butler. Where Renno building now is was a small frame built for a postoffice by, we think, the late Mr. David A. Agnew, who became postmaster in 1845. Its gable end was to the street, with a recess or porch in front. After Mr. Agnew's time it was used for various purposes until present buildings were erected. A barber shop stood next to it, occupied for a long time by the late Major Richard Hughes, father of present Richard and Samuel G.

Hughes. This was about where the present Frank Drug Store stands.

Next to this was the well known office of the late Robert Carnahan, Esq., who was a justice of the peace in the town for many years, elected first in 1840 and doing much of the business in that line. His widow, a daughter of Mr. Potts is yet living at the age of 86 and is said to be the oldest citizen living who was born in the then town. Where the Esquire Carnahan office stood now stands the Krug meat shop.

Next to this and where now stands the newly erected and fine brick store house of Mr. Henry C. Heineman, stood the residence of Mr. Potts. It was a log-framed house, only removed last summer, and said to have been one of the very oldest of the old houses of the town. On the corner where is the large Heineman brick stood a frame one of Mr. Potts, used as a storeroom within our recollection. When Daniel Heineman, father of present Henry C. came to this place, 1842, he purchased this corner lot and in 1849 erected the two storied brick, which a few years ago was raised to three stories by Mr. H.C. Heineman. It was first used by them as a restaurant or general refreshment stand. The late Dr. Isaiah McJunkin had his office in part of it between the fifties and sixties. Part is now occupied for mercantile purposes and Mr. H. C. Heineman has his residence in part. The present block of two brick buildings is now one of the largest and finest in the town.

Of the elder John Potts we have but a slight recollection. He died between the thirties and forties. He had been a postmaster of the town and was at one time a member of the legislature. Of his sons, George, John, James and Wilson K. Potts, but one, James is now living, and who resides at present in Johnstown, Pa. He was postmaster of the town at one time. George died a few years ago at Altoona, Pa., to where he had removed and lived. He was a member of the legislature, about the year 1836. John, Jr., who owned or lived upon the farm on top of hill north of town, Mercer road, died some years ago. This farm is same now owned by Mr. Charles Duffy. Wilson K. Potts, the youngest son, died also here about 15 years ago. He at one time owned a part of the Potts lot. He will be remembered by some yet living as a very active man in the political affairs of the town and county.

Jan. 31, 1891                                                    J. H. N.

## GILCHRIST-BEATTY SQUARE

Across Main Street from last described Potts and DeWolfe square is what we will call the Gilchrist-Beatty square of 50 years ago. John Gilchrist owned two of its lots and the late Hon. William Beatty the other one. Mr. Gilchrist built and lived in what is now the greater part of the Vogeley House property. He built all of the large brick from and including the present Morrison bakery and grocery up to and within 25 or 30 feet of the upper corner. On this upper corner stood one of the first and oldest public houses of Butler, a log frame, which was removed, about 1863, by the late William Vogeley, and in its place erected the brick now attached to the main brick erected by Mr. Gilchrist, both together composing what is now the Vogeley House. The old log-frame on corner was said to have been erected by Mrs. Collins in her day here. Our first distinct recollection of it commences with the time the late Michael Zimmerman began keeping hotel there, about 1843. Mr. Zimmerman kept there as a renter until 1848, when he bought and removed to what is now the Williard House, heretofore spoken of. Mr. William Vogeley succeeded him shortly after, probably in 1848, buying from Mr. Gilchrist the old log-frame part and keeping hotel in it alone until he purchased the balance, or larger part. This larger part had been purchased of Mr. Gilchrist, about 1852, by the late William Bell, the contractor and builder of the old courthouse that a few years ago was destroyed by fire. Mr. Vogeley came to own this part through Mr. Bell. Mr. Gilchrist had himself kept public house there and was followed in same, 1846 and 1847, by our present Mr. James Borland. Professor Borland was followed 1848, by the late Mr. William B. Lemmon, who afterwards removed to Beaver Falls and died there some few years ago. Mr. Bell removed from the county and is also deceased. He was the father-in-law of our present L. P. Walker, Esq. A front room of this larger part, on street, and where is now the parlor of present hotel, was used for years as an office, one of its present windows being then a door. Doctors Agnew and McJunkin had their office there, about 1845; and the late General Purviance had his law office there in 1856 for a number of years. Mr. James A. Negley, Mr. M. Schneidenan, and others, had stores in the room where now is the bar-room of the present Vogeley House, between 1860 and 1870. Mr. Vogeley removed the old log hotel part in 1863, down to Washington Street where and in which his widow now resides. The whole of the Hotel Vogeley is now the property of his widow and heirs. He died in Oct. 1873, aged 50 years.

Where present Campbell hardware store is was part of the Gilchrist lots and purchased of him by the Messrs. Campbell about 1838, which is still carried on by members of that family in the name of J. G. & Wm. Campbell, and is now one of the best and largest hardware stores of our town. At first it was a dry goods and general store. Mr. John Gilchrist, after or about the time of disposing of his above property, removed to Brady's Bend, Pa. where he kept a hotel for some time. He returned to Butler and shortly afterwards, about 1853, removed with his family to Wheeling, West Virginia. His son, John Parker Gilchrist, is said to be a very successful business man in Wheeling. Another son, Christy, went to California. No other member of his family is living that is now known of by any of our present people. Mr. Gilchrist was a hatter by trade and for many years had a hatter shop where now stands the Campbell hardware store, spoken of. He was an active and enterprising man in the business of the town in his day here, and its postmaster at one time. He was rather tall in person, had a hesitancy in his speech, and was very apt to defend himself with vigor if occasion required him to do so.

## BEATTY LOT

The old Beatty Hotel building disappeared only last summer. Few now here knew it by such name, or would have called it by that name. Where it stood is the new three-storied store house of Mr. Adam Troutman & Sons, the largest and finest single store house in the town. When the old two-storied brick was built by the late Hon. William Beatty, is beyond our recollection, but we recollect him in it there more than 50 years ago. The Beatty Hotel was in some respects the leading one of Butler for many years. The stages of past days stopped there; prominent visitors to the town generally put up there; it was Democratic headquarters for years and drew to it the leading men of that party in and out of the county. Mr. Beatty kept a good hotel and there would be no disorder about it if he was there. His stern manner would soon quell anything like disturbance about his house. The barroom was where the present Williams' Music-organ room is, and Mr. Beatty would stand at the bar, easily seen from the street and by all passers-by, and there attend to his customers. There were no stained glass windows or doors to hide them nor screens to shelter from view those going in or going out. All was open to view.

And nothing perhaps so illustrates the great change in public sentiment of the drink question, then and now, as this matter of stained glass and screens in bar-rooms. Now at even licensed houses customers are hid from view by the screen and stained windows, as if ashamed to be seen there. And so indeed they are, a large majority of men now would not be seen entering a bar-room.

Mr. Beatty kept this public house until he bought the farm west of town and built the residence there for himself, about 1840. Our present Col. Alexander Lowry bought it in 1850, and came here to keep it in the fall of that year, and continued there for about 15 years. Mr. Jordan Eyth afterwards kept it for a few years when we believe it was sold to and owned by Mr. Mark Schneideman. Mr. Jacob Reiber, cousin to present Jacob, also was there at one time. When finally it ceased as a hotel it was rented out and used for law and other offices, and for dwellings. J. David McJunkin, Esq., George C. Pillow, Esq. and other attorneys had their offices in rooms there within recent years. The corner room was occupied by present Dr. H. C. Linn as a drug store for a number of recent years. Mr. C. W. Coulter had preceded him there with a drug store. Dr. Linn had years before, been engaged in the drug store business here probably at the old Boyd or Dougal corner and until he removed to the village of Sunbury, this county. He returned here some years ago to enter the same business and continued there until Mr. Troutman tore away the old hotel stand. The late Capt. Jacob Ziegler, however, had bought a part of the Beatty lot, or buildings, where he removed the *Herald* printing office to when he purchased that paper in 1867. This part, on front still standing, is where present music store is and is now, we believe, the property of Mr. John S. Campbell.

## HON. WILLIAM BEATTY

As stated above, Mr. Beatty bought the farm and erected the brick residence on the hill side west of town. This was shortly after his retiring from congress, to which he had been elected in the years 1830 and 1838, serving two terms in congress (*House of Representatives*). This was during the administration of President Martin Van Buren and when, as now, there were exciting and important questions before congress. Nothing will illustrate better the character of Mr. Beatty for courage than his declaration in congress when a certain bill was up that created much debate and opposition. When others were timid as to their votes and doubting as to the propriety of the measure, he arose and said that he was not afraid "to take the bull by the horns," and voted accordingly. This expression, while not the most elegant, yet gained him a very wide reputation for courage. He was as unyielding in his views as he was brave and honest in the expression of them. And while for years a leader of his party in this county he never practiced, indeed did not know of any of the tricks of modern politicians. Mr. Beatty's strength with the people came from an inate force of character, and this, added to his honesty of purpose in all things, gave him the great influence he had over his fellow men. He was upright as well as stern, and men went to him because they relied upon and trusted him. He was a man of strong and good common sense and while austere in look and brief in speech he was as kind and tender hearted as a child. No one failed to excite his sympathy when appealing for aid, and this as much as anything else kept him in constant financial trouble. He was public spirited, lending a hand to every enterprise and improvement for the benefit of the town. Personally he was a very fine looking man, a little above ordinary height and well built.

His appearance and manner wherever he went would attract attention and he was generally chosen to preside at meetings and conventions. While rigid in his political views yet men of all parties respected him. Had he been an educated man he would undoubtedly have risen to still greater distinction. Not a son or daughter remains behind him here, and scarce a blood relative in the county that we know of. Wm. McNair, Esq., a prominent lawyer of Oil City, is a grandson as is Mr. John B. McNair, late of this county and C. C. McCarnes, Esq., late of this place is a great-grandson.

Mr. Beatty died in April, 1851, being suddenly seized with sickness on the road when going from town to his farm home spoken of. He was in the 64th year of his age. The late Hon. John Duffy and present Hon. E. McJunkin were his executors. The farm that he had spent so much labor and expense in improving was sold after his death to Capt. James O'Donnell of Pittsburg, a steamboat or river man, who had been raised or had relatives in this county. After Capt. O'Donnell's death his widow married Mr. John Groutt, of Pittsburg, and after his death Mrs. Groutt removed to Butler and lived upon this farm until her death. This farm is now the property of Mr. Charles Duffy. It embraced what is now that growing part of our town called Duffyville, and which by the energy and liberality of Mr. Duffy, has perhaps a hundred houses recently erected upon one of its hills facing the old town.

## COLL-STEWART SQUARE

Crossing Cunningham Street and continuing on down Main on same side we come to what we will call the Coll-Stewart square of fifty years ago. There were, perhaps, other old occupants on it who are as much or more entitled to the old name, but they were on or about the middle of the square, and so far we have been designating the squares by the names of the old owners at the ends of them. The late Daniel Coll lived at the one end of this square and the late Hon. William Stewart, at the other. Mr. Coll was at upper corner. He was a merchant and kept a store in a frame where present Berg brick is now occupied by Messers. Graham and Hafele as a store. The old frame is said to have been erected by the late John Sullivan, Esq., and sold by him to Mr. Coll. About 1849 this corner became the property of the late John Berg, Sr., and his brother, present Herman J. Berg, who carried on a hardware store there for many years since. This corner lot is still the property of the heirs of the late John Berg. The Berg banking house was first established in one of the rooms of this building in 1876, and continued there until Mr. John Berg, Jr., bought a few years ago, the old National Bank building, to where he removed and is still carrying on the banking business. The "Racket Store" now occupies the room where the original Berg bank was. John Berg, Sr., died in June 1884.

Mr. Daniel Coll in his day was one of Butler's very best citizens. He was proverbial for his honesty, his name, indeed, being but another for honesty itself. All spoke of him as a man of the utmost integrity and correct principles in all his transactions. In addition to keeping store he followed droving cattle, in which it was said he met with frequent losses. He was elected county treasurer, about 1840, and was appointed postmaster of the town in 1853. He had five sons who were regarded as very talented and scholarly. Francis, the oldest, was a member of the Butler Bar and his early death was much regretted by all who knew his worth and learning. James also died when a young man, much also regretted. Of Cornelius we have elsewhere spoken. John and Samuel, younger boys became the proprietors of the *Democratic Herald* of this place in July, 1858, and continued to publish the same until 1867 when it was sold by them to the late Hon. Jacob Ziegler, who removed it to part of the old Beatty building spoken of, and continued it there to his death near three years ago.

The next building to this Berg property, and where now is the bakery and confectionery store of Mr. John A. Richey, was another frame one, until the present brick was erected by the late John Sweeny, then owner. The first recollection we have of this old frame is when occupied by the late Anthony Faller, Esq., and family. Mr. Faller and family came here from Germany about 1830. They were an interesting family, having brought with them from Germany various musical instruments, among them two large musical clocks, which they exhibited to the citizens and caused to play for their amusement. These clocks were a wonder to the large crowds who called to see and hear them. When set to music, soldiers and other personages or figures would appear and disappear on their face part, in regular order and with great precision. The clocks were perhaps eight feet high and were something never seen here before the advent of Mr. Faller and family. They kept also a bakery there, about the same as Mr. Richey keeps now. Shortly after coming here they bought from the late John Negley, Esq., a piece of land south of the creek, about ten acres, on which they built two buildings, one the cluster of frames across the creek on plank road and near the residence of present Mrs. Muntz. Here Mr. Anthony Faller kept a hotel for many years. The other building was stone and further up the hill there and stood near where is now the residence of the family of the late Mr. Samuel McClymonds. Here they established a brewery and bakery and carried on same for a number of years. This old stone building became the property of the writer of this and was torn away within the past twenty years. The other frame hotel stands yet and is the property of Mrs. Faller's heirs, among whom are our present Jacob and August Faller, his sons. Mr. Faller became a prominent man in this community, was active in political affairs and had great influence with his German fellow citizens. He was a justice of the peace for his township, then South Butler Twp., for many years. He was an intelligent man and one of very decided opinions. He died about 1850. His widow, the late Mrs. Faller, will be remembered by many of our citizens as a woman of great worth and usefulness. She died in 1880. When Mr. Faller bought this land, Mr. Negley took one of the clocks spoken of in part payment for the same.

Feb. 6, 1891                                                                                    J. H. N

We closed our last recollections of the house which stood fifty years ago where the present John A. Richey bakery is. The next lot to this, and where now stands the Aland merchant tailor shop, we will call the Thompson blacksmith lot. Our first recollection of it is in seeing a blacksmith shop there. Five brothers of the name of Thompson are said to have lived on it in the early days of the town. James Thompson, spoken of in the history of the borough as the "sturdy blacksmith" of the town, we suppose was one of the five. We do not recollect him, nor two of the others,

John and Joseph. But another one, Samuel P. Thompson, we recollect well. He removed from here down to Middlesex Township where he died but a few years ago. He will be remembered as a very good, honest and inoffensive man. Another, Dr. Wm. C. Thompson, now of Indianapolis, Ind., we have met. He is yet living and last visited Butler about three years ago on business and to see old friends here. He is said to be a very successful physician in Indianapolis at present, and is the only one of the five brothers known by any of our citizens to be yet living. Where this old blacksmith shop once stood a brick was erected, owned at one time by Mr. Christian Otto, yet living. The late Robert and James Cunningham had their store there for a while, about 1845. A Mr. Douglass followed with a drug store there and had as clerk a young man named Wythe who is said to be now a successful manufacturer of drugs in Philadelphia. Dr. R. L. McCurdy followed with a drug store here. The *Democratic Herald* was published there from about 1850 to March 1855.

The Stehle new brick now adjoining the Aland one was erected in 1874 by the late Mr. Thomas Stehle, who became the owner of same. Mr. Stehle died 1887. The Aland new building was

built only a short time before the death, October 1888, of the late Mr. William Aland. Where the Stehle one now stands was a brick erected or owned by our present Mr. Conrad Smith, in which late Hon. William Beatty lived for a short time and in which also the late National Bank had its first origin and was first kept, 1864. The Producers Bank of Butler County was also kept there for a short time afterwards. The next building to this is the present Mr. M. Buchele one, shoemaker and now barber shop. Mr. Buchele bought this from the late Michael Zimmerman, Esq., who lived there at one time. Our first recollection of a building there, or about there, was an old frame one in which, a Mr. Samuel Johnson lived and had a candy shop. He and his family were a rather queer set, having a good deal of trouble with their neighbors. Where they went or what became of them we suppose no one now living here knows or cares very much.

**STEWART LOT**

Next to this is the present Mr. Harvey Colbert's fine hat and cap store on part of the old Stewart lot. Mr. Colbert bought this of the late William Stewart, Esq., or his agent here, about 1865 and carried on the hatting business there in connection with his father, the late Mr. Isaac Colbert, from that time to 1869, when the partnership ceased. An old frame also stood there fifty years ago. Mr. Harvey Colbert erected the present brick one. Mr. Isaac Colbert, his father, was a hatter by trade and came to Butler about 1836. He manufactured hats and had his shop in several other places before being in with his son Harvey, the last of which was nearly across the street from there in a small shop erected by him where present A & H Reiber store now stands. Hatting in his day here and before was a very different business from what it is now. Within our recollection almost every man got his hat made at home here, generally of the old stove-pipe fashion. The hatters, therefore, were more numerous in those days than now and the business was among the chief industries of the town, three or four shops being carried on at the same time. If you wanted a hat made or dressed up, you went to the Gilchrist shop, the Ben Niblock shop, the Frank Gilmore shop, or in later days to Mr. Colbert's shop. Mr. Colbert, we believe, was the last manufacturer here of hats. Now we have the fine hat and cap stores, made and brought from abroad, the derby and the soft felt being the ruling fashions.

Mr. Isaac Colbert was known by all as a strictly honest man. All we have said as to the character of Mr. Daniel

Coll in that respect would apply to Mr. Colbert. They were both chosen treasurers of the county on account of their honesty of character. Mr. Colbert followed Mr. Coll in that office and we well recollect the arguments made use of for electing him about 1845, were the same he used for Mr. Coll, to-wit, his sterling integrity. About 1842 Mr. Colbert bought the property down North Main Street, where he lived and which is yet in the possession of his heirs. He died July 1872.

The John Bickel boot and shoe store comes next. Where it stands was a frame in which the *Sentinel* newspaper was published, first by the late Moses and John Sullivan, Esqs. then by late Wm. Stewart, afterwards by late George W. Smith, Esq., and Parker C. Purviance, 1840 and last, we believe by John B. Butler, Esq. Mr. George Frederick became the owner of the lot and erected the present brick there, on which he had his boot and shoe store for some years previous to his removing to Ohio. When sold as the property of Mr. Frederick, it was bought by Mr. John Berg, who in turn sold the same to present Mr. John Bickel.

The corner house of this square, now owned by Messrs. J. and B. Kemper with their fine saddlery shop and business was built by the late Hon. William Stewart. We do not recollect the date, nor the different owners of this property before being purchased by present Messrs. Kempers. Mr. Stewart once lived in it and afterwards the late Hon. Wm. Haslett lived there for some time.

**MR. STEWART**

Mr. Stewart was an active citizen of the town fifty years ago. He had been prothonotary of the county and in 1853 was elected to represent it in the legislature and re-elected in 1854. While there he was one of about thirty members who stood out and prevented the election of the late Simon Cameron in one of his early efforts to get to the United States Senate from this state. Before that Mr. Stewart was associated with the late Hon. Charles C. Sullivan in the ownership and improvement of what is known as the Hickory Mills of Slippery Rock Twp. this county, to where he removed in 1844 and remained until 1850. From there he went to Roy Furnace, Lawrence County in which property he was interested and where he lived some time. From there he removed to his Winfield Furnace property in Winfield Twp., this county, where he lived for some time, and which, we believe, is at present the property of his heirs and considered quite valuable for its rich deposits of iron ore and lime stone.

A railroad to reach these is now being constructed from a point on the West Penn road. When the West Penn road was being located Mr. Stewart made an earnest effort to have the route pass by the Winfield Furnace instead of its present location. From Winfield Furnace Mr. Stewart removed to New Castle, and from there to Pittsburg, where he lived for some years, and from there back to New Castle shortly before his death, which event happened in June 1888, in the 80th year of his age.

From the above it will be seen that Hon. Wm. Stewart was a very enterprising man, not only in the affairs of this county but in neighboring Lawrence County. At the iron furnaces he had the native ore taken out and made into pig iron, an industry quite extensive in this section of the country fifty years ago. He was at the same time active in political affairs and religious works. In 1841 he was cashier of the state treasury, the late Hon. John Gilmore of this county being then the state treasurer. He was one of the founders of the Methodist Church of this place, occupying a leading position in it for years as a teacher and local minister. In a word he was an active man in all good works. He was buried at New Castle where he died among relatives and his memory is respected by all who knew him.

**HAGERTY-SULLIVAN SQUARE**

Across the street and opposite the last described square is what we will call the Hagerty-Sullivan square. On the corner where now stands the large Reiber business block stood fifty years and more ago, an old log frame house, used as a hotel [*Woolworth's site*]. This was known as the Hagerty property and on it a hotel known as the "Black Horse Hotel." A sign stood in front on which was the picture of a large black horse and hence the name. Three men by the name of Hagerty said to be among the very earliest comers to the town owned it sat on two lots of this square. They were Patrick Hagerty, the father, and Alexander and William, his sons. We have no recollection of the father and but little of the sons. But we well recollect the widow and family of Wm. Hagerty keeping hotel in the old Black Horse, after we suppose his death. After they left it was kept by the late Samuel Craig , some members of whose family, we believe, are yet living about Millerstown. Mr. A. L. Craig, late county treasurer, is a grandson of said Samuel. Our present Mr. Christian Otto lived there and kept the Black Horse at one time. Mr. Martin Eyth kept it for a time, and others may have occupied it, but about 1858, it became the property of the late Patrick Kelley Jr., who kept the old Black Horse for a number of years. It was finally torn away in part by him and a frame erected, facing Cunningham St., in which a Mr. John Hackett kept some kind of a public house there until happened, 1878, one of the most extensive fires Butler was ever visited with. This fire swept away the Hackett house and all that remained of the old "Black Horse Hotel" besides burning up two small buildings

adjoining on Main Street, and reaching to and somewhat damaging the Rockenstein buildings and also threatening for a time to consume the Sullivan residence. This was the last of the old Black Horse Hotel. After Mr. Kelley died, 1885, the present Messers. Reibers became the owners of the lot and erected the fine large business building that now covers the whole lot. This building at once afforded convenient rooms for many offices and societies and has proven a great benefit to our town. It is the largest business building in the town and reflects great credit upon its builders.

Next on Main Street were the two small shops mentioned as destroyed by the above fire, one a butcher's shop where present Mr. Henry Krug. Sr., for a long time sold meat, and the other the shop heretofore mentioned as one in which the late Mr. Isaac Colbert had at one time his hat shop. The late Edward M. Bredin, Esq., had his law office in this for some years. Thomas B. White, Esq. kept the postoffice there for a short time when he was appointed postmaster, 1870. The ground upon which both stood is now covered by the Reiber building. Next to this on the middle lot, and where now stands the John N. Patterson clothing store and the Miss Rockenstein's millinery and ladies furnishing store, stood fifty years ago a rather large frame, one of the few in the town that was painted white. The late Mr. Oliver David was the first owner we recollect of this. The late Mr. John Berg, we think, was in it for a time. The present Mr. Feigel had his carpenter shop therein for some time. Finally, 1852, the late Mr. Anthony Rockenstein became owner and lived and had his shop there until a disastrous fire in 1859, burned it down. Mr. Rockenstein immediately after this fire erected his present brick, a part of which was purchased lately by Mr. John N. Patterson and where is at present his clothing and gentleman's furnishing store. The other part remains in the family of Mr. Rockenstein and is occupied as mentioned by daughters of his as a millinery store.

Mr. Anthoney Rockenstein came to Butler about 1841. He was a tailor by trade and for some years had his shop in the south end of town in part of the present residence of Mrs. Wm. Aland. He was an industrious and very quiet man in his ways and as honest a man as we ever knew. Of all the old citizens whom we have spoken of as good and honest none surpassed Mr. Rockenstein in those traits of character. He died in October 1880, and his worthy wife followed him only about two months after.

Next to the Rockenstein was fifty years ago, another frame, first occupied within our recollection by a Mr. Hecker, a stone maker, and then by a Dr. Dockaliere, a Frenchman. When the fire that burned down the Rockenstein house took place in 1859 this Dr. Dockaliere lived in this adjoining one also burned down then, and there were very strong suspicions that he was the cause of the fire. He had his property insured in four or five companies as appeared after the fire, but failed to recover any insurance money from any of them. He was a desperate kind of a character and generally dreaded. Various stories were told of him in the practice of his profession as a doctor. He left here shortly after the fire. The late Nicholas and Lewis Miller bought this Dockaliere lot, about 1860, and built the present brick upon it. They were butchers by trade and built it for a meat market, for which purpose it has been used almost ever since, at present by the Messrs. Hale, Clark and Wick. Mr. Lewis Miller, however, lived in part of it, and died there, about 1871. Messrs. Nicholas and Lewis Miller were brothers and came to Butler about 1853. When their property was sold it was purchased by Mr. John Berg, Jr., who is present owner. The Miller brothers had also purchased a part of the late Joseph McQuistion square in the south end of town, Main Street, where Mr. Nicholas Miller removed and was living at the time of his death, 1874. A daughter of his, Mrs. Christian Harley, now owns and lives there.

The next lot of this square is that upon which stands the present residence of Col. John M. Sullivan. It was erected by his father, the late John Sullivan, Esq., in the year 1842, almost fifty years ago, and thence we call it by the name we do. The residence of Col. Sullivan is the first and only one that has ever been on this lot. Therefore, we cannot say of it as we have of many before, that an "old frame once stood there" unless indeed, we apply that term to a blacksmith shop. The first building we recollect being on this lot was a blacksmith shop that stood just about where the residence of Col. Sullivan stands. It was carried on by Andrew Sproul and John Howe, under the firm name of Sproul & Howe. And here it will be observed that this is the third blacksmith shop we have spoken of as being on Main Street fifty years ago, one of them on a prominent part as the Diamond. Should one now be planted upon Main Street it would create general alarm and be declared a public nuisance by general consent. But times have changed, and so have blacksmith shops. Now they are ordered to the rear, to take a back seat, as the saying is, on the alleys or cross streets. However, the blacksmith business cannot be robbed or squeezed out, as has been the hatter, the tanner, and some other of the industries of the former days of the town. The blacksmith shop is a necessity and it has come to stay. Hats and leather may be supplied from abroad, but nothing yet discovered can supply the horses with shoes or drive them upon their feet except the hammer of the home blacksmith. In this respect that worthy trade would seem to have a local advantage over some others, in that it cannot be supplanted or competed with from outsiders to the same extent that other trades can. [*Until Henry Ford came along*]

Mr. Andrew Sproul in his day here was a good and useful citizen. After leaving the Sullivan lot he removed his shop to Water Street, at the foot of West Wayne and there built a shop and a house where the family of the late John F. Manny now resides. From here he removed to Tarentum, Allegheny Co., at least 40 years ago and is long since deceased. What became of Mr. John Howe, his partner, we do not know.

Feb 18, 1891                                  J. H. N.

## MCLAUGHLIN-FRAZIER-BOYD SQUARE

ED. CITIZEN—Continuing on same east side of Main Street from last square we come to the one we will call by the above name. If we gave it the name of the George Vogeley and George Reiber square no doubt our present citizens would more readily recognize it. But we have to keep in mind that we are giving our recollections of 50 years ago, and contrasting houses and persons on the squares then with houses and persons today. Fifty years ago where now stands the well known cigar factory and tobacco shop of Mr. George Vogeley stood a rather neat frame house owned and occupied by the late Dunlap McLaughlin, Esq. And who was Dunlap McGlaughlin many will ask. Dunlap McLaughlin was a son of the late Mr. Hugh McGlaughlin who lived in his day at the northwest corner of Cunningham and McKean Streets, and was a brother of the late Mr. John B. McGlaughlin, who was a sheriff of this county, elected in 1839, and of the late Mr. James McGlaughlin, who was a prothonotary of the county, elected in 1845. Dunlap their younger brother was district attorney of the county between those above two dates, appointed in 1842. So it will be seen that fifty years ago they must have been a family of some importance. James was one of the founders in 1842, and early publishers of the present *Democratic Herald* and was a man of very considerable influence and of many good traits. John B. after being sheriff removed down into now Clinton Twp. and died there not many years ago. Dunlap it will be noticed was a member of the bar. It will also be noticed that he dropped a letter "G" out of his name, that the others always retained.

Whether he did this, from choice or for convenience in writing his name we do not know, but as the G is a pretty hard letter to make, some said it was to save the labor writing it. In person he was a tall, slim man, somewhat stooped, of good moral character and gentlemanly in deportment. During his time as district attorney Mohawk the Indian was tried. After selling to George Vogeley in 1852, he bought of the late Samul M. Lane the property which is now the residence of W. D. Brandon, Esq. and family. About same time he had an interest in the orphans home property. About 1855, Mr. McLaughlin became engaged with the late Hon. Alfred Gilmore, Mr. A. N. Meylert, and others in the purchase of some coal lands in the eastern part of the state, to where shortly after he removed. He died in Philadelphia in 1860. He was one of the early opponents of slavery, abolitionists, as they were then called, and acted with a small body of that party in this county for many years.

Mr. Hugh McGlauglilin, father of above mentioned, lived as stated, on corner of McKean and Cunningham

Streets which is now owned by one of the Messrs. Kempers. We make mention of him from one particular fact, that his house was known as the place where to get your tame pigeons, fifty years and more ago. It was the headquarters for pigeons, and it was said Mr. McGlaughlin was the first to introduce that handsome domestic bird into the town. Here at least, was where the tame pigeons most did congregate, starting out from there in the morning and assembling back there in the evening, to roost. The house had a large upper porch fronting on Cunningham Street and there in boxes with holes for nests provided for them, the pigeons were bred and reared. They flew over the whole town. But the small boy would have to go there to buy his pigeons, as they were all claimed as the property of Mr. McGlaughlin. Now there does not seem to be the same property right in them and the owners of pigeons are now much more numerous.

Mr. George Vogeley purchased this lot from Mr. Dunlap McLaughlin in 1852, and in 1874 erected the brick in which he until lately lived and is part of which he yet had his fine tobacco shop and cigar factory. The property we believe now belongs to Mr. D. L. Cleeland.

The next building to this is the Berg one, in which is the hardware store recently known as that of Berg & Cypher. Where it stands fifty years ago stood a frame. Shortly after the late Mr. John Berg came here, about 1835, he bought this lot and there about 1841 is the first place we recollect of him doing business. He was a baker by trade and carried on that business there in connection with what we now call a restaurant, oysters and refreshments being the specialties. From this small beginning he rapidly increased in means and soon went into that of the hardware business, heretofore spoken of. He was known as a strictly correct business

## A Credit To Butler

The new store room of Mr. C. N. Boyd in the Diamond block and the display of goods made by him are so very handsome that they must be seen to be appreciated. The storeroom itself is the handsomest in the town and Mr. Boyd's selection and artistic display of the goods usually found in a first-class drug store is a revelation to our citizens. The granulated masses of alum and blue vitriol in his show windows are novelties here, and were made expressly for him by the leading manufacturing chemists of the country. The crystals are very handsome and very costly.

His store is full of show cases filled with perfumery, toilet articles and special holiday goods, but the case which attracts the most attention is a plate glass one which cost more than all the rest together. At a distance of ten feet you would say there was no glass in it, it is so fine and clear. The prescription desk at the end of the store is what attracts most people's attention. It is of solid cherry, carved from Mr. Boyd's own designs and is certainly a work of art. A large beveled plate glass mirror is placed in the centre of it and finds a ready use among the ladies. Behind, the scene is changed, poison cases, shelves filled with drugs for prescriptions, drawers full of labels, etc., meet the eye. The principal sight though is his prescription scales which are the finest in town by far. They are sensible to a weight of one-sixteenth of a grain. Of course you can't imagine what that is anymore than we did, but here is an illustration. Mr. Boyd took two pieces of paper of the same size and placed one in each balance-pan. The scales balanced precisely. We then wrote our initials with "Butler, Pa." in addition and replaced the paper. It went down like a shot, not quite so fast perhaps, but just as surely. Mr. Boyd informed us that he means to make a specialty of filling prescriptions and from the appearance of his prescription desk, we think he will. His store is certainly worth seeing even if one does not intend to buy. We looked around for a couple of hours, taking no note of time, and were treated most courteously by Mr. Boyd. We must confess that his display of holiday goods indicates unusually good judgement and taste.

Mr. Boyd came to Butler some years ago from Somerset, Pa., where he had been engaged in the drug business and was known to be a reliable druggist and a good citizen. He purchased property here and now has the handsomest store in town.
*Butler Citizen*, 12-16-1887, pg. 2

man and we do not know of any one coming here who prospered so speedily in business. He at one time, we think, owned where present Stehle toy store is and where present Rockenstein building is. At the time of his death, 1884, he was the owner of various valuable properties in the town and the farm north of town about a mile on Mercer road and perhaps others. In 1875, he erected the present large brick on the lot we are now speaking of, the lower part used as a hardware store and the upper rooms for offices.

The middle lot of this square is the property of present Mr. Andrew Miller. The frame house on it, next to the Berg hardware store and now occupied by Mrs. Marks and daughters, for their millinery store, was built by Mr. Miller The brick there was built, we believe, by the late Mr. David H. Potts, at least he lived and had his shoe making shop there between 1830 and 1840. Dr. James Graham was the next person we recollect of there and who became owner and lived in this brick. Mr. Miller became owner afterwards and had a brewery there until late years. Dr. James Graham came from Ireland and besides practicing his profession here he taught school in town. His first school was kept in the house immediately opposite the present Rink building on McKean Street, between 1830 and 1840. We were one of his pupils. He brought with him from the "old country" some of the old methods of school teaching. One of them was the use in his school of taws, otherwise called "cat of nine tails," as a whip or instrument of punishment for the bad boy. These taws were composed of a round wooden handle, about a foot long, something resembling a rolling pin and to one end of which was tacked nine leather straps of about three feet in length. On the end of each of those nine leather straps was a knot. This was his whip and it hung upon the wall of the school room as a warning to all scholars to beware of its use. He frequently did use it, and sometimes with terrific force and effect making the offender to fairly jump up every time the "cat of nine tails" would descend upon him. To use such a school whip now would likely enhance interest in the debated question of the use of any corporal punishment in our present schools. Dr. Graham afterwards taught in the old Butler Academy. In person he was short but heavy set, fat and sassy, and quite strong, as any of his pupils who had any experience with his "cat of nine tails" could testify. He was very fond of reading novels and would borrow and read all the books of romance he could get. He died about 1843, in the brick house we have been telling about, being found dead in his bed one morning. His habits were unfortunate in respect to the use of strong drink, but he was regarded as a very learned man and had always a quite extensive practice as a physician. He had no children. His widow survived him a long time living in the house opposite the present Rink. He was in no way related to our present Dr. Samuel Graham or any of our other Graham people.

The next lot of this square is now the property of Mr. George Reiber. On the Main Street part of it now are the business places of the Smith Bros. restaurant, the W. M. Nickle Ten Cent Store, and the Jarecki Manufacturing Co. On the corner where the Jarecki Co. stood fifty years ago was a brick in which the late Mr. James Frazier and his son, the late Isaiah N. Frazier kept a dry goods and general store. It was a three-storied building and the first persons we recollect of doing business in it were the Messrs. Fraziers mentioned. Mr Isaiah N. Frazier kept the postoffice there for a term when he held that office. About 1845 the lot upon which it and the others above mentioned stood was purchased by the late Mr. William S. Boyd. Mr. Boyd tore away the old buildings upon it and erected another and larger three-storied brick there, which he had ready for business and went into in 1848, his family moved into part of it also in 1849. On this corner would thus seem to have been the first three-storied building in the town. The one built by Mr. Boyd, however, did not remain long for in about ten years after, 1859, it was burned down. Then he erected, 1861, the present two-storied one which has since been enlarged and had other buildings attached to it on Jefferson Street by Mr. George Reiber. Between the date of its building in 1848 and burning down in 1850, there were several persons associated with Mr. Boyd in the drug and grocery business on that corner. The late Mr. Samuel Marks was with him in 1848, going with him there from the Dougal corner. Mrs. Marks, his widow, with her daughters are now living a few doors above on this same square. She is a daughter of late Mr. James Frazier mentioned above and one of the names we choose to call this square by. In 1852, the late Mr. Albert G. Boyd was in partnership with his brother William there. Mr. Joseph Earhaft was with him there for a while. Present Mr. James Dunlap was connected with Mr. Boyd in business there in 1861.

The late Henry N. Boyd did not accompany his brother when they left the Dougal corner nor was he with him at the Frazier corner at any time. They left behind them at the Dougal corner some in the same drug and grocery business, among them the late Andrew Carnes, already mentioned, and with whom, we think, the late Patrick E. Bey, Jr. was associated for a time. A Mr. Wm. Cheesman was also there, probably with them, and probably with Mr. Boyd. Mr. Cheesman, we believe, went or was with Mr. Boyd after he went to the Frazier corner. Mr. Samuel Marks was also with the Messrs. Boyd at the Dougal corner while business was carried on there. And here we wish to make a correction as to the business first done by Wm. S. and Henry N. Boyd at the Dougal corner. We have spoken of it as being that of a grocery and restaurant. This last one was an error, a slip of the pen, and should have been drug instead of restaurant. We probably fell into the error from recollecting of Mr. Wm. S. Boyd inviting some friends into his store and furnishing them with "cheese and crackers." But he and his brother Henry never kept anything like the modern restaurant. They were both men of good works and of high moral character. Our attention has been called to the error by a daughter of Henry N. Boyd, Mrs. Julia Evans, widow of the late Wm. V. Evans, Esq. of Tarentum, Pa., where Mrs. Evans is yet living. She is favorably remembered here as Miss Julia Boyd and it gives us pleasure to make the correction referred to. She states that the third story rooms of the first building erected by her uncle, Wm. S. Boyd, on the corner were occupied by the first Good Templars Lodge of Butler. When Mr. Wm. S. Boyd quit business there he sold out his merchandise to Mr. George Weber and Mr. Adam Troutman, and at a later date he sold the building to Mr. George Reiber, the present owner. The date of Mr. Boyd's death has been given before. Mr. Henry N. Boyd died here August 4, 1845. Mr. Samuel Marks died in Freeport, Pa. in 1881. Mr. James Frazier died here in 1839. His son Isaiah died in New Wilmington, Pa. about 1873.

## OLIVER DAVID-SCOTT-MCKEE SQUARE

To the square on the opposite side of the street from the last one we give the above name. Like all the original squares it had three lots, which in early days were generally owned by three different persons. The late Mr. Oliver David owned the upper one, the late Robert Scott, Esq., the middle one and the late Hugh McKee, Esq., the lower one. Where the Pape store and the two Grieb ones now stand were store and house of Mr. David. Our first recollection of Mr. David is in his keeping a store where the Pape one now is. His store was the largest one in Butler for many years. It was a general store, dry goods, hardware, queensware and almost every other kind of ware. He did an extensive business and this corner became noted for the number of persons keeping there and changes made in firms after him. The first partner Mr. David had there was the late Mr. Samuel M. Lane, who came to Butler from Huntingdon County, about 1832, and about 1835 became connected with Mr. David under the firm name of David & Lane.

Then the next firm there, we think, was that of Lane, Campbell & Yetter, the late Mr. James Campbell and the late Mr. Henry Yetter going in with Mr. Lane and Mr. David probably going out. It was probably carried on as Lane & Campbell for some time after Mr. Yetter left here. Then next we think that Col. George S. Hays, of Allegheny Co. and Col. Wm. F. Rumberger, now of Armstrong Co., became connected with the store. Col. Hays had been prothonotary of Allegheny Co. and we believe is deceased. Col. Rumberger we believe is still living. Then next we think was the firm of Hall & Bastian. Mr. John Hall came from Portersville and Mr. Wm. Bastian about Zelienople. Mr. Hall went west and died there. Mr. Bastian died in Zelienople some years ago. Before their time however the late Wm. L. Spear & Bros. kept a store there for a time, probably succeeding Mr. Lane or Mr. Campbell in the business. Hall & Bastian were succeeded in 1859 by our present Robert C. McAboy and his brother the late J. Lynn McAboy, who kept a store there until about 1872 when they sold the property to the late Mr. D. T. Pape. whose widow and family are still doing business there in their dry goods and ladies furnishing store.

So it will be seen that this corner was a rather celebrated business one. The present Grieb stores occupy the remainder of the old David lot. The Mr. John R. Grieb Jewelry store part was but very recently sold by the owner Mr. Charles Duffy to Mr. Smith of the "Racket Store." Mr. Charles Grieb with his hat and gentleman's furnishing goods store occupied the other part. Both these last compose a part of what is known as the "Union Block".

Mr. Oliver David came here from Middlesex Twp. where he carried on the tanning business and also had a tannery here for a time. He was a hard working industrious man and as a merchant he was very successful. While attentive to business and careful of his accounts yet we never heard his honesty called in question. He died here in 1871.

Mr. Samuel M. Lane was a very successful business man here fifty years ago. He became owner of several properties and erected several houses among them the one now occupied by W. D. Brandon, Esq. and family. He represented this county in the legislature of the state for a term being elected in 1841. He removed to Philadelphia and died there on January 1, 1884.

The late Mr. James Campbell died here so recently, 1886, as to be remembered by all. An extended obituary notice of him appeared at the time of his death. Mr. Henry Yetter we believe is long since deceased. Mr. Pape is deceased. Mr. J. Lynn McAboy commonly called Lynn is deceased. So that of all the men who were engaged in business at that David corner within the last fifty years but one, our present Robert C. McAboy, Esq., remains or is living here now.

Feb. 25, 1891                                                    J. H. N.

## OLIVER DAVID-SCOTT-MCKEE SQUARE (Continued)

The middle of this square is first recollected by us as that of the late Robert Scott, Esq. Upon it at present stand the fine store buildings of Mr. Al Ruff, Mr. D. H. Wuller and Mr. F. P. Baldauf. Where they stand fifty years ago stood small frame or brick buildings. The late Mr. Philip Bickel became owner of the one where Mr. Ruff has his shoe store and had his shoe making shop there, near fifty years ago. He was followed by Bickel and Schenck in the same business. Mr. Adam Schenck was father to present Schenck enterprising citizens. Mr. Adam Schreiber followed Bickel and Schenck in the same business. So it will be seen that this particular place has been occupied from the time of Mr. Philip Bickel down to the present by men engaged in the shoe trade or business, Mr. Al Ruff being the present one with his fine boot and shoe store, composing a part of the Union Block, erected since the fire of 1878 that burned the old buildings there.

Where Mr. D. H. Wuller's fine drug store stands the late Mr. William Criswell had his saddlery shop fifty years ago. Mr. Criswell was a prominient citizen of our town for many years. He was one of the earliest and best saddlers in the place. In his latter days he had connected with him in business the late Mr. Curtis Smith, and Mr. Smith probably carried on the saddlery business there himself for a time. David H. Mackey had his marble shop there at one time. Wm. S. Ziegler, Esq. had his tin shop there at one time. Present Drs. Graham and Zimmerman had a drug store there for a time and we believe sold out same to present Mr. Daniel H. Wuller. His building is part of Union Block erected to replace those burned down by the fire there in 1878.

Fifty years ago where now stands Mr. Baldauf's shoe shop and store stood a small building which has had many occupants, "too numerous to mention" as they say in vendue bills. It is longer ago than that since our present Gen. George W. Reed had we think his first saddlery shop there. Present William S. Ziegler, Esq. afterwards had his justice of the peace office there. This part of lot finally became the property of Mr. John Greer of Prospect, from whom we believe Mr. Baldauf obtained it and upon which he has erected the fine brick now standing there, in upper rooms of which is located the office of the Western Union Telegraph Co.

Robert Scott, Esq. who owned above lot of this square was in his day one of Butler's prominent citizens and an active and influential man in its political affairs. We have but a faint recollection of him. He was the principal justice of the peace of the town for many years, and was at one time a commissioner of the county and also its register and recorder for a number of years. He was the father of ex-Sheriff John Scott, whose widow is still living here, and the grandfather of our present Robert Pressley Scott, Esq. of the Butler Bar. He died in the latter part of 1830.

**McKEE LOT**

The late Hugh McKee, Esq. was the owner fifty years ago, of the lot on which now stands the Savings Bank, the Schneidenian clothing store and the former National Bank, now Berg Bank Building. Where the Savings Bank is formerly stood a small brick, generally used for a butcher's shop. Our present Mr. Christian Otto

Pharmacist G. Harry Davey

had his meat shop there and probably owned the property for some time. When Nicholas and Lewis Miller first came here they had their meat shop there. The late James Glenn had his tailor shop there in former years and the present Mr. Nelson McCandless had his tailor shop there for some time.

Where store of Mr. Herman Schneideman now is was a frame which was part of the residence of the late Mr. McKee. Mr. John A. Sedwick, about 1865, had a saddlery shop there. Present Mr. Joseph Reckenstein followed him with his saddlery shop there. It finally became the property of present Hon. Charles McCandless and Mr. Charles Duffey, from whom Mr. Schneideman purchased same.

The corner, where present Berg Bank stands, was also a part of the McKee residence, or used rather by him as the drying part of his tanning shops. After Mr. McKee's death and about 1846, this whole lot became the property of his son, Doctor J. Cooper McKee, now of the United States Army. About 1871 the part where stands Berg Bank was purchased by Col. John H. Thompson for banking purposes, paying $12,000 for same, soon after which, 1872, the construction of what was known as the National Bank building was commenced and completed in same year. It did business there to the time of its failure or being closed up by the government in 1880.

The late Mr. Hugh McKee was one of the early and enterprising citizens of Butler. Our recollection of him is slight, but he was always spoken of as a most worthy man and excellent citizen. It is said that the present prosperous U. P. Church of this place owes more to Mr. McKee than to any other of its early members for its origin and success. He was regarded by all as a good man. In person he was tall, quiet in manner, cool of head and collected in speech. He was a tanner by trade and his tannery was the most extensive one in town for many years. His shops and business extended down Jefferson street, from Main, and the tan bark after being used was thrown upon Jefferson. This tan bark deposit and place was a favorite one for exercise to the small boys of the town, particularly in the exercise of jumping, and many were the contests there in "running jumps" in the "hop, step and jump," and all the then other kinds of jumps. The leaps that were claimed to be made there far exceeded the one made by the celebrated Samuel Brady when pursued by the Indians. The springy nature of the tan bark and the soft places it afforded for leaping and landing were however better than Brady had. But none who ever exercised on Mr. McKee's waste tan bark yards will forget the excitement and fun of the running, leaping and jumping done there.

In connection with his tanning business Mr. McKee also had a meat market which was a great convenience to the people of the town at that day. He acted as a justice of the peace for some years and filled other places of trust. His family although large became scattered and no child of his is now living in or about Butler. Doctor J. Cooper McKee, surgeon in the United States Army, is probably his only child living. He visits Butler occasionally and was last here two or three summers ago. Some grandchildren of Mr. McKee however are still here, being the children of his daughter, the late Mrs. Alexander McBride.

**KEARNS-STEIN-CARNAHAN SQUARE**

Crossing Jefferson St. and continuing on west side of Main, is the square to which we give the above name. The late Mr. Patton Kearns owned the first lot on corner of which is now the large dry goods, carpet and furnishing store of Ritter & Ralston, and on the remaining parts, the fine shoe store of Mr. B. C. Huselton and the drug store of Mr. Joseph L. Wuller.

The first recollection we have of this corner is a tin shop being on it, kept by the late William B. Lemmon, fifty years ago at least. The late George C. Roessing Esq. shortly after coming here was in part of this at one time with his cabinet maker shop, which part was moved away and is now the house, or part of it, in which Dr. Pillow lives at present.

Finally the ground was leased of Mr. Kearns by the late Mr. Eli Yetter, who under a ten years lease erected the brick store house there, lately much improved and extended by the present Ritter & Ralston firm. Messrs. Reiber and Yetter kept a store there during their lease of the ground. Mr. Patton Kearns followed, keeping a store there until he sold to Ritter & Ralston, 1871. The *Citizen* was published in the upper story of this Kearns store house from 1864 to spring of 1872, the three last years of which time by the writer of this, when it was removed to its present place of publication on Diamond.

Where Mr. Huselton's shoe store stands was a small frame in which Mr. Kearns, who was a tailor by trade, kept his tailor shop for many years and until the same was sold by him to Mr. Huselton, who erected the brick now there.

Where the Mr. J. L. Wuller drug store stands was also a frame in which we think the late Mr. George W. Crozier had his paint shop at one time.

In the middle lot of this square now stands the fine dry goods store of Mr. Lewis Stein & Son and the residence of Mr. George Reiber (blacksmith). Formerly the late Samuel C. Stewart, Esq. had his cabinet making shop there. Two merchants named Parker & Donelly who came from Indiana, Pa., had a store there about 50 years ago. We believe Messrs. Parker & Donelly when they left here returned to Indiana. Mr. Stein and Mr. Reiber we believe bought this lot from the estate of the late Hugh McKee but before that it was probably part of the estate of the late William Kearns, father of Patton and the present Mr. James Kearns, Gen. Reed had his saddlery shop there for a time after leaving the Scott lot. Mr. Stein came to Butler about 50 years ago and was first in business with the late Mr. Bernard Roessing.

The remaining part of this square was, 50 years ago, and more, the property of the late Robert Carnahan, Esq. and hence the name we have given it. Squire Carnahan was a cabinet maker and carried on his shop here previous to becoming a justice of the peace. The present extensive tin and hardware store of Messrs. Biehl and the present grocery store of Mrs. Koch & Sons now occupy this lot. Mr. Henry Wagner became owner of the corner and built the brick there, now the Koch store. The late Thomas Burton & Sons, we believe, purchased it from Mr. Wagner, and kept store there for a number of years. It is now the property of Mr. Charles Duggy who obtained it from the Messrs. Burtons. The Biehl part came through Squire Carnahan either in his life time or through his estate. Both the Biehl and the Koch stores are now among the largest and best in the town of their kind.

## McBRIDE-LANE-DUFFY SQUARE

Across Main Street is the square to which we give the above name. That of McBride will no doubt be as new to most of our present citizens as some of the names we have given to other squares. But fifty years ago, and more, the late Col. Francis McBride owned the lot where now stands the Lowry House, and the first persons we recollect of living on this corner were him and family. The house that then stood there was a rather large log frame, used as a hotel and one of the oldest hotel stands of the town. Col. McBride, we believe, kept hotel there between 1830 and 1840 and probably after he was sheriff of the county. The next persons we recollect living there were Messrs. Marquis and Kelker, who kept a hotel there about 1840. They came from about Harmony.

Main Street, looking North from Jefferson Street. Butler, Pa.

The present Mrs. Edward Mellon of Zelienople is a daughter of Mr. Marquis. Two of the Kelker girls married two of the late Pearce men west of town, Silas and John. Between 1840 and 1850 Mr. Benjamin Niblock kept that house for a time, and probably some others before or after him. About 1846 it became the property of the late Mr. Samuel M. Lane and soon after the property of the late Mr. Martin Reiber, who bought it of Mr. Lane and in turn sold it, about 1850, to our present Mr. H. Julius Klingler. The late Mr. Jacob Reiber kept hotel there during ownership of his brother Martin and when he left there went to and kept the late Beatty House and after keeping it a time went to New Castle. He is deceased for some years. Mr. Klingler removed the old frame and in 1850 erected there the present three storied brick on the corner, being the first three storied hotel erected in the town. When the old courthouse was being built, 1853, the courts were held in the basement of the Presbyterian Church, and rooms for the juries to meet in or retire to when making up of their verdicts were obtained in the new Klingler hotel. We recollect, as the then district attorney, of climbing up the stairs with a grand jury to one of the rooms on the third story of Mr. Klingler's new hotel, not then entirely finished. Away up there the jury deliberated, with the late Hon. Samuel Marshall acting as its foreman. Mr. Klingler kept there until he sold to Col. Lowry about 1864 and Col. Lowry was there until he sold to Mr. G. J. Cross, when it was kept by Cross and McOmber until again purchased by Col. Lowry and kept by him and son Mr. John F. Lowry until recently sold to present owners, Mr. Howard Campbell and Mr. John D. Brown. It has been known as the "Lowry House" since Col. Lowry first went there and still retains his name. Last summer it was enlarged by him and his sons and now covers the whole of this lot on Main Street.

To the middle lot of this square we give the name of Lane, the late Mr. Samuel M. Lane being the first person we recollect of owning it. He erected the house there, now the property of Mr. B. S. Roessing, in front of which he has recently built his saddlery shop. Mr. Lane lived there about 50 years ago, and sold the property to the late Mr. James Campbell, who lived there until he sold to Doctor Stephen Bredin, who lived there until he removed to Franklin, Pa. The late Doctor J. S. Lusk then lived there until his recent death. Mr. Roessing, present owner, now lives there.

The Doctor J. C. Redick drug store occupies the remainder of this old middle lot. The building on it was erected by Doctor R. L. McCurdy when living here. It is now the property of Doctor Redick and in which he continues his fine drug store, being one of the principal drug stores of the town for many years.

The remaining lot of this square will readily be recognized by the name of Duffy. It has the same name now it had more than 50 years ago, being one of the few original lots of the town of which this can be said. While it did not receive its name from its present owner, Mr. Charles Duffy, yet the large brick block standing upon its whole front is due to his enterprise. In 1854 he build part of it and 1868 enlarged it to what it now is. His large dry goods and general store occupy two parts of it and the large clothing and gentleman's furnishing store of Mr. D. A. Heck the other part.

Where this large building now stands, 50 years ago, stood a low-one story frame, in which a store was kept by the late John and Peter Duffy. As has been stated heretofore, they first built and kept a store on one of the Dougal corners when they came to the town. On leaving there, they went down to the present Duffy lot, building and keeping a store there for many years. They were recognized by all their fellow citizens as honest men in business and fair men in all the walks of life. There are few men in this life who entirely escape enemies or censure but we do not recollect of ever hearing the name of either John and Peter Duffy spoken of in any other than that of respect.

Mr. Peter Duffy was the father of present Charles. He died as late as 1883, at the age of 85 years, and is remembered as a good man. He was prothonotary of the county for a term of that office, appointed 1833, and was previously the postmaster here for a term of that office. He held other offices and posts of trust, always filling them with fidelity to duty.

Hon. John Duffy, older brother of Peter and uncle to present Charles, was an associate judge of the county for ten years, appointed in 1842. We recollect seeing him on the bench with the late James Bovard, the other associate. Judge Duffy was appointed to fill the vacancy created by the death of Judge John Parker, father of the late George Parker of Parker Twp. this county, and of Fullerton Parker, of Parker's Landing. No man ever questioned the fairness

## When Streets Were Mud

It was not an uncommon sight in the early nineties when the Thorn Creek and Petersville oil excitements were in full swing to see the old tortoise shell bus sink in the mud on Main Street in the winter months.

There were no paved streets in those days and during one particular winter, 1890 and 1891, Main and Jefferson Streets were nothing but a sea of mud. Women and children as well as men wore rubber boots when they went shopping or to church. Boiler trucks and lumber wagons bound for the oil fields with four or six horses attached sank to the axles.

Men attired in hip-length rubber boots gallantly carried the women across the streets on the stepping stones or boldly waded to the middle of the street and carried passengers from the stalled omnibus to the sidewalks.

Butler was then a typical oil country town. Oil country teamsters traveled in pairs between Butler and Petersville, and if a horse got down in a mudhole, as frequently happened, a helping team was always handy to pull him out.

It was about this time that the paving of Main Street from the courthouse to the foot of cemetery hill was started. Many of the old residents and businessmen thought that the town would be ruined financially when the borough council proposed to pave Main and Jefferson Streets, but after the jobs were completed they turned in and heartily supported all public improvements, including sewers and street lights.

*Butler Eagle*, April 16, 1925, James A. McKee

or honesty of Judge Duffy while on the bench. He died in 1864 at the age of 80 years.

March 25, 1891
J. H. N.

## DUFFY-NEYMAN-SEDWICK SQUARE

To the next square on same east side of Main Street, we give the above name. The first lot, on passing over the alley from Mr. Charles Duffy's store, might with properity be given the name of Walker, as the late David Walker, Esq. is said to have been its owner within fifty years. But our first recollection of the persons living on that corner was the late Mr. Peter Duffy, and as his son Charles is now its owner we give it the name above.

Mr. Anthony Rockenstein with his tin and hardware store is the present occupant of this Duffy part of this lot. Mrs. E. Greib is owner and occupant of the next part, with her fine jewelry store on same. Mrs. Julia Niggle is present owner and occupant of remaining part. The late Mr. Andrew Marshall, among others, was owner or lived at one time where either Mrs. Greib or Mrs. Niggle now live.

The next and middle lot of this square is the Doctor Neyman one. Fifty years ago and more his mother with her family lived in a small brick which stood where the large one erected by the Doctor now stands. The gable end of this small brick stood to the street. In it at one time it is said the late Mr. Mark McCandless was there with his shoe making shop. Mr. McCandless afterwards removed to Cherry Town-

## OLD LIVERY BARNS

Who remembers the old livery barns which adorned West Jefferson Street, Cunningham Street, Wayne Street, and the alleys of the town 20 or more years ago? With very few exceptions all of them have given way to garages, just as gas has taken the place of old Dobbin for motive power.

For almost 50 years West Jefferson Street from the Lowry House corner to Church Street was a sort of horse traders' emporium. More horses were bought and sold in that area than in any other part of the town, or the county for that matter.

Buyers for the Pittsburgh and eastern markets made periodical visits to purchase horses. Several carloads of horses, the pick of the county, then noted for its good horses, would be delivered in a day. Traders were always present every day in the week and always ready for a "swap."

Many a horseman who thought himself a shrewd dealer had his "eye teeth cut" and used horrible language after he got home and found in a day or two that his new horse had developed a case of the "thumps" and that the animal's handsomely braided tail, tied up with red and blue ribbons, was false hair ingeniously done up in a way that would fool the elect.

The old-time horse trader was no "cribber." If he was beaten in a deal, he took his medicine and awaited his chance to come back. They seldom got into court over their deals.

Old livery barns recalled by some of the middle-aged residents were McBride's on Jefferson Street next to the post office building. Henry Bickel and William Kennedy were in the next block toward Main Street in the days of the oil excitement. Bickel was regarded as the "king bee" of the horse traders. Thirty-five years ago, two livery barns located in what is now the Duffy block, burned and a number of horses perished. One was a valuable horse owned by the late Julian A. Clark, a former register and recorder of the county.

Bickel and Kennedy and Flick and Kennedy held sway during the nineties when the oil business was at its height. Then it took nerve to run a livery barn and a neck yoke was a handy thing to have around when trouble started. For twenty or more years William Kennedy, afterwards burgess of the town during the typhoid fever epidemic, was one of the striking figures seen on the streets, especially about the Lowry House corner. He was a large man, always faultlessly dressed and was known to everybody.

Other livery barns, competitors of the Jefferson Street row, were the Wick house barns on West Clay Street [now Brady], where George Ross was the presiding genius for 25 years, the Schreiber barn on East Clay Street at the rear of the municipal building, conducted by Martin Schreiber and a number of successors, the Lowry Hotel barn on Cherry Alley and East Mifflin Street, the barn of John and Jacob Lowell on the site of the Union trolley station, West Cunningham Street, the Kramer barn on East Wayne Street, the Gregg barn on Vogeley Way at the rear of the Arlington hotel, the Wise barn, at the rear of the Park Hotel; the Butler House barn and half a score of small barns in the alleys, were run on a small scale.

In addition to the private stables, many contractors engaged in teaming in the oil country, had stables in the back alleys where they housed their own stock and boarded horses. The alleys were full of wagons, buggies, buckboards, torpedo wagons used by oil well shooters, boiler wagons, and like as not a few cases of nitroglycerine.

Saddle horses were much in demand by oil scouts in the early days and many high-headed, Kentucky-bred animals were to be seen on the streets ridden by the picturesque characters known as the "scouts." Butler at one time had better driving and saddle horses than any town of its size in this part of the state.

Today there are only two livery stables which make a business of hiring out horses for any use, and privately owned driving and saddle horses can be counted on the fingers of one hand."

*Butler Eagle*, April 14, 1925

ship.

The post office has been moving southward and more towards the center of population. Mr. Eastman is now postmaster under a recent re-appointment to the office.

The old Sedwick lot is now owned by Mr. Charles Duffy, and Mr. Sam Teung Hop has his Chinese Laundry there in the corner part. These Chinese names by the way are queer and often made to spell like English ones. "Sam" in this case is peculiarly English and "Hop" is a very American word. However we have no reason to doubt but that "Sam Teung Hop" came by his name honestly in China and brought it over here in as good shape as he could.

That part of the buildings on this lot next to Doctor Neyman was the

Stable of Eli May on Jackson St.--the 100 block--Grandfather of Dick May

property and residence of the late Rev. Mrs. Niblock, who lived there until her recent death. The first recollection we have of this was the living there of a Rev. Mr. Hilton of the Episcopal Church. Afterwards the late Mrs. James Bredin and family who come from Carlisle, Pa. lived there for some years. The present Rev. Mrs. William White, Mrs. Elizabeth Porterfield, Mrs. John Graham, Esq. and their brother James Bredin, Jr. deceased, were members of this family. In later years Ex-Sheriff John Scott and others lived there. This is now the property of Mr. Charles Duggy. Mr. John Hildebrand and Son have now a meat shop in the front room where Mrs. Niblock might often have been seen setting. Another meat shop, that of Mr. Blymiller, is between there and the laundry of Mr. Sam Hop.

## WALKER-HASLETT-PURVIANCE SQUARE

On opposite side of the street is the square to which we give the above name. The late David Walker, Esq., father of present Lewis P. Walker Esq., owned the ground 50 years ago, where now stand the store lately occupied by Mr. Adam Troutman & Son, and the house, shop and office of Jacob Keck, Esq., and the house and saddlery shop of

Mr. Joseph Rockenstein. About 1847 Mr. Walker erected on this ground the block of buildings now standing there. It was called Walker's Block, extending from the corner of Mr. Troutman to the then residence lot of the late Hon. Samuel A. Purviance, now Col. John M. Thompson. When this block was erected it was considered the largest and finest in the then town. Mr. Walker had enlarged Mifflin Street [New Castle], then an alley, by adding 20 feet to same from his own ground.

He owned at that time the lots or ground on Mifflin Street, north side down to where he then lived, the present James Borland property. This enlargement of Mifflin made the corner lot more desirable as a business place. The first store on this corner we think was that of present Mr. L. Stein and late Bernard Roessing. Then the late James Campbell and present H. J. Klingler had a store there. The late Mr. Charles Wiseman was there with a jewelry store and shoe shop. Following him were Mr. Adam Troutman and Mr. George Weber. Mr. Jacob Boos bought out Mr. Weber and the firm became Troutman & Boos, who kept a store there until Mr. Troutman purchased the interests of Mr. Boos, since which time this corner became and is now the property of Mr.

Adam Troutman. It is now occupied by Messrs. Campbell & Tempelton as a furniture store.

Jacob Keck, Esq. is present owner of the greater part of the middle lot of this square. Mr. Joseph Rockenstein is the owner of the other part. Mr. Walker himself lived for a time where Mr. Keck now is. The late Hon. William Haslett lived there in part of same for some years. His paper, *The Whig*, was published for some years in the upper story of what is now Esquire Keck's merchant tailoring shop. Mr. Haslett removed *The Whig* there from the south wing of the old [first] courthouse, where about 1850 he published it after leaving the south end of town, spoken of. *The Whig* continued to be published there until changed into *The Butler American*, also published by Mr. Haslett for a number of years, between 1853 and 1864. About 1867 Mr. Haslett established another paper called *The Press* which he published a short time, when its material was sold by him to the writer of this, who in April 1869, had purchased the *Citizen*, then called the *American Citizen*. Mr. Haslett had been an active journalist for near twenty years. As an editor he was able and wrote with a great deal of elegance and clearness. As a man he was a warm friend, liberal, generous and open handed. He exercised a strong political influence in the old Whig Party of this county and was sent to the state senate by that party, in 1840. In 1863 and 1864, he was elected to the house of the legislature by the Republican Party.

From the above it will be observed that about 1853 there was a change in the names of newspapers, the name of "American" becoming fashionable about then. The reason for taking the name may be of interest to some at present. It arose from the breaking up of the Whig Party in 1852 and the rise of the American party upon its ruins. The cause of the breaking up of the Whig Party was the defeat of General Winfield Scott, its candidate for President in 1852. And the cause of this defeat was the abandonment by the Whigs of their position on the slavery question, then greatly agitating the country. When they nominated Gen. Scott they put him upon a "milk and water" platform on the slavery question. It was said at the time that it was no better on that question than was the Democratic Party and platform. This so disgusted the great mass of the Whigs that they became lukewarm and indifferent and the result was the defeat of Gen. Scott and the election of Pierce the Democratic candidate. Gen. Scott received the votes of but four states, and the effect was an immediate effort for the formation of another party to take the place of the former great Whig one. The name American was given the new party. Just where it was formed, or how, or when, nobody seemed to know or could tell. It had a secret feature in it as to membership, and it spread "like wild fire" over the whole nation. Candidates of both and all parties rushed to get into it. Its meetings were held in out of the way places and its members were initiated in barns, stables and even in coal banks, it was said. They would not acknowledge being members and if asked if they were their general reply was that they "knew nothing about it." Hence they came to be called "Know Nothings" and the party the "Know Nothing Party." But people, tired of the old parties, joined it and it swept nearly every state in the union during the years 1853-4 and 5. It obtained a majority in congress and governors and state and county officers were elected by it during those three years. Some amusing things might be told of its effects in Butler County on candidates. A Democratic candidate, for instance, who had quietly joined it was elected by nearly 2000 majority over his old Whig opponent who had declined to join it, and a Whig who had quietly joined it was elected by about the same majority over his Democratic opponent who refused to join it. It began to break up in 1856 and the Republican Party rapidly arose in its place, gathering to its ranks many old Democrats who were dissatisfied with the position of their party on the slavery question. The name "American" for papers began to drop off with the dropping out of the American Party, otherwise called the "Know Nothing Party." Its principles were hostility to Catholics and foreigners in general and their holding office in particular.

Where Mr. Joseph Rockenstein has his present fine saddlery shop, part of the old Walker block, were many stores within the last 50 years. The first there we think was that of a Mr. Ormond, followed by the late Charles Wiseman, the late Sheriff John Scott, and the late Campbell E. Purviance, Esq. Mr. Jacob Boos became owner of it and lived and kept store there for a short time. He probably purchased it from Mr. Wiseman and sold it to Mr. Rockenstein, who is present owner of this part of this square.

## PURVIANCE LOT

This brings us to the lot and former residence of the late Hon. Samuel A. Purviance, now the residence of Col. John M. Thompson, who bought it of Mr. Purviance, about 1859. Mr. Purviance erected the large house standing there about 1840. He also erected the office there used by him as his law office for many years. Col. John M. Sullivan was a law partner with him between 1846 and 1853. Then Col. Thompson was partner with Mr. Purviance. They were followed by Mr. Thompson and Hon. John H. Mitchell, present United States Senator from the state of Oregon. Mr. Mitchell left here about 1860. Col. Thompson with his son continued to practice law there until they removed to the Diamond, where they now are. The office is at present occupied by Doctor W. H. Titzel as his medical office.

## SAMUEL A. PURVIANCE

Much has been spoken and written of the Hon. Samuel A. Purviance since his death, but no word of praise or encomium of him, has ever been too great. He was a citizen of Butler whom all respected and all knowing him will continue to respect his memory. This respect arose from the high character of the man, his pure life, his private integrity, his public service, and his honorable bearing in all his intercourse with his fellow citizens. Mr. Purviance was a good man, an honest man, and an enterprising, useful citizen in and to Butler. His character was appreciated by the people and they made him their representative in the state legislature in 1838. Previous, 1837, he was chosen a member of the convention to reform the state constitution, which gave us the constitution of 1837-1838. Then he was twice elected to congress, 1854 and 1856, serving with credit and distinction. He was attorney general of the state for a time. When the state constitution was again reformed, 1872, 1873, he was sent as a delegate to that convention by the people of Allegheny County, in which he then resided. He also filled other positions of trust and honor. In political and public affairs he was always active and influential. In the practice of his profession of the law, he was always honorable. As a man he was always a gentleman, pleasant, and agreeable. After serving his term in congress Mr. Purviance removed from here to Allegheny City, about 1859, where he practiced his profession and lived until he died in February, 1882, in the 74th year of his age.

**DAVID WALKER ESQ.**

A word is due to the memory of Mr. David Walker who we have seen was closely identified with this square, building all the houses upon it except the Purviance, now Thompson one. Mr. Walker was a plasterer by trade and also carried on brick making. He was industrious, and about 1850 was one of the largest property owners of the town. He was a justice of the peace in the town for a time. When he left the house he lived in below Klingler's Mill and now the property of Mr. James Borland, as stated, his brother the late Mr. Nathaniel Walker, went to live there and also carried on brick making there. Mr. Nathaniel Walker was the father of our present Capt. Samuel Walker and Clarence Walker, Esq. Shortly after this the project of building the ill fated North Western Railroad began, about 1853, and Mr. David Walker undertook the contract of excavating the deep and long cut on same about a mile or two west of town. This railroad enterprise was unfortunate and fell through, about 1855, involving Mr. Walker in its failure to such an extent as to result in the loss of all his property here. He returned to and worked at his trade until the war of the late rebellion broke out, when, 1861, he accompanied the Butler boys, Company 11 of the 78th Regiment, to Kentucky and Tennessee. Here he was in charge of the sick in the hospitals and was otherwise attentive to and useful to the soldiers. He was a charitable man and always good and liberal towards the poor. He died while in the army at Bowling Green, Kentucky, in 1862, in the 59th year of his age. His remains were brought home here for interment.

The date of last weeks "Recollections of Butler" should have been March 5 instead of 25.

March 12, 1891                                        J.H.N.

**STEVENSON-MILLER-REED SQUARE**

Passing over North Street and continuing down west side of Main is the square we give the above name. Within our recollection from north down to the old limit of the borough now Penn Street was known as the "Gilmore Meadow." Some citizens yet living can recollect when the cows were turned into pasture at the corner where now is the Acme Candy and Confectionery store of Mr. David Scott. The lot on this corner fifty years ago was the property of the late Mr. Abraham Stevenson, who about that time built the house now standing there, embracing the Haslett part, now owned and occupied by the heirs of the late Hon. William Haslett. Mr. Stevenson sold it all to the late Mr. William Miller and from Mr. Miller came the Haslett part. The corner part now occupied by Mr. David Scott, became in recent years the property of the late Mr. Thomas Stehle and is now the property of his daughter Mrs. Aland.

The late Mr. William Miller owned also the middle lot of this square. He was a cabinet maker and had his shop and carried on that business in the buildings there until his death about 1880. He was succeeded there by his son, present Mr. William F. Miller, who had his cabinet making shop there until recently. This lot and buildings are now the property of the heirs of Mr. Miller and are at present occupied as boarding and eating houses.

The next lot is that of present Gen. George W. Reed on which is his comfortable residence. Gen. Reed bought this about 1839, and built and moved there in 1840, now more than 50 years ago. He also bought the adjoining lot of the next square, now owned and lived upon by Mr. Alfred Wick. Here he built and had his saddlery shop from about 1850 to 1861. Previously he had his shop in places heretofore mentioned. In 1863 he ceased working at his trade and has lived since then in his present house.

**GENERAL REED**

All things considered Gen. George W. Reed is the most interesting citizen of our town at present. He is perhaps the oldest, being, if he lives to July coming, 86 years of age. He came to Butler, it is stated, in 1824 and while therefore not one of the very early comers yet he is perhaps the closest connecting link between them and the present of any of our other old citizens. He has always been an active, correct and industrious citizen, of good moral habits and honest in all his ways and walks. In military affairs he has been a most prominent and conspicuous character. He at one time was the captain of the "Butler Blues," a militia company of the town. Soon after he was a major in the militia, then an adjutant to a battalion, then brigade inspector, from 1835 to 1842, then brigadier general until 1848. During part of this time, Butler was connected with Beaver County in military matters. In all these positions General Reed was every inch a soldier. No more gallant or soldier like man ever sat in saddle. When on horse back to this day he sits quite erect, and rides with ease and grace, commanding the attention and admiration of all. His services are still called for upon Decoration Days, reunions of regiments, and other military occasions.  He retains to a remarkable degree all his faculties except that of hearing, and if it were not for this loss of hearing he says he is as good a man as he ever was.

In 1845, Gen. Reed was elected sheriff of the county, over the late Gen. Robert McNair, and in 1862 he was elected treasurer of the county.  In politics he was a very ardent and active Whig during the days of the party, and since then has been an equally ardent and active Republican, always exerting an influence with the people surpassed by few if any of our older or present citizens.  He yet takes a lively interest in all public affairs and is respected by all.

## MECHLING MEADOW

With this last square ends what were the built up squares of Butler 50 years ago.  On the opposite, east side of street from this last one was what was then known as the "Mechling" meadow on which were no buildings of any kind.  The "Gilmore" meadow on the west side was built upon a little earlier than the Mechling one.  The present residence of W. D. Brandon, Esq. and family was the first break made on the old Mechling meadow.  This meadow extended from Main Street east to McKean and North to the old borough line, now East Penn Street, containing six or eight acres. it was the favorite place for football games or playing, 50 years and more ago.  About the holidays every year there was sure to be a football match in the Mechling meadow, largely attended by the scholars at the old Academy and many others.  The meadow was divided by a line as near the middle as could be.  Two parties were made up, with captains and rules for the play.  Both parties assembled at this middle line.  The ball, a large one, was tossed up in the air and the contest began at its fall, the struggle  being on each side to get the first kick and the objective points being the fences at the north or south ends of the meadow.  Which ever party got the ball to the fence of the other first were the victors.  These matches were often exciting and hotly contested, some times ending in a row, possibly in a fight.  The penalty paid by the defeated side was a treat for all of apples, gingerbread and cider to wash it down.

The Brandon residence was as we have said, the first building put on this meadow.  It was built by the late Mr. Samuel M. Lane, about the year 1847.  Mr. Lane sold the lot and house to the late Dunlap McLaughlin, Esq., 1853, and he sold same to the late Mr. James Campbell, about 1855.  Mr. Campbell lived here until his recent death.  His son T. Chalmers Campbell, Esq. and his son-in-law, J. D. McJunkin, Esq. have their fine residences on parts of this lot on North Street.

### WITHERSPOON INSTITUTE

The Witherspoon Institute was we think the next building on this old meadow, the Schreiber House being built after it.  The Witherspoon was erected about 1853, under the auspices of the Presbyterian Church.  The late Rev. Dr. Loyal Young was its first principal.  Rev. David Hall followed Dr. Young as its principal.  Then followed Rev. J. R. Coulter, Rev. Martin Ryerson, Rev. John Smalley, Rev. J. S. Boyd, Rev. Jesse Wells Hamilton and finally the late Rev. W. I. Brugh, all as principals of this institute.  During their time the Witherspoon was a widely known and useful educational one, turning out many scholars who have risen to distinction in many of the professions, especially in the ministry.

In 1876, the Witherspoon was purchased by the English Lutheran Church of this place, where that congregation worship at present and whose property it still is.  Mr. Brugh made an effort to have erected a more extensive Institute than the old one for that purpose purchasing ground on what is now called "Institute Hill."  But the project failed for want of financial aid.  A building however was erected in which schools were held for some years, when it became the property of the Catholic Church and a seminary of that church is there at present.

From the old Witherspoon, or now Clay Street on the old Mechling meadow are now the residences of Mr. Henry Miller, Mr. Kerr McBride, Mr. Dal Harvey, Dr. Zimmerman, Hon. Charles McCandless, Theodore Huselton, John Huselton, Esq., and Capt. Samuel Walker, all built in recent years.

Crossing now East Penn street was another meadow known as the Sullivan meadow, being the property of the late Hon. Charles C. Sullivan, originally a part of the Graham land.  On it at present is the residence in which Mr. Gib Linn resides and the residences of R. P. Scott, Esq., John S. Campbell, W. S. Ziegler, G. Wilson Miller, F. M. Eastman, Esq., the late Capt. James B. Storey, in which Mr. D. Osborne resides, and the residence of Hon. A. L. Hazen, all built in recent years.

From there up on former Graham ground is the Mr. John B. Graham former residence, now we believe the property of Mr. Charles Duffy and the residences of Dr. J. C. Redick, Rev. W. E. Oller, Joseph G. Vanderlin, Esq., J. R. Grieb and the Henry Eitenmiller property, formerly that of Mr. Ebenezer Graham, all constructed in recent years.

## ROBERT GRAHAM AND RESIDENCE

Crossing over the road, now Main St., stood the residence of the late Mr. Robert Graham.  On its old foundation now stands the residence of Mr. H. W. Christie.  This was built in recent years by Mr. Bernard Dougherty and when built was considered the most costly and elegant residence in the town, and is perhaps yet.  It passed from Mr. Dougherty into the hands of Mr. John Berg, who sold same recently to Mr. Christie.  The old house there was also a brick one and Mr. Graham lived there 50 years ago and for a period beyond our recollection.

With the exception of the Cunninghams, the late Mr. Robert Graham gave more of his property for the

## Three Horsemen

Twenty-five years ago West Jefferson Street was decorated with at least three livery stables. Several horseshoeing "emporiums" were within a stone's throw, and dealers visited Butler several times a year, making Jefferson a horse street.

Some old-timers will recall three brothers, Uncle John, Jimmie and Archie, who owned a stable on Jackson Street and were trainers and dealers in horses for 50 years. Uncle John was a veterinarian: Jimmie was a horseshoer, and Archie was the horse trainer.

The brothers were known among horsemen from New York to Chicago. If Wilsons of Pittsburgh, or Hildebrands of Lancaster, or McGown of Chicago, or some of the big dealers in New York or Philadelphia wanted a team of horses for a special purpose they wrote the three brothers in Butler, giving specifications. The horses would be selected, matched, and shipped and the price asked was paid without quibble. If the horses came from the three brothers in Butler they were "right."

The brothers were Irish and had some peculiarities. For instance, Uncle John never told what ailed a horse he was treating, nor what medicine he gave, and he was famous over the country as a horse doctor. What's the matter with McBride's horse, a shrewd jockey would ask. The noncommital response would likely be, "He's sick." Another shark after information would take a different track and inquire of Uncle John, "What are you giving Bickle's mare for distemper?" The response in a soft and mellow voice would be, "some medicine." The conversation usually stopped there.

Hundreds of horses were bought for the eastern markets every year by dealers who came to Butler several times during a season to purchase from the farmers. The three brothers were always conspicuous figures at these sales.

The three brothers were absolutely square with their friends. Theirs was the last word in judging a horse. A neighbor youth took a fancy one time to a driving horse that had everything in the town, then full of good horses, shaded for class and appearance. The brothers wouldn't sell—they wouldn't even set a price. The young man wanted the horse for his mother and sister to drive and he was inclined to get peeved over the refusal to deal. One day the horse was sold to a city dealer and the young man was sore over the turndown.

"Why didn't you sell me that horse," he demanded of one of the brothers the next day. "The horse is gone and we'll tell you," replied the brother. "No one knew it here, but that horse had a bad fault. If we sold him to you and he would run off and kill your mother or sister, we could never look you in the face. We'll get you a better horse by far that is safe."

Butler Eagle, 4-6-1925, James A. McKee

founding of Butler as the county seat than any of its other early citizens. To his liberality, it is recorded that the early town owes much for its location and growth. He was among the very earliest settlers and became the owner of the tract of land, 300 acres immediately north of town. He did the teaming or hauling between here and Pittsburgh for many years. We recollect his team of four bays and the old fashioned wagon in which he hauled goods for the merchants here from Pittsburg. This wagon had a covered bed, curved up high in front and rear, resembling somewhat the high old bonnets the women used to wear. It was to Butler then, as in the transportation of goods, what the modern railroad freight cars are now. Everything was sent to and from Pittsburg by Mr. Graham and his wagon. Before the time of the stage coaches, citizens even traveled as passengers in it being then no other mode of conveyance, and we have heard some of our late citizens say they went to Pittsburg and back in Mr. Graham's wagon, and were glad of that chance to do so.

Mr. Graham was a respected citizen, a good, benevolent, kind hearted, obliging man. He raised a large family, of whom, our present aged Mr. John H. Graham, Mr. Ebenezer Graham and their sister Mrs. Mary Heiner are the only surviving ones, all now living here. Mr. Ebenezer Graham is we believe the youngest of that family. Present Walter B. Graham, Esq., and Dr. Samuel Graham, are grandsons. Mr. Robert Graham died in 1849 at the age of 81 years.

Passing down from the old Robert Graham place, now H. W. Christie, are the fine residences of Mr. Joseph L. Purvis, Mr. H. C. Haselton and C. G. Christie, Esq., all of recent date. Next is the large residence erected by Walter L. Graham, Esq., about 1870. This became the property of Ex. Judge James Bredin, then of Mr. Howard Thompson, and now of Mr. Wilson E. Reed, present owner. Crossing Pearl street the next properties are those of Mr. D. H. Wuller, Ex-Sheriff, Thomas Doneghey, Mr. G. W. Ziegler and the late General John N. Purviance residence. These are all upon former Graham land or meadow. General Purviance was among the first to buy and build out there. He erected his residence about 1841, near 50 years ago. It is now the property of his son John Purviance, Esq. and other heirs. General Purviance died so recently, 1885, and his useful life and good character have been so fully made known that we deem unnecessary any further presentation of them here.

Crossing West Penn Street, the old borough line, that divided former Graham and Gilmore meadows, is first, the Colbert property, heretofore spoken of and where Mr. Harvey Colbert now resides. Then is the present Mr. W. N. Hardman fine residence, formerly that of late Andrew Carnes, Esq. heretofore spoken of. Then is the fine residence of S. F. Bowser, Esq. formerly that of the late Samuel C. Stewart, Esq. who built same about 1850. He and Mr. Andrew Carnes built their houses in same year. Mr. Stewart was a treasurer of the county, elected about 1848. He came from

44

about Portersville, this county, was a cabinet maker by trade, and a man of excellent character in every way. He removed from here to Beaver County and is, we believe, deceased. The only child of his we know of now, is a son, Mr. Newton Stewart, of Brady's Bend, Pa..

The next residence is that of the widow and heirs of the late Mr. Martin Reiber. This was originally the property of the late William B. Lemmon, before spoken of. It has been greatly improved and is now one of the finest looking in the town. Mr. Martin Reiber in his day was one of the best, most useful and enterprising citizens of Butler. He owned several properties. He was father to present Ferd, Albert, Martin, Howard and Aaron E. Reiber. He died 1882, aged 71 years.

The residence of late John Scott, Esq. is next, and then the houses of Mr. Joseph Elliott, Mr. J. M. McClung and the store building of Messrs. Reed & Kirkpatrick. Crossing Clay street is the popular Wick House, now owned and kept by Mr. J. S. Wick. The Mrs. William Miller residence is next and then the residence of Mr. Alfred Wick. Mr. George Weber erected this house, 1872. This whole square was at one time owned by the late David Walker. The late Samuel G. Purvis, Esq. was owner for a time of the Wick House and that lot. The late Mr. William Miller was owner of the other two lots. Gen. Reed bought the one next him and sold same to Mr. George Wever, all heretofore spoken of.

### Four Of A Name

The name Graham seems a favorite one for the ministry by our people. Butler last Saturday had four ministers of that name here. Three of them were born and raised here and two of these returned to visit relatives and friends.

First to come this vacation season for the preachers, was the Rev. John Graham, son of John Graham, Esq. deceased. He is on a visit to his mother, Mrs. Catharine Graham, living on the Diamond here. His father whose memory is respected by all who knew him came of the Graham people who were Scotch and early settlers of this county in and around Petersville, Connoquenessing Township. John is now a minister in the Episcopal Church and preached for his people while here.

Next to come is Rev. Loyal Young Graham D.D., born and raised here and now a very prominent minister in the Presbyterian Church and located in Philadelphia for the past twenty odd years. He is a son of the late James H. Graham, one of the very early settlers of Butler and therefore cousin to Doctor Samuel Graham and Walter L. Graham Esq. of this place. His two sermons to the people here on last Sunday were to crowded houses and are highly spoken of for their eloquence and interest. He is a credit to this the place of his early days and our people honor him. With him this time he brought his son Rev. Loyal Young Graham Jr., also now a minister in a Presbyterian Church in Philadelphia and who assisted his father in his church services here. He has also another son in the ministry in Philadephia.

Rev. Ernest O. Graham of this place, born here and son of the late Ebenezer Graham and therefore cousin to above Rev. Loyal Young Graham, is now a minister in the English Lutheran Church and assisted in the cornerstone laying ceremonies of the new English Lutheran Church here on last Sunday.

Thus we had the four clergymen of the name of Graham with us here last Sunday and all doing duty in their line.
*Butler Citizen*, date unknown

This now brings us to where we left when crossing from Gen. Reed's to "Mechling meadow" and completes both sides of Main Street, from where we first commenced. And it would complete the task we had in view if it were not that something should be added as to the south end of present town, not before mentioned, and of one or two points or places not on Main Street but now within the town limits.

In the last article one place where Mr. Thos. B. White kept the post office in year 1872 was omitted, to wit, where present Krug Meat Shop is. From there he removed it to Cunningham street, in 1873. We also omitted to state that the late Capt. Edwin Lyon was associated with late William Haslett in the publication of the "Butler American" for a short time, and also with Col. John M. Thompson for a time in the practice of the law. Capt. Lyon was also cashier of present Saving's Bank for a time about 1868. He died in 1872 at age of 43.
March 19, 1891.                                            J. H. N

### CUNNINGHAM - NEGLEY MILL

In the first article of "Recollections of Butler" we spoke of "the commons" in the then south end of town and as being a part of the donation of John and Samuel Cunningham to the county of Butler for the county seat. We also referred then to the piece of ground south of the commons and between them and the Connoquenessing Creek, some six of eight acres, not in the original town, but as the property fifty years ago and more of the late John Negley, Esq. This piece will now be best recognized when stated it is the same upon which is the flouring mill of present Mr. George Walter--old Cunningham mill--and upon which also is the residence of Mr. Walter, a house and lot of Mr. Jacob Boos, the old mansion house of the late John Negley, a fine new residence recently erected by Mr. and Mrs. Wm. Ritter, the residence of Mr. George McCandless and two or three houses recently erected and owned by Mr. John N. Patterson, all now standing there.

For some reason this piece was not included in the grant made by the Cunninghams for the county seat, probably because their mill was upon it. But it was part of their 300 acre tract of land, which they had procured before the formation of the county and which they called "Butler" and which covered nearly all of our old built up town and a good part of our present one. In the bend of the creek about the middle of their tract, they built their celebrated mill; the first flouring mill, according to history, built upon the waters of the Connequenessing. They came here, the chronicles state, in 1797, and built their mill about that time. The late John Negley first appears upon the scene there in 1800 and becomes for a time their miller. They seemed to have had an idea from all we ever learned from our father that the future county seat of the county would be where it is. But their hopes of prosperity were soon shattered by the death of John Cunningham in 1805, according to the chronicles. His remains were interred in the old burial ground of Butler and "now no man knows his grave," is the brief record concerning him in the recently made history of our town.

This is a sad reflection to our citizens as to the grave and end of the man who as his share gave about 77 acres of the ground upon which Butler stands, embracing probably this very burial ground in which he was laid, and of the place in which it must now be written, "no man knows his grave." But perhaps the then citizens of the town likened Mr. Cunningham to Moses who saw but did not enjoy the land he sought and therefore desired that the place of his burial should be like unto that of Moses, of which we are told no one knew the place. Of what became of his brother Samuel we never learned. In the year following 1806, we find the mill and the balance of the 300 acre tract becoming the property of the late Mr. Negley. Samuel probably returned to Lancaster County, from where they are said to have come. Samuel Cunningham, the history of the county states, was the foreman of the first grand jury ever convened in this county.

## DEPRECIATION LANDS

The 300 acre tract of the Cunninghams was one of what were known as "depreciation lands." These depreciation tracts or lands have an interesting history. They covered about half of our county. The lands themselves were not depreciated or poor, but were so called because the script or certificates that thestate had issued to her soldiers of the Revolutionary War became depreciated. The state, to relieve and pay its then needy soldiers, ordered these lands in the western part of the state, to be surveyed into tracts and sold, the proceeds to go to paying off and redeeming the depreciated script held by the soldiers for their services in the Revolution. Hence the name "depreciation lands." James Cunningham, a brother of John and Samuel, it appears was a surveyor and was appointed by the state, one of its surveyors to run off these lands. The district he surveyed passed through or into part of what became Butler County and hence the name of "Cunningham's district of depreciation lands." James Cunningham seems to have been acquainted with Robert Morris of Philadelphia, the distinguished patriot of the Revolutionary War and General Washington's secretary of the treasury. Whether through the influence of James Cunningham, or through his own desire to aid the soldiers, we have never been able to learn, but Robert Morris, history tells us, purchased a great many of these tracts, about 100 of them in Butler County, containing perhaps 90,000 acres of land. One thing seems pretty certain and that is that John and Samuel Cunningham came out west here either through their brother James or through Robert Morris. Robert Morris, we are strongly inclined to believe, aided them and in the interests of his lands, probably sent them here resulting in locating the town of Butler where it is. The first road made from Pittsburg to Butler was made by John and Samuel Cunningham. It was a direct straight up and down road going up and down the hills without turning to right or left. Its old track can be seen here yet on south of town; passing near the present barn of Mr. Hugh McCrea on top of the hill south of town. There were some other very steep places on it that we know of and have seen. We mention the above to show the probable connection of Robert Morris with the Cunningham, afterwards Negley mill property. We have but little doubt that it was by his money or aid that John and Samuel Cunningham came out here and founded the mill at the point they did.

Through his sympathy for the soldiers in buying these lands and thus enabling the state to redeem its certificates issued to the soldiers and thus paying them the debt it promised them, Robert Morris involved himself and to such an extent, history tells us, that he became financially embarrassed and died poor although being previously a wealthy man. All his lands were sold at the city of Philadelphia in 1807. Stephen Lowry, of Maryland, became the purchaser at this sale of the Morris lands in Butler County. He was the father of the late Mrs. Sarah Collins and in his will devised them to her. From Mrs. Collins they came to her daughters, the late Mrs. Judge McClure and present Mrs. Judge Wilson McCandless of Pittsburg. So it will be seen that the old Cunningham, afterwards Negley mill property, came through Robert Morris, as came the titles of many farms in the county through Lowry, the successor to his lands.

## JOHN NEGLEY

From the above it will be seen the late John Negley was the direct successor to the Cunninghams in this first mill property, purchasing same as apprears in 1806. He owned and carried it on for nearly thirty years. During this time he added to it a large woolen mill which was operated by a brother-in-law of his, the late Mr. Malachi Richardson, favorably mentioned in the early history of the town. He also established near this mill a cabinet making shop in which we have been told the late Robert Carnahan, Esq. and the late Mr. Norbert Foltz were his principal workmen for some years. He engaged also in different other kinds of businesses among them the mining of coal. The mill at the time of this purchase and during the time of the Cunninghams appears to have been the center place of business for the town. Public meetings were held there. The first public sale of lots in the town, 1803, was held or made at this mill. The Cunninghams and their successor it is said were hospitable and entertained people when coming to the mill. A rather large and good frame house had been built by them across the creek west of the mill, situated among or near to large rocks. The creek at this point had, and has yet to a certain extent, a very peculiar formation. Very large rocks, by some great convulsion or upheaval in the earth would seem to have been hurled down into or what became the creek there. The channel at a certain point there was very narrow and could be spanned by a single timber reaching from this side to one of the rocks. Over this narrow, deep channel a foot walk afforded communication between the mill and the house spoken of. The track of the recently constructed Pittsburg and Western Railroad passes over where some of these large rocks stood, causing the removal of those near the old house. Mr. Negley lived in this house for a time, between 1816 and 1826, and until he erected the one on this side of the creek, already spoken of. Where the old house stood can yet be seen. We have spoken of his many enterprises, but there was one that deserves special mention. This was an effort to manufacture salt here.

## THE OLD SALT WELL

About 1832 he commenced the drilling of a well for salt water on the south side of the creek below plank road bridge on now property of his daughter, Mrs. Mary B. Muntz. In those days salt wells were drilled by hand or foot power rather a lever being used, upon the end of which two men tramped and worked the rods up and down. These rods were of hickory and similar to those now used at our oil wells for pumping purposes. They required frequent repairing. The hole drilled was only about two and a half inches in diameter. The depth of the well, it was supposed, would have to be about the same as that at which salt water was then obtained at the salt wells on the river about Freeport, to-wit, about 800 feet. That distance was drilled, after much labor and expense, and some salt water was obtained, but not in sufficient amount to justify operating. This distance would be at about where present oil producers get what they call the "mountain sand," in which it appears some salt water is generally found. The present theories and knowledge of "second sand," "third sand," "fourth sand," "hundred-foot sand," and "gas sand," were unknown to the drillers for salt water fifty years ago. And all recent experience derived from the oil business shows very clearly that had this salt well been drilled but a little deeper an abundance of salt water would have been obtained, as witness the great flows of it found at from 1100 to 1200 feet in the "hundred-foot field," and in fact at all oil wells hereabouts. The immediate and pressing question just now is, how to "shut off" or "head off" the salt water, and the oil producers would now rather know how or where not to find it than how or where to find it. The flow of it is so great in the "hundred-foot" field that legislation is just now being sought for to prevent our streams being "salted down." The old salt well enterprise of Mr. Negley had thus to be abandoned for want of obtaining sufficient water to make salt "in paying quantity," and after his expending about $8,000 in the effort to find it.

## SALE OF THE MILL

In 1832 the mill and some three acres of the ground surrounding it were sold to the late General Robert McNair and brothers. These brothers were the late Thomas, James, William and Alexander McNair. These men were quite prominent here for a time, particularly in political affairs. A daughter of Thomas, widow of the late Mr. Peterson Pearce is living on the farm immediately west of town. Mr. Thomas S. McNair, living here, is a son of James, who was a justice of the peace in the town about 30 years ago. William, a single man went, we believe, south. Alexander was quite a cripple, but notwithstanding his greatly crippled condition he studied law and was admitted to the bar here. Robert the elder and leading one, died recently near Petersville--this county. They carried on the mills for some 12 or 15 years. During this time they were entirely destrtoyed by fire in 1842. They rebuilt the flouring part which is partly the present structure there. About 1848 it became the property of the late Hon. William Beatty, through his executors, were conveyed to the late Jacob Walter and present John C. Grohman who carried it on until the death of Mr. Walter in 1865. Mr. Walter was succeeded by his son, present ex-Sheriff George Walter, and the firm became Grohman & George Walter, until Mr. Grohman sold his interest, about 1872, to present Mr. Jacob Boos. It has since been carried on by Messrs. Walter and Boos, either jointly or separately until last year when Mr. Boos sold his interest to Mr. Walter who is entire owner at present and is now carrying on this old and noted mill. His father, the late Mr. Jacob Walter, was in his day one of the best and most influential citizens of our town. He was a blacksmith by trade, and for many years, in connection with present Mr. George Reiber, had a shop were the present residence of Levi McQuistion Esq. now stands. Their shop was about 50 years ago, the principal one of the kind in town, having the custom of the Beatty stables, which then included the custom arising from the stage coach company and its horses. Mr. Jacob Walter died, as stated, in the year 1865, at the age of 50 years.

In further reference to the late Mr. John Negley it may be stated that he was the first treasurer of the county; its third prothonotary; 1817-1820; one of its earliest representatives in the general assembly of the state, 1809; and twice afterwards in the same, 1821 and 1822, all matters of record. His charitable and benevolent nature, especially to the poor or needy, are matters also well known and spoken of often. He died August 11, 1870 in his 93rd year.

## JOHN McQUISTION-ARCHIBALD McCALL and others

March 26, 1891.                                    J. H. N.

Fifty years ago there were some prominent men living close to the town but seen so frequently in it that they might be considered a part of it and therefore worthy of mention. Among these was the late Mr. John McQuistion Sr. of Butler Twp. who lived in the large stone house on the old Freeport road on the hill a mile southeast of town. The present owners and occupants of the house and the large old McQuistion farm there are the widow and heirs of the late John Doerr who became owner of same. Mr. McQuistion in his day also owned several other tracts of land adjoining where he lived being of the Morris-Lowry depreciation lands already spoken of. He also owned several of the lots in the borough of Butler, and was considered quite a wealthy man. His farm was noted for its large amount of fruit trees particularly of the apple upon which the boys of the town made frequent raids, sometimes by night. He defended his fruit on such occasions by some large dogs he had. Besides his extensive farm he carried on tanning and shoe making and many of the people of the town went to his shop a mile of nearly uphill travel [*Center Ave.*] to have their shoes repaired or mended with him. He was one of the early commissioners of the county and for years one of its principal citizens. Nearly all of that name now living near or about here are grandchildren of his. He died in 1841 at the age of 74 years.

James McQuistion, one of his sons, who lived...?... noted for its good fruit. His son ? now lives in the brick house there built by his father. Two of his sons in law, Joseph B. Mechling, Esq. and Thomas B. White, Esq. have their fine residences on part of his farm. James McQuistion was known as a good citizen and personally was a very kind hearted and benevolent man. One illustration of his humanity is worthy of mention.

## A NOTED PAUPER

A queer character by the name of Ross Gattley became a charge on Butler Township as a pauper and was cared for by James McQuistion and his family for many years. Ross Gattley was a man of a very peculiar make-up, both mentally and physically. In body he was tall and very slim, being of about the same thickness from head to foot. It by no means could be said of him that he was as broad as he was long, being all long. He was said to have been part Italian, and by some means the toes of his feet had been frozen off, making him walk lame. He was a great reader however, and always could be seen carrying a book of some kind. He was cross and surly in disposition and few cared about keeping him, but paupers had to be sold under the law in that day to the lowest bidder or who would agree to keep them. Ross would be put up yearly for sale and Mr. James McQuistion would be the lowest bidder to keep him, and his family did keep him until he died about 1809. They were the only family who could manage Ross, bear with him, or induce him to do any kind of labor. Mr. James McQuistion died in 1831 at the age of 45 years.

## ARCHIBALD MCCALL - ORPHANS HOME

Mr. Archibald McCall was a Philadelphia merchant and a man of wealth. He became owner at an early day of a large body of land in this county, some of it laying near Butler. To look after his possessions here brought him frequently to our town, between 1830 and 1843 and probably before and after those dates. On his visits here, always in the summer time, he would be accompanied by his family. This family coinsisted, as far as we can reflect, of two or three daughters and a son. They would stay in the then old Mechling Hotel on the Diamond. They were very nice, well dressed, well behaved, and cultured people, and great attention was paid to them by our people on their summer visits here. Mr. McCall took quite an interest in the welfare of the town, bringing or sending here at times some improved animal stock and perhaps other things valuable to our citizens and farmers. He built the mill up the creek from town, now known as the George Reiber mill. He desired also to have a summer residence for himself and family when they came here, and for this purpose erected what is now the Orphans Home building on the hill, northeast of town. When it was built about 1836, it was the wonder and admiration of our people. He and his family inhabited it on several of their visits here. It has been enlarged by more recent owners, but the large and broad porticos around it and other of its features are the same as put there by Mr. McCall. After several changes in ownership, this property became that of the Reformed Church, the present owners, and was turned into an Orphans Home, now successfully carried on by Rev. Plugh. The Mr. A.M. Meylert, with a Mr. Clymer of the eastern part of the state, became the purchaser of all the McCall lands in this county which included the farm upon which this house, now Orphans Home stands. These parties are all, we think, deceased. Mr. McCall died in Philadelphia, but in which year we cannot now state. It was however after 1843, as in that year his son General George A. McCall was in Butler with the family. The summer of that year, 1843, was the one in which the attempt was made to take the Indian Mohawk from the jail and General McCall being here and being a distinguished soldier in the regular army, was consulted by the sheriff and citizens as to how to best defend the jail in case of an attack upon it. Gen. McCall made suggestions or gave the sheriff pointers in the proper military defense which suggestions were acted upon but he declined to take any open part in the suppression of that rebellion. He however was a brave soldier and afterwards bore a conspicuous part on the batlefield of Gettysburg and through the late Civil War.

## REV. WHITE RESIDENCE

Near to this orphans home and on the hill to the east, a little beyond is the residence of our present worthy Rev. William White and family. This residence must be mentioned for two reasons, first as being the best fruit on any of the hills around the town and second for its peculiar shape by the person who is said to have built it. We do not know the date but that house is one of our earliest recollections and was built no later than about 1830. The late Evan R. Evans Esq. is said to have erected it. Evan R. Evans was a lawyer practicing at the Butler Bar about that time. He was a son-in-law of the late Mrs. Sarah Collins who then owned that and adjoining hills. This may account for Mr. Evans coming to Butler. The unique structure of this house has always been a subject of remark and would indicate that the builder intended adding more or other buildings to it. Mr. Evans however left here about that time on account of his health and is said to have gone to and died in Texas. Rev. White became its owner about 1860 and has with his family since resided there. Its prominence commands a pleasant view and it and grounds have thus become a valuable property. Rev. White came to Butler more than 50 years ago and is the survivor of all the ministers to that date. He is now, we believe, about 80 years of age and in his declining days has the respect of all our citizens.

## HON. JAMES MITCHELL

We could not close these recollections without mention of the Hon. James Mitchell and his brothers, Samuel and John. While their old farm residence is not within view of town and is a little farther out, we have noticed yet they have been and are so identified with...?... interests and with our citizens so as to make them almost a part of the town. For 50 years or more they have been mingling with our citizens and participating in their public affairs and have always been considered as honest, useful and obliging men. James Mitchell's worth has been recognized by his fellow citizens. He was elected in 1851, one of the commissioners of the county and was such at the time of the erection, 1853 of its second court house, burned down in 1883. Two of his sons, Alexander Mitchell Esq. and James B. Mitchell are among our best business citizens. His brother, Samuel S. Mitchell has been ill for some time and is not now a very frequent visitor to town. Ex-Sheriff John Mitchell, his other brother is now living among us and like all of the others takes an interest in the welfare of the town.

In our article last week in speaking of the patriot, Robert Morris, the expression "and General Washington's secretary of the treasury" should have read "and the friend and...?... of General Washington's secretary of treasury." Mr. Morris was never himself secretary of treasury but aided the government in providing for its dcbts in thc manner we spoke of. He was however a signer of the Declaration of Independence and was a member of the Continental Congress of the United States. In speaking of the Cunninghams the word "leased" should have been printed "learned".

## CONCLUSION

When we commenced writing these recollections of Butler we thought they could be embraced in three or four articles of the length made them. But this is now the fourteenth article and much more could be written. We had but little idea they would create the interest among our citizens that they immediately did. We were encouraged by the flattering words spoken of them and the frequent commenting of the good object we had in view. All seemed to think that now was the time to preserve much concerning our town of the past 50 years which if not written now might otherwise be lost. If we have supplied this link between the past and the present we will feel fully paid for our labor. A good part of our time for the past three months has been given the task. The 14 articles contain about thirty thousand words, or about four thousand lines as published and there was scarcely one of these four thousand lines but was a subject of care and study to us. We desired to be as correct as possible as to the dates and events referred to, but doubtless there are some errors. We would liked to have extended the scope laid out and to have spoken of other streets than Main; but Main Street 50 years ago embraced nearly the whole town. We have however either directly or indirectly, made mention in some way of all the old families of the town. We found that about 50 years ago, 1840, was a turning point in the habits and affairs of the people of the town. About that time the spinning wheel and the weaving loom began to disappear and the linsey-woolsey dresses then worn to be supplied by a more costly and fashionable material. The first photograph artist came to Butler since 1840. And now we have telegraphs, telephones, railroads and other things unknown 50 years ago. We desire to return our thanks to all friends who kindly tendered or gave us any information they had as to persons or events written of or who by suggestion or otherwise in any way aided us in the preparation of the work we now bring to a close.

March. 31, 1891          John H. Negley

copied from the *Butler Citizen* dated 1890 and 1891 by Audrey Fetters
edited by Dave and Audrey Craig

# DU-CO CERAMICS COMPANY

P. O. Box 568 • 155 South Rebecca Street

## SAXONBURG, PENNSYLVANIA 16056

Phone: 724-352-1511   FAX: 724-352-1266   E-mail: duco@nauticom.net

## Manufacturing Technical Ceramics in Butler County
## Since 1949
## Celebrating Butler County's Bi-Centennial Year

## Reldon W. Cooper, President and CEO
## Founder of Du-Co Ceramics Company

Technical ceramics for electrical, electronic, refractory and mechanical usages.
Steatite - Cordierite - Porcelain - Magnesium Oxide - Alumina
http://www.ceramics.com/duco/

# Main Street

If you are more than slightly interested in local history, John Negley's recollections of Butler's Main Street should have been quite enjoyable. Wouldn't it be exciting to go back in time to the turn of the century and take a stroll down Main Street—hear the sounds, smell the smells, and best of all—watch people? Main Street was thronged with all kinds of folks—shoppers, clerks, business people, families, farmers, street vendors; you name it.

As informative and interesting as Negley's account is, his remembrances were almost entirely of people, their buildings and businesses. The old man didn't have much to say about the ambiance of the street itself. There was usually a great deal happening out on the street. Fortunately some information has been found which gives us sketchy details of these scenes. Sande Cristofano found a dozen or more newspaper articles which enlighten us a bit. These articles were written in 1925 by James A. McKee, the historian who wrote one of my favorite early Butler County histories—*20th Century History of Butler and Butler County, Pennsylvania and Representative Citizens*. McKee was born in 1865, wrote his history book in 1909, and was still documenting history in 1925. I have quoted McKee's articles extensively in the early sections of this tome; each is documented and easily recognized by the smaller number ten font.

At the turn of the century, Butler's Main Street and several adjoining streets were the stage for a raucous choir of street vendors. As was typical in any thriving-northeastern city of that era, the medley of noises went on until well after dark—no nine to five hours for those Main Street merchants. Most businesses closed when the crowds thinned, regardless of the hour.

Pushcart men sold every item imaginable from clothing to vegetables. Young boys sold newspapers and candy; young women sold hot ears of corn from tin boxes—and yes, a few sold themselves. One could buy a tin cup of lemonade from the bucket of a street vendor. Once in a while a sandwich man with his gaudy placards strapped on front and back would shuffle by with slow-exhausted steps. Sandwich men, you know, were the dregs of the street vendors.

Butler's littered streets resounded with the chant of the vegetable salesman. Noisy competition was provided by the very vocal "clothes man" who wore as many as six coats and a teetering stack of ten hats. There was a traveling salesman by the name of Simon. He was familiar to most Butlerites and his clanking graniteware pots and pans announced his arrival. Any townsperson who kept Simon overnight and fed him received a gift of one of his pans. Another traveling salesman named Louie Davis carried, strapped on his back, a pack of clothing about four to five feet square. The person hospitable enough to give Louie a bed for the night received a pair of socks for his trouble.

According to James A. McKee, one of the harbingers of spring, in addition to the appearance of the robins, was the arrival of Honest John, the street fakir who held forth at the corner of Main and Jefferson Streets or near the courthouse. Honest John sold a variety of goods ranging from pins and needles to gold watches and chains. His biggest seller was a surprise package done up in a sealed envelope. The package contained finger rings, ladies-neck chains and an assortment of writing paper, pencils, pens and small knickknacks; he sold the entire collection for a dollar. After John had been back in town for a week or two, numerous men and women might be seen at church on Sundays wearing

Many readers who have reached the half century milestone, will remember John and Leon Allshouse, better known as the "Pickle Brothers," who worked all their lives picking up and hauling trash and rubbish. Their route included Main Street so they were very well known to Butler County residents. The Allshouse brothers lived in the city on Madison Avenue but later moved to Cosco where they conducted their hauling business.

Shoppers were lured into several Main Street stores by the sounds of piano music. Just inside each open door was a high-circular platform which was completely surrounded by sheet music. Someone who had achieved a high degree of musical ability, commonly referred to as a song plugger, played songs by request, or merely performed to practice and at the same time, entertain. The store owner's objective was of course, to sell music sheets to some of the usual group of half-a-dozen listeners who would courteously applaud after each song. Some people weren't interested in purchasing music but would nevertheless request songs and enjoy the free entertainment. It was a cheap night out and it always included a bag of peanuts and a walk up and down Main Street. People who are fifty years of age or older may remember piano playing "song pluggers" of more recent days. Harvey C. Trader's, Steadman's, G. C. Murphy's, Miller's Music Store and F. W. Woolworth's all had such talented pianists. Woolworth's kept their piano and sheet music in the back where the cacophonous sounds from the street did not interfere with the music making.

Some of the most popular songs in Butler County around the turn of the century were a result of the Spanish American War. Marches such as "The Stars and Stripes Forever," and Sousa's "El Capitan" were very popular for several years after 1898. Other widely loved songs of that era were, "Animal Fair," "I Don't Want to Play in Your Yard," "After the Ball," "The Girl I Left Behind Me," "Sidewalks of New York," "Daisy Bell," "A Hot Time in the Old Town Tonight," "Anvil Chorus," and that everlasting charmer, "Home Sweet Home." Songs then remained popular much longer than do today's tunes. During the 1920's and 30's some big hits were, "Yes Sir That's My Baby," "Yes We have No Bananas," "My Old Kentucky Home," "Old Black Joe," "Beautiful Dreamer," "Columbia the Gem of the Ocean," "Old Oaken Bucket," and "Red Wing." Remember, before the phonograph and the radio, people had no other options when it came to music—it was only performed live. Even the organ grinder's tunes were enjoyed and appreciated. If one prefered dancing to the music, in 1900 the cakewalk was Butler's most popular dance.

We know there was a bicycling craze occurring around the year 1900, but information on the pastime is elusive other than a few photographs of Main Street which show several bicyclists.

Many will remember the central bookkeeping office in Offut's and Troutman's. The sales person put the money from the customer, along with a sales slip, into

## MILITARY BANDS

In the summer of 1876 the city of Butler sent a band and a military company to Philadelphia to participate in the centennial celebration of the Declaration of Independence. The members of the band and military company spent three weeks on the exhibition grounds and had the time of their lives. The only survivor of the band [in 1925] is Barney Kemper of Franklin Street, who played second coronet. Later Barney gave up the cornet for the bass drum, which he played for many years in the Germania band which was the successor of the old military band which was attached to the Thirteenth Regiment of the National Guard. The Butler company of this regiment was known as company A and was organized by Captain J. B. Story, who was later promoted to colonel.

In the Spanish-American War the Butler unit volunteered as Company E. Fifteenth Infantry. In the re-organization of the National Guard after the Spanish-American War, the Butler unit was assigned to the Sixteenth Infantry, National Guard as Company L. Sixteenth Infantry and entered the World War as Company 5, 112th Infantry. The successor of the first regimental band was the Germania Band organized about 1881 from the membership of the Germania Orchestra, which had been organized and trained by Prof. Von Meyerhoff, a well-known music instructor of that time.

Leonard Wise and Jerome Staley were early leaders of these bands and for twenty years William G. Ziegler was director of the Germania Band, which was finally merged with the Sixteenth Regiment Band. Butler was without a military band until 1903 when the Sixteenth Regiment Band was organized and made its first appearance at the National Guard camp at Somerset. Eugene Morrison was principal musician and A. J. Bowser was director. This band held a front line position among the regimental bands of the state for ten years.
*Butler Eagle*, May 26, 1925, James A. McKee

## Still Booming

Butler is still booming in the building line, and in increase of population and in business generally. Particularly is this the case in the Southside or end of town. One of the most unique buildings about finished there is that of Mr. Bole, south end of Main Street [Kenmac building]. It has a form and fashion of style that is peculiar—none like it yet erected. Something like the spring bonnet of the young ladies, it aims to go up higher, with angles upon angles, and one section differing from another. It attracts much attention and is regarded as quite an interesting improvement upon the old style of house building.

The excavation for the new John Stein store house, near the Willard House, south end of Main Street is about completed. The stone foundations of the new Schenck building, corner of Diamond, are about completed and brick work is soon to commence. Also for the large addition to the Eitenmiller Hotel.

The old tenements on the west side of the Dougal lot have been removed and the rubbish cleared away, previous to the large business block to be erected conjointly by Mr. Ketterer, Miss Gilkey and Messrs. I. J. McCandless and A. Perry Stewart, Esq.

Many other buildings of various kinds are going up in diffferent parts of the town.

*Butler Citizen, 5-27-1887*

a metal basket which was attached to an overhead-moving wire. A pulley system whizzed the basket along the wire to a cashier on the mezzanine. It is difficult to forget the sound of the moving wires. A few moments later the basket came sailing back on the wire with the customer's change and the bill which was stamped "paid." Sometimes the system broke down and the clerk had to walk up to the mezzanine. With some of these systems the wires moved continually; with others the clerk yanked a bell chord which hung from the ceiling. This alerted the cashier on the mezzanine to start the machinery. Troutman's replaced their wire system with a vacuum operated one much like that found at today's drive-in bank windows.

Churches had gospel concerts, ice cream socials, strawberry festivals and other social events where young men and women could meet. Ladies' prayer circles had countless bake sales. Many of these activities occurred on Main Street.

One of Butler's senior citizens showed me a handwritten description of the Nixon Hotel which opened on the Diamond in the summer of 1906. "In the city's newest hotel a man at the desk was smoking a strong-smelling cigar—the aroma was very pleasant. He was not in a cage as were the hotel clerks and bankers we had observed in larger cities. The bellboy directed us to the elevator which was in the main lobby. We took it to the third floor where we stepped out into a foyer. A well-dressed man standing in the hallway spat tobacco juice into a ubiquitous spittoon. His aim from six feet was deadly. The bellboy replied, 'This is your private bathroom. You won't find another hotel in Butler with these fine accommodations.'

The small room, although very hot, was well decorated and furnished with a patterned carpet, a bed with clean sheets, and a writing desk. Through the open window we felt a faint breeze and heard the sounds from the street below. A small bedside chest of drawers held a phone and a paper fan which advertised Berkhimer's Funeral Home. The room was lighted by a ceiling fixture which contained three electric bulbs--two more flanked a large wall mirror. The room had a

## Veteran Barber

Fifty years a barber is the record of William A. Spingler, 334 East Jefferson Street, who celebrated his fiftieth anniversary Monday in much the way he has celebrated every other March 4th the past half century, by devoting his talents toward improving his customers tonsorial appearance. "Bill," as he is familiarly known by his associates, can be seen any day of the week at his chair in the Kemper shop in the basement of the Butler County National Bank.

Modest and unassuming, Spingler is none too anxious to discuss his achievement. "Why, take Freddie Krause, he's worked at the barber trade longer than I have," he will say. "You'd better see Freddie. Why he taught me the trade." He was referring to Fred L. Krause, 248 East Fulton Street, a barber in the McCrea shop.

Since he first entered the shop of Joseph Wagner under the old Berg Bank on the fourth day of March, 1885, Spingler has worked in only one other shop, the one in which he is now employed, to which he came about a quarter of a century ago.

And if this is not enough to cause posterity to remember him, it might be added that he was born within a stone's throw of where he now resides, and has lived continuously in that vicinity.

No one, it seems, ever could quite figure out why the average man will discourage a child from following the avocation of his father. But Spingler is no exception to the rule. He frankly admitted he would have been tempted to consider taking drastic steps had ever a son of his even casually remarked he thought he would become a barber.

But nevertheless, he sticks to the trade. One of the reasons he has done so, he says , is the Depression. "If the Depression had not come along," he mused, "I might have—" but that is as far as he went. Then after a pause, "But then—what could a fellow do when the bottom fell out of everything but stick to his job?"

Expecting to celebrate his sixty-eighth birthday next August, he said he was nearing 18 years of age when he became an apprentice and attained that age the following August. His father had spoken for a place for him in the Wagner shop about a year before. There were no barber schools in those days. One learned by serving an apprenticeship, and when one had done so, the shop simply took on another apprentice.

The veteran recalled with a chuckle how barbers in those days after a hard week's grind, wound up on Saturday night by cleansing the individual shaving cups and brushes of their customers. Now that has all been done away with, and the once familiar sight, a cupboard filled with shaving cups of various colors and designs, is to be seen no more in the modern shop.

Spingler derives considerable satisfaction from the fact that many of his first customers are his customers still: among them is Edwin S. Riddle, the court stenographer, one of the first men he ever shaved. Then there's Attorney Albert C. Troutman and other familiar figures about Butler who still hunt out Spingler's chair.

He and a sister are the only survivors of a large family. The veteran occupies his own home on Jefferson Street, which he shares with his wife.

The history of Butler for the past half century is like an open book to him. Butler was a town of about 4,000 population when he began his apprenticeship, and natural gas was unknown here. In fact the first gas used in Butler was of the artificial kind, and in its wake came natural gas and the oil excitement which stamped Butler indelibly on the map.

"But," he insisted, "You'd better see Freddie Krause. He's the one who deserves a writeup. He'll give you quite a story. I went into the business after he did. Oh yes, by all  means, see Freddie."
*Butler Eagle*, March 1935

radiator, which would certainly not be needed tonight. I handed the bellboy a quarter as he deposited the luggage on the bed. As the boy turned to leave, he smiled and thanked me warmly."

Many of the new arrivals to Butler, especially factory workers, rented sleeping rooms and ate all their meals out—this was strictly a "room." Some of the large houses in the western area of Butler were built as boarding houses for Standard Steel Car Company workers. A meal or two a day and even a packed lunch was included in the agreement—this was known as "room and board." Most of these houses included facilities for bathing, but the occupants of apartments and/or sleeping rooms needed to make a weekly visit to a public bath house on South Main Street.

The end of the century was a patriotic time in Butler's history. We "Yankees" had not been on good terms with the south since the Civil War. But the Spanish American War united the people of this nation as we had never been united. After the war we were suddenly a world power with possessions and protectorates that sprawled from the Caribbean to the China Sea. The American flag sporting just forty-five stars was prominently displayed at many homes and businesses along Main Street and throughout the county. School children wrote patriotic essays as part of their assignments. Veterans of the war were respected and venerated during their waning years. They were recognized at county fairs, churches and other events. They ran for political offices and won.

The Spanish American War not only influenced our music, it even dictated our fashions. The was—riding pants flared at the sides. Later these were called Jodhpur trousers. Black boots and a khaki shirt went well with the trousers and a cowboy hat was a necessity. Many a young man, especially the veteran, sported the polka-dot bandana of the Rough Riders around his neck. He was making the statement, "I'm proud to have ridden with Teddy."

In 1923 there were forty barbershops listed in Polk's City directory; nine of them were on Main Street. I asked some "old timers" how barbershops have changed in the past fifty years and found that many men have detailed and fond memories of those old havens of male dominance.

As late as the 1940's some barbers used hand clippers. A few still used an aparatus which hung from the ceiling. It was attached with cables to an electric motor which usually sat in one corner. Most men sixty and older today would consider the sound of those moving cables to be quite nostalgic.

Many barbers aren't so anxious to change the methods they used for years. It was yet possible in the 1990's to get a shave with hot cream and a straight razor; the later was sharpened on a leather strap. Older shops had mugs lined up on a shelf or two. Each was individualized with the customer's name. If the customer was a lodge member, an emblem on his cup announced the fact to anyone who cared. Some displayed the name of a company such as Armco or the Standard Steel Car Co. It was considered hygenic that the customer got his own mug each time he visited the barber. Upon completion of the hair cut and/or shave the barber had tall bottles of bay rum and other fragrant colognes he splashed on the customer's face and neck. There were also many advertising posters on the wall of the shop—Noxzema, Burma Shave, Moxie, Brylcream, and Peach Pomade.

Most of today's barbers are known as "hair stylists." They cut, dye, shampoo and style hair in trendy mall salons while the customer enjoys a manicure.

Sometimes it is difficult to accept change. The animated, colorful scene on Butler's Main Street decades ago was an attraction in itself--it conveyed a carnival-like spirit. The street was a happening and people warmed to it--to the crowds and the excitement of variety. Retrieving that environment is impossible; those days are gone forever.

## The Town Pump

It wasn't more than a generation ago that the "town pump" graced the sidewalks on the business streets of the city. The town was three-quarters of a century old before the old-fashioned water wells were discharged and some of the unfailing springs which oozed out of the side of the hill were condemned as unsafe for public use.

Time was when the water wells were dug out of the solid rock near the Diamond about the court-house, Main Street, Jefferson Street, and North Street, McKean and Washington Streets. Some of the dug wells were equipped with the old fashioned windlass and bucket and the old oaken bucket—the iron bound bucket, that hung in the well was very much of a reality to the school kiddies 40 years ago.

After the well with the iron bound bucket and its back-breaking windlass with long chain or rope, came the pump. The early pumps were often constructed of logs which were bored out for the purpose and the pump handle was usually made of iron with a big knob of iron on the end of it. The public used a common dipper tin cup sometimes, to drink water from the wells, and no one died of poison, either. Occasionally there would be a spurt of fever but it was generally agreed that the infection didn't come from the deep-dug wells.

Probably the oldest and the deepest of the dug wells is located on the Mrs. William A. Lowry homestead on East Diamond Street. The well is about 100 feet deep and was dug considerably more than 100 years ago for the late Judge Gilmore, who owned the property at that time.

The history of the well is that when the workmen had dug down to a solid rock there were no indications of water. It was decided to go through the rock and a heavy blast of powder was set off. The workmen decided to allow time for the gas fumes to disappear before resuming work and did not return until the next morning. To their surprise they found ten or fifteen feet of water in the well and their tools with which they had been working submerged.

The tools are in the hole yet, for the well has never been pumped dry. During the lifetime of Col. W. A. Lowry a pump was installed and for more than half a century persons have taken cooling draughts from the "old wooden pump" and carried glass jars and buckets full of drinking water away. During the driest of seasons, when wells and springs went dry all over town "Old Faithful" remained steadfast, no matter how much of a demand was made upon it.

During the hot summer weather persons walked from all parts of the city to get a drink from Lowry's well and the handle of the pump could be heard squeaking all hours of the night. During more than half a century that the family has lived there no one has been turned away, and it is not likely that they will, so long as the present owner is mistress of the mansion.
*Butler Eagle,* 5-6-1925, James A. McKee

Sadly, at least for those who want to preserve the old central business districts, the decentralization that Butler has experienced has happened in most small towns. The crowds that once thronged downtown shops are now drawn to the malls and other suburban retail outlets, or they drive long distances for a day or two of shopping. A very few individual stores or entire downtowns which specialize in certain products and/or services are yet successful at attracting large numbers of customers, but they are rare. To yearn for the return of "the good old days" is futile. Be that as it may, most would agree that it was a very exciting era.

**Dixon's Pharmacy**

**Guaranty Safe Deposit and Trust Company**

## John Autenreith's Armchair Tour of Downtown Butler

John Autenreith was born in 1916 and has lived his entire 83 years in the city of Butler. He became interested in local history around the time of the sesquicentennial and has, for the past fifty years, been observing and documenting local events and details. At the present time, John is not very ambulatory as he lives alone in the house of his youth, but his recollections are absolutely amazing.

When John was eleven years old, he and his brother had a morning and an evening newspaper route with customers "all over Butler." To further complicate such a young boy's busy schedule, his task involved the delivering of several newspapers simultaneously i.e., the *Pittsburgh Gazette Times,* the *Pittsburgh Post,* the *Pittsburgh Chronicle Telegraph,* the *Pittsburgh Sun,* A Pittsburgh German newspaper, late stock market reports, and also Butler newspapers.

He and his brother, William, ate an early breakfast at 4 o'clock a.m, delivered the morning papers, then ate another breakfast before they went to school. They walked home at lunch time and ate their third meal of the day. After school they delivered the evening papers, had a bit of free time, only if there was no homework, then ate the evening meal. By this time they were ready for bed. John did this until he was eighteen years old. He says, "I was lucky in that I didn't get sick much but when I did, my brother either helped me or I struggled along feeling weak and miserable as I completed my job." Little did John know that the observations he made on that paper route would one day be enjoyed by the descendants of many of those very customers.

John Autenreith began to purchase real estate in 1936 and this line of work eventually became his livelihood. The impetus which thrust him into the life of a landlord was somewhat unusual. Here is how it happened. John had reached the age of twenty and was still living at home with his parents on North Bluff Street. He found that he could acquire some extra cash by repairing automobiles; he had always been interested in mechanical devices and in figuring out what made things work. As he spent more and more time at this task, his parents' basement was becoming increasingly crowded with auto parts and tools. John's mother could hardly make her way through the basement to do the washing. He says that his "mother got fed up with my auto parts in the basement. One thing led to another and I found myself kicked out of the house. She had a right to do it. I realized that later."

A temporarily homeless Autenreith put fifty dollars down on a five-acre piece of property which was located on the back road to Chicora, not far from the Oneida Dam. Realtor, C. H. Rodgers had found the property for Autenreith and had arranged for the financing. The struggling young auto mechanic got some rough lumber, built a shed on his new property, and began to haul the auto parts from his parent's basement out to his new place. However, within the month, C. H. Rodgers approached John and made him an offer that he couldn't refuse. Someone was willing to pay five thousand dollars for the five-acre plot! Well, naturally the young man could not turn down that kind of money, especially when had invested such a small sum. He sold the land and even after paying the Realtor's commission, John realized a very nice profit. It was easy money and he had hardly lifted a finger—he was immediately hooked. He didn't take the money and run, but rather he told Rodgers that he enjoyed making money this way and that he would like the Realtor to invest his profits in other properties which he could rent out. Within the year Autenreith had bought and sold six, separate properties and was the proud owner of twenty garages which he continues to own today. He had a "heck of a bank account," and it had all started with just fifty dollars.

John told me that since his humble beginnings with C. H. Rodgers, he has made over one hundred real estate transactions involving properties in or near Butler. Owning rental properties all over town for over sixty years has been an excellent type of work for John Autenreith, the historian, in that it has involved him with countless bankers, attorneys, and contractors as well as the renters, their families and neighbors. He has always walked from one end of town to the other because he never had a driver's license. This is surprising considering the fact that he was an auto mechanic; nevertheless, it's true. Frequent visits to his rental units allowed him, without realizing it, to monitor the changing pulse of downtown Butler. Today he owns approximately twenty buildings in the city and is a millionaire on paper, yet he lives very austerely in the house in which he grew up—the house his mother expelled him from when he was twenty. John describes himself as hardworking and frugal.

In 1891, John Negley, editor of the *Butler Citizen,* took a stroll down Butler's Main Street and recorded his recollections of early businesses, buildings, people, and even bits about their private lives. I hope that you enjoyed that account in chapter two. As I read it with much enthusiasm, I thought that it had been, and is yet today, a very nice gift to the community. It dawned on me that a wonderful complement to the

Negley recollections would be a present-day trip down Main Street by John Autenreith during which he would comment on the years that few people remember i.e., the1920' and 30's.

When I visited John, it was a ninety-three degree, June day. He was sitting at his desk in front of a small fan, clipping coupons for grocery bargains. I subtly asked him whether he liked air conditioners. He answered, "If an air conditioner goes bad, the service technician wants about fifty dollars just to come and inspect it. Then the new parts and labor are outrageous. I can buy one of these fans for twenty dollars and if it breaks, I simply throw it away and buy another."

John was very much in favor of the Main Street project as I explained it. He said "This information should be recorded while I'm still able to remember it. I could go on for a couple of days talking about the downtown Butler of yesteryear. But when I'm gone, I'm afraid that much of the information will also be gone with me." I wiped the perspiration from my brow and we got down to business.

I'm calling this chapter appropriately, "John Autenreith's Armchair Tour of Downtown Butler." What you read here is largely from the remembrances of Mr. Autenreith although I have enhanced his report with my own related findings as well as the recollections of several other older Butlerites who contributed to the chapter.

If one wants a list of all Butler businesses for a particular year, then a perusal of Polk's City Directories would be in order. I wanted information on the buildings, the businesses and the people who lived there and/or ran the businesses—the kind of information which isn't available in Polk's—the kind of information which is very difficult to find. I wanted stories and John had plenty of them.

We began at the top of North Main Street hill and our easy chair tour took us south along the west side of Main Street all the way to the top of South Main Street hill. Then we returned to the top of North Main Street hill and repeated the jaunt, this time considering and discussing the east side of Main. It took several two to three hour sessions to complete the armchair tour of Main Street. When we finally finished John said, "Now we'll have to do Jefferson Street starting at North Butler, going all the way down to the West End and then down Hansen Avenue." I plan to interview him again, soon, but I'll have to put the information on the back-burner perhaps for another time.

## John Autenreith's Armchair Tour of Downtown Butler

At the very top of North Main Street hill we find St. Peters Catholic Cemetery. Butler's first aviator, Leo McElligott, who met an untimely death at the young age of twenty-seven, is buried here. Leo M. Stepanian, well-known Butler attorney, was named for McElligott; his mother, Mrs. Steven Stepanian, was Leo McElligott's sister.

Behind St. Peter's Cemetery was the location of the pest house. During the first decade of the twentieth century the pest house was used as an isolation ward for the old Butler County General Hospital. Patients who had, or were suspected of having contagious diseases were treated in this facility. The building has been gone for many years, even before Autenreith was born, but "old Doctor Ritchie, who made false teeth," took a young John Autenreith for a Sunday walk and showed him the site of the former pest house—it was by that time just a grassy area.

The Israelites were a "religious group" who, at the end of the nineteenth century, dressed in gowns and trekked to the top of North Main Street hill where they awaited the end of the world. Many curious Butler residents were there observing the Israelites who, as many groups before and since, had obviously miscalculated.

The trolley's regular route took it up and down North Main Street hill several times a day. There was a small shelter of sorts, just large enough to keep a few people out of the rain and cold, at the intersection of Main Street and Belmont Road. And it wasn't just the commuters who took the trolley. Many caskets made that last ride up to the cemetery on the rails of the Butler Traction Company. Other funeral processions walked up the hill—all the way from Butler's Southside—some of those were followed by Professor Nick Siriani's Italian Band. Such a procession was similar to a New Orleans funeral.

The street car needed no roundhouse or turn around. The operator merely unhooked the lever, walked to the back of the car, made the attachment and the back of the trolley became the front for the return trip.

Continuing down the hill we arrive at St. Paul's Cemetery, also known as Calvary Cemetery. Many members of the Duffy family are interred here. The Duffy family was discussed to some extent in *Butler*

*County, the Second Hundred Years.* They owned a great deal of land on the West End of Butler, from Hansen Avenue out to Duffy Road. They also owned Duffy's store at the corner of Main and Mifflin [New Castle] Streets; this was the source of some of their wealth. The Duffy's are remembered for their generosity. They gave the land for St. Paul's Church and rectory.

[There will be more information on the Duffy family when the "armchair tour" gets to East New Castle Street.] Duffys lived at the top of North Main Street hill back near the end of Germaine Road. At another time the family lived at the northeast corner of East Pearl and Franklin Streets. The large brick Duffy house which is yet standing there is over one hundred years old. Father Nolan, the Irish Priest at St. Paul's many years ago, and a contemporary of the early Duffys, is buried in St. Paul's Cemetery. The road surrounds his grave in a large circle.

Headed south, the next cemetery is North Cemetery. Many of Butler's prominent family members such as the Phillips, are buried here. Near the Phillips' mausoleum is the grave of a young lady. Several people who have visited the cemetery at dusk reported that smoke or a vapor rising from her grave eventually takes the shape of a woman, sits on the grave stone for a while, and then floats away. [Mr. Autenreith believes in ghosts—we'll leave this story in our narrative for your consideration and/or investigation.] Another famous Butlerite buried in North Cemetery is Washington D. Brandon, who lived to be 105. After his first wife died, he remarried. A visit to the grave site reveals that his two wives are buried, one on each side of Mr. Brandon.

Dr. Purvis is buried in North Cemetery. His home was directly across McKean Street from the library—the middle house of the three on that block. The Nixons, famous Butler

## St. Peter's Cemetery

For a quarter of a century after the settlement of the town, the old cemetery on North McKean and East North Streets, where the Junior High School stands, was the only burying ground in a radius of seven or eight miles. It was kept up at public expense for the common use of all and controlled by the borough council.

St. Peter's Roman Catholic congregation was organized about 1882. Soon after the first stone chapel was erected on the hillside outside the borough limits between what is now East Locust and East Jefferson Streets on a tract of land called "Newry," obtained from the heirs of Stephen Lowry. Lowry had obtained the land by purchases from the bankrupt estate of Robert Morris, the Revolutionary patriot, who at one time owned practically all of the depreciation lands in the southern half of Butler County, including what is now the city.

Thomas Collins, agent for Stephen Lowry, lived in Butler during the first two or three decades of the town's history. His wife was Sarah Lowry, a daughter of Stephen Lowry, and the couple had their home where the new Memorial Hospital now stands. Collins and his wife had been very kind in helping the St. Peter's congregation acquire land for a chapel and a cemetery.

On January 15, 1820, Mrs. Sarah Lowry Collins, deeded to the Right Rev. Henry Conwell, D. D., Bishop of Philadelphia, in trust for St. Peter's Catholic church of Butler, one acre and seven perches of land located at what is now the head of College Street and between East North and East Jefferson Streets, near the top of the hill, with the right of way from the tract to the "Butler and Kittanning pike." This was a part of the "Newry" tract mentioned, patented by the state to Stephen Lowry and bequeathed by the latter in his will to his daughter, Mrs. Collins, in 1821. The only reservation mentioned in the deed on 1829 is that which reserves to Mrs. Collins and to her heirs the right to bury in the Collins tomb in the cemetery relatives by blood or marriage.

The cemetery was enlarged to two acres and 100 perches in 1830 by a donation of land made by Mrs. Valeria Evans, a daughter of Mrs. Sarah Collins, in consideration that the trustees of St. Peter's congregation build a fence around the chapel and cemetery grounds and finish the chapel which had been commenced several years before. This was a parol contract. The trustees carried out their part of the agreement, but Mrs. Evans died before a deed was executed. In 1831 her husband, E. R. Evans claimed all his rights to the entire amount of land within the fence.

The Collins tomb mentioned in the deed is located in the northeast corner of the old cemetery. The only member of the Collins family to be buried in the tomb was Thomas Collins, husband of Mrs. Sarah Lowry Collins, who resided in Butler and was the agent of the Stephen Lowry estate at the time of his death.

Collins was an Episcopalian, but permission was granted by the officials of the Catholic church to bury him and other members of Mrs. Sarah Lowry Collins' family and relatives by blood in the cemetery as an appreciation of kindness and services rendered St. Peter's congregation.

The stone chapel erected by St. Peter's congregation served its purpose until the present brick church was erected on Franklin Street in 1840, when it was dismantled. The burials in the cemetery were discontinued in 1880. Subsequently all of the bodies in the old cemetery were removed to the new St. Peter's cemetery on the north hills. The only remaining tomb in the old cemetery is that of Thomas Collins.

*Butler Eagle,* May 12, 1925, James A. McKee

County hotel operators, are also buried here. Their story was presented in *Butler County, the Second Hundred Years*. Alfred G. Reed, Civil War Adjutant from Butler who was just twenty-one years old when he died, is buried in North Cemetery. The cannon in Diamond Park bear his name. He was wounded in the battle of Fredricksburg in 1862 and lived only fifteen days after the incident. Reed left a wife and young son. His body was brought back by train to Pittsburgh then by wagon to North Cemetery. A soldier was commissioned to bring Reed's horse back to Butler.

Reverend Fetter, of St. Mark's Lutheran Church, is also buried in North Cemetery. On his tombstone is the following: "Here rests Reverend William A. Fetter. For almost sixteen years, the pastor of St. Mark's Church of Butler, where he had hoped to rest from his labors—driven thence, not by the congregation—but by a few men of the same— he now rests here in peace." Reverend Fetter left St. Mark's during the Civil War and became pastor of a Lutheran Church near Chicora.

Many members of the Lowry family are buried in North Cemetery. Porter Lowry was an attorney who made his home at the southwest corner of Bluff and Pearl Streets. Porter had a daughter Jeanette Lowry who was a secretary for many years at the First Presbyterian Church on East Jefferson Street. Porter had a photographic memory. He could go to the courthouse and read three or four pages of legal records, go back to his office, and remember it verbatim. Part of his business included the investment of funds for others. He bought mortgages or otherwise invested money, then passed the accumulating interest along to his investors. In a few cases, instead of investing the money, he kept the principal and made the small interest payments to the investors out of his own funds. He was eventually caught and sent to the penitentiary for a short sentence. While in prison, he became the prison librarian. After he was released he was not allowed to practice law. This event happened over 100 years ago. It was related to Mr. Autenreith by his parents.

Gardner Lowry, a banker with the Butler Savings & Trust, lived on West Penn Street directly across from Emily Britain School. It's the oldest brick house in that area. Gardner's mother died in 1903 and is buried in North Cemetery, a victim of the typhoid epidemic. His father was proprietor of the Lowry House, one of the oldest hotels in the city. Some of the Lowrys lived in a substantial house on East Diamond Street, site of the present day municipal parking lot. This house was built by Jacob Ziegler who married one of the Lowry girls. Judge Purvis also lived in that house for twenty-

---

### Albert Waters

Tomorrow the surviving members of old Company E. Fifteenth Pennsylvania Volunteer Infantry in the Spanish American War, will turn aside from the ordinary beaten paths in the North Side cemetery to mark the grave and pay tribute of respect to a negro soldier.

There is nothing peculiar or significant about the grave. It is just like hundreds on the North hill. The name of Charles Albert Waters on the tombstone, however, will be enough to bring a flood of memories to the war veterans of 1898.

The skin of Albert Waters was black. Ask any of the members of old company E. Fifteenth Infantry, and they will with one voice declare that Albert Waters was the finest black man they ever knew. He was the only negro soldier in the Spanish American War who served in a white regiment. He was the only soldier from Butler to make the supreme sacrifice in that war. He fell a victim to typhoid fever at Fort Washington, August 8, 1898, and he was buried with military honors in the North Cemetery, this city.

The funeral of Albert Waters, August 12, 1898, was the talk of the town for weeks. The services were held in the Methodist Episcopal Church. All of the ministers in the city and several from the county attended. The pastor of the church presided and the only negro minister in the town sat on the platform and had a part in the services.

The procession from the church to the cemetery was headed by the Germania band. The relatives of the dead soldier rode in carriages. The hearse carrying the body was followed by A. G. Reed, Post No. 105. G. A. R.: Camp 45 Union Veteran Legion: Company G, Twenty First Regiment Provisional National Guard: six companies of the volunteer fire department and hundreds of civilians. The hillside about the grave was crowded with people of all walks and vocations in life in our city. Hundreds were there from curiosity. Many others were there because they knew Albert Waters and respected him.

Albert Waters had lived most of his life in Butler. He was first employed at the camps of the National Guard as a cook. He had an ambition to be a soldier and the captain of the company finally yielded to Albert's importunings and enlisted him as a member of the company, after he had been voted on by the members. When the call came for volunteers in 1898, Private Albert Waters went along with his company to Mt. Gretna. The enrolling officers of the regular Army haggled some about enlisting a negro with a white unit in the service. It was then that members of old Company E stood up on their feet and declared that if they were taken into the regular establishment, Private Albert Waters would go along. The mustering officer finally yielded a point and gave the Butler company a unique place in the history of the volunteers in the war.
*Butler Eagle*, 5-29-1925, James A. McKee

two years. Autenreith remembers three Lowry girls living in that house—Jenta, Maude and another whose name he cannot remember. Polk's Directory for 1923 lists Bertha, Blanche, Annie and Jenta living there at 136 E. Diamond.

Jacob Ziegler ran away from his home in Gettysburg when he was just a boy. He arrived penniless in Butler but he was a very intelligent lad. He soon acquired a position as a printer's devil and prepared a contract wherein he was to be an indentured servant. The unusual thing about the contract was that Ziegler was guaranteed a good place to sleep and he was to eat at the table with the family—not off by himself in another room as was common with most indentured servants. Jacob Ziegler would have the same privileges as family members. In addition to being clever, he was motivated, and this combination usually leads to success. Ziegler started a printing company which he operated on East North Street directly across from T. W. Phillip's Gas and Oil company until about 1928. The former indentured servant by then could afford to construct his own building—which he did on the southeast corner of Cunningham and Bluff Streets. The building was designed and built by local architect George Clobus and yet bears the Ziegler name at the top. George I. Woner became general manager of Ziegler's operations.

Continuing our tour down Main Street hill, the congregation at St. Andrew's United Presbyterian Church had its beginnings just south of the cemetery, where Heckett Division Of Harsco Corp. is located today. When the weather permitted, the Presbyterians met under the trees and used logs for seats. In 1891 they were able to build their present sanctu-

## Leo E. McElligott Falls To His Death At Rodgers Field
*Lieut. Charles S. Tygard, in Plane With McElligott, Also is Victim*
*Tragedy Occurs When Take-Off is Attempted*
*Young Flier Was Graduate Of Butler High and Grove City College*

Full military honors will be accorded Lieut. Leo Eugene McElligott, aged 27, of 428 Liberty Street, Butler's first air crash victim and one of the district's earliest pioneers in aviation, who was killed, together with his companion, Lieut. Charles S. Tygard, aged 25, of 2819 Crosby Avenue, Dormont, at Rodgers field, Pittsburgh, late yesterday, when the small monoplane in which they were flying slipped out of a bank as the pilot was attempting to avoid colliding with a tree in taking off, and crashed to earth. Both victims were members of the 324th Observation Squadron.

It is believed Lieut. Tygard was at the controls when the accident occurred. Persons who saw the crash told Sergt. Leo I. Herman, who was on duty at the field, that the monoplane banked vertically at an altitude of 200 feet to avoid striking a tree, when it slipped out of the bank and crashed to the ground in a field opposite the hangars.

The engine of the monoplane seemed to be working perfectly, but the pilots were unable to bring the ship back to an even keel after the bank because of insufficient altitude, witnesses said. The engine crashed to its side, a portion of one wing and the engine striking the ground simultaneously it was said.

A few hours before the tragedy, McElligott had spoken at the weekly luncheon of the Aero Club of Pittsburgh, of which he was a member, telling of his flying experiences at Langley Field, Va., recently during a two week's training which Observation Squadron officers underwent with army planes. He returned from Langley Field Monday. Tygard had been instructing flying students at the field for the last few days.

The body, burned beyond recognition, was brought to the Harvey J. Geibel undertaking establishment on East Cunningham Street last night.

Military funeral services will be held from St. Peter's church with solemn funeral mass, Monday morning at 10 o'clock, and interment made in the St. Peter's cemetery. Army officers from Pittsburgh will participate in the services, and flowers will be dropped over the cemetery from the air by aviators who knew the late Butler youth.

McElligott is survived by his mother, Mrs. Laura McElligott, and two sisters, Mrs. Steven Stepanian of Charleroi, and Miss Mildred Alice McElligott of Butler.

A graduate of Butler High School in 1918 and of Grove City College in 1922, young McElligott became interested in aviation shortly afterward and left for Love Field, Dallas, Tex., where he began his training as an aviator. He purchased a Travel-Air plane, and in April 1927, flew from Love field to Butler, where he landed at the Headland Airport a short distance out of Butler on the New Castle Road.

Last winter he flew from Rodgers Field to Mexico City and then back to Pittsburgh, landing at Rodgers Field, where his first plane is still being quartered. The young reserve officer was the second Butler civilian to own his own plane. Robert S. Headland, proprietor of the Headland Lunch on West Jefferson Street, being the first.

Besides being a member of the Pittsburgh Aero Club, he was a member of the Butler Council No. 866 Knights of Columbus. Butler Elks Lodge. He was unmarried. He founded the Lee McElligott Tree Surgery company, a few years ago, and did considerable work for the Bell Telephone company by contract, as well as for private individuals.
*Butler Eagle, 9-6-29*

ary at the corner of McKean and East Jefferson Streets.

Mr. Autenreith has patched a large number of roofs in his lifetime and has become very cognizant of roofs. He says that Heckett's has an unusual roof on their building. It has no rainspouts but rather, features a soft, tar covering. They always keep the tar covered with water to keep it soft, otherwise it would crack and leak.

Mr. Autenreith remembers, as a boy, how at times, the hillside seemed to be aflame with burning crosses. When he and his friends tried to get a closer look they were always kept back by KKK patrols on Fulton Street. The Ku Klux Klan had a chapter here and from time to time they

held a rally or a funeral on the hillside in the cemetery. The Klan also met in the old silk mill on Institute Hill. In Autenreith's opinion Butler's version of the Klan was mostly social. Members openly discussed their affiliation with the organization. According to Autenreith, "If a husband was being unfaithful, the Klan would show up during the wee hours of the morning, kick the door in and confront the man while he was yet in bed. 'We didn't come here to harm you but we know what you're doing and we want it to stop. This is just a friendly visit—a warning. We won't hurt you this time, but listen to us or you'll be sorry.'" He remembers by name, many of the Klan members including a former Butler County Sheriff.

John Berg came to Butler in 1835 and opened a general store at the corner of Main and Cunningham Streets. Around 1860 he opened a grocery business on Main at Wayne Street in the present Natili's building. Mr. Berg was a very active businessman who was also involved in oil and banking. His financial success allowed him to build, on the present site of The Towers, on North Main Street, a very impressive home and carriage house. The 1896 drawing of Butler by James Moyer, includes an accurate sketch of the Berg mansion. The mansion, which Autenreith says "dated back nearly to Civil War days," had a castle-type tower on the top—a good example of the Queen Anne architectural style. Behind their home the Bergs had a large apple orchard; those old, gnarled trees continued to produce fruit long after the Bergs were gone.

The John Berg & Co. Bank, a large contributor to the Berg family's wealth, was founded and was doing business in the building located at 318 East Jefferson Street. It was not the first bank in Butler but it is the oldest, bank building yet standing. Before world War II, Pfisters had a tire shop in the building. When it was built as a bank in 1870 it was a three-story, brick building—for some unknown reason the top floor was later removed. The Berg Bank business relocated to the corner of Main and Jefferson Streets where National City Bank is today. That site was the focal point for downtown Butler. It was at the main crossroads in the county and was the best location for business. Bergs knew that and it was undoubtedly the reason for their move. However, the bank went out of business about 1922-23 and members of the family stored their extensive bank records as well as business machines and bank furniture in the large horse and carriage barn on their North Main Street property. Butler Savings & Trust Company was built on the Main and Jefferson site.

According to Mr. Autenreith, Bergs' carriages were elegant and better built than most automobiles of that day. Unfortunately, burglars broke into the barn and stole many of the items the Bergs had stored there. On Halloween, kids would steal one of the carriages, ride it downtown and abandon it on Main Street. Today it is all gone—the mansion, the barn, and the materials which had been stored in the barn. Autenreith's final comment on the Berg family is "They were of Nordic descent and were of the Roman Catholic faith."

John Autenreith remembers some of Butler's earliest electric automobiles. One was owned by Louis B. Stein of the Butler Savings & Trust Co. He lived near the Washington Street postoffice and drove the car all around town. Frank Troutman who lived across from the Bergs on North Main Street was also the proud owner of an electric car. He was chairman of the board at the Standard Plate Glass Co. and was a partner in Troutman's department store. He had facilities for charging the electric car's batteries at his home as well as at the glass plant. Mr. Troutman's son, John Henry, was much envied and admired by his peers because "he was a rich man's son." Diehl's bakery had ten or twelve, electric, delivery trucks around 1930. They operated throughout the year. These electric vehicles were not very fast. Autenreith compared their speed to that of a bicycle.

Continuing south on North Main Street we arrive at the site which was once the home of Judge Wilson. The judge had a barn in back of the house where Mr. Billy Boettner, a State Trooper, kept a white horse. Billy rode the horse around town—he was a very good horseman. Billy and his brother live in the Slippery Rock area yet today. They should be about eighty years old. Mr. Boettner in his official role as a state trooper, went to South Dakota to track down Irene Schroeder [See *Builders, Dreamers, Scandals, Schemers*] and brought her back to Pennsylvania.

Located at the north corner of West Pearl and Main Streets was the home of Henry Berg and his son Henry Jr. who would be in his 90's today. Patricia Berg, a sister, married William Kinzle who was associated

with the Berg Bank. Henry was very talented in radio in those days. He also liked to ride a motorcycle and was once involved in an accident in which he landed on his head. He survived but had to go through the rest of his life being unable to straighten his neck.

Autenreith does not remember every family along Main Street; he skipped a house here and there and told me that I could find the names of the people he forgot in Polk's City Directory. The next family he remembers was the Troutmans, owners of Troutman's store. Their home, much later became the Butler offices of AAA. John remembers one of the Troutman girls, Gertrude, who married Jack Campbell. Mr. Campbell was part of the Campbell family which owned the farm which was razed for the Clearview Mall. Part of their varied farming specialties involved the raising of Jersey cattle. The Campbell family sent milk into Butler where it was sold at many retail outlets. The Campbell family's businesses also included oil; they had a foundry under the Main Street Viaduct and a hardware store on Main Street. The foundry building is yet standing across from Spang's—It's presently the location of Barnsteel [Butler Rotoblast].

At their home on North Main Street, Jack and Gertrude Campbell owned two new Duisenberg automobiles which they kept in a garage at the rear of the house. They had, living on the premises, two mechanics who were trained at the Duisenberg factory. Autenreith recalls that one of the mechanics was named Charlie Fair. These men not only made repairs and maintained the cars, but were also chauffers and caretakers of the Campbell property. The mechanics had families living in Butler, but their responsibilities often dictated that they stay at the Campbell residence. They received a monthly salary rather than hourly compensation. Jack and Gertrude didn't like the Duisenbergs; they referred to them as "gas hogs," so they took the cars out to their Clearview farm and stored them in a barn. They eventually sold the two Duisenbergs for thirty-five dollars each and replaced them with two, brand-new Chevrolets.

From time to time, Autenreith digressed from his armchair trip down Main Street. But his digressions were very interesting. He told me that young people used to ride bobsleds down both North and South Main Street hills. The bobsleds held from ten to fifteen people and reached phenomenal speeds. And while he cannot recall of a single accident in Butler, he heard of a bobsled accident in another town in which a girl passenger was thrown from the sled, smashed into a telephone pole and her teeth were embedded in the pole.

Another bobsled accident on Pittsburgh's Northside killed several riders. In Butler they did most of their bobsleding very late at night and always had guards posted at the street crossings to hold back the traffic.

But getting back to our armchair tour, the house south of Troutman's was occupied by a Miss Jennings who taught mechanical drawing at Butler Junior High School. She was related to Dr. Atwell. On the northwest corner of Main and Penn Streets lived the Lutton family. Mr. Lutton was part of the management at the Valvoline Oil Co. in East Butler. A son, Dick Lutton, would be about eighty-five today.

Crossing Penn Street takes us to the E-Z Stop food mart. The Richard Matlack family lived on this corner. Mr. Matlack was a supervisor at the Standard Steel Car Company. Mrs. Matlack was an invalid who never left the house. There were two boys—Richard Jr. and Norman who was a friend of Henry Berg Jr. and was also very good at the early technology associated with radio—he even broadcast out of his home.

The widow, Mrs. Howard, lived in the next house with her father, a prominent Butler attorney named Bowser. The Howards rented the house from Richard Matlack. These last two houses mentioned were removed for the Sinclair station which was built there.

The house which is now occupied by Home Realty was built before the Civil War and is one of Butler's oldest houses. It contains a sky parlor in the upper reaches. Dr. Armstrong lived in the next house which is today, the office of Dr. T. T. Channapati. There was a carriage house in the rear where doctor Armstrong kept his horse and buggy. Hay was stored on the second floor of the carriage house. The next house, at 340 North Main, features solid stone construction from top to bottom. Autenreith says it was the Howard Reiber house. Polk's 1923 City Directory shows Martin H. Reiber as the occupant at that time. Autenreith says that whenever they set the table for meals they always set a place for all the members of the family who had passed away.

The next house in our southerly trek was owned by Dr. Wm. Leroy Eisler. He was a well-liked doctor with a large practice. He had very old antique furniture in the offices and waiting room. The next building held the offices of Dr. May the dentist. A son, Bill May, is a teacher and is well-known because of his involvement in a Civil War reenactment group and his strong interest in local history.

We now arrive at the Flowers apartments. In the building at the northwest corner of Brady and Main Streets, Bill Flowers had thirty apartments which occupied the building all the way back to Friedman's. Mr. Flowers was of German ancestry and came to Butler from Evans City where he had been a barber. The building was built in 1909 by a Kirkpatrick who had a general store in the front and it was he who converted the entire building to apartments. The Flowers real estate office faced Brady Street and the sign on the wall displayed "William J. Flowers Mortgages." Mr. Flowers had the reputation of being strict and quick to foreclose on any mortgages which were late. According to Autenreith, it was easier to deal with Flowers' two sons, Bob and Bill. Tony Monday also had one of his earlier shoe repair businesses in this building before he moved to his present location at 208 North Main Street. Cunningham Shanor owns the building today and continues to rent the apartments.

The south side of the Brady Street corner was the site of the Wick Hotel. At the rear of the hotel was the usual livery stable. Next to the hotel was the Butler Play House which featured live plays in the 1920's. The Monday boys remember when their father's shoemaking and repair business was in the Wick hotel. A large stairway divided the front lobby into a north and a west section. To the north, was a fruit stand which was run appropriately by Jenny Cherry. One of Ms. Cherry's most grueling jobs was that of carrying the fruit outside to display cases in the mornings and then moving it back in at evening times. She got the bright idea to build wooden frames and to cover them with chicken wire. At the end of her working day, the frames were set in place over the fruit, thus protecting it from anyone who might be tempted to help himself. It also served to eliminate the daily movement of the fruit. On the other side of the stairway was Tony Monday's shop.

The Daubenspeck apartments occupy the next building. The date on the facade says 1909. On the first floor was J. G. Heist's grocery store. The next building at 218 South Main where it intersects with Locust was the home of the Lindsay Pontiac Sales. By 1930 Lindsay had moved the business to 102 East Brady Street, but earlier, in the 1920's, in his Main Street location, Lindsay sold Oaklands and Wippetts, in addition to the more popular Pontiacs. Lindsay's business was famous locally for its unique advertising gimmicks. One promotion, for example, featured a marathon piano player. The musician had a "good ear" and could play most requests. He played day and night for nearly a week. People checked in the dead of night and the man was always playing. His wife was a nurse and fed and attended to him during the ordeal. Even when the musician needed to use the restroom, his wife put a screen around him, which afforded the necessary privacy. As part of another Lindsay promotion, "Pontiac Chief of the Sixes" coins were distributed as good luck pieces. The

Indian chief Pontiac's likeness was engraved on each coin. Autenreith remembers a common joke which made the rounds in Butler: "If you want a job, go to the Pontiac dealership and stand out front and bend over with your bare butt sticking out, and as people go by, yell Wippett." They enjoyed a different kind of humor in those days.

The Burger Hut building is not very old. It was built in the front yard of a house which is yet standing—the house is over one hundred years old. The first floor contained an Alderman's office and the second floor housed an apartment which was believed to be haunted. [Can you take another ghost story?] Jesse Ryan lived there. He would go off to work in the mornings and his wife would lock all the doors because she spent the days alone doing housework and cooking. Several times she saw a man walking around from room to room. Upon investigation the doors were locked and she never found anybody. Autenreith says, "many people would have quickly moved to another apartment, but the Ryans weren't scared by the ghost—they stayed."

Crossing the alley, Locust Street, takes us to a business that many people remember—Bill's Bargain Barn. [Photo-*Butler County, the Second Hundred Years*, pg. 58] This building was constructed in the 1920's and first housed an A & P Store. This particular A & P was Butler's first authentic "supermarket" and did a phenomenal business. After the A & P moved to the Island section of Butler, Bill Mattheis opened "Bills Bargain Barn." At different times Mr. Mattheis operated a clothing store and a paint and hardware store adjacent to his Bargain Barn. Mr. Mattheis was quite the diversified businessman—he also had a used car lot in what is now Friedman's parking lot.

Polk's City Directory for 1930 lists thirty-one dealers and repairers of shoes and among these businessmen was Tony Monday at 208 North Main Street. Autenreith remembers Monday's advertising Korry Krome soles and Cat's Paw heels. He also remembers that Mr. Monday spoke very good English as well as his native tongue which was Italian.

In the 1920's, Yee Wing Lee's Chinese laundry was located at 212 North Main Street. Mr. Lee was brutally murdered in 1930. During the investigation the murder was suspected to have been the result of a "tong war," however it was discovered that robbery was the real motive. This murder has been documented by Molly Woodroofe in *Builders, Dreamers, Scandals, Schemers.*

The building that houses Natili North was formerly the location of John F. Truman's general bake shop. Truman was especially known for his donuts and French pastries. South of Truman's is Keffalis' bar, which has been there for a very long time. The Keffalis building was also the location of a general store. Julius Yoos, a German barber, had a shop on the second floor. His daughter also cut hair in the same establishment. During World War II, rumors circulated that Yoos was a German spy, to the extent that it hurt his business. Of course, the rumors were false.

As we cross North Street, we notice by the date at the top of the corner building that it was built in 1929. This was the location of Grohman's Drug Store. Edward John Charles Grohman, at the turn of the century was in business with a man named Reddick. E. J. C. Grohman's son Earl followed in his

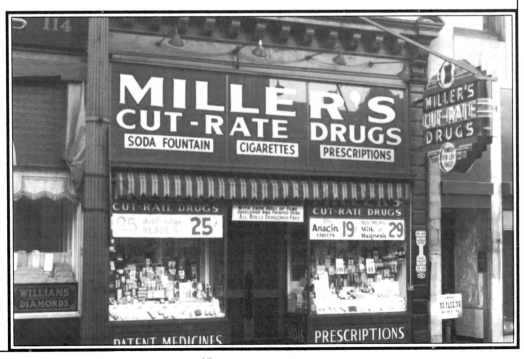

67

father's footsteps, studied pharmacy at the University of Pittsburgh and worked for his father eventually becoming the proprietor of the business at 158 North Main Street. Earl had two sons and three daughters; he discouraged them from going into the pharmacy business. Jean, presently works at the library.

Many pleasant odors seeped from the apothecary jars in the back of the store where Mr. Grohman mixed his remedies. In the line of over-the-counter drugs and medicines, Grohman sold Beecham Pills and Citrate of Magnesia for constipation. Other over-the-counter remedies included Castor oil, Lydia Pinkham's Compound, Vick's salve, Bromo-Seltzer, and Sloan' Linament which some Butlerites liked to mix with green oil and rub on their sore museles. A type of cough medicine in a tall bottle showed a giraffe on the label and proclaimed that even if your throat were as long as this giraffe's, this medicine could cure your cough. If none of these products was suited to your particular problem, Mr. Grohman, an excellent pharmacist, could mix up something special for you based upon his own vast knowledge of various powders, solutions, and drugs.

A joke which had Mr. Grohman as one of the major characters is yet remembered by many who knew him. It was related to me by Tony Monday Jr. "If you didn't feel well and none of the over-the-counter medicines was what you needed, you sat down and in a matter of five or ten minutes Mr. Grohman had something custom mixed just for you. A man who lived on Institute Hill walked into Grohman's complaining of a terrible, stomach ache and asked the druggist to mix something special for him. Grohman told him to take a seat as he began to pull bottles off the shelves and commenced to create a mixture. Grohman said, "by the way, where do you live?" The man answered, "Second Street up on Institute Hill." Grohman then asked, "Are you going to walk home or are you going to drive?" The man said, "Neither, I'm going to take the trolley." Grohman then asked, "How far is your house from the streetcar station?" The man answered, "Just about a block." Grohman bottled the concoction he had just created and handed it to the man, and one of the instructions was to take a dose immediately, which the customer did. Two weeks later the man came into the store and said, "Mr. Grohman, I have to commend you. The medicine you prepared for me did a wonderful job, but you miscalculated. Just as I stepped on my front porch, nature called with a fury. You came pretty close." In spite of this slight miscalculation, Grohman was respected for his understanding of pharmacy.

Mr. Grohman was just one of thirty hard-working druggists who made their livelihood in the city in 1930. The Grohman family lived in a brick house at the southeast corner of East Penn and North McKean Streets. The house, yet standing, has seventeen rooms. The Grohman children received no allowance but were paid ten cents an hour for working in the drug store. When they entered high school their wages jumped to fifty cents an hour. Grohman's was somewhat diversified as drug stores go. For example, they sold Burpee's Seeds. Jean remembers the time a farmer came in and purchased a one hundred pound bag of seeds—she tried to lift it to carry it to his vehicle but it wouldn't budge. The farmer hoisted it easily laughing all the way to his truck. Earl was interested in photography, sold cameras and photographic equip-

Miller's soda fountain

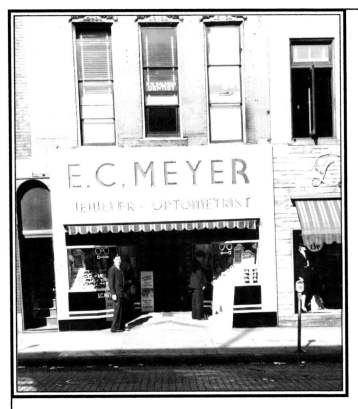

ment and also had a developing studio in the basement of the store. The drug store even had a book-lending library. It was a real coup when they were the first place in town to have *Gone With The Wind*—in fact they had seven copies which they loaned for five cents a day. Earl Grohman retired and closed the drug store in 1954. After he "retired" he worked in thirty different drug stores around Chautauqua Lake, NY where the Grohman family always spent their summers.

A business a door or two south of Grohman's Drug Store was Crawford's Jewelry Store. Crawford's opened in 1924 and continues in the same location today.

Cummings Candy Shop is about half way between North and New Castle Streets. Pete Cummings established Cummings Confectionery in 1905. The business, at the outset, was located in the one hundred block of South Main Street. In 1919, brothers William and Eugene joined forces with Pete who had relocated to the present location. The name of the business was changed to Cummings Candy Shop at that time. The hand-made, mahogany-cherry, wood booths, polished black marble table tops with the letter "C" etched on the surfaces, the custom made white marble soda fountain, the hand cranked cash register and the mirrored walls are just as they were in 1924. Entering Cummings Candy Shop is like stepping back in time. In 1946, William Cummings' son Tom, took over the business and continues to provide Butler with chocolate treats made with the old family recipes. Cummings Candy Shop is already a three generation business since Tom's son, Barry, has assumed a major role in the business—they've now expanded their daily fare to include coffees.

Upstairs was the office of Dr. John Aver, dentist. His home was on the northeast corner of Brady and Cedar Streets. Autenreith tells that Dr. Aver pulled two of his teeth about 1930. He used novacain and the patient did not feel the teeth being extracted but says that the dentist nearly twisted his head off in the process.

Dr. Aver drilled more than just teeth. He had worked extensively in the oil business and it was this sideline that brought about his gruesome death. He was out servicing one of his wells on a cold winter day. He started a gas engine which powered the well and his long overcoat became caught in the flywheel. The machinery pulled the dentist around and around battering his body and killing him instantly.

The corner of Main and New Castle Streets was the location of Jake Winter's Drug Store. Winter's was just one of several favorite meeting places for Butlerites. The typical drug store featured about eight, wire stools along a marble, soda fountain. The fountain was usually near the front of the store but at Winters' it ran parallel with New Castle Street on the north side of the store. It was argumentive as to which fountain was the best place in Butler for ice cream sodas, floats, milkshakes and sundaes—Winter's was certainly a contender. If one was in the mood for candy, the drug store sold everything from gum drops to licorice sticks. Customers often sat at the soda fountain conversing or reading the latest editions of Harper's Weekly or the Police Gazette.

Another meeting place was Barney's near the present intersection of Route 8 and the West Sunbury Road. The building is yet standing. At night, especially after sporting events, crowds also congregated at Cozy Corner on Institute Hill, the Inn at the corner of Brady and Franklin Streets, Cummings Candy Shoppe on North Main Street, the Hot Dog Shop on East Jefferson Street, Davy and Hilliard, and the Dixon Pharmacy, both on the Diamond.

Getting back to John Autenreith's armchair tour, the first business encountered as we cross New Castle Street is Decker McBride's store where one could purchase curtains, blinds, rugs, linoleum and similar products.

The Capitol Theater was a door or two south of the McBride's. In the late 1920's, world famous magician, Harry Houdini came to Butler and performed. Autenreith says they had the magician hanging upside down in front of the theater. He was blindfolded, handcuffed and perhaps in a strait jacket. Nevertheless, he was able to free himself within the short time he had predicted. Later on, Capitol Cleaners was so named because it

was located beside the theater. The cleaner is now located on Center Avenue and is spelled Capital Cleaners. Some time after the Capitol Theater closed, Eat' N Park Restaurant occupied the building. Today it is another one of Main Street's many unoccupied buildings.

The State Theater was located just south of the Capitol. It featured movies and live plays. The early silent movie theaters always employed piano players. He or she was located near the stage close to the screen and improvised as the movie progressed. The pianist watched the screen and played background music to match the mood—exciting, fast, mellow, romantic, happy, or whatever. It was too dark to read music so the only pianists who could handle such engagements were those who could "play by ear." Talking movies came in around 1930 and forced all these pianists to look elsewhere for employment.

The Jay Shoppe was a door or two south of the Capitol Theater. Taper's and later King's jewelry stores were next in line. On the corner was I. M. Jaffe's ladies clothing store, but before Jaffe's, Zimmermans had a ladies and children's clothing store at the corner location.

Attorney Norman Jaffe is the son of I. M. Jaffe. The Jaffes lived directly across from Emily Brittain School next to the old Lowry house which we discussed earlier. The house is approximately one hundred years old. Later the Jaffe family had a very impressive home built on North Duffy Road. It was built by George Schenck. Some of the Jaffes remembered by

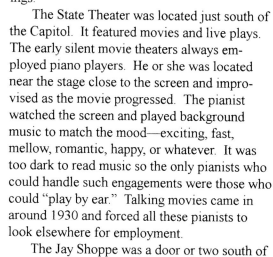

Autenreith were the father, I. M., and Sydney, the oldest son and at least two other boys, Norman and Richard. Beulah was a daughter. "They were a nice family."

Across Jefferson Street from Jaffe's was the Butler Savings and Trust Co. It has long been Butler County's highest building. There is a mural inside which depicts God holding the world in his hands. The building was built in 1923 by contractor Harry Wimer whose story is found in chapter fifteen. Autenreith remembers when "human flies" climbed up the facade of the building to the top. These people came to Butler with the circus or carnival and at the time, such daring events were being staged all across the country. Spectators assumed that the climbers had suction cups on their stomachs, or hands and feet but no one was quite certain as to how they did it.

The present "Store on Main" at 103 North Main was the location of Douthett and Graham, men's clothing store, which business had previously been located in the Woolworth building. A drug store occupied the next site. Irene Forcht worked there and out front was a newspaper stand run by Peter Hamder. Milo Williams has been located in the next store since approximately 1912.

Next to the alley was the G. C. Murphy Co., for many years one of Butler's major department stores. Across the alley, Birch Street, was Koch's Hardware Store. On the second floor Dr. Williams had his office for the practice of homeopathic medicine and two floors below, in the basement, was Corbett's Barber Shop. To enter the barber shop, it was necessary to descend a stairway which stuck out into the alley. The city made Corbett remove the stairway for obvious reasons. Corbett's had two white barbers and one "colored" barber. But there was no discrimination. The building burned in the late 1940's.

South of the hardware store was a business called Colbert & Matlack. Isaac Colbert was a hatter and a retail outlet for Mallory hats. His partner, Matlack, sold radios, phonographs and related equipment. Colbert and Matlack built the building their business occupied and part of the cement which bonded the two men was the fact that Mrs. Matlack was a Colbert. Mr. Colbert never married. Gaudino's purchased the building and subsequently opened a shoe store at this site. Today Ron Bennett has his photography business in the building.

William Aland built the next building in 1888. It is today, probably the oldest original facade on Main Street. Unfortunately, Aland's Toyland closed a couple of years ago. Interestingly, when the building was built, Alands were not in the toy business. William was a tailor and sold bolts of cloth and made custom suits and coats. His son Joe Aland continued in the tailoring and clothing business but Joe Jr. did not enter that profession. He liked fireworks, toys and such things and opened a toy store in the building. The tables used by William and Joe Aland in their tailoring business were later used in Joe Jr.'s toy store.

Benjamin Beetle occupies the building which previously housed the Hub, men and boy's clothing store. The Hub had earlier been located across Main Street south of Cunningham Street.

The Comique Theater was located on the corner of Main and Cunningham Streets, where Sun Drug later located. Today the Wishing Well Gift Shop conducts business on the site. The side entrance to the theater was on Cunningham Street; that fact is yet evidenced in the old brickwork pattern visible on the wall. The Comique showed silent pictures—"flickers"— and after 1930, of course, "talkies." Autenreith says the Comique specialized in coyboy movies which featured early stars such as Ken Maynard, Tom Mix, Gene Autry and later the Durango Kid and Roy Rogers. Weekly serials were very popular with the hero finding himself in a seemingly impossible situation at the end of each week's episode. Somehow he miraculously escaped and continued the action the following week. Butler's theaters were full of kids on Saturday mornings, kids who would shriek and whistle and were caught up in the excitement as they ate their popcorn and peanuts.

As we cross Cunningham Street we see the century old building which held Butler's largest department store—Troutman's. A. Troutman and son occupied the building at 136 North Main Street in 1888 but needed more space. In 1890 the Beatty House was razed and the present Troutman's building was erected. The business remained in the family as long as it remained open. Several name changes indicate the involvement of sons and uncles i.e., Troutman's Department Store, A. Troutman's Sons, and the A. E. Troutman Company. According to Rebecca Cammisa, writing in *Builders, Dreamers, Scandals, Schemers*, "By the early 1960's Troutman's had become a member of Allied Stores Incorporated of New York, the second largest chain of department stores in the world." Alas, as has happened to so many downtown businesses, competition from the shopping centers, malls, and big-box retailers sounded the death knell for Troutmans—it closed its doors forever in 1987.

Just south of Troutman's was Mardorf's store where one could purchase crocks, kegs, earthenware, flatware, tools, and other hardware. Mardorf's had big glass jars full of peas and lima beans. These vegetables were dried and very hard. They had to be cooked a long time before they could be eaten. Mardorf's also sold cider in season and there was a good reason for that. Mrs. Mardorf had been an Eisler and Eislers owned Treesdale Farms. In the fall, they would bring barrels of cider into town and sell it. Billy Eisler stood outside Mardorf's store and offered passers-by free samples of Eisler's cider in paper cups. Mardorf's earlier store was on the corner of Main and Wayne Streets where the postoffice is today. Billy is also remembered for the free samples he passed out at that location.

Just north of the alley, Vogeley Way, was the Arlington Hotel. The story of Butler's hotels was covered in *Butler County, the Second Hundred Years*. The Arlington Hotel was torn down in 1936 for the construction of a large Montgomery Ward store. Since then Montgomery Ward has moved to the suburbs and the Main Street building has been converted to offices. Just across Vogeley Way was Ketterer's Furniture Store. Autenreith remembers that Ketterer's used a Huselton truck which was built in Butler. See *Butler County, the Second Hundred Years*, pg. 119.

In 1923 Lizzy Young had a millinery shop on the second floor of the building at 136 South Main. As her business grew she moved to 232 South Main where she was able to rent the main floor. In 1906 she made another move, this time to 127 South Main Street. Today, Lloyd Johnson's store occupies the building at 232 South Main Street; they were preceded by Lichty's Book store. The dates at the top of the facade show "Lichty 1880 - 1954. The old building yet sports a latice work fence on the very top. Lloyd Johnson's has a

second store where they sell office furniture; it is just south of the main store in the old Farmer's National Bank building. The sign at the top of the facade has been removed.

On the corner of Diamond and Main Streets was Pell's Restaurant; previous to that in the 1930's this corner spot was the location of Dean Phipp's Auto Parts. Later Dean Phipp's business moved across the street.

The first building south of the Lafayette Building is well remembered by Autenreith. On the first floor was Whitehill's Plumbing shop. They owned the building and rented the second floor to Autenreith's mother and two uncles. John's mother's maiden name was Greot and the two uncles were her brothers. The two Greot brothers had an agency for all of the magazines and newspapers which came into Butler County. Newspaper boys would pick up the papers there for delivery to their customers.

The next building houses the office of attorney Joe Gillott. Prior to Mr. Gillott's tenure here the address was the flower shop of Anton Krut. The next stop on South Main Street is the Olympic Diner. Autenreith says that the Leras family operated the Rainbow Restaurant but when those buildings were taken by the Urban Redevelopment Authority, the Lerases moved across Main and opened the Butler Diner which was a predecesor to the Olympic Diner. Next to the alley was the location of Chris Stock's Hardware Store. His brother is attorney, Robert Stock. When Chris Stock retired

his building became available for Camissa's House of Style, which was also forced to move from its previous location across Main Street.

On the south side of the alley, Brush Street, was the Butler Hotel. Autenreith remembers a sign, "body shop," mounted near the front entrance. He didn't remember what the sign meant because the building housed only a hotel at the time. Perhaps it had something to do with a business which was conducted at the rear of the hotel. Frenchy Grosclod and another Frenchman named Grolemund repaired cars and did autobody work there.

Just south of the Butler Hotel was a one story A & P store. It was built during World War II. There was also the previously mentioned A & P store on North Main Street across the alley from the present Burger Hut and a third, smaller A & P was doing business on the southside. The latter wasn't a supermarket, but rather the clerk took the customer's order and filled it himself. The customer's bill of purchase was written by hand on the back of one of the grocery bags. The Masonic Temple was built in 1911. Montgomery Ward operated on the first floor of the Masonic Temple until the business moved to the site of the former Arlington Hotel in 1936. Autenreith's brother William, worked at Montgomery Ward in the tire and battery department.

The history of what is now the Natili building was covered in *Butler County, the Second Hundred Years*, pg. 50. It is a very old building which was long ago used as a general store. Mr. Autenreith remembers an army surplus store, which I cannot confirm in Polk's Directory, which sold items from the battlefield i.e., helmets with bullet holes, bayonets, U.S. and German army rifles, and other military surplus items until 1939 when John A. Natili opened his popular restaurant in the building.

Across Wayne Street, Butler County Ford has occupied the corner since 1918. Prior to 1918 the business was conducted by a man named McIntire, but not on Main Street—it was operating at the corner of Cunningham and Monroe Streets—the building which presently houses Sutton Tire Service. The Monroe Street business had been basically a carriage repair shop before they started selling Fords. At the Monroe Street location, the company was very demanding of its employees. Mechanics were not paid by the hour but rather by the job. For example, if the work order involved changing the engine in a Model T, the mechanic had a certain length of time in which to take the old engine out, dump it on the floor, put a new engine in and make all the connections. If the task wasn't done within the time limit the mechanic may find himself looking for another job. Tony Johns explains that repairs and replacements are done in a similar fashion today. There is a flat rate charged per hour and each job has a time rating. If a particular mechanic has too much trouble doing the job within the alloted time, then perhaps auto mechanics is not his forte. L. J. Forcht worked at the Monroe Street shop before he left and started his own Lincoln-Mercury, automobile dealership.

In 1919 McIntire built the present Main Street Ford building and opened the McIntire Motor Company. The business went bankrupt in 1922, then Tony Habrell took over the business and also went broke in 1929. At that time the business was assumed by the Union Trust Company, which appointed Walter J. Cramer to manage the dealership which was now called the Butler County Motor Company. Prior to his appointment, Cramer had been office manager. After a couple of years of showing a profit, Cramer purchased the business from the Union Trust Company. Tony Johns, who was married to Cramer's daughter joined the organization in 1948 and today serves as the corporation president.

At the rear of the "Ford Corner," on Jackson Street, was a streetcar station for the Butler Traction Company. That story was covered in *Butler County, the Second Hundred Years,* chapter 13. Masseth Machine Shop, which was owned by T. W. Phillips, was also located behind the Butler County Motor Company.

Before the Red Head Service Station opened, the building just south of the Ford dealership was the M. A. Berkhimer Funeral Home. Autenreith remembers well the funeral of his eighteen year old sister. The procession began at his North Bluff Street home and traveled all the way to Pittsburgh's north side where she was buried. Berkhimer made all the arrangements.

Mr. Berkhimer had a son named Marshall Berkhimer who began to work for his father at about age twelve. Marshall was a prankster. One of his more memorable practical jokes was somewhat morbid. Some of his friends put Marshall Berkhimer in a brand new casket, powdered his face, and put him on display in one of the viewing rooms. A few people got a quick glance at the boy and soon the story spread all over town—Marshall Berkimer had died! People sent flowers, food, and their condolences. A day or two later Marshall walked from one end of Main Street to the other—people thought they were seeing a ghost. Mr. and Mrs. Berkhimer were out of town during this fiasco but as you might expect, Marshall found himself in big trouble when his parents came home.

The next house which is the present location of Ken-Mac Rentals, was the home of Edgar C. Huselton, the manufacturer of the Huselton automobiles. [*Butler County, the Second Hundred Years*, chap. 17.] At the rear of the Huselton home was a large warehouse used by Ketterer's Furniture. The building was later converted into apartments. After the apartments were closed, the building became a hardware store. A man named "Rock" sold tools, including electric drills, power saws, drill presses, nails, bolts and other general hardware. He was able to get genuine Stanley tools, which were seconds. The Stanley name was ground off, although on some tools it was still legible.

### The Story of Six West Diamond Street

Located just behind the Lafayette Building and just south of the Butler County Courthouse stands one of the most beautiful Victorian houses in Butler County. Just like a page out of the history books, a person with a good imagination can stand in front of her and hear the clopping of horses' hoofs on brick roads, and the laughing of children.

John Quincy Adams Kennedy was born in 1828 and raised on a Winfield Township farm. He became a military man and in 1860 got involved in the oil business. This involvement made him rather wealthy and he decided to use some of his newfound riches to purchase a house in Butler. He fell in love with the three-storied, red-bricked, Victorian house on Diamond Street and was able to purchase it from Clint Wiser on March 14, 1885 for $8,000. The house sported a mansard roof that was outlined by iron palings. Around the small yard an iron fence surrounded the house while maple trees and mock orange framed it. In back stood a very large barn, a chicken coop and the ubiquitous outhouse.

Six West Diamond Street was a great place for Helen Pride, great-granddaughter of J. Q. A. Kennedy, to grow up. Not only was it just across the street from the courthouse, but it was in the heart of the city. Within a block one could enjoy Diamond Park, take care of the banking, buy groceries and baked goods or visit the tailor. There was also a drug store with a soda fountain. Surprisingly, little Helen loved most to visit the tin shop of Chris Stock.

"Every weekday I would crawl through the board fence that surrounded the backyard. One board had been removed for some time so that we children could visit the tin shop down the alley. Each time I went, I climbed a set of rickety stairs to the back of the shop. Every afternoon, the shopkeeper's wife, Mrs. Stock, would put on a fresh apron, her hair neatly in place, and would sit down to mend a basket of socks. She sat at a table in the back waiting for the faint tinkle of the front door. The bell indicated that a customer had come in. Her husband was always out installing tin rain spouts that he had made in the mornings.

When a customer came in, I followed Mrs. Stock to the front of the store. Oh, there were so many interesting things for sale, but the bins of quarter-penny, half-penny, and penny nails were the most fascinating. I loved to run my little fingers through the bins until I heard a startling yell!

'Get out of those nail bins!' It was Mr. Stock standing there with a great big smile and a nickel in his hand. 'I'm sure you'd much rather have an ice-cream cone.' Then it was off to the pharmacy down the street."

When Kennedy purchased the house he collected the finest furniture money could buy—afterall, he could afford it. He hired decorators from New York City and himself traveled to Grand Rapids to buy furniture at the source. The rooms of his home became adorned with beautiful curtains, floral carpets, and lovely furniture. The curtains that hung in the parlors were made of red velvet and had golden fringes. The davenports and chairs matched the curtains. All the bedrooms had hand-carved wooden bed frames, dressers, and wash stands which were decorated with pitchers and linens.

The front room, where most guests were greeted, had a grand-white-marble mantel with a mirror over its top. The mirror was so large that the entire room could be seen in its reflection. In the corner of the room, by a window, stood a Jerusalem Cherry Tree.

In the dining room, the furniture appeared to be massive. A walnut table, perfectly restored, sat in the center of the room. It had the capacity to seat as many as twelve guests. On the side of the room, a server extended from the floor to the ceiling with its carved wooden head and another mirror. A dumbwaiter journeyed from the dining room to the kitchen below. Food was made there in the huge oven and gas stoves which lined one wall, then it was lifted to the dining room on the next floor. On one side of the kitchen there was a row of shelves for dishes, but on the other wall sat a table in a bay window. The windows overlooked the herb garden and provided a beautiful view of the morning. Behind the kitchen there were two more rooms—the furnace room and the ice house. The ice house stored perishable foods such as fruits, cheese, and butter. The other room which contained the furnace, provided the heating system for the entire house.

When the Kennedy's first moved in, they had come from a farm. Hannah Kennedy did not want to leave her horses, and since there was a barn behind the new house, she convinced her husband to let her bring a few animals with them to Butler. Naturally she brought horses, but she also brought a few cows for fresh milk, some chickens, and two pigs. Pigs seemed to be very common in Butler's back yards.

"One afternoon, just after school was dismissed, some girls were walking home. Among them was Mary Pride. As the girls were leaving the school in the distance, they heard a great commotion. Everyone in the vicinity had stopped all activity to watch a thirteen year old boy chase a pig down the street. All the girls laughed hysterically except for Mary—the boy was her brother and she was humiliated.

She finally began to calm down as she prepared for a dance outing later that evening. She became so caught up in her preparations that she forgot about the pig incident. She had been invited to the dance by a very debonair young man who had recently returned to Butler from Paris. Mary spent hours preparing for the dance and just as she was making a few last minute adjustments, there was a knock on the door. She warned her younger brother and sister that they had better not embarrass her, then she answered the door.

Mary's date was a very tall gentleman dressed in tails and a cape. he handed her a bouquet of flowers and a box of candy. As she took the gifts, another knock was heard at the door. Mary opened the door, and there standing in front of her was the town drunk with the pig underneath his arm saying, 'Excuse me ma'am, but I believe this pig belongs to you.'"

Six West Diamond yet stands across from the courthouse; it is now a home to lawyers and their staffs. It is becoming a bit worn. The iron fence is gone as are the iron palings. The old house seems to be crowded by the large business buildings around it. However it still remains one of the most beautiful buildings in Butler and has long been the author's favorite.

(As told to John Wimer by his grandmother, Mary Pride Wimer)

The South Main Street Viaduct was built in 1927. Autenreith says the remains of the first bridge are yet visible under the Viaduct. Search as I did, I could not find any such ruins. Kesselman Machine Shop was also under the viaduct. The Muntz family lived in a very large house on the south end of the old bridge—it was down closer to the Connoquenessing Creek. If one walked along the new Viaduct it was possible to reach down and touch the roof of the Muntz home. Muntz mined coal in that area. Some of his mine shafts extended under the cemetery—others entered the hillside above Coal Street.

Autenreith says the famous Federal Spring is still there. It comes out of the bank under the old hospital and from there it is piped under Route 8 and cascades down the bank into the Connoquenessing Creek. Several houses under the viaduct were rented out by John Negley. The Solari family lived in one of Negley's houses. Autenreith remembers two of the several Solari boys—Merle and Lido, who were stone masons and brick workers. Their building skills kept them quite busy.

Starting up the hill, South Cemetery was owned by the German Lutheran, English Lutheran, and Presbyterian congregations. John's father's first wife, Emma is buried there near the foot of the hill. She was a Mueller. About half way up the hill are buried Jacob and Magdalena Mechling who were the proprietors of the Mansion House where Lafayette stopped for lunch in 1825. The Reibers are also buried here. There is a very unusual grave there, the headstone resembles the headboard of a bed. There are also concrete siderails and a footboard. Someone planted red, white, and blue flowers on the grave every spring and during summers the floral display resembled a quilt.

Near the top of the hill on Muntz Avenue is the old home of Bill Jahnig who built dozens of houses in that area. He built a very high tower, "higher than an oil derrick, which enabled him to look all over Butler through a telescope." He drove around town in a pickup truck which had a minature house built on the back; it was a good advertisement. He carried his tools, nails and other construction equipment in the back of his pickup in the minature house.

When we reached the southern limit of our tour we took a short breather, then imagined ourselves back at the top of North Main Street hill, ready to begin our trip down the eastern side of Main Street.

John didn't have much to say about Ritz Park so we quickly found ourselves near the bottom of the hill.

There were many apple orchards around that area of Butler. Elm Court, the Phillips' Mansion had the best apples because they pruned their trees. The local boys, of course, used to steal a few bags of apples. John says they "just let them rot anyway." The purloined apples made very good apple sauce, dumplings and pie.

Andersons lived across Main Street from the Berg Mansion. Mr. Carl Anderson worked in one of the local banks and had a son, Carl Jr. who was nicknamed Bus. Bus was a very fine horseman. His horse was also kept in Judge Wilson's barn. A sister, Dorcy Anderson, was about six feet tall and very athletic. She was highly skilled at tennis and could outplay all comers, including the men.

The Vanderlyns lived at the south corner of Polk and Main. As their name suggests, they came here from Holland. The house has windows which are ten feet high. The family lived as though they had money. Continuing down the hill brings us to the Jewish Synagogue. The north end of the Synagogue was once the home of Washington D. Brandon who was mentioned earlier in this chapter. His son J. Campbell Brandon was also an attorney and as was stated earlier, wrote *A Concise History of Butler County, Pennsylvania 1800 - 1950.*

The large office building at 457 North Main Street, which is presently owned by Servistar, was the site of the large-stone home of Alf M. Reiber. It was torn down for the Farm Bureau Insurance Company building. After that it was occupied by Nationwide Insurance. Behind this building on McKean Street was home of J. V. Ritts and Elias Ritts who were among the founders of the Butler County National Bank on the Diamond.

The present day Sterling Apartment building has an interesting history. The Sterling Club at 415 North Main Street was a popular social organization. Its members enjoyed banquets, dances and other events in the building. The hall on the first floor was rented out for high school proms, company dances and such events. Dr. Robert Bruce Greer lived on the next corner at 371 North Main Street. In addition to his private practice, he was the company surgeon for the Standard Steel Car Company, the Butler Bolt and Rivet Company, and both the Pennsylvania and the Baltimore and Ohio Railroads. His biography is in *Butler County, the Second Hundred Years*, pgs. 201-202.

Rosenblums bought a private residence and founded radio station W.I.S.R. in 1941. It was Butler's first radio station. They also owned three stores on Main Street—S. Rosenblum & Son operated a dry goods store and women's apparel at 127 South Main. D. Rosenblum had a department store at 207 South Main; and the Rosenblum Furniture company was doing business at 323 South Main Street. Rosenblums also owned the Paradise Shop which was a more recent vintage of a ladies clothing store.

Judge Aaron Reiber lived in a substantial stone house just south of W.I.S.R. at 351 North Main. The

---

### Old Cemeteries

Most of the present generation recall the old public cemetery at the corner of East North and north McKean Streets, on the site of the Junior High-School building. Most of them can remember the stone wall that surrounded the cemetery, the iron gates on North Street, and the inscriptions on the tombstones.

At a public sale of lots held August 15, 1803, two lots located at the corner of North McKean Street and East Mifflin Street were sold to John Cunningham and Abraham Brinker for $10 each and donated by them to the town for a public burial ground.

In 1828 Norbert Foltz bought the adjoining lot on the north and donated it to the borough of Butler. The borough council erected the stone fence with the aid of contributions by the people of the community.

In 1856 the council passed an ordinance forbidding further burials in the cemetery after the cemetery on the Southside and the North Cemetery had been established and many of the bodies had been removed from the old burial ground to the new cemeteries.

In 1866 an attempt to condemn the old public cemetery for school purposes met with a storm of indignation and the scheme was abandoned by the school board. A similar attempt made in the middle of the 80's was frowned down.

In 1902 when the school board began to look for a location for a high-school building and started condemnation proceedings to get the burial ground there was no protest offered.

After considerable preliminaries in court title was passed to the school district of Butler, one of the conditions being that the board remove all of the graves to a new location at its own expense. This was accomplished in 1905 and 1906 and the erection of the present Junior High-School building was started...The wife of Hon. Walter Lowrie of Butler, who was United States senator from March 4, 1819, to March 4, 1825, was buried in the old cemetery, as also were two soldiers of the revolution and one of the first ministers of the Methodist Episcopal Church in the county.

More than 700 graves were opened and whatever remained of bones and dust was removed to the North cemetery in 1905, but of the whole number only 84 could be identified by markers or monuments. The names of John and Samuel Cunningham, founders of the town are perpetuated by bronze tablets placed on the wall of the Junior High-School building.

*Butler Eagle*, May 11, 1925, James A. McKee

Judge was a widower who lived there with his bachelor son, Martin and a daughter Mary. Polk's 1923 Directory lists both children as students. The Reibers had a live-in mother and daughter housekeeping duo who were from Lyndora. There was another Reiber house at the northeast corner of Washington and Walnut Streets where the Y. M.C.A. parking lot is now located. It was the home of Howard Reiber. George Reiber lived in the beautiful home at 412 North Washington Street. The present owners are Dr. and Mrs. LaMonte Crape.

At 327 North Main Street, Dr. Clarence E. Imbre, had a tonsil and adenoid hospital. The strong smell of ether permeated the area near the house, especially in back near the sun porch. Patients usually recuperated for a day or two on this sun porch. Autenreith remembers when the school nurse sent him home with reports that his tonsils and adenoids were "enlarged and diseased—must be removed." He thought that the "good Lord put them there for some reason" so he ignored the advice to have them removed. He has his tonsils and adenoids yet today.

At the northeast corner of Main and Brady Streets, Cheeseman and Watson ran the Standard Motor Company, often called the "Buick garage." Joksters around town sometimes referred to the business as "Cheat-em and Watch-em." A man named Kamerer was one of Standard Motors' mechanics. In the rear of their spacious building they had a paint shop. Some cars, especially trade-ins, were taken from the Standard Motor Company directly to the junk yard. Autenreith recalls watching George Soles open the hoods of many of these cars and smash the engines to pieces with a sledge hammer. When John inquired as to why he was doing such a thing, Soles replied, "so nobody can buy used parts at the junkyard; they'll have to buy new ones from us."

Henry Boyer, who lived in Bon Aire, had two sons, George and William Henry. They all worked for Standard Motor Company. When Bantams came out, the boys each purchased one; at that time the purchase price was about three hundred dollars. The Hoffman boys from Hoffman Auto Parts also purchased and drove Bantams.

Across Brady Street is the English Lutheran Church which was previously the location of the Witherspoon Academy. The Academy moved to "Institute Hill." That story is covered in *Butler County, the Second Hundred Years*, chapter 11. One hundred and fifty years ago, the Lutheran minister, Gotlieb Bassler converted Sam Mohawk before the Indian was executed. Bassler came up to Butler from Harmony and preached at the English Lutheran Church as well as St. Mark's Lutheran Church. There is more detailed information on Sam Mohawk's conversion in chapter seventeen.

The municipal parking lot across Main from the Burger Hut was the site of the city building. It was originally a two-story, brick hotel and was built around the time of the Civil War—it was known as the Schreiber House. After it became the city building, it housed the Mayor's office, the police station, city treasurer and other city offices. The city purchased the Troutman house on North Street and tore down the old office building for the construction of the parking lot. As recently as the late 1940's, the area between T. W. Phillips and the Lutheran Church was used as the farmers' market.

Around 1902, when the Standard Steel Car Company was having such an impact on the local economy, an apartment building was built on the northeast corner of North and Main Streets. The apartment building was

Duffy Flats

78

appropriately known as the "Duffy Flats' and while the use of that name slowly disappeared, the apartments are still there today. Early in the century the upper floors of such tenements usually housed the poorest people. There were no elevators in such buildings; the upper floors were very hot in summers and drafty in winters. Reports handed down by word of mouth tell that the roof of the Duffy Flats was sometimes a sort of park and promenade for all the residents of the building and their friends and neighbors. Women hung the wash out to dry on the roof. Occasionally a gardener cultivated a few plants in some soil which had been carried to the roof. Today tenement roofs are seldom used for these purposes but during the early 1900's these practices were common.

Just before the turn of the century, Sam Teung Hop rented space on the corner lot—before Duffy Flats was built. Chinese laundries such as Hop's and the previously mentioned business at 212 North Main Street were part of the scene in Butler for many years. The typical Chinese laundry was a small room or two with a counter just inside the door. On the counter was a bell which summoned the laundry operator from his living quarters which were either in the back or in the basement. The typical Chinese proprietor could not speak English but it wasn't necessary. The customer brought in his laundry to be washed and ironed and after examining it the launderer would write in Chinese on two, small pieces of paper. He did not ask for the customer's name but rather identified him in some way in written Chinese on the two papers. One paper was given to the customer and the proprietor would say, "Tuesday, two dollar." He would put the other paper in with the dirty laundry. The washing was done in a boiler which was heated by a three-burner hot plate. City gas was used to heat the water. The earlier Chinese launderers such as Sam Teung Hop heated the water in large tubs outside over an open fire. After the laundry was cleaned, ironed, and folded, the paper with the Chinese message was placed in the finished bundle. When the customer returned to pick up his laundry the proprietor would match the two papers, collect his money, and thank the customer.

Today, A. E. Worsley Wallpaper and Paints occupies addresses 155 though 161 North Main Street. Worsley's business was founded in 1927 by Albert E. Worsley Sr. Mr. Worsley began his operations as Empire Wallpaper and his original location was on Cunningham Street in the basement of the Troutman building. Sometime later he moved the business to the southeast corner of Washington and Cunningham Streets. In 1964 Mr. Worsley purchased the corner building at 159-161 North Main Street and located his business there.

An investigation of Polk's City Directory, 1934 shows Reynolds Brothers Furniture operating in the old Duffy building. Harry Wishnev, known affectionately as "Loonie" because he sold aluminum pots and

---

In 1912, George J. Krug had a meat market at 107 South Main Street. He and his wife Marie resided at 311 East Pearl Street. The Krugs owned two ice dams and a barn on Penn Street Extension near Alameda Park. The breast works may yet be seen today during the winter season, even though Butcher Run creek has completely eroded through both the dams. Word of mouth has it that the dams were built around 1895. Krugs also owned a slaughterhouse near the creek at 411 Maryland Avenue. Water used in the slaughtering process came from a spring, which still flows at 410 Maryland Avenue.

During cold winters when the impounded water froze to a sufficient thickness, workers cut the ice into large blocks and floated to the shore where it was transferred to the ice barn. The ice barn had double outside walls; the opening between the walls was filled with sawdust for insulation. During a cold winter enough ice was harvested to keep into the summer season. When the ice ran out, most butchering stopped for the summer. People ate smoked, pickled and salted meats. Cold packed meat was also very popular.

Krug's ice was delivered by horse drawn wagons to meat markets, private homes, and restaurants. The ice deliveryman had a regular route much like a newspaper boy. Ice companies had a unique method of saving the iceman a trip to the door to find out how much ice was needed. Customers had a square piece of paper or cardboard; each of the four corners had a number—25, 50, 75 or 100. The paper was hung on a nail or the doorknob in such a way that the top number told the iceman just how much ice was needed. The Butler Ice and Coal Company, on North Monroe Street, used red papers, which also advertised the company name, its officers, and the company address. The Crystal Ice Company used yellow.

The iceman used an ice pick to break off the correct sized block and he took it in the kitchen and put it in the icebox. Ice companies gave free ice picks inscribed with the company name as another form of advertising. The ice business was a source of enjoyment in more ways than one. Children flocked around the iceman for the chips which were enjoyed much like ice cream. Ice skaters used the ponds in winter and swimmers used them in summers. (John Autenreith as related to the author)

St. Paul's Church, Rectory and Charles Duffy Home

pans, among his other household fare, used part of the old Duffy building as his headquarters. Mr. Wishnev motored around the county selling a variety of items out of his car—a traveling salesman at a time when they were fast becoming a thing of the past. Old timers say Mr. Wishnev conducted his business in the 1940's. Apparently he used just a part of the old Duffy building because the city directories tell us that in 1936 Reliable furniture occupied the site and continued to do business there until the early 1950's. By 1956 the main floor of the Duffy Flats building was vacant; Reliable Furniture had moved to South Main Street adjacent to Troutmans.

The building just north of New Castle Street which presently houses the Book Nook was, in 1923, the site of Hildebrand's Meat Market. Their slaughter house was located at Bon Aire but they sold the meat at their downtown Butler store. Hildebrand's had large ice boxes which enabled them to sell fresh meat nearly all year if the ice held out. They were especially known for their German bologna. One of their butchers was a man named Blymiller—a big powerfully built man. He and his son Clifton worked for Hildebrand's for many years. Clifton had a sister, Viola, who was "a very pretty girl."

Duffy's store was located on the southeast corner of Main and New Castle Streets. John Negley discussed the Duffys at length in his 1891 remembrance, but since the original recording of Negley's lucubration there is more to tell. By 1891 practically all of the Duffy block in addition to the store became the property of Peter Duffy's son Charles. According to Autenreith, who knew the Duffys quite well, Peter's father wanted to be certain that the Duffy name remained prominent in the area and as a means to that end, offered a sum of $5,000 for every child born to Peter and his wife. Autenreith reports that ultimately fourteen children were born to the couple, and most were boys. Grandfather must have been very happy. Two of Peter Duffy's

sisters married well-known Butler personages—John Pillow and Lemoyne Graham. Charles, the last proprietor of Duffy's store, was not very business minded. Business declined and the old store eventually closed. Offut's then opened a store in the old Duffy building. It burned after

World War II and never reopened as Offut's. J. C. Penney opened their store in a new building which they had constructed on the site. Today the Dollar General Store occupies the location.

The northeast corner of Main and Jefferson has been occupied by a succession of banks since the

Lowry House was razed in 1920 for the construction of the Guaranty Safe Deposit and Trust Company. For a considerable length of time in more recent days the corner site was the location of Pittsburgh National Bank. Across Jefferson, the corner lot has housed one drug store after another. There was a second floor on the previous building which, as was the case with most Main Street buildings, housed several offices.

Even though it's a bit off Main Street, we can't exclude the Hot Dog Shop from our armchair tour. It has been located at 107-111 East Jefferson since it opened in 1912. [The author has relatives who live in Akron, Ohio who from time to time, hop in their car and come to Butler for hot dogs at the Hot Dog Shop. While they're in town they stop at my place and say, "Since we were in town we thought we'd say hello." That's the kind of drawing power Butler's Hot Dog Shop enjoys.]

Matthew McConnell wrote a chapter on the Hot Dog Shop for *Builders, Dreamers, Scandals, Schemers*. In it he reports that when Anthony Klutinoty opened the business it was "little more than a small hallway with a few stools, a hot plate, and a shoeshine stand...The Hot Dog Shop was closed for eighteen months in 1945. The excessive time for remodeling was required because of a wait for a shipment of material from about twenty states." McConnell's chapter details many features of the restaurant which would go unnoticed by the average, hungry customer. For example, "Pink and black marble-like slabs were shipped in by the carload from Cold Springs, Minnesota. A bakery on the second floor has the capacity for baking over five hundred pies a day in addition to other breads and pastries. "During the 1950's the Hot Dog Shop was open twenty-four hours a day, seven days a week, and employed eighty-five people."

Schoener's Bakery was located just east of the Hot Dog Shop. One of the boys, Otto Schoener, became a Lutheran missionary. His sister, Elsie, worked in the bake shop. They had a very good business—bread and buns, cream puffs, chocolate eclairs, ladylocks, cakes, pies and cookies. The family's work day began shortly after midnight in order to be ready with fresh bakery items by opening time.

John Dillon's meat market was located on the southwest corner of Jefferson and Cedar Streets. His slogan was, "We trim our meat, not our customers."

Getting back to Main Street, John didn't have much to say about the one hundred block until we arrived at the Woolworth building. He was anxious to discuss it—the building which collapsed on May 18, 1999. It was a Reiber building. At the turn of the last century the first floor of the building was the home of the Douthett and Graham clothing store. There were twenty-one offices on the second floor and Polk's City Directory shows that nearly all were occupied. In this busy building one might visit his dentist, doctor, or music teacher, buy or sell real estate or purchase some insurance. Several attorneys including the Reibers, Judge Aaron Reiber, Saul and Ruth Campbell Bernstein had their offices on the second floor. In 1923 the building held the offices of five coal companies and one gas and oil company. The Reibers were attorneys as well as major stock holders for many of the coal companies. For a time, the office of the International Correspondence School was located on the second floor; the Bell Telephone

exchange was also there as was Russell Bennett's photography studio.

The third floor of the Woolworth building was mostly occupied by Reiber Hall. Many lodges and civic groups rented the hall for meetings and banquets. The local Jehovah's Witnesses also met there. Homer Smith, the janitor, lived in a third floor apartment. Autenreith was fascinated by the large number of antique office machines and antique furniture found on the upper two floors of the building.

Woolworth's occupied the first floor and the basement and sold everything from gold fish to office supplies. Mr. Autenreith remembers a news stand outside Woolworth's at the curb. It was run by a sixty year

### Briar Hill

Many of the coal companies were one-man operations. Do you remember the two coal mines which were over on the hill above the Bonnybrook Creek, facing East Butler? Well, when I was just a kid those mines were already history. We used to go over and step inside the dark openings—we could hear water dripping but weren't foolish enough to venture inside. A man named Imbre operated those mines. He also owned what they called the Briar Hill mine. It was out the East Butler road just on the Butler side of International Staple & Machine Company. The entrance to the mine was on the west side of the road and the mine shaft went under the road. A great many farmers found a coal outcrop on their land somewhere. If it were on a hillside they merely began to extract the coal as they needed it. If the owner got into the coal business in a big way, he would rent an office on Main Street in the McClung building or nearby and hire someone to answer the telephone and take orders.

A rule of thumb was that if the vein of coal were not more than two feet thick, it didn't pay to mine it. The vein at Briar Hill was just eighteen inches which made it, at best, a questionable business venture. Pete and John Kopie worked for Mr. Imbrie. They couldn't speak much English—just enough to get by. The brothers were both married. I think that John had about four sons. They lived in East Butler up the hill where Stoner's used to live. They walked all the way to the mine, carrying their big coal miner's lunch buckets. On payday they cashed their single check at Glenn's store. Either Mike Glenn or Brady Fair divided the money for the two Kopie boys.

There was also a coal mine up near the "reservoir" on Valvoline Oil Company property. The shaft ran directly into the hill. Fred Shoup operated it for awhile. A man named John something, I can't remember his last name, had a mine up on Mitchell Hill. It was a one man operation. If a family needed coal they would notify John to deliver twenty-five bushels. As soon as he got to it he would dig the coal in the mine, haul it out, shovel it on to his truck, deliver it to the customer's house and then shovel it off the truck. Many people had a coal chute down which the coal slid to a pile near the furnace. John lived next to George Church, superintendent of the Fretz-Moon Tube Company, who hired him. From that time on the coal business became a sideline.

( As related by Ralph E. Goldinger Sr. to the author)

old man known affectionately as "Al Capone."
He also recalls that when Butler was hit with
three feet of snow in 1950, that Martin Reiber
hired anyone who had a shovel and was willing,
for a fee, to remove the snow from the building's
flat roof. Hindsight proved that the snow removal
was a costly mistake—the roof was very well
enforced and would have had no trouble carrying
the weight of the snow. It should have been left
alone because the snow shovelers tore off the
roofing and caused some bad leaks. It took about
ten men and a large amount of money to make the
necessary repairs.

Autenreith likes to talk about the Reibers
because he knew them well. They did the legal
work associated with his real estate interests from
1936 until about 1990. He made frequent visits
to the Reiber offices in the Woolworth building.
Autenreith relates that he visited Judge Reiber on
a Saturday evening about 1946 to discuss some
legal matters. When John said that he was going
to window shop on Main Street, Judge Reiber
said, "John, please stay and talk with me; I am
very lonely." That stuck with John all of these
years. It surprised him that such a prominent man
could feel lonely.

Miller's shoe store opened in 1893 and is
probably oldest business establishment in the city.
It has been at the same location for over a
century—215 South Main Street. John Chiprean
joined the business in 1916, at the age of ten. His
major responsibility was to act as an interpreter
for Mr. Miller and his Italian shoe maker. In 1934

Mr. Chiprean became the proprietor of the store, a position he filled until his retirement in 1991. the Chipreans are proud of their long tradition in the shoe business. They cherish the words of John Negley who said of the business in 1900, "C. E. Miller is the proprietor of Butler's progressive shoe house, and by fair dealing and untiring efforts to please the trade, he has pushed to the front and stands second to none in the shoe business in Butler today."

The present day Unicorn Gift Shop at 221 South Main Street is on the first floor of a very old and unique building. A shaft, which is actually a skylight, exists in the center of the building. Everybody taps into that shaft, and even if there are two or three floors above, every room which is adjacent to the skylight is able to experience the sunlight. Natili's restaurant also has such a skylight.

The McClung building, just north of Vogely Street had more than a dozen offices and in 1923, coal companies occupied eight of them. Many of these coal companies were small operations and the office contained not much more than a clerk, desk, file cabinet and a telephone.

The mention of Rockenstein's Restaurant, now the location of Sir Speedy Printing Center, brought back many gustatory memories for John. In earlier years diners at Rockenstein's could be seen wolfing down Mrs. Rockenstein's German cooking. With a name like Autenreith it is no suprise that German cooking is John's favorite. Their homemade, mashed potatoes and gravy were in a class only with John's mother's. He liked to mix his peas, corn, yellow and green string beans with his potatoes and gravy and he especially liked the endive which was prepared with little pieces of crisp bacon.

This section of Main Street was a real mecca for the hungry. If Rockensteins were full, one could continue a few doors up the street to 247 South Main where the Crescent Restaurant was serving tempting fare—especially deserts. Some may remember the large stone porch in front of the restaurant—downstairs was a barber shop. The Crescent sold cigars and tobacco and "the men smoked as they ate." Many diners actually enjoyed the pleasant fragrance of the pipe tobacco and cigar smoke. As John went through a litany of pies served at the crescent my mouth began to water. "They even served rhubarb pie. One big meal on Sunday— all you could eat—cost less than a dollar."

There were several additional restaurants in downtown Butler. Also catering to the throngs on Butler's Main Street were the drug store fountains where one could purchase sandwiches, hamburgers, or hot dogs as well as banana splits, sundaes and ice cream cones, and wash it all down with a favorite soft drink. One must consider the fact that the city of Butler had more than ten thousand people in 1900 and that the number grew until it peaked in 1940 at 24,477. Many of these folks worked, shopped and did business downtown. The city was flourishing—it was one of the fastest growing in the entire state.

Continuing down South Main Street just south of the Dixon Pharmacy was the location of the Butler Business College. It was on the second and third floors and was run by a man named Regal. Down in the basement was Herbert Frazier, a man who could fix anything.

Next was Benny Gluckman's clothing store. Benny was over six feet tall and a very gentle man. His prices were reasonable. Autenreith claims that Gluckman was the first merchant in Butler, perhaps anywhere, to put a display of shoes out on the sidewalk—all left shoes. Nobody would steal a pair of shoes if they were both lefties. Benny's father helped out with the business; they spoke in German to each other but used English when addressing the customers. The Gluckmans lived on West Penn Street near Mercer Street and usually walked back and forth.

Right next to the alley, Weber Way, which is now Citizen's Bank drive-through, was the location of the Sport

## Roessing Meadow and Neighbors

Ritts creek starts at Ritts Park and ends at Broad St. School. In 1925 the creek had willow trees all along its bank. The open field which is now the site of Emily Brittain School at that time belonged to the Roessings, who were undertakers by trade. Max Ureaugh, aged 12, who lived on Amy Avenue spent a large amount of time playing on the creek bank that ran through the Roessing property. Max had a box of tools and a bag full of clean tin cans. If any boy wanted a small boat to float in the creek, Max would strike up a bargain—cash or barter. Max would then cut up a tin can with tin snips until he had a flat sheet of metal. Next he folded it and bent the two ends shut. Then he spread it open and the boat or canoe was complete.

In 1925 street cars ran along West Penn Street. There were several bill boards flanking the street. The large Roessing house stood on the northeast corner of the lot facing North Washington Street near several smaller houses. All were constructed of wood. Where North Church Street meets West Penn Street on the Roessing property, there was a horse shoe court and a baseball diamond. Flying kites was a popular pastime in that meadow. Eventually the Roessing family sold the land to the local school district and the school was built. The creek is now buried underground, but it is open at the Broad Street School and Ritts Park. Contractor Norman Boyer buried the creek using a coal fired steam shovel and six foot high concrete sewer pipes. Manholes were placed along the line and the creek flowed underground from West Penn Street to North Bluff Street at State Street.

Shortly after World War I ended some young veterans brought an army kite to the Roessing meadow. It was the type of kite used by our military for observation during World War I. It looked much like an airplane and took about four men to control. A winch was staked to the ground and a rope was used instead of lighter kite string. The men put a ten year old boy in a harness sling under the kite and the strong west wind soon had him high in the air above the East Jefferson Street and Franklin Street area.

Emily Brittain lived at 427 North Bluff Street with her sister and a man they called Uncle Archie. Ms. Brittain had a brother who operated a drug store on Center Avenue. Joe Brittain lived next door at 425 N. Bluff Street.

A sister, Lillian Heck, another early, well-known Butler educator, lived at 444 North Bluff Street. She was married to Marcus Heck, and they had two sons: Marcus Jr. and Richard. Also living with them was Lillian Heck's sister, Jane Loutzenhiser. Lillian Heck's maiden name was Loutzenhiser. Jane had a brother, Chauncey Loutzenhiser, who was a Butler dentist. The Loutzenhiser home was just half a block away from Emily Brittain's. Ms. Brittain and Lillian Heck were both elementary school principals. The neighborhood was well represented with teachers; Eunice Turner and Grace Patterson, Butler teachers, lived on the northeast and southwest corners of North Bluff Street and West Penn Street.

Emily Brittain had a two-story, wood barn in the back yard where she kept a horse and buggy on the first floor and stored hay on second floor. She and her family are buried in North Cemetery. (As related to the author by John Autenreith)

Shop. Where the postoffice sits now was a row of old, four-story buildings. There were offices and apartments on the upper floors and retail shops on the main floors. At 331 South Main Street was Mrs. Louisa Kummer's meat market. She had a small stockyard in the back where live animals were kept. Campbell's Good Furniture store was located at 337 South Main. It was a large operation with eight or ten employees. Behind Campbell's store, O. H. Nicholas sold Packard automobiles and trucks. At the turn of the century the corner building was the site of DeArme's Bargain Store—dry goods, notions, hardware, wall paper, and household supplies. Polk's City Directory shows The Mardorf Company twenty-five cent store at the corner location in 1923. Records show that the building was vacant in 1936. The Rainbow Restaurant became a fixture on the site for quite a few years. However, when John F. Kennedy visited Butler in 1960, many photographs of the Senator show the restaurant in the background, and it was then called People's Restaurant.

In the 1960's, this area on the east side of Main Street was becoming blighted, and since it was one of the first sights encountered by northbound visitors to Butler, it became the first project of Butler's Urban Redevelopment Authority. The newly formed Authority [1965] purchased the properties using the power of eminent domain, razed the buildings and had the new postoffice constructed. Originally the postoffice was owned by a man who lived in New Jersey.

The Williard Hotel was discussed in *Butler County, the Second Hundred Years*, pg. 41. Most Butlerites mourn its passing. Autenreith remembers when somebody operated a church in a Quarry Street home. If one attended this church and took a course, one could be ordained a minister and start his own church. It was probably non-denominational. The Bessemer Railroad owned some houses under the viaduct, which they rented out. These small houses have all been torn down.

After the final three hour session, I thought John was wrapping things up. "Most of the buildings from the bottom to the top of South Main Street Hill are residences. It looks like we're finished with Main. Would you like to start at North Butler and discuss Jefferson down to Pillow Street then clear down Hansen Avenue to Armco?" I replied, John, I would love to but allow me to put all of this in the computer and begin to work with it first—I'm being overwhelmed with local history. Let's put the armchair tour on the back burner for now. Speaking of a burner, John, do you realize that it must be at least ninety degrees in here?

[John Autenreith's armchair tour of Jefferson Street and Hansen Avenue will never become a reality. Mr. Autenreith died on September 7, 1999. Many stories and information associated with local history died with him. John's love of local history was evident to all who knew him and enjoyed his recollections. He will never read his "armchair tour of downtown Butler," but would be happy to know how much delight it will bring to others. John--may you rest in peace.]

# Cunningham's Mill

When in 1769 the State of Pennsylvania opened the area between the Appalachian Mountains and the Ohio River, many pioneering families and individuals eagerly took advantage of the opportunity to get a place of their own. By the end of the century there were 3,916 adventurous settlers living at various locations throughout Butler County. [The county did not become an official entity until 1800; it had previously been part of Allegheny County.] John and Samuel Cunningham, the brothers who founded the city of Butler, settled here four years earlier, in 1796. [*Butler County, the Second Hundred Years, pg. 2*] For the sum of $158.00 the two brothers purchased a 300-acre tract which today comprises most of downtown Butler. The site chosen by the Cunninghams was on a direct route between Pittsburgh and growing areas to the north such as Franklin, Meadville, Mercer and Erie. Their newly acquired acreage was centrally located and was ripe for settlement. The Cunninghams were very confident that with all its assets, their town would someday become the county seat.

The location had another important advantage and being millers, the Cunninghams were very cognizant of it. The bend in the Connoquenessing Creek on the south end of town flowed in a western course until it reached an area of large boulders where it turned to the north. The rocks caused a channel, which was very narrow yet deep—perfect for a gristmill. A forty-foot tree was felled and the improvised bridge quickly made both sides of the creek very accessible.

Brown reports in his 1895 history that when Lasher's mill was erected on Buffalo Creek in Millerstown in 1803 that his biggest competitors were the Neyman mill at the mouth of Bonny Brook, the Sarver mill on Sarver's Run and the Cunningham mill in Butler. The early histories verify the fact that there were dozens of gristmills in the county prior to 1810. People were pouring into the new county.

The town of Butler began in a manner which was similar to that of many villages of that era. First, a gristmill was constructed near a stream, in this case, the Connoquenessing Creek, and because area farmers were willing to travel a considerable distance to get stone-ground flour, the new mill was soon busy. In areas where no gristmill was available within a reasonable distance, families ground their own grain by means of either horse-power or hand mills; the process in either case being one that was very unsatisfactory. Hence the building of a gristmill was a matter of community interest and the builder was often looked upon as a benefactor to all.

Workdays found a small crowd of people milling around while waiting for their flour to be ground and bagged. These people had money or would soon have valuable flour to trade. They were also hungry and thirsty. Often an enterprising person, seeing the potential, would open a general store or trading post. The next business to appear was usually a blacksmith shop which was then followed by several homes and a church. If the site were on a busy route, such as Butler was, someone would construct a building, get a liquor license and open an inn—presto we have the beginnings of a town. Butler conformed to this pattern only as far as acquiring a gristmill. Since the Cunninghams together with their first neighbor, Robert Graham, owned four hundred acres of land in the vicinity of the mill and covering what is now the main area of Butler, these acres were not available for development in the usual manner.

But John and Samuel Cunningham set aside about 77 acres of their 300-acre tract for the purpose of founding a community. They, along with neighbor Robert Graham, in the late summer of 1803 conducted a public sale at the mill of lots covering the entire town of Butler. Each surveyed block was divided into three lots. Five of these lots were set aside for the county. John Cunningham kept lots 44, 78, 86, 87 and 142; Samuel took lots 21, 155, 156, 157 and 162. Prices of the individual lots ranged from $20 to $126. David Dougal, whose story is found in *Builders Dreamers Scandals Schemers*, purchased the first lot—number one for $103. A cursory look at the map on page 42 of *Butler County, the Second Hundred Years*, shows that lot number one is located at the northeast corner of Main and Diamond Streets. Lots 149, 150 and 151 were set aside as the town cemetery.

A payment plan was devised for prospective buyers—a third of the money down, a third after nine months and the final third after eighteen months. The above mentioned map shows most of the original purchasers at Butler's first land sale. Many of the names on this map are not familiar to local historians because most of the original purchasers did not settle in Butler. Some had bought lots merely as investments; this of course, was the reason for the large number of early property transfers. Other property owners sold as they became discouraged or changed their plans for a multitude of reasons.

John and Samuel Cunningham and Robert Graham named their new town Butler to honor the Indian fighter, General Richard Butler, who had been killed in the Battle of St. Clair, just twelve years earlier in 1791. They named two of the streets after early presidents of our nation—Washington and Jefferson. We can only speculate as to their reason for excluding Adams, our second president. Monroe Street was originally called Lookout Avenue; it was not named for President Monroe until much later. The founders also named McKean and Mifflin Streets after the first two governors of Pennsylvania. Wayne Street was named after the Indian fighter, "Mad Anthony Wayne" and Penn Street was named for William Penn, founder of Pennsylvania. Main Street was originally called High Street for obvious reasons. Perhaps some people thought it presumptuous that the Cunninghams named a street after themselves, but they certainly deserved this token recognition considering their gifts to the county and the town. Today Cunningham Street is the only remembrance we have of the brothers inasmuch as neither married nor left any descendants here.

Most new towns in this area were not planned, surveyed and laid-out on paper as was Butler. The typical western Pennsylvania town began and grew haphazardly, filling in the areas between rivers and hillsides. John and Samuel Cunningham deserve credit for the forethought they put into the birth of their community.

Granted, we cannot give the Cunningham brothers credit for fighting the Indians, and/or taming the wilderness, but it is certainly fitting that they receive our respect and admiration for another reason and that was the fact that they were millers. The milling vocation required an amazing amount of skill and hard work. And since their mill was a successful business for over one hundred years, we must give the Cunninghams our accolades for they were not only millers, but were very good millers.

The location they chose for their gristmill was ideal for water impoundment. A millrace tapped the creek approximately where Main Street crosses the Connoquenessing today. When this proved to be insufficient the creek was dammed and the accumulated backwater better served the purpose. The mill was washed away by a flood in 1812 after which time it was rebuilt and enlarged.

Most gristmills of that

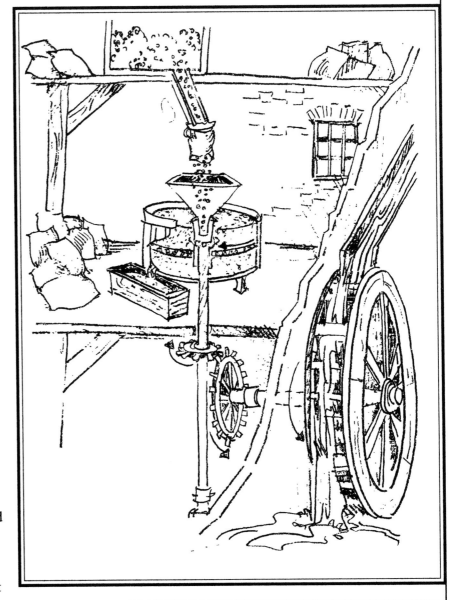

era contained three floors. The third floor was used to store the grain and flour that the millers kept as payment for their labor. The actual grinding was done on the second floor and the bottom floor housed the gears. The mill wheel was outside, and in the case of the Cunningham mill, was an overshot type which meant that the water which turned the wheel was channeled through a millrace and was directed to flow over the top of the wheel. This was the most efficient type of waterwheel. The miller had some control over the amount of water that reached the waterwheel by opening and closing the sluicegate.

Millers needed a great deal of knowledge and experience to construct, operate, adjust and repair the machinery in the mill. The grinding procedure was different for each grain--i.e., wheat, corn, rye, oats, barley, and eventually—buckwheat. After a length of time, the miller knew his machinery so well that he could sense a problem by listening to the sounds of the machinery and by feeling the texture of the flour.

Early gristmills such as the Cunningham's had wooden gears. The gear wheel attached to the waterwheel was large, whereas the gear that turned the millstone was only about one-fourth its size. The millstone rotated four times for every single rotation of the vertical gear wheel. Early millers used animal fat, for obvious reasons, as a lubricant on the gears. Most people are not aware of the volatility of flour. One spark can cause an instant inferno, a danger which was constantly on the mind of the miller.

The millstone was often made from many smaller stones and was fitted together at the mill. The miller had to be very careful that when operating, the millstones never touched; this could cause a spark. It might also ruin the batch, as bits of stone contaminated the flour. Every few weeks the millstone needed to be dressed. The miller usually did this himself with an iron tool similar to a pick. As a result of this dressing, splinters of stone would imbed themselves in the miller's hands and remain lodged beneath his skin for a time. This is where the expression, "show me your mettle," originated. [*The Gristmill* by Bobbie Kalman]

John Negley, whose recollections were presented earlier in this treatise, in a *Butler Citizen* article dated 1906, described the area around the old Cunningham mill and house. "Near [the house] stood large oaks, one of which can yet be seen. A cluster of butternut trees also stood near and close to the big rock yet in the creek. But one of them yet remains. Other wild native trees, ferns and wild flowers were profuse around. Small berry trees, the plum and the cherry prevailing, were plentiful, but these have long since disappeared. The old Cunningham homestead, the first house of Butler, also disappeared about 1836. It was of frame construction, square, rather large and well built. Where it stood, the foundation of it can yet be seen, between the two railroad tracks passing there. A mother's kind hand probably caused the peppermint to grow and spread around this old house, and growths of that pungent and aromatic plant can yet be found in or near its old foundation. For many years the large rocks in and near the creek were a favorite place for the boys of the town, particularly on Sundays. Boys of every age made it a special point to have their initials or their entire name carved into the rocks. Most of the rocks on the south bank of the creek were taken away when the Pittsburgh and Western Railroad was constructed through the site in 1880. The Bessemer Railroad's construction workers removed the rest of the rocks in the creek when that railway was built along the creek in 1896."

We know that the old original mill was built on the north side of the creek, at the south end of Washington Street where Fuelgraf's Electric is now located, and the previously mentioned forty-foot log was used to cross back and forth between the house and the mill. The house was built on the south side of the creek because of the spring that existed there. The spring was well-known and was named the "Federal Spring" in honor of the politics of the days of General George Washington. Indians passing through Butler, years before the Cunninghams settled here, made it a point to visit the spring to quench their thirst and perhaps to lie in the sun and rest awhile. The spring later became the property of John M. Smith who closed it to the general public.

The spring may have closed but the mill operated well into the twentieth century. Nearly a dozen different men owned the mill outright or were involved in partnerships between 1832 when Mr. Negley sold the mill until 1880 when Jacob Walter bought it. When Mr. Walter died in 1903 his sons operated the mill.

## BIG FLOUR MILL NOW READY FOR OPERATION

Among the big improvements to Butler's manufacturing plants this year is the completed change in the Geo. Walter & Sons flouring mills. The change amounts to the entire making over of the whole milling plant—the wheat flourmill, the buckwheat mill, the corn meal department and the feed department. Besides this, a handsome new office is being built and a new warehouse in which to store, ready for shipment, the immense quantities of flour and feed that the increased capacity enables the management to get out.

Seventeen years ago this firm commenced to expand, and more warehouse room has been added from year to year, until today they have a floor space of over 30,000 feet. Fifteen years ago a new system of flour milling was installed with a capacity of about 4,000 sacks of flour a week. This improvement added very materially to their already rapidly increasing trade. But, like other improvements, they soon outgrew it. The handsome new mill just installed has a capacity of almost 10,000 sacks a week of the very highest grades of spring and winter wheat flour. The system of milling is the very latest, placing this firm in the very front rank of flour millers in the United States.

Preliminary runs of the new mill have been made and everything is working as smooth as silk. All of the changes are now completed excepting the finishing touches to the office and the installing of the large motor for driving the flourmill which has been delayed in shipment. When completed the entire plant will be driven by electric motors, excepting the buckwheat mill; the present steam outfit will be used for it.

The basement has been very much improved and enlarged. In it will be found the steam plant, the electrical motors, four in number, bottoms of the elevators, the main shafts and almost innumerable numbers of pulleys for driving the various machines on the floor above. On the ground floor are six double stands of very large rolls, twenty-four in number for grinding the wheat: also a wheat tempering machine. Besides these there are also 12 large rolls for grinding the buckwheat flour; also flour and feed packers for both wheat and buckwheat mill, the rolls for grinding graham flour, corn meal and feed, and buckwheat drier.

The second floor contains the wheat tempering bins, automatic scales which weigh every pound of wheat before it is ground. We also see wheat-cleaning machines for the most thorough scouring and scrubbing of every grain before grinding. We also find on this floor purifiers, these machines are equipped with fans and long silk cloth sieves to remove the small brown specks which have a tendency to make flour dark and heavy. On this floor are to be found two immense Universal bolters. These are wonderful machines and are literally filled with hundreds of sieves covered with all grades of silk cloth. They perform the immense task of separating the large amount of flour, 1,600 sacks a day. Numerous buckwheat flour machines are also on this floor, as are also bins for wheat flour, buckwheat flour, middlings, bran and various grain bins.

On the third floor are located the tops of the numerous elevators, more cleaning machines for wheat and buckwheat, dust collectors and a large number of buckwheat flour machines. Electric elevators for both passengers and freight, reaching all floors, have been installed.

This firm has developed a very extensive trade in both wheat and buckwheat flour, but, in addition, has a very extensive trade in the following lines: many grades of feed, grain, seeds, salt, cement, lime, sand, gravel, building block, tile and coal. In order to properly care for the increased out-of-town business, an office has been opened in Pittsburgh.

This firm employs many men. Two motor trucks, besides several horses and wagons, are needed to deliver the vast amount of merchandise about town and the small local shipments to the depots. Large shipments are loaded into the cars at the mill.

Pennsylvania Railroad Station and P. J. Oesterling's grain elevator

Altogether this mill is one of the most modern and complete in the state and is a very important addition to Butler's industries. No one should fail to inspect it who can arrange to do so.
(copied from the *Butler Citizen* dated July 7, 1914 by Dave and Audrey Craig)

## H. J. KLINGER

Harry Samuel Klinger was born in Butler, July 3, 1856, and was the son of Herman Julius Klinger. He was educated at Capitol University in Columbus, Ohio. After his graduation from college in 1875, he entered into the milling business with his father and in 1878 became general manager of the concern known as H. J. Klinger & Company. When his father died on March 3, 1910, Harry became head of the firm.

In the thirty-seven years of his business career he gained a wide reputation as a practical miller and has contributed much to the literature of the trade. Some of his papers, read before the Pennsylvania Millers' Association, were subsequently published in the national trade journals and given wide circulation. In July 1883, he won the prize offered by the *American Miller* for the best essay on "The Handling of Middlings and the use of Purifiers." He contributed other

P. J. Oesterling's Elm Street operation

90

articles to that paper in 1884 and 1885, and for four years after was a contributor to the *Milling Engineer*, besides writing for other trade journals. For a number of years he conducted a column in the milling trade journals entitled "Random Reflections," that attracted considerable attention among members of the trade. In December 1886, he was one of the prime movers in organizing the Pennsylvania Miller Fire Insurance Company and was a long time member of the board of directors.

In 1900, Klinger's plant consisted of two mills and an elevator. They were located at 117-125 South Monroe Street and 240-248 Mifflin Street with the main office at 139 East Jefferson Street. Klinger's wheat-flour mill was called the "Oriental Roller Mill" and was unique in that it milled no other grain but wheat. Winter wheat was grown mostly by local farmers; spring wheat was shipped in from the "west." The modern machinery in the mill was capable of producing two hundred barrels of flour per day. "Klinger's Pure Pennsylvania Buckwheat Flour" had a national reputation. The firm advertised "absolute purity" in its buckwheat flour. Klinger was a member of the Anti-Adulteration League of the United States and offered a bond of one thousand dollars as a guarantee that it would manufacture only pure flour. Klinger's company also manufactured whole-wheat products and feed of all kinds. Negley's *Butler County Centennial Souvenir* contained a photograph of a railroad shipment of Klinger's buckwheat flour, which was leaving Butler in eighteen, railroad cars of about thirty thousand pounds each. Such was the efficiency of his operation that this large shipment was loaded in one day. According to Negley, "No other private industry in Butler has as much capital invested in its manufacturing plants or has done so extensive a business in the past year as the firm of H. J. Klinger & Company."

## EXIT OIL—ENTER RAILROADS

As the nineteenth century was drawing to a close, Butler was experiencing a glowing economy. The area's intoxication with petroleum had waned but had certainly not become a hangover. The number of pumping wells in the county had diminished from its peak of the 1880's, but was yet significant—many men and women still owed their weekly paychecks to petroleum. The number of service industries associated with oil was, in fact, continuing to increase. Kesselman & Co., Spang & Co., Evans Machine Co., and Keystone Pipe and Supply were a few of the many Butler County companies which were manufacturing and repairing all kinds of well-drilling tools, machinery, pumps and a plethora of petroleum related equipment. Some of these businesses boasted of customers as far away as Texas and Oklahoma. As a result of these oil-related and many other industrial opportunities, Butler continued to be a magnet for many of the nation's hopeful who were wishing to find the good life and to ride the wave of prosperity into the twentieth century.

Butler's healthy economic condition prompted the *Butler Citizen* to report in its April 15, 1897 issue: "Butler is apparently in its heyday. All of its people are benefited directly or indirectly by the oil business. We don't believe there is a town in Pennsylvania in which the people seem more prosperous and in better circumstances than in our own Butler. We venture to say that we have less real poverty here than has any other town of equal size in the state." But also a warning—"If the oil production of the surrounding regions ever becomes exhausted Butler will receive an awful backset. And there is a possibility and a probability that the oil production will play out. [Butler County produced over 60,000 barrels of oil a day in the 1880's; by 1909 that daily figure had fallen to 3,500 barrels.] Then where will Butler be? Of what use will our fine big business buildings be if there is no business to transact in them?

In order to secure the town's prosperity and business for all times we must have more manufactories. This seems to us the proper way to invest surplus oil earnings. What's the use in trying to induce outsiders to come in and build and run factories? Why not do it ourselves? Plenty of able businessmen in Butler who have been fortunate in oil have the time, talent and capital necessary for new industries. Why not decide which would be most preferable and then go at it? Go at it to win. No one will ever help Butler if Butler doesn't help itself. New works of whatever sort you desire to go at, backed by home labor mean permanent security to Butler's prosperity."

But even if the demise of Butler County's oil industry was under way, the savior had already arrived in the form of an iron horse. The first public steam railway in the world was known as the Stockton and Darlington and made its appearance in England on September 27, 1825. The railway was horse powered with stationary steam engines for inclines. Five years later, on September 15, 1830 the first full-fledged, steam-powered railway opened—no horses involved. On that fateful opening day, the train stopped for water, the passengers alighted on the opposite track when another train came along and killed William Huskisson. Was this perhaps, a harbinger of things to come?

Railroad cut on the Bessemer north of Butler

Very early, in 1836, just six years after the opening of the world's first railway, a group of Butler businessmen saw "the handwriting on the wall," and began a grassroots movement toward bringing a railroad to Butler. A committee of concerned citizens was formed and a survey was completed for a railroad route from Freeport to New Castle through Butler borough. [This early attempt to procure a railroad adds credence to our statements about the vision of our Butler forefathers.] As an aftermath of the 1836 survey, meetings were held, agreements were reached and contracts were signed. A couple of cuts were made, one in Clay Township and one in Summit Township [Euclid Cut, 6700 feet long and 60 feet deep – Muddy Creek Cut, 4000 feet long and 54 feet deep] but both these operations failed and resulted in financial disaster to those who had put up money. The only thing everyone seemed to agree upon was— "Railroads are the future and Butler needs a railroad."

It was 1871 before Butler's dream became reality. That year, the West Penn Railroad was constructed from Freeport into Butler. The new railway terminal was built along Jefferson Street just west of Monroe Street and became the city's first railroad station. Another station was built along the West Penn line at Cabot which was called Saxony Station at that time. (*Historic Saxonburg and Its Neighbors*, pg. 93) The opening of the new railroad was the occasion for a great celebration throughout the county.

Two years later a separate railroad was completed from Parker to Karns City and in 1876 that Karns City-Parker Railroad was extended south to Butler thus becoming Butler's second railroad. According to Brown's *History of Butler County*, the "Karns City and Butler Railroad operated until 1881. It had a good patronage, and paid its projectors a handsome profit upon their investments...It was a common remark among the patrons of the road that there was no danger of being hurt by a train leaving the tracks, as that part of the road never had a serious accident to its passenger trains, and never killed anybody." The Karns City and Butler Railroad was consolidated with the Pittsburg and Western Railroad on June 10, 1881. The following year the railway was leased by the Baltimore and Ohio Company and the tracks continue to serve Butler today.

The era between the opening of the West Penn Railroad and World War I was one of railroad dominance. The relatively new form of transportation became an integral part of the delivery system of agricultural products, petroleum, and raw materials for Butler's growing industries. The importance of railroads was now well understood by all of Butler's business community as well as by the general populace. Railroads brought in raw materials; railroads shipped out finished products. Railroads brought prosperity and railroads with greater tonnage showed greater profits.

Since tonnage equaled profit, all the railroad entrepreneurs had their eyes focused upon the Pittsburgh region. The *Butler Citizen* reported in its August 22, 1883 edition "The tonnage of Pittsburgh is acknowledged to exceed that of any other city in the United States, and consequently all the great carrying companies are anxious to receive their share. This fact within the past few years has inaugurated a regular railroad boom in the attempt to reach this city and the coal territory contiguous thereto. Coal furnishes one great part of the immense tonnage, and a number of lines have been in contention to reach after it, but the great majority have ruled that to come thus far means to come entirely. Today there is hardly an accessible avenue between the hills leading into Pittsburgh and Allegheny but that is occupied, if not with a railroad, at least with a charter for a railroad."

The old Pittsburg, Shenango and Lake Erie Railroad had been constructed from Shenango to Pardo in Mercer County in 1869 and extended to Harrisville in July 1872. It was originally constructed to be a coal-hauling road from the mines of Butler and Mercer counties to the Atlantic and Great Western Railroad which ran north of Butler County. On August 9, 1883 a twenty-mile extension of the Shenango & Allegheny railroad was completed from Hilliards to Butler. The Shenango & Allegheny now offered a connection between Pittsburgh and northwestern Pennsylvania and the east and it ran right through Butler. The new railroad followed the Connoquenessing Creek into Butler. In fact it was originally called the Connoquenessing Valley Railroad Company but the name was changed because it was so difficult to spell.

Shenango & Allegheny trains made connections at Butler Junction (North Butler) with the Baltimore & Ohio which was already at Butler. So when the Shenango & Allegheny Railroad roared into Butler it was the county's fourth railroad. Butler was now connected by rail and its locational possibilities were being examined by manufacturers from all over the United States.

## RAILROAD WORKERS

E.S. Milligan, of Clearfield Township was in town Tuesday for a load of Italians to work on the railroad cuts on his place. The laborers in his vicinity are behaving themselves but in some other places the contrary is reported. A gang of Italians is taking out stone on the Graff farm and they make good music evenings. The new railroad is graded through the farms of P. Fennel in Clearfield Township, and the grading is progressing rapidly on the farms of widow McDevitt and Agnes Green.

At the summit, near the pump station, at Carbon Center a large force is working in both directions with steam shovels etc. "Work was commenced in earnest on Monday on the foundations for the new railroad bridge across the Allegheny at Mosgrove. There are 400 Negroes working on one side of the river and 400 Italians on the other side of the stream. Derricks, steam shovels, pumps and all kinds of machinery for this work are on the ground and it is a scene of the liveliest activity and the work at that place is being pushed along at high speed. Unless a tight rein is kept on these foreign workmen by the authorities of that section it may prove a second Unity."

*East Brady Review*, July 1898

The camp life at the summit and at the other locations is interesting. All of the hard working Italians live by themselves in bachelor fashion. Some live in mud dugouts, others in tents and many in rough board structures. All are living frugally with but one ambition and hope—that of returning to Italy with a fortune. Some manage to live all week for seventy-five cents. The Americans live more pretentiously. At the summit they were camped in a beautiful grove in neat frame dwellings erected by the contractors. They live well, are happy and the caterer of the camp, Jim Noss, is their guardian angel. I did not see a woman in one of the camps nor a child. It is a great village of bachelors.

Every comfort and convenience is furnished on the summit. It costs the contractors ten dollars a day for water alone and twenty-five dollars more for fuel, but they have each in abundance. An abandoned water well was leased and the water pumped from this to large reservoir tanks.

Each camp has its company store, operated by the contractor, and a blacksmith's forge is kept busily running. At the summit, A.W. McDonald keeps his blooded horses, two cows and everything that will cater to his enjoyment. It is an ideal outdoor summer life.

*Butler Citizen*, October, 1, 1896

The dark side to the construction of this great railroad is the horrible vice and depravity rampant in the construction gangs. Scores of murders and other numberless crimes have been committed. The record of these crimes has attracted as much attention as has the building of the road itself.

*Butler Citizen*, October 1, 1896

The following newspaper article indicates the excitement generated by the completion of Butler County's fourth railroad:

### THE NEW RAILROAD REACHES BUTLER

"Last Thursday and Friday were days of interest to our citizens. The fourth railroad had reached our town and there was general rejoicing. The "Connecting Link" was made. The last spike being driven on Thursday evening Aug. 9. On the event being known, a general salute was given from the whistles of the locomotives of the other roads, by the ringing of bells and other demonstrations of joy. On the next day the new road carried a large number of the State Militia to Greenville, on the way to their encampment at Conneaut Lake.

This has opened another important route to and from this place. The connecting link connects us with the main branch of the Shenango and Allegheny Railroad, near New Hope this county. This opens up to trade and travel what is supposed to be the richest part of our county in coal and other minerals. In coal especially, large fields will undoubtedly now be developed and much additional business be done in that line. It will also give a speedy and cheap communication with Butler to the citizens of about ten of our townships. The very heart of the county it may be said is now penetrated by railway.

A glance at the map and a calculation show that to any one going north to Mercer, Greenville, Meadville or Erie, the connecting link shortens their travel about twenty-five miles. Greenville can now be reached in about sixty miles, or less. By New Castle, or any other present railroad route it takes about eighty-five miles travel to reach that point. As Greenville is on the direct way to Meadville and Erie it will consequently shorten the route to those places about the same number of miles. To Oil City, Corry, Titusville, and other points north it will be just about as short a route as any other that can now be traveled

Much credit must be given to the managers of the Shenango and Allegheny for their energy and untiring efforts to hasten the completion of this road to Butler. Mr. Steele, the President, and Mr. Blair, the General superintendent, were frequently with their men as the road approached this place, giving matters their personal attention and taking a lively interest in seeing the last spike driven. They are the right men in the right place for railroading.

We presume a formal opening of this new road will be had some of these days soon, when we will have more to say. In the meantime we rejoice with our citizens at this increased evidence of business and future prospects.

## Can Come by Rail

The making of the connecting link now leaves less than a half dozen of our townships and towns but can come to Butler by rail. The first road made, Butler Branch, from Freeport here, accommodated to a greater or less extent the citizens of Buffalo, Clinton, Jefferson, Winfield, Summit and Clearfield Townships, in coming to Butler. The second road made, the Karns City extension, accommodated Allegheny, Parker, Fairview, Donegal, and Oakland townships, with their towns as well as parts of Clearfield and Summit townships. The third road made from Butler down the Connoquenessing to near Evansburg, [now Evans City], and now known as the Pittsburgh & Western, connecting at Callery Junction with trains for either Pittsburgh or New Castle, accommodates, more or less, the citizens of Adams, Cranberry, Middlesex, Forward, the Jacksons, the Connoquenessings, Penn, Lancaster and Butler townships, with the towns of Zelienople, Harmony, etc. The fourth and last one, connecting the Butler Branch, or West Penn, with the Shenango and Allegheny road, will accommodate, in coming to Butler, in whole or in part, the citizens of Venango, Marion, Mercer, Slippery Rock, Cherry, Clay, Center, Brady, Concord, Washington and Worth Townships, with their numerous towns and villages. This leaves in fact but the townships of Muddy Creek and Franklin that it may be said are not as yet convenienced by the construction of railroads to Butler. Their time will come next.

## Now for Manufactories

Now is the time for our people to turn attention to manufacturing businesses. All we need is the introduction of some good manufactories. We have everything else. Four railroads now enter Butler and our population must rapidly increase. The manufacturing establishments that now exist are doing an excellent and extensive business. The more recent one established, the Glass Works, is doing a business beyond expectations. A large lumber business is done. The firm of the Purvis Bros., bring in and sell an immense amount of all kinds of lumber for building, fencing and other purposes. But we need other kinds. A paper mill, it is thought, would pay well. We have all the material, and now all the facilities for iron manufacturing. But there are other kinds that might be profitable. Our object now is to direct attention to this matter, and we hope soon to hear of some new establishments being introduced.

## By Way of Butler

The completion of the connecting link, and of the Pittsburgh & Western roads to this place, not only make Butler a central point, but shorten the former uses of travel from Pittsburgh and this point to points directly north of here. Heretofore the two routes from Pittsburgh north, were either by the Allegheny Valley road or by the Pittsburgh and Erie road. The following show the distances that can be saved now to some of the principal

## ANNANDALE STATION
### 1884

Messrs. Eds:—If you will allow us the space in your valuable paper we will give you a small history of the beautiful little town called Annandale Station.

On last Wednesday morning about two o'clock a.m. the alarm of fire was heard, the fire department responded promptly but the flames had gained such headway that they could not be extinguished until the entire building of George P. Christie's coal house had been destroyed. George, in the future be sure your ashes are cold before barreling them.

The Sproull Brothers are doing an extensive business in the flouring mill at this place. Their flours are giving unbounded satisfaction everywhere, which fact is plainly apparent from the number of teams we see going to and coming from the mill daily. They say they cannot be beaten in Butler County on a straight grade of flour and that is what the farmers want.

Annandale Station is one of the greatest tie and stave shipping stations on the S. & A. railroad. There are about twenty teams hauling ties and staves daily. Mr. Small is our station agent and you will find him the right man in the right place.

The young people still carry on the singing at the M.E. Church at Annandale. They are so far advanced they can carry on the singing themselves with the assistance of Mr. E.G. Sproull. They expect to have a grand concert about September next.

Mr. S.S. Crawford still works on the railroad. Sam is a good section hand, especially at pumping the handcar home in the evening. Our genial friend Mr. Lisney looks quite sad for a few days past, his wife has gone away on a visit to her mother's at Pulaski, Lawrence Co., Pa. But cheer up Levi, she will be glad to come back ere long. Our Hotelkeeper Mr. J.H. Kelly has removed from midst. He has gone to Altoona, Pa. We were sorry to lose John but as fast as one leaves another steps in to take his place. James A. Sproull has moved into the Central Hotel building, formerly occupied by Mr. Kelly, you will find Jim an obliging landlord, give him a call. H. Baldwin, our village blacksmith, has just completed a new veranda and picket fence in front of his dwelling and intends putting down a new sidewalk which will add greatly to the beauty of his dwelling. Our obliging storekeeper, Mr. Mabold is getting very industrious this summer. He is clearing a piece of land and leaves his store in charge of his lady clerk through the day. Our wagon maker, Mr. Burkhart, has been wearing a very pleasant smile for sometime past. It is a bouncing baby boy.
The Jolly Two, *Butler Citizen*, June 18, 1884

places north of Pittsburgh and of this place.

From Pittsburgh to the city of Corry, for instance, the miles to be traveled from Pittsburgh by way of the Allegheny River valley road, are 177. By the Pittsburgh & Western and connecting link, by way of Butler, is but 162 miles.

From Pittsburgh to Oil City by the Valley road is 132 miles. By Butler, as aforesaid, is but 114 miles. To Greenville, from Butler, by way of New Castle is 82 miles. Now by the connecting link and Mercer is but 57 miles. From Pittsburgh to the same point a still greater distance will be shortened by coming by way of Butler.

The above are only a few of the points north of here that the distance is shortened by way of this place. To go therefore now from Pittsburgh to points north, the traveling public will soon learn to ask for tickets 'By way of Butler.' And the same will be the case in going south from points north of here."
*(Butler Citizen, August 15, 1883)*

## THE BESSEMER AND LAKE ERIE RAILROAD

At this time Andrew Carnegie was building his giant industrial empire. His U.S. Steel Corporation was destined to become the world's first, billion dollar business. The three basic raw materials needed to make steel at that time were iron-ore, coal, and limestone. Carnegie's unique Bessemer steel-making process required phosphorous-free iron ore which was available in Michigan and Minnesota. So Carnegie set about making the connection between his steel mills in North Bessemer, Allegheny County and locations of the aforementioned raw materials.

The previously mentioned Shenango & Allegheny Railroad had deteriorated quickly and the company was nearly bankrupt. The Carnegie interests in 1896, purchased the line, improved it and extended it to Conneaut Ohio. Then the old line from Shenango to Butler was totally rebuilt with 100 pound, per-yard rails making it a double track road. Screened gravel and crushed slag replaced ash and mine refuse. These improvements would enable the rails to handle heavier loads. At the same time, an extension of this railroad was built from Butler to North Bessemer in Allegheny County. The Bessemer's entire length, when finished, was 214 miles with Greenville at the halfway point. Some of the really long trains of the Bessemer, were 600 cars in length and were pulled by several engines. When a train left North Bessemer it could go as far as Branchton before replenishing its coal and water. The entire project was finished in 1897 and Carnegie called his new railroad the Bessemer and Lake Erie.

The connection was now complete: ore was shipped on 600 foot steamers from western Lake Superior to the port at Conneaut—a distance of 900 miles. At Conneaut the ore was transferred to ninety-ton-hopper-railroad cars and then transported to Carnegie's steel mills in Allegheny County. The train would then head back to Conneaut filling its hoppers with coal as it headed north. At Conneaut the coal was dispersed to freighters which took it to a number of Great Lakes steel mills. There were at times, eight million tons of coal waiting at the dock at Conneaut. [The fact that much more coal than iron ore is used in the manufacture of a ton of steel, argued for the movement of the ore to the coal rather than the opposite.] For a considerable time, the Bessemer and Lake Erie hauled more tonnage than any railroad in the United States. According to Jean Dreher, author of *Iron Horses, Iron Men*, the Bessemer was only 91st in length of all United States railroads, but of Butler's five railroads, It certainly had the greatest economic impact on the county.

The Mercer Mining and Manufacturing Company had long operated coalmines in Pardoe and several other locations in northern Butler County. They had been shipping over railroads which were predecessors of the Bessemer, since the Civil War. Now that it could be accessed, coalmines were opening all along the Bessemer's route and small towns were growing rapidly around the mines. Branchton, about twenty miles north of Butler was so named because of the number of railroad lines that branched off the main line. These branch lines were built to access coal and iron ore. Have you ever heard of Gomersal, Burnett, Roy, Ferris, Kiesters, or Hilliards? These were all coal towns which developed almost overnight around the new coalmines. One three-mile branch line ran from Branchton to Coaltown, a small community of 75 dwellings, stores, a church, school and a town hall. Burnett had a coal crusher and 250 coke ovens. Much of the coke was shipped from northern Butler County to mills in Shenango, Youngstown, Loraine, and Chicago. Because the coal along the Bessemer, north of Allegheny County was not of a metallurgical quality, much of it was shipped north to Ashtabula, Ohio for steam power generation. The coal in southwestern Pennsylvania and northern West Virginia was better suited to Carnegie's steelmaking process and therefore ended up at North Bessemer.

The first railroad cars of Mesabi Range iron ore, so important to the Bessemer steelmaking process, began to pass through Butler in 1897. A large limestone quarry opened at Kaylor in 1903 and another one at Annandale in 1907. This limestone was all shipped by rail. Limestone from Michigan was also shipped to Conneaut and transferred to railcars for the rest of the journey to Carnegie's mills.

Some products Carnegie may have never anticipated were being shipped on his railroad. Conneaut Lake ice was harvested by hundreds of men and shipped in insulated boxes and refrigerated cars to customers all along the line. And before a pipeline took the business away from the railroad, a considerable amount of oil was shipped in railroad tank cars. Add finished and semi finished steel, cement and miscellaneous manufactured products and Mr. Carnegie had a very busy railway. According to Joe Benson, Bessemer and Lake Erie engineer, now retired, the railroad's main cargo today is coal most of which is headed north to two Canadian hydroelectric plants.

The Bessemer never offered sleeping, dining or lounge cars. Although, a large numbers of passengers traveled by train, especially to and from Conneaut Lake Park. Passenger traffic on the Bessemer peaked in 1913 at 1,140,000 for the year. After this a decline set in; in 1935 only 35,000 passengers took the Bessemer. 1954 was the last year that the line offered passenger service. Joe Benson, remembers the annual Bessemer picnic at Conneaut Lake. It was a very big day for the employees and their families. The railroad had to rent passenger cars from another railroad since the Bessemer had halted its passenger service. The company soon found that it was easier and more convenient to use busses.

Ms. Dreher describes the wrecker. It had a short heavy boom attached to a platform of one car. There were also a tool car, another car with extra parts, of course an engine, a caboose and a cook car. The wrecker was kept at Greenville. And when not in use, Bessemer's wrecker helped clean up wrecks on other railroads.

The following newspaper article gives a very good description of the excavation and construction of the Bessemer line:

### ALONG THE NEW RAILROAD

*A correspondent of the Pittsburg Dispatch who followed the line of the new railroad from a point on the Allegheny River to Saxonburg last Tuesday, writes as follows:*

"The only tunnel on the road is a small one 350 feet long, which is being driven by contractor Simon Herrold under Brimstone Corners. This hamlet is the only town on the road between Butler and the river, and its sulphurous name was occasioned by the collection of roughs that once infested it, the farmers say. It seems peculiar and fated that the Butler and Pittsburg Railroad should avoid it by tunneling fifty-five feet beneath it.

This tunnel is one of the most important contracts on the line. It is almost two miles long, with its approaches, and 75,000 feet of earth and rock will be taken out of the approaches alone. Work has been begun from both ends, and a monster steam shovel, with its great steel teeth, has been tearing its way into one end. All the earth from this excavation is hauled one and one-half miles to a deep ravine toward the river.

Little steam locomotives were puffing hastily about yesterday, and I gained some idea of what the finished road will look like. The ravine is bridged with a high rough trestle, and the earth is dumped from this until the woodwork is buried.

C.I. & A.W. McDonald, the general contractors, have a cut thirty feet deep and 500 feet long at Brimstone Corners, over half-finished, and the digging is being pushed with great speed. Spellacy & Ellwier, of Columbus, who have almost two miles of digging, have 150 men at work with scrappers and D.A. Sanders has 140 men and forty horses taking out the earth from his half mile of work. The cuts in these portions are heavy, deep and rocky, and the advance made is necessarily tedious.

The greatest and most important contract on the entire road is that at the summit end, which contractors McDonald are themselves doing. Over 162,000 cubic yards of earth will have to be taken out, and 200 laborers are employed night and day. It is at this point that the best idea can be obtained of the progress made on the line. This cut, with a few breaks, is three and one-half miles long, fifty-five feet deep and has fills eighty-five feet high. The organization of the men and the equipment could not be surpassed.

Great long trenches, sixteen feet wide at the base, 170 feet wide at the top and 20 feet deep have been gouged out of the solid rock by two monster steam shovels, and the work is only half complete. Temporary tracks have been laid for four and one-half miles to the great ravines at either end of the work, and four little steam locomotives are kept constantly hauling back and forth the eighty-five cars loaded with earth. And still another twenty feet deeper must be dug. One and one-half miles in this cut alone will cost over $100,000.

### DYNAMITING BURGLARS

The little burglarproof safe in the office of the Penn's R.R. Co. at the station here had a remarkable experience last Friday night. Some fellows, who got into the room through a window, placed a large dynamite cartridge underneath it, lit the fuse and then went out—went out of the room or they would likely have been there next morning. The explosion that followed shook that whole section of the town and tore the bottom of the safe into fragments which shot out in all directions, but as the floor under the safe offered but little resistance. The explosion spent part of its force in that direction, and the safe was not split open—as the operators, no doubt intended. Fragments of the safe were shot into the wall and ceiling, and one piece ricocheted from the wall to the window frame and then across the yard and street to the front of the Davidson & Gilghrist grocery where it made a big hole in the plate glass window, and another piece is imbedded (flat) in the pine lining of the room and will be left as a curiosity. The explosion occurred about two a.m. but very few people knew where, until next morning. The safe is completely ruined: it dropped into the hole made in the floor and was pulled out with block and tackle next day.
*Butler Citizen*, May, 25, 1899

The camp seems like a small city, and the bustle and activity only strengthen that impression. One of the great steam shovels worked for a time yesterday, the earth for several rods before it had been loosened to a depth of twenty feet. Holes had been drilled to this depth, and powder placed. The charge was only sufficient to increase the size of the hole to that of a barrel. Five kegs of powder and dynamite were then lowered in this well, tamped, and exploded. The earth for rods was lifted ten feet in the air in one mass. As it fell the rocks were shattered and the earth loosened.

The steam shovel began its work. Great wagonloads were taken at one mouthful and loaded in the long train of cars waiting. They were filled in a few minutes and the little engine puffed away with them almost two miles to the big fill at Davis run. Another train was ready for its load as soon as the first left, and it was not many minutes until more dynamite was necessary to feed the greedy monster. Over 150 workers are deprived of a living by its work, and its average daily duty is 1,000 yards of earth and rock....Only last week one of the miniature engines backed over the high bridge with its train and crew. One of the brakemen was killed and another probably fatally injured. The engineer escaped only by jumping down the steep embankment....Two contractors have the last fourteen miles of the road, and both are rushing ahead. Breen & Butler have four miles of work of 175,000 cubic yards, and keep one hundred men employed. At the Butler end the Ferguson Contracting Company has ten miles, with 500,000 yards of excavation. Over five hundred men are at work, and the place is more than half-done. Every employment is at hand, although cut up by trestles and fills, it is now looking as if this strip will be finished first.

Crane used in building the Bessemer Railroad

The scenery along the route was grand. The leaves were just turning yesterday, and the wild country added beauty. I saw but few places suitable for village sites. This will probably be just to Chairman Reed's liking. He wants freight exclusively. The line was either above or below grade for the first fourteen miles, but at the summit the location is admirable. The country is flat and rolling, and the land rich. It was the prettiest place on the entire line.

The grade is wonderfully low for the hilly country. It will doubtless startle those who have claimed success for the road impossible. It can scarce be surpassed for fast, through freight service and Pittsburg may expect a revolution in freight business on its completion.

(*Butler Citizen*, October 1, 1896)

**Two Railroads Prepare To Erect Stations in Butler in Near Future**
**B. & O. Takes Initiative by Ordering Chief Engineer to Borough,**
**And Pennsylvania Line Follows Closely—To Construct Boulevard**

Butler will have two new depots in the very near future, the first one to be started at once. Word was received in Butler Saturday by the attorney for the Baltimore and Ohio Railroad that the plans recently drawn up for approval of B.& O. officials at Baltimore, for a handsome new station at Butler have been definitely decided on and the chief engineer of the company has been directed to proceed to Butler and begin operations at once. The Pennsylvania Company also will begin soon.

Plans for the new station at Butler for the B.& O. call for a two story pressed brick building with brown stone trimmings. The new building will be on the site of the present building, except that it will occupy more space.

The first floor of the building will be fitted up with ticket office, lady's and gentlemen's waiting rooms, toilets and retiring rooms. These will be located in the east end of the structure. The part west or next to Center Avenue, will be only one story and will be occupied by the baggage rooms, checking rooms and express office. The building will have a tower, in which a large clock will probably be located.

Ground will be broken for the new structure just as soon as weather permits. It will probably be built in sections, but as yet that is not an assured fact. The office may be removed to the room now occupied by the restaurant, and the west end of the structure may be erected first.

The building will probably cost $60,000 and other improvements are either now under way or contemplated by the B. & O. in Butler for early spring, that will run the cost of the improvements to more than $100,000.

A 40-foot boulevard is now under construction in the B. & O. yards, extending from Center Avenue through the yards to Lookout Avenue. This will greatly relieve the congestion caused by heavy traffic on Center Avenue, as all hauling from the B.& O. to the Pennsylvania railroad will be done by way of this boulevard.

The freight station at the B. & O. will probably be moved several feet to make room for additional tracks necessary to handle the large and steady increasing traffic.

The Pennsylvania Railroad Company will not be far behind the B. & O. in extensive improvements. Butler officials were in conference with head officers of the Pennsylvania in Pittsburg, Saturday. The result of the conference is that the Pennsylvania Company will begin in the near future, the erection of a new depot on plans mentioned some time ago in the citizen.

It is not certain when work will begin, but plans are approved and an appropriation is well under way. The fact that it is the supposition that the Pennsylvania Company has been waiting on the B.&O. to do something in the way of a depot for Butler, and that a conference in regard to this matter was held last week, is direct assurance that early spring will see two new depots under construction in Butler. It has been the desire of Butler people to have a union depot for several years, but since the different railroad companies cannot get together, residents of the city will be gratified to know that conditions, which have existed for many years, will be much improved.

The plans given out by officials of the Pennsylvania, Saturday, call for rebuilding the present passenger depot into a handsome structure. The present freight depot will be torn down and the passenger depot will extend westward a considerable distance. The structure will be a one-story affair, built of brick, with stone trimmings. The new station, as stated in this paper some time ago, will be located across the street, on company property near the intersection of East Jefferson and Kittanning streets.

The freight station will be a two-story, brick building. The first story will be used for freight and the entire second floor will be used for offices of the company. Plans have been completed for a high retaining wall to be built along the grade of Kittanning Street, extending from Monroe Street to about 300 feet along Kittanning Street. This improvement will take considerable work, as much cutting into the hill will have to be done.

The present Pennsylvania station is a disgrace to any city and especially in this kind of weather, when it is next to impossible to get from the station to trains."
(copied from the *Butler Citizen* dated Feb. 21, 1910 by Dave and Audrey Craig)

Confirmation of the report published two weeks ago in the *Citizen* that the Pennsylvania Railroad Company would make extensive improvements in the local yard and build a passenger station and freight depot this summer, was made yesterday by J. J. Daniels, assistant trainmaster of the division, who, with several members of the engineering corps was in town looking over the ground.

The proposed improvements will include a new steel water tank in the yard, a new round house, a passenger station, a freight depot and warehouse, additional trackage in the yard, and the grading out of ground owned by the company lying between Monroe Street and the Bessemer Railroad up to Kittanning Street.

In the city yesterday with Mr. Daniels were G. C. Walter, chief inspector of equipment, and A. H. Ream, assistant master mechanic of the Butler division, who will have charge of the preliminary arrangements in advance of the construction work.

Mr. Daniels stated that the Pennsylvania Company not only intended to make improvements this year out that construction work had already been started. The foundation work of the new all steel water tank has already been started. The tank itself will be constructed at the local plant of the Standard Steel Car Company. The tank is located at the western end of the yards.

The railroad company owns the ground from Monroe Street along Jefferson Street west to the Goebring and Richards store, and the improvements in this part of the yard, will include the removal of the old station and the grading of the yard up to the street. A cut 15 feet deep will be made at the Geobring and Richards property and a retaining wall put in.

The exact location of the new passenger station and the warehouse and freight depot were not

Around 1911 the Pennsylvania Railroad had a program which was designed to increase crop production along the railroad by promoting scientific farming. The "Pensy" supplied literature and advice to prospective crop growers. The railroad also drained swamps and dynamited stumps for their removal. At an experimental plot, the railroad took ten acres that hadn't been farmed and was considered infertile. They applied manure and lime and several varieties of fruits and vegetables were planted. A profit was realized. Lima beans were the most profitable, then cucumbers, watermelons, muskmelons, radishes, leeks, onions and sweet potatoes.

designated by the officials of the company yesterday. He said that the company had the plan under consideration for the improvement of the Butler yard for some time and that there would be no delay, after the work had been started. (copied from the *Butler Citizen* dated Feb. 12, 1915 by Dave and Audrey Craig)

## OTHER RAIL LINES

The Buffalo, Rochester & Pittsburgh railroad entered Butler from the east in 1899 and eventually, in 1931, it too became part of the Baltimore & Ohio system. In 1904 another railroad, the Western and Allegheny, was built for the purpose of accessing the coal lands in northern Butler County and Armstrong County. A line was built from Queen Junction in Clay Township through Concord and Fairview Townships to Kaylor and on to Brady's Bend in Armstrong County. The railway was then extended from Queen Junction west to New Castle. These new rail lines along with the Bessemer made Queen Junction a focal point—a major rail crossroads and as you may have guessed, the small village drew a great deal of attention from industrialists. Queen Junction is located about seven miles north of Butler and was believed to have a great future as an industrial site. We will cover that story in the following chapter.

The railroad was the principal mover of both people and goods from the post-bellum period until after World War I. It was not only the cheapest but it was also the fastest form of transportation. For most of this era, Butler had five railroads in addition to two interurban trolley lines. [The trolley story is told in *Butler County, the Second Hundred Years*, chapter 13.] Because of these rail transportation links to the rest of the country, Butler's industrial base experienced phenomenal growth. After about 1925, however, other forms of transportation gradually became more competitive than railroads. The interstate highway program, begun in 1956 during Eisenhower's administration proved to be the death knell for many of the unprofitable or marginally profitable railroad lines. Railway companies, in order to compete, had to trim staff and modernize. They were forced to sell off or close many of their freight lines. They kept open only the highest-priority linkages. Crew sizes on the trains were cut usually to an engineer and a conductor from the old norm of four or five—a conductor, flagman, brakeman, engineer and sometimes a fireman. Of course the old four or five man crew didn't have computers and other high-tech devices such as are available today.

Big railroads have in the past, antagonized smaller customers by dictating schedules and cutting loose businesses that weren't large enough. Today's railroad companies, unlike some of their predecessors, have started catering more to customers. In short-line marketing the rail people get to know the customers personally. Short-lines can make a profit where the large rail companies cannot because they often have lower labor costs and can be more flexible at scheduling.

Railroads in general have countered the competition from the trucking industry in both pricing and

---

### RAILROAD STATION NAMES

It is said "there is nothing in a name." But it is a mistake. There is much in a name. While one, like a rose, "may smell as sweet by any other name," yet it may not sound as sweet. The names on the new extension or connecting link near Butler and up along the road are very nice, but they don't seem appropriate, and the "oldest inhabitant" would not know where certain stations were unless told. For instance the first station after leaving Butler is called "Oneida." This is generally known as "Pine Tract," where the road leaves the Connoquenessing and goes up the McGrath or Stoney Run. Why not call it one of those local names and then all would know just where it was? Or some other appropriate local name such as Robb, whose lands adjoin and who is an old and respected citizen. The Oneida were a tribe of Indians, we believe, away up in "York State," and it is a common name up there, but appears out of place down here in Pennsylvania. The next station is Jamisonville, at the farm of Mr. Samuel Miller, Centre Township. This is in honor or Mr. B.K. Jamison, of Philadelphia, who has aided much by his means and liberality, in the making of the extension. A station named, in compliment to him was deserving. But the next station, where you get off for Sunbury, is called "Euclid." It will be some time before all traveling on the road will understand that Euclid means Sunbury. At least it will take some training to learn that you get off there to go over to the flourishing town of Sunbury. If a local name can be found that will indicate that it is the station nearest Sunbury, we think it would be advisable to also change that. The other stations, up to the junction, Hallston, Kiesters, etc., are local and appropriate and you know just where you are when you hear them called out. We have merely thrown out these remarks as to the stations referred to, in order to direct the attention of the management of the S & A to the subject and to any relief that they may be able to afford in the matter. *Butler Citizen* (no date available) sophistication of equipment. Lighter-weight, freight cars and more efficient locomotives have improved the fuel efficiency of rail-roads and with the advent of "clean air" laws the railroad's popularity should increase.

According to an article in the *Butler Eagle's* August 22, 1993 edition, "Three railroad lines still play an important role in moving goods and supplies to twenty Butler County businesses...The Buffalo & Pitts-burgh, the Bessemer & Lake Erie and CSX operate trains through the county, and some of those tracks are used by other companies on long trips—for instance, Amtrak's passenger train from Chicago to Washing-ton D.C. runs along some CSX track in the Zelienople-Harmony area.

The Buffalo & Pittsburgh alone—

## Paul Whaley

In 1932 the Whaley family moved from Albion to Queen Junction. Mr. Whaley worked for the railroad and was transferred by his employer. Son Paul, acquired a job on the Bessemer Railroad in 1949; he worked in the car department. It was shortly after Paul became a railroad man, in the very early 1950's that railroads were making the change to diesel engines.

Paul remembers taking the train to high school in Butler in the late 1930's and early 40's. The trains picked up students at Branchton, Halston, Kiester, Claytonia, Euclid and Queen Junction every morning. At five o'clock they caught the train for the trip back home. If one's dad worked on the railroad one could get a free pass, so Paul rode free. If one wasn't so lucky, one could purchase a monthly ticket which the conductor punched daily. The availabilty of railroad service opened up many areas to people of that era. Paul and his mother regularly took the train to East Pittsburgh to visit his uncle. Paul remembers large numbers of people who took the train north from Butler to Queen Junction then transferred to the Western Allegheny and traveled to New Castle to Cascade Park.

The Western and Allegheny went under the Bessemer bridge. Their trestle was built right in the creek and was attached to the stone walls of the Bessemer bridge. When the creek was high, the steam engine would splash through the high water create large clouds of steam. Kids used to congregate at the bridge to see and hear the hissing sounds of the steam.

Paul became a member of the railroad police department in 1960. I asked Paul, "I've seen many movies where hoboes jumped on to the trains and rode free. In fact, I did that myself as I grew up in East Butler. We used to hitch rides up to the 'swimming hole.' Did many people jump on trains and ride free?" Surprisingly, Paul told me that very few people did that for the simple reason that the Bessemer hauled mostly coal. There was so much coal dust blowing around that any illegal riders would be black, their clothes would be covered with soot, including their lungs, when they reached their destination. Most of his police work involved investigation of people's shooting out of lights etc.

One caboose is yet being used on the Bessemer Railroad. When they take the cars to Armco, they shove them. If the engine was leading the way, they would pull them, but since they are shoving them, they need a man in the caboose. When they approach the Center Avenue railroad crossing, a man has to toot the whistle to warn people of the approaching train.

There were originally two men in the caboose—the flagman and the conductor. The conductor now rides up front with the engineer. When the train stopped for any reason, the flagman walked down the track with a flag or a lantern to make sure no other train would come along and run into the stopped train. Today, with the electronic circuit set up, another train cannot get into the occupied track. It's operated much like a toy electric train.

I asked Mr. Whaley about the Pennsylvania station near the corner of Monroe and Jefferson Streets. Did the track just end there?" "How did they get out of there? Did they back out?" He answered, "No, they backed in. They had a "Y" under the Bessemer bridge on Kittanning Street. The train would pull up, then back into the Pennsylvania station." That answered a question I had wondered about for a long time.

"We had a big wreck in Claytonia in 1982. Two engines collided head-on. One man was killed. I was called out and had to work twelve hours in the below zero temperature. That's when I decided to retire."

(As related to the author by Paul Whaley)

formed in 1988 when CSX sold off some of its track—hauls steel coils and slabs for Armco Advanced Materials Inc., plastic pellets for Napco Inc., steel shot for Ervin Industries, wood for Lezzer Lumber and paper for Butler Color Press...'People think of the railroad as a dying industry. But we're hauling more freight than ever before,' says Harold Kaufman, assistant general manager of the railroad's yard in Butler.

When Butler County's Community Development Corporation worked with the state to bring Napco Inc., an aluminum siding manufacturer, into Butler Township, state agencies contributed $111,000 to build a railroad spur from the main line to service the plant."

The *Butler Eagle* further reported that "Armco's use of rail transportation has tripled or quadrupled in the past five years. Armco has one in going and one out going train each day. The company receives large shipments of scrap metal by rail and uses trains to send out unfinished products to plants in Ohio,

Kentucky and New Jersey.

All of the nations thirteen class-one-freight railroads—those that haul trains of 100 cars or more over long distances—reported record profits last year, said Larry Malski, chairman of the Pennsylvania Rail Freight Advisory Committee. CSX is the only class-one railroad that cuts through Butler County. CSX is a global company that owns barge lines and ports around the world, and they don't want to worry about keeping a marginally-profitable rail line open to a local sawmill that may ship only fifty cars a year. It costs too much to maintain lightly used track. So they sell off the short line. The number of small railroads has exploded, Malski said, from about 200 in 1980 to more than 500 today. 'The industry hasn't been this healthy in maybe the last 100 years,' he said.

Punxsutawney is the regional headquarters of Genesee & Wyoming Industries Inc., the largest operator of short-line industrial railroads in Pennsylvania. The *Pittsburgh Post-Gazette* reported in its June 16, 1996 issue that "Little lean railroads are flourishing as bigger railroads shed short lines to concentrate on profitable longer routes. These are feeder or farm-to-market lines of less than 350 miles that tie into one or more of a big railroad's long-haul routes, comparable to interstates…Five GWI railroads operate in Pennsylvania and New York. The lines run northeast from the Beaver-Butler County line…the biggest of the bunch, the Buffalo & Pittsburgh, extends 350 miles from the Niagara frontier at Buffalo into Western Pennsylvania. It carries scrap steel for Armco, oil from refineries in northwestern Pennsylvania, paper from Willamette mill in Johnsonburg, in Elk County plus coal, glass and forest products. Automobiles move down the line from Canada."

Railroads in Europe and Japan have made a comeback with their high-speed trains. Many experts believe that such trains would revitalize railroad passenger traffic in the United States. At this point there is a great deal of discussion on the topic with some actual experimental lines under construction. The day may come when we board a train in Pittsburgh and arrive in Washington D.C. in less than two hours. That would certainly revolutionize the railroads but whether or not it will happen, only time will tell.

# QUEEN JUNCTION

As we saw in the previous chapter, railroads had become a very important factor in the development of our county. Butler's five railroads brought a great deal of prosperity to the city as well as to suburban towns such as East Butler and Lyndora. Investors and developers always seem to be the first to recognize places with potential and by 1909 the junction of the Bessemer and Lake Erie, and Western Allegheny Railroads, just a few miles north of the city, was causing speculators to salivate. They were calling that railroad crossroads "Queen Junction" and were planning great things for the area.

### Contract For Shops Was Let
### Mars Company Will Build Works At Queen Junction

The S. H. Robert's Boiler & Tank company, which contemplates the erection of immense shops at Queen Junction has awarded the contract for the work to John Eichley, Jr., and Company of Pittsburg. Material for the main building, which will be built of structural steel, and will be 160 by 110 feet in size, is now on the ground and work will be pushed as rapidly as possible.

The work on the new shops has been somewhat delayed on account of the inability to get material on the ground, but the work will now be pushed as rapidly as possible. The machinery and equipment of the factory is now arriving and will be placed as the erecting of the new building progresses. The Robert's company has been located at Mars for some time, but will remove all machinery to the new location. It will continue to conduct a tank and boiler repair shop at the old location.

(copied from the *Butler Citizen* dated June 2, 1910 by Dave and Audrey Craig)

### ANOTHER MILL FOR NEW TOWN
### Keystone Tube Company Will Erect New Mill At Queen Junction
### Work Will Be Rushed On Plant

The Keystone Tube Company, of Pittsburg has purchased land at Queen Junction and will next week break ground for a mill which will employ, when completed 100 men. The new works will be rushed to completion as rapidly as possible, and it is expected that it will be ready for operation by the first of October.

The fact that manufacturers are beginning to invest in real estate at Queen Junction is an indication that it will soon become one of the leading towns of the county. The recent acquisition of a large acreage there by the Electric Steel Company, of

Queen Junction Station

Cleveland, and the announcement that work would shortly be commenced on the erection of a large steel mill, the story of which was told in the *Citizen* two weeks ago, clearly demonstrates that the place is soon to become a factor in the manufacturing line in this part of the state. It is reported on the best authority that the Electric Steel Company has let the contract for 2,000,000 cubic feet of excavating for the big works which the company will erect. This work will be done by a New York contractor. Just when the start will be made on the steel mill has not been made public, but the letting of the contract for the excavating is an indication that the work will not be long delayed.

With the tube mill and the steel works in operation, the next year will witness a big boom for the new Butler County town, and will incidentally be of considerable advantage to this city, which is the natural center for the additional business which will be created. It is rumored that other manufacturing concerns are investigating sites at Queen Junction and the new

town promises to rapidly become an important industrial center.
(copied from the *Butler Citizen* dated July 30, 1909 by Dave and Audrey Craig)

**TO CELEBRATE BIG OPENING**

**REALITY FIRM WILL GIVE AWAY LOTS AT QUEENS JUNCTION THURSDAY SALE**

The launching of a new town in a western state would not be considered an unusual feature although many of the wonderfully successful communities of the region west of the Rockies have gained their wide popularity on account of the fact that they "sprung up over night." But when, within the Commonwealth of Pennsylvania and upon a tract of land not ten miles from Butler, the launching of a town is announced it is worthy of more than a passing notice.

An enterprising reality firm of Pittsburg; The R. C. Johnston Company, announced that they will, with due ceremony, open the new town of Queen Junction next Thursday by giving away of $2,500 worth of lots. A balloon ascension, band music and an auction will also be part of the festivities.

Excursion rates are promised all that desire to attend and in a large advertisement in today's issue of the *Citizen* the firm states that plans are under way for the erection of manufacturing plants that will employ at least 1,500 men. Among the industries being erected at Queen Junction is a sheet bar, and skelp mill, a tube works, boiler and tank works and railway terminals.
(copied from the *Butler Citizen* dated Oct. 12, 1909 by Dave and Audrey Craig)

The day after the sale and festivities, the *Butler Citizen* reported that "Junction City is now a reality. Queen Junction became a reality according to the plan of the Pittsburg reality firm, which is promoting it yesterday. More than 2,000 people attended

the sale of lots, enjoyed the music and awaited with interest the awarding of plots. Many Butler County people were among the purchasers and it is estimated that between twelve and fifteen thousand dollars worth of property was bid by prospective purchasers. A.F. Shaner, of Portersville was the buyer of the first lot for $125. Other purchasers were Andy Zillion, Ellwood City, four lots: WA Coulter, Grove City; Graham Bros., Butler; H.H. Heilman, Ford City; K. Weiss, Lyndora, Mrs. Jacob Schumaker, East Brady; Mrs. Elizabeth Norton, East Brady; Mrs. Kalina, Butler; J.A. Monroe, Wellsburg, W. Va.; Josiah Adams, Slippery Rock; E.S. Sager, Greece City; J.S. Pisor, Enon Valley; Mrs. Mary Meier, Branchton; F.M. Strecker, of Pittsburg, who is manager of the S.H. Roberts Boiler and Tank Company; Mrs. Mary Walrabenstein, East Brady; N.S. Snow, Butler; R.J. Whitmire.

The women of the Queen Junction M.E. Church conducted a lunch sale which was liberally patronized and the

Sixteenth Regiment Band, of Butler furnished music before and during the sale of lots. The giving away of lots was the most interesting of the day's proceedings to the general public. Tickets with coupons attached were distributed to all present, and the coupon bearing numbers were deposited in a box from which was drawn at intervals during the sale. The following were winners: W.W. Mechling of Munhall, Pa.; C.B. Kelly, Grove City, Pa.; A.L. Rider, Mt. Chestnut, Pa.; A. Smolovits, Butler, Pa.; C.R. Perry, Grove City, Pa. It seemed that Queen Junction was off and running!"

### GREAT INDUSTRIAL REVIVAL HAS CENTERED IN BUTLER COUNTY
### MILLIONS TO BE SPENT IN NEW INDUSTRIES DURING NEXT YEAR
### INDICATIONS ARE THAT THIS SECTION WILL RAPIDLY BECOME A
### LEADING CENTER OF THE STATE——EXCELLENT RAILROADS FACILITIES AND NATURAL
### RESOURCES HAVE ATTRACTED BROAD ATTENTION——QUEEN JUNCTION FACTORIES TO BE
### ERECTED AT ONCE

That this section is soon to enjoy a business revival which has never before been equaled, has been indicated for some time, and the amount of work projected in Butler, and Butler County by manufacturers is evidence that Butler is soon to become one of the largest manufacturing centers in Western Pennsylvania outside of Pittsburg. A considerable portion of the work on new manufacturing plants in Butler has been started, and Queen Junction, 10 miles north of the city, workmen are engaged in the construction of one works and others will soon be started.

Among the new projects at that place is now a new specialty steel works, which is to be erected by a steel company of Cleveland, as account of which was given in the *Citizen* three weeks ago. Another newspaper in this city, which never neglects an opportunity to attempt to discredit the news published by its contemporaries, took occasion to refer to the *Citizen* account of the locating at Queen Junction of the steel mill as "a newspaper splurge," and stated positively that no such works was in contemplation there. Yesterday the same paper published a reprint from a Pittsburg paper which told the story of the preparations for the building of the works.

The steel works will be built at Queen Junction just as the *Citizen* said it would, and in addition to it, several other large industries will be established at that place. Work has been started here by the Standard Steel Car Company on the construction of the large open hearth malleable iron works which is to be completed by that company by the first of the coming year, and the company has in contemplation the erection of a billet mill to supply steel for the Forged Steel Wheel Works of the corporation. It is very likely that the billet mill will also be completed early in the new year, as the plans for it have been drawn and estimates taken on the cost of material for the construction of the mill.

Excavations for the piers on which will rest the steel work of the malleable iron foundry of this company have been started, and a large force of men are engaged in the work. The site is being fenced with a tight-eight foot board fence, and the work will be pushed as rapidly as possible as it is the desire of the company to have the foundry in operation not later than January 1 next.

Regarding Queen Junction and its outlook, the *Pittsburg Dispatch* yesterday contained the following: "Pittsburg real estate men are manifesting considerable interest in the new industrial town site at Queen Junction, Butler County. Within the next three months, that will be the location of nearly a score of manufacturing and industrial concerns, while plans are now under way to extend new railroad tracks through the town. Several hundred houses and other buildings will be erected in the near future. Real estate men declare that the town will attract hundreds of home seekers, as many thousand men will get good employment. The town is on the Western Allegheny and the Bessemer and Lake Erie Railroads and ten miles north of Butler. It is rich with gas and coal.

Local real estate men have visited the new site since the beginning of the present work and speak well of the prospects. The Keystone Tube Company, which will employ more than 250 men, has already let contracts for its buildings and equipment; the Robert's Boiler and Tank Company, which will employ more than 300 men, will start building in probably less than 30 days, while a number of manufactures of oil well equipment and boilers will locate there probably before the close of the present year. A steel manufacturing concern, which will make specialty steel will begin to build in a month.

These interests, it was stated by real estate men yesterday, will not build "company" houses and it is because of this fact that they are displaying so much interest in the new town. They say there will be a spurt of building before the next 60 days. Houses and shops are going up every day on the new site. In addition to the industrial plants and dwelling houses to be built, the Western Allegheny Railroad headquarters and shops will be located there. This line extends from Kaylor, Pa. to New Castle, connecting with the Bessemer and Lake Erie at Queen Junction, built four years ago by Pittsburg capitalists. At first the line operated as a part of the Pittsburg and Lake Erie, but is now independent. This road will be extended with the New York Central Railroad. Thus the new industrial town will have a railroad outlet to all parts of the country, a decided advantage over many other towns in Western Pennsylvania.

The Standard Steel Car Company is in the market for a large quantity of basic iron for the open hearth-malleable-iron works is evidenced by the following from the *Pittsburgh Gazette-Times*:

"An indication of the early starting of construction work on the new mills and open hearth furnaces for the Standard Steel Car Company interests at Butler is apparent in inquiries sent out by the company for 100,000 tons of pig iron. The requirements of the company call for delivery during the coming year and in periods of months, according to the building and completion of the furnaces.

"While the order for 100,000 tons is not a year's supply of iron nor even four months' supply under full operation of the plant, the order is taken to mean that the company will start very early in 1910. In round figures the value of the first order for pig is about $1,400,000."

The *Iron Trade Review* of Cleveland, issued yesterday, says: "Continuous ordering of many locomotives and cars by the railroads indicates that they appreciate the necessity of large increases in equipment, but it is doubtful whether car building companies will be able to fill orders rapidly enough to prevent a serious car shortage before the beginning of the new year.

The Standard Steel Car Company has not succeeded in covering its requirements for the next year, and its inquiry for 100,000 tons of basic is still pending."

(copied from the *Butler Citizen* dated August 20, 1909 by Dave and Audrey Craig)

### A NEW BOILER SHOP

### QUEEN'S JUNCTION SITE

### COMPANY WITH SHOPS AT MARS TO REMOVE TO NEW LOCATION

Ground was broken yesterday for an extensive boiler and tank works to be built at Queen Junction, by the Robert's Boiler and Tank Works of Mars. The new plant will consist of a large building of iron and steel to be used for the factory, and a boiler house and a large office building. When completed, the new works will employ 150 men, and will mean much to the industrial importance of the new little town. Work on erecting the buildings will begin as soon as the excavating is completed, and the company expects to be turning out work by the first of May.

The Robert's company has large shops at Mars, but all the heavy machinery at that place will be removed to Queen Junction, but the company will retain a repair shop at Mars. The general offices of the company are in Pittsburg. S. H. Roberts is president of the company, and Mr. Brecker is general manager.

The Keystone Tube Company, who are erecting a large tube mill at Queen Junction have the buildings almost completed, and expect to be turning out material in a month or so. This company will manufacture special tubing, such as trolley poles, bedstead tubing, etc, and will employ about 200 men.

(copied from the *Butler Citizen* dated March 5, 1910 by Dave and Audrey Craig)

### ANOTHER INDUSTRY MAY BE SECURED

### ATTORNEY J. C. GRAHAM BOUGHT QUEEN JUNCTION PLANT

The Robert's Boiler and Tank Company's plant at Queen Junction was sold yesterday to J. C. Graham of Butler for a price approximating $15,000. The plant consists of a new steel building, 90 x 160 feet, which is full of equipment and machinery for constructing boilers and tanks, and a small building 30 x 80 feet, which was established at Queen Junction at a cost of about $32,000 a little more than a year ago.

Owing to lack of funds to carry on the business and mismanagement, the company got into deep water and last August one of the stockholders presented a petition in the courts asking for the appointment of a receiver. This of course brought on executions by the creditors and bankruptcy proceedings, which ended in the sale of the property. When asked yesterday by a *Citizen* reporter what disposition would be made of the plant, Attorney Graham said that if the Butler Chamber of Commerce would secure him a site of about two acres with a railroad frontage in Butler and pay for the moving of the building and machinery, the plant would be moved to Butler.

With the outlook of the iron and steel business in as promising condition as it is, the plant would employ about 40 men, with excellent prospects that the business could be increasing in the near future and the plant enlarged.
(copied from the *Butler Citizen* dated Dec. 6, 191 1 by Dave and Audrey Craig)

## STEEL TIRE FACTORY IS PROBABLE
## ROBERT'S PLANT AT QUEEN JUNCTION MAY BE UTILIZED FOR THE PROPOSED INDUSTRY
### SUCCESS SEEMS ASSURED FOR THE NEW AUTO TIRE

From official information given out Saturday, it is learned that the Butler district is to get the new factory of the Miles Motor Tire Steel Spring Company, which if the present plans are consummated, will be located at Queen Junction. President F. H. Miles of Wilkinsburg, Secretary and Treasurer Z. A. Zelwarte of Braddock and several other members of the official board of the company were in Butler last week looking over the ground and Saturday. It was announced that an option had been secured until the first of June on the plant of the defunct Robert's Boiler Company at Queen Junction, which is at present controlled by Attorney John C. Graham of Butler.

To carry out its plan of organization and start the work here, the board of directors last week appointed a committee of three of its members to solicit subscriptions for stock in the Butler district. As soon as the stock is subscribed, the work will be commenced at the Queen Junction site, and a factory put in operation that will employ a large number of men at the start and eventually, its owners believe, develop into one of the largest manufacturing plants in the Butler district.

The Miles Motor Tire Spring Steel Company is incorporated under the laws of Delaware and capitalized at $200,000. The business men of the Butler district are asked to subscribe for $30,000 of the capital stock in order to locate the plant here. The board of directors of the company named a Butler banking house trustee to hold the money of the subscribers to the capital stock until such time as the list can be closed and the option on the Queen Junction plant taken up.

The directors of the company are delighted with the prospects of locating in the Butler district. The plant of the Roberts Boiler Company at Queen Junction consists of a steel building 120x140 feet, fully equipped and six acres of land having a frontage on two railroads. The machinery and equipment of the plant is such as will be needed by the motor tire spring company and in the event that the deal is closed up, the company can go to work at once on orders that is already on hand.

A proposition was considered to move the plant to Butler but the cost of tearing down and rebuilding was considered too high and the project was abandoned. The motor tire spring that the company proposes to manufacture has been on exhibition for several weeks in Butler and is of much interest to owners and operators of automobiles. If the owners of the patent realize their claims for it, the tire spring will revolutionize the pneumatic tire business and the development of business at the Queen Junction plant would be unlimited.

A factory that will employ 500 to 600 skilled mechanics in the next few years is not improbable. The addition of a factory of that dimension to the Butler district would mean much. It would mean another town the size of East Butler and a plant of the size of Pittsburgh-Hickson or the Standard Plate Glass Company. It would mean more than half a million dollars added to the pay roll in the district. It would mean the same amount of money distributed among merchants for dry goods, provisions and supplies, and to the real estate owners for rentals. It would mean extension of the trolley systems, additional tonnage for the railroads, better markets for the farmers, an increase in bank deposits and more money for everybody.

The plans for starting the factory are to be pushed as rapidly as possible. The company is receiving orders and inquiries every day for its tire and the advance orders will keep the plant running for some time.
(copied from the *Butler Citizen* dated May 6, 1912 by Dave and Audrey Craig)

### Butler Attorney Sells Boiler Works At Queen Junction

A deal was completed last Wednesday whereby John C. Graham disposed of the property known as the Robert's Boiler and Tank Works at Queen Junction to Tarentum capitalists. The plant will be dismantled and removed to Glassmere and will be rebuilt and started as a foundry and machine company. A charter will be applied for under the name of the Allegheny Valley Foundry and Machine Company. Under the arrangement, Mr. Graham retains a large interest in the new organization.

The Robert's Boiler and Tank company was organized in 1910, and after the completion of a new plant at Queen Junction at an expense of over $30,000 and operating for nine months the company became financially embarrassed and was landed in the bankruptcy courts. In order to protect himself, Mr. Graham had to sell the property.

During the last eight months he, at different times, made proposals to the Butler Chamber of Commerce to remove the plant to Butler, but was unable to make terms, consequently the plant now has to be removed from the Butler district.
(copied from the *Butler Citizen* dated Aug. 15, 1912 by Dave and Audrey Craig)

### QUEEN JUNCTION PLANS OBSERVANCE INDEPENDENCE DAY

The biggest and best 4th of July celebration in the northern end of Butler County will be held at Queen Junction. The location is ideal, being easily accessible by train from the north, south, east and west. There is plenty of good water, good shelter and a beautiful grove. The arrangements are being completed by the enterprising people of Queen Junction for handling and entertaining the crowds which will doubtless be present.

This is to be the first annual basket picnic of the Sunday schools of the third district of Butler County, including Washington, Concord, Clay and Cherry Townships. Each school in the district will endeavor to have the largest delegation present. The speakers will include some of the most up-to-date Sunday school workers in the county. Among them will be Rev. S. I. Louden, president of the county Sunday school association, Dr. B. F. Rhoads, pastor of the First M. E. Church, Butler, and Rev. H. C. Miderbrand of Haysville.

The West Sunbury band and the drum corps of Queen Junction will furnish the music. The program of sports will begin at 9:30 a.m., with two ball games; one by the ladies and the other by boys under 14. Other baseball games to be played will be: West Sunbury Stars vs. Queen Junction Athletics, and Queen Junction Athletics vs. Story Run Giants. The songs and exercises by the Sunday scholars and the various track events will be interesting features of the day. All are invited to come and bring a full basket for a sane 4th celebration.

(copied from the *Butler Citizen* dated July 3, 1914 by Dave and Audrey Craig)

### LUCY AND TWILA

As the news articles indicated, expectations for Queen Junction were very high. Imagine! Five hundred homes were needed at once as several factories were on the drawing boards or already under construction—factories which were expected to employ as many as 6000 men! At the inaugural opening of Queen Junction a balloon ascension, parachute drop, and brass bands were all part of the hype. Two hundred and fifty business and residential lots were put on the block and all were sold immediately.

Most people I talk to have never been to Queen Junction; they probably couldn't find it if they tried. However, if one is persistent and checks a map or gets directions, Queen Junction is accessible. When I drove to the village I expected to see the rusting remains of old factories and perhaps a few still operating, but I was very surprised. There are about eight houses and absolutely no factories; there are no ruins or abandoned industrial buildings. There is only part of an old wall which may have been an industrial building.

As near as I can tell, at its peak, Queen Junction had fourteen houses. The anticipated growth never took place. What happened to change the course of events in Queen Junction was a question which proved very difficult to answer. The newspapers of that day are strangely silent, especially after they had made such a big to-do about the future of the railroad crossroads. I searched and investigated but I could not find the answer to this mystery. Since the event happened approximately ninety years ago, the grim reaper has taken his toll of all eyewitnesses. My hope was that I might interview some former or present Queen Junction resident who may remember hearing the story from his parents.

I knew that the Porterfields were long time residents of Queen Junction. I called Dick Walker, who is Lucille Porterfield Walker's son and found to my good fortune that the Porterfield family had an upcoming reunion of sorts—Lucille's sister Twila Porterfield Kaiser was coming all the way from Alaska where she had been a missionary for forty-nine years. Brother Orville Porterfield was also coming in from Edinboro. Their get-together was just two weeks away and they would be happy to have me come and discuss Queen Junction with them.

I felt that surely they would know what had happened to all of the proposed industries and the expected population growth; but I was wrong. They remembered many details of life in Queen Junction but as far as industries--they knew nothing. Lucy and Twila gave me the names of some old-timers who had lived or live yet in Queen Junction. I contacted several but they were not able to help me. I was striking out on this one. Several of the former residents of the town said that the only evidence of any of these proposed factories was a big cement wall which is down along the railroad tracks. Apparently construction of at least one of the buildings was begun but never finished—part of that old foundation remains as a testimonial to what Queen Junction might have been.

Several months later, after I had nearly given up on the Queen Junction mystery, I was interviewing

Paul Whaley, who worked in security on the Bessemer and Lake Erie Railroad for many years. He was telling me several interesting stories related to his career, when it dawned on me that the Bessemer ran right through Queen Junction. I guess I had not given up on

Porterfield's Store

finding the answer the mystery. When he paused, I asked him, "Do you know anything about Queen Junction?" He answered, "I lived there for many years and my work took me through the village daily." I then asked if he had ever heard of the proposed industrial growth which never came to pass? His smile convinced me that he had the answer--I felt as though I was about to solve a difficult puzzle! He told me the story just as he remembered hearing it when he was a boy. "R. C. Johnston & Co. of Pittsburgh was promoting Queen Junction. They had a man from Slippery Rock survey the lots. A company even started construction on a boiler factory, which of course, made everything look secure and gave people confidence in the new town. But it wasn't secure because either the agent or the sales manager absconded with the money. It was a major rip-off." Well, that would explain it. I cannot document Mr. Whaley's story but when I mentioned it to other Queen Junction residents they vaguely remembered--it was a story they had heard many years ago.

Queen Junction never became an industrial center, but according to the Porterfield girls, it was a pretty good place in which to grow up. Here is their story:

There were four Porterfield men in early Queen Junction: Clifford, John, and Harry were all uncles of the girls and Billy was their father. Billy and his wife, Blanche, made their livelihood by running Queen Junction's general store. The store building had six bedrooms on the second floor while the living room, kitchen and store occupied the first floor. Lucy, now 89 and Twila 83, naturally have many memories of the small village. Their father, Billy was quite industrious—in addition to the general store he owned the town water well. Water was piped to all the buildings in the town and the customers paid three dollars a month for this service. Local farmers brought produce and animals to Porterfield's for shipment to Butler. Porterfields also raised and sold chickens. Mr. Porterfield, a man of varied economic interests, ran a coal mine and used eight ponies and a mule to pull the coal cars in and out of the mine. There was a tipple on a siding, which allowed the coal to be transferred to railroad cars for shipment out.

Mrs. Buckham opened a restaurant between the two railroads and her meals were very tasty—she was especially well-known for her pies. Hungry, railroad workers were her main customers. Uncle Clifford Porterfield married one of the Buckham girls.

There was no feed mill in Queen Junction but feed and grain could be purchased at Porterfield's general store. Grain, oil, coal were just some of the products which arrived on the railroad. Porterfields had a railroad siding behind the store and an adjacent building they called the "feed house." The corn and oats were shipped in loose and had to be bagged by the Porterfield family before it was sold to local customers. This bagging was done at the feed house. When the feed house was empty it occasionally became a dance hall on Saturday nights. The fathers, mothers and children came in after the work was done and square danced and round danced to the music of the fiddle and the piano. The neighbors brought sandwiches and refreshments and such occasions offered a bit of excitement to the hard life in Queen Junction.

Lucy and Twila remember the following families as being residents of the village: Porters, Millers, Buckhams, Riders, Cochrans, Browns, Campbells, Rays, Stoughtons, Bakley's, Youngs, Ralstons, Kaufmans, and Sandersons. Mail arrived daily by train. It was sorted and placed in the proper mailboxes by postmistress Nannie Cochran. Patrons had to go to the post office to pick up their mail—it wasn't delivered. When the post office closed, father Billy bought the small building and moved it to a location adjacent to the store where it became a wash room.

Typical of that time period was the one-room schoolhouse. The school's water supply came from a deep well and the restrooms, were of course, outside. Lucy especially remembers two of her teachers, Pearl Day and Mildred McCall. Mildred taught eighth grade. If one passed the eighth grade exam, which Queen Junction residents took at West Sunbury, one qualified for high school. Lucy took the daily train back and forth to Butler High School until she earned her high school diploma in 1928. The township picked up the tab for such ambitious students. (*Butler County the Second Hundred Years*, pg. 90).

Church meetings were held in the cool basement of the large building next to the store. The itinerant minister, Jim Wagner, had no license to preach but was remembered as dedicated, eloquent and inspiring—he was also blind. Services were held about twice a month. The group was not affiliated with any larger denomination but the congregation was loyal and God-fearing. Baptisms, marriages and other official religious functions were usually solemnized at Rider Lutheran Church in nearby West Sunbury.

Groups and individuals would arrive at Queen Junction on the Bessemer and Lake Erie where they could switch trains and travel to New Castle on the Western and Allegheny Railway. Idora Park in New Castle was a popular destination but not so much for the people of Queen Junction. They had too much work to do and they couldn't afford an amusement park more than once a year--if that. On rare but memorable occasions, the Porterfields packed a picnic basket and took the Bessemer excursion to Conneaut Lake Park.

From time to time, crime visited Queen Junction. Being so accessible by rail, many transients passed through the village. Traveling Gypsies visited the area about once a year. Everyone was terrified because they had heard stories that the Gypsies stole children. And to add credence to the rumors, some things seem to disappear when the Gypsies' were in town—but never children. One day mother Blanche had canned and when evening came, the weather being nice and the family so weary from a long and difficult day that they left rolls of wire and other products which had been on display outside the store—surely no one would bother these things. Unfortunately their assumption was wrong. Thieves stole everything that was left outdoors and Twila remembers it as "quite a large amount." Porterfield's general store was also broken into and burglarized several times. A window was smashed, the money drawer was emptied and various items such as cigarettes were missing.

Twila remembers the time when, up the road from Porterfields, a woman was running a brothel. Her own daughters were the "main attractions." The sheriff came one evening with several deputies and

Queen Junction Store, Postoffice and Feed House

surrounded the house demanding that the occupants appear and face the charges. The law, however, mistakenly had the wrong house—there was a great deal of confusion and excitement for a few hours but no arrests were made. We can only imagine what the innocent occupants of the "wrong house" thought.

During the depression Porterfields lost the general store. Too much credit had been extended and out-of-work customers just could not pay. The family moved to Butler and Billy Porterfield did what he could to provide for his family. He cut hair and even helped a couple of Butler funeral directors prepare the deceased for burial. Mother, Blanche Porterfield, of all things, attended Universal Chiropractic College in Pittsburgh, traveling back and forth on the streetcar. She became the first chiropractor in Butler County when she set up her practice with Dr. Frazier in 1924. It wasn't exactly easy street. In fact the authorities forced Blanche to shut down her business because at that time the State of Pennsylvania did not license chiropractors—she was forced to turn to practical nursing, a profession she followed for several years. During these tough times, the kids had to baby-sit, iron clothes and perform assorted odd jobs to help with family finances. Twila worked at Isalys for three years to help support the family before she went to Bible School and became a missionary to Alaska. Those were difficult days; the girls would not want to go through the experiences again but at the same time, they wouldn't trade them for anything. Tough times build character.

Queen Junction remains a small hamlet with fewer than ten houses. The Western and Allegheny railroad is gone forever and the Bessemer is down to just one track and only about fifteen trains a week. Queen Junction is the town that almost was.

**It's Where Your Friends Are**

## The Butler Mall

It is the mission of The Butler Mall to provide the Butler community with a safe, reasonably priced market place where daily needs may be fulfilled. The Butler Mall, with its central location and easy access, shall endeavor to serve the Butler community as a focal point for activities and cooperative growth. Accordingly, the Butler Mall will seek out retailers who wish to be an integral part of the growing, Butler community.

Promotions at the Butler Mall reflect not only management's commitment to their tenants, but to the area residents who gather here to shop, eat and attend to many of life's necessities.

Churches and non-profit organizations are welcome to use The Butler Mall, free of charge, for fund-raising events.

William L. Casey          General Manager
(412) 261-9008           (724) 282-2250

# COSCO

When I was growing up in East Butler, Cosco was a place to be feared. While it was only two or three miles as the crow flies, we didn't go there. Pete Kline says that "If a stranger came through Cosco he'd better be a good man or he would suffer a beating." Those rough and tough coal miners and their sons were always ready for a fight, or so we thought. About the only time we made a visit was to play their team in a baseball game and even as we played we were intimidated—afraid that if we won the game we might take a physical beating. Now it may not have been that bad but in our minds it was.

After I co-authored *Butler County the Second Hundred Years*, several people told me that if I ever wrote another book on Butler County that I should include a chapter on Cosco. So when the time came I began to research the area. I found very little in the existing history books and not much more in the old Butler newspapers so I thought it would be a good idea to line up some interviews with old-timers who had lived in or knew something of the Cosco area.

My first interview took me to Route 38 to the home of Pete Kline. Mr. Kline was anticipating my arrival and told me that we were going to walk to Fred Dellen's house where the three of us could talk. Mr. Dellen invited us into his living room. I turned on my recorder, sat it on the coffee table and didn't have to say much more. These two former coal miners began to reminisce about their years in the mines, the village, the railroad, church and the old one-room school.

One of the first things I learned was that Cosco did not refer to the entire Oneida Valley area along route 38. Cosco was the unofficial name of two of the coalmines, which were owned by the Consolidated Coal Company, and to the row houses which were adjacent to those mines. Those particular mines were called Cosco I and Cosco II. So there were actually two Coscos.

Coal had been mined in the Oneida area as early as the 1850's. It was of a very high quality, very hard and yielded up to sixty-percent coke. Information on those very early mines is sketchy. Cosco I and Cosco II were operating at full capacity in the 1920's and 30's. In addition to the two Cosco mines there were also the North Butler, Zenith, and Victoria mines. When Fred Dellen moved to his present house in 1978 most of the mines in the Oneida valley had been closed for twenty years or more--the coal had been mined out. The two men discussed the years when the mines were in operation. The Zenith mine had been across the railroad tracks from the present, water-company building and the entrance to the Victoria mine was near the Cosco I operation. Some of the mineshafts went under-ground to the Clearview Mall area and actually passed under Route 8. Kline remembers working in the mineshaft and easily hearing traffic passing overhead on Route 8.

The actual mining involved digging tunnels sixteen feet wide, fifty feet apart. The area between the tunnels was called the stump and it was left to support the roof and prevent cave-ins. Side tunnels were dug to connect the sixteen-foot openings. This was good for safety inasmuch as there were always two or more ways out of the mine. In some coalmines, before government regulations, miners would mine the stumps as they retreated from the mine. This of course often led to mine subsidence. The stumps were left in all of the Oneida Valley mines but generally speaking the coal has been mined—it's depleted. Some eighteen-inch veins remain but it doesn't pay to mine a vein unless it is at least twenty-four inches thick.

The coalmine shafts were about four and one-half feet high, which meant that the men had to crawl and stoop constantly. At times they had to actually swing the pick from the prone or kneeling position. "They called them entries. You'd take coal out, you'd drill holes through the rock and shoot it leaving posts on both sides, then shoot that rock down and after you took the coal out you put the rock in where the coal had been. That was work and we didn't get paid very much." When the car was loaded with coal it was the miners' responsibility to physically push the car, often through water, fifty to seventy-five yards out to the main track where the same pushers emptied the car into the larger railroad car. Then the car had to be pushed back to the actual site of the digging. "It was no picnic."

Coal mining was very hard work--that goes without saying. One hard-working, coal miner could mine about six tons of coal a day—contrary to Tennessee Ernie Ford's popular song. The miners used dynamite to break up the coal veins, then the chunks that were too big to lift were smashed with a sledge or a pick and it was all loaded by shovel into a coal car. Kline and Dellen remember when the mining operations used ponies, then later, electric motors, to pull the loaded railroad cars out to the main line. For this hard labor the men were paid ninety cents a ton. If one did not work, one was not paid. If the miner reported to work and for some reason loaded only one car, that's all he was paid for. The harder the miner worked the more money he made. Seven dollars a day was about tops. Many days, after work, Kline and Dellen walked up to Hendrick's dairy farm near the present Clearview Mall on Route 8 and put up hay and did other rigorous farm work, sometimes until ten o'clock at night. They were often paid in milk and butter. Kline, for a time, lived in North Butler and walked along the tracks every day to Stover's mine, worked all day then made the walk back home. He said that many days his pants were frozen stiff when he got home. He never hopped on any freight trains for a free ride. The trains moved too fast.

Dellen says that when he came to the area at the age of nine, [1929] there were only five houses between Karnes Crossing and the Victoria mine, and only one automobile that he knew of. That very year Dellen lost a finger, but not as a result of a mining accident—the finger was sliced off as he folded up an old army cot. Dellen tells that when he was seventeen "I drilled a hole, put black powder in it, nothing happened. Then it exploded and put my eye out. I was in the hospital for over a month and have had a glass eye ever since." Dellen received $2100 for the loss of his eye. "If someone was killed in the mine his widow was lucky if she got two or three thousand dollars, and even to get that you had to get a lawyer and fight for it." Back in those days, companies rarely gave any kind of remuneration for injuries or death; it was looked upon as an admission of negligence and responsibility. Dellen had to retire at the age of fifty-five with black lung. Kline also suffers with the malady.

Dellen remembers when one man was electrocuted in the Stover mine but, as far as he knows, no one ever died in a cave in. That was because there were always alternate exits. The worst case scenario meant digging fifty feet to the next shaft and freedom.

Fred Dellen began work in 1935 at age seventeen. Kline actually went into the mines and worked with his father while he was still in high school. When the North Butler mine was in operation near the location of present day Vin and Joe's, Kline lived just up over the hill. He and his father drove ponies at the North Butler mine for awhile. Then he went into the mine with his father and actually started to load coal. The elder Kline said, "Now that we're both working, I'll buy a car then we'll get one for you." His father realized his ambition, bought a nice Willys, and Fred got a chance to drive it but then the mine shut down and he never did get his car.

The average working day was eight hours and often the workweek included Saturday. Joe Benson, former engineer on the Bessemer, remembers seeing those hard-working miners of Oneida walking along the Bessemer to and from work--the worn kneepads testified as to the difficulty of the labor.

The coal vein at the Victoria mine was a rich one, between twenty-eight and thirty-six inches in thickness. The Oneida Valley mines weren't deep mines; their horizontal shafts entered the hillsides. Cosco I entered the hillside where Millich's junkyard is today and extended underground all the way to Thorn Run Dam. Another shaft made its way to the area where Offstein's junkyard is today.

The Bessemer came through about three times a day and loaded the coal onto railroad cars. The Butler Water Company took one flat of very fine coal each week. They burned it at their North Butler location and used the power to operate their machinery. Most of the coal was shipped to destinations which were, for the most part, out of Butler County.

The Bessemer ran a passenger train through Cosco twice a day. The railroad station there was called Victoria Station. The Stover family who owned the Victoria mine had a general store which could be considered a company store for those who worked at Stover's mine. The weekly purchases were deducted from the miners' checks. Montgomery's also had a store in Cosco just about where the Oneida Valley firehall sits today, and Watson's had a store at Cosco I. So there were three stores operating in the area. There were a large number of company houses on both sides of the highway.

The boundary line between Oakland and Center Township ran right through the heart of Cosco. If students were lucky enough to live on the Oakland side of the line, their school was right across Route 38. But the kids who lived on the Center Township side were required to walk to a different school which was near the present Clearview Mall. It was quite a hill to climb every morning. First graders made the two-mile walk unescorted. Dellen remembers a couple of teachers in the Oakland one-room school. Miss Murphy rode the Muscatello bus down from Hooker. Fred Dellen also remembered Miss Shanor. Her family owned much of the land where the Clearview Mall is today. If one wanted to further his education beyond eighth grade it was necessary to make the trip to Butler every day. Most of the girls did so but the boys practically all quit after eighth grade. Kline says, "I quit after eighth grade. You didn't need any education to work in the mine. Anybody could do that. All you needed was a strong back."

The two men continued with their reminisces. "There was no church so to speak, however church services were held in the township school building. Catholics used the school building on Sunday mornings and the Protestants had their services on Sunday evenings." Ethnically, the area was a mixture of Italians, Polish, Germans and a few blacks.

There were many strikes—some became violent with stone throwing and name-calling but nobody was ever hurt. Strikes were commonplace in many industries back in the first half of the century.

Dellen remembers the days when Route 38 was unpaved. When the paving occurred the road machines were pulled by mules and horses. Cosco residents enjoyed watching the workers pave the road. The state police, on their daily patrols, traveled on horseback through Cosco and on out to Oneida Dam.

Kline remembers a Cosco family named Otto who were garbage collectors. They rode in to Butler on Saturday nights and picked up old produce at stores and hauled it to Cosco in horse drawn wagons. The rotting produce served as feed for some of Cosco's pigs and chickens.

There wasn't much time left for leisure activities but when possible, one of the favorite pastimes was hunting. Many days after work, a gang including girls, would jump in the truck and drive to some good, rabbit-hunting area. Chuck Reep, who grew up in Cosco, remembers seeing hunters walking out of the woods with more than a dozen rabbits hanging from a rope. Racoon hunting was done at night with dogs and flashlights. The animals were not wasted; they became the main courses on Sunday's dinner tables. On Saturdays when the men weren't called to work, Kline would load up his old Chevy truck with half-a-dozen friends and drive all the way to Cochranton for a day of fishing.

Not many residents of Cosco owned motor vehicles--it wasn't necessary. Cosco was always centrally located. It has the best of both worlds at hand. It is close to town, and today, the malls and shopping centers just "over the hill." At the same time, it is quiet and rural. At one time the Cosco shopper had his choice of Muscatello's bus or the train. They both ran to and from Butler several times a day. The bus seemed to be the choice of most because it was cheaper and it dropped its passengers off right downtown whereas the train trip necessitated a walk to and from the Center Avenue station. Today, the bus is long gone and the train doesn't offer passenger service but it's no problem as virtually every family has a vehicle.

The area we know as Cosco lost much of its economic importance when the mines closed and the business on the railroad dwindled. Some of the children of those hard-working miners continue to live in the Oneida Valley but they drive elsewhere for their employment. Many second and third generation Cosco residents have built new homes where row houses once stood. Not all of the old row houses are gone. Most of those which survive however, are not easily recognizable with their new porches, windows and vinyl siding. The residents who live in Cosco would be reluctant to move to any other part of the county.

# Real Estate and Shields
## Synonymous In Butler County

In 1933 Carl E. Shields & Co. was established in Butler as an insurance office on Diamond Street. In the 1940's the business was expanded to real estate and moved to 408 North Main Street where it flourished for over 40 years. Carl Shields became a leader in real estate brokerage in the area. He was selected to be a State Real Estate Commissioner where he helped formulate many procedures which are still in place in Pennsylvania today. He was also active in the International Real Estate Federation.

In the late 1940's he began writing a well-known advertising promotional called "Chili" (hot news). This column appeared successfully each week in the local newspaper for over 15 years. In 1950 he became involved in real estate development and construction. Some of the better known residential plans designed and completed by Mr. Shields are McQuistion Manor, Northvue Farms and Meadowood. Carl Shields was recently honored as Realtor-Emeritus by the local, state and national associations of REALTORS®

Currently the Shields traditions in real estate are being continued by his son under the name of Ed Shields REALTOR® at 364 Pittsburgh Road (Route 8 south) Butler, PA 16002. Both Carl Shields and Ed Shields have served their profession as vice president of the Pennsylvania Realtors Association. Ed has earned several professional real estate designations, and has been REALTOR®-of-the-Year in Butler County on two different occasions.

Carl Shields is officially retired, but maintains his broker's license with son, Ed. Their slogans are well recognized in the area: "From Cabins to Castles . . . See Shields," and "List With Shields and Start Packing."

# BUTLER'S WORK ETHIC AND SELECTED BUSINESSES

Today as bulldozers are cleaning up the site of the former Woolworth building, John L. Wise III, of the *Butler Eagle* editorializes his dreams of what a reborn downtown might become. He also laments, "Nearly everyone can agree the Main Street area has been slipping. Where agreement becomes more difficult is when it comes to deciding what should be done and how to pay for it...But renewal does not happen spontaneously. It takes cooperation, a shared vision, hard work and money. Even with all these ingredients, it is still not a sure thing." *(Butler Eagle,* Aug. 10, 1999)

Butler is not alone in its frustrating attempts to counteract competition from malls, shopping centers, and large-box retailers such as Wal-Mart and Lowes. As previously noted, the forces, which have led to Butler's demise, are at work all across our country.

Deteriorating U.S. communities have tried a multitude of tactics to reverse the erosion of businesses and customers to the suburban shopping centers. Some central-business districts have been transformed into pedestrian malls. Unfortunately, it's not guaranteed to bring the customers back. Many cities have developed festivals which are designed to pack their streets with shoppers and tourists. Nearby Clarion has its "Autumn Leaf Festival," and Myersdale celebrates an annual "Maple Festival." Thousands of people flock to Tionesta for the "Indian Fest," and in Franklin the "Applefest' helps fill local coffers. Farther afield, a city in Canada has an annual "Shakespearean Festival" which attracts busloads of potential customers from all parts of the U. S. as well as Canada. The list of such attractions is quite lengthy and the increased business is a real plus but even these events, as successful as they may be, bring prosperity for only a week or two. Butler could create such a festival, but at this point it looks as though it will take much more to reverse the demise we are experiencing. We should not lose hope as many creative Butler residents are pondering the problem. As John Wise III suggests, perhaps with everyone working together some remedy will be found to rejuvenate our downtown. But we can't sit back and wait for someone else to do something.

In this chapter we are going to look back to a time when Butler was thriving--between 1890 and 1930 the entire area was experiencing unprecedented growth. The population of the city tripled from 8,734 to 24,477 as thousands of people moved here to find the good life in Butler's growing industries, businesses and/or retail establishments. Granted, that was a different era; it was before interstate highways, suburban shopping areas, the internet and the relocation of U.S. industries far from our shores. But I think the attitude Butlerites had toward the local economy was very admirable and effective, as you will see.

Our analysis of "turn of the century" Butler is based upon a compilation of newspaper articles which deal mostly with businesses. The articles are included in their entirety, just as they appeared in the old newspapers. Not only do these articles reflect the economic boom Butler was experiencing at that time, but they also give considerable insight into the positive attitude and work ethic which was common at that time. I will even venture to say that these newspaper articles can teach us some valuable lessons. For example: Butler's customers purchased locally and patronized Butler businesses as much as possible—regardless of the costs. And when Butler's entrepreneurs founded new businesses and expanded existing ones they used local money if at all possible. If the county's people adopted these policies today, many of Butler's economic problems would dissipate. The twenty-first century mind-set however, makes it very difficult or even impossible to apply these lessons. One can get it cheaper at Wal-Mart or over the internet. That notwithstanding, it certainly is inspiring to read the details of "the way Butler used to be."

## The Board Of Trade

Community leaders were continually striving to bring new industry to Butler. They formed an organization called the Board of Trade. In 1899 a yearly membership cost five dollars which would be the equivalent of $350 today. The board had regular meetings and did whatever they felt necessary to reach their goal--that of "making Butler what her natural advantages entitle her to be, namely, the best town in western Pennsylvania." The board advertised in newspapers around the nation proclaiming the merits of Butler. They went so far as to offer land, buildings and even money to industries which were contemplating moving and as you will see, their efforts were rewarded.

"An organization that has done more to bring about a greater Butler than any other agency is the board of trade. If in any mind there existed a doubt as to the practicability and the immense benefit of such a movement, that doubt must long ago have been dispelled. By their works ye shall know them. Since the inception of the project and the consequent concerted efforts of this body of public-spirited and far-seeing business men, there has been secured for

Butler a number of important industrial establishments of which further mention is made in detail in another part of this paper.

And the good work still goes on. Negotiations are now pending with a number of manufacturing enterprises which are in search of an advantageous location, and there is every prospect that these negotiations will eventuate in bringing Butler several more factories and mills which will almost double the present investment in industrial plants...it was decided to advertise the advantages of Butler, and the fact that she had inducements to offer the prospective investors. The following newspapers were selected for this purpose: *Pittsburg Dispatch, New York World, Philadelphia Ledger, Baltimore Sun, Cleveland Leader, Toledo Blade, Buffalo Courier, Cincinnati Enquirer, Chicago Times, St. Louis Globe-Democrat, Wheeling Intelligencer, Columbus Journal, Indianapolis Journal and Philadelphia Evening Telegram...*During the year there were a great many communications from iron, glass, steel, engine, brick and all kinds of manufacturing plants known to be in existence...many propositions were made in good faith. However, each case was carefully considered and not droped till the board was satisfied it was not desirable...We think it but proper to commend the liberality of those of our citizens who helped make it possible to secure this great plant [Davis Lead Works]. First the generous offer of Mr. Duffy, donating five acres of valuable land; then thirty-two of our citizens contributing the sum of six hundred and ninety-eight dollars...At the meeting of the directors of the board of trade last evening arrangements were consummated for the locating in Butler of a silk mill and a factory that will manufacture shirts, overalls, muslins, underwear, etc...A garment factory is to be located on the Southside, and a new building...will be erected...At the meeting on Monday night, two glass concerns, a pickle factory and an iron works asked for Butler's best terms.

*(Butler County Centennial Souvenir*, the Hon. John H. Negley, Chairman of the Executive Committee, 1900, pgs. 10-11)

### Butler Booming

The influx of people to this place is remarkable. So many new faces are among us that the old citizens seem as if they were among strangers. Business is also correspondingly increasing. A large number of new buildings have been erected and many others are being built. They are going up in all parts of the town but principally in Springdale. This may be attributed to the erection of the large glass works being built there. These works will be as large as any in this country of the kind and will employ it is said near a thousand persons. Other new works are contemplated. The railroads are all doing a good business. The stores are thronged with purchasers and in fact in every line of business there is increased activity.

*(Butler Citizen*, May 6, 1887)

### Butler Is Riding On Crest Of Wave Of Prosperity And Healthy Growth
### Demand For Rental Houses Is Greater Than The Supply Available

Butler real estate developers are now experiencing the greatest demand in the history of the borough for houses of four, five,and six rooms to rent at from $16 down. An idea of the commercial and industrial situation may be given when it is said by house renting agencies that they cannot near supply the demand made for houses of this size.

"There is promise in sight for someone with capital who will erect a number of houses of small size in desirable locations," said a real estate man Saturday. There is also money in it for a man who will build on the outskirts of the city a settlement where the houses have conveniences and rent for from $8 to $12. These settlements would have to be rented to Americans only."

"The high price of lumber is practically responsible for conditions and a man can build a brick house at practically the same cost that he can a frame dwelling when everything is considered, such as durability, etc. There is plenty of ground on the outskirts of the borough and the trolley service is as good as in larger cities and the low taxes make a house a profititable investment for the man investing his money."

Several real estate dealers interviewed Saturday concurred in the opinion expressed by the man quoted that houses for the working classes are scarce, rentals too high and that a profititable investment is in sight for the first capitalist to see the opportunity who will build a number of houses to rent for a reasonable sum of money.
(copied from the *Butler Citizen* dated Nov.22, 1909 by Dave and Audrey Craig)

### New Section Is To Be Opened For Residences
### Ground to be Converted Into Residential Lots on Mercer and Pearl Streets

There is a new section of the city to be opened up and beautified, to be laid out in lots, sewered, houses built, sidewalks laid. Two enterprising citizens of the city, Elmer Schenck and Edgar H. Negley, have purchased from D. C. Wick, of Pittsburgh, 13 acres of ground, lying east of Mercer Street, between Mercer and the A. M. Christley property at the end of West Pearl Street and laid the same out in 120 building lots. They have also purchased from F. J. Holt, about three acres, with the old greenhouse and four other houses, making about 14 building lots. Much of the ground purchased is in the city, but extends into Butler Township. They will open up a street the entire length of the valley, put a bridge over Sullivan Run which runs through the valley, sewer it and build sidewalks as well as erect a number of houses, beginning their work as soon as possible. The houses will be either for rent or sale as the demand dictates. (copied from the *Butler Citizen* dated Jan 22, 1919 by Dave and Audrey Craig)

### Butler's Prosperity Seen By Men Of Other Cities
### Pittsburgh Man Comments on Business Condition In Borough
### And Says It Leads Western Pennsylvania Cities Commercially

So noticeable has been the prosperity of Butler that even persons from other cities are beginning to comment on the stability of the borough as a commercial and industrial center. Tuesday, T. A. Wright, a Pittsburg insurance agent was in the borough on business. He expressed surprise at business conditions that exist in Butler now. According to Mr. Wright it exceeds that of any other community of like size in western Pennsylvania. To bear out his assertions, Mr. Wright showed figures that the Butler business of his company had increased 35 percent in a very short time. His figures were a comparison with those of November, 1908, and most of the business has been given his company lately, showing that merchants and investors are beginning to experience a return to normal.

The oil fields of the county are now producing from 3,500 to 4,000 barrels of oil and this is considered heavy production for a field as old as that of Butler County's. In the days of the Thorn Creek field when gushers were comparatively plentiful, the production rarely averaged more than 60,000 barrels. This one industry alone is turning thousands of dollars into the channels of trade weekly and citizens are beginning to realize this and do all they can to foster the industry.

With prospects as bright as they are now and the information becoming generally scattered throughout the state, indications are that new investments will be made in the borough in the near future and that they will not be small. This means dollars to the merchants and good wages to employees together with a better and larger Butler in every sense of the word.
(copied from the *Butler Citizen* dated Nov. 24, 1909 by Dave and Audrey Craig)

### Manufacturers To Look Butler Over
### Men From All Over United States Will Inspect Factories Especially Pittsburg-Hickson

Butler industrial plants will be seen today through the critical eye of manufacturers from all parts of the United States and the Pittsburg-Hickson plant will receive special attention. This plant is the largest of its kind in the world.

The Metal Bed and Spring Association of the United States closed a convention held in Pittsburg this week, and about 75 of the manufacturers will come to Butler today as guests of the Pittsburg-Hickson Company. They will arrive at East Butler this morning at ten o'clock by special train over the Baltimore & Ohio Railroad, and be immediately shown through the immense plant of the Pittsburg-Hickson Company. They will have luncheon at the Hotel Nixon at one o'clock, as guests of the East Butler company. At three o'clock they will leave in a special car over the Pittsburgh and Butler trolley for Pittsburgh. [The city added the 'h' shortly after the turn of the century; many companies maintained the older spelling.]
(copied from the *Butler Citizen* dated Dec. 8, 1909 by Dave and Audrey Craig)

### Butler Citizen A Home Paper That Goes Into The Homes Of Butler County People
### Butler Enters On New Year With Prosperity Looming Like A Beacon 2c A Copy 10c A Week

**Banking**

Butler banks have all added to their surplus and undivided profit funds in the year 1909. In addition all have declared an extra dividend. These dividends range from six to 13 percentum annually and show that no large dividends are being paid indicating that the banks are careful of the investments made with depositors' money and prefer the safe and sane to the risky, paying high returns. A banker interviewed yesterday said, the banking houses of Butler have deposits on hand equal to those of banks of any city of the size of Butler in the country and the coming year looks to have an even brighter outlook. I can say that the banks of Butler are on solid footing and that the clearing house returns would surprise the bankers of most cities of our size. I can see nothing but a cheering outlook for the year of 1910 and considering conditions, Butler has been fortunate in the year just gone.

**Oil Production**

The oil fields of Butler County are as important as any fields in the country according to a statement made by as oil producer familiar with conditions in the entire country. Butler County produced more oil in 1909 than in several years previous. The average monthly production of the county is 90,000 barrels or 3,000 barrels a day. The oldest producing well in Butler County today is the Big Medicine well, in Black Hills, near Ralston's Mills, Troutman, Pa. This well is 37 years old and today is producing about two barrels of oil daily.

The decrease in the price of oil will have a tendency to stop the amount of new work done in the county the coming year. The price of crude oil is about 36 cents a barrel lower than it should be. "However, with the handicaps placed on the oil business we look for a good year," said a producer.

**Railroads**

Officals of railroads entering Butler are very much pleased with business conditions of 1909. One official

A little daughter of John Sutton of Martinsburg, [Bruin] was burned to death in a peculiar manner. The child was gathering potato bugs and burning them in the fire. To make the fire burn better she poured on oil from a can. The oil exploded setting fire to her clothing and burning her fatally. Nellie Burton of Allegheny was drowned in Connoquenessing creek near its confluence with the Slippery Rock creek, July 4.

**Twenty Years Ago**

Butler celebrated the Fourth of July in a fitting manner. The soldiers monument on the diamond was dedicated in a fitting manner. Newton Black was chief marshal of the civic and military parade. D. Swain of Harmony, president of the soldiers monument association made the presentation address.

(copied from the *Butler Citizen* dated July 4, 1914 by Dave and Audrey Craig)

## MUCH BUILDING IN PROSPECT
## CONSTRUCTION WORK IN BUTLER INCLUDES SOME LARGE CONTRACTS
## PLANS FOR AN ARCADE ARE BEING DISCUSSED

Considerable activity is noticeable the past few days among the contractors and builders of Butler and the general outlook for the building trade has been more encouraging than it has been for the past year. The leading architects of the city have a large amount of preliminary work on their hands and are waiting for orders to prepare specifications and take bids. This work includes building houses of the better class and some business blocks running into large sums of money.

One of the largest contracts for the season will be that for the building of the new Lyric Theater. The details of the building have not yet been worked out for the contractors, but work on razing the old buildings and preparing the ground for the new structure will be commenced in a few days.

Edward Weigand and son closed the contract yesterday for the construction of the new bakery for Phil Diehl and Sons on the corner of Center and Lookout Avenues. Work on the building will be commenced in a day or two. Plans for the building were prepared by architect George Kline, who will have supervision of the construction. The plan calls for a three story brick and steel building with a finished basement, steam heating plant, elevators and an up-to-date equipment for a bakery. The plant will include a battery of continuous bake ovens with a capacity of 10,000 loaves of bread a day. The latest improved machinery will be installed, making it one of the largest as well as the most complete bakeries to be seen outside the big city. The cost of the plant will approximate $30,000.

Rumors were revived on the street yesterday to the effect that negotiations were pending for the purchase of a site for an arcade building to be located in the business center of town. The building, according to reports, may be erected this summer and will cost approximately $150,000.

Contractors yesterday began the work of remodeling the front of the old Troutman store building at the corner of Main and Mifflin streets, now occupied by Patterson Brothers furniture store. The store will be occupied after the first of April by Jamison's Pharmacy, which will move from its present location in the Graham block on North Main Street.

Patterson Brothers expect to have their new building on Mifflin Street ready for occupancy and will move their stock of furniture from the Troutman building the first of the month.

(copied from the *Butler Citizen* dated March 19, 1914 by Dave and Audrey Craig)

### What Is Butler?

On the accepted and approved theory that an ounce of prevention is worth several pounds of cure, Butler is taking stock of its civic and industrial conditions. What it is hoped will result in remedial measures has been instituted by the chamber of commerce by their present campaign to quicken the pulse of the community. Just what is Butler? It is not the streets and bridges, not the fine public and semi-public buildings, not the banks, repositories of wealth nor the splendid churches and schools.

We have splendid up-to-date retail stores, fine hotels, factories, fair railroad accommodations, and other things that go to make a center, but that isn't what makes a city great. It wasn't the physical frame on any of the world's great men that made them great. Undoubtedly there were many men in their time just as perfect physically as Caesar, Hannibal, Alexander, Napoleon, Demosthenes, Cicero, Shakespeare, Mohammed, Mozart and other geniuses. And many, many of these physically great were slaves.

It is the mind or soul that makes the remarkable difference between men who are alike physically. And cities and communities have souls as much as individuals have. A city's soul is the composite soul of the men, women and children who by living together in one place constituting a community.

Probably there isn't much real difference between the souls of the cities located in widely separated parts of the county. But the impulses or actions of these communities of souls may have been quickened or restrained by varying influences.

Too many men lack imagination and are unable to look into the future. Tomorrow is but another day and progress is marked by the excess of this year's profit over last year's. How many of us take intelligent interest in our public schools or even the general scheme of education? Vastly too few. Some of our most successful men in commerce or in industry may be our most marked failures as parents, as producers of the country's richest resources—children.

Butler has a vital, pulsing soul. Its people are noted for their hospitality, their courtesy, their cooperation in good works. The right touch at this palpitant juncture is setting that soul's current to coursing toward a realization of the fondest hopes of our idealist and without idealists any dormant community would be quite inanimate.

Butler's finest asset and her greatest need is unswerving loyalty to Butler. Every dollar sent elsewhere by a citizen of Butler for merchandise that can be bought in Butler is a knock to the city. The cardinal tenet of a city's success is home trading. There need be no cause for worry about the future of this community, if the people in it will awaken to a realization of our needs and buckle to the task of developing a greater energy in the work for their city. We must consider the community interest and not individual interests. The most rapid knockers must become ardent boosters and the desired need will be accomplished.

What is Butler? Not merely a city of brick and mortar and stone and timber but the people who live here. The way to build up Butler is to build up its civic consciousness and arouse a wide awake, fighting spirit for the city, as an inspiration to those who are here now, and those who will come here later because Butler is a good place for men, women and children to live, a city with a soul that surpasses its surface.

(copied from the *Butler Citizen* dated June 1919 by Dave and Audrey Craig)

## PITTSBURG-HICKSON COMPANY IS GROWING RAPIIDLY

The receipts in the past week of orders for two car loads of brass beds from dealers in Puerto Rico by the Pittsburg-Hickson Company of East Butler is one of the indications of the manner in which this company has increased its business since coming to the Butler district and the extent which Butler made goods are being shipped to foreign markets.

Last Saturday the 18 representatives and traveling salesmen of the company completed their fall inspection of the factory and conference with the heads of the company at East Butler and departed for their respective fields to close the year's work with another trip to their customers. There were representatives present from all over the United States, Canada, Mexico and Cuba. The business of the Pittsburg-Hickson Company the past year has been the largest in its history, the volume of trade showing a steady increase every month this year.

The company is at present carrying 500 men on its payroll, exclusive of the sales force. The company has been exporting goods extensively and at present has orders booked for Puerto Rico, Cuba, South America, Mexico and Canada, as well as initial orders for other foreign countries.

The rapid growth of this company's business, in view of only fair business conditions over the country, is due to a number of patented articles on the market which were originated and are controlled exclusively by this company. So popular have these articles become that the company has been obliged to increase its capacity of brass beds many times over the capacity of the initial plant.

At the East Butler factory, the company has just completed installing an additional unit to its power plant consisting of a Parker and Wheeler generator and a large Fitchburg engine. The additional power will enable the company to operate its factory to its full capacity.

The volume of freight out of East Butler yards for the past four months exceeds by 100 per cent any preceding four months in the history of the East Butler office. The Pittsburg-Hickson Company is preparing for the semi-annual exhibition, held in Chicago in January of each year, when new models and patents and samples of the product of the factory will be displayed to the trade. The outlook of the local factory is for the most prosperous year in the thirteen years of its xistence.

(copied from the *Butler Citizen* dated Oct. 30, 1911 by Dave and Audrey Craig)

## EAST BUTLER FORGES TO FRONT AS A MANUFACTURING CENTER
### Thriving Suburb Strives to Keep Pace Industrially with Booming Butler and its Progress is Marked

East Butler, one of Butler's thriving suburbs, will enjoy the greatest industrial boom of the century this summer. The two large plants located at that place are running full capacity, and furnish constant employment for many hundred men.

Many new houses are in course of erection and many additional ones will be built in a short time. The demand for homes at East Butler was never greater, and at the present time there is much need for at least 50 homes for men who are employed at the factories there. The Butler Land and Improvement company has a large number of lots on the market, desirably located for home seekers, and these are selling rapidly. Material is now on the ground for the erection of a large reservoir to be located on the Heinzer farm at East Butler, with a capacity of 50,000 barrels of water. This will supply the town with the best water attainable, as the supply comes exclusively from drilled wells.

Residents who are interested in the welfare and growth of this prosperous and thriving little town, are considering the erection of a sewage disposal plant, a definite move in that direction is only a matter of a very short time. All in all the town of East Butler has a brilliant future, and with street car connections with Butler, will make it a most desirable location for home seekers, both those who are employed in the immediate vicinity and men who are working in Butler, as the town is only a 10 minutes ride in the cars from the industrial center of the city. The town has recently completed and dedicated a handsome church. The congregation, the East Butler Presbyterian, has a large and continually growing membership. It also has two school houses and several up-to-date stores.

The Pittsburg-Hickson Company, located at East Butler, is one of the largest and most modern plants for the manufacturing of iron and brass beds, sanitary couches and bed springs in the United States. The plant consists of 10 large modern buildings, with seven and a half acres of ground under roof. The plant is running full capacity, and furnishes steady employment for

more than 400 workmen, a large number of whom own homes of their own in East Butler.

The company has started work on a large addition to be built to one of the present buildings, to be used as a store house. This building will be 170 feet in length, two stories high and built of sheet iron. The output of the Pittsburg-Hickson factory for every ten hours is 2,500 iron beds, 300 brass beds and 600 sanitary couches and davenports. The company has an excellent future and will mean much toward the development of the town.

Located near the Pittsburg-Hickson company's plant is the Valvoline Oil refinery. This is one of the largest refineries of crude oil in the world. The Valvoline company control three refineries, one at Edgewater, N. J., one at Warren, Pa., and their main plant in this city. The many buildings at this plant are built of the best material, and are strictly modern in every respect.

Many additions and improvements are being made to the Valvoline works at the present time. A large building equipped with some of the most modern appliances known to the oil industry was completed last week. This new addition is for sweating paraffin wax, and is a comparatively new process.

A new building is being rapidly rushed to completion called the filter building. It is a two story brick structure, 35 by 50 feet, and when completed will be used as a filtering plant, for filtering oils. Another improvement which will soon be in running order is the bone burning house which will be operated in connection with the filter plant. Animal bone will be burned in the building, a substance used in filtering oils.

A new steam still was recently completed, which has a capacity of about 800 barrels. Ten stills are now in operation at the works with combined capacity of 25,000 barrels a month. The barrel factory, which has been in operation for some time is turning out 500 barrels a day.

The Valvoline Oil company has about 110 large oil tanks, with a capacity of more than 155,000 barrels. The capacity for storing crude oils is 95,000 barrels, for refined oils 20,000 and for unfinished oils about 40,000 barrels. (copied from the *Butler Citizen* dated March 21, 1910 by Dave and Audrey Craig)

# THE PITTSBURG-HICKSON COMPANY HAD SPECIAL TRAIN FOR VISITORS
## ABOUT 100 DELEGATES TO CONVENTION AND CITIZENS OF BUTLER VISITED THE BED
## FACTORY AT EAST BUTLERBUTLER IS JUSTLY PROUD OF THIS INDUSTRY

About 100 men and ladies, delegates to the Merchants Convention and residents of Butler, took advantage of the offer of the Pittsburg-Hickson company, yesterday made a trip to East Butler to visit one of the largest bed manufacturing plants in the world. The company provided a special train for its quests, leaving the Baltimore and Ohio station at 8:30 a.m. and returning at 10 o'clock. The visit to this well known company's immense plant will long be remembered by those who accepted the generous offer of the managers. The members of the party were shown through all departments of the works and were, very much edified by the knowledge gleaned of the manufacture of brass and iron beds and the other products of the company.

The reader of the *Citizen* cannot fail to be interested in a brief dissertation of the Pittsburg-Hickson company's great industrial plant and the processes through which the material must pass before it reaches the buyer in its attractive and useful forms.

The metal bed industry has witnessed some kaleidoscope changes during the brief period of its existence. Metal beds were first made in England something over 50 years ago. They were novelties and did not meet with great favor for many years. The manufacture of iron beds in America on a large scale does not actually date back more than a dozen years. Even ten years ago, if you had asked a well-posted furniture dealer where the largest iron and brass bed factory was located, he probably would have answered that there were no large ones.

When the industry began to grow, it grew at what some seemed to consider an alarming rate. Plants began to spring up rapidly all over the country. The manufacture of iron beds threatened to become largely a local business, and an overproduction seemed imminent. But of late a reaction has taken place. Many small plants have disappeared. Others have consolidated. Today it seems that the tendency is toward a limited number of very large plants, instead of a growing number of small ones, for the manufacture of iron beds is peculiarly a business in which a plant of meager capacity cannot successfully compete with one enjoying the many advantages of production on a large scale.

These considerations justify us, we believe in declaring that the opening of the immense Pittburg-Hickson plant was an epoch-making event in the history of the iron bed industry. For be it noted the Pittsburg-Hickson Co. begins it career as the largest exclusive bed manufacturing concern in the world. Its capacity is 5,000 beds every twenty-four hours.

Such a large capacity is made possible by an equally large plant. The site includes 20 acres of ground, the main buildings alone covering 5 acres. The construction of the building required over thirty trainloads of material. The shop floor space 220,000 square feet. The steam heating and electric systems utilize 9 miles of iron pipe and 15 miles of wiring. But the size of the plant alone would lose much of its significance were it not reinforced by that exquisitely perfect and unique equipment, and the through and admirable system which makes the Pittsburg-Hickson plant a marvel of modern manufacturing.

There are ten complete departments, exclusive of the offices, including the drafting and designing rooms, power house, foundries, machine shops, brass works, rail department, enamel and paint mixing plant, ovens, warehouse and packing and shipping departments. These departments are operated as distinct units, each being a factory in itself. The coordination of the different departments is secured by nine general systems, centrally controlled.

The electric system utilizes a 400 horsepower Westinghouse generator with twenty-five motors in different parts of the plant. All power generating machinery is installed in duplicate thus obviating any chance of delay on account of a possible breakdown.

A complete private pumping and water system is another feature. The reservoir has a capacity of 1,000,000 gallons. The overhead ball-bearing trolley system is one and one-half miles in length. There are also complete telephone, heating, watermain, paint-conveying, and other general systems binding the different departments together.

It would take one a long time to walk through the Pittsburg-Hickson plant at the pace of a professional pedestrian. It would take one a day to explore the plant for the purpose of learning how iron beds are made, and an absorbing interesting day's experience it would be.

This concern is fortunate in its location in the heart of the Pittsburg district. That wonderful region made famous by its products of iron and steel. All of the heavy materials used are within easy reach and can be had without delay. Its location is also most advantageous by reason of the equalization of freight rates to all points in the country. The new and improved melting furnaces or cupolas in use are most interesting in their never failing supply of liquid metal, brass as well as iron. Thousands of brass and iron bed parts are moulded and welded here each day. Every bed made in this plant is subjected to a chemical process or treatment, which renders it practically rust proof. This process is attended with some degree of danger, so that special precautions are needed to guard against accidents.

The paint mixing department is the soul of the plant. Numerous vats housed in separate buildings hold the various paints, lacquers, varnishes and enamels. Each vat being equipped with a special apparatus for thinning its solvents. All mixing is thus done on the spot, so that the company always has an exact knowledge of every composition used, and can guarantee every mixture of paint to hold its color tone. The vats which terminate at numerous outlets, are each controlled by a novel cut-off automatically, which permits the flow to be started, stopped, or regulated instantaneously. The painting, enameling, and finishing constitute the most important part of the process of making an iron bed. It is the finish that forms the chief element in the appearance of an iron bed on the dealer's floor, and nothing is so well calculated to catch the eye of a customer. In the Pittsburg-Hickson plant, very few beds are painted by the old process of dipping, in fact this process is used on extremely low priced beds, all others are painted by hand, and this work is entrusted only to expert workmen. After being painted, the beds are placed in ovens, the intense heat thoroughly baking the channels and rendering them smooth and durable. At the Pittsburg-Hickson plant there are thirteen fireproof ovens each 16 by 80. They are built of brick, cement and steel, heated by steam, lighted by electricity, and enclosed with steel fireproof doors.

From one end of the plant to the other, all beds are handled by means of over-head, ball-bearing trolleys. These overhead trolleys are to the modern bed plant what a system of trucks is to the modern wood-working plant. There are a vast number of minor details in the making of iron beds, but many of these are not comprehensible to those lacking a technical knowledge of the industry and want of space forbids our elaborating the above meager outline.

The Pittsburg-Hickson company is to be congratulated. No prophecies need be made as to its future. Located in the heart of the iron region, on four great trunk lines of railroads with a plant such as above described, the accomplishment of its promoters' ambition is assured. But in addition to those advantages it is fortunate in having at its head a man of through experience, a man of brains and of energy, a man who has played no small part in bringing the manufacture of iron beds to its present enviable state as an industry. Every furniture man in America knows E. J. Hickson, and we are sure that they all join the *Citizen* in wishing for him and his great plant that which we all desire in the world, that which we all strive for and live for success.
(copied from the *Butler Citizen* dated Aug. 19, 1910 by Dave and Audrey Craig)

## PITTSBURG-HICKSON WILL ENLARGE ITS POWER EQUIPMENT

The Pittsburg-Hickson Company of East Butler closed the contract in the last few days for a large addition to its power plant. The contracts include a battery of two 250 horse power boilers, a 350 horse power engine and an electric generator. The additional power was made necessary on account of the large amount of new machinery that has been installed in the plant within the last two years. The present power plant is inadequate to run all of the machinery in the day turn. Part of the plant has to be operated at night in order to oblate the difficulty. On account of the rapid increase in the business of the plant it is expected that other additions to the power plant will be made in the near future. The new generator, engine and boilers ordered will be installed and ready for use by July I st.
(copied from the *Butler Citizen* dated May 13, 1911 by Dave and Audrey Craig)

## VALVOLINE OIL LOST BUILDING
## FIRE DESTROYED BONE HOUSE AT EAST BUTLER SATURDAY MORNING

### FIREMEN PREVENTED EXTENSION OF BLAZE

Fire caused by the explosion of an accumulation of gas in the bone house at the Valvoline Oil works in East Butler destroyed the building Saturday morning and entailed a loss of $3,500. There was no one in the bone-house at the time the explosion occurred. The workmen in other parts of the factory quickly responded to the alarm and found the interior of the building in flames. The fire fighting apparatus of the company was soon at work and a line of hose was laid to the Pittsburg-Hickson factory, which is about 300 feet from the Valvoline works.

A call was also sent to the Butler fire department and the auto truck and crew from the Southside station were sent out. The services of the crew were not needed. The fire was confined to the one building though it was feared for a time that flames would spread to some tankage where a large amount of refined oil and gasoline was stored.

The building destroyed was a three-story structure, 50 by 80 feet in size and located at some distance from the other buildings of the plant. The first story was brick and the succeeding stories corrugated iron. There was no oil in the building that was burned. It is used for preparing a mixture of ground bone and other ingredients used for filtering oil. There was considerable machinery in the building that has been ruined by the fire.

The falling in of the roof of the building caused a spectacular display that gave rise to the report on the streets of Butler that the entire factory was on fire and that the plant of Pittsburg-Hickson company was in danger.
(copied from the *Butler Citizen* dated Nov. 25, 1912 by Dave and Audrey Craig)

### PITTSBURG-HICKSON COMPANY ADDS TO FACILITIES

The Pittsburg-Hickson Company has about completed a two story, 60 by 80 brick addition to the brass bed department at its factory at East Butler. The addition is the fourth that has been built to this department in the last four years and when the machinery is installed will increase the output from 500 to 850 brass beds per day.

Other additions and improvements to the equipment of the factory are the installing of a Crocker Wheeler direct current electric generator and a 100 horse power Fitchburg engine in the power plant. The additional power units will furnish ample power for all departments in the plant. Each department can run full capacity without hampering other departments in the big factory. Yesterday the factory turned out something like 350 brass beds, 1,500 iron beds, 100 bed springs, and 200 children's beds and baby cribs and when the new building is in operation the capacity will be increased to 500 brass beds, 2,000 iron beds and 300 children's beds per day. The most satisfactory part of the announcement is that the company has orders in advance for all of the goods it can make and can't get them fast enough.

**Damard Lacquer Brass Beds**

At present the company is having a big run on brass beds and cannot fill the orders fast enough. This branch of the business has grown by leaps and bounds. When the factory was started at East Butler, brass beds were a sideline. Now they are rapidly forging to the front as the principle line. The Pittsburg-Hickson Company is the first in the United States to take up the manufacture of the Damard Lacquer Brass Beds. Every owner of an old fashioned brass bed knows the difficulty that is experienced in keeping it from tarnishing. The Damard Lacquer Brass Beds of the Pittsburg-Hickson company are guaranteed for five years and a surety bond is given with each bed. The Damard Lacquer finish is guaranteed to be impervious to moisture, acids, soap and water, alcohol, and can not be affected by cold, heat, gas or coal fumes.

The Damard Lacquer is the discovery of Prof. A. W. Raikens of London, England, and has been used by the principle bed manufactures of the country for a number of years. The Pittsburg-Hickson company is the first to use it in the United States and with a success that is phenomenal in the manufacturing business.

**What Becomes of the Beds**

With an output of almost 3,000 beds and couches a day the question arises in the minds of the average layman, what becomes of the beds? The day of the four poster bed with cords as springs and feather ticks as matress, as well as the modern wooden bed, with its accompaniment of vermin is past. The iron and brass beds are taking their places all over the country

The Pittsburg-Hickson Company has 13 salesman who travel all over the parts of the United States, Canada, Mexico and the West Indies and the product of the East Butler factory is shipped to all of these countries in car load lots. The largest domestic shipments are to the Pacific coast and in recent months there is a growing demand in the large cities of the East.

The railroad shipments show that a daily average of 20 cars of material are recieved at the East Butler plant and 20 cars of finished products were billed out. The company is employing at present 660 people at the factory full time and much of this summer different departments have run overtime to keep up with the orders.

(copied from the *Butler Citizen* dated Aug. 12, 1912 by Dave and Audrey Craig)

## EAST BUTLER BED FACTORY WILL BE GREATLY ENLARGED

## PITTSBURG-HICKSON COMPANY WILL ADD TO CAPITAL STOCK

A special meeting of the stockholders of the Pittsburg-Hickson Company, who own the brass and iron bed manufacturing plant at East Butler, has been called for December 2, when a proposition will be made to increase the capital stock of the company from $500,000 to $1,500,000.

The Pittsburg-Hickson plant is one of the largest in the country and the rapid increase in the business done by the company makes enlargements of the works quite necessary. During the past four years, extensive additions have been built, but further work along this line cannot be done until the capital stock is increased, and for this reason it is believed that no opposition will be encountered when the vote for increasing the capital stock is taken next month.

The tripling of the capital stock of this concern means much for Butler, as in addition to increasing the capacity of the mills already in operation, additional plants for the manufacture of brass bed accessories are said to be contemplated, which will give employment to a large number of men. The beds manufactured by the East Butler concern are well-known all over the country and it is quite common to see their beds advertised extensively in the catalogs issued by the great furniture dealers of this country. They give their beds a lacquer finish which is guaranteed for a number of years, and the most prominent wholesale household-goods concerns are giving this particular feature a great boost in the advertising line.

The improvements to the East Butler concern, in addition to the new mills to be erected by the Standard Steel Car Co., will mean a great increase in the force of men now finding employment in Butler, and the outlook for a bigger, better and more prosperous Butler was never better.

(copied from the *Butler Citizen* dated Nov. 20, 1912 by Dave and Audrey Craig)

# LOCAL MANUFACTURING PLANT MAKES GOVERNMENT OFFER

Butler manufactures were among the first to tender their services to the government after the break with Germany in the event that hostilities finally come. Among the list of prompt offers reaching the war department at Washington Monday was one for the Pittsburg-Hickson company of East Butler. The following telegram was dispatched by the company to Secretary of War Newton D. Baker and Secretary of Navy Josephus Daniels: "Our plant is capable of furnishing 1,000 steel hospital or army beds per day. We offer our entire assistance to the government when needed.

Pittsburg-Hickson Co. E. J. Hickson, President

In answer to the offer sent to the war department the following telegram was received by the Butler company yesterday afternoon:

Mr. E. J. Hickson, Pres. Pittsburg-Hickson Co.

Your patriotic offer has been received and it is much appreciated. Very Sincerely,

Newton D. Baker

The offer to make 1,000 steel hospital or army beds per day is a conservative one, an official of the Pittsburg-Hickson Company said today. He explained that such an order could be handled without in any way interfering with the regular business. Working on a war basis, 24 hours a day, the local concern could turn out between 3,000 and 4,000 beds daily, it was stated.

Another highly patriotic offer, which will be commended by all right-thinking people in this community, was contained in a telegram sent yesterday by Attorney John C. Graham of Butler to President Woodrow Wilson at Washington, D.C. Attorney Graham is vice president and one of the principal owners of the Allegheny Foundry and Machine Company, whose plant at Tarentum was recently moved there from Queen Junction, Butler County. The telegram reads as follows:

"Having one of the largest foundries in the Pittsburgh district, working at full capacity, we place same at your disposal in case of war."

(copied from the *Butter Citizen* dated Feb. 7, 1917 by Dave and Audrey Craig)

## TO HAVE CHARGE OF LOCAL BED FACTORY

At a meeting held before Commissioner James W. Hutchison Tuesday, the creditors of the Pittsburg-Hickson Company selected Grover Higgins of Pittsburgh, as trustee in bankruptcy to take charge of the East Butler plant of the company. The bond of the trustee was fixed at $100,000 and he is authorized to run the business of the plant until further order is made.

(*Butler Citizen*, Oct. 11, 1917)

### Pittsburg-Hickson Affairs Examined

### Creditors of Company Meet at Hearing Before Commissioners in Bankrupcy

The business affairs of the Pittsburg-Hickson Company were given an airing yesterday at a meeting of the creditors and attorneys concerned in the bankruptcy proceedings held before James W. Hutchison, commissioner in bankruptcy for this district, in No. 2 court room of the courthouse. The meeting is being held for the purpose of ascertaining what became of the assets of the company and accounting for the indebtedness which amounts to upward of $1,000,000.

The principal witness yesterday was E. J. Hickson, president of the Pittsburg-Hickson Company. It was brought out in the testimony that one of the subsidiary concerns operated by the company was a bank brokerage company of Pittsburgh. Mr. Hickson explained the purpose of the brokerage company, which was placing notes of the Pittsburg-Hickson Company, and also explained how the business was conducted.

The hearing before the commissioner had not been concluded yesterday evening and an adjourned meeting will be held this afternoon. (copied from the *Butler Citizen* dated Oct. 18, 1917 by Dave and Audrey Craig)

## PITTSBURG-HICKSON COMPANY IS THROWN IN RECEIVERS HANDS
### Changed conditions caused by war responsible for difficulties of concern
### Reorganization and refinancing planned, company employs about 350 people.

On the petition of a number of the creditors and preferred stockholders, Judge I. W. King, of Kittanning, specially presiding in the common pleas court here late yesterday afternoon appointed J. F. Anderson and Attorney C. H. Hosford, Jr., of Butler, and Attorney Grover Higgins, of Cleveland, temporary receivers of the Pittsburg-Hickson Company, of East Butler, pending the serving of notice to creditors and the hearing of the petition for a permanent receiver to be held August 18, 1917.

The temporary receivers were authorized to operate the plant located at East Butler, and pay employees, pending the adjudication of matters before the court. The purpose of the proceedings, as stated last night by the receivers, is to protect the interest of the creditors and the stockholders, pending investigation of the affairs of the company and a reorganization.

The petitioner for the receivers was presented by J. Henry Troutman, J. F. Anderson, John S. Campbell, the Butler Savings and Trust Company, the Merchants National Bank and other creditors, and the preferred stockholders of the Pittsburg-Hickson. Company.

Attorney T. C. Campbell and J. 0. Campbell appeared for the petitioners and Brandon and Brandon appeared for the Pittsburg-Hickson company in the proceedings.

The reason given for the proposed refinancing of the company is that the Pittsburg-Hickson Company, like many other manufacturing concerns, has been working under changed financial conditions caused by the war, and a readjustment and reorganization is made necessary to save both creditors and stockholders.

The company is capitalized at $1,600,000 and employs about 350 people, mostly skilled labor at its plant at East Butler.

(copied from the *Butler Citizen* dated August 7, 1917 by Dave and Audrey Craig)

### WILL ERECT WINDOW GLASS FACTORY IN EAST BUTLER SOON
### Work begins in August on $250,000 plant to employ 250 or 300 men
### C. Stock convinced new machine will revolutionize glass industry

C. Stock, of this city, interested in the Mechanical Glass Company, formed in Pittsburgh, and was capitalized at five million dollars, with stock of $30 par value, has received definite information that East Butler has been selected as the location for a great glass plant to be erected without delay. Four other sites were considered, one of them carrying a bonus offer of $50,000, but the company after carefully canvassing the field came to the conclusion that the natural advantages to be found in East Butler overcame all other inducements offered by other cities. Good railway facilities, a good supply of coal and plenty of good quality and availability were some of the inducements that caused the concern to locate here.

The company expects to break ground for the East Butler plant about the middle of August; the initial cost of which will be about $250,000 and which will employ 250 to 300 men. George C. Tebay, the inventor of the machine used by the Mechanical Window Glass Company, is a native of Belgium who has devoted many years of study to the industry. He has invented a marvelous labor-saving machine that saves from 35 to 50 per cent of the cost of production; it controls a steady motion of blowing the cylinder, which does away with pulsations, cockles and other window glass defects. The glass is considered to be the equal of plate glass and far superior to window glass manufactured by the old methods.

Mr. Stock has seen demonstration machines in action and is thoroughly convinced of the claims in its favor. An ideal site has been secured in East Butler, he says, and construction work on the plant will be under way with in the next few weeks.

(copied from the *Butler Citizen* dated June 21, 1917 by Dave and Audrey Craig)

### CONCRETE PLANT TO BE ERECTED ON THE ISLAND
### BUTLER CONCRETE MFG. CO. BUYS GROUND ON WHICH TO EXTEND WORKS

Ground has been purchased by the Butler Concrete Manufacturing Company for a plant which will be erected adjoining the Wood Fiber Plaster Works, on the Island. The building will be erected on concrete and cement blocks with steel trusses and a fire-proof roof. The plant will have private sidings connecting with the Bessemer Railroad.

The plot of ground purchased is 100 by 115 feet in dimensions and faces on the Bessemer tracks. In the near future another building will be erected. The building now planned will be used for the manufacture of the water-proof vault now used extensively in western Pennsylvania and Ohio and composition gravestones, which will be put into the market soon, will also be made in it.

The building contemplated will be used for making the double air space concrete blocks and other products, such as chimney caps, fence posts, sewer pipes, etc. The erection of those buildings means employment of additional labor in the near future and an increased payroll which will redound to the benefit of the business interest of the borough. The building to be erected for which plans have been drawn, will be 40 by 80 feet in demensions, while the one contemplated will be of about the same size.
(copied from the *Butler Citizen* dated Aug. 1910 by Dave and Audrey Craig)

## GLOVE FACTORY TURNS OUT FIRST PRODUCT

The first product of the reorganized Butler Glove and Mitten Company, whose factory is located on Bluff Street, was completed yesterday. The total number of gloves finished Wednesday was 90 dozen, and of this quantity one girl made 20 dozen.

About a dozen persons are now employed in the factory, and it is expected that this number will shortly be increased. When the factory is running to its full capacity it is expected that the output will reach 200 dozen pairs per day.
(copied from the *Butler Citizen* dated May 5, 1910 by Dave and Audrey Craig)

## GLOVE FACTORY IS PROSPERING

The Butler Glove and Mitten Company recently reorganized into a stock company, with a capitial of $2,500, is running full capacity now, and is turning out about 115 dozen pairs of canvas gloves a day. The plant has been equipped with modern machinery, and electric power is used. The equipment consists of an electric hand cutter, turning machines, electric cutting machine and a packing machine. Twelve sewing machines, all run by electricity are used. Twelve girls and several men are regularly employed.

Although the plant is running in full, the output will be increased to 175 dozen pairs of gloves a day, when the employees become more familiar with the machinery. Four different styles of gloves in four different weights are manufactured.

The Butler Glove and Mitten Company was reorganized into a stock company some time ago. The stock is all owned by Butler businessmen, with J. H. Altman manager of the concern. The company is enjoying an excellent run of business, and the gloves are sold as fast as they are completed. Many mail orders are arriving daily, and Butler merchants, almost without exception are liberally patronizing the home industry.
(copied from the *Butler Citizen* dated May 17, 1910 by Dave and Audrey Craig)

## CLOTHING FIRM TO OPEN STORE ON MAIN STREET

The People's Credit Clothing Company, with headquarters in New York City, will open a store in Butler about the middle of March, at 247 South Main Street, corner of Wayne. The room is part of the store now occupied by Templeton and Company, who will remove to the new Masonic Temple in a short time.

The new concern will be permanently located in Butler. They have 34 stores in different cities in the country, and have three factories where they manufacture their own goods. The store will handle a complete line of men's and boy's clothing, ladies' suits and ready-to-wear garments of all kinds.

The store will be run on the credit system, on a plan that has never yet been introduced in this city. On account of the great purchasing power of the concern, they say they will be in a position to sell goods on credit, as cheap as elsewhere for cash. In view of the fact that the company controls 34 large stores, they will show latest styles just as soon in Butler as they do in the larger cities.
(copied from the *Butler Citizen* dated March 1, 1910 by Dave and Audrey Craig)

## PLANT HAS BEEN ENLARGED
## NEW EQUIPMENT HAS ALSO BEEN ADDED

The reduction plant of H. C. and Curtis Bricker on the old Mercer Road, north of Butler, has been enlarged and the capacity increased by the addition of an evaporating machine for the purpose of making glue, tankage water, ammonia and other by products of offal and refuse material.

The company has, for several years, been conducting an abattoir where old horses and diseased cattle that were not fit for the dairy or market were converted into fertilizing material. No attempt was made to extract the by-products until this year, when the new machine was installed. The new machine is a ten-ton, odorless evaporator and has a capacity of five gallons of liquids a minute. With one exception it is the largest machine of its kind in the United States, and it is the only one in operation in western Pennsylvania, outside of Pittsburgh.

It is proposed at the present time to manufacture concentrated tankage, fertilizer, glue and ammonia. The capacity of the plant will be increased to meet the requirements of the trade, and it is only a matter of a little time until the reduction plant will be one of the important manufacturing enterprises of Butler.

The present establishment is due largely to the enterprise of Curtis Bricker, who is associated with H. C. Bricker in the Butler Hide & Fur Company as salesman.

(copied from the *Butler Citizen* dated Oct. 17, 1910 by Dave and Audrey Craig)

### Corona Tire Co. Now Has 135 Employees

The importance to the city, of Butler's newest industry, is illustrated by the fact that on January first the Corona Cord Tire Company employed but 45 operatives while now they have 135 on the payroll. On June first, when the plant will have reached capacity, 200 men will be necessary to operate the plant, Manager H. B. Callahan said this morning.

Nearly all the stockholders of the company were present at the annual meeting of the company yesterday. The following men were elected to serve on the board of directors during the coming year: T. W. Phillips, J. V. Ritts, B. D. Phillips, Samuel Sherwin, H. B. Callahan, Elias Ritts and A. C. Fisher.

The report of operations for 1920 was exceptionally favorable and the report of operations since January first of this year even more so, in light of developments in the affairs of other large producers of automobile equipment and accessories. The report submitted at the meeting included the information that since January 1, 1921, the plant showed orders for over fifteen thousand tires and a corresponding number of tubes. Shipments to date exceeded ten thousand tires and sales for the month of April amounted to $107,483.90. A check of the orders on hand showed a total of five carloads for shipment between now and June 5. Production at the plant on May 2 was registered at 225 tires, compared to an average production of last week of 190 tires per day. Mold equipment and deliveries of raw materials are scheduled for an average production of 350 to 400 tires per day by June 12. This schedule will be maintained throughout the sumer months. Officials of the company commenting upon the price reduction of twenty per cent announced last saturday by the larger tire companies, explained that they were in excellent shape to meet this cut in price. In fact, Butler consumers have been enjoying a twenty per cent

THIS IS ·
**CORONA WEEK**
INTRODUCING
**NATIONAL STANDARD TIRES**
*"Made to United States Government Specifications"*

The Bureau of Standards of the United States Government at Washington writes specifications for many articless. Among these are Tires, of which the Government purchases ... ... ... ands each year.

We manufacture a tire in accordance with these government specifications and as a guide to the tire buying public, market it under the very appropriate name of "NATIONAL STANDARD."

WE SOLICIT YOUR PATRONAGE:

First: On the basis of a quality product at a reasonable price.

Second: On the basis of a Home industry employing over 200 men with an annual payroll of more than $240,000.00.

**CORONA CORD TIRE CO.**

*Ask Your Dealer for National Standards*

reduction on Corona Cords since last fall, and it is expected that this policy will be continued and local consumers can still obtain their tire needs at twenty per cent off the new lists of other companies.

In explanation of the optimistic outlook as evidenced by the increased production schedule the management explained that the company was in the enviable position of having no losses to write off from last year's operations; no high-priced raw materials to carry over into this year and that they were protected on purchases for the balance of the year at very favorable prices. This puts the company in position to meet the keen competition of the trade without loss and as was aptly stated, the firms who are in position to meet the economic demands of the trade today from a price standpoint, without jeopardizing the quality of their product are the firms which are going to forge ahead and benefit their communities as well as themselves.

A number of the stockholders present expressed themselves as being agreeably surprised at the progress made by this new addition to Butler's industries.

*(Butler Citizen,* May 1921)

### Trip Through East Butler Tire Plant Revelation To Unitiated
### Company Heads Guide Guests Through Factory This Week During Open House
### This Is Corona Cord Tire Week

Every day this week visitors at the tire plant in East Butler will be piloted through the big plant and will see the process by which raw rubber is converted into automobile tires, to be used throughout the country and abroad, and incidentally to carry the name of Butler to remote climes.

Started here by local capital in 1919, the company has weathered what has proved to other independent tire companies a rough, tempestuous sea, for since that year when there were approximately 360 plants in the United States all have quit the field but sixty-two, including the East Butler concern.

Its daily output is 1,450 tires, but within the next few weeks this will be increased by 400 or 500 tires. The first shipment of tires left the local plant in 1921, and ever since that time it has been one of the busiest industrial establishments in the Butler district.

Two hundred and forty men are employed by the firm, and if the number of automobiles, and the type thereof can be taken as a criterion, any visitor who espies them as they stand parked outside the factory will immediately arrive at the conclusion that employees of the Corona Cord Tire Company are indeed prosperous workmen.

Henry B. Caliahan, vice president and general manager of the company, and former Mayor Joseph A. Heineman, escorted a reporter through the big plant the other day, and the trip proved both interesting and instructive. After a trip of such a character, one is almost inclined to exclaim to the world, "See Butler First."

Heads of the company have so arranged their plant as to bring about the highest possible production, for once the rubber starts on its round trip from the freight car which brought it to East Butler, it never turns back until it reaches the opposite end of the factory, and then backwards it comes, resembling a tire more and more at each successive operation.

Finally it is wrapped and labeled, then thrown on a hugh heap to be loaded for shipment. The former mayor has been added to the company's force as its new sales manager, and already he has accomplished much in introducing the company's newest creation the "National Standard Tire," to the public.

One of the most interesting processes that will be explained to the visitors this week will be the manner in which inner tubes are shaped. Into a machine resembling a hugh sausage-grinder is fed a reddish substance, which issues from the end of the machine like a continuous rubber hose of the diameter of the average inner tube, which are cut into the proper lengths, glued together, and mounted with valves.

Although various grades of tires are made, the company will feature the National Standards, a tire that was only recently perfected after considerable experimentation by the local laboratories.

*(Butler Eagle,* April 18, 1927)

### Corona Tire Will Move Sales Room

The sales room of the Corona Cord Tire Company which has been located at 127 East Cunningham Street will be moved to 110 East Diamond Street beginning August 1, it was announced by H. H. Callahan, sales manager for that company today.

The new location will give a suitable outlet for the company's business and a service station will be constructed at the rear of the location, at which place all the work which had formerly been done on Cunningham Street will be performed. Work on remodeling the building began today and the showroom will be ready for occupancy by the first of next week.

*(Butler Eagle,* July 27, 1927)

### Construction Of Plant Will Begin In Near Future
### Principal Product of New Organization Will Be Retreaded Tires
### Corona Core Tire Expects Busy Year
### Intend To Exceed Last Year's Production of 209,000 Tires And 184,000 Tubes

Ground Will Be Broken within the next several days for a new rubber plant in East Butler, to be known as the Stetson Rubber Company. It will be a $25,000 organization incorporated under the laws of the state of Pennsylvania.

Organization of the new company is headed by H. B. Callahan and stockholders will be practically the same as those interested in the Corona Cord Tire Company, with the addition of a few individuals in East Butler. The new plant when finished will consist of three units each measuring 40 by 100, one-story-mill type construction and will be located on land adjacent to the East Butler B. & O. siding.

The charter calls for the manufacture of practically all kinds of rubber goods, yet the principal product will be retreaded tires. With the introduction of balloon tires, it has been found that due to certain conditions, tread wear is very rapid. The carcass of the tire may be good as new, but with the tread worn away it is useless unless retreaded. Retreading of tires is almost as old as the industry but in the past has been carried on in very small repair shops with equipment having a capacity of only two or three tires per day. The labor cost of operating such equipment makes the process of doubtful economy. It is the intention of the new firm to equip the plant for a capacity of over 200 retreaded tires per day as the processes and system to be used are along the same lines as used when building the tire new. The new plant will employ twenty-five men and will be a nice addition to the group of successful industries already located in East Butler.

Operations at the Corona Cord Tire will be resumed next Monday after a ten-day shutdown for necessary repairs. Prospects for a busy year are good, according to Mr. Callahan, who also believes Butler will have a splendid business year.

The Corona concern last year manufactured 209,000 tires and 184,000 tubes. When the plant resumes operations Monday 180 men will be on the payroll. This number will be gradually increased. The average number of men employed for six months' summer average last year was 250 men.

(*Butler Eagle*, Mar. 9, 1928)

### Property Of Corona Tire To Be Sold

Marking the passing of an East Butler industry, a public sale of all the physical property of the Corona Cord Tire Company will be held at the company's property in that place June 12, beginning at 9 a.m. The following property will go under the hammer: office furniture and fixtures, garage and service station equipment, machine shop equipment and tools, power house equipment, electric equipment, pipe and pipe fittings, and miscellaneous articles. [The East Butler tire company was another casualty of the Great Depression.]

(*Butler Citizen*, June 4, 1930)

## Hilliard Canning Company

Some Butler residents remember stories which their parents or grandparents told about a canning factory in Butler. A canning factory did open here in 1912. The *Butler Citizen* in its April 23, 1912 issue reported that the C. M. Hilliard Company, with assets of $50,000, had acquired a location for a building and a shipping facility and expected to hire several hundred people. The company leased the Muntz garage building on South Main Street and equipped it with a first-class canning plant. A large amount of tomatoes, corn, and fruits were packed in 1912 but the plant never approached capacity production. The fledgling canning company purchased all the local tomatoes which were available and Butler County farmers were encouraged to raise more. The company itself planted a large number of acres of tomatoes on a farm near Butler. Unfortunately the C. M. Hilliard Canning Company of Butler declared involuntary bankruptcy in December of 1913. The general manager gave the reasons as a failure to procure sufficient tomatoes and a lack of sufficient working capital. Ironically, one of Hilliard's reasons for choosing Butler in the first place was his belief that the county was situated in the heart of the best fruit and vegetable growing land in western Pennsylvania.

### CANNING FACTORY MAY BE ADDED TO BUTLER CONCERNS
#### Chamber of Commerce Has Offer from National Concern

The chamber of commerce was asked by a member of the National Canner's Assocation to secure a sufficient acreage of tomatoes (500 acres asked for) to make it worthwhile locating here and as Butler is an ideal location for a cannery, it is hoped we will be able to secure the necessary acreage within the next ten days.

The company agrees to furnish the seed, lend assistance in growing crops, contract to pay $8 per ton for the crop delivered to the factory in Butler. We all know, tomatoes will grow as well in this locality as any place in the United States, and the average crop report for the United States is six tons to the acre and as there are farms where tomatoes have grown on the same ground year after year without much fertilizer added and have commenced to run down so they do not produce more than three tons to the acre. It is easy to be seen that we can increase the yields from six to twenty to the acre. It would be safe to guarantee $50 to $75 per acre with no more expense than a crop of corn and not half as hard on the land and as the company will buy all kinds of fruit and vegetables, it is easy to be seen what a plant of this kind will mean to Butler.

It will mean $25,000 to $50,000 for the farmers and Butler. It will benefit every businessman in town and during the busy season will employ over 100 people and will pay for help from $40,000 to $60,000.

If there is any kind of business that will benefit more people in Butler County, we would like to know what it is. We earnestly solicit your support and would kindly ask all growers who will promise to grow tomatoes, to write to chamber of commerce, Butler, Pa., stating number of acres you will grow, if everything is satisfactory to you.
(copied from *Butler Citizen* dated Jan. 23, 1912 by Dave and Audrey Craig)

### CANNING FACTORY WOULD BE BENEFIT TO MANY GROWERS

The canning factory proposition for Butler is not dead by any means and we wish to have the farmers who have not given us an estimate of acres which they will grow to communicate with us at once if they want a cannery located in Butler. A cannery without stuff to can is a poor proposition, so if the farmers of this community do not show interest enough to raise the stuff to can, we will not get a cannery.

Our informant who is looking after this proposition finds that the average price for tomatoes paid by the canneries of the country is $9 per ton and the Butler cannery is willing to pay as much as they pay in other places. The following letter from a representative of the canning factory is self-explanatory. Would be pleased to have any farmer interested in this proposition to communicate with the Butler Chamber of Commerce at once. The cannery is a profitable market for fruit and vegetables, better by far than sending the produce to a commission man to sell for whatever he can get for your goods. With a cannery you know that if you agree to plant and tend a number of acres of tomatoes, that you have a ready market for all you can raise, which in this locality will be above the average and it will be easy to figure counting 2,178 plants to the acre set 5 by 5 feet and only one peck to a plant and we all know tomatoes will do better than that here, for it is not uncommon to get as much as a bushel to a plant where they get special care, but for a safe estimate,

134

2,178, one peck each, would be 544 1/2 bushels at 27c, $147 per acre and no more trouble than a crop of corn and not nearly so hard on the ground.

There have already been a number of acres signed up and it is expected that the necessary acreage will be secured within a few days and we have the assurance from the canning company that the plant will be located in Butler and we would appreciate your support by letting us know soon as possible how many acres you will grow.

After making a careful investigation, the canning company has learned that some of the canners are paying $9 per ton and they agree to pay the same, the highest average price paid in the country. Besides, tomatoes, it is learned that there will be packed all kinds of fruit and vegetables and will make a ready market for all kinds of fruit thus, heretofore has been allowed to go to waste for lack of a market.

It is not necessary to tell what can be done and what benefits a canning factory will be to Butler and surrounding county that is easily figured. It you will give it a second thought if there is anything you do not understand do not hesitate to write for further particulars. Show you are interested by writing to the chamber of commerce.
(copied from The *Butler Citizen* dated Feb. 16, 1912 by Dave and Audrey Craig)

## WORK SOON TO BEGIN ON CANNING PLANT

C. M. Hilliard, who has charge of the canning factory that is to be located here, announced Saturday that negotiations were closed for the Breaden and McCoy property at the corner of Main and Quarry Streets for the site of the factory.

It is expected that the factory will be in operation by June 1, and will employ fifty to sixty people when in full operation. The building to be erected will be three stories high, and work will be commenced about March first.

Before entering into the contract with the local people to start the factory, a canvas of the farmers in the Butler district was made and enough contracts secured to guarantee the success of the enterprise.

The principal thing canned will be tomatoes, though, and other vegetable products will be utilized.
(copied from The *Butler Citizen* dated Feb.21, 1912 by Dave and Audrey Craig)

## CANNERY WILL BECOME VALUABLE PLANT FOR BUTLER

The charter has been received for the C. M. Hilliard Company, with C. M. Hilliard, M. G. Bishop, Dr. Guy A. Brandberg and others named as incorporators. Mr. Hilliard, who for the past six years has been manager for the People's Ice Company will now devote all his time to the canning business, beginning today, and the success he has had in the management of the ice business in a manner satisfactory to all concerned. Mr. Hilliard has been following the canning business very closely for the past 15 years; has been attending the meetings of the National Canners' Assocation, of which he is a member and in which he has a host of friends, all of whom will lend their assistance at any time required, thus helping to assure success.

We understand the canning company will put up a line of goods similar to the famous concerns in Pittsburgh and it would look as though in a short time it will be possible to get all canned food from the Butler cannery. The factory will be located on site purchased, corner of Main and Quarry Streets, will be brick, two stories and basement and will have a frontage on Main Street of 100 feet and will be built along the Bessemer 100 feet and will have about 23,000 square feet floor space of reinforced concrete. The equipment will be the latest improved machinery and when completed will be one of the finest plants of its kind in the United States and will be a business Butler can be proud of.

It is hoped the farmers will see the benefit to be derived from a plant of this kind and will give it their full support by growing the necessary fruit and vegetables to keep the plant running. If you cannot see your way clear to grow five acres make it two; even half an acre will help some and after the first year you will grow all that is asked for.

The canning company agrees to furnish the seed free and if you will write to or call the C. M. Hilliard Company at the People's Ice Company, Butler, Pa., stating you are interested they will be glad to take up the matter with you promptly and will deliver the seed so you can get the plants started early thus assuring a full crop and a paying one as well.
(copied from the *Butler Citizen* dated March 1, 1912 by Dave and Audrey Craig)

## CONSTRUCTION OF CANNING FACTORY WILL BEGIN SOON
### Farmers Near Butler Urged To Grow Tomatoes On Large Scale

Construction on the canning conpany which was recently organized in Butler due to the efforts of C. M. Hilliard and the chamber of commerce, will be commenced within a very few days. City Engineer Carson, assited by G. W. Pillow were yesterday surveying the lot which was chosen for the site at South Main and Quarry Streets. Architech O. C. Johnson is now completing the plans, and it is expected that ground will be broken within the next few days.

From that time, construction will be pushed as rapidly as possible in order that the plant may be in full operation by June 1. The confidence that the backers of this company have in Butler is readily seen when it is known that the entire amount of acreage that is desired has not been subscribed. These men feel so sure that through the efforts of the chamber of commerce they will be able to secure enough farmers who will guarantee to grow certain amount of tomatoes that they are going ahead with their plans to seem as if the entire capacity of the plant was already provided

for. It is the earnest wish of the chamber of commerce that farmers who have not already signified their intention of growing fruits and vegetables especially tomatoes, communicate with the secretary at once in order that the backers of this enterprise may be informed as to just what to expect. If the farmers cannot grow an acre or two let each lend a hand and grow as much as he can. As soon as it is definitely known how many acres will be grown the C. M. Hilliard Company will provide seeds free of charge to those who propose bringing their product to the cannery. This method of distribution of seeds assures a uniform growth of tomatoes that are all especially adapted to canning purposes.
(copied from the *Butler Citizen* dated March 9, 1912 by Dave and Audrey Craig)

## PROMINENT BUSINESSMEN ARE INTERESTED IN CANNING PLANT

After several months of active work, during which time the efficiency of the canning plant located on Main Street, between the Bessemer and B. & O. railroad tracks, has been absolutely proven. C. M. Hilliard has succeeded in satisfying a number of the leading citizens of Butler that, with proper financial backing, this enterprise will soon grow to such proportions as will net those becoming interested in large returns.

During the past week by request, a number of gentlemen visited the factory and made a thorough investigation as to the equipment, etc., the result being that twelve representative businessmen of Butler have become personally interested to the extent of becoming stockholders, and arranging to finance the company with sufficient capital to make the business a success, providing, however that an additional five thousand dollars worth of the treasury stock shall be subscribed for by the people of Butler. Mr. Hilliard, the manager of the company spent 19 years on the farm and for the past 15 years has been making a study of the canning business by attending the national canners conventions each year, of which assocation he is a member, in addition to which the information gleaned through the trade journals, together with personal visits to a number of factories has practicularly suited him for this work. The superintendent processor in charge of the factory has had 15 years experience and thoughly understands the packing of high grade goods for which the market is unlimited.

The plant can be operated during the entire year and with the exception of the beans, all of the raw materials will be furnished by the farmers in this section of the country. This means an unlimited market for their various products, thus giving them the opportunity of using their entire acreage, without any element of risk in disposing of their material. Such assisstance rendered the farmer will enable him to increase the value of his land at least 100 percent within the next few years, and will also be an incentive for the improvement of much farm land now being idle.

During the next three months, berries, peaches, plums, rheubarb, etc. will be prepared for the market and the following two months, September and October, will see the factory being operated to its full capacity of 20,000 cans of tomatoes per day, while the remaining two months of the year will be devoted to the preparation of apples, cabbage, etc.

With the present capacity of the factory, the production of 150 acres of tomatoes can be utilized. This should mean an average return of one hundred dollars per acre to the farmer.

Considering the earning capacity of the plant and the number of people it will benefit, this enterprise is not equalled in Butler, therefore those desiring to secure a portion of the treasury stock which is now being offered for sale, this being limited to $5,000, should call upon or communicate with the manager of the company at once. People's phone1294, Bell phone 466.
(copied from the *Butler Citizen* dated Feb. 8, 1912 by Dave and Audrey Craig)

## THE C. M. HILLIARD COMPANY BUTLER, PA.
### GUY A. BRANDBERG, PRES. M.S. BISHOP, VICE PRES. C.M. HILLIARD, SEC. & TREAS.

The C. M. Hilliard Co. is a duly chartered company authorized by laws of the state of Delaware to conduct all business pertaining to the canning industry. It is organized by Butler men who have at heart the welfare of the community and whose desire is to bring before the people of Butler, a business which will reward the stockholders and be a lasting benefit to the farmers and the businessmen of the town and all property holders. Below we propose to set forth a few established facts concerning the industry.

First: Butler County is situated in the heart of the best fruit and vegetable growing land in western Pennsylvania. All kinds of choice fruit such as strawberries, apples, peaches, raspberries, currants, cherries and pears are easily cultivated and yield prolifically, under care and with little attention. Many vegetables suitable for canning purposes are grown at present under discouraging marketing conditions. Tomatoes, corn, stringbeans, and peas flourish and afford a good yield and with suitable market bring large returns.

Second: The canning industry is an established industry in this section of the state. The H. J. Hienz Co. of Pittsburgh has made a world wide reputation from Pennsylvania grown and canned articles, and throughout the eastern part of the state are to be found many prosperous establishments. Indiana, a state much of which lies north of our own section is noted for its canneries and vegetable growing and government statistics show that the soil and altitude of Butler make it an ideal place for extensive cultivation.

Third: The C. M. Hilliard Co. is organized upon a conservative basis the object of growing and canning fruits and vegetables. The capital stock of the company is fifty thousand dollars. The stock is divided into five thousand shares with a par value of ten dollars each, stocks to be non-assessable. The business of the company is to be transacted through a medium of a board of directors which is elected by direct vote of the stockholders at regular stated elections. These directors shall choose from time to time such officers as the business may demand.

Fourth: The C. M. Hilliard Co. has secured the best location with regard to shipping facilities, accessibility for growers and patrons, possible to be secured. Plans and specifications have been prepared and are open for inspection, for a building with approximately 3500 square feet of floor space. This building to be a four-story building consisting of 3500 feet of floor space. We court an investigation as to character and standing; we desire your co-operation, both as investors and friendly supporters.

For further information, address the C. M. Hilliard Company, Butler, Pa.

Or call at office, 501 South Main St. Peo. phone 1294, res. 1136

## OFFICERS CHOSEN BY CANNING COMPANY

The annual meeting of the C. M. Hilliard Canning company was held last night at which a board of directors was elected for the ensuing year. Reports of the business since the factory started were read and the stockholders decided to put the concern on a good financial business for the next season.

The directors elected are; Porter Scott, C. E. Detter, M. G. Bishop, C. M. Hilliard and Ethel LeVier. The board organized by electing Porter Scott, president; M. G. Bishop, vice president; and C. M. Hilliard, secretary and treasurer.

The company shipped a car load of tomatoes to Chicago yesterday, and is now starting to can apples, and sauerkraut. The machinery has been received for taking care of the cabbage and from 800 to 1,000 heads an hour can be utilized. Pork and beans and maple sugar will be among the products of the factory this winter and it is expected to get enough raw material to keep the factory running all winter.

(copied from the *Butler Citizen* dated October 23, 1912 by Dave and Audrey Craig)

## HILLIARD CANNING COMPANY IS MAKING PROGRESS

Farmers in the Butler district will find something to their interest by inspecting the factory of the C. M. Hilliard Canning Company of Butler. This concern has been in operation a month and is already doing a nice business in the canning line.

Fifteen people are employed in the factory, while the concern has a capacity to employ fifty people and turn out 20,000 cans a day, if it could get enough raw material to keep it going full time. At present the factory is running on tomatoes and apples. The tomato crop has been somewhat of a disappointment on account of the weather, but with good weather the next two weeks the pack will prove satisfactory, though not up to the expectation in size. Most tomatoes received are from Zelienople, Harmony and Saxonburg, outside of the company's own farm of 30 acres near town. From 50 to 100 bushels are received daily from the farmers. The farmers are paid at the rate of $9 a ton for the tomatoes and as an acre will produce from six to 20 tons, varing with the season and the condition of the soil, there is a good profit in the business for the farmer.

The canning company is making a speciality on apples this season and has already packed over 2,000 bushels. It is expected that the factory will be run on apples, apple butter, apple jelly and sauerkraut after the tomato season is over. The company has secured the entire crop of the H. E. Taylor orchard near Chicora and is purchasing fruit wherever it is to be had in the county. The apple crop will keep the factory going until February, when another line of work will be taken up. Canned pork and beans is a commodity that has a large sale and the managers expect to keep the factory running on the line of goods until the fruit season opens in the summer.

The manager of the factory Mr. Detter has had considerable experience in the canning and packing business in Ohio and western states. He is much pleased with the outlook of Butler. The factory here is one of the most complete in the country and has a capacity that will be able to take care of the raw material for several years to come, or until the fruit and vegetables growers of the county get educated up to producing goods for the factory. Under favorable conditions and the proper encouragement the factory will be running its full capacity next year and continuously. The company expects to increase its own acreage next season and promises have been received from farmers in the Butler district of increased acreage. The factory will be of immense advantage to fruit growers as it is in shape to take the entire yield of an orchard and work it up into marketable goods, canning the best quality of apples and using the culls for apple butter and apple jelly.

## CANNING COMPANY CLOSES ITS DOORS

Announcements were sent out Saturday by the officals of the C.M. Hilliard Canning Company of Butler that the concern had failed and had gone into voluntary bankruptcy. A statement of liabilities and the assets of the company was not given in the letters sent to the creditors and others interested.

The Hilliard Canning Company was organized in 1912 and capitalized at $50,000. It is understood that only $8,500 of stock was issued and most of this amount was held by Butler people. The company leased the Muntz garage building on South Main Street and equipped it with a first-class canning plant. A large pack of tomatoes, corn and fruits was put up in 1912 and this season efforts were made to secure a pack of tomatoes that would run the plant to its capacity. The company planted a large acreage of tomatoes on a farm near Butler and bought the crops of all the farmers that raised tomatoes but was unable to get a supply sufficient to make the plant a success.

C.M. Hilliard, who is the general manager of the company and the organizer of the company, stated that the cause of this failure was due to a failure of the tomato crop the last season and to lack of sufficient working capital. Mr. Hilliard stated last night that he would undertake a reorganization of the company after the present difficulties were straightened out and either start anew in Butler or move the plant to a new location where conditions are more favorable in the way of securing capital as well as a large acreage of tomatoes and other vegetables that can be utilized by a canning plant.

(copied from articles from the *Butler Citizen* 1912 and 1913 by David and Audrey Craig)

## DEVELOPMENT OF NEWSPAPER
## BUSINESS IN BUTLER COUNTY

It is a long cry from a four page weekly distributed intermittently to a modern eight page daily laid at the door of the subscriber in the city before breakfast and on the dinner table of the country subscriber on the same day of issue. Journalism had its inception in western Pennsylvania, July 22, 1786 when John Scull issued the first number of the *Pittsburgh Gazette* in Pittsburgh. Butler County had not then been organized and there were no white settlers within its borders.

For more than two decades the *Gazette* was the official organ of the district. The paper had a few subscribers in Butler County. These were supplied by the mail carrier who rode horse back from Pittsburgh to Erie and carried all the mail in his pockets or in a sack and made distribution at various log cabins, hollow trees and other convenient depositories along the route. If a subscriber missed his *Gazette* one week, it was considered no great hardship, and he waited patiently until the return of the carrier, which might be ten days or two weeks, depending on the condition of the roads and the weather. It was not considered a great affliction by the settler either if he had to walk five or six miles to the post office for his paper, which he did at least once a month unless he had business that required his attention at the office at more frequent intervals.

### A PRECARIOUS BUSINESS

Journalism in the early days of the county was a precarious way of earning a living and a thorny path to public favor. The men who entered the profession did so for the love of it and a strange adherence to principals of party and they usually increased the individually of the journals they published.

The pioneer paper of Butler County was the *Palladium and Republican Star* which was established in March 1818 by John Galbraith. Previous to this time the official printing of the county as well as all of the job and book printing was done in Pittsburgh. The editor of the *Palladium* afterwards turned his attention to the law and when he died in 1860 he was president judge of Erie County.

There is no official record of where this pioneer printing plant in Butler was located. Presumably it was in one or more of the log buildings that decorated Diamond square in the vicinity of the court house.

Old files show that the editor of the *Palladium* and his successors as well as the competitors in the business encountered serious difficulties in issuing their papers regularly. These difficulties were sometimes financial, at other times inability to get white paper delivered in time accounted for missing an issue for which apologies were made to the subscribers.

### A LINE OF INHERITANCE

The *Daily Citizen* is the legitimate descendant of all the Federal, Whig, American and Republican papers published in Butler prior to 1870.

The politics of the *Palladium* was Whig. In 1820 the name of the paper was changed to *The Centinel*. In 1824 the ownership changed and the paper was issued as *The Sentinel* by William Stewart and Joseph Buffington. The latter gave up newspaper work for law and became president judge of Armstrong County. The policy of the paper was anti-Jackson.

In 1830 George Smith, a prominent attorney was associated with Parker Purviance in the publishing of *The Sentinel*, and was a dominant factor in its policy through what is known as the "Know Nothing" period of the county's history.

In the decade or so previous to the Civil War the original plant established the *Whig*, under Captain William B. Hazlett, and *The American* under William B. Lemmon, the latter being combined with the *Whig* later under the title of *The Star Spangled Banner*.

### THE DAILY CITIZEN

The *Daily Citizen* as it is known today was established by the late John H. Negley from the wreck of two of its predecessors, *The American Citizen* and the *Butler County Press*. In November 1872 John H. Negley and his son William C. Negley became sole owners and editors. The name then changed to *The Butler Citizen*.

There have been few changes to ownership since William C. Negley succeeded his father as editor and owner in 1884 and in 1908, the plant, subscription list and good will was sold to A. M. Christley and I. E. Christley. The latter organized the Citizen Printing Company, of which A. M. Christley is president, N. C. McCollough, Secretary and I. E. Christley, treasurer.

The Citizen Printing Company established the daily and suspended the weekly in May 1909. The wisdom of the course of the owners in establishing a morning daily that covers the news of the county as well as giving the best of the general news to the readers has been fully established. The *Daily Citizen* has long ceased to be an experiment and has become an established institution, covering field exclusively its own.

**A MODERN PLANT**

A comparison of the pioneer plant with the modern equipment of the daily newspaper is an interesting study. The outfit of the first newspaper office in Butler was brought from Pittsburgh the winter of 1818, either on a sled or a wagon drawn by a team of oxen.

The outfit consisted of a "Washington" hand press, capable of printing a four column page a little more than half the size of the page of the *Daily Citizen* of today. A few fonts of type not exceeding two or three hundred pounds completed the outfit. All of the white paper and other supplies for the office were hauled by wagon from Pittsburgh.

The first home of the *Butler Citizen* was in the Reiber building on East Jefferson Street. From there it was moved to the old Negley building on West Diamond Street. The next move was to the *Eagle* building on Main Street.

In 1900 the plant was moved to the present location on South McKean Street, where it occupies the first floor and basement of the three-story, brick building with the largest newspaper and job printing equipment in Butler. In its early history, when in the office on West Diamond Street, the *Citizen* was the first local paper to install a cylinder printing press in the town and use steam power to operate its plant.

When the daily was established and the plant moved into the new building on South McKean Street, the old system of hand setting type was discarded, and modern machinery was installed.

The newspaper is now equipped with a modern high-speed Duplex printing press, capable of turning out ten pages. The special news features of the *Citizen* commend it to its readers. These are timely and prepared by the best talent obtainable. Its policies commend it to the favorable consideration of the best home in the county. Its editorials on local, social, civic and religious topics meet the approval of the best element of our citizenship and are widely quoted by contemporary journals.

**THE JOB PRINTING DEPARTMENT**

The history of the job printing, ruling and book-binding business in Butler is contemporary with the growth of the newspaper business. In the early days in the special ruling and larger contracts for blank ledgers, special ruling and catalog work was all done in Pittsburgh. In the last two decades surrounding cities bid for the work. It is only within recent years that the town can boast of an up-to-date printing establishment capable of handling any kind of job and book printing and contracts of any size. The job printing department of the Citizen Printing Company is the largest and best equipped in the county and is capable of turning out the highest grade of work.

It is equipped with a large Optimus high-speed press, a Colt Army press, two Gordon platen presses, power paper cutter, book folder, ruling machine, bind and punching machines, capable of turning out high-grade work in the speediest manner possible. All of the power machines in the department are operated with electric motors.

This department has turned out many large contracts since its organization that could not be attempted by any other plant in the town. At present it has advance orders that will keep it running its full capacity for several months.

**PHENOMENAL GROWTH**

The Citizen Printing Company takes pride in the growth of its business. In a few years it has become the leading newspaper of the city, as well as the leading job printing plant. It employs 30 people the year round, all skilled labor, and its annual pay roll is a very substantial item in this business of the community. Satisfied customers are the best evidence of the material success of any financial or industrial institution and the Citizen Printing Company can boast of more of these than any of its competitors. Its patrons and the public generally are always welcome visitors and are invited to inspect the plant and its work

(The last known address for this company was 309-311 South McKean Street.)

**FIFTY-FIVE YEARS OF PROGRESS**

**The Butler Citizen Only Morning Daily in Butler Co., Celebrates Its 55th Birthday**

**by Installing New Newspaper Printing Outfit**

From equipment valued at a few hundred dollars to a printing plant valued at between $50,000 and $60,000 and from a yearly business which could be counted in the hundreds of dollars to one aggregating many thousands, is the story of the evolution of the *Butler Daily Citizen* from the time of its beginning eight years ago to the present date. No other Butler newspaper plant has experienced such a rapid growth as the only morning sheet in this thriving community. It has grown rapidly year by year until it is now considered one of the leading morning papers in this section of the country, and indications at the present time are that within a few years the *Citizen* will lead all other competitors in this field.

Synonymous with this rapid increase in business and in popularity, a change has been necessitated in the newspaper printing plant. The old duplex-flatbed press which has served for the past eight years is being discarded and a new modern up-to-date printing plant installed in its place. This outfit got under way this week and readers, advertisers and all interested in the paper will be better and more expeditiously taken care of than ever before. The new press is one of the latest and most modern to be found on the market. It was manufactured by the R. Hoe Printing Press Company of New York City and will print from eight to 16 pages, turning out several thousand every hour. The press has been installed together with the stereotyping and is already in operation for the betterment of the appearance, and salability of the *Citizen*.

The constant increase in the business of newspaper and job department and bindery has necessitated an increase in floor space and that now occupied by the plant is many times larger than when the present company took charge of the building and the plant. The present crowded condition is evident to any visitor and will soon require further increase in the size of the *Citizen's* quarters.

At the present time the Citizen Printing Company is one of Butler's most prosperous concerns and at the same time boasts of the largest and most up-to-date printing plant in this part of the state. The present company, instituted and incorporated just a few weeks over eight years ago, numbers among its 73 stockholders many of Butler County's most successful business men.

Journalism had its inception in western Pennsylvania July 29, 1786, when John Scul founded the *old Pittsburgh Gazette*, which was the first newspaper west of the Allegheny mountains. Butler County had not then been organized and there were no settlers within its limits. North of Pittsburgh the first newspaper enterprise was *the Weekly Messenger* of Crawford County, published at Meadville in 1905, now published as a daily. The *Messenger* was followed by the *Mirror* published in Erie by George Wyeth, and in 1811 the *Western Press* was started at Mercer by Jacob Herrington. This paper probably had some circulation in the northern section of Butler County and after a checkered career of more than 100 years, is still one of the leading weekly papers of this part of the state.

The pioneer newspaper of Butler County was the *Palladium and Republican Star* and was first issued August 17, 1818. Previous to this time Butler County depended on Pittsburgh for enlightenment, current events and political information, and that the legal printing was all done in Pittsburgh. Job printing for the county offices and the merchants went to Pittsburgh.

The readers of the Pittsburgh papers were satisfied with the *Gazette*, which they received once a week, often by a postman who rode horseback or walked carrying the small amount distributed to the settlements between Butler and Pittsburgh. As likely as not, the mailbox was a hollow tree, log or cranny in a rock beside the road.

Journalism in the early days was a precarious way of making a living and a thorny path to public favor. The men who engaged in the business did so from the love of it and a strong adherence to principles for party, and they usually impressed their individuality on the papers they published. Thus it happened that the patrons of the old times weeklies subscribed to the paper because it was Uncle Jake Ziegler's paper, Tom Robinson's paper or Clark Wilson's paper, and they wanted to know what these particular editors had to say of the political question of the day, whether they belonged to the same party or not.

Some of these pioneer editors and those who came fifty years later are worthy of mention in this article because of the fact that they were Butler County men and after leaving the then quaint little village in the hills for the larger spheres of endeavor, made state and national reputations as jurists and statesmen. One of these was John Galbreath, born in Center Township, pioneer editor of the county, who at the time of his death in 1860 was president judge of the courts of Erie County, and a leader in political affairs. Another was James W. Thompson, born in Middlesex Township, who learned the printer's trade and was the first printer's devil employed in the office of the *Palladium and Republic Star* in 1818, afterwards became Chief Justice of the Supreme Court of the state and one of the most distinguished jurists the state ever had.

Joseph Buffington, father of the present Judge Joseph Buffington, of the United States district court, was associated with William Stewart in the publication of *The Sentinel* in 1824. Later he moved to Kittanning, became a prominent lawyer and filled the position of judge in that district for many years.

One of the most distinguished men of the early days was Capt. Jacob Ziegler, known from coast to coast as "Uncle Jake" Ziegler, who was for more than 30 years connected with the *Butler Herald* as printer's devil, editor and manager, with the exception of a few years when he was engaged in public duties in Harrisburg and Washington. He

140

studied law but gave up active practices for journalism. He served in the legislature several terms from this county and wrote a book on parliamentary law, upon which he was a recognized authority. It may not be generally known that Mr. Ziegler was the originator of the Credit Mobeller, known in financial history, and that from his fertile brain sprang the plan to raise funds for the construction of the Union Pacific Railroad. So wide was Mr. Ziegler's reputation for some years that he was once mentioned by the *New York Herald* among the prospective candidates for president. The *Herald* dates back to 1842 as the Democratic organ of the county, and preceding that date was known as the *Repository*.

A hundred years of journalism in Butler County marks a long period in the development of newspaper making. The initial plant, brought here by John Galbreath in 1818 consisted of a Franklin hand press and a few fonts of type, assorted sizes, with which he laboriously turned out a small column folio. The white paper question was a serious one at that time as it is now, various issues of the *Palladium and Republican Star* as well as the *Sentinel* and old *Repository* mentioned the fact that the editor was obliged to omit an issue occasionally because of inability to get white paper from Pittsburgh.

The news printed in the paper of that day was all clipped from Pittsburgh, Philadelphia and Boston papers and related to politics, national and state and European war news, all of it from two to three months old. Of local and county news there was none, except the notice of a death or some political meeting.

The advertising was as quaint as the paper itself. The merchants were apparently satisfied with spring and fall announcements. Some of them crowded a curious condensation of information into a small space. In one instance a merchant in the western end of the county advertised in a four-inch-single-column space that he had secured for the spring trade a "fine assortment of calicoes, domestics, prints, groceries, hardware, gun powder and whiskey." The editor was hard up for cash in the early days as may be judged from the appeals made in the old *Repository* and *Sentinel* and offers to take in trade, bees wax, tallow and bacon on subscription accounts.

Whig and Republican papers had a hard time of it in the early days of the county. The *Palladium and Republican Star* was federal. After two years Moses and John Sullivan became the owners and editors and the name was changed in 1920 to the *Butler Centinel*. William Stewart and Joseph Buffington bought the plant in the fall of 1824, and the name was again changed to the *Sentinel*. Mr. Buffington retired in 1826 and Mr. Stewart declared a strong predeliction for the Democratic party. For the four succeeding years the Democrats of the county had it their own way so far as controlling the two newspapers, the *Sentinel and The Repository* was concerned.

In May 1830 Parker Purviance and George W. Smith, then a leading attorney of the county, bought the *Sentinel* and Mr. Purviance, as managing editor, cleaned house of all democratic tendencies. From that time on the paper was run as pro-Whig. The successor to the *Sentinel* was the *Butler County Whig* published in 1846 by William Hazlett. In 1855 Mr. Hazlett sold the *Whig* to William B. Lemon and the paper eventually lost its identity in the Butler *American*. The new editor of the *Whig* appeared to have different political opinions from Mr. Hazlett, for he had no sooner purchased the paper in April, ___up to 1865, when the plant was purchased by Thomas Robinson and moved to the office of the *American Citizen*. Two years after he sold the *American*, Mr. Hazlett established the *Butler County* and became owner and editor of the paper in 1866, when he purchased the interest of Thomas Robinson and continued to publish until 1869. April 7, 1869 John H. Negley purchased the *American Citizen* from Major Anderson and the following month purchased the *Butler County Press* from William Hazlett. He then combined the two into *The Butler Citizen*. The Butler Citizen is the lined *Republican Star*, and all of descendents of the *Palladium* and the *Federal, Whig, American* and Republican papers published in the county prior to 1870 including the *Centinel* of 1829, the *Sentinel* of later years, the *Butler County Whig*, the *Butler County American*, the *Star Spangled Banner*, the *American Citizen* and the *Butler County Press*. The original owner and editor of the *Butler Citizen* was a man of strong character. Appointed state's attorney for the county by a Democratic governor, he became a Republican when the party was formed in the early 50's and was the first district attorney of the county elected under the constitution. Later he was elected to the legislature several times. How Mr. Negley bluffed the vice president of the Pennsylvania Railroad and secured a signed agreement that the company would build the branch from Freeport to Butler within a certain time is a bit of history that the vice president did not preserve in the files of his office.

Mr. Negley was a member of the legislature at the close of the war and his colleague from Butler County was William Hazlett, also a newspaperman. The Pennsylvania Railroad Company wanted a piece of legislation passed that concerned Philadelphia City, but did not effect the western counties. The railroad official needed votes from the "county cousins" to pass his bill. Butler had been trying to get a railroad for years but the Pennsylvania officials turned a deaf ear and would not make the promise. Mr. Negley saw a chance to get something out of the hard-headed-railroad lobbyist and he went to the vice president with a proposition. The proposition was simple. The Butler members were in position to defeat the railroad bill. If the railroad company would sign an agreement to build the line to Butler in five years, the Butler members would help his bill. Otherwise the bill would be defeated. The railroad manager turned, ranted and swore and made all kinds of verbal promises. It was either a signed agreement or have his bill defeated and the manager finally affixed his name to the agreement.

W. Negley took his son, William C. Negley into partnership with him in 1872 and in 1888 the latter became sole owner. He continued to publish the paper until November 1, 1908, when the plant, subscription list and good will of the *Citizen* were sold to A. M. Christley and L. E. Christley and W. C. Negley retired from the business.

The present officers of the company are A. M. Christley, president and editor-in-chief; N. C. McCollough, secretary, L. E. Christley, treasurer. The above named, together with T. M. Baker, and Hunter Coulter, compose the board of directors. Walter E. Baker general foreman mechanical department; Herman Elliott, managing editor; James A. McKee, city editor; Charles R. Morrison, assistant manager of the advertising department.

When the Citizen Printing Company bought out the previous owners, the business was merely in its infancy. Since the present company has had charge it has made big yearly increases in the volume of business taken care of, until at the present time in the neighborhood of 40 employees are busily engaged day and night in turning out job printing and the daily newspaper.

(copied from the *Butler Citizen* dated June 22, 1917 by Dave and Audrey Craig)

## THE SHORT LINE THAT MAKES TRAVEL BETWEEN
## PITTSBURGH AND BUTLER SAFE, SPEEDY AND PLEASANT

The building of the Pittsburgh and Butler Short Line not only lessened the distance between Pittsburgh and Butler, but opened up forty miles of the richest country on the American continent. This county was traversed more than a century ago by the Butler Plank road, but it was not until the Pittsburgh and Butler passed through it that it attained its present prosperous conditions.

Its numerous truck farms are now able to ship their products to Pittsburgh and Butler with promptness and those nearby markets have given an impetus to the industry. No more desirable sites for the location of light manufacturing can be found anywhere than are available along the route of the Pittsburgh and Butler Railway, while the frequency with which passenger cars run between Pittsburgh and Butler has made this territory a mecca for the over crowded population of the "smoky city" and picturesque towns dot the distance along the route between the two cities. The most important of these are Etna, Undercliff, Glenshaw, Allison Park, Valencia, Mars, Renfrew, Odell and Lyndora.

No finer district could be desired than the beautiful country opened up by the Pittsburgh and Butler line which going to the north is free of the smoke and cinders produced by the belching chimneys of the numerous factories that girdle Pittsburgh.

There are numerous available town sites along the Pittsburgh and Butler railway that are equally as desirable as those that have already been selected for suburban towns and the opportunities for development are unsurpassed.

About twenty miles from Pittsburgh, the oil country is reached and from this point on into Butler, the oil development is almost continuous. Last year witnessed a phenomenal exhibition of this industry. Several gas and oil wells were struck and a number of big gas producers. The two biggest producing 300,000,000 and 23,000,000 cubic feet respectively. Oil and gas were first discovered in Butler County in 1859, since then it has been the center of the western Pennsylvania oil and gas industry.

The headquarters of the Pittsburgh and Butler Railroad is at Butler, but its extensive car barns, repair shops, dispatcher headquarters and other operating departments are at Mars.

The company has recently expended over $100,000 in making its equipment the most modern in existence and is now operated by 1200 volt dc equipment. The speed, safety, comfort and frequency of its service makes it by far the best between Pittsburgh and Butler for both passengers and freight. On account of its increased freight traffic the company was recently obliged to buy a new 54-foot freight car which enables it to handle freight with increased promptness.

The rigidity of the steam railroad makes it incapable of competing with the flexibility of the trolley. The latter can be easily adapted to make prevailing local conditions, quickly overcomes disturbing natural forces and is capable of maintaining a continuous service under any and all conditions with the least effort and at the lowest price. The big double truck, high speed Pullmans with smoking compartments, lavatories, plush upholstered seats and all the comforts and conveniences of expensive railroad trains, make travel over this road a delightful pastime that is less expensive than that by steam railroads, takes no longer time and requires less wait on account of operating with much greater frequency. This road not only operates the handsomest and most complete cars built, but has the most up-to-date road bed it is possible to construct.

It uses the standard rails adopted by the American Society of Civil Engineers, ties of the best white oak, ballasted with stone and track work built by experienced steam railroad mechanics after the grading had been solidified by time, weather and the continual operation of construction trains. The possibilities of accident have been eliminated where possible; all bridges are of steel and concrete and the high road bed is above the reach of floods.

The power-house is at Renfrew, where enough water can be obtained to supply power for all time. It is five and one-half miles from Butler and is connected with the Baltimore & Ohio and the Bessemer & Lake Erie railroads, whereby fuel can be obtained at the lowest cost.

The overhead construction is known as the catenary system. The electrical system is of the latest type, 200 volt direct current. It insures safety and reliability by preventing breakdowns or accidents. It is the finest work of its kind in existence.

A complete steam railroad train order system is employed in the operating system. The cars are all controlled and are in charge of the most trustworthy and experienced men it is possible to employ. Stations with comfortable seats are at all regular stops and every convenience that experience could suggest or capital command for ensuring the comfort and safety of passengers and the efficiency of the service has been adopted.

The officers of the company are: George Heard, president, Chas. C. Tennis, vice president, and R. E. Sprenkic, secretary and treasurer.

## T. W. PHILLIPS GAS AND OIL
### ITS FOUNDER A PIONEER IN THE OIL AND NATURAL
### GAS AND OIL PRODUCERS IN WESTERN PENNSYLVANIA

Oil was discovered on Oil Creek in 1859 and the oil and gas fields were soon after developed from the north through the entire length of Butler County in which thousands of wells have been drilled making it for a long time the center of the oil industry. Shortly after the discovery of oil, Hon. Thomas W. Phillips (1835-1912), the founder of the T.W. Phillips Gas and Oil company, went to Oil Creek, became fascinated with the oil industry and in 1861 with his brothers, became active in the oil business, in which business he remained until his death. The longest term of active service that the oil industry up to that time had seen.

The firm of Phillips Brothers, composed of Isaac, John, Charles and Thomas was formed and it was on the flood tide of fortune when the Jay Cook panic occurred (1873-74) simultaneously with the discovery of great deposits of oil and the unprecedented drop in its price from $4.55 to 65 cents per barrel which involved the firm in debts totaling more than half a million dollars, a large sum in those days. To the paying off of that debt, which with interest finally amounted to $800,000, Thomas W. Phillips devoted the next fourteen years of his life and before the debt was paid his eldest brother, Isaac had died and the firm of Phillips Brothers had been disolved.

The oil industry in Pennsylvania probably benefited more by the presence of Thomas W. Phillips than from that of any other one man. He was a leader in every movement for its protection and improvement. In 1866 he was directly responsible for the removal of the internal revenue tax on oil of $1.00 a barrel and he was at the head of the committee formed in 1879 to oppose a tax on oil well rigs of $1,000 or the alternative tax of 10 cents per barrel proposed in the Pennsylvania Legislature. In 1888, when a move was made to restrict production he refused to curtail his own operation until satisfactory provision had been made to compensate and protect the laborers engaged in the industry who would be thrown out of employment by the "shut-in" and his production at that time was so large that he dominated the situation.

After the debts incurred by Phillips Brothers were all paid he devoted the major portion of his time and energy to work connected with religious, educational and political questions rather than to business, so that his activities and attainments might be placed under the heads of religion, politics and business and he considered his accomplishments in the political field secondary to those in the religious field and his business attainments of less importance than his political attainments. In 1890 he was nominated for congress, but owing to the presence of two Republican candidates in the field he was not elected. In 1892 he was elected by a very substantial plurality and in 1894 re-elected by a plurality of nearly 12,000, larger than that ever before received by any candidate in the 25th district. He introduced into the 53rd congress an important bill authorizing the appointment of a non-partisan commission to collate information and to consider and recommend legislation to meet the problems presented by labor, agriculture and capital. This bill did not become a law during his term in congress through the failure of President Cleveland to sign the bill which was passed just before congress expired. He had the bill introduced in a latter congress and largely through his influence had it passed and was appointed a member of the commission by President McKinley.

In 1896 the Phillips Gas company, a Pennsylvania corporation, was formed, the name of which in 1904 was changed to T. W. Phillips Gas & Oil company. Its capitalization increased and in addition to taking over the holdings of T. W. Phillips Sons company, a co-partnership, it purchased all the stock of and merged with the Home Natural Gas Company of Butler, the Enterprise National Gas Company of Freeport and the Mahoning and Citizens Natural Gas companies of Punxsutawney.

The T. W. Phillips Gas & Oil Company, now being conducted by T. W. Phillips, Jr., and B. D. Phillips, is one of the largest gas companies in western Pennsylvania. The company now owns more than 800 gas wells, 180 oil wells and 900 miles of gas lines, employs on an average 500 men and has more than 150,000 acres under lease for oil and gas purposes in the counties of Allegheny, Armstrong, Butler, Clarion, Indiana, Jefferson and Westmoreland. During the last five years it has delivered on the average more than 6,900,000,000 cubic feet of gas per year. During the year 1913, its deliveries were 7,219,000,000 cubic feet of which amount 6,024,000,000 or 84%, was used by manufacturers or other large consumers and 1,194,00,000 or 16% was used for domestic purposes. Last year this company delivered to its customers in Butler and vicinity almost 2,000,000,000 cubic feet of gas produced largely outside of Butler County, which, however, was only 26 percent of its total deliveries. Gas is piped to Butler through five main lines; one 12 inch, one 10 inch, one 8 inch and two 6 inch.

In order to maintain this supply of gas during these years the company has found it necessary to drill more than 100 wells per year for gas and in addition a considerable number of wells were drilled for oil. Last year the total number of wells drilled for gas was 168, many of which were more than 3,000 feet deep, the total number of feet drilled being approximately 300,000, or over 56 miles.

The officers of the company calculate that in order to maintain a sufficient supply of gas for its growing trade it will within a very few years be required to drill from 150 to 200 wells per year. At present the company is supplying 12,700 domestic consumers and during the last five years the average gain per year in the number of domestic consumers has been 761, the gain for last year being 659.

While Butler County has been a prolific producer of oil and gas, yet unfortunately few of the large producers located their principal offices in Butler. It has meant much to Butler that since 1883 Thomas W. Phillips and his companies have maintained their principal offices here, necessitating the locating in Butler of large numbers of superintendents, foremen and employees and also their machine and repair shop. At present the T. W. Phillips Gas and Oil Company has branch offices in Punxsutawney, Kittaning, Freeport, Tarentum and New Kensington.

It is hardly necessary to speak of the advantages of natural gas as compared with other kinds of fuel to citizens of Butler where it has been in use in ever increasing quantities since it was first introduced in the early 80's and where it is used for domestic purposes almost to the entire exclusion of coal for both heating and cooking purposes.

At the present time much of the gas used in Butler is piped long distances and the expense incurred in transportation including returns on the necessary and ever growing investment has steadily increased during the last decade, yet the price charged for natural gas has advanced less that the price of almost any other commodity in general use and natural gas is today, all things considered, one of the very cheapest commodities for sale.

Although natural gas might be considered a luxury yet its price and dependability are such that none are barred from its use in this, one of the cheapest coal markets of the world. During the year 1913 the average domestic consumer in Butler supplied by the Phillips company used a trifle less than 115,000 cubic feet, the net price of which was $28.75. No doubt if there were a way of dividing the community into two classes, equal in number, based on their yearly incomes, we would find that the poorer class would on the average use about $24.00 worth of gas and not having in most instances their houses equipped with coal furnaces or electric light installed, this expenditure of $24.00 per year (less than 7 cents per day) being only 3 percent of a yearly income of $800 would represent on the average practically their total expenditure for heating, lighting and cooking. Certainly the present high cost of living cannot be charged to the gas companies, but rather the high prices of other commodities force an undue economy in the use of gas, the efficacy of natural gas being so great that a very little can be made to go a long way. The additional comfort and satisfaction that could be secured from the careful use of 150,000 or 200,000 cubic feet per year instead of 100,000 cubic feet would in many cases more than justify the additional expenditures involved.

Natural gas is a highly combustible gas made by a secret process of nature. It is the most perfect fuel known and has never been equaled by any man-made product. The smoke nuisance in the average city is not caused alone by the factory but in a very large measure by the total smoke from the homes and therefore, natural gas adds much to the beauty and cleanliness of a city as well as to its prosperity and the convenience, comfort and happiness of its citizens. The public does not always fully appreciate:

1. That natural gas is a service as well as a commodity. A commodity may be manufactured at a uniform rate of production and then placed in storage until it can be sold to advantage; while on the other hand a service must be available at the moment it is required and in the case of natural gas the service is paid for only when used, although the patron whether he uses much or little of the available service enjoys.

2. That the requirements of natural gas users vary so much between certain days of the year and certain hours of the day that the expense and investment involved in rendering the service demanded are enormous.

3. That a very large investment is necessary to transport gas from distant gas fields to the consumer's premises. The major part of which is under ground and therefore unappreciated.

4. That the depletion of all gas fields is very rapid and therefore the expense (not investment) in drilling any wells is large and continuous.

5. That the life of a gas plant is limited by the commercial life of the gas field. The depreciation of a gas field is very great because upon its inevitable dismantlement at no very great distant day its value will be small compared with the original investment. Gas fields or gas deposits are continually becoming exhausted which necessitate the taking up or the extension to more distant fields of lines that were laid to the exhausted fields.

6. That a large investment in nonproductive leased ground is necessary in order to maintain an adequate supply of gas for

future use.

7. That there is a large shrinkage in the volume of the gas produced due to leakage in transmitting gas from the well to the consumer.

8. That the fixed charges involved in domestic service during a large portion of the year are greater than the gross receipts from the domestic trade.

9. That the average price of artificial gas in the United States is over 85 cents per thousand cubic feet and that natural gas on a heating value basis, volume for volume, is worth 20 per cent more than artificial gas.

10. That the positive meters used for measuring gas for domestic purposes register correctly to within 1 or 2 per cent when they come from the manufacturer. That when through use or misuse they become inaccurate fully 90 per cent of the time they under register. That in case of under register the meter may register but a small part of the gas that passes through it, frequently registering no gas at such times when but a small amount of gas is being used. That in case of over registry, on account of the very nature of the mechanism of the meter, the amount in every case is very small. That, therefore, the losses to the company from inaccurate meters exceed the gains from the same source in a ratio of fully 100 to 1.

11. That the developed natural gas supplies of this country are capable of serving less that 8 per cent of this developed supply of natural gas is not readily available for domestic service due to the fact that many of the most prolific fields are located great distances from centers of population.

12. That a city is to be congratulated which is so fortunately located that nature and man make possible a good supply of gas for domestic purposes and that city is to be twice felicitated if gas can be had for industrial as well as for domestic purposes. Therefore, the T. W. Phillips Gas and Oil Company takes this occasion to congratulate and twice felicitate Butler and to express its most sincere wish that it will long continue to be favored with an abundance of nature's most wonderful and useful products.
(copied from the *Butler Citizen* dated July 11, 1914 by Dave and Audrey Craig)

## INDEPENDENT NATURAL GAS COMPANY OPERATES MORE THAN SIXTY GAS WELLS
### Distributes Gas all over Butler County for lighting, heating, cooking and power purposes

The Independent Natural Gas Company, whose main office is at 117 East Jefferson Street, operates

more than sixty gas wells and distributes gas all over the county. Its main honeycomb is in Butler and places within the reach of her citizens a convenient and economical method of lighting and heating their homes. Natural gas, while in every way as good as manufactured gas, costs less and is a very desirable fuel for lighting, heating, cooking and power purposes. The Butler County home that is not equipped for burning natural gas is being deprived of one of the greatest blessings that a residence in this part of the state confers. Burned with a Welsbach burner, natural gas gives a clear, steady light of great brilliancy that almost equals sunlight in brightness and white effects, and its cost is below that of kerosene per equal candle power, while for cooking and heating purposes there is no fuel that can compare with it. A cold room can be warmed in five minutes with a gas stove, while it would take almost an hour to do so with a coal stove, as the fire has to be built and given time to ignite before it throws out any heat.

For cooking purposes natural gas is unsurpassed and especially so in summer, as it dispenses with keeping a fire all night and yet in case of sudden sickness during the night can be instantly lighted for hot water, hot poultices or anything hot that may be needed. Gas stoves for cooking can be used year round. In summer they keep the kitchen cool and comfortable, while in winter they are appreciated for the quickness with which they enable the morning breakfast to be prepared. A match is struck, a valve is turned and the stove is ready for use; there is no chopping of wood and saturating it with kerosene to make it burn; no fetching of coal from the cellar; no dirt, soot, smoke or ashes, but if the wind is blowing in the wrong direction it does not refuse to burn, as is the case when a coal stove is used, and besides, the flame of a gas stove can be raised or lowered to as produce an intense or low heating.

For power purposes a gas stove is compact, clean and convenient and is in every way more desirable than a steam engine. Aside from supplying gas for households, office and store uses, the Independent Natural Gas Co. can supply it in all parts of the county for power purposes. It is an ideal source of power for industries of all kind, as it dispenses with the drayage, handling and storage of coal, as well as the dirt, waste, ashes, smoke, soot and cinders that result when coal is used.

The company has at its head a capable and efficient management that has spared no expense in providing every facility and convenience for ensuring a satisfactory service. Its affairs are closely identified with the development of the natural gas and oil interest upon which the prosperity of Butler and Butler County largely depends, and contributes toward the general welfare of the entire county.

The officers of the company are: Henry Reiber, president; Edward Reiber, secretary; George L. Reiber, treasurer. The territory over which the company's mains extend is one of the largest in the gas fields. The company will be pleased to hear from parties who are using the system and wish it extended, as well, as from those residing near its mains who are not using the gas but wish it installed. It keeps in its employ a large force of skilled gas fitters and gives prompt attention to complaints and endeavors to accommodate its customers in every way it possibly can, that is consistent with the best interests of the people of the entire county. It is a company operated with Butler County money and by Butler County businessmen, and conducts its business in an enterprising and progressive manner. It places at the service of its customers all the privileges and advantages that are derived from ample capital and unsurpassed natural facilities, and aims to give them a service that is unsurpassed in efficiency and economy.

The company is made up of public-spirited enterprising businessmen of Butler County, who are identified with some of the most important industries in this section of the state and who conduct their affairs in a capable and efficient manner and have spared no expense in providing every convenience and facility for ensuring a satisfactory service.
(copied from the *Butler Citizen* dated July 11, 1914 by Dave and Audrey Craig)

## EVANS MFG. CO.
### One of Butler's Successful Industries

In 1893 Evan Evans who had been engaged in the manufacture of brass fittings and valves at Chicora removed his shop to Center Avenue, Butler and commenced the manufacture of oil well supplies. Later he invented clutch pulleys and gas engines and in 1896 the present plant at McKean and Wayne Streets was erected to meet the growing needs of the business.

In 1898, Mr. Evans went into partnership with C. A. Templeton under the firm name of Evans-Templeton. Two years later the Evans Manufacturing Co. was organized. Mr. Evans died in 1906. In addition to a large and well-equipped machine shop, The Evans Manufacturing Co. has a metal foundry and makes castings of all kinds for the oil well trade and also builds gas and gasoline engines, clutch pulleys and a general line of oil well supplies. The company does business throughout the oil country and enjoys a reputation for the high grade quality of its products that places it at the head of manufacturers in its line.
(copied from the *Butler Citizen* dated July 11, 1915 by Dave And Audrey Craig)

## SUPERIOR ICE CREAM
## THE KIND MADE BY THOMPSON BROS.
### At Their New Factory

Some years ago Thompson Bros. commenced the manufacture of ice cream in a modest way and made it so well, that the demand for it soon outgrew their small factory with the result that the Thompson Bros. Ice Cream Co., was organized and its present fine factory at 400 West North Street erected and equipped in the most up-to-date manner. Two large modern brine freezers were installed and ice cream flavored with genuine-fruit flavors has since been made in sufficient quantities to meet all demands. The plant has a capacity of 1,000 gallons a day and Thompson's ice cream, sherberts, water ices and frozens custards are not made in a dark, damp cellar, but in a well-lighted, properly-ventilated and throughly equipped factory, provided with every convenience for ensuring the production of a high grade assortment of frozen dainties.

A service room has been provided at the factory for the purpose of permitting the public to become acquainted with the delicious quality of the frozen dainties made by the company. It is handsomely fitted up with marble-top tables, comfortable chairs and an elegant-soda fountain. Here ice creams, sherberts, sundaes, sodas, etc., are served, at all hours of the day and evening.

The company manufacturers it own ice obtaining its water from a drilled well on the premises. It also makes its own flavoring and keeps its fruits and raw cream in a storage room that is kept at a temperature of 20 degrees all through the year, while the hardening room in which the ice cream is placed as fast as made is kept at a temperature of 5 to 10 degrees. The huge mixer in which ingredients are mixed before being placed in the freezer holds 150 gallons.

The ice creams and other frozen dainties are made fresh daily and are served to customers as fast as two-auto-delivery wagons can deliver them. The factory is open for inspection at all hours and the company takes pride in having visitors inspect its throughly sanitary conditions. All containers are throughly scoured and sterilized before they are filled.

On the second floor of the factory, the company has installed a large-automatic-cone machine which does all the work of making the cone with the exception of mixing the batter. The company also makes a very superior quality of brick ice cream. The factory is operated by electricity on account of it being cleaner and more convenient than steam.

All departments of the business are supervised by Mr. Charles Thompson and Mr. Orville Thompson, both of whom are brimful of energy. The Thompson Bros. Ice Cream Co. has developed a large business which covers a wide territory. It is the largest producer of ice cream in the county and no better ice cream is made anywhere than is manufactured by it.
(copied from the *Butler Citizen* dated July 11, 1914 by Dave and Audrey Craig)

146

# J. T. & A. HAMILTON
## Manufacturers of Flint and Amber Glass
### Bottles of All Kinds

One of the successful industries of Butler and one that is contributing to her general prosperity in a very substantial way is that of J. T. & A. Hamilton manufacturers of all kind and sizes of flint and amber glass bottles. The firm operates two plants, one at Butler and another at Pittsburgh and their combined output is sold in all sections of the country.

An industry of the character is of great advantage to Butler as it brings considerable outside money to the city a large portion of which is paid to employees who circulate it among merchants. Both plants of the firm are throughly up-to-date in every respect and their output is unsurpassed in quality.

This business has been established in Butler for years and the firm enjoys a reputation with the trade that keeps their goods in constant demand. J. T. & A. Hamilton have at their command every facility for keeping their products up to the highest standard of merit and take pride in the fact that a great deal of their business comes from repeated orders. They personally supervise all departments of their factories and aim to give their customers a service that cannot be surpassed in any way and they are succeeding in doing so, the demand for their goods gives ample proof.

The firm makes bottles of all kinds, sizes and shapes for every purpose for which bottles are needed and are always pleased to hear from persons who have need of goods in their line.

(copied from the *Butler Citizen* dated July 11, 1914 by Dave and Audrey Craig)

## TWENTY-FIFTH ANNIVERSARY
### Of the Masseth Packer and Machine Works

This year the Masseth Packer and Machine Works round out their twenty-fifth year of existence. The business was established in 1889 B. Masseth, who owned patents for oil and gas well packers and other valuable inventions. He established a machine shop on Wayne Street with J. R. Sherman as partner, and later D. W. Black, an inventor and machinist, also became a partner. Shortly after Mr. Sherman retired the firm became Masseth & Black. In 1903 Mr. Masseth died and Mr. Hyle became owner of his interest. The business is now conducted as the Masseth Packer and Machine Works by J. N. Hyle and D. W. Black, who manufacture the Masseth patent self-supporting wall packers and all kinds of machinery for oil, gas and artesian wells, gas pumps, engines, etc.

The Masseth trade mark is an oblong square with the word "Masseth" in the center. This trade mark is a valuable one for the goods it represents and is known not only throughout this country, but in foreign ones also, and represents the highest achievement in the construction of the goods for which it stands. The works also manufactures gas pumping powers, gas pumps, sucker rod sockets, sand reels, fishing tools and oil, gas and artesian well supplies. Repair work is given prompt and careful attention. The works are located on Wayne street.

(copied from the *Butler Citizen* dated July 11, 1914 by Dave and Audrey Craig)

## CAST STONE BUILDING BLOCKS
### And Other Goods Made by the Butler Plaster and Cement Company

The Butler Plaster and Concrete Company, whose office is in the Reiber building have a large plant on Negley Avenue, for the manufacture of neat or sanded-hard-wall plaster, cement-building blocks, concrete-burial vaults, etc., and also handles Universal Portland cement, Sackett plaster board, wood and metal lath, Tiger finish, Alca lime, sand and gravel.

The company is one of the largest manufactures in the state of a strictly high grade quality of cast stone for building purposes. It is a reliable and economical stone that is adapted to every purpose for which stone is used and is rapidly taking the lead in the market. Cast stone makes a building that will stand for years without discoloration or disintegration like ordinary stone. Its handsome appearance, cheapness and durability make it an ideal stone for building purposes and it is very popular with contractors who have had experience with it. Houses built with it are sanitary and hygienic, warm in winter and cool in summer. Masons work more rapidly with cast stone than with ordinary stone, as there are no rough edges to be chipped and it does not have to be shaped in order to fit as is the case when ordinary stone is used.

The company is making a very attractive, soft-gray-trimming stone for sills, lintels, arches, base courses, sill courses, brackets, ornament, coping, caps, columns, cornices, steps, paving blocks, etc., also for churches, schools, public buildings, residences, factories and other purposes. It is always pleased to correspond with architects who wish stone made for any special purposes.

Cast stone is durable, efficient and economical, and buildings constructed with it always present an attractive appearance. Its light-grey color is pleasing and soothing to the eyes and cannot be surpassed by any tints or shades produced by the most expert painter.

Concrete cast stone is one of the most wonderful products of the age and is adapted to any climate, as neither heat nor cold, dry nor damp atmosphere affects it. It will outwear iron, steel, terra cotta, brick or lumber and its low price places it within the reach of everyone.

Everything that goes into a building is carried in stock by this company, including building tile of all kinds, and silos in tile, cement and wood.

The officers of the company are: J. F. Anderson, president: John Younkins, vice president, and F. C. Anderson, secretary, treasurer and general manager.

(copied from the *Butler Citizen* dated July 11, 1914 by Dave and Audrey Craig)

### The Butler Sheet Metal and Steel Welding Company

The Butler Sheet Metal and Steel Welding Co., whose plant is in the rear of the Guaranty Safe Deposit and Trust Co., is quite busy getting out several orders. The company welds cast iron, wrought iron, steel, brass, copper, and other metals, so neatly that it is impossible to see where the welding has been done and the article mended is much stronger at the place where the welding has been done than it is in any other part. The company does considerable work in the welding of broken automobile parts. It also manufacturers cornice, skylights, gutters, conductors, metal ceilings, warm air heaters, ventilators, blast pipe and does repair work. It uses tin with a genuine-charcoal- iron base guaranteed to last from 15 to 20 years. Mr. E. E. Coffman, the manager, is throughly experienced in all departments of the business and gives personal attention on the proper filling of all orders. The company guarantees all work it does and gives prompt attention to orders. Its plant is throughly equipped for ensuring high grade work in all departments.

(copied from the *Butler Citizen* dated July 11, 1914 by Dave and Audrey Craig)

### BALL STEAM AND GAS ENGINE
### BUILT BY THE BUTLER ENGINE AND FOUNDRY CO.

The Butler Engine and Foundry Co., whose plant is on Lookout Avenue, between the B. & O. and the B. & L. E. R. R., makes a specialty of building the famous Ball steam and gas engine for oil country purposes. These engines are the oldest and best in the oil country and have been in service for 35 years. Their efficiency and reliability has been fully proven and they are being shipped to all parts of the world. The Ball gas engines are of the most improved type and large numbers of them have been sold in the gas belt. They are simple, strong, economical and reliable and are always ready. The company also has a well-equipped foundry and makes machinery, casting of all kinds. Prompt attention is given to repair work and an old machine after it has been repaired at this plant will give as good service as a new one. The company has at its command every convenience and facility for ensuring high grade work. It has built up a large business by giving satisfaction to all who have dealings with it and is working as hard to maintain its reputation for doing good work as it did to earn it.

The officers of the Butler Engine and Foundry Co., are: Harry B. McKinney, president; and Mortimer M. McKinney, treasurer and manager.

(copied from the *Butler Citizen* dated July 11, 1914 by Dave and Audrey Craig)

### A MODEL LAUNDRY
### That is Noted for the High Grade Quality of its Work

The Butler Steam Laundry, which occupies a large, well-lighted and throughly ventilated building at 217 West Cunningham Street is noted for the high grade quality of work it turns out and one reason why it does better work than is done by the average laundry is due to the fact that its employees do not have to work in cramped quarters and a close atmosphere but in large, well-lighted and properly ventilated apartments, the floor space of which gives an abundance of room for doing the work without crowding. (photo on pg. 60, *Butler County, the Second Hundred Years*) The equipment is of the most up-to-date character and the employees are throughly competent. The proprietor, Mr. George Ketterer Jr., has spared no expense in providing his laundry with every convenience for ensuring a high grade quality of work and the fact that his enterprise is appreciated by the public is shown by the liberal patronage given his laundry.

Its collection and delivery wagons go to all parts of the city and housekeepers who wish to avoid the troubles of wash day have merely to telephone and a wagon will call for their work. There is nothing in the laundry line that cannot be done at the Butler Steam Laundry in the highest style of the art. In the rear of the laundry is another building devoted exclusively to the cleaning of garments by the French-dry-cleaning process. It is equipped with the most up-to-date machinery for the purpose and does exceptionally fine work in the renovation of the garments of men, women and children.

(copied from the *Butler Citizen* dated July 11, 1914 by Dave and Audrey Craig)

### Pure Milk Co. Explains the Reasons Why Superintendent Shanor Says Cheese Makers Are After Output Of Faithful Bossy Dealers Pay Higher Rate

The advance in the price of milk at the Pure Milk Company on Sunday, to take effect on September 1, was the cause of considerable discussion in the city yesterday. Most of the patrons of the company are, of course, inclined to the belief that the raise was not justified, but the officials of the concern contend that if the move had not been absolutely necessary that it would not have been made.

To the citizens yesterday John J. Shanor, general manager of the Pure Milk Company said: "I am a believer in keeping the prices of the necessaries of life as low as is possible and still enable the dealer to make a fair profit. We have followed this policy consistently and have met several raises in the price of the milk which we are compelled to buy to supply our customers without making a corresponding increase in the retail price. We held off as long as possible in announcing the advance, hoping that there would be a downward tendency in the wholesale market, but the hoped-for drop did not come, and in justice to ourselves we were compelled to increase the price of milk to our customers a cent a quart.

A large portion of the milk which comes to Butler is secured by us in Crawford County, where we buy from 400 different farmers and dairymen. This section is a cheese-making locality, and cheese has advanced 2 1/2 cents per pound wholesale during the past year. It requires a little over a gallon of milk to make a pound of cheese, and of course the cheese makers are paying more for their milk than they were when the prices were lower. The producers of milk will sell to the party paying the most for his product, whether it is for the making of cheese or what not, so it is up to us to pay the price for the milk we need or do without it.

Butter has also advanced materially during the past year, and the indications are that the high prices will remain on this product of the dairy, so that all around the price of milk had advanced. We are compelled to make the increase in price, else it would not have been done you can rest assured."

In the circular issued to its patrons the Pure Milk company makes the following quotations as the prices which will prevail after September 1st:

bottled milk, 8 cents per quart
bottled milk, 4 cents per pint
bottled cream, 32 cents per quart
bottled cream, 16 cents per pint
bottled cream, 8 cents per half pint
bottled xxx cream, 40 cents per quart
bottled xxx cream, 20 cents per pint
bottled xxx cream, 10 cents per half pint

The company explains the advance in the price of milk in the circular as follows:

"This advance of price that we are compelled to pay has been continual for a number of years past, and while we hoped that conditions would change so as to enable us to continue to supply our customers at present prices, the proportionate increase this year has been greater than heretofore. We were therefore compelled to either reduce the quality or increase the price."

"Our trade is the highest quality and our aim has always been to satisfy this demand. While we regret that conditions are such as to necessitate an increased price, we assure you that we will continue the high standard and the uniform quality of our goods at all times."

Other dealers in milk seen yesterday were noncommittal as to whether they would follow the Pure Milk Company in advancing the retail price of their product, but the indications are that they will fall in line, and the people of the city will be compelled to pay the difference in the price for the milk which they may require.

(copied from the *Butler Citizen* dated Aug. 24, 1909 by Dave and Audrey Craig)

### Steen Creamery Sold To Butler Pure Milk Company

Negotiations were completed yesterday by which the Butter Pure Milk Company absorbs the J. H. Steen Creamery. The transfer goes into effect at once, and today former milk customers of Mr. Steen are being supplied by the Butler Pure Milk Company.

The business formerly carried on by Mr. Steen was extensive, he having supplied dairy products to about 500 customers. The entire Steen business was taken over by the Butler company, including horses and equipment of the Steen Creamery.

The Butler Pure Milk Company is making extensive improvements to their plant on South McKean Street to enable them to handle the added business. Officers of the company have been removed to the second floor. The sterilizing plant is being enlarged and additional machinery for washing and sterilizing milk bottles is being installed. When present additions to the ice cream factory are completed, its capacity will be more than doubled.

With the additional business absorbed, the Butler Pure Milk Company will be supplying almost the entire city with dairy products, and when contemplated improvements are completed, the company will have one of the largest and best equipped plants in the state. The dairy is located at 417 South Main Street, Butler, Pa.

(copied from the *Butler Citizen* dated Dec. 21, 1909 by Dave and Audrey Craig)

### Condensed Milk Plant Completed

### Conneautville Creamery Was Built By Butler People

J. J. Shanor & Company of the Pure Milk Company have completed their large condensed milk plant at Conneautville and the plant was put into operation several days ago. The capacity of the factory is 20,000 pounds of condensed milk every ten hours.

The plant is one of the largest of its kind in the country and is thoroughly modern in every respect. The plant consists of two large buildings, a main building and a power house. The pan holds 10,000 pounds of milk and is about ten feet high. This equipment was furnished by C. T. and R. Rodgers Company of Detroit, Michigan.

Besides making condensed milk, the company sells cream, milk, and ice cream. It is exclusively wholesale and furnishes Erie, Franklin, Oil City and many other cities in the northern part of the state. Most of the condensed milk is shipped to Pittsburgh via the Pennsylvania Railroad. The plant was built and equipped by the Butler company consisting of Mr. Shanor and his sons, at a cost of more than $10,000. The condensed milk is only sold in ten gallon cans and is used mostly by ice cream dealers, hotels and bakers.

(copied from the *Butler Citizen* dated May 5, 1910 by Dave and Audrey Craig)

## A MODEL CREAMERY
### The Butler Pure Milk Co., Corner of McKean and Wayne Streets

The Butler Pure Milk Co. represents the most up-to-date idea in conducting a dairy business on a high plane, and its plant on the corner of McKean and Wayne Streets is an object lesson of the progress that has been made in an industry that is of vital importance to the public by whom its food products are consumed.

The company's plant is equipped with the best machinery and apparatus required in one of its character and its sanitary arrangements are perfect in every detail. The company also makes an exceptionally fine brand of rich-creamery butter which is served on the best appointed tables over a wide territory. It also manufacturers the celebrated Shanor's ice cream, which is unexcelled for its purity, smoothness and delicious flavor. It uses the choicest ingredients in making this ice cream, which is flavored with genuine-fruit flavors.

The company does both a wholesale and retail business and has developed a large business by supplying its trade with the highest grade of goods in its line. Its plant is a model one in every respect and no expense has been spared in its equipment.

The company has at its head gentlemen of ability and wide experience in its special line. The officers are: J.J. Shanor, president: D. A. Shanor, treasurer, and George Varum, secretary.

(copied from the *Butler Citizen* dated July 11, 1914 by Dave and Audrey Craig)

## New Owners Plan for Butler Concern
### Extensive Alterations In Local Plant Will Be Commenced At Once
### Business Taken Over formally this Morning
### New Modern Sanitary Machinery To Be Installed--Announce Larger Facilities

A consolidation of business interests was announced today by which the Butler Pure Milk Company is merged with the Reick-McJunkin Dairy Company of Pittsburgh. The new owners took over the business and property this morning.

Extensive alterations in the local plant will be commenced at once. Modern-sanitary machinery will be installed and as soon as it can be rushed to completion, Butler will have one of the most complete milk and ice cream in this section of the state according to an announcement by the owners.

**Large Concern**

The Rieck-McJunkin Dairy Company is one of the largest

and most active concerns operating in the dairy business. Its plant in Pittsburgh is nationally known both for the excellence of its operation and the constant high standard of product. At the same time by the establishment of a great system of county milk stations in the best dairying sections of Pennsylvania and Ohio. The company has built up for its customers a practically limitless supply of fresh, pure milk and cream.

The Pittsburgh concern has taken over the property of the Butler Pure Milk Company at Wayne and McKean Streets. A new delivery system for the city will be inaugurated immediately it was stated. Speaking of the consolidation, a Rieck-McJunkin Dairy official said, "We are planning to supply Butler with dairy products of the highest possible quality and we are in such a position that we can remodel and reorganize this local plant almost immediately." D. A.

Shanor, former manager, will continue to be in charge of the plant.
(copied from the *Butler Citizen* dated May 1, 1922 by Dave and Audrey Craig)

### Company To Hold Public Reception

### Rieck-McJunkin Dairy Company Invites All To Test Its Cream Products

Next Wednesday the Rieck-McJunkin Dairy Company will be open for inspection by the people of Butler and the surrounding district. It is one of the most complete milk and ice cream plants in the country. From 1:30 in the afternoon until 5 o'clock open house will be maintained and everybody in town is invited to come and see how ice cream is made on a large scale. Incidentally, the public will also be invited to sample the delicious product and an adequate supply will be ready for all comers. Incidentally, the new plant is unique in one feature, the fact that it has been built entirely, literally from the ground up, and yet has continued daily operation during the whole time of building.

The site at the corner of McKean and Wayne Streets, was originally occupied by a dairy plant and was purchased in the spring of 1922. Almost immediately construction was started and today not a single vestige of the old plant remains except the four standing walls. Every bit of machinery is spic and span new, every known sanitary device has been installed, every mechanical improvement that goes to make better ice cream is in place and the institution, as it stands, represents an outlay of about $500,000.

Butler now has one of the best dairy plants in the country, a plant designed to handle every phase of dairy manufacture, milk, cream, cottage cheese, butter and the best known products of them all, ice cream. When all departments are in full operation the capacity is 50,000 pounds or 6,000 gallons of milk every day. The entire city of Butler can be supplied with fresh butter, milk, and cream from this plant.

Perhaps the most interesting department in the new plant is the portion given over to the making of ice cream. Five giant, shining freezers are geared up to produce 360 gallons of America's favorite dessert every hour and it is easily possible in this department to produce in a given year as much as 500,000 gallons of ice cream. Great glass-lined tanks, sanitary to the very last minute, hold the mix until it is ready for freezing, and hardening rooms, capable of almost unlimited storage, receive the product from the freezers and maintain it at even temperatures until delivered to dealers. A complete ice plant, producing forty-five tons of crystal-clear ice every day, a condensing plant which will deliver 100 gallons of condensed milk every two hours are in operation.

Milk sold in quantity to bakers and confectioners, as well as a butter and cheese department with a capacity of 600 pounds of sweet-fresh butter each churning, are all part of this complete enterprise which is to be shown to Butler people when they come on Wednesday.

One important feature of Rieck-McJunkin operations in Butler is the fact that all the milk used in the operation of the plant is secured from farmers living within a few miles of the city. This gives the producer a wonderful, steady market for his product, encourages him to extend his operation and stock his farm with higher grade cattle. Butler now becomes a distributing center. In addition to supplying the city itself with milk and ice cream, large refrigerated trucks serve ice cream daily to neighboring towns like Zelienople, Harmony, Chicora, Grove City, Tarentum, Prospect and shipments are made to Punxsutawney, Dubois, Falls Creek, Clarion, Vandergrift and many other towns in this section of the state. An up-to-date repair garage, equipped to take care of all cars and trucks and a modern, sanitary stable is part of the equipment of the new plant.
(copied from the *Butler Citizen* dated May 12, 1924 by Dave and Audrey Craig)

### Public Inspects $600,000 Plant Of Big Milk Company

### Thousands Pass Through Departments Of Rieck-McJunkin Dairy Building

### 2,500 Gallons Of Milk Are Pasteurized Daily

### Concern Also makes Quantities of Ice Cream, Butter, Cheese and Ice

Thousands of persons, including what seemed to be all the kiddies of Butler, yesterday afternoon were guests of the Rieck-McJunkin company at the public inspection of their new dairy plant at McKean and Wayne Streets.

The public was shown the numerous processes through which the milk must pass from the time it leaves the farm until it is ready to be delivered to your doorstep in an absolutely pure and wholesome form.

Clyde Fowler, manager of the local plant, saw to it that everyone was cordially welcomed, saw everything and left the premises with an ice cream cone in one hand and a souvenir in the other. Mr. Fowler said the attendance and general interest shown in the workings of the plant exceeded his fondest expectations. Folks attending the Rieck-McJunkin opening who heretofore gave little thought to what is back of the routine job of picking up the milk from their doorstep each morning, now realize it is a great industry, requiring a great deal of planning, constant vigilance to keep the product pure and a large investment of capital.

**Plant is Model**

The plant is a model of cleanliness and sanitation. The workers are dressed in white aprons. Human hands never come in contact with the milk and cream as it passes through the many processes. New and expensive machinery does everything, even putting the caps on the filled-milk bottles and tying the string around a package of brick ice cream.

Having seen what lengths the company goes to insure a pure and healthful product, patrons of Rieck-McJunkin's know they are getting the best that human ingenuity and mechanical skill can produce.

The company makes milk and cream, condensed milk, ice cream, butter, cheese and ice. Two years ago they purchased the real estate and business of the Butler Pure Milk Company. Since that time they have been busy building additions and installing new and up-to-date machinery. Nothing of the original investment remains today except the four walls of the building that stood at the corner of McKean and Wayne Streets.

The plant today represents an investment of nearly $600,000. There are seventy-six men and women employed by the company, requiring a weekly payroll of about $3,000. Many Butler County farmers and those in surrounding counties sell their product to the Rieck company. Every day in the year 2,500 gallons of milk are bought from these farmers. The plant is equipped, however, to handle 6,000 gallons a day.

**Business Grows Rapidly**

Mr. Fowler told an *Eagle* reporter that the business of the company has gained amazingly during the past years and as an illustration cited the figures in the making of ice cream. "In 1922 was sold 79,000 gallons of ice cream and last year the amount leaped to 152,000 gallons." He said, "This year we expect to sell something like 250,000 gallons."

One of the most interesting parts of the three-story plant which visitors were shown yesterday are the vats and machinery where all the milk received from the farmers is pasteurized before it is cooled as it passes down through a series of pipes. All milk is kept at a temperature of 142 degrees for a period of at least thirty minutes as the first step on its way toward the public's doorstep. This insures the consumer that all bacteria has been killed.

In addition to the departments for the producing of milk and cream, ice cream, butter and cheese, there is a good sized ice plant, capable of producing more than enough for the company's needs. The rest is sold at wholesale. Every day forty-five tons are manufactured in blocks, each weighing 400 pounds.

A visit through the power rooms will show what an impressive array of machinery is necessary to keep such a plant in operation. Giant motors furnish the power to drive machinery and the means by which numerous pipes are kept frosted. Ice cream is frozen and rooms are kept at a temperature of below freezing throughout the year.

**Delivery System Extensive**

People who never realize what a task it is to get that milk delivered early and promptly get some inkling of the problem when they visit the garage, and stables. Large five-ton trucks are there to make large deliveries, while fifteen horses are used in the house-to-house deliveries in the city. Oddly enough in the center of the company's plant is to be found a giant hay mow, protected from the hazard of fire by solidly built brick walls.

One of the fifteen horses is a real veteran, having taken a milk route for twenty-six years. He knows the way better than the driver for he has been on the job longer. He never hesitates, nor has to be told. He knows to stop and when to start. This dobbin likes his work, apparently, for after all these years he is in prime condition and hasn't missed a day or taken a vacation.

This afternoon doctors, nurses and school teachers were the special guests of the company for an inspection of the plant they were interested in the fact that all milk is carefully analyzed by a chemist both before it is pasteurized and after it goes

through the various processes.

(copied from the *Butler Citizen* dated May 15, 1924 by Dave and Audrey Craig)

### A. H. COHN
#### Has Extensive Coal and Transfer Business

When hauling of any kind is to be done it will be to your interest to at once ring up A. H. Cohn, who recently moved from 130 Monroe to East Cunningham Street and notify him of your needs. Mr. Cohn operates one of the best transfer services in western Pennsylvania and his moving vans and teams are adequate in all demands that may be made on him. There is nothing too heavy and cumbersome or dainty and fragile that cannot be moved by him without sustaining the slightest injury. He employs careful and expert handlers and drivers who have had long experience in doing this kind of work and know how to do it properly. Household furniture, pianos, safes, or anything that needs moving is transferred from one place to another in safety. Mr. Cohn's equipment includes wagons for doing both light and heavy hauling, trucks, moving vans, riggers and everything needed in the business.

He also operates an extensive coal yard where all grades of coal are kept in stock and delivered to its customers properly screened. Mr. Cohn receives his coal direct from the mines and stores it in huge bins which are kept under cover, and coal delivered to customers is dry, clean, full weight and of the best quality. Telephone orders are promptly and carefully filled. Mr. Cohn enjoys a reputation for fair dealing that has largely contributed to his success and is working hard to maintain it.

(copied from the *Butler Citizen* dated July 11, 1914 by Dave and Audrey Craig)

### LARKIN & CO.
#### Manufacturers of Fishing and Drilling Tools

One of the oldest, largest and best known establishments in western Pennsylvania engaged in the manufacture of fishing and drilling tools, packing, sand pumps and a general line of oil and gas well supplies, is that of Larkin and Co., on Center Avenue. The business was established by Thomas and G. W. Hays in 1883. In 1887 Larkin, Warhus & Co., bought out the Hays Bros., and in 1890 Mr. Warhus sold his interest to Mr. Larkin, since which time the business has been conducted by Larkin & Co.

The firm does an extensive business throughout the oil country and their name has become a valuable trade mark for the sale of oil and gas well supplies of all kinds. Mr. Larkin, head of the firm is a veteran in the business and his thorough knowledge of conditions in the oil and gas territories enables him to keep the products of his firm up to a high grade of efficiency. The plant of the firm covers several acres and is

provided with every convenience and facility for enabling it to produce a strictly high grade quality of goods. Larkin & Co., take pride in the fact that their large trade has been built up through the thorough satisfaction their goods give to all who purchase them. The firm is working hard to maintain the reputation it has earned for making dependable and high quality goods.

(copied from the *Butler Citizen* dated July 11, 1914 by Dave and Audrey Craig)

### QUALITY ICE CREAM
#### The Kind Made At Limberg's New Ice Cream Factory

F. W. Limberg is producing a high grade quality of ice cream at his new factory at East Penn and Cliff Streets. It is unexcelled for its purity, smoothness and delicious flavor and is made with pure-country cream and genuine-fruit flavors. It is a rich, wholesome cream that appeals to the taste of all who eat it and is made under the most thorough sanitary conditions.

153

Mr. Limberg supplies freshly made ice cream to residences, hotels, drug stores, picnics, weddings, banquets and social occasions of all kinds and if you are not a patron of his, you are depriving yourself of a delicious treat. Orders sent in by Bell phone 342-J and Peoples phone 347-A are given prompt attention. Limberg's brick ice cream is also quite popular. Mr. Limberg personally supervises all departments of his factory which is thoroughly equipped and provided with every convenience for keeping its product up to a high standard of quality. Mr. Limberg invites trail orders from all who have not tasted his ice cream and feels confident that its delicious quality will ensure their future trade with him.

(copied from the *Butler Citizen* dated July 11, 1914 by Dave and Audrey Craig)

## STAUDACHER REFRIGERATORS
### Built in Butler and Sold Everywhere

The Staudacher Refrigerator which is built in Butler by its inventor, Joseph Staudacher, who patented it a few years ago, is a decided improvement on the old style refrigerator made as it develops more cold with less ice than any refrigerator made. The factory is on Etna Street near the B. & O. R. R. and each refrigerator is built under the personal supervision of Mr. Staudacher. This refrigerator is in service in a large number of business places and is giving thorough satisfaction.

It is built in sizes adapted to any business and also for family use. Mr. Staudacher also takes orders for cabinet work of all kinds and the facilities of his factory are adequate to all demands that may be made on it. He uses only the best quality of throughly seasoned lumber in the manufacture of his refrigerator and cabinet work. Staudacher refrigerators are in great demand and are sold as fast as built. Orders are filled direct from the factory and the price charged is always as low as good material and workmanship will permit.

(copied from the *Butler Citizen* dated July 11, 1914 by Dave and Audrey Craig)

## SILK MILL HAS BEEN REMOVED TO NEW JERSEY TOWN
### OWNER SAY PLANT HAS BEEN OPERATED IN THIS CITY AT LOSS

Butler lost one of its industrious plants this week when workmen dismantled the silk mill on First Street and shipped the machinery to Paterson, New Jersey. The silk mill had been operated by the Butler Silk Mill Company for the last 15 years and employed from 20 to 30 operators the greater part of the time.

According to the statement of members of the company, the factory had been operated at a loss the past few years and the owners decided to dismantle the plant and quit business. The plant had not been in operation since last September.

It is understood that the company will sell the building and plot of ground attached which fronts 100 feet on First Street and extends through to Second Street.

(copied from the *Butler Citizen* dated Feb. 18, 1916 by Dave and Audrey Craig)

## GOOD WORK
### CAN ONLY BE DONE WITH GOOD MATERIAL

The man who builds wisely, builds well. To build wisely the quality of the material used has to be considered. Shufflin and Green, whose office, warehouse and tipples are on Lookout Avenue, have earned the good will of contractors and builders who have had experience with them selling only the best quality of cement, lime, plaster, tile, sand, gravel, crushed slag and other builder's supplies. The firm is a recognized leader in its special field and handles only such goods as experience has taught them will prove satisfactory.

Shufflin and Green also receives coal direct from the mines. They handle several grades and can supply coal for either cooking, heating or power purposes. All coal is properly screened before delivery. They sell clean coal that burns freely and evenly and they give full weight. Prompt attention is given to orders sent in by either phone.

Shufflin and Green aim to make a friend of every customer, and people who buy goods of them can rely upon getting the best quality, full quantity and lowest price. The firm sells in both job and car load lots and makes prompt deliveries.

(copied from the *Butler Citizen* dated August 22, 1917 by Dave and Audrey Craig)

### Drop Forge Plant At Spang's Will Prove Big Asset
### Work On New Building Is Being Pushed To Completion, A Peace Time Industry

The drop forge plant of Spang and Company will in all probability, prove one of this city's greatest industrial-peace time institutions. The company is pushing the work on its forge plant which is located at the extreme end of the large institution, to speedy completion. The plant and part of the machinery and material have already been moved from the old location to the new building.

The new building will, when completed, be connected with the main building of the Spang and Company's plant, which is now engaged mostly in the making of shells. The latter work is proceeding on practically as large a scale as of the past several months. The large cores for the shells are being unloaded from freight cars onto the conveyors and started on their journey through the plant where their progress never permits the iron and steel to touch the ground until it is a perfect shell and is ready again to be loaded onto a car for shipment.

However, the work of arranging the drop forge plant is of unusual moment and importance at the present time. This plant operates in war or in peace and in the future will prove one of this city's most active industries. The new building is constructed of steel and concrete. Its height varies. The lower part of the roof starting at a height of about thirty feet and begins rising until it reaches approximately fifty or sixty feet. The floor space is several hundred feet. There are numerous windows and skylights making the structure a pleasant and inviting place to do one's work.

The writer observed one great detriment and deplorable condition. This was the matter of roadway. The street running parallel with the railroad being a sea of mud. Trucks, wagons and other vehicles found it rough going to navigate this street. Not a few were "stalled" in the attempt to get through with loaded trucks and forced to make detours.

That Spang and Company intends to progress in peace times as well as in war periods is plainly foreseen by a visit through this immense plant which employs hundreds of men and has a weekly payroll which totals many thousands of dollars.
(copied from the *Butler Citizen* dated Dec. 10, 1918 by Dave and Audrey Craig)

## GUARANTY SAFE DEPOSIT AND TRUST COMPANY
### Healthy Growth and Steady Progress as Indicted by its last Statement

Organized in 1903, the Guaranty Safe Deposit and Trust Company has during the eleven years of its existence, accomplished more than most institutions of its class succeed in accomplishing in a quarter of a century, and the reason why it has done so is due to the fact that it has at its head is capable and efficient management, who know how to safeguard its interest and at the same time develop its usefulness to the fullest extent.

The resources of its banking department amount to almost one and a half million dollars, and the business of its trust department to almost one and three-quarter million dollars. It has paid six per cent interest on its capital stock from the first year it commenced business, and has up to the present time accumulated a surplus and undivided profits. This is a showing that is highly gratifying not only to its management and stockholders, but to all who have dealings with it, as it is an indication of the capable manner in which its affairs are managed.

The company transacts a general banking business and affords to its customers all the privileges of an up-to-date banking institution. Interest is paid on time deposits, which can be withdrawn at any moment without notice, and working people who wish to invest their surplus earnings with safety and profit and at the same time have them available in case of need, will find it to their interest to open an account with the company.

The Guaranty Safe Deposit and Trust Company also acts in a fiduciary capacity and accepts trusts of every description. It acts as guardian trustee, administrator, executor or agent, manages properties in the interest of owners, minors, etc. and takes charge of wills, which are properly indexed, and upon death of the testator, are delivered to the attorney, executor or other person named by the testator. The company gives much more capable and economical service as the administrator or executor of an estate, owing to its experience in handling such matters, than it is possible for an inexperienced individual to give, and besides there is always the risk when an individual is named executor, that such individual may die before the estate is settled, a contingency that can never occur when a trust company is named as executor.

The Guaranty Safe Deposit and Trust Company places at the service of its customers the same experience and wisdom that has guided its own affairs and resulted in its success. Its management is made up of men who command the respect and confidence of the public. Its officers are: Hon. A. E. Reiber, president; W. G. Douthett, Frank Koch, vice presidents; T. M. Baker, treasurer; George C. Stewart, secretary. Its directors consist of the above named gentlemen and J. V. Ritts, Daniel Younkins, A.I. Reiber, William Watson, Geo. A. Schaffner, Z. P. Lauffer and W. H. Larkin.

The Guaranty Safe Deposit and Trust Company is a member of the Butler Clearing House Association and identifies itself with every project that has for its object the growth and prosperity of Butler.

## Zuver Studio
### Produces High-Grade Photography Of A Distinctive Quality

The Zuver Studio, 215 South Main Street, is noted for the high grade quality of the work it produces and is a recognized headquarters for everything in the line of photography, miniatures, antique frames and framing. It has a method of mounting and finishing photographs that results in getting the soft subdued effects that only skilled photographers know how to obtain.

"It requires a technical knowledge of both chemistry and art to produce photography that is above the ordinary," said Mr. Lewis W. Zuver to a representative of the *Butler Citizen* who recently visited his gallery, "and the reason why I take such excellent photographs is due to the fact that I not only possess this knowledge, but have the equipment for doing so."

## R. WILLETTS & SON
### Garage, Repair Shop, Accessories And Supplies

R. Willetts and Son whose garage in the rear of 315 and 343 North Main Street is complete in its appointments, provides everything needed by motorist, and is a headquarters for accessories, supplies, storage, overhauling, repairing, welding and free air. R. Willetts and Son maintain a staff of competent repair experts who are familiar with the mechanism of all makes of cars and who make repairs skillfully and quickly. Welding is done in aluminum, brass, bronze, cast-iron, copper, rolled steel, sections, steel plates, wrought iron, cast steel, forgings and malleable iron. Magnetos are delicate instruments which when broken can only be repaired by experienced experts. R. Willetts and Son make a speciality of doing such work. The Stromberg carburetor, the best, strongest and simplest made can also be obtained at Willetts. Car cylinders are cleaned by the best method, at one dollar a cylinder.

Mr. Rueben Willetts, the senior member of the firm of Willetts and Son is the pioneer automobile man of Butler County. He became identified with the industry when it was in its infancy and a Winton which was the first automobile handled by him, is now retained by its owner as a relic. Mr. Willetts was for some time in the employ of the Braden Gas Engine Co., and did most of their drawing and designing. He is also the inventor of the Bessemer Gas Engine, now being made at Grove City by the Bessemer Gas Engine Co., to whom he sold his invention.

His son Elwood Willetts is an expert mechanic who has been familiar with automobiles from his childhood days.

Both father and son give their personal attention to all details of the business and enjoy a reputation for fair dealing that has largely contributed to their success. They extend a cordial invitation to car owners to make Willetts' Garage their headquarters. Cars left in their care will be properly looked after and customers may always rely upon receiving a service that will be satisfactory in every way. R. Willetts and Son are well-known to motorists and the large quantity of repair work done in their shop shows that owners of cars recognize and appreciate the good work they do.

(copied fron the *Butler Citizen* dated July 11, 1914 by Dave and Audrey Craig)

## REFRESHING BEVERAGES
### Made by Chas. H. Kennedy 158 Race Street

For years Chas. H. Kennedy has made it his business to supply thirsty people with drinks that refresh but do not intoxicate. Cool, sparkling and delicious, his ginger ale, soda and mineral waters stand at the head of goods in their line. They are made in a factory, the sanitary arrangement of which is perfect in every detail, and water used in making comes from a 90-foot-deep artesian well on the premises. Kennedy's ginger ale not only pleases the taste and quenches the thirst, but tones and settles the stomach. It aids digestion and possesses old-tonic properties which make it a valuable hot weather drink. A case of it should be in every home.

Mr. Kennedy makes delivery by auto truck over a wide territory. People who drink his beverages not only find them wholesome and refreshing, but much purer than ordinary drinking water. All bottles are throughly scoured and sterilized before they are filled, and Mr. Kennedy's goods are of such a high-grade character that other bottlers will have to step lively to equal them.

(copied from the *Butler Citizen* dated July 11, 1914 by Dave and Audrey Craig)

## "THE BIG BANK"
### The Butler County National Bank

Throughout its history the Butler County National Bank has been closely identified with everything that has contributed to the growth and prosperity of Butler. It has encouraged home enterprise, fostered home industries and rendered substantial assistance in the development and improvement of the natural resources of the county, and because of its strength and the largeness of its operation, and its ability to finance big undertakings of a sound and legitimate character, has become known as "The Big Bank by the Court House."

The Butler County National Bank has a capital of $300,000, a surplus and profits of $569,547.61, and resources amounting to over three and one-half million dollars, while the wealth of its stockholders amounts to over $20,000,000.

It transacts a general banking business and the service it renders its customers extends to all parts of the world. It issues letters of credit and sells travelers checks that are payable in all parts of the world. It rents boxes in its safe deposit vaults, loans money on approved securities, and is at present receiving interest on two and one-third million dollars of their loans. It pays interest on time and saving deposits and up to its last statement the interest it had paid on said deposits amounted to $596,023.93.

The Butler County National Bank has as its head an able and efficient management who safeguard its interests in every possible way. Its officers and directors have been selected from prominent men conspicuous for their ability and wide financial experience, many of whom are identified with some of the largest industries in this section of the state. Its officers are: A. L. Reiber, president; J.V. Ritts and T. I. Mifflin, vice president; John G. McMarlin, cashier; Albert C. Krug. W. A. Ashbaugh, assistant cashiers; W. A. Ritts, teller; G. K. Haslet, L.C. Ritts, general bookkeepers; R. H. McClester, corresponding clerk; J. H. Stewart, Geo. G. Smith, J. H. Forcht, A. B. McClester, individual bookkeepers; S. R. Hill, proof clerk; W.P. McCandless, discount registrar; W. M. Kaufman, collector. It board of directors consists of Leslie Hazlett, W. H. Larkin, Alphonse Krause, A. I. Reiber, Harry Heasley, T. P. Mifflin, Joseph Hartman, Jr., Dr. J. J. Schultis, Dr. W. C. McCandless, A. E. Russell, Blair Hooks, M. Henshaw, E. M. Bredin, M. N. Heinzer, H. McSweeney, R. A. Marks and J. V. Ritts.

The bank at present occupies temporary quarters on South Main Street, opposite the bank's building, which is now being remodeled. The entire first floor of its building will henceforth be used for banking purposes and this ample floor space permits of every convenience, being provided both for the working force of the bank and its customers. These improvements will be completed about November 1, when the Butler County National Bank will have one of the most modern bank offices in the state.

The Butler County National Bank was established in 1890 and will soon be a quarter of a century old. It had been a success from the day it opened its doors, but especially so during recent years, in which time it has almost doubled it's business.

All business transacted with it is considered as being of a strictly confidential nature, and courtesy, promptness and accuracy are characteristics of all its transactions.

### Has A Record
### For High Class Plumbing and Heating Work

Mr. R. J. Kleemann, 491 W. Wayne Street, has made a record for the high grade plumbing and heating work he does. He insists the most up-to-date systems of steam, hot water and hot air heating and does plumbing work of all kinds in such a careful and conscientious way that it always proves satisfactory. He carries a full line of plumbing material and bath room fixtures and is prepared to give prompt attention to all orders.

(copied from the *Butler Citizen* dated July 11, 1914 by Dave and Audrey Craig)

### A Full Line Carried By The Auto Tire And Supply Company

The Auto Tire and Supply Co., whose store is on the Diamond Square near the Nixon Hotel is showing a large and attractive stock of automobile supplies of all kinds and there is nothing that may be needed by motorist that cannot be found at their store. The company handles the well-known Kelly Springfield and Diamond tires, which give service for every dollar paid for them and are quite popular with motorists. Messrs. H. C. Johnson & Son, proprietors of the business, aim to give their customers a service that will be satisfactory in every way and with this object in view make quality a first consideration and handle only such goods as are made by manufacturers who have a reputation to sustain. The company extends a cordial invitation to owners of cars to call at their store and inspect their large and attractive stock. The company keeps in close touch with producers of automobile goods and their store is a recognized headquarters for goods in its line. Their prices are always as low as quality will permit and goods ordered by mail or telephone are promptly shipped.
(copied from the *Butler Citizen* dated July 11, 1914 by Dave and Audrey Craig)

### Butler County Light Company
### Supplies Electricity For Any Purpose For Which It May Be Needed
### and Equip Buildings For Its Use

The Butler County Lighting Co., 101 East Diamond Square, supplys electricity and equips buildings for its use in every way. The company makes a specialty of wiring houses at a normal cost and handles electrical supplies of every description. All work is done under the supervision of an electrical engineer of experience and ability, who frequently suggests improvements on the plans of customers that not only result in the increased efficiency of the work, but in a lowering of its cost.

For lighting purposes electricity is the ideal light, as it is not only the most brilliant, but safest. When it is used the walls of the room are not defaced by having matches scraped on them and the risk of fire is less, as fires are frequently caused by lighted matches thrown on the floor. Moreover, electricity consumes no oxygen and for this reason is the best all night light as well as the best light for places in which there are larger gatherings, as it requires as much oxygen to feed any other light as it does to sustain a human being.

With electricity in the home, the washing, ironing, sewing, sweeping, cooking and other household work can be done by merely connecting the requisite appliance for doing either to an ordinary lamp socket. Electricity is also in great demand for decorative purposes and is extensively used in social functions of all kinds. Amusement houses recognize its value in drawing trade and make lavish use of it. Some merchants do also and reap a harvest of trade in consequence.

The merchant who clings to the old-fashioned idea of not using more light than is needed to see with is saving pennies and losing dollars by his lack of enterprise. People like to patronize well-lighted stores, and a store cannot be properly lighted without the use of electricity, which has the same effect on a display of goods that moonlight has on a pretty girl in the eyes of her lover. It heightens effects and imparts a charm that creates an irresistable desire to possess.

Every property owner is interested in the use of electricity, for the more of it used, the greater will be the volume of business transacted. The Madza lamp, the latest improved tungsten incandescent lamp gives a light almost equal to sunlight in brilliancy and white effects and does so at less than one half what it costs to produce a much inferior light with other lamps.

The factory that uses electricity for power, saves time, labor, trouble and expense. The electric motor is small, compact, quiet, safe and clean and power can be developed with it in an instant, whereas with a steam engine a fire has to be built and time allowed for the steam to generate.

The Butler County Light Co. does the wiring, installs the equipment and supplies the electricity and keeps in its employ a large force of electricians, so it can at all times give its customers a prompt and efficient service.
(copied from the *Butler Citizen* dated July 11, 1914 by Dave and Audrey Craig)

### INTERIOR DECORATION
### Artistic Work That Will Appeal To the Most Fastidious

Lovers of harmony in colors and the beautiful in art are delighted with the decorative work that is being done by the Butler Decorating Co. 236 North Main Street. Through the creative ingenuity and original conceptions of its management the humblest apartment can be converted into a bower of beauty. Expertness in the blending of color tints in striking contrast and bold relief makes it decorative work the acme of perfection. A full line of domestic and imported wall papers of the latest and most attractive designs together with paints, oils, varnishes, pictures, etc., are kept in stock and attention is given to picture and mirror framing.

The Butler Decorating Co., has done considerable work in and out of the city and enjoys a reputation for skill and efficiency in its particular line of business that is bringing it considerable trade. Home should be the most attractive place on earth for every member of the family and this company can do considerable toward making it so. Housekeepers who visit the salesroom of the Butler Decorating Co. will find much to interest them. The stock carried is one of the largest and most attractive for decorative purposes in the county and the company knows how to make the interior of a home as attractive and inviting as it is possible for human ingenuity to make it. Its business is conducted by Joseph B. Olmsted and his son Joseph G. Olmsted.
(copied from the *Butler Citizen* dated July 11, 1914 by Dave and Audrey Craig)

### Butler Buick Co.This Year The Most Prosperous One In Its History

It has always been claimed by the Buick Motor Co., of Flint, Mich., that when better cars are built, the Buick Co., would build them and its present 1914 models which can be seen at the garage and salesroom of the Butler Buick Co., Diamond Square, appear to sustain this claim.

Up to the present 32,000 Buick cars have been built and sold and this fact is convincing evidence of their popularity. More than 450 of these cars are at present in service in Butler County and thus far this season the Butler Buick Co., has already sold more than ninety, eighteen of which are of the six cylinder type. One never hears of a worn out or broken down Buick car and yet quite a large number were built and sold before any of its present competitors were in existence or their builders knew how to construct an automobile. The first Buick was built strong and durable as those made today. One reason why the Buick is such a general favorite in Butler County is due to the fact that it is an extra good car for the hilly roads that abound in Butler. An underpowered car with a load of five passengers is no more fit for traveling over the Pennsylvania hills than a team of ponies would be to haul their truck load any distance over them. The ponies might haul their load over a hill or two but would soon show the effects of the strain and become incapable of proceeding.

There are five distinct types of Buicks which sell at prices ranging from $950 to $1,985. The Buick Motor Co., has always enjoyed the distinction of being the foremost manufacturer of medium priced cars, and is working as hard today to maintain this reputation as it did to earn it and in spite of the most strenuous competition is meeting with the success that its energy and enterprise deserve.

(copied from the *Butler Citizen* dated July 11, 1914 by Dave and Audrey Craig)

## Huselton Automobile Company
### Handles The Famous Hudson Car And Everything In Automobile Supplies

The Huselton Automobile Company, whose office and showroom are at 180 North Main Street, has the agency for the famous Hudson Car, the easiest, light running vibrationless, high powered automobile built. This car is said to make a greater mileage per gallon of gasoline than any other car built. So gentle is its motion that the passengers reclining on its soft cushioned seats feel as though they are floating in the air as they see the trees and buildings glide swiftly by. The Hudson is made by skilled workmen from the best material, and is one of the strongest, handsomest and most dependable cars made.

Mr. E. C. Huselton commenced selling cars in 1908. He recently erected a large fireproof garage and repair shop at 111 and 115 West North street, just around the corner from his store, and it has become the home of many of the handsomest automobiles to be seen on the streets of Butler. Cars stored at this garage are properly cared for and kept in first class condition. The repair department is in charge of skilled mechanics and is provided with every convenience for enabling work to be done quickly and throughly.

Mr. Huselton also has a large paint shop at 515 North Washington Street, where cars are cleaned, painted and varnished. The stock of supplies carried is one of the largest and most complete to be found anywhere in the state and covers everything needed for motoring. Mr. Huselton's success is largely the result of his wide awake, progressive business methods and the fact that he makes quality a first consideration with all goods he handles.

(copied from the *Butler Citizen* dated July 11,1914 by Dave and Audrey Craig)

## Slentz Auto Company
### Has Moved Into The New Addition To Their Garage

The new fire-proof addition to the garage of the Slentz Auto Co., Cunningham and Cherry streets, give their garage a floor space of 5,000 square feet. The new addition is used exclusively for storage and exhibition purposes and the ample floor space permits the company to house quite a large number of automobiles without crowding.

The Slentz Auto Co. are agents for the "Maxwell 25," the car that beat sixteen foreign and nine domestic cars at the Indianapolis races. It has a record for speed, endurance and ease of management and is an excellent hill climber and well adapted to the hilly ground of Butler County. It sells for $750.00. The company will be pleased to demonstrate its efficiency to all prospective purchasers.

The Slentz Auto Co., make a specialty of overhauling and repairing automobiles in an expert manner and their repair shop, which adjoins their handsome new garage is throughly equipped for doing work of this character in a high grade manner. All three members of the company are expert motorists and mechanics, and understand the mechanisms of all makes of cars. They know how to do repair work in a way that will prove satisfactory and their charges are always reasonable.

The company consists of A. J. Thompson, George R. Slentz and R. I. Burtner, who take pride in the fact that a great deal of work they do comes through the recommendations of old customers. The Slentz Auto Co. can be consulted by People's phone 1461-X and Bell phone 84-J.

(copied from the *Butler Citizen* dated July 11, 1914 by Dave and Audrey Craig)

## Steady Growth Of the Farmers National Bank Of Butler

The Farmers National Bank, during the fourteen years of its existence, has experienced a steady and healthy growth and today with assets amounting to one million dollars, presents an aspect of strength and responsibility that commands the confidence of the public.

It carries the account of a large proportion of the corporations firms and individuals doing business in Butler, together with a large number of individual accounts, and places at the service of its customers all the conveniences and privileges of a strictly up-to-date banking institution.

In addition to transacting a general banking business, it also operates a savings department and pays interest on savings and time deposits, which are not tied up like other interest-bearing investments, but are subject to withdrawal at any time. The Farmers National Bank is a member of the Clearing House Association and the National Reserve Bank of the United States, and has at its command every convenience and facility for ensuring to its customers the most complete and efficient banking service it is possible to obtain anywhere.

Its management is made up of citizens who have made their own successes in life and who have demonstrated their ability to make a success of any undertaking in which they engage. Its officers are: John Younkins, president: A. H. Sarver, first vice president: E. W. Humphrey, second vice president: R. W. Dixon, cashier: A. R. Williams, assistant cashier: its directors are: John Younkins, B. F. Shannon, Daniel Younkins, Henry Miller, D. B. Campbell, E. Abrams, C. N. Boyd, Thomas Hays, A. H. Sarver, Levi M. Wise, E. W. Humphrey, R. W. Dixon and John R. Henninger.

The Farmers National Bank is identified with all that makes for the prosperity of Butler and Butler County, and uses its funds in assisting such industries as are large employers of labor whenever it can do so under safe banking methods. Its officers and directors have an abiding faith in the future of Butler and Butler County, and aim to give the public a banking service that is complete and efficient in all its departments, and that they are succeeding in doing so is shown by the general popularity and steady growth of the bank.

Preferring small profits with safety to large ones with risks, the Farmers National Bank transacts a safe business and its investments are all of a gilt edge character. Persons having dealings with the bank may rely upon their business being regarded in a confidential nature. Loans are made on approved securities and an effort is made to accommodate customers in every possible way.

The Farmers National Bank invites the accounts of both business concerns and individuals, and is always pleased to open accounts in both its checking and savings department. The home of the bank is 242 South Main Street.
(copied from the *Butler Citizen* dated July 11, 1914 by Dave and Audrey Craig)

### Home Photography
### The Latest Fads in Photographing Family Groups

The latest fad in photography is the taking of family groups in familiar home surroundings. Children are taken playing with their toys and grown people seated in their favorite chairs at their homes. This gives a naturalness to the photographs that is impossible to obtain in the average studio. The pleasing effect produced by the home atmosphere improves the appearance of the portrait over one-hundred per cent as the familiar home surroundings impart a softness to the picture that completely effaces the rigidity of the studio photograph with its unfamiliar and somewhat artifical surroundings. The naturalness of the pose of both children and grown people who have been photographed in their homes is in marked contrast to the constrained pose of the studio.

Miss Della R. Hayes who has an elegantly appointed studio at her home at 241 W. Jefferson Street makes a speciality of home portraiture and your photograph or that of your family can be taken at her home or your home in the most effective manner. Miss Hayes has had years of training in studios at Washington, D.C., Memphis, Tenn., and Butler, Pa. She uses the most up-to-date photographic apparatus and her skill in producing high grade photographs has resulted in making her studio one of the most popular in Butler.
(copied from the *Butler Citizen* dated July 11, 1914 by Dave and Audrey Craig)

### Lot Recently Secured On East Wayne Street Will Be Improved

Plans for the new business block on East Wayne Street for the Lloyd Company Incorporated will be ready this morning for the contractor's bids. The structure will be three stories with basement and will be constructed of brick, stone and steel and will be modern in all its appointments. The building will front 41 feet on East Wayne Street and have a depth of 100 feet.

The plans for a tenement in pleasant, well-lighted rooms in the front basement, extending under the side walk. The front of the second floor will be arranged for offices or may be converted into flats and the owners hope to interest some of the fraternal societies in the third floor for lodge rooms.

The business of the Lloyd Company Incorporated was organized at Apollo, Pa., 1893 by W. E. Lloyd. Two years later it was transferred to A. N. Lloyd and R. R. Lloyd and was conducted as a partnership under the name of Lloyd Brothers. In September, 1902, the business was incorporated as the Lloyd Company Inc., and in the same month the main store and office was transferred to Butler, leaving the branch store at Apollo.

At the time the company was incorporated the wholesale tobacco business of D. D. Lloyd, father of the family, that had been established in Beaver Falls in 1887, was merged with the business of the Lloyd Company Inc., and when the main store was opened in Butler by R. R. Lloyd, D. D. Lloyd was left in charge of the Apollo branch.

In 1904 the Apollo store was abandoned and since then all the business of the company has been conducted at the Butler store. The company was first located at the corner of West Jefferson and Washington Streets in the building now occupied by the People's Telephone Company. About five years ago the store was moved to the Elk's Home building on East Cunningham Street, its present location. The business of the Lloyd Company Inc., has grown rapidly since it was established in Butler and the concern is now one of the largest wholesale dealers in tobacco and confectionery in the western part of the state.

Work on the new building will be pushed rapidly as soon as the contract is let and it is expected that it will be ready for occupancy the early part of next year.
(copied from the *Butler Citizen* dated June 9, 1915 by Dave and Audrey Craig)

## Chamber Of Commerce Begins Move To Secure Armory For Butler
### Committee Will Investigate Assembly Act Regarding Erection Of Such Buildings

The chamber of commerce last night began agitation of a movement to secure for Butler a convention hall with a seating capacity of several thousand persons. The attention of members was called to such a move by E. I. Brugh at the meeting held in the court house last night.

Mr. Brugh pointed out that the state, under a recent act of assembly, had power to erect an armory building, provided the borough donates a site. An armory, such a the state would erect, could be used as a convention hall as well as quarters for the National Guard.

The matter was left in the hands of the legislative committee with power to investigate and report back to the January meeting. "Fake investments" were discussed along the lines of devising means of proctecting residents of Butler County from wily promoters. Publicity through the daily newspapers, it was agreed on by the speakers, is the best method of reaching the people and warning them against such schemes and educating them to recognition of alluring investments which have no solid base. It was left to the education committee to devise ways and means of checking the fake investment evil and report to the chamber at the next meeting.

Speakers on this subject were John V. Ritts, W. B. Purdum, T. W. Ruff, C. A. Templeton, E. I. Brugh, William Graable, Charles Barnhart, Clarence B. McMillan and Levi M. Wise. About 100 persons attended the meeting.
(copied from the *Butler Citizen* dated Dec. 10, 1909 by Dave and Audrey Craig)


## Pioneer Buggy Maker Enters New Industry
### W. C. Laderer Soon To Open New Rubber Plant In This County
### Zelienople Plant Will Make Rubber Electrician Gloves
### Plant to occupy Building Formerly Used As a Carriage Shop
### Stock to be Sold Soon   Company Plans Other Industries

Prominent in business circles in Butler County is W. C. Laderer of Evans City, for years one of the best known vehicle manufacturers in western Pennsylvania, and president and general manager of the W. C. Laderer Carriage Company operating large carriage factories in Zelienople.

The name of the W. C. Laderer Carriage Company is known from coast to coast and its products have always been held to a high standard of quality. It is only during the past year that Mr. Laderer has decided to discontinue manufacturing horse drawn vehicles, and by late in the spring or early summer he expects to build his last vehicle. It is generally known that the automobile is fast replacing the horse drawn vehicle throughout the country and it is with sincere regret to Mr. Laderer that he is discontinuing a business he has spent twenty-eight years in bringing to a point where he expected to turn over to his sons a large and well established trade. It is also with sincere regret to Mr. Laderer that in the passing of the vehicle business he is obliged to sever his connections with the large producers of raw-vehicle materials, as well as his business connections with all of his customers throughout the country.

The passing of the W. C. Laderer Carriage Company has come about through no fault of Mr. Laderer, in fact the passing of the vehicle business is a general condition throughout the country, and it is Mr. Laderer's every hope and desire that in entering a new field he will be able to continue to do business with a big percentage of the firms and individuals from whom he purchased raw materials, as well as the firms and individuals to whom he sold his finished products in the past.

A few years ago he established and still is sole owner and proprietor of the W. C. Laderer Company, a large Overland and Willys-Knight automobile distributorship, located at Butler, and operating branches at Evans City and Zelienople, and he now intends to embark in a new manufacturing venture, however at the same time continuing the automobile business.

With the opening of the spring Mr. Laderer will begin construction of additions to his present large plant at Zelienople, which will be devoted exclusively to the manufacture of rubber-electrician gloves. The company which is to be formed will be known as the W. C. Ladder Rubber Products Company, with factories and main offices at Zelienople and large distributing branches in New York, Chicago and San Francisco. It is Mr. Laderer's desire to make his new company within the next several years, the largest electrician glove manufacturer in the world, and it is with this in view that he hopes to re-establish the pleasant business relations he has always enjoyed with those with whom he did business while manufacturing vehicles.

As Mr. Laderer puts it, he is only fifty-eight years young and it is now his every desire to build up a new business that he can turn over to his sons and grandsons, when he becomes the age that he wishes to retire, and have an organization big enough to require the services of his three sons and three grandsons at the head of important departments.

Mr. Laderer was born at Zelienople in a quaint-old-log cabin fifty-eight years ago, his father and mother having immigrated from Germany, locating at Allegheny and later at Zelienople. A few years ago they moved to a farm in Lancaster Township where his father put the boys to work running the farm and himself operating a general store at Middle Lancaster, where he for many years was postmaster.

At the age of seventeen Mr. Laderer went to Rochester, Pa., to learn the wagon makers trade. After spending three years at learning the trade, for which his wages were $50 a year and board, he went back to Middle Lancaster and started a small,wagon shop where he built a few wagons and buggies and did general repair work. After his first year's business he realized that he could sell more buggies and wagons than he could build, and his limited capital permitted him to do business in only a very small shop for which he paid a dollar per month rent, so he purchased several car loads of buggies and wagons from a manufacturer at Youngstown, Ohio. When the thirty to forty odd vehicles reached destination at Harmony, Mr. Laderer trailed them to his place of business at Middle Lancaster. Every one in the community felt sorry for him, feeling that he had bought enough vehicles to supply the trade of the county and that he would be years disposing of such a large shipment for at that time were retailed at a price from $175 to $200 each. However, before the end of the summer he had bought and sold six additional car loads of horse drawn vehicles.

After several years of successful merchandising of vehicles and manufacturing of wagons at Middle Lancaster, Mr. Laderer at the age of twenty-six married Matilda Wahl of near Evans City. Several years after their marriage he located at Evans City purchasing the retail business of Wahl, Bishop and Company. For a few years he continued as a dealer in light vehicles and heavy wagons, but later on he enlarged his factory buildings and manufactured all of the vehicles he sold. For a long time Mr. Laderer continued the building of additions to his plant each year. Several times his factory buildings were partially destroyed by fire and finally in 1913 practically the whole plant was destroyed by fire at the busiest season of the year, just at a time when his books were filled with orders and his large plant was taxed to its capacity in its every effort to keep the production up to the demand for his vehicles. He immediately rented every available building in the town, purchased new material and left his sons to fill the orders on his books, while he spent all of his time in constructing his present large plant at Zelienople, where the vehicle business has been continued ever since. With this successful career of one of Butler County's most prominent men it can be appreciated by every one that Mr. Laderer regrets the passing of the vehicle business, and it is the wish of all his friends and wide acquaintances that his new venture will be even more successful than his vehicle business and it will be his pleasure to hand down a big business to his sons and grandsons, when the time comes that he wishes to retire from active business.

Mr. Laderer has always devoted his every effort in increasing his business, very progressive in all of his undertakings, and in addition, has placed his efforts in building his business in such a way that it found employment for his entire family and has the satisfaction in addition to always having been successful, of having kept his family together and at home, by being able to keep his business increasing sufficiently to have his sons at the head of each important department.

The assistance secured along these lines from Mrs. Laderer was invaluable. Her sincere regard for the higher things of life, together with her economical ideas of home life, being very essential in bringing the success Mr. Laderer now enjoys.

## NEW RUBBER PLANT TO BE STARTED THIS SUMMER AT ZELIENOPLE

Following immediately the discontinuing of his successful career in the vehicle business, which has come about through no fault of his own, but on account of a general condition throughout the country in which the automobile is fast replacing the horse drawn vehicle business. Mr. Laderer will equip his present carriage factory at Zelienople with the very latest type machinery for manufacturing electricians rubber gloves.

Following the policies of his entire career, Mr. Laderer intends starting this new manufacturing business at the foot of the ladder. He spent the past year and a half thoroughly investigating the demand for this product, as well as securing a man of unexcelled ability and experience to manufacture the gloves. After finding that the demand was far in excess of the supply, and that on account of the electric industry being just in its infancy, he realizes that the demand for an electrician glove of superior quality and merit will increase by leaps and bounds.

He has been fortunate in securing a man for the manufacturing end of the business who has made a life study of the rubber business and who in his whole career has been connected with only one concern. This man's experience in the rubber manufacturing business is going to ensure the success of Mr. Laderer's new venture, for his knowledge in the mixture of rubber and chemicals and producing a finished product is unexcelled by the best men in the largest rubber factories in the country. Just recently, on account of his inability to secure German chemicals for the mixing of his compounds, he discovered that by the use of several American chemicals he could make electricians rubber gloves that would stand a 10,000 higher voltage test than any other electrician's glove on the market. This glove can be produced and sold at a price not higher than the next best electrician's glove on the market and still carry the same profit. Since tendering his resignation to his present employers to take effect July 1, they offered to double his salary to induce him to continue with them, which further assures Mr. Laderer that he has been fortunate in securing a man of unexcelled ability.

After having all of these tests made Mr. Laderer immediately placed the sample gloves in the hands of the largest jobbers in the United States for inspection and one jobber alone has agreed to take the entire first year's output of the new plant, of six hundred gross pair and totaling $180,000.

The new company will be capitalized at $100,000.00 of which $80,000 will be sold immediately and $20,000 held in the treasury. Of the amount to be sold immediately, Mr. Laderer will take $55,000, the remaining $25,000 to be issued to friends of the Laderer interest who may wish to associate themselves with this new enterprise. A prospectus showing, the probable profits of this particular rubber product will be mailed to anyone on request, as stated in the W. C. Laderer Rubber Products Company's ad on the following page.

In achieving success Mr. Laderer traveled over the usual rocky road, experienced by most business men, the worst of which were fires which several times practically destroyed his plants. With his untiring ambition he would rebuild his plants and start manufacturing his products with renewed energy.

Mr. Laderer always realized that knowledge and ability brought no results without work, and from the very beginning of his business and up to the present day it is not unusual to find him at his place of business from six o'clock in the morning until late at night. During the regular working hours he is usually found in the plant working and mingling with his employees as one of them, and by whom he has always been held in the highest esteem. Many of his employees have been with him from the time they learned their trades in his shops and it is now his desire to have all of his employees continue with him in the new enterprise. After the closing of his plant in the evening he is most always found at his desk in the office or home until the wee hours of the morning. "Work" is his middle name and seems like play to Mr. Laderer. He belongs to two unions and labors two eight hour shifts every day.

## LADERER AUTO INDUSTRY LARGEST IN THE COUNTY

Just four years ago, last August, Mr. Laderer established an automobile agency at Evans City and contracted for twenty-five cars to be sold during the 1913 season. A small room in one corner of his old carriage works at Evans City was used as a salesroom. After the fire in April 1913, which practically destroyed the entire carriage plant, a new location for the automobile business had to be found. A small two story frame building on Washington Street, where the present Evans City branch is located was purchased. For the 1914 season larger quarters were necessary and the present two-story-brick salesroom and garage was built early that year.

From the very start Mr. Laderer's automobile business, like his vehicle business, grew with leaps and bounds. The contract for twenty-five Overland cars totaling approximately $25,000 for the 1913 season has grown to a contract for the 1917 season for over two hundred Overland and Willy-Knight cars, totaling approximately $200,000. In addition his automobile accessory, tire, oil and grease department will increase the total business approximately $60,000 for this season. At the Evans City and Zelienople branches a contract for fifty Chevrolet automobiles has been made which will increase the total business for 1917 to over $300,000. This unparalleled growth of an automobile agency, comprising a territory of only one county, is all due to the fact that Mr. Laderer has applied the same business principles of honesty, integrity, and fairness that made him successful in the carriage business to each individual deal, in addition to being certain that he had secured the leading lines of merchandise for his business.

The present salesroom in the Kirkpatrick building, Butler, by July 1, will be used exclusively for the handling of accessories, tires, oil, grease and gasoline, while the main offices, salesroom, public garage, Overland and Willys-Knight service station will be moved to the new Kramer building being erected on South Main Street directly adjoining the Hotel Willard. This building, which is to be finished some time in June, will be one story with basement fifty by one hundred and eighty feet, with a storing capacity of practically eighty to one hundred automobiles and for which Mr. Laderer has secured a ten year lease.

This new building is the first step of a series of important improvements and enlargements of Mr. Laderer's automobile business. Plans and specifications as well as contracts, are being prepared by Mr. Laderer, which will give Butler, within the next year, the only arcade in the industry devoted exclusively to the automobile business and operated by one organization, the complete details of which are given in another column in the texture section of this paper. In addition to this the opening of new branches at Cumberland, Md., and Johnstown, Pa., is being contemplated. These two cities control a territory in which over four hundred Willys-Knight and Overland cars will be sold this season.

When you drive or walk into the Laderer Automobile Arcade at Butler, you will find magnificent store fronts and shop fronts for each department. Each store and shop is managed separately by experienced and competent men. The following stores and shops will be found in this magnificent arcade, and the equipment throughout will be such that automobile owners can have anything done to an automobile of any make, no matter what nature of work is required, from tires to top and radiator to tail lamp.

## Department

No. 1. Overland and Willys-Knight salesroom equipped with turn table. Also ladies rest room. The finest salesroom outside the largest cities.

No. 2. Accessory, oil and grease store where a full line of all necessary automobile accessories, oil and grease are displayed.

No. 3. Tire store, where all makes of tires and inner tubes and tire accessories are displayed and sold. Also all kinds of casing and inner tubes are vulcanized and casing retreaded.

No. 4. Battery store and service station, where the best makes of storage batteries and dry cell are displa ed and sold. Also, competent and experienced battery service men are in charge. Storage batteries of all kind are repaired and rebuilt here. All makes of electric starters, generators, coils, distributors and magnetos, in fact every electric appliance used on automobiles are repaired or replaced.

No. 5. Parts store, where all Overland and Willys-Knight parts are displayed, stored and sold.

No. 6. Repair shops, where all Overland and Willys-Knight cars are repaired, including machine shop for taking care of all kinds of machinery. Also the Overland rapid service car used as the Overland emergency road car free to Overland-Knight owners.

No. 7. Repair shop, where all makes of automobiles other than Overland-Knight cars are repaired, including machine shop for doing all kinds of machine work, such as straightening front axles, making springs and leaves for springs, making rear axles. This shop is equipped for machining any part for any make of automobile.

No. 8. Wood shop, where new wood wheels are made as well as spokes put in broken wheels. Where new wood bows are put in tops, where all makes of bodies are equipped and new doors are made, including sheet steel body construction. New pleasure car and truck bodies both wood and sheet steel are made here.

No. 9. Upholstering shop, where all kinds of upholstering is repaired and new upholstering made. Also new tops and curtains are made here and old tops and curtains repaired.

No. 10. Paint shop, where all makes of cars are repainted to the taste of individual owner.

No. 11. Storage room, where only Overland and Willys-Knight cars are stored by their respective owners.

No. 12. Storage room, where all makes of cars are stored by their respective owners.

No. 13. Storage room, where transient storage is taken care of for all makes of cars.

No. 14. Wash racks, where an artillery of wash racks used for polishing and washing all makes of cars is found.

No. 15. Dead storage room, where the big stock of new Overland and Willys-Knight cars are stored, as well as the big stock of all automobile accessories, oils, tires and grease.

No. 16. Dead storage room, where all makes of cars are stored during the winter months by owners who do no winter driving.

No. 17. Print shop, where all of the printing and advertising matter of the W. C. Laderer Company and its branches will be printed and a monthly publication issued. In addition all kinds of printing of the Laderer customers will be taken care of.

No. 18. Convention hall and gymnasium. The entire upper floor of the new building will be equipped with an auditorium and stage, bowling alleys and billiard tables, a hall where basket ball and all indoor sports, as well as reading and rest rooms will be furnished for the comfort and pleasure of Laderer employs and customers.

In erecting this new building Mr. Laderer has placed at the service of the public an automobile salesroom and service station unexcelled anywhere in this country or abroad and it no doubt will be the means of many tourists routing themselves through Butler. This service station is equipped with a number of gasolines and oil so that all owners can have their gasoline tanks and oil reserves of their automobiles filled promptly. The building has a capacity for storing three hundred cars. In all this new arcade is one of the latest steps in the advancement of the automobile business.

(copied from the *Butler Citizen* dated March 8, 1917 by Dave and Audrey Craig)

### Auto Salesroom To Be Formally Opened

What will resemble as automobile show as far as display, decorations and the like are concerned will be the formal opening of the new salesroom of the Diamond Motor Sales Company, located next to the Hotel Nixon on the square from January 19 to 26, inclusive. The complete lines displaying all the models of the Chevrolet and Maxwell automobile and trucks are to be exhibited.

Not to be outdone by the opening held by W. C. Laderer company, Overland and Willys-Knight dealers, there no doubt will be many interesting features, including music and everything for the convenience and entertainment of their customers and friends, so that all who visit the new salesroom during this opening week will have no regrets. The Diamond Motor Sales Company is a new sales agency organized recently by the W. C. Laderer Company and is in complete charge of Mr. J. H. Welsh, a well known businessman of Slippery Rock.

(copied from the *Butler Citizen* dated Jan. 18, 1918 by Dave and Audrey Craig)

### Basket Grocery Will Be Opened In Butler Tomorrow

The "Basket Grocery" is a new establishment that will be opened for business tomorrow morning by L. H. Hilliard on West North Street, adjoining the Central Fire station. Mr. Hilliard has remodeled the old Hilliard residence by building a store room at the front and remodeling the second story. The store room will be used as a combined grocery and meat market.

The grocery will be what the name implies. Mr. Hilliard expects to sell for cash and buy for cash and each customer is expected to carry his purchase home with him in his own market basket. There will be no delivery wagon, except for articles that are too heavy for a basket.

One of the chief causes of the high cost of living today is the expensive delivery system that the grocer and provision dealers are obliged to keep up to accommodate their customers. The practice of ordering by telephone and often causing the delivery wagon an extra trip for a twenty-five-cent purchase contributes to the cost.

While the basket grocery is an innovation in a sense, its manager expects to make it profitable for the customers who patronize it by selling at prices that will be an inducement for cultivating the habit of carrying a market basket.

(copied from the *Butler Citizen* dated July 2, 1912 by Dave and Audrey Craig)

### NEW BUSINESS BUILDING WILL BE BUILT SOON
### KIRKPATRICK BLOCK WILL BE ORNAMENT TO MAIN STREET

Architect W. G. Kline, Butler County National Bank building has the plans ready for the contractor's bids on a three-story brick and stone store and office building for Robert A. Kirkpatrick, the South Main street jeweler. The new building is to be located at 132 South Main street on the site of the building now occupied by the Racket store.

The building will cover a ground space of about 20 by 160 and will extend through from Main Street to Jackson Street. The building will be practically four stories high at the rear, as the basement floor will be close to the street level on Jackson Street. The building will be completed in modern style, steam heat, elevators, and electric lights, and will have an ornamental front that will greatly enhance the appearance of that part of the street. The first floor basement, and rear of the second and third floors will be used for a general store. The front of the second floor will be fitted up for dental offices and the front of the third floor as a photograph gallery.

The construction of the new building will be commenced early this spring and the building will be ready for use the coming summer. Bids will be taken the coming week.

(copied from the *Butler Citizen* dated Jan. 30, 1912 by Dave and Audrey Craig)

## Empire Glass Company

The Empire Glass Company of Zelienople was built on land purchased on May 4, 1899, form Steven and Frances Lockwood. John A. Gelbach was president and Louis E. Phillis, treasurer.

The two buildings, one the mixing room, the other the decorating room, were situated along the railroad tracks where Penn Power is now located. Milk bottles and decorated glassware were made. A few pieces of Empire decorated glassware and milk glass plates in white, torquoise and black are on display at the Zelienople Historical Society Passavant House on Main Street, Zelienople, Pa. The business failed and was sold by the sheriff on June 10, 1904 to Jacob Gelbach, who did not continue with the glass manufacturing business. The company employed 23 people.

Glass Blowers: Frank Smith B. 1879, Edward Dietz, 1874, Patrick J. La'y, 1863 Ireland, John Beck, 1855 Ohio, Alonzo Miller, 1865 Va. Glass gather: Louis Brunner, 1877 Switzerland, Bronzing: Harriet E. Shaffer, 1880, Decorators: Emma Garmen, 1884, Mary Fogel, 1880, Moldholders: Adam Rape, 1883, Harvey Rape, 1885, Laborers: Joseph Linn, 1886, Phillip F. Gloss, 1885, Joseph B. Powell, 1875, John Heilman, 1877 Ohio, Fred Fitch, 1862 N. Y., Packers: John Synder, 1855, Charles Rogner, 1882, Pearl M. Lutz, 1883, Sara A. Hays, 1884, Robert J. Hays, 1881

## Salesman Buys Local Auto Concern

### W. H. Smail, 505 Fifth Street, New Owner Of Butler Paige Automobile Co. Business

Mr. W. H. Smail, of 505 Fifth Street, Butler, has purchased the interest of T. H. Frederick and S. J. Keck in the Butler Paige Automobile Company, located 128 Mifflin Street, and took charge of the same Saturday. Mr. Smail has for the past 12 years been a commercial traveler out of Butler in the biscuit and confectionary line. He was with the Peerless Biscuit Company of Pittsburgh, and left them to become a member of the Dixon-Fisher Company, which was engaged in the same line of business. When this firm sold out, Mr. Smail went on the road for the Heim Confectionary Company, of Pittsburgh, and did a very successful business for his company during the past four years.

As representative for the Paige Automobile Company, he will control its sales in Butler, Armstrong and part of Clarion County. It is his intention to make some changes and extensions, due notice of which will be given the public. In the meantime Mr. Smail will endeavor to give the same prompt and efficient service characteristic of the Butler Paige Company.

(copied from the *Butler Citizen* dated Jan. 14, 1918 by Dave and Audrey Craig)

## BUTLER SOON TO HAVE ANOTHER NEWSPAPER IN EVENING FIELD

### Application For Charter Will be Made by Local Men, March 18.

### FIRM TO BE KNOWN AS PRESS PUBLISHING CO.

Butler is going to have another daily newspaper. This information was contained in a notice of application for charter, handed the *Citizen* last night for publication in this morning's edition. The company will be known as the Press Publishing Company, and although the notice does not specify what the name of the publication will be, from the name of the incorporation, it is presumed the paper will be known as the *Press*.

In the notice, it is pointed out that W. Z. Murrin John H. Wilson, C.E. Walter, George Ketterer, Jr., and C. F. Hosford, Jr., all of Butler will make application to the governor of Pennsylvania, Monday, March 18, under the provisions of an act of assembly, entitled "An Act to Provide for the Incorporation and Regulation of Certain Corporations," approved April 29, 1874, and the supplements thereto, for a charter for an intended corporation, to be called the Press Publishing Company, the character and object of which will be the publication of an evening democratic newspaper in the city of Butler.

The company also, will operate a printing establishment for general job printing, ruling, book binding and the like. It was not announced last night just when the company hopes to publish its first edition. With the introduction of another evening publication in the local field, Butler will have four daily newspapers three evening and one morning journal.

(copied from the *Butler Citizen* dated Feb. 7, 1918 by Dave and Audrey Craig)

## BUTLER SAVINGS AND TRUST BANK BUYS PROPERTY

### Deal Closed in Which Financial Concern Becomes Owner Of Property Occupied by Samuel Cohn, Clothier, Embracing Frontage of 24 Feet, One Inch

A real estate deal, involving the transfer of one of the most valuable frontages on South Main Street was completed yesterday afternoon, when the Butler Savings and Trust company purchased of the Wuller heirs the property occupied by Samuel Cohn, Clothier. The deal was completed early in the afternoon, but did not become generally known until several hours later.

The newly acquired property of this progressive financial institution has a frontage on Main Street of 24 feet, one inch, and a depth of 150 feet. The present frontage of the Butler Savings & Trust is 18 feet, with a depth of 105 feet, and with an annex facing on Jefferson Street. The total frontage, therefore, of the bank will be 42 feet and one inch.

No statement was made, last evening, as to when the new owners are to take possession of their newly acquired property or the purchase price in the transfer but inasmuch as this is one of the most valuable sites on South Main Street, it is reasonably certain that the transfer would involve many thousand of dollars.

The Butler Savings & Trust Company has been located in its present quarters some thirty-five years. During that time it has been found necessary to enlarge the room three times, the latest change being made seven years ago when the room was enlarged to its present capacity.

The business of the bank is constantly increasing in volume, so that the seventeen employees are kept busy continuously. Recently it was found necessary to have the entire bookkeeping department removed to the annex facing on Jefferson Street in order to give additional facilities in the main room for the handling of trade. The statement of the Butler Savings & Trust company published elsewhere in this issue of the *Citizen* shows the largest business in the history of the bank and because of the continued increase in the patronage, the directors deemed it advisable to secure the additional frontage so that still more commodious accommodations could be provided for its customers.

It is reasonably certain that when the bank takes possession of its new property and reconstructs; or builds anew it will have a banking property in which will be embodied all the modern facilities for conducting and handling a modern banking business.

**Officers and Directors**The officers and directors of the bank are well known men in financial circles, and are as follows: J. Henry Troutman, president: John S. Campbell, vice-president: Louis B. Stein, secretary and treasury; C. E. Cronenwett, assistant secretary and treasurer. Directors are: J. Henry Troutman, W, J. Breaden, William B. Purvis, John S. Campbell, George Worrall, Theodore Vogeley, W. D. Brandon, Porter Wilson, F. C. Vanderhoof, Robert Krause, Dr. L. R. Hazlett, and R. O. Wood.

(copied from the *Butler Citizen* dated June 7, 1919 by Dave and Audrey Craig)

## BATTERY SERVICE STATION OPENS IN THIS CITY

### Butler Battery Company Ready to Serve Wants of the Local Automobile Trade

A new storage battery service station has opened in Butler, known as the Butler Battery Company. They are located at the comer of the Viaduct and Center Avenue, and handle the "Exide" battery, The famous "Giant that lives in a box." This is a well-known battery of excellent quality, made by one of the oldest battery manufacturers in the United States, backed by thirty-one years of battery specialization and experience.

For the last year this battery has been hard to obtain, owing to the fact that the U. S. Government took nearly the entire output of the Electric Storage Battery Company, the manufacturers of the Exide battery and they were unable to fill their orders for automobile starting and lighting batteries.

About 80 per cent of the U. S. submarines were equipped with Exide batteries of the same type of plates and cell construction as used in the automobile starting and lighting batteries. They also built batteries for government trucks, airplanes and wireless stations.

The Electric Storage Battery Company is very careful in selecting its distributors and service stations, and will sign contracts only with such as are fully equipped and thoroughly capable of handling any kind of battery service or trouble.

The new service station is fully equipped and competent to give any kind of service and advice on all makes of batteries. Inspection and testing are done free of charge. Butler car owners who have cars equipped with Exide batteries will now have the opportunity of availing themselves of this service.

(copied from the *Butler Citizen* dated March is, 1919 by Dave and Audrey Craig)

## OVERALL FACTORY IS IN FULL OPERATION

### Spaide Shirt Company is Now Operating Becker Brother's Overall Factory

The Spaide Shirt Company which has been in operation in this city for the past four or five years, has taken over the Becker Bros. Overall factory and is now manufacturing overalls from the plant. In addition the shirt concern continues the operation of its plant and with the ending of the war the trade has not declined but has increased considerably. The overall factory has been overhauled and improved and the daily capacity increased. Additional labor is being employed from time to time as conditions warrant. The two manufacturing plants are two of the fastest growing industries of the city and the demand for goods made by them come from all parts of the country.

(copied from the *Butler Citizen* dated Jan. 18, 1919 by Dave and Audrey Craig)

(note: Armco, the Standard Steel Car Co., Standard Plate Glass Co., Du-Co Ceramics and other Butler County industries are found in *Butler County, the Second Hundred Years*. Penn United Technology Inc., II-VI Incorporated and Saxonburg area industries may be found in *Historic Saxonburg and It's Neighbors*.)

# NEW FACTORY IN SIGHT FOR THE CITY

## INVENTOR OF NEW PROCESS FOR MAKING LAMP BLACK IS ORGANIZING COMPANY SITE WITHIN EASY REACH OF CITY IS DESIRED

### Under Moffow process, Production of Material is Reduced by Less Than Half- Local Men Interested

Plans for the establishing here of a carbon black manufacturing plant are now being perfected and it is possible that on next Saturday evening the company will be organized and a site for the factory selected.

John Morrow, an Ohio man, has a patent process for the manufacture of this important commercial product which he claims will reduce the cost of production to less than half that of the present methods of manufacturing the product. He has been in this city the past few days in the interests of his process, and has succeeded in bringing it to the attention of a number of people. He desires to locate somewhere in the gas producing regions of the section and prefers Butler to any place which he has visited. Mr. Morrow was so encouraged here with assurances of support for his proposed company that he left yesterday for Pittsburg to secure prices on the necessary machinery, so that he will be able to report to those interested the exact amount of cash which will be required to put the plant in operation. It is proposed by Mr. Morrow to organize a stock company with sufficient capital to carry the project along, with a possibility that the par value of the stock will be $10 a share and the amount to be sold to any one person will be limited. These are questions, however, which will be determined at a meeting of those interested, but is the idea of the inventor of the process, who is confident of the success of his plan, and desires to place the stock so that no one person can monopolize the business.

A meeting of the parties interested will be held at the office of Justice of the Peace James M. McNally, of Lyndora, on Saturday evening, when the plans will be further outlined and the character of the organization probably determined. It is believed that a capital of $5,000 will be sufficient to equip a plant under the Morrow process which will turn out a sufficient quantity of the black to make it a paying investment. A site between Lyndora and McCalmont has been examined by those interested and they have been favorably impressed with it. The location contains a producing gas well, and there is ample room to drill other wells as the occasion would demand after the plant was in operation. This site can be obtained at a reasonable figure, and will without a doubt be selected by the company when it is organized.

The carbon black industry of the United States is said to be controlled by two firms, one of which has a plant at Cabot, on the West Penn Railroad in this county. Mr. Morrow's system of converting the gas to carbon black is said to differ very materially from that used by other firms, and the reduced cost which he claims for it places it in the money making class from the start. Carbon black is the fine impalpable soot obtained from the smoke of natural gas, and there is always a market for it as it is used in different articles of every-day consumption, such as printer's ink and various black pigments and cements. One of the firms now manufacturing carbon black was so much impressed with Mr. Morrow's system that he offered him $10,000 for the use of it, but he declined the offer, believing that there were greater possibilities in the manufacture of the black himself or by a company of his organizing. It is claimed for his system that it has been tested thoroughly and has fully demonstrated that it will do all that he represents.

(copied from the *Butler Citizen* dated July 1, 1909 by Dave and Audrey Craig)

## Standard To Enlarge Car Wheel Plant Soon
### Forged Steel Wheel Company Takes Over Many Acres South Of Plant
### New Wheel Is In Demand

With a view of enlarging their plant, the Forged Steel Wheel Company, a subsidiary of the Standard Steel Car Company has acquired seventy-three acres of the Pierce farm, lying to the south of and adjoining their present buildings. The land was owned by the Pierce heirs, one of whom is a lunatic, Miss Effie Pierce, and owing to the fact the transfer cannot be completed for a period of ten days, Judge James M. Galbreath Saturday afternoon, made an order authorizing the sale of Miss Pierce's share, through her trustee, Edward H. Negley, attorney, and the transfer shall become absolute at the expiration of the stated period. The consideration was $20,887. The nogotiations for the property have been on for several weeks.

The Forged Steel Wheel Company manufactures steel wheels under a new process. The present plant was erected over a year ago and several months was devoted to the testing of the wheels, which now bid well to prove the most successful car wheel made. Already the larger railroad companies, all of which have experienced costly trouble from the old cast wheel are demanding the new wheel. Since the testing of the new wheel was conducted for several months, the demand for the new wheel was immediate and it became apparent that to meet the demand a larger plant was neccessary. It is understood that an addition to the present plant will be started in the near future.

It is stated on good authority that when the present plans of the Forged Steel Wheel Company officials are carried out, the Butler plant will be one of the largest in the world

(copied from the *Butler Citizen* dated July 19, 1909 by Dave and Audrey Craig)

## Local Car Company Acquires More Land

Confirmation of the sale of the Davis White Lead property, containing fifteen acres, the Charlers Duffy tract, abutting on Fairground Avenue, and including the Butler Baseball Park, containing fourteen acres, and a fraction less than three acres of the Vogeley tract abutting on Pillow Street, to the Standard Steel Car Company, was had at the *Citizen* last night, the authority being Attorney W. D. Brandon, counsel for the company. The sale of the Pierce heirs farm, containing seventy-three acres, lying to the south and west of the southern extremity of the origninal Standard holdings, was comfirmed Saturday. The publication some days ago, by an afternoon contemporary, in which it was claimed the Standard Steel Car Company has purchased the Pierce brother's property lying to the west of Pierce Avenue, and the gate of which it was claimed, had been confirmed, was without foundation. The Standard Steel Car Company does not own this property, nor does it expect to at this time. To what use the newly acquired holding will be put by the company is not made public for publication.

Rumors have been current and published frequently during the past few weeks, in which expansion of the local works, already the largest of their kind in the world was exploited; but in no case have the officals of the company given out any information whatever. That the property has been acquired with an object is obvious; just beyond this, what will result is purely problematical, despite published reports.

The real estate deals just closed by the big company constitute the largest transfers, from the point of money involved that have been made in the city for several years.

(copied from the *Butler Citizen* dated July 20, 1909 by Dave and Audrey Craig)

## Standard Car Co. To Move Into New Offices This Week

### Building, Handsomest In Western Pennsylvania, Erected At A Cost Of About $175,000, A Marvel Of Beauty

General offices of the Standard Steel Car Company will be removed this week to the handsome new building just completed by the company on Pierce Avenue. The new office building is one of the handsomest and most expensive of it kind in the country and cost more than $175,000 to erect.

The main building is 180 feet long and 48 feet in width. The building was designed by Architect Thomas Scott, of Pittsburg; C. O. Markhart was architect in charge.

The building is a three story steel structure, veneered with stone, with terra cotta trimmings. The approach is a flight of many white marble steps. The interior of the building is furnished in the most expensive and elaborate manner. The plumbing, which was furnished by Moot and Company, of New York, is the best, and most modern to be had. The lavatories, two on each floor, are all marble wainscotted, and are of plate glass. The building is heated by low pressure steam and the entire structure is regulated at a uniform temperature.

A vacuum cleaning apparatus will be used in the building, operated by electricity. This will do away with all brooms and dusting. On the first floor will be located the offices of the manager of the works, the treasurer's and auditor's offices. The second floor will be used for the purchasing department, offices of the different agents, and offices of the chief engineer. The third floor will be used as the engineering offices and the drafting rooms. It is subdivided into two main drawing rooms, one for the passenger car department, the other for freight cars.

The head of each department will have an office, located in the center of the rooms, built entirely of glass and is so situated that each manager will have every man in the department under his direct supervision. There are three other offices on this floor, one for the chief of the dye department, the other for the chief of motor trucks.

The drawing rooms are fitted out in a most expensive manner. All the furnishings, being finished in flumed oak. The rooms will be lighted with Cooper-Huet lamps. The thrid floor has 48 of these candle power lights. The other floors are lighted with 100 candle power-tungsten-electric lamps.

More than 350 men will go into the handsome new building this week. The building is conspiciously situated and is a great credit to the company and to the city of Butler.

(copied from the *Butler Citizen* dated Feb. 21, 1910 by Dave and Audrey Craig)

## Contract For New Building Let By The Standard Works

### Addition To Car Works Plant Means Much To Butler District

Announcement was made yesterday that the Standard Steel Car Company had given the contract to the McClintic-Marshall Construction Company for the erection of a new addition to the open hearth mill in Lyndora. The plans for the building and the machinery and equipment have all been prepared, so that no delay will arise after the work has been started. The plant will require about 2,000 tons of structural steel.

Statements differ as to the kind of a mill that is to be erected. One is that the new mill is to be an extension of the billet and slab mill of the open hearth and the other that a new mill is to erected on the David Pierce property for the manufacture of channel iron, angle bars and other parts used in the construction of steel cars.

When the road supervisor of Butler Township asked for a closing of a part of Standard Avenue from the Zambo store to the Pierce property and for the opening of a new street or road to take the place of the highway closed, it was presumed that the intention of the Standard Steel Car Company was to enlarge the open hearth mill or to build a new sheet mill. It was given out at the works that the ground obtained by the change in streets was to be used for yards and sidings.

The erection of a new plant will mean employment for a large number of men and will be a substantial increase for the Butler district.

(copied from the *Butler Citizen* dated Nov 19, 1912 by Dave and Audrey Craig)

## Packing Houses To Be Opened, Will Lower Prices And Employ Many Men

Butler meat prices are slated for a drop. Application for a charter which will give the capital stock at $50,000 has been made by the Butler Beef and Provision Company, composed of Butler and Punxsutawney people.

Negotiations are in progress to buy of D. H. Campbell, the brick building in West View district, formerly used by the Thorne Planing Mill and Lumber Company. Contracts have been let for remodeling the building and contracts let for the machinery which will be operated by gas engines. Several large boilers will also be installed. The company expects to be ready to deliver its product by January 1 and will give employment to about 20 men. The capacity will be 5 carloads a week. The floor will be cement and everything will be along strict lines in regard to sanitation. As far as possible, purchases of cattle will be made from Butler County persons.

William Heckendorn and John A. Philliber, of Punxsutawney, are behind the movement. Mr. Heckendorn says Butler meat prices will take a drop after the plant is put in operation. It is possible that after the company begins putting its product into the market a fertilizing plant will be added.

(copied from The *Butler Citizen* dated November 1, 1909 by Dave and Audrey Craig)

## Butler Firm Gets Large Contracts
### Phillips Mfg. Co. Gets Bulk Of $10,000 Equipment For Plant Of Butler Packing Co.

The Butler Provision and Packing Company yesterday awarded contracts for about $10,000 worth of equipment for their new packing house, now under construction near the Butler Brewery. The Phillips Manufacturing Co. of Butler was awarded the bulk of the contracts. The Phillips Co. will furnish several boilers, gas engines and a complete plant for the manufacture of ice for the new plant.

Work on remodeling buildings of the old Thorne Planing Mill property, which the packing company recently purchased, is well under way, and as soon as the buildings are completed, new machinery will be put in place.

(copied from the *Butler Citizen* dated Dec. 10, 1909 by Dave and Audrey Craig)

## Where All But The Squeal Of The Hogs Will Be Used
### Butler's Packing Plant, Nearly Completed, Has Facilities Equal To The Best In The Country

A new industry which will mean much to the people of Butler in general will be ready for business in a short time. It is the Butler Beef and Provision Company, located on the old Thorne property in the Island district, between Negley Avenue and the Bessemer & Lake Erie railroad tracks. The company, which is composed of several of Butler's most prominent men, and W. H. Heckendorn, of Punxsutawney, will do a general wholesale meat business.

Honorable Ira Mujunkin, of Butler, will be president of the company; S. T. North, of Punxsutawney, vice president; T. M. Baker, of Butler, secretary, and W. H. Heckendorn, of Punxsutawney, treasurer and general manager.

The board of directors is made up of Ira McJunkin, J. Henry Troutman, Harry S. Klingler, T. M. Baker, of Butler, and W. H. Heckendorn, Irvine Simpson, S. T. North, J. A. Philliber and James Lockard, of Punxsutawney.

The plant consists of two large buildings. The main building is a two story brick with a basement 70 by 110 feet. The other is a frame building 48 by 55 feet. A private switch has been put in by the Bessemer Railroad company. The switch runs into the cattle yards, which have accommodations for several car loads of cattle. The cattle are first run into the yards, and then direct to the killing room, which is located on the first floor. The cattle are first weighed and then killed, dressed, put on a track and sent to the chilling room where they are kept for some time and then run to the cooling room. These rooms are all located on the first floor.

When hogs are killed they are dropped into a large scalding vat, located in the killing room. They are then dressed and the refuse material is thrown into a rendering tank, which is in the basement, but has an opening in the killing room. The hogs are then sent to the cooling room, where they are kept until they are ready to be put on a track and delivered to the shipping room.

The large rendering tank into which refuse material from the hogs is thrown is one of the most modern pieces of machinery known to the packing industry. After this material has been kept in the rendering tank for a specified time, the tallow is drawn off and the residue left is made into fertilizer. The gases from the rendering tank are conveyed to a point below the boiler furnace and consumed as generated, thereby obviating all possibility of the slightest odor to be detected in the entire plant. On the first floor is the sausage room. This room is located between the killing room and the offices. In this room lard agitators, rendering machines, power sausage machines and cooling tank will be located. Adjoining the sausage room are two large smoke houses, which have a capacity of a car load of hams. The pickling room is also on this floor. The flooring is all cement. The main hall, running the entire length of the building is 14 feet wide. More than 1,000 feet of track is used to take cattle from and to the different departments.

The second floor will be used as a storage room. It is one large room. The ammonia pipes for cooling the different rooms are on this floor, there being 2,200 feet of two inch ammonia pipes. The floors of the cooling room are covered with two layers of two-ply paper, two inches of cork and four inches of cement. The brick walls are covered with three inches of cork and cement plaster. The machinery for the plant was furnished by the Phillips Manufacturing Company of Butler. Besides manufacturing the equipment, this company placed all the machinery and contracted for all the engineering work. The work was in charge of A. F. Clarke, chief engineer of the company. The machinery is all the best and most modern known to the packing industry, more than $20,000 being invested in machinery alone.

The refrigerator machine or ammonia compressor has a capacity of 40 tons and is driven by a 75 horse power Phillips type B gas engine, thereby making it possible for keeping the different storage and cooling rooms in any temperature in the warmest weather.

This ammonia compressor does away with the necessity of using ice. A 50 horse power Phillips steam engine is used to drive the many different machines in the sausage room.

The boiler used in the plant is a 150 horse power Phillips return tubular boiler, connected to a stack to be constructed on the outside wall of the building. This stack when completed will be one of the largest in Butler, being 150 feet high. The building is heated by steam.

The company will have its own water supply. One well is already completed, and another is being drilled. These wells will be pumped by steam driven pumps, and will have a capacity of 250 barrels an hour.

The frame building, which is located near the main structure, is being remodeled and will be used as cattle pens. It will also be used for stables for the company.

The Butler Beef and Provision company was granted a charter some time ago, and is capitalized at $50,000. The company owns an acre and a quarter of land surrounding the buildings. The directorate and stockholders are mostly local men, all of which are substantial businessmen of the city. The plant has a capacity of handling two carloads of cattle daily, and will be ready for business within a week or so.

(copied from the *Butler Citizen* dated March 14, 1910 by Dave and Audrey Craig)

## PROVISION COMPANY IS DOING BUSINESS

## MODERN MEAT PACKING HOUSE IS IN OPERATION

The Butler Beef and Provision company, which recently completed a large packing industry in the island district began to operate the plant for the first time on Monday. Several carloads of beeves and hogs arrived at the plant last week, and the first killing was done Monday morning. Many visitors visited the new industry and watched the operation from the time the cattle leave the yards until they are killed, dressed, cut and sent to the different cooling rooms.

The new plant will have a capacity of two carloads of cattle and hogs a day. The company will sell exclusively to the wholesale trade and no doubt Butler County meat dealers will liberally patronize the home industry.

(copied from the Butler Citizen dated May 18, 1910 by Dave and Audrey Craig)

### Butler Brick And Tile Company To Make Improvements Costing $10,000

Improvements which will aggregate more than $ 10,000 are being made to the plant of the Butler Brick and Tile Company, at North Butler. The yearly capacity of the plant has been 3,000,000 bricks, and when contemplated improvements are completed the capacity will be increased to 6,000,000.

George E. Howard, of Butler, is at the head of the works, and says that orders are now booked to keep the plant running in full for six months, and that inquiries are coming in daily in regard to Butler brick. One order was received by the company a few days ago for 2,000,000 bricks for immediate delivery. For more than a year the company has been adding machinery and equipment to its producing capacity, but have not had facilities for handling the output. One of the recent additions to the equipment is a power conveyor, for handling refuse material. One of the advantages of this new conveyor is that it is a great labor saving device. They also have under construction a new-waste-heat dryer to utilize the heat which is ordinarily wasted.

The most important of the improvements now being added is a continuous kiln. This kiln is one of the most modern additions to the brick industry. Out of the 6,000 brick plants in the United States only eight of the largest factories have installed it. As the name implies, it operates continuously, and bricks are being put in, burned, cooled and taken out, all at the same time. This is not only a modern way of burning brick, but it increases the quality of the product as well as decreasing the cost of the brick. The kiln consists of a series of chambers, and while one chamber is being filled another one is being emptied, and another contains brick being burned and cooled.

The demand for the product of the Butler Brick and Tile Company is increasing daily, and when these improvements, which are being pushed as rapidly as possible, are completed, Butler will have one of the largest and most modern brick plants in the country.

(copied from the *Butler Citizen* dated Feb. 5, 1910 by Dave and Audrey Craig)

## Ice Will Be Made In Large Quantities

Butler is to have an up-to-date cold storage house, according to the plans which have been started by Joseph and Peter Schlicht, the well known poultry and fish dealers. Work was commenced on the plant Saturday and it is expected that the building will be ready to install the machinery by the middle of June.

The Schlicht brothers recently purchased from Henry Berg, the old Patton livery barn on the corner of Monroe and College Streets and will begin the construction at once of a cold storage and ice plant.

The work of tearing down the old livery barn was begun Saturday morning and contractor Albert Kutsch will begin work this week on the foundations and cement construction of a building 36 by 60 feet and two stories high that will be used as an ice manufacturing plant and cold storage ware room. The brick work of the superstructure will be done by contractor McKay and the building is to be rushed to completion by the middle of the coming month.

The contracts for the machinery have been let to the York Manufacturing Company of York, Pa., and include ten-ton compressors, ice manufacturing plant and all the necessary equipment for a first class storage plant. A special engine for the plant will be built by the Butler Engine and Foundry Company.
(copied from the *Butler Citizen* dated May 29, 1911 by Dave and Audrey Craig)

## New Ice And Cold Storage Plant Ready For Operation

With the opening of the cold storage rooms and ice manufacturing plant of the Standard Ice Company Monday, Butler will have a new industry inaugurated that will furnish employment to at least 15 men and also have one of the finest storage plants in the state.

It is worthy of remark too, that the new industrial institution was financed and set in operation without the aid of the guarantee fund of the chamber of commerce or any stock jobbing schemes. All that the people of Butler are asked to do is buy ice and patronize the cold storage department of the plant.

The head and manager of the Standard Ice Company is J. A. Schlicht, the well-known poultry and fish dealer, of 112 South Main Sreet. Some time ago he foresaw the need of a cold storage house in Butler and set about to secure a plant. The result of his investigations and enterprise is not only a cold storage warehouse, but an ice manufacturing plant second to none in the state.

The plant is located on College Street, near the corner of Monroe and College Streets, and occupies a ground space of 60 by 80 feet. The building is constructed of brick and concrete work and the lumber was furnished by the S. G. Purvis company.

The storage part of the building is divided into five compartments, which will be used for the storage of perishable goods. The division walls, floors and ceiling are lined with seven inches of specially prepared cork, covered with cement, and are perfectly fire-proof. Three rooms are kept at a temperature of 20 degrees below freezing, and used for storage, one room will be used as a freezing room and one room will be used for packing and storing furs. This last feature is something that Butler has never had and will be a great convenience to people who have valuable fur goods they wish to store for the summer months.

The ice manufacturing plant was installed by the York Manufacturing Co. of York, Pa., and is the most complete plant of its kind in the state. The equipment consists of a 65-horse power boiler, one 35 ton compressor, one 15-ton compressor, a steam dripping compressor, electric light generator and two engines for driving the machinery. The machinery was installed and is in charge of Frank Hoover, a representative of the York Manufacturing Company.

Two water wells at the plant, one 158 feet and the other 125 feet deep supply the water for the plant. All of the water used in the manufacture of ice is distilled. It is first run through the boilers, generating steam, reboiled, distilled and cooled and stored in tanks before it is run into freezing cans.

The plant has a capacity of 20 to 25 tons of ice daily, besides keeping the cold storage rooms going. The plant will employ two firemen, two engineers and six helpers in the operating of the ice plant and cold storage department, and as many more men in the delivery department. Delivery will be made by auto trucks, two three-ton trucks have been ordered, to be here the first of the week.

Operations at the plant will begin today and the company will be ready to make deliveries Wednesday of next week. The public is invited to inspect the plant any time during the day.
(copied from the *Butler Citizen* dated Sept. 2, 1911 by Dave and Audrey Craig)

## Contract Was Signed

At the meeting of the board of directors of the chamber of commerce, held last night, the contract with the Natioal Hydro-Carbon Company was closed and the papers signed by the officals of the company and the attorneys in fact for the guarantor of the loan.

A representive of the National Hydro-Carbon Company stated last night that the company would proceed at once to sell stock that is expected to be subscribed in Butler and vicinity and as soon as the finanical details are arranged proceed to erect a factory in Butler that will cost approximately $200,000 and will furnish employment to from 400 to 500 men.

The capacity of the plant and the number of men employed will be increased as the business enlarges and it is expected that the local plant will develop into one of the largest in the country. The company is capitalized at

$3,500,000 and has assets in the shape of raw materials variously estimated from $300,000,000 to $400,000,000.

The company has been operating a small plant near Pittsburg, which it is understood will become a part of the Butler plant. A site of 10 acres of ground will be required for the initial plant and this will be increased to 25 acres. The initial plant will make what is known to the trade as shoddy rubber and coating materials. Other products of hydro-carbon will be manufactured, including hard rubber for insulating, automobile tires and all of the hydro-carbon products of which there are over fifty. [This plant was never built for unknown reasons.]

(copied from the *Butler Citizen* dated June 20, 1911 by Dave and Audrey Craig)

## Traction Interests Get plant
### Butler Electric Lighting and Power Equipment Has Been Sold
### Plans For Extensive Improvements Likely
### Transfer Has Revived Talk Of Traction Road From The River

The negotiations between the Butler Light, Heat and Motor Company, and the Kuhn interests of Pittsburgh for the sale of the local electric light and power plant to the West Penn Traction Company were concluded Saturday morning. The West Penn Traction Company will take over the entire holdings of the Butler Light, Heat and Motor Company, including its power plant on Spring Street and the plant of the People's Ice Company adjoining the power plant and the office building of the company on Mifflin Street. Surrounding the power plant is a large plot of ground which can be used for the enlargement of the plant.

The new owners of the plant will assume charge today. It is announced that there will be no change in the working force. John Humphrey will remain as superintendent and J. L. Flack in charge of the office. The other employees will retain their old positions.

### Interests Important

For the development of Butler, the control of its electric light system by the J. S. and W. S. Kuhn interests means much. These interests have large properties. They control the Butler Water Company and the water companies in forty other cities in the United States, the holding company being the American Water Works Company. Another large property of the Kuhns' is the United Coal Company of Pittsburgh, the third largest coal company in western Pennsylvania. Its property is valued at nineteen million dollars. In connection with the local deal it is announced that plans have been worked out for a system of dams and reservoirs on the Cheat River just across the line in West Virginia, by which one of the gigantic power plants in the world will be developed. This system for the generation of electricity will rival Niagara in its proportions. It is significant that Butler will have the benefit of this big power system.

The promoters of the Cheat River power system expect to develop 160,000 horse power. The power plant on the Youghiogheny River is a small affair as compared with the new project in West Virginia. It is announced that as a result of this big power system, electric power will be funished to the people of western Pennsylvania much cheaper than at present. This has in prospect cheaper light and power for Butler, a fact which greatly interests Butlerities.

### Properties are Gilt Edged

The financing of all these properties is in the hands of the Kuhns. The bonds disposed of by this concern are held all over this section and they are regarded as gilt edged. The local representative is C. P. Marshall, among the bonds that are held by many Butler County people are the American Water Works bonds, the Twins Falls, and Sacramento Valley Irrigation bonds, West Penn Traction and other bonds. The Twins Falls proposition is a large one, over 400,000 acres having been irrigated. This acreage is now producing. The Sacramento proposition includes 250,000 acres. The work of irrigating this land is now going on.

The Butler Light, Heat and Motor Company's plant will now become one of the many gilt-edged properties which secure the bonds issued by J. S. and W. S. Kuhn..

### Plan Big Extensions

The Kuhn interests are the largest holders of traction and electric power plants in the United States. Their main power plant is located at Niagara Falls and they are also the owners of practically all of the traction lines in the Allegheny and Kiskiminitas Valleys, including the West Penn Traction Company.

**May Mean Much For Butler**

The acquisition of the local electric power plant by the West Penn Company may mean much for Butler. It is said that the company will expend $200,000 in improvements and enlargements of the plant and the belief is that there will be improvements in the way of additional traction facilities. The company supplies power to manufacturing concerns and it is said that it will run a trunk-power line through Butler to the Beaver Valley and supply the towns in the Lawrence and Beaver County districts with power. The belief is current that it will be only a short time until the company will extend its traction lines from some point in the Allegheny Valley to Butler, probably Tarentum by way of Saxonburg. The approach of a new electric line from the southeast will be incentive for Butler borough to get busy in the viaduct matter as the traction company will be obliged to get into the business center of the city by some route that will eliminate the grade crossings over the railroads.

The Butler Light, Heat and Motor Company has been in operation for 22 years. The original electric light plant was erected on South Washington Street in 1885 by Kerr McBride and John S. Campbell under the title of The Butler Electric Light Company. This company was in existence for five years when it was taken over by the Butler Light, Heat and Motor Company with the following officers - President; John S. Campbell; vice president, W. D. Brandon; secretary, J. H. Troutman; treasurer, L. R. McAboy. Those officers with A. C. Troutman composed the board of directors of the company at the time the plant was disposed of.

The announcement of the sale Saturday caused considerable surprise in business circles. The negotiations were carried on through Messrs.: Campbell, Brandon and Troutman directly with the purchasing company. The papers were closed Saturday morning and the matter was given out to the newspaper at noon.

(copied from the *Butler Citizen* dated Apr. 1, 1912 by Dave and Audrey Craig)

## COMPANY ORGANIZED TO START NEW INDUSTRY IN THIS CITY

The Butler Portable Steam Hammer Company has been organized with a capitalization of $59,000. All of which has been subscribed. The company will engage in the manufacture of the Shearer hammer for dressing drilling bits on oil wells especially in deep hole territory.

The company has a number of hammers in successful operation and the practicability of the hammer has been fully demonstrated. At present the company is getting its machines made by contract in the local machine shops but as the business develops it is the intention to erect large shops in the Butler district for the manufacture of special hammers and other oil well tools.

The hammer is the invention of the late Theodore M. Shearer, of North McKean Street who perfected it shortly before his death and had plans started for the organization of a company to manufacture it. The hammer is the result of 20 years work on the part of the inventor. More than 20 years ago hammers were invented for the purpose of dressing oil well drilling bits in the derrick but they failed because they were stationary and the position of the bit could not be changed to get the right angle.

The new hammer can be changed in its position to strike at any angle while the bit remains stationary on the anvil. It is especially useful in deep hole drilling territory where the large drilling bits require much heavy sledging by hand. It can be so adjusted as to make welds on auger stems and other drilling tools in the derrick, thereby saving much time and expense when breakdowns occur.

The company just organized, already has orders for the portable hammer from West Virginia, Ohio, Oklahoma and California and will place with one of the local shops this week an order for 25 machines to be completed at once.

The directors of the company are A.L.Reiber, George E. Stewart, Mary Shearer, N.C. McCollough and J.C. McKee. The board organized by electing A.L. Reiber president, Mary Shearer secretary and N.C. McCollough treasurer.

(copied from the *Butler Citizen* Butler, Pa. dated Oct. 1912 by David and Audrey Craig)

### Organizations Mean Extension Of Electric Lighting In County
### Butler Short Line To Supply Current

On Saturday, six charters for electric companies to operate in Butler County were granted at the state department in Harrisburgh, Pa. The companies take the name of the district where they are to operate, being Cranberry, Center, Chicora, Oakland, Fairview, and Parker. These companies will purchase their power from the Butler Short Line.

By the middle of 1913, the Short Line will be furnishing power to light and power companies which have been organized in all towns and townships along the line from Butler to Pittsburgh. The interest and appreciation manifested by all of the residents along the line has encouraged the companies and they are sparing no expense in installing every modern improvement to secure reliability of service. A great number of farmers are taking advantage of the opportunity, particularly in view of the fact that rural communities are furnished with 24 hour service, the same as towns.

At Butler, the Butler County light company has installed frequency changers in its substations which will convert the 25 cycle current generated at the main power plant station at Renfrew, to 60 cycle at 2300 volts. Voltage regulators are used to maintain and have uniform voltage on lighting lines.

Although the new light company in Butler has been furnishing current for only a short time, it has secured a large number of patrons and new business is being very rapidly acquired. The Butler County companies were chartered by E. C. Carpenter, R. E. Sprenkle and C. R. Bartley of Butler, their companies being Cranberry, Center, Chicora, Fairview, Oakland and Parker.
(copied from the *Butler Citizen* dated March 17, 1913 by Dave and Audrey Craig)

### Charters Issued for Electric Companies

Charters for electric companies covering the different townships and boroughs in the county through which the Harmony trolley lines pass were filed for the record with Register and Recorder W. W. Crawford yesterday. The following are the companies: Butler Township Electric Company, Lyndora Electric Company, Zelienople Electric Company, Harmony Electric Company, Callery Electric Company, Evans City Electric Company, Jackson Township Electric Company, Forward Township Electric Company, Connoquenessing Township Electric Company, Cranberry Township Electric Company, and Butler ElectricCcompany.
(copied from the *Butler Citizen* dated Aug. 1, 1913 by Dave and Audrey Craig)

### Wishbone Steel Wheels for Automobiles and Trucks To Be Manufactured in This City

The Wishbone Auto Steel Wheel Company of Butler, Pa. was organized Saturday, March 28 under the laws of the state of Pennsylvania, and under the legal direction of Attorney W. D. Brandon, with an authorized capital of $100,000, divided into 10,000 shares, at a par value of $10 a share.

A large number of stock subscribers were present at the meetings and the following were unanimously elected to serve as a board of trustees for the first year of the company's corporate existence: H. W. F. Graham, J. F. Anderson, J. E. Forsythe. W. S. Watson, A. P. Starr, Frank W. Badger, George G. Stuart, all of Butler, Pa. J. W. Carnahan of Washington, D.C., W. C. Schafer of Chicago, Ill., C. P. Young of New York City, J. J. Angel of Cleveland, Ohio, W. H. Gelbach of Zelienople, Pa., A. E. Remaley of West Winfield, Pa., G. F. Reznor of Mercer, Pa., and J. M. Gastmann of Apollo, Pa. All stockholders present attended the first meeting of the board of trustees at which officers of the company were elected

J. W. Carnahan, one of the inventors of the Wishbone Auto Steel Wheel, who has devoted time and money during the past two years in demonstrating the practicability of this wheel for use in connection with the automobile and truck industry, was elected president of the company by acclamation. Mr. Carnahan accepted the position and proposed to serve the company without salary until such time as the board of trustees can agree upon some practical man to fill the position. W.S. Watson was elected vice president, H. W. F. Graham, second vice president; A.P. Starr, treasurer; J. M. Gastman, secretary; C. P. Young, auditor, and George G. Stuart, factory superintendent. With the exception of the secretary and superintendent, all of the said named officers agreed to serve the company without any fixed salary.

This factory is to operate under a license granted by the owners of the patent rights in the premise, and will be one of a series of factories to be located throughout the United States. All stockholders in this, the initial factory, will participate in the profits of all other factories. It is largely due to the efforts and influence of Mr. Watson, and his previous acquaintance with Mr. Carnahan, that Butler was selected as the home of the initial factory of this steel wheel enterprise.

Many prominent and conservative investors of Butler and vicinity are stockholders in this company, and it is the general opinion that this enterprise will prove an exceptionally good manufacturing proposition. There seems to be a universal demand for the Wishbone steel wheel, and it is claimed that the initial capacity of the Butler factory is already contracted for. The success of the company is therefore apparent. The Wishbone steel wheel is particularly adapted for use in connection with motor propelled vehicles, and can be used in connection with any style of tires, solid, cushion or pneumatic. Its resilient steel spokes are so constructed that they serve as cushioning means for the wheels so that nonpuncturable cushion tires can be substituted for the well known pneumatic tires, thus avoiding punctures and blow outs.

It is claimed that by the use of this wheel the life of the motor and transmission as well as the durability of pneumatic or cushion tires will be greatly prolonged, in as much as the strain and vibration will be largely absorbed by the resiliency between the hub and the felly.

It is further claimed that this construction of the wheel solves the problem of resilient transmission and that it is unsurpassed by any wheel on the market for use in connection with the automobile and truck industry.
(copied from The *Butler Citizen*, Butler, Pa. dated March 30, 1914 by Dave and Audrey Craig)

### PEARL BUTTON FACTORY PROBABLE ADDITION TO INDUSTRIES OF BUTLER
### FIRST CONTRACT UNDER GUARANTEE PLAN SIGNED BY CHAMBER OF COMMERCE
### WORK OF ORGANIZING COMPANY WILL BE COMMENCED AT ONCE

Those who are interested in finery and the use of genuine pearl buttons, will be interested in the proposed plant of W. S. Watson of Memphis, Tenn., who closed a contract with the Butler Chamber of Commerce to erect a factory in Butler for the manufacture of pearl buttons from the soft water shells that are found in shell zones of the Ohio and Allegheny Rivers.

Mr. Watson will proceed at once to organize and charter a company capitalized at from $75,000 to $100,000. A good share of the capital stock will be owned and controlled by Butler people. A site will be selected for a factory in a few days and a special building of steel and concrete construction will be erected. The inital factory will have a capacity of 200 machines and will employ about 100 men, at least 25 helpers, and if a carding department is established, employment will be furnished to fifty women and girls.

The special machinery to be used in the factory has been designed and patented by Mr. Watson, and it is believed will revolutionize the pearl button business in the United States. The capacity of the plant will be 2,500 gross of buttons per day, and this capacity will be increased. This looks like a big lot of buttons, but when it is considered that the output in the United States is 110,000 gross per day, the ordinary layman begins to wonder about the extent of the button business.

The *Commerical Appeal* of Memphis, Tenn. published the following account of the shell gathering industry, much of the data for which was obtained from the factory at the location in which Mr. Watson is interested. "The annual production in the United States is now about 20,000,000 gross. This, at producers prices, amounts to approximately $6,000,000 per annunity, a very neat little slice of the total annual production of this country. So large has the production become indeed, that there is an oversupply for the home market, and pearl buttons are now regulary recognized as an article of export. As to the present geographical distrubution of the business, a town in N.Y., is the principal center in the United States.

Undoubtedly the most picturesque features of the button industry are those which have to do with the gathering of shells from the lakes and bayous and rivers and sea coasts. Here is no creaking of pulleys or whirling of spindles and growling of surly sailors. Vanished are factory walls, and in their stead stretch blue heavens and leafy trees, instead of a pine floor is the laughing surface of the water rippled now and then in the light breezes that play across the scene and blow gratefully upon the bare arms and sweating brows of the sturdy laborers heaving at the 'crow-foot' or delving with long-handled tongs among the treasures of the smiling depths below.

Yonder you see barges, laden with the gathered spoils, ready to be towed to the nearest factory or railway siding whence they may be shipped to the factory. There great steaming receptacles into which the gathered muscles are thrown to be boiled until the valves fly apart and the flesh slips easily from them. Close beside the vats are groups of other laborers searching the boiled shell for the pearls which are to be found now and then, and stripping them of the flesh before casting them into heaps to be transported to factories.

Pearl hunting, by the way, is for the most part regarded as merely an incident to the mere prosaic worth of gathering shells for the button factories, but on certain rivers and bayous it has proven so incentive that it may fairly be said to take precedence in those places. Pearls of great value are discovered sometimes, their initial price running up to thousands of dollars.

It is the possibility of discovering a 'pearl of great price,' however, which lends to 'clamming' its chief romantic interest. There is something in that possibility which appeals compellingly to the gambling instinct which exists in active or latent form in the blood of every man, woman and child. Watching a winner poke his nose across the wire is tame sport compared with the sensations which chase each other through the excited consciousness of the lucky finder of a big pearl.

There are two methods of gathering shells from the rivers and bayous and lakes of the south, the depth of the water determing which shall be employed at any given place. In comparatively shallow waters longhandled tongs are employed. These have shanks five or six feet long and wide-spreading jaws. By means of them the shell-gatherer combs the bottom of the mussel-bearing water and brings the bivalves to the surface by scoopfuls, but where the water grows too deep for the use of tongs, and frequently even in shallow water, the device known as the 'crow-foot' is used. This is simply a big rake, having inumerable small grapple hooks attached to its prongs and dragged over the mussel-producing beds by long ropes attached to its two ends. The hooks engage the mussels, which lie habitually edging out of the mud and slightly open, feeding and when dragged a sufficient distance the crow-foot is brought to the surface, usually with from twenty to sixty pounds of mussels clinging to the hooks."

(copied from the *Butler Citizen* dated June 12, 1911 by Dave and Audrey Craig)

## BUTTON MAKING SOON TO BEGIN
## BUTLER BUTTON COMPANY HAS ERECTED LARGE BUILDING FOR PURPOSE
## FRESH WATER SHELLS WILL BE UTILIZED

A mortage for $27,500 from the Butler Button Company to Butler Savings and Trust company was filed for record in the register and recorder's office yesterday. The mortage is given to cover a bond issue made by the company, which is starting a factory to manufacture pearl buttons in Butler.

The company has its factory erected at the intersection of Negley Avenue and Sullivan Avenue and will be ready for operation about the first of the month. But for an error that happened in shipping the machinery for the factory last May, the plant would have been in operation three months ago. Two carloads of machines made in Cincinnati, were wrecked on the way to Butler and when the cars arrived here nearly all of the machines were broken. The machines were shipped back to Cincinnati to be rebuilt and word has been received from the shops that they are ready for shipment. Manager Watson of the button company was in Pittsburgh this week conferring with the managers of the railroad companies in regard to the settlement of the claims for damages and replacing the damaged machines.

A car load of fresh water shells arrived at the factory this week and two more cars are expected today. Mr. Watson expects to have a stock of material on hand on which to work as soon as the machines arrive and can be set in place.

An addition to the main building has been erected to take care of the stock and for use as a warehouse. The plant itself is brick and steel construction with concrete floors with a two-story office department facing the street. It will be one of the most complete and best equipped plants of its kind in the country. It will furnish employment to 50 to 100 people and will be a valuable addition to the manufacturing interests of the town
(copied from the *Butler Citizen* dated Sept. 20, 1912 by Dave and Audrey Craig)

## BUTTON PLANT IN OPERATION

Can you sew a button on straight or can you arrange 12 buttons on a card, four buttons in a row and three rows, so that the rows will be straight and the eyelets of the button perfectly aligned? If you can do more than nine out of ten women can do you can make money.

It may be of interest to know that the Butler Button factory, which began operations a few days ago will employ a number of girls and women to card the buttons. It is also of interest to know that with all man's ingenuity he has never invented a machine that will sew buttons on a card as you find them in the dry good store. Whenever you get a daintily colored card with a dozen pearl buttons on it, or a dozen overcoat buttons for that matter, the buttons have been sewed on the card by hand one at a time. The trick is to get the buttons on the card in straight lines both ways. The buttons are strung on one thread and it is an exceedingly nice operation to do the work perfectly and rapidly.

Manager W. S. Watson of the local button factory says that nine out of ten of the girls who begin the work can't sew the buttons on straight. Most of them learn quickly but some never learn. It is true that overall factories and shirt factories have machines that will sew buttons on at a rate of two or three a minute, but the buttons are placed one at a time and ten threads are used in the operation. Machines have been invented to card buttons, but none of them have proven successful and are not saving in time and labor over the hand operation.

Mr. Watson has invented a device which he expects will materially increase the output of the hand operation and at the same time insure the perfect alignment of the buttons on the card. The device is simple and easy to operate. It is estimated that it will save one-half cent a gross in the cost of carding, which is quite an item in a factory that is turning out from 2,500 to 3,000 gross of buttons a day.

### Factory Operating

The factory of the Butler Button Company is getting under way and will have a full force of operators employed in a few months. One of the difficulties encountered by manager Watson is to get enough men to operate all of the machines and run the factory to its full capacity. All of the machine operators have to be trained and it takes two weeks to a month for a "green" operator to become sufficiently skilled to make any money for the company or for himself.

There are at present 17 men employed in the factory. Twelve of these are working on the machines cutting blanks and the others are engaged in the machine shop and in the operation of the plant. The machine operators are turning out an average of 25 gross of blanks a day each and the daily output is about 300 gross. When the 200 machines in the factory are in full operation the plant will employ 100 men cutting blanks besides the additional help required to run the polishing and finishing departments and the girls employed in the carding rooms.

The men employed on the machines are paid piece work and make good wages, once they have acquired a certain degree of skill. The average output of two machines operated by one man is from 25 to 30 gross a day and the daily output is about 300 gross. It is estimated that it pays the operator from $12 to $15 a week.

The process of making pearl buttons from common fresh water mussel shell is an interesting one. The company has in stock enough shells for 100,000 gross of buttons. This is a small item of 14,400,000 buttons. The shells used in the Butler factory are brought from the Ohio valley and as far west as the Mississippi and are the common mussel shell found in the sand bars of the river. Before they are sent to the factory the shells are soaked in water for four or five days. Then they are sorted and distributed to the machines where the blanks are cut.

The man who sorts the shells and makes the distribution has his weather eye open usally for any pearls that may be sticking to the interior of the shells, but the shell diggers usally see that few of these valuable items escape them. Once in a while the man who sorts the shells at the factory finds a small pearl and occasionally he finds one of considerable value.

After the blanks are cut and the face put on them, which is done by one operation on the Watson machine, they are sent to the backing machine, which trims the blank down to an even thickness. These machines are automatic feeders, the blanks being placed on a belt face up by the operator. From the backing machine the blanks go to the drilling machine where two or four eyelets are drilled in each blank as required. After this process the rough buttons are placed in a churn like arrangement filled with water and pumice stone. The machine is agitated like an old fashioned barrel churn, and when the buttons come out all of the rough edges have been trimmed off. The next process is another churning in a solution of hot water and muriatic acid. This is the finishing touch. When the buttons come out of the bath they have a bright, glossy finish that distinguishes the pearl button from all other buttons. The final operation is the carding of the buttons, which is done by girls and is practically the only hand operation in the entire process.

Manager Watson is breaking in new men in the factory as fast as he can get them and in a short time expects to have all of the departments running full. The factory will furnish employment to a large number of people at wages the equal of any of the manufacturing concerns in the district. (The Butler Button Factory was located where Hutchinson's Cleaners is now on Negley Ave.)
(copied from the *Butler Citizen* dated April 3, 1913 by Dave and Audrey Craig)

## Mitchell Insurance, Inc.

Mitchell Insurance, Inc. is one of the oldest businesses in continuous operation in Butler County, dating back to the middle of the last century, before the Civil War. The agency was started by James McJunkin, on East Jefferson Street, just off Main. He was followed into the agency by his sons, Loyal and Ira McJunkin, operating as I. S. McJunkin & Co. In 1894 they hired George Mitchell, son of a pioneer New Castle family, as a policy-writer because of his beautiful handwriting. He became a full-time employee, then a partner, and later bought out the McJunkins when they retired. George Mitchell was joined in 1936 by his son, Loyal, and the name of the business was changed to Mitchell Insurance Agency at that time. In 1976 Loyal's son, William, joined the agency, which incorporated in 1981 with Loyal as president and William as vice president. The agency's phenomenal growth of over 400 per cent in premium volume necessitated the hiring of more employees. To accomodate the increased business, the agency in 1985 purchased the office building at the corner of Brady and Washington Streets.

Loyal and Catherine Mitchell reside in a wonderful old, Queen Anne-style, tower house at 434 North McKean Street. The oldest part of the house was built in 1890 by Mrs. Sophia Burchfield. She sold the house shortly thereafter to Mrs. Eliza Blakslee. Mrs. Blakslee was the mother-in-law of J. V. Ritts, founder of the Butler County National Bank and prominent Butler businessman. What was the J. V. Ritts home sits next door on the corner of Fulton and McKean Streets. Mrs. Blakslee moved here from New York state to be near her daughter and son-in-law. Mrs. Blakslee planned a large addition to the house in 1898 but died before it was completed. In more recent times, the Mitchell house was the residence of Dr. Atwell and his wife, parents of J. Clinton Atwell, county coroner and owner of the Atwell Funeral Home.

Loyal and Catherine purchased the house about ten years ago in order to save it from becoming a parking lot. The house became their personal residence about a year ago. Of special interest to lovers of old houses are the complimentary stained glass windows, original Lincrusta wainscoating, a servants call system and the combination electric-gasoliers. The Mitchells who love and appreciate history have collected many antiques over the years, including Catherine's collection of glassware designed by her maternal grandfather, J. E. Miller.

## H. L. Raabe, Motorcycles

The Harley-Davidson motorcycle company had its beginnings in 1903. At that time the typical automobile was much too expensive for the average American which fact probably accounted for much of the popularity of motorcycles. Those early motorcycles were not much more than converted bicycles; they weighed less than 125 pounds. Many handymen fabricated their own "motorcycles," put a name on the tank and had a personalized bike--one of a kind. During the first ten years of the 1900's there were as many as 250 such brands of motorcycles in the U.S.

In 1914 Butler's Harley-Davidson distributorship was owned by the Diamond Garage. The garage was located on East Diamond Street and was owned by the Willetts brothers who are mentioned earlier in this chapter. In 1915, that Harley-Davidson dealership was acquired by Herbert Leroy Raabe. The Willetts brothers closed their Diamond Street business and moved their operations, sans Harley-Davidson, to Route 68 just a few miles north of Butler. Mr. Raabe ran the motorcycle dealership until 1917 when he took on a partner, Arthur Dumbaugh. Raabe and Dumbaugh sold and serviced Harley-Davidsons in their shop behind the Cleeland building in the alley at the corner of Cedar and Birch Streets. The site is presently the location of Alley Antiques. After 1918 Raabe and Dumbaugh each gravitated toward other business pursuits. Arthur Dumbaugh was a very fine mechanic and became involved in selling Hudson automobiles. [Incidentally, Arthur's brother, Earl, was the founder of Dumbaugh Electric and another brother, C. T. Dumbaugh, became one of Butler's best known contractors.] H. L. Raabe began to work full-time as an auto mechanic. There is a void in the record of Harley-Davidson sales in Butler until Dom Zanotti acquired the franchise from the Harley-Davidson Company in 1950.

## Zanotti Harley-Davidson

In 1925, Dominick Zanotti moved his toolbox into a shed in his North Vandergrift back yard and hung out a sign. He and his friends needed a place to meet and work on their Harleys and Indians. Dom had the shed, the tools and the mechanical ability. He was a full-time coal miner but loved motorcycles and spent as much time with motorcycling activities as his busy schedule allowed. It wasn't long until his riding buddies and their acquaintances found that Dom was a mechanical expert when it came to motorcycles and his part time hobby was growing into a full time opportunity. He made a decision right then and there. He applied for and got the franchises for both Harley Davidson and Indian motorcycles. He quit mining coal and the North Vandergrift shop became his livlihood.

In the spring of 1936, the Kiski River swelled above its banks and destroyed the Zanotti home and shop but Dom didn't quit. The summer of 1936 was spent rebuilding the home and shop on the original foundations. By autumn his new shop was opened and his life was back to normal.

In 1947 Dom moved the Indian franchise to Butler. His first Butler location was at the famous "pickle gate crossing," under the current Lyndora Viaduct. In 1950 Dom acquired the Harley-Davidson franchise for Butler and opened a shop on the south end of the Main Street Viaduct. Dom formed the Sunset Riders during that era.

Andy Zanoti was discharged from the army in 1954 and entered the growing business. It was necessary to expand their facilities so construction began on a new building at 171 Pittsburgh Road, directly across Route 8 from the present location.

Doris Doerr was a high school senior working part-time at Zanotti's. Andy proposed and they were married in 1958. Son, Dean, was born a year later. In 1963 Harley Davidson expanded into the golf car business. Andy brought the franchise to Butler and Zanotti's have been leasing and selling golf cars throughout the tri-state area ever since. Andy purchased the Kiski Valley Cycle Center in 1963; his brother Don became the general manager. The business flourished. The franchise for Artic Cat snowmobiles was acquired, then the Yamaha franchise was added in 1968.

Huck Davis' Indian motorcycle shop on Jackson St.(dedication of new police station--1960)

During the freezing, pre-dawn hours of February 11, 1970 four businesses located between Zanotti's and the Greater Butler Mart were simultaneously ablaze. Zanotti Motor Company was a total loss. Every motorcycle, both customer and company owned, burned; the fire was fueled by the gasoline in their tanks. Even the entire parts inventory was melted or destroyed by the intense heat. All of the office records were lost. It was an administrative nightmare that lasted for years, but rebuilding began the following day. Grand opening festivities were held in the spring of 1971. The new, larger facility enabled Zanottis to add pleasure boats, travel trailers, motorhomes and fishing boats to their inventory. Mercury Marine and Holiday Rambler units were now available. The Honda marquee came on board in 1976.

The 1970' were tough times for Harley-Davidson sales. Foreign motor-cycle sales soared.

Zanotti's shop on the east side of Route 8

They were cheaper and were earning reputations for dependability and quality. Harley-Davidson sales plumeted. If it hadn't been for Honda and Yamaha sales, Zanotti's may have gone bankrupt. But during the 1980's employees bought the Harley-Davidson company and made some needed changes. This along with a government induced tariff on foreign motorcycles started to turn things around. Harley-Davidson sales began to soar and after three years into the tariff, Harley-Davidson CEO, Vaughn Beals, told President Reagan, that the government could lift the tariff, that Harley-Davidson was competing in the world market and making a profit.

The "reborn" Harley-Davidson company required much more of its dealers. Sales staffs, technicians and administrators had to attend school. All received job specific training as well as marketing and customer relations classes. Computers were introduced and store image became an issue.

In the spring of 1990 Zanotti's current store was remodeled. Over 20,000 square feet was added to the showroom and the shop. It is a very complete facility and with a staff trained in marketing and customer relations it looks as though the Zanotti family will be serving their customers well into the new millenium.

**Standard Motor Company - Corner of Main and Brady Streets**

## A LOAF OF BREAD

In the early 1900's the mother of the house or a servant baked all the bread that the family ate. Every kitchen had a trough in which the dough was mixed, kneaded and formed into loaves by hand. Many enterprising people even made their own yeast. They purchased only the flour, salt, sugar, and perhaps milk because many who lived on the edge of the city or in one of the rural communities also had a cow or two. The flour was, in most cases, a product of the family's hard work. Farm families harvested the grain then hauled it to a local mill to have it ground into flour; some ground it at home with a hand grinder. As recently as the 1950's there were, within a few miles of Butler, several feed mills which ground grain. Polk's City Directory for 1950 lists nine such establishments for the county.

Before 1900 most villages had a community bake oven. It was built of stone and wasn't much to look at, but was certainly put to good use. Approximately once a week, usually on Saturdays, the women of the town met and baked enough bread for the week. A roaring fire was started in the oven, then after a while the burning wood, charcoal and ashes were pulled out and the bread was put in. The heat from the stones baked the bread. The aroma of the freshly baked bread carried for a considerable distance. This was a real treat considering the foul smells that so often pervaded those back yards and alleys. One of the continuing discussions among housewives was how often a woman ought to bake to be sure that her family had fresh bread. In addition to the community ovens, fussy cooks baked every day in their own kitchens, except on the Sabbaths. Today very few households do their own baking. Nearly all the bread consumed in this country is baked by commercial bakeries.

### Diehl's Bakery

One of Butler's earliest and most successful commercial bakeries was the Diehl Baking Company which was located at 361-63 Center Avenue. An in-depth look at the Diehl operation will shed considerable light upon Butler's bakeries in general.

Philip Diehl was born in Pittsburgh in 1868. He married Catherine Nuesser, also a Pittsburgh native,

### SHERMAN BAKING CO.

We wish we could show you through our big, bright, busy bakery, that you might learn why our baked goods sell so fast. Baking bread with us is a science. We have been in the business more than 20 years; and our goods are recognized as standard. One bite of Sherman's bread tells why it is best.

Its distinctive taste and appetizing flavor appeal to all who eat it. It is made with care from the choicest flour and with a skill that only long experience makes possible. It is mixed in large electric mixers, made up in electric driven machines and baked in modern ovens in a throughly equipped bakery, the sanitary arrangements of which are perfect in every detail. Sherman's bread is all quality and purity and is bought and eaten daily by thousands in western Penna.

It is sold by all grocers and we ask you to join the large army of quality bread consumers; you get the best bread baked and it costs you no more than the ordinary kind.
(copied from the *Butler Citizen* dated July 11, 1915 by Dave and Audrey Craig)

[Sherman's Bakery was located just off Brown Avenue in the building which later housed the Dixie Bakery. Mr. and Mrs. Joe Sherman and their three children, Joe Jr., Casper, and Mary ran the family bakery. Sherman's was especially known for its bread. Another family member, George, had a blacksmith shop which was located in the building which may yet be seen in the Cunningham Street parking lot of the Terrace Apartments. Today the building is owned by the Butler County Housing Authority and is used for residential purposes. Mr. and Mrs. Sherman lived in a house on Cliff Street where the main entrance to Terrace Apartments is today.]

and the couple became the parents of four children. As an aspiring young man, Mr. Diehl learned the baking trade and opened his own bakery in Pittsburgh but he didn't feel that he would make his career in the old-mill town. He had dreams of locating in a thriving town where his business could grow along with the community. The young family followed their vision and relocated to Curwensville, Clearfield County where Mr. Diehl opened and operated a bakery, but after six years Curwensville left something to be desired. The family had heard a great deal of positive news concerning the burgeoning town of Butler, just thirty miles north of Pittsburgh. It was growing rapidly and seemed to show a great deal of promise. It would be a good place to raise children—a good place to open a bakery—a good place to make a life. The Diehls came to Butler in 1901 and never regretted their choice. Philip initially found employment with the Sherman Baking Company which was then located on Brown Ave (*Butler County the Second Hundred Years*, pg. 25) and continued to work toward the day when he could open his own bakery.

That day arrived on May 20, 1910 when the bakery and confectionery of Philip Diehl & Sons opened at 319 Centre Avenue. Philip was the president, son Gilbert A. became the general manager, treasurer and secretary, and son Philip J. served as vice president. Advertisements were placed in the local newspapers and visitors were cordially invited to visit and inspect Diehl's new bakery, and an impressive facility it was. The salesroom with a large display window faced the street. It was equipped with shelves and cases for showing cakes, pies, bread and confectionery. Most bakeries also made candies at that time.

Immediately behind the salesroom was the bakeshop where the Diehls utilized the latest machinery available to the baking industry. The bread dough was placed in the humidity and warmth of the steam room for raising. The bake oven, which was next to the steam room was fourteen by sixteen feet and had a capacity of three hundred large loaves of bread at a time. After the bread was baked it was placed on galvanized bread racks to cool prior to wrapping.

A company named Day's at that time manufactured and sold bakery equipment. Diehls purchased and installed one of Day's "cookie machines." The dough mixture was put into the machine and soon the baked cookies were rolling off the line at a rate of 150 a minute. Diehls also acquired the latest model of Day's "egg beater and cake mixing machine." On the second floor the business had a large space which was divided into two rooms. The smaller of the two rooms was used as a storeroom for pans, baskets and assorted containers, and the larger room was where the bread dough was mixed. This operation was also done with a Day's "bread mixer." After mixing, the dough was put into a chute and sent downstairs to the steam room for raising.

### Southside Bakers Will Construct A Big Modern Plant

One of the largest real estate transactions of the year was closed yesterday when Phillip Diehl and son, the Southside bakers, took over the vacant lot at the corner of Center and Lookout Avenues owned by J. H. Harper. The lot faces 96 feet on Center and 125 feet on Lookout Avenue and is the largest and most desirable building lot in that part of city. The consideration was not made public.

The new owner will occupy the entire grounds space with a three-story, brick building which will be used entirely as a bakery, stock rooms and sales room. The building will probably be the largest devoted exclusively to the baking business in the city and will be equipped with up-to-date machinery for mixing, weighing and handling the dough, as well as handling the bread as it comes from the ovens.

Diehl and son have had remarkable success in Butler since they started in business a little over three years ago. Their trade has grown by leaps and bounds until they are among the largest producers in the western part of the state outside of the city of Pittsburgh.

They started with a one-horse, delivery wagon that put in its time delivering freight from the depot when not used in delivering bread. In the past year the business has grown until an auto, delivery truck was added to the equipment and within the past few days an order had been placed for an additional auto, delivery truck.

Phillip Diehl, the senior partner of the firm, stated last night that work on the new plant will be commenced as soon as the details of the building and equipment can be worked out.

It is expected that the building will be completed and the machinery installed for business the early part of the year. The new plant will furnish employment to quite a number of people and will be a substantial addition to the industrial interests of the city.

(copied from the *Butler Citizen* dated July 25, 1913 by Dave and Audrey Craig)

In opening such an elaborate bakery in Butler, Mr. Diehl and his sons knew they were taking a risk. They invested a great deal of money in a new town where they weren't well-known, and there was also the competition from a dozen other bakers to consider. The Diehls however, as many other entrepreneurs before them, were convinced that they could capture a large share of the growing market in the Butler area, and capture it they did.

They had started with one oven and a horse-drawn, delivery wagon. The increase in business had been phenomenal. A second wagon was soon needed and it wasn't long before four trucks replaced the horse-drawn, delivery wagons. Their gamble was paying off—within four years Diehl's business had outgrown their 319 Center Avenue facility and they were looking for a new location. A news article in the *Butler Citizen* on July 25, 1913 announced plans for a new Diehl's bakery at the corner of Center and Lookout Avenues.

Since the opening of their first Butler operation four years earlier, the entire baking process had become so highly mechanized that from the moment the grain was harvested until the loaf was on the supermarket shelf, no human being had touched it much less done any handwork on it. Flour, water, and the other ingredients were tossed and mingled in big, mechanical mixers, conveyed by machinery to fermenting rooms, separated into balls and shaped into loaves by other devices, baked on trays that moved automatically through tunnel-like ovens, and finally wrapped by a packaging machine. Trucks then rushed the bread to market.

Diehl's introduced such mechanized baking to Butler with the opening of their new operation in 1914. As they had done when they opened their first bakery just a couple of blocks away, Phillip Diehl and his sons held an open house for their customers and friends—an invitation to all to inspect their new facilities. Consider the following description of their modern operation: "The mixing room was on the third floor. Sacks of flour were taken off the elevator and dumped into the electrically powered mixer. From the mixing room the dough traveled down to the second floor through a steel tube. There it was taken up by an automatic dividing and scaling machine, formed into loaves of a predetermined size, passed on to the steel proofing cabinets and from there into the molding machine where it was made ready for the ovens. Similar automated machinery used in making cakes, pies and doughnuts was located on the second floor. One continuous oven, which was used for baking bread, had a capacity of 12,000 loaves in a twenty-four hour period. Another identical oven on the second floor was used exclusively for baking pies and cakes. The combined weight of the two ovens was over one hundred tons and they contained enough bricks to build a six-room house."

Polk's City Directory for 1898 lists five bakeries for Butler. By 1915-16 Butler's population had grown to over 20,000 and there were fifteen bakeries doing business in the city. By 1930 the economic effects of the Great Depression were taking their toll in so many ways: only ten bakeries continued to operate. But 1940 found the economy rejuvenated, the city's population had climbed to an all-time high of 24,477 and sixteen bakeries were open and doing business in the city. 1950 found the city's population to have dropped about a thousand souls to 23,482 and the number of bakers in turn, declined to thirteen.

**Butler Facing Bread Famine--World War I Rationing**

District bakeries may exhaust flour supply in three weeks unless the government steps in to relieve the present flour shortage. Butler may be in the throes of a bread famine within another month, Gilbert A. Diehl, of the Diehl Baking Company predicted today.

" I have been in business thirty-six years," said Mr. Diehl, "and I have never seen the outlook before as dark as it appears to be today. I am hoping the government will do something about it." Many of the bakeries will be out of flour within three weeks, Mr. Diehl predicted, and over half of the bakeries in this district may be out of business by that time.

The Home Town Bakery closed last week for lack of flour. Many others are said to be considering similar action. Fortunately for the Diehl Bakery, it has about a six week supply on hand, but it is rationing its flour in an effort to make it last as long as possible.

Mr. Diehl explained that the mills have not been able to buy any wheat for the past several weeks, as the government has been paying the growers a thirty cent bonus over the OPA ceiling price, ostensibly to swell the nation's supply of wheat for shipment to war-torn Europe.

The government bonus ended May 25, but by that time considerable damage had been done from the bakers and consumer public's point of view. "The mills have not been able to buy wheat since the lifting of the bonus," Mr. Diehl said he had been informed.

**Wholesalers Affected**

"The mills couldn't give me any definite idea as to when they would be able to furnish us additional flour," he said, "as they do not know when they can get wheat, wholesalers are about out and bakeries are running out." The Butler baker said he believed that most of the bakeries in Butler have a three-week supply, while most of the bakers in Grove City have only a two-week supply.

The government called upon the mills to sell it seventy-five percent of their wheat for April, May and June, offering them the thirty cent bonus. At the same time the government asked the mills to buy no more wheat.

Bakeries for many months have been limited to seventy-five percent of their former flour supply, and many did not fare even that well. Neither is the cereal outlook any better. Many grocers' shelves are low, and no relief can be seen for the next several weeks.

(copied by Dave and Audrey Craig from the *Butler Eagle*, date unavailable)

**Cheaper Bread In Butler To Become Effective Dec. 10, 1917**

**Local Bakers To Co-operate With Government Under New Food**

**No More Icing On Rolls Will Be Permitted**

Reduction of the wholesale and retail prices of bread will be made Monday, December 10, by the Butler bakers who expect to cooperate with the government under the new federal food laws. The Diehl Bakery, Center Avenue, announced yesterday that a reduction would be made on the price of the pound and the pound and a half loaf. The wholesale price of the pound loaf will be seven and one-half cents and the pound and a half loaf will be eleven cents. Retail prices will be nine cents for the pound loaf and thirteen cents for the pound and a half loaf. The bread loaves will be sixteen and twenty-four ounces baked. All bread rolls will be made under government formula, which will not permit icing on bread and rolls.

The Sherman Baking Company of Butler has issued notices to its customers that it will comply with the government regulations as to size of loaves and retail and wholesale prices.

**NO MORE SWEET DOUGHS**

The bakers themselves will not be regulated as to the use of wheat. The consumption of this commodity is to be regulated through the mills. Heretofore the finest kind of flour has been about 96 percent hard wheat and 4 percent spring wheat and other ingredients.

The new regulations will require the millers to grind only 65 percent hard wheat, 30 percent spring wheat and 5 percent what is known as "durum," which is used in the manufacture of macaroni. The bakers will not be allowed to mix the so-called sweet dough used for buns and other sweet breads. Consequently, those articles will disappear from the bills of fare of hotels and restaurants, unless they are baked by those concerns. Neither can the bakers put icing on their rolls and cakes and otherwise sweeten their breads as has been customary in many instances. Heretofore six pounds of sugar and six of lard were used to each barrel of flour in making bread mixture. The new regulation reduces the amount to two of sugar and two of lard to the barrel of flour.

(copied from the *Butler Citizen* dated Dec. 6, 1917 by Dave and Audrey Craig)

**Baking Company Of Butler Announces New Loaf Of Bread**

**Diehl Baking Company Gives Out Statement At Last Night's Banquet**

A banquet was held last evening at the Nixon Hotel at 6:30 for the salesmen of the Diehl Baking Company. It was announced by management that plans were completed for the marketing of a new loaf of bread, to be known as "Betsy Ross" bread, which will be placed on sale at all grocers' Thursday morning, April 5. This new loaf 'Betsy Ross' is the result of considerable research work and experimenting, G.A. Diehl stated, and we feel that we have perfected a loaf as near like the bread our mothers used to bake as is possible to manufacture. In fact it was that elusive, old-fashioned flavor that we were striving to secure and we believe that 'Betsy Ross' bread has that flavor.

The advertising and merchandising plans were outlined by O.W. Keene, who represents the W.E. Long Company, a bakery service organization of Chicago. Mr. Keene stated that this company was interested in watching the reception this new loaf received in Butler and vicinity, and feels that a real, old-fashioned loaf, baked with a mother's care, would be welcomed by the public.

Phillip Diehl, the founder of the business, stated that he felt "Betsy Ross" bread was the finest he had ever produced in his forty-five years of experience and that every care and attention would be given this loaf to maintain a uniform quality. Mr. Diehl and his son, P.J. Diehl spend their time in the production department, while G.A. Diehl acts as general manager of the company.

(copied from the *Butler Eagle* dated April 4, 1928 by Dave and Audrey Craig)

## Common Wheat Diet For Allied Powers
### All Bread Used In America To Correspond With That Used Abroad

Washington: Aug. 27, 1918

The allied nations go on a common wheat and bread schedule after September 1st. America with a great harvest coming, has enough grain to care for the deficits of all, if all maintain a "victory bread and flour" system.

That was the announcement from the food administration today.

### Common Wheat Diet

All the wheatless days and meals for America are abolished, but all bread in this country must correspond with the bread to be used abroad. It must not exceed 80 per cent wheat. "It has been agreed that the wheat bread of the allies shall contain 20 per cent grain other than wheat, and it is only just that we should bear our share in this savings, that our bread at least should be universal with those who are suffering more greatly from the war than ourselves," says the announcement from Herbert Hoover's office. Exact proportions for mixing victory flour are given. Four pounds of wheat flour to one pound of barley; four pounds of wheat flour to one pound of corn flour; eight pounds of wheat flour to one pound of barley flour and one pound of corn flour; three pounds of wheat flour to not less than two pounds of rye flour.

Whole wheat, entire wheat, or graham flour or meal must contain at least 95 per cent of the wheat berry. Dealers may sell these flours without accompanying substitutes, but where straight wheat flour is sold 20 per cent substitute must be sold coincidentally.

(copied from the *Butler Eagle*, dated Aug. 27, 1918 by Dave and Audrey Craig)

### Bread Loaves And Wheat Mixtures

A loaf of bread weighing one and one-half pounds was adopted today by master bakers as the standard for this city, following the establishment of a uniform price yesterday. The price is reduced from 18 to 17 cents a loaf because of the standardization. There will be other sized loaves put out by some of the bakers and prices will be made accordingly. Prices on cakes and pies remain the same.

(copied from the *Butler Eagle*, dated Mar. 5, 1920 by Dave and Audrey Craig)

## Bill To Fix Size Of Bread Loaves
### Measure Is Designed To Regulate Sale And Fix Weight

Harrisburg, PA Feb. 16, 1921

Standardized loaves of bread in sanitary packages would be required if a bill introduced in the house by Walker, Philadelphia, passes the legislature.

### Fine of $25

A fine of not less than $25 nor more than $100 is provided for violators of this act. The bill is designed to regulate the sale and fix the weight of bread as follows:

1. Standard weight for each loaf made twelve hours after baking fixed at one or more pound weights
2. Wrapped in a package stamped with net weight
3. If not wrapped must be conspicuously tagged. It would be unlawful under this bill to qualify the statement of net weight by words or phrases to show that the law is being complied with.

(copied from the *Butler Eagle*, dated Feb. 16, 1921 by Dave and Audrey Craig)

## Morrison's Bakery

Certainly one of the most enduring and successful baking operations Butler ever had was the Thomas A. Morrison bakery. For more than seventy-five years, Morrison's bakery was located in downtown Butler. Mr. Morrison founded his business in 1881. By 1895 his bakery was located at 212 South Main Street. Originally it was known as the Morrison Bakery and Confectionery Company; later it was named Thomas A. Morrison Manufacturing Confectioners. Morrison's always had a stand at local fairs and carnivals where they sold their products including homemade lemonade. In addition to the bakery and candy interests Mr. Morrison was the first president and one of the founders of the Butler Coin Club, which was organized in 1947 and had its early meetings at his candy factory on Jackson Street.

Sometime just after the turn of the century, Thomas Morrison moved from his Main Street location to 112 West Cunningham Street. Morrison's remained at the West Cunningham Street location until the family closed the business. They owned or at least occupied all the buildings on the north side of West Cunningham Street between Main and Jackson Streets. They occupied those buildings along Jackson Street as far as the rear of the former Aland's Toy Store. The Morrison family rented the corner building to Sun Drug on Main and had their bakery retail outlet where Matthew Fischer's law office and Pepper's Flowers are today. Before the Wishing Well Card Shop, which opened after Sun Drug closed, the Comique Theater was on that corner.

Morrison's did all the baking as well as the candy making on the premises. They baked bread, cakes, pies, and were especially famous for their ladylocks, chocolate eclairs, and Christmas candy canes. But their most successful product was without a doubt, Morrison's giant, souvenir lollipops, which were shipped all over the country. The business prospered considerably after their introduction in the early 1950's.

Morrisons hired a few high school students; only those who could handle a rigorous regimen lasted very long. Starting time was 3:00 a.m. and they worked until time to go to school. It made for a very long day but the extra money made it worthwhile for some of those hard-working boys.

Morrisons lived at 115 South Washington Steet. They are remembered by older Butler residents as a hard-working family who walked the half block to work with their lunch bags under their arms—even as they reached advanced years. They must have loved their work because they always sang as they walked the short distance up Washington Street to Cunningham Street. When they left their place of employment to return home, it was easy to guess what their jobs were—they were covered with flour from head to toe.

The Wings were related to the Morrisons and are responsible for the "candy cane" house on Standard Avenue. It was built after World War II.

Mr. Thomas A. Morrison had been born in Hadley, Crawford County, on January 8, 1870. He died at the Butler County Memorial Hospital April 10, 1964, of complications from a broken hip, at the ripe old age of ninety-four. His son, Horace W. Morrison and his wife, Lenora Woods Morrison, closed the bakery but continued to operate the candy company. For more than thirty years she managed the office while her husband managed sales; her father-in-law supervised the candy-making business.

## Bush's Bakery

Luther M. Bush and Hulda I. Anthony were born in Jefferson County. Each attended Slippery Rock Normal School and taught in the public schools for about two years. After Hulda became Mrs. Luther M. Bush, the young couple relocated from Jefferson County to Butler. The year was 1918. Mr. Bush found employment in one of East Butler's several factories. Things seemed to be going well but the Great Depression was lurking on the horizon. In 1927 the factory closed; Mr. Bush found himself unemployed and the depressed economy at that time made any hope of finding a job rather bleak.

Hulda, who was one of ten children, naturally learned considerable kitchen skills while helping raise such a large family. Her mother was a wonderful cook and baker and one of Hulda's sisters and her husband, using some of the family recipes, had opened and operated a bakery in Punxsutawney. With money being so scarce during the depression, Mrs. Bush thought that she might earn some extra cash by using the old family recipes and selling baked goods to her friends and neighbors in the south hills area of Butler. Word spread quickly and in spite of the bad economy, her business grew to the extent that she soon needed help. At this time the family lived in a three-bedroom house and all of the baking was done on the family oven and range.

The nation was caught up in the throes of the greatest, economic slowdown in history, but Bush's bakery business was nevertheless flourishing. Luther and Hulda found it necessary to move to larger quarters. They purchased a building on North Cliff Street, between Penn and Walnut Streets, which had formerly housed a small neighborhood store and the Limberg Ice Cream Company. Martha Bush Noble and and her sister, Peggy Bush Sherrod, still remember one of the back rooms on the first floor of their new building--it was completely lined with cork. The room had been specially constructed by Mr. Limberg to keep the ice cream cold. Luther and Hulda located their bakery on the first floor in the back of the Cliff Street building. The new occupants added to their capacity by purchasing another home-style oven/range and two, large, bread ovens. The bakery eventually housed four ovens. They also operated a small, general store and used a large display window in the front to service the store as well as the bakery. The family lived upstairs—mom, dad, three daughters and one son.

It was at that time that Luther learned to bake. He made the bread and rolls while Hulda specialized in making homemade pies. Mrs. Bush made as many as one hundred pies a day, particularly when they had an order for a Rotary club or Lions club function. "These special days," said Martha, "saw about one hundred pies coming out of those ovens." Business continued to increase necessitating the hiring of a woman to make the cookies; the kids helped with the clerking and some operations such as shelling walnuts.

Mr. Bush never worked elsewhere after settling in to the bakery business--The bakery became the family's full-time occupation and livlihood. "We weren't rich but my parents were able to raise four kids," said Martha. The family never vacationed; they were too busy to go to Conneaut Lake or any of the other parks. The only thing that resembled a vacation was when the hard-working family traveled back to Jefferson County to visit with relatives.

When I asked Martha Bush Noble what were the most popular or famous of their baked goodies, she immediately replied, "We baked bread and buns, cookies, cinnamon rolls, clover-leaf rolls and coffee cakes, but I think the pies were most popular. People came from as far away as Pittsburgh to get mom's pies." But when I asked some of the people who were once customers of Bush's, they unanimously answered, "The sticky, cinnamon buns." I have a feeling that all of Bush's baked goods were delicious.

Some days work at the bakery began at 3:00 a.m. Luther and Hulda must have been exhausted long before quitting time, but in spite of the demanding work days, Mrs. Bush always had a home-cooked meal on the table at suppertime.

Martha remembers seeing her father mixing fifty loaves of bread at a time. Luther became an expert at 'pinching' cloverleaf rolls. He started with a small ball of dough and squeezed it just right. The pinched rolls were remarkably all uniform.

The flour, sugar, yeast and other ingredients used in their baking business were all purchased at Rom's Wholesale Products on South Cliff Street. When I asked the girls if they would share a favorite recipe with the readers of this book they graciously approved, but added that the ingredients alone do not make a great, baked good. It takes a touch too, because the ingredients weren't always the same; the lard was not always of a uniform texture and even the milk differed from one season to the next. "And any good baker," says Martha, "knows that a good pan makes a big difference."

Hulda Bush died in 1950 at age fifty and Luther kept the bakery going for several

## Hulda Bush's Delicious Cinnamon Rolls
### (Makes 10)

3    cups sifted flour
6    tsp. baking powder
2    tbs. sugar
1    tsp. salt
3    tbs. butter (or other shortening)
1    egg
¾    cup milk

### FILLING

2    tbs. butter, soft but not melted
1    cup brown sugar
2    tsp. cinnamon
(option - 3/4 cup seeded raisins)

### OVEN

Preheat to 425

### BAKING PAN

4    tsp. butter
½ cup brown sugar
Mix butter and sugar together until creamy.
Then spread all over bottom and sides of baking pan.

### DIRECTIONS

Sift flour, baking powder, sugar and salt into a large bowl. Stir around to thoroughly mix. Add butter and cut into small pieces with a knife. Then completely mix in the butter with the hands.

Beat the egg thoroughly and add the milk. Then slowly pour this into the flour mixture, stirring with a large spoon while the liquid is being added. (There should be just enough liquid to combine the ingredients into a dough.) If a little more liquid is necessary, add a very small amount of milk. Knead the dough slightly with the hands.

Sift some flour on your table or pastry board and roll the dough into an oblong about 20 inches long by 9 inches wide.

When rolling, keep the corners as square as possible and the edges of the dough straight. Do this by working the dough with the hands and pressing it wherever necessary.

When the dough is rolled out, use the filling mixture as follows: Spread the butter over the dough just as you would spread butter on bread. Over the butter, sprinkle a layer of the brown sugar and cinnamon (mixed well). Now roll the dough from the long side into a roll 20 inches long. Roll it just as you would a jellyroll.

Cut with a sharp knife into pieces about 2 inches long. Place the cut pieces of rolled dough in the prepared pan cut side up and let stand 15 minutes. The rolls should loosely fill the pan.

Place the pan in a hot oven (425 degrees), as near the center as possible. Bake for 25 minutes. Remove pan from oven and immediately turn the buns out upside down on a large plate, intact. The buns will all bake together in one cluster, and can be separated as needed.

(Recipe given by Martha Bush Noble)

years until he eventually sold the building. Mr. Bush lived with Martha and her husband until he passed away in 1976 at the age of eighty-six.

## Other Butler Bakeries

Some of Butler's sages whom I interviewed remembered other bakeries around town, which for one reason or another were not listed in Polk's directories. In a few cases, a bakery had an official name for official purposes but was commonly referred to by another name--often that of the owner. John F. Truman as early as 1915 had a bakery on the west side of North Main Street between North and Locust Streets. Mrs. Ralph's Bakery was located at 227 North Bluff Street around 1930. She baked and sold all of the typical bakery products. Lyndora boasted five bakeries— (1) Krienbucher's, (2) Markiw's, (3) Semanco's, (4) John Isaac's, and the (5) Lyndora National Baking Company. The Dellotto family operated a bakery on the south end of Cliff Street. (*See Butler County, the Second Hundred Years*, page 74)

The Jenkins Bakery was located on the north side of New Castle Street near Pillow Street in the three-story, brick building which presently houses the Brookside Apartments. The Jenkins bakery establishment was located on the first floor and the building housed several apartments on the upper floors. Mr. Ed Jenkins, the proprietor, had been a coal miner in Wales before migrating to the United States. He opened his bakery about the time that the Standard Steel Car Company opened for business. There were many apartments and hotels in the West End of town, which provided hungry customers for Jenkins' pastries and bread. In later years Mr. Jenkins had a fleet of Model A Ford-panel, delivery trucks. He delivered all over town and became quite prosperous.

Schoerner's Bakery was located just east of the present Hot Dog Shop and was owned and operated by the widow Schoerner. Her two sons, Wilhelm and Otto worked in the bakery. They spoke German to one another in the shop but when addressing customers always used very good English.

The telephone book for 1999 lists just a dozen bakeries for the entire county and only two in the city. Of course, most of the larger supermarkets have in-house bakeries. This is no doubt, one of the major reasons for the decline of the small, family-owned and operated bakeries. Many of the mom and pop operations, which survive today, whether they be bakeries, grocery stores, or other retail outlets, are a result of inertia. They're trying to keep the business going because their parents or grandparents started it. They feel bad about closing the shop after two or three generations so they keep it open on a very small profit margin in the hope that things will get better.

**South Main Street Bridge Before Viaduct - 1916**

# A PAIR OF SHOES

In the very early years of the village of Butler, tanneries were among the most important industries in the community. The pioneers needed leather to make shoes, harnesses and other articles. Hugh McKee owned and operated a tannery at the corner of Main and Jefferson Streets. The Butler Savings and Trust Company was later built on part of the tannery site. For twenty-five years this tannery was the largest industry in the town. Another tannery was located on East Jefferson Street near Franklin but details on that business are very sketchy.

George Mardorf's tannery on West Cunningham Street and Roessing's tannery on North Washington Street, between Clay and Penn Streets, were operating until the closing decade of the nineteenth century when they went the way of all small tanneries. They were practically forced out of business by larger concerns.

For more than seventy-five years farmers could make a little extra money by peeling the bark from hemlock, chestnut, and oak trees, from which tannin for treating leather came, and hauling it to the tan yards in Butler. [A chemical which could be produced more cheaply was discovered about 1880.] Stacking the bark in piles about the yard or storing it in sheds was the work of many a schoolboy who took the job during the summer months. Tanbark walks were much in evidence around the town until paved streets came into vogue, and the city fathers issued an edict calling for brick or stone pavements. Before the modernization of the streets, the bark, after it had been used, was thrown out on the street and became a popular place for young boys to run, jump, and frolic. The springy nature of the tan bark and the soft places it provided for jumping and landing were excellent.

In 1898 there were six makers and repairers of boots and shoes in the city of Butler. In addition to these businesses, Butler had eight, retail-shoe outlets. Polk's City Directory for 1915-16 listed thirty-one shoemakers for the county. Eighteen of those were in the city of Butler. There were nine shoe stores on Butler's Main Street and six shoe-shining parlors on or near Main Street. From these statistics it is plain to see that during the first few decades of the century, a considerable number of Butlerites made their living by either making, selling or shining shoes. These shoemakers often lived in the back or upstairs of their shops. The shops generally faced the streets and featured large display windows. Some of the larger operations hired extra workers, journeymen [men who had mastered the trade but did not have shops of their own] and three or four apprentices.

The shoemaker did every bit of work that went into making a pair of shoes. He cut the leather into uppers, inners, soles, and heels, and stitched or tacked them together; all the work was done by hand. The shoemaker could purchase all of his raw materials from a few suppliers such as a leather merchant, a thread maker, a cutler for tools, and a nailmaker. Most

## POLK'S CITY DIRECTORY
## BOOTS AND SHOES—MAKERS
## AND REPAIRERS
### 1898

Borland, A.M., 233 Centre ave.
Harley, Chris, rear 323 S. Main
Kemper, B., Jr., 347 S. Main
Schenck, Leonard, 113 E. Jefferson
Schmoker, Wm., 310 Elm
Walter, G. H., 239 S. Main

### SHOEMAKERS
### 1915-16

Aldinger Charles F, Chicora
Catalano Tito, 105 Elm
Ciciotti Victor, 201 S Chestnut
Climenti Samuel, Zelienople
Duell Alfred E, Mars
Field Alfred J, 119 S Main
Fleissner Frederick, Mars
Hindman Adelbert G, Evans City
Kacpevski Stephen, Standard Av cor Penn Av, Lyndora
Kellenbaugh Adam, Evans City
Kapecki Tom, Standard Av opp Kohler Av, Lyndora
Kern Frederick, Callery
Little John, Evans City
Martin Fred, 330 E Jefferson
May Wm L, 122 Hazel Av
Milleman George, Harmony
Miller Samuel F, 115 New Castle
Pilat Frank, Harmony
Renzetti Vincenzo, 475 W Wayne
Saashuf Michael, 107 W Jefferson
Sassone Nick, 214 N Main
Schiavo Antonio, Evans City
Scialabba Gondolfo, 125 E Jefferson
Scialabba Joseph, 353 Miller
Scialabba Peter, 97 Mercer
Scialabba Salvatore, 106 W Cunningham
Sowash Peter H, Slippery Rock
Triccasi Joseph, 355 Center Av
Tritt Joseph J, Slippery Rock
Walter G H & Co. 303 S Main
Wyschka John, 323 E Jefferson

### SHOE REPAIRERS
### 1930

Abraham Saml 2 Hansen Av (Lyndora)
Berardelli Angelo 413 (725) Eau Claire
Catalano Alf 106 W Cunningham
Chiprian Michl 327 Locust
DePaolis Jas 222 N Main
Giacomo Andrew 223 Center Av
Kurvnski Felix 7 Main (Lyndora)
Lankewicz Frank 305 Hickory

of the shoemakers either made their own cobbler's benches and the wooden forms on which shoes were shaped, or they used such equipment as was handed down by a father or some close relative. A shoemaker might spend several days on a particularly fine pair and could seldom turn out more than two or three pairs of hand-made shoes a day. He was his own designer and stylist, salesman, and accountant. When the customer picked up a pair of shoes, they weren't wrapped or in a box. Nearly everybody bought his shoes locally; a wealthy person might order his from a fashionable shoemaker in a larger city.

By 1930 there were eighteen men who called themselves shoe repairers and there were twelve retail outlets for shoes in downtown Butler. Handmade shoes by this time were becoming very rare. Certainly a few of the shoe repairmen could have made shoes by hand but there was very little demand for the product. The shoemaking business had become totally mechanized. Machines capable of making thousands of pairs of shoes a day had completely taken over. The quality of machine-made shoes was high and the price was less than the shoemaker was forced to charge. The shoemakers gradually found out that they could not compete with quality and price. Many retired or found other employment.

### Tony Monday

I spent an enjoyable Saturday afternoon interviewing Tony Jr., Henry, and Nick Monday. The Monday boys are not sure as to the exact year of their parents' migration from Italy to the United States. The ship's manifest in their possession reveals such information as what their parents ate on the way over, but surprisingly, it doesn't tell the year of their arrival.

Stories handed down by word of mouth indicate that, on the trip over, their father met a man from Scotland who taught him some English. One of Butler's older citizens told me that he was impressed with the "good English" spoken by Tony Monday.

After he arrived, Tony worked on the railroad for a time before opening his shoemaking shop. He had attained the age when most young men were starting their work careers, but he chose to get an education at a school on Institute Hill in spite of the fact that it was required that he begin in first grade with kids much younger than himself. Tony Monday entered first grade as a young man. He was a good student, advanced rapidly and soon understood the American system. The Monday boys believe that much of their father's success was due to his attitude. He believed strongly that he could go in only one direction—up. That was the way many immigrants looked at their situations.

Polk's City Directory for 1915-16 lists thirty-one Butler County shoemakers—It was about the time Tony Monday opened his shop. The humble shoemaking business Tony started in the teens hasn't moved more than a few doors from its original location which was in the Wick Hotel. When the Hotel was torn down, Mr. Monday moved his shoemaking and repair shop was located

Shoe Repairmen cont'd.
Maddalena Angelo 315 (475) W Wayne
Martin Fred 415 Locust
Monday Antonio 238 N Main
Monfre Chas 330 E Jefferson
Monfre Tony 307 ½ Mitchell Av
Rosenberg Abr 126 W North
Salvano Michl 135 E Jefferson
Sassone Nickolas 504 (144) W Cunningham
Scarpitti Frank 719 (219) E Brady
Scialabba Gandolpho 97 Mercer
Szostak Albin 40 Hansen Av (Lyndora)

### SHOE REPAIRERS
### 1940

Aquilino Nicholas V 237 S Main
Cammisa Hector 315 W Wayne
Cassese Adam 223 N Chestnut
Catalano Tito 356 E Jefferson
Catalfamo Jos E Wayne nr Center Av
Depaolis Jas E 222 N Main
Gaudino Frank 135 E Jefferson
Gerhart Jules P 331 ½ Locust
LaBella Paul 201 Morton Av
Maletta John 105 Hickory
Monday Antonio 208 N Main
Monfre Chas 330 E Jefferson
Morabito LeRoy F 246 W Jefferson
New York Shoe Repair 116 W Cunningham
Scarpitti Frank 721 E Brady
Szostak Albin 40 Hansen Av (Lyndora)
Tiberi Angelo 312 Eau Claire
Torok Emory J 35 Bessemer Av (Lyndora)

### SHOE REPAIRERS
### 1951

Cammisa Hector E 315 W Wayne
Catalfano Jos 374 Center Av
Dennis Shoe Repair 115 E Jefferson
DePaolis Jas 222 N Main
Gaudino Arth G 135 E Jefferson
Monday's Shoe Service 208 N Main
Morabito LeRoy F 234 W Jefferson
New York Shoe & Bicycle Repair 134 S Washingt. n
Sam's Shoe Repair 100 4th Av
South Side Shoe Repairing 105 Hickory
Szostak Henry B 40 Hansen Av (L)
Tiberi Angelo 312 Eau Claire
Torok Emory J 388 Chesapeake Av (L)
Zaccari & Rapone 237 S Main

one door south of Monday's present location—the door to that establishment may yet be seen between Monday's Boots and Shoes at 208 North Main Street and Keffalas' Bar on the corner.

Tony Monday Sr. was the first local shoemaker to mechanize. Up until the 1970's it was relatively inexpensive to start a shoe factory, because it was nearly impossible to buy the machinery. A single company, the United Shoe Machinery Corporation, which only leased its machines, made ninety per cent of the shoe making and repairing machinery in this country. Eventually the hold of the United Shoe Machinery Corporation was broken, but during the early part of the century, it was the only way to get machinery. Tony Monday leased machinery from the company. The boys remember the details. For one thing, one had to show proof of insurance. In case of a fire or theft the United Shoe Machinery Corporation wanted to be sure they were paid for any losses. There were odometers on the stitching machines, which counted each stitch. The shoe repairman paid by the stitch. The company gave each dealer a stack of penny postcards with the leaser's name stamped thereon. Once a month the leaser read a number from the odometer, recorded it on the postcard and mailed it in with his payment. Every six months there was an audit in which an official company representative visited and read the odometer, in case a customer had reported the numbers a bit on the low side. The company took care of any maintenence-type problems with the machinery.

In spite of the monopoly and the strict regulations used by the United Shoe Machinery Corporation, one thing is certainly true—the new, machine-made shoes were high quality and they were much more inexpensive than handmade footwear. This is when people stopped buying custom made shoes. Tony Monday's business and that of all other shoemakers gradually changed. The only people who bought custom made shoes were those with handicaps—those who could not be fitted with factory made shoes; for example—those who needed one thick sole.

## LeRoy Morabito

LeRoy Morabito never intended to become a shoe repairman. It was during the Great Depression in 1932 and jobs were difficult to find—to say the least. His father made arrangements for the 18 year old Morabito to become an apprentice shoe repairmen under Angelo Madalena and Nicholas Sassone in their West Cunningham Street shop. LeRoy didn't like the business and after a short time, quit. But jobs were very scarce so it was difficult for him to turn down the chance to learn the shoe repairing trade and get paid while doing it. In 1932, with some training completed, he opened his first shop, Center Shoe Repair on Center Avenue, with a man named Viccari.

Leroy was not following in his father's footsteps. His father wasn't a shoemaker but rather worked in the mines, on the railroad and finished his career at Armco. At that time Armco, the Standard Steel Car Company, and the Bantam were operating, but work in these factories was at best, sporadic. One might work a couple of days, then be laid off for a week or two. Learning a trade seemed to be much more secure.

Despite his dislike of the trade and the lack of a shoe-repairman role model, the young Morabito opened his own shop on Mitchell Avenue in 1937. Tony Monfre had a shoe shop in that location, and before him, one of the Scialabbas ran a shoe repair business there. By 1939 Morabito had moved his business to a West Jefferson Street location where he paid thirty dollars a month rent; it was two doors west of his long-time location at 234 West Jefferson Street. He never dreamed that his business would last sixty-two years.

Morabito remembers the early days. He replaced heels on ladies shoes for a nickel. He did repairs for most of the shoe stores in the city and the outlying malls and shopping centers. During World War II he was under contract with the U.S. Army to repair shoes for Deshon Hospital on the New Castle Road. "They used to come in here with big boxes of shoes," he said. "I had to have my father-in-law come in to help." Other clients included Armco and a couple of dance studios.

"At one time, I opened at 7 a.m. and worked until six at night. I worked all day six days a week," he said. "I earned so little that I had to work that long to earn a living." Morabito was the first Butler shoe repairman to stock and sell new shoes. He first purchased shoes wholesale on Pittsburgh's Fifth Avenue. He also sold cancellation shoes, which were discontinued shoes or shoes which stores had returned. The seller used to slash the shoes with a knife so a customer could not take them back to a store for a refund. Eventually Mr. Morabito offered the Crosby Square and the Endicott Johnson lines. Business was better than ever—in 1950 he was able to purchase a new Oldsmobile. The news of the Oldsmobile purchase spread like wildfire and soon many of Butler's shoe repairmen "jumped on the bandwagon." Before long, most of Butler's shoe repair shops were selling shoes but Morabito had been the first.

LeRoy and his wife, the late Olive Tiberi Morabito, raised and educated two sons. This is probably the thing of which Mr. Morabito is most proud. Both sons have graduated from college and are successful today.
(As related to the author by LeRoy Morabito)

Many shoemakers tried to hang on as business declined. Others conceded and began to sell the factory made shoes.

Most shoe retailers employed a "shoe shine boy." Even dry cleaning establishments had a couple of shoeshine chairs. Kids were hired to do the shining. The establishment got ten cents a

Left to right: Leo Zachari, Yanotti boy, Tony Monday

customer, the kids weren't paid; they kept only the tips. Tony Jr. recalls his stint as a shoe shine boy. "Spats were very stylish for a time. Before I shined the customer's shoes, I had to remove the spats. Removing the spats required a buttonhook." "What are spats, I asked?" Tony Jr. explained, "During the transition time between the six inch shoe and the oxford, men were not accustomed to having their ankles uncovered. Their ankles actually felt cold, so a woolen cover was worn to insulate the ankles. Those were spats."

As factory-made shoes increased in quality and became more expensive, the repairman again began to experience an increased demand for his skills. Things were going full circle. People who wore the expensive brands found it economically sound to have the shoes repaired a time or two before discarding them.

I asked the Monday boys why nearly all of the shoemakers in this area, perhaps across the nation, were Italian. "If you were Italian you either became a barber, a shoemaker, or a stone mason. Many men of Butler's Italian community also worked on the railroad. Some worked here for several months and went back to Italy where they were able to live in luxury. They did this annually." We got off the subject and I still don't know the answer to the question.

Some of the reminisces of the Monday brothers had very little to do with shoes. "People used to shop at the A & P, leave their cars parked behind the Mobilgas Station across Main, and load the front of Monday's store with packages while they took care of other business in the area." Sometimes Monday's couldn't close until after midnight and all the packages had been retrieved. "Butler's streets were thronged with people on Saturday nights. Kids went to the movies; dad went to one of the local watering holes, or stood in front of the bank talking and "people watching." Mom window-shopped or if she were lucky, actually bought a few items."

The Monday boys have fond memories of their boyhood days in Butler. During summer vacations the boys went to work at the shop with dad. At noon they would go home and eat lunch then carry dad's lunch back to the store and help out while he ate. Along the way they enjoyed watching blacksmiths use the bellows, heat the iron and form it into horseshoes or whatever tool the blacksmith may be creating. They remember the blacksmith shop which was located on Cliff Street behind the beautiful home of Dr. Schultz. The Doctor's home was on the corner, which is today the site of the Terrace Apartments. Blacksmiths, of course at that time, were a dying breed, as were shoemakers. Dr. Schultz had a small fishpond in his front yard. Some of the local kids would catch fish and frogs and sell them to the Doctor who would add them to his pond. The Doctor loved to hear the croaking of the frogs at night. I don't know of anyone who doesn't.

Today, Monday's business has changed with the times; it now supports five families and has been in the Main Street location since the removal of the Wick House.

### Orlando Pride

At a time when shoe repairmen are nearly a thing of the past, Butler County has one exception to the rule. It was only eighteen years ago that Orlando Pride became a shoe repairman. Surprisingly, he does not come from a long line of shoe repairmen. He had been working at Pullman Standard as a welder and had been moonlighting as a dental technician. Pullman closed its doors forever in 1982 forcing Orlando and many others who were too young to retire, to find other employment.

Orlando told his wife he wanted to become, of all things, a shoemaker. He had been motivated by stories of a shoemaker Bernhardt who was at one time a very skilled, German shoemaker. "Shoemaker Bernhardt spent many years in America honing his skills," said Orlando. "Eventually he retired and went back to Germany hoping to enjoy the autumn of his life but it didn't happen that way—within a year he was dead. You never know when your time is up; you could drop over tomorrow. When you look at it that way you'll get your priorities straight. Enjoy every moment of your life."

It is obvious that Mr. Pride enjoys coming in contact with people. He enjoys dispensing a great deal of his philosophy during his workday. As I was interviewing him, several customers came in and I noticed that he greeted them in German and Russian. I said, "Orlando, you know that most of Butler's earlier shoemakers and repairmen were immigrants and had some difficulty with the English language. You were born and raised in the United States, have spoken English all of your life and yet, you greet your customers in a foreign language. Isn't that rather unusual?" He responded, "I like to have a good time with people; it breaks the ice and makes them feel at ease. Also, you'd be surprised to find out how many people understand German and/or Russian."

Orlando learned his trade from a man named Vince Capawano. Mr. Capawano had a busy and profitable shop down near Route 8 just below the Pennsylvania Turnpike and was willing to teach the trade. After three months of intensive training with Capawano, Orlando felt that he was ready to open his own shop. Mr. Capawano, as one might expect, had some friends and business associates in the business and was able to steer Orlando to a shoe-repair shop in Carnegie which was closing. Orlando examined the equipment, machinery and supplies, made an offer which was accepted, and had it all shipped to Butler.

I asked Orlando where his customers come from. He immediately responded, "Louisiana is the farthest." "This particular customer drives bus for a rock group or some kind of an entertainment show. Every time he comes through here he leaves a pair or two of boots. If you do good work, the word gets around. Business is good—I'm doing well but there's another way of looking at this job. I work all day, take supper between 5:00 and 6:00 then return to the shop until 10:00. If I worked only eight hours a day I could not make ends meet."

Orlando, at his age, is putting in some very long hours. He says that hard work keeps him young; while that may be true, I think that it also has much to do with the philosophy that he dispenses.

 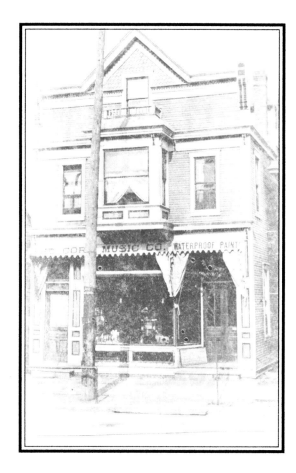

Above left: Marshall Cochran's watch repair shop was located on West Brady Street.

Above right: Butler also had many female entrepreneurs, one of which was Mrs. N. C. Core. She began her career as a teacher in the Parkersburg, West Virginia public schools. In 1867 she married Nathaniel Core. Mr. Core was involved in the oil business at the Tarr farm near Oil City. Mr. and Mrs. Core followed the oil excitement to Greece City in 1877 and then on to St. Joe in this county. The year 1882 found them in Millerstown.

After so many moves, the couple settled in Butler. Mrs. Core opened a music store in the Armory building on Butler's Diamond. In 1898 Mr. and Mrs. Core built the residence shown above at 313 South McKean Street. The music store was relocated to that location.

Mrs. Core's business interests were not limited to music. She became a travel agent of sorts. She was the first woman to conduct excursions to the World's Fair in Chicago in 1893. She also conducted several excursions down the Ohio River on Pittsburgh and Cincinnati packets. Mrs. Core was one of the original members of Butler's Women's Christian Temperance Union.

## SOAP BOX DERBIES

In the early 1930's Myron E. Scott was working as a photographer for the *Dayton Daily News*. One day as he was crossing a Dayton street he had to do some very nimble pirouetting to avoid being run down. He found himself dodging several young boys who were speeding downhill in strange looking homemade vehicles. His ensuing investigation found that the vehicles were made from orange crates and soapboxes with baby buggy-wheels and other improvised materials. Mr. Scott was so impressed by these boys' creativity and the excitement that the race generated that he suddenly got a bright idea—to organize this type of homemade car race and make it a citywide event. His boss at the *Daily News* agreed that the idea had merit and within a short time the *Dayton Daily News* sold the idea to the Chevrolet Division of General Motors. The national soapbox derby was born.

The first sanctioned race was held in 1934 in Dayton. When young boys from thirty-four cities participated it was considered to be a very good response to a new event. That first race went well; it was a fun day and everyone agreed that it should become an annual happening. The following year, with more exposure and advertising, boys from fifty-five cities competed. In 1936 the race was moved to Akron to take advantage of the hilly terrain, Dayton being rather flat. The Akron race was such a success that civic leaders there built an official soapbox derby track and increased efforts to make the annual race an event of national importance.

Sponsors around the nation began to hold local races with prizes for the hometown winners and if the local races were affiliated with the National Soapbox Derby, the winners were given the opportunity to travel to Akron to compete in the All-American Soapbox Derby. Prizes at the national race consisted of merchandise, scholarships and a trip to Europe.

Butler's first derby was held on Labor Day, 1946 and was sponsored by the local Optimist club. The Butler event was not affiliated with the National Soapbox Derby and therefore could not be called a "soapbox derby." Local officials instead called the Butler race the "orange crate derby." Cliff Street was chosen to be the first racecourse for the new event; it was not a major thoroughfare and traffic would not be disrupted during the races. The course extended from Cunningham Street down Cliff Street for a distance of 600 feet.

Rules were decided upon and explained to the entrants and the spectators. A process of elimination would determine the winners of the race. All contestants were paired, and the winner of each heat would stand aside until the next round, and those who won the preliminaries advanced until only two contestants remained. The winner of the last heat was declared the winner of the derby; the contestant he had defeated won second place and the one eliminated in the last preceding heat was declared winner of the third prize.

Thirteen years old Robert Kiddle, of Columbia Way, Butler won the maiden race with a time of twenty-two seconds, which calculates to a speed of approximately eighteen miles per hour. In addition to the honor of winning Butler's first orange crate derby, the champion received a $100 savings bond. Jack Uber of Butler RD 6 was the winner of the second prize, a boy's bicycle. Lou Muti of Fairview Avenue won third prize, a wristwatch. Every boy and girl who competed in the Butler derby won a prize; the main prizes were bestowed at a dinner hosted by the Optimist Club in the Hotel Nixon, Butler's finest hotel. John McKool was the owner of "Tip Top Signs" during those derby years, and used to set aside one day for

nothing else but painting the orange crates. He did this as a service to the boys. Generally the sponsor's name was painted on the front of the car. Mr. McKool relates that one particular year Bob Kaufman, who was for many years the voice of WISR radio in Butler, asked him to be sure he attended the banquet at the Nixon Hotel. It was a nice evening with a fine meal and many awards to the derby competitors but that evening they also awarded Mr.

McKool with a plaque for his help. He cherishes that plaque yet today.

The *Butler Eagle* provides us with details of the races. "At that first orange crate derby Police Chief Charles J. Miller was the official starter. He had to pull the trigger repeatedly as the blank cartridges in his gun failed to fire…D. J. Angeloni served as chief announcer and stood on a truck bed outside the Wise Machine shop about mid-way along the racecourse. He announced that the Optimist Club proposed to make the derby an annual event, and to make the next one in 1947 even bigger and better…The sponsors obtained both public and personal liability insurance for the event, at a cost of $185. There were no claims so the insurance company made a nice profit for the day."

Robert Fisher, age eleven, was probably the most frustrated boy in that first race. He pushed his forty-three pound racecar "Spooky" into Butler from Jefferson Center on Saturday morning. Imagine! When his turn came and he lined up to start he discovered that he was having steering trouble and had to withdraw. "Spooky" was quickly repaired, or at least Robert thought so, and the boy made a second attempt, but the problem recurred a short distance down the course. In spite of his determination, Robert wasn't able to compete that year.

There were two major changes for the third running of the annual classic in 1948. The course was moved from Cliff Street to East Jefferson Street with the start at the intersection of Franklin Street and the finish line at Monroe Street. Also the date of the derby was changed from Labor Day to July Fourth. Stephen Lowe of Mercer Road won both the 1947 and 1948 derbies.

The crowd in 1948 was estimated at 2000. The weather was fine again for the third year in a row as the

Lyndora Drum and Bugle Corps escorted the contestants from Hoch's motor garage to the race site. One accident marred the serenity of the day but it was not of a serious nature. During the second heat the cars driven by Leonard Pintell and Billy Sechake collided a short distance into the race. Both vehicles were damaged so badly they could not be driven again but fortunately the boys escaped uninjured. The only derby injury that ever required a trip to

the hospital took place during the final race in 1959. "William Bridenbaugh, 12, of 432 N. McKean St., suffered injuries to his right ankle and leg when a racer piloted by Rue Snider, 14, of 429 Federal St., went out of control and crashed into the curb. Officers said Bridenbaugh was taken to Butler County Memorial Hospital for examination and treatment." I called Rue Snider who has just retired from teaching. He had been a music teacher in the South Butler County elementary schools and a fine musician and teacher he is. Rue remembered the day like it was yesterday. Snider relates, "My father had drilled out an axle; parents were allowed to assist with the vehicles that year. He must have drilled out too much for as I got going down Cunningham Street the axle broke, and I lost control. I slammed into the curb and ran into a friend of mine. He kind of flipped up over and landed on the hood of my car. I can't remember his name right now, but he wasn't hurt. His father requested that he be taken to the hospital merely for observation. He was O.K."

In 1949, the Mayor's Fourth of July committee instituted a "stay at home and enjoy a safe and sane Fourth" program. The objective was to keep people off the highways and it was felt that the festivities here would promote camaraderie among the local residents. It was a good idea and very successful. Nearly 7,000 people jammed Pullman Memorial Park to witness a two-hour show which was then followed by a brilliant fireworks display. A crowd of approximately 3,000 had attended the annual orange crate derby earlier the morning of the Fourth and breathed a collective gasp as they watched young Joe Nowakowski turn over his crate in the middle of East Jefferson Street. Fortunately young Joe was not hurt. Cloyd Smith

of East Jefferson street was the winner of the race that year and his younger brother Ronnie kept it in the family by winning the following year, in 1950. Succeeding winners were John McIlvain of East Jefferson Street who won in 1953 and 1954. Marlin Sarvey of Prospect took home the prize in 1955 in near 100-degree heat. In spite of the temperature the crowd was numbered at near 5000 and very enthusiastic. David Johnston of Greenwood Village was the champion in 1956. The 1957 race was a dead heat and an extra race was required to determine the winner. It was the first time this had happened. In the tiebreaker, Robert McGarvey of Summit Street edged out Tom Miller of West Brady Street. However, Miller got his revenge the following year when he took first place. The last race held in Butler was in 1959 and the winner was Richard Swidinski of Mercer Road.

Not all of those races were on Cliff and East Jefferson Streets. In 1954 the race was moved to North Main Street. The new course ran from King David Court to Fulton Street and was 250 feet longer than the previous courses.

The Optimists were considering becoming affiliated with the National Soapbox Derby and as a means of evaluating the merits of the national organization, took the eighteen Butler entrants to the Ellwood City "soapbox derby" which was affiliated with Akron and was held on July 21, 1954. The boys were then taken to the All-American Soapbox Derby at Akron, Ohio on August 15. It was a positive experience; they liked what they saw and the following year Butler became affiliated with the National Soapbox Derby. This meant that winners here were eligible to compete in the Akron race and would be eligible for the more impressive prizes. The "orange crate derby" had become just a memory. The annual race was now called the "Butler Soapbox Derby." Expenses were greater and it was becoming too much for one sponsor so for the first time, beginning in 1955, Butler's Soapbox Derby was sponsored jointly by the Optimist Club, Standard Motor Company and the *Butler Eagle.*

Interestingly a derby spokesman boasted in 1955 that Butler had had ten derbies and it hadn't rained on a single one. His statement was printed in the *Butler Eagle.* One should never make statements like that—we all know that. You guessed it; the following year "intermittent rain put a damper on the derby crowd and forced a fifteen minute delay in the action shortly after 11 a.m." It also rained on the derby the following year, in 1957. Two rainy events in a row prompted the *Butler Eagle* to announce that "The race is held annually, even if showers arrive before or during the event. Only in the case of a downpour is the race discontinued."

According to the *Butler Eagle*, D. J. Angeloni was the regular master of ceremonies. He presided at the microphone for the first eight derbies and always kept the crowds entertained "with his announcements and inimitable line of chatter." He must have been a priceless character because each year the *Eagle* described him as such.

The derby was originally open to boys ages six to sixteen but later changed to ages eleven to fifteen. Entrants could not spend more than $10 on materials and until the 1950's, could not have help from adults in the building of their vehicles. All cars entered had to be built according to specifications and had to pass rigid safety inspections. There was a weight limit of 250 pounds for car and driver combined. This often caused anxious moments. Some boys had to diet and exercise before the weigh-ins. One Butler boy and his car weighed in at 249 and one-half pounds. Another boy asked to be locked in his room at night so he wouldn't raid the refrigerator and go over the weight limit.

As we look back through reading the news of those days and discussing the races with some of our older citizens, there is no doubt that the local and the national derbies were exciting events. A crowd estimated at 8,000 to 10,000 turned out for Butler's first race and every year but one; crowd estimates were in the thousands. Most of the derbies were family events with picnics, games and parades. On the morning of Butler's first derby the Meridian Fife and Drum Corps led a parade from the Butler Motor Company garage at Main and Wayne Streets to the scene of the race. The many-colored racecars were ceremonially unloaded from trucks at the Cunningham Street starting line. The parades became a tradition—usually the Meridian Fife and Drum Corps, the Lyndora Drum and Bugle Corps, or the Catholic Daughters of America, sometimes all three, marched and performed in the parades.

Some major changes took place in the derbies as the years passed by. In 1964 time trials were included which gave the boys a chance to get the feel of the track. The cars became sleeker, ran on ball-bearing wheels and glistened with metallic paint. Drivers had to lie down in their cars rather than sit. Kids were generally larger in the 1970's than they were in the earlier years of the derbies so weight limits were raised. Several inches were added to the length of the cars and kids could now spend up to $40 on materials.

Dolores Korb attempted to be the first female to enter the Detroit Derby in 1967. She was ruled ineligible because the rules stipulated that only boys between the ages of eleven and fifteen could compete. As a concession to Dolores, officials allowed her to open the event. Butler, on the other hand, allowed girls to compete from the beginning. In the 1946 derby, Marilyn Uber, daughter of the Optimist Club secretary, seemed to be the favorite as she took her position for the first heat, competing against Donald Grystar of Lewis Avenue. Marilyn won the heat but lost in the semi-finals. Girls weren't allowed to race in the national competition until 1971. In 1975, Karen Snead, an eleven year old from Morrisville, Pa., was the first girl to win the All-American Soapbox Derby in Akron with a photo-finish victory.

Scandal rocked the national derby in 1973. It was discovered that the winning car had electromagnets embedded in its fiberglass body, allegedly giving it a starting advantage. It was estimated that $10,000 to $20,000 had been spent building the car. It sent shock waves through derby fans, caused many sponsors to withdraw their support and was the beginning of a decline in interest. By 1974, for example, the number of entrants in the Detroit-area Derby had dropped to thirty, compared to 526 in 1956. Chevrolet withdrew its national sponsorship and the Akron Chamber of Commerce dropped its participation in the national derby.

Today the derbies continue to be staged in some American cities. Probably the most important local derby in the nation is the one in Detroit. The name has been changed to Autorama Metro Detroit Soapbox Derby. Even though today's soapbox cars are more high-tech, the derby continues to be a wholesome activity that teaches the value of hard work, craftsmanship and competition. (On page 150 in *Butler County, the Second Hundred Years,* we mistakingly identified one of the orange crate derby photographs as being Route 8 north. It was actually a few miles south of Butler on Route 356.)

# GASOLINE STATIONS

Before the automobile, nobody knew what to do with gasoline; it was a dangerous by-product of the cracking process and was often thrown away. By 1905 however, motorists were filling their tanks with the fuel by pouring it from cans directly into the cars' tanks. Some more enterprising drivers would buy a large drum filled with gasoline, take it home, and store it someplace accessible to the car. If the barrel had a spigot at the bottom, the gasoline was drained into a can, then poured through a chamois filter into the car's gas tank. Many motorists bent a piece of tin and used it as a channel; the well-prepared used a funnel. Some creative gasoline salesmen delivered the fuel to the customers in horse-drawn tanks. Transferring gasoline by these primitive methods was not only inconvenient and messy but also very dangerous as the fuel routinely spilled. An inventive person in St. Louis gets credit for attaching a flexile piece of rubber tubing to an upright gasoline storage tank thereby creating the first gasoline "pump."

Burkett's in Hooker

Standard Oil of California opened the first "filling" station in Seattle in 1907. By 1915 just about any business owner could make arrangements, have a pump installed outside his establishment, and sell gasoline and many were doing so. Refineries installed the pumps, delivered the fuel, and collected their profits leaving a share for the retailer. By the mid 1920's over 250,000 gasoline stations were operating in the United States. Today nearly all of those early stations are closed or have been replaced by convenience stores.

Until 1915 automobiles were not enclosed so they weren't driven in bad weather. Motoring was almost exclusively a warm-weather activity. Most automobiles were merely stored away during the winter season. The earliest gas stations were sheds, converted livery stables and other makeshift outbuildings. The pump was located at the curb, very close to the street and as one would suspect, it was not at all unusual to hear of a vehicle running into a pump. Another disadvantage of the curbside pump was, of course, the traffic congestion created by the lines of cars waiting to "fill-up." Filling the tank was a slow process so the traffic jams did become lengthy. But, Jinks Cirillo explains that there weren't many cars back

Orchard Inn on Saxonburg-Butler Road

English cottage on Center Avenue, built by Harry Wimer for Penn Drake

then so the traffic jams are myths. He remembers playing base-ball on the street at the intersection of Kittanning, Monroe, and Jefferson Streets and says, "we'd have to put the game on hold when a car came along—the game wasn't inter-rupted that often."

But as the sale of gasoline and other petroleum products grew, refiners began to improve and upgrade their retail facilities. They wanted to present a more dignified image. During the later 1920's it became stylish to build imagina-tive and impressive gas stations. Some were constructed in shapes such as windmills, castles, dinosaurs, lighthouses and even giant, gasoline pumps. Standard Oil used a low hip roof; some stations sported pilasters at the corners, which simulated pillars and were quite attractive. Gable roofs also became popular. Gulf stations featured tile roofs for awhile. Cupolas were added to old stations and incorporated into the designs for new stations. The buildings were cleverly painted to match the company's signage, at the same time; every effort was made to avoid gaudiness. Pure Oil Company stations of that era were built to re-semble small English cottages. Several other companies followed their lead. For easier recognition Pure built all its stations the same and saved money with the use of standardized designs, materials and equip-ment. They were tasteful and attractive and fit nicely into middle-class residential neighborhoods—these stations drew few if any complaints from home owners.

Some station attendants of that era dressed totally in white, with polished shoes, matching shin guards, Jodhpur trousers with waist jackets, an eight pointed garage cap, and the ever-present, black bow tie. The company logo was very visible on the hat and on the breast pocket of the jacket. This display of sartorial comeliness was an attempt to shed the "grease monkey" image. And these splendiferously attired attendants performed more services than just filling the tank—they checked the oil, cleaned the windshields, fixed flat tires and even did mechanical work. In fact it was because of these extra services that in the 1930's the "gas station" came to be called the "service station."

During the depression the average price of a gallon of gasoline dropped to just ten cents. Millions of people couldn't afford to drive even at those prices, so they parked their cars and gasoline sales plum-meted. Gas station owners in an attempt to bring in more revenue began to sell tires, batteries, antifreeze, fan belts, and other auto parts. And since more women were now driving, the oil companies met this potential market with a line of such products as furniture polish, glass cleaner and other cleaning fluids.

Early on, listening for the sloshing of the gasoline was one of the methods used to alert the driver that it was time to "fill-her-up." Before there were gas gauges in cars, drivers would verify their suspicions by checking the gasoline level with wooden dipsticks. Many gas stations gave these devices away as an advertising tactic—they generally had their name and some catchy slogan printed on the dipstick. These dipsticks are valued collector's items today.

Pumps were, of course, very primitive by today's standards. A hand crank or electric motor was used to pump the gasoline into the transparent glass cylinder which was atop the pump. The attendant used the "eye measure" method of filling the tank to one of several marks on the cylinder. Then when the proper amount of gas had been pumped into the cylinder, a hose was inserted into the automobile's gasoline tank and the fuel drained into the car by the process of gravity. The entire process was much slower than present day methods but the wait was good

Old, hand-operated oil pump at Jefferson Center

in a way--it gave the attendant time to check the oil, windshield, tires and most important, to talk to the customer. Most station owners believed that the relationship with the customer was what would bring him back regardless of price or anything else, therefore a great deal of time and effort was spent fostering that relationship. Life was lived at a slower pace back then and the visit to the service station was an event.

The mechanical "Wayne Honest Measure Gas Pump" was introduced in 1932. For the first time neither the customer nor the attendant had to figure how many gallons one received for his money. These Wayne pumps measured the amount of gasoline and also calculated the price to the penny. In addition to the meter on the pump, a bell rang as each gallon was dispensed. To provide convenience in adding oil, a sixty-gallon tank was positioned near the gasoline pumps. The attendant took an empty glass bottle, which was usually stored in an eight-container pack, and filled it with oil using a hand pump. He then poured the oil into the car's engine. Cars were much simpler mechanically, and even if the attendant was not so inclined, he learned to do a surprisingly large number of repairs.

In 1933

there were 170,000 gasoline stations in the United States. Most offered a grease job at a cost of about fifty cents. Gear lubricant was fifteen cents per pound, and when warm weather came it was necessary to drain the ninety-weight lubricant and replace it with 140 weight—this became a spring ritual for most automobile owners.

Not much happened in the service station business during the war years of the forties. In fact almost no automobiles were built during the war. But after the war the nation experienced an economic boom and the prosperity was reflected in automobiles and the stations that serviced them.

During the 1950's automobiles displayed higher and higher tail fins, much more chrome, and were generally more streamlined. If your car were a few years old it was suddenly very dated, in fact, obsolete. Old cars did not have the allure they command today. The old was out; the new was in. Gas station construction also exhibited a trend in a similar direction. The unique stations built to resemble windmills and English cottages had gone by the boards in favor of uniformity. Hip and gable roofs were replaced with flat roofs and much more glass was visible. Texaco built streamlined stations to match the cars of the day. Their architects promoted the concept that white, oblong boxes gave the impression of speed, modernity and progress. Shell too, adopted the oblong box but modified it with towers or pylons. The new stations featured more glass, gloss, glitter and glare. The baked enamel and porcelain, usually white, needed very little upkeep. Yes they clashed with their surroundings, but this was now considered to be an asset—it attracted attention. To appease zoning boards, some of which were now furious, service station designers backed off a bit and added features such as cedar shingles, used brick, overhangs and darker colors. These concessions allowed the stations to "blend in" much better.

Gasoline did not have octane ratings until the mid fifties and there was actually very little difference between brands, but it had become time to specialize now that engines were "high performance." The Sun Oil Company was the first to introduce octane ratings. Then Standard Oil added tetraethyl as an anti-knock additive. Texaco divided the U.S.A. into twenty-five weather areas and offered a different blend of its Sky Chief gasoline, for each area. Texaco also was the first to offer the public "registered rest rooms." This policy caught on and before long the most refiners were offering clean restrooms for their customers. Some hired "checkers" to drive around the country and visit and examine their particular service station restrooms--incognito of course.

In 1947 George Urich dreamed up a revolutionary new concept. His California customers were allowed to pump their own gas and pocket the savings—self-service. His three Los Angeles stations immediately became so very busy that his idea spread like wildfire—he had set a new trend. He forever changed the nature of gasoline stations. Many people speculate that the next big change in the gasoline dispensing business will be "pay at the pump" which is, of course, already here. But as John A. Jackle pointed out in his book *The Gas Station in America*, "If gasoline customers can pay at the pump, the business loses the

201

opportunity to make other sales inside."

As the turn of the century arrives, most of the gasoline sold in Butler and Butler Township is via the convenience store. There are more traditional service stations in the rural areas of the county. Service station enthusiasts mourn the passing of the old stations and would agree that the convenience store has taken the heart, soul and pizzazz out of selling gasoline. Nearly every station had its share of loafers. Males congregated at gas stations in ways reminiscent of the old livery stables and blacksmith shops. Many service station operators would hire one of the loafers to keep an eye on the cash register when the attendants were pumping gas or doing repairs. Gas stations of old were intimidating places for most women— remember the calendars? Today the merger of the gasoline station and the grocery store has spawned places where both men and women are comfortable.

Hi Way Oil Co, "small box station" on Route 8 south of Butler

Following convenience stores, the second most prevalent gasoline retailers in the Butler area would be service stations, a majority of which are hangers-on from the oblong box era. At most of the convenience store and oblong box locations the gasoline pumps are located under canopies. Since the customer pumps the fuel himself, the canopy is good business on rainy days. The third most common gasoline retailer in the Butler vicinity would be what service station zealots call "small box stations" such as the Hi-Way Oil Co. on Route 8 just south of Butler. These particular small box operations were usually operated by independents who weren't affiliated with a name brand but rather, purchased gasoline from different suppliers and sold it at very competitive prices. The small booth didn't contain much more than an attendant and a cash register and was often flanked with billboards, which gave the illusion of a larger operation. Where feasible, the independent station owner would arrange for a railroad tank car to be parked obviously on a nearby railroad siding. The tank car conveyed the idea of "no middleman" and therefore cheaper prices. Francis Conerty who had worked for Esso, built and operated the Payless gas station at the top of McBride Hill. His operation was a good example of the independent, small-booth station. The Falcon Station at the bottom of Armco Hill was another. According to Arnold Karnes, there was a railroad siding behind the Falcon station where a gasoline tank car was at times connected and sat indefinitely as the gasoline was being sold through the pumps.

In 1972 there were yet 226,459 "service" stations in the country. Places like Jiffy Lube and Midas undercut the cost of certain repairs and service so that by 1990 the number of "service" stations had dropped to 111,657. It is also a fact that newer cars require less maintenance—older cars used a great deal of oil. Station owners had to adapt to expensive environmental regulations for example: storage tanks need to be replaced and new underground piping had to be installed to accommodate the new vapor recovery nozzles. A cursory search for Butler's popular stations of earlier days yields a multitude of real estate offices, gift shops, barbershops, beauty parlors and residences.

The gasoline station, much like the shoe repair business, and the railroads, has come full circle.

## ARNOLD KARNES
Over the years during the 1940's 50's and even 60's I repeatedly heard the names of certain Butler-

area service station operators i.e., Merle Sarver, Ray Andre, Jinks Cirillo, Harold Erhman, Bill Puff, Don Black and Arnold Karnes. I made a few inquiries and checked the telephone book to see if any of these men were still in the area. Fortunately, several of them are, and without exception they very graciously allowed me to interview them. My first interview was with Mr. Arnold Karnes. We had never met face-to-face; I telephoned Mr. Karnes and made arrangements to meet at the Summit Dairy Queen where we could talk over coffee. I arrived a few minutes before our 10:30 a.m. meeting time and noticed several cars in the lot. One white-haired gentleman was checking the air in the tires of his car—I immediately suspected that it was Arnold Karnes, and sure enough, I was right. At age eighty-eight he is still servicing automobiles!

We got our coffee, sat down in a corner booth, and I turned on my recorder. Mr. Karnes began his story by giving me a brief background. He had grown up in the Parker area and after graduating from high

Arnold Karnes' Brady Street station

school, moved to Butler and acquired his first job at Putt MacDonald's gasoline station which was located at the corner of Brady and Franklin Streets, directly across from the Inn. The year was 1930 and Karnes' starting pay was just $75 a month. Mr. MacDonald was basically in the coal business and had only recently purchased the gas station from Fred Harper. As fate would have it, Paul Fair, a very fine mechanic, had worked for Harper and stayed on when MacDonald purchased the business. He "knew his stuff" and became Arnold's mentor. Mr. Karnes learned the mechanics of motor vehicles from Harper but especially remembers one difficult lesson he learned the hard way. A customer, Mrs. Lydecker, accused Arnold of leaving her valve caps off after her car was serviced. Arnold became a bit irate at the accusation and replied, "No, I'm sure I put them on!" Paul overheard this and "jumped all over Arnold" saying among other things, "Whether the customer is right or not, you never talk back to a customer." This was a memorable lesson for the young Karnes.

When he started with MacDonald the old gas pumps were still being used. The service station attendant pumped the gas up into a marked five gallon container then let the gasoline flow into the car's tank by gravity. He related that MacDonald had seven different brands of gasoline available; each had a separate underground tank.

The Great Depression was under way and business was lean. All the men at MacDonald's station were paid by the month and it was necessary to cut their wages. When Paul Fair's pay was cut by $30 a month he promptly quit. The vacancy was filled by Arnold Karnes—he moved up to manager and received a $5 a month raise. Eventually Mr. Karnes was taking home $120 a month.

In addition to his hours at the station, Karnes worked part time as a substitute mail carrier for the Butler Post Office. He soon had to make one of the big decisions of his life when the post office offered him a full time job. He mulled it over and decided that he liked the service station business better— he never regretted his decision to stay. After sixteen years of working for others, Arnold Karnes stepped out and made arrangements to run his own station. The Kendall station at 113 East Brady Street was available; it had previously been operated by Merle Sarver whom Karnes remembers as "a very fine and knowledgeable man who was aggressive and moved around more than most." Karnes' new Kendall station covered the entire lot between Cedar and McKean Streets and consisted of two buildings, one was the office and the other had a washing bay with an automatic washer and a second bay where mechanical work and inspections were performed. The architectural style featured a hip roof.

At that time most of the oil companies built the stations and leased them to dealers. Karnes leased the station for one year; from then on his leases covered five-year periods. During our interview he conveyed a great deal of interesting information on some of the "service station men" around town and the ins and outs of running a station. Karnes became a certified mechanic and specialized in motor overhauls, tune-ups and clutches. He also had a state inspection license and had the reputation of being somewhat strict with inspections. He told me that he loved to make cars run better. Bill McClain was running AAA at the time and wanted Arnold to do AAA service calls, but Karnes realized that he would be called out during the worst weather and at all hours of the night. This he didn't relish, but McClain took him on anyway, calling him only during the hours that his station was open—no night-time, road service.

I asked Mr. Karnes if he ever operated more than one station at a time. He said that he had many offers over the years but never diversified in that manner. The opportunity to run the Sterling station at the corner of Main and Penn Streets was offered to Karnes. He was tempted but to meet the company requirements he had to agree to stay open twenty-four hours a day--he reluctantly declined. The station later became a Quaker State and was run by Frank Hilliard. By this time Karnes was retired and collecting social security but agreed to help Hilliard a couple of days a week. Mr. Karnes had retired in 1973 at age 62. At the time he had six men working for him—his station was then affiliated with Sunoco. Sunoco signed a lease with Lou Lahere who worked at Armco but also wanted to run a station. Harold Irvin, one of Karnes' best men stayed on to work for Lahere but after just one year Lahere gave up the station and Gary Schultz became the new proprietor. The building stood vacant for a time until Ron Fudoli purchased it and opened it as a music store.

### RICHARD CUPPS

Richard Cupps' service station experience began away back in 1928 when Penn Drake hired him. At that time Penn Drake was a part of the Beck brothers' Pennsylvania Refining Company which had its home base in Karns City. Desiring a retail outlet in the city of Butler, Pennsylvania Refining built a service station near the corner of First and Locust Streets in the Institute Hill section of the city. The station sat directly in front of the old silk mill which had been the former home of the Witherspoon Institute. In addition to selling gasoline, Penn Drake manufactured fly spray and toothpaste at the First Street location. One of Cupps' jobs was to work on the assembly line where the spray cans were filled. The Beck brothers opened an office in Butler in 1930. In addition to the Institute Hill interests, Penn Drake had service stations at 121 W. North Street, the present location of Bill Steiner's station, and a larger station at the corner of Brown and Center Avenues; Ralph Dreher was the manager there. Richard Cupps at one time or another worked at all three Penn Drake stations.

Cupps tells and interesting story related to one of the very early "gas wars." Penn Drake had three stations in Erie where this gas war began. The market

Cupps' Sunoco station on South Main near the viaduct

## POLK'S CITY DIRECTORY
## GASOLINE SERVICE STATIONS
### For Selected Years

1912
Atwell Auto Co., W. Wayne
Butler Buick Co. E. Diamond
Longwell, Arthur E., 151 Etna
Willetts, Reuben, rr 340 N. McKean
1915-16
Huselton Automobile Co., 150 N. Main
Callihan & Co., 330 N. Jackson
Atwell Auto Co., W. Wayne near S. Main
1920
Butler-Paige Co., 128 Mifflin
McIntire Auto Garage Co, cor. E. Cunningham and S. Monroe
"The Inn" auto Sales Company, cor. Franklin and Clay
Willetts, R. Garage, rear 340 N. McKean
1930
Andre Service Station S. Main cor Etna
Butler Oil Sales Co 110 S. McKean
Campbell's Auto Supply & Service Station, Lincoln Ave and S. Monroe
Central Parking & Supply Co. 125 E. Jefferson
City Service Station Roosevelt Blvd cor S. Main
Gulf Refining Co. 129 Pillow, N Main cor E. Fulton 417 S. Main and
W. Cunningham cor W. Jefferson
Inn Service Station 300 E. Brady
MacDonald Gasoline Oil Co 301 E. Brady
McKissick Guy 1101 Center Av
Mifflin Street Service 507 New Castle
Peerless Gasoline & Oil Co Service Sta W. Cunningham cor Fourth
Pennzoil Service Sta 222 W. Jefferson
Sterling Service Sta 141 W. Jefferson
Sutton Gasoline Co. Inc. Kittanning rd nr rr and cor Monroe and Cunningham
1940
Andre Ray 459 W. Cunningham
Andrews Roy A 109 Roosevelt Av
Archer & Marra 352 Center Av
Armstrong & Kidd 915 Center Av
Barnhart Edgar E 232 Pillow
Barto H Leroy 330 Center Av
Betres Service 5 Bessemer Av
Boettner's Gulf Service 501 N Main
Butler Edgar H 581 W Cunningham and New Castle and Fourth
Central Parking & Supply 125 E Jefferson and 225 N Main
DeCoux H Douglas 417 S Main
DeWoody Carl H 130 E Wayne
Dinstbir's Service Station 104 E. Brady
Douglass Lauren N 515 W Jefferson
Ehrman Harold B 141 W Jefferson
Elliott Oil & Gas Co 501 W Cunningham
Geibel Wm J 110 S Mckean
Green Simon P 203 Kittanning
H & A service 240 N Main
Hume Bros 422 W Jefferson
Hummel's Service Station 425 S Main

price for gasoline had been holding steady at around thirty-one cents a gallon. A competing business in Erie dropped the price to twelve cents and the war was really on! Penn Drake called five men from its Butler operation, one was Cupps, to help pump gas and service cars in Erie, where Penn Drake had retaliated by lowering the price to just six cents a gallon! Cupps remembers lines of cars five to six blocks in length. "One guy took the money, others pumped gas and we gave full service; checked tires, oil, water and cleaned the windshields."

Cupps and another service station enthusiast, Ray Martin, worked together and were partners in several Butler stations. In the 1930's the two men were employed by Central Parking & Supply Co., which had two stations in downtown Butler. One was at 125 E. Jefferson Street across from the old Butler Theater, where the city has a parking lot today. A canopy covered the pumps at the Jefferson St. station, and surprisingly the building had an indoor horseshoe court on the second floor. The other Central Parking & Supply Co. station was at 225 N. Main, across from the present Burger Hut; the present location of another city parking lot. George Sprankle was the boss of both stations. Eventually the station was razed; Mobile purchased the site, and built a new three bay station there. Cupps and Martin managed the new Mobile station and this was without a doubt the zenith of their service station careers. For one thing, the location was great; it was directly across Main Street from the A & P store and at that time people from all over the county came to Butler to get their groceries. Cupps and Martin could park forty to fifty cars, mostly A & P shoppers', behind their station at twenty-five cents a car. Many of the shoppers had their tanks filled and their car serviced while they shopped. It added up to good business. Another reason for their prosperity hinged around the fact that they were able to service large, road-building equipment. The state was rebuilding Route 8 north of Butler at the time and Cupps and Martin landed the contract to do the tire and battery work on the state construction vehicles. Some of the tires weighed as much as 3000 pounds so it was a job that not every service station could handle. Their reputation preceded them and when the Greater Pittsburgh Airport was being built the two men serviced those construction vehicles in much the same way as they had the highway equipment. And if that were not enough to keep them busy, the two men had a contract to service all of the Bantam's vehicles.

The Hume brothers had a station at 113 Brady Street. It was torn down in the late 1930's and a Kendall station was put in its place. Hume brothers moved to 422 W. Jefferson St. then after a few years to 228-30 New Castle St. Cupps and Martin

Inn Service Station 300 E Brady
Jack Lewis E 204 E Brady
Johnson H C & Son 115 Roosevelt Av
Johnson Service 250 W Jefferson
Lindsey & Slupe Co S Monroe nr E Cunningham
Maker Peter 2 Main Lyndora
McCullough's Friendly Service Station S Main and Roosevelt Blvd
McKissick Guy 1101 Center Av
Metropolitan Petroleum Corp 118 N Monroe
Mifflin Service 505-07 New Castle
Noble & Eakin 232 W Jefferson
O'Neil's Service Station 127 New Castle
Pennsylvania Refining Co 340 Center Av and 121 W North
Pennzoil Super Service Station 222 W Jefferson
Puff's Bill Esso Station cor W Cunningham and Pillow
No 2 Station cor Third and E. Jefferson
Rockenstein, Vincent 101 Franklin
Rodgers Herman M 41 Bredinville
Sarver Merle J 235 E Jefferson
Scialabba Jos R 314 E Jefferson
Smitty's Service Station 333 E Jefferson
Spino Jos 322 E Jefferson
Stanfield Arth E 400 W Jefferson
Stewart Jas J 203 Fourth
Sutton Sales Co Inc 150 Kittanning and 520 E Jefferson
West End Garage 541-43 W Cunningham
Wilson Gilbert L Kittanning nr limits
1951
Amoco Service 240 N Main
Anderson Atlantic Service 400 W Jefferson
Andre Ray C 459 W Cunningham
Archer's Service 352 Center Ave
Bardocz Esso Service US Highway 8 North RD 5
Barnhart Service 232 Pillow
Barto H Leroy 330 Center
Bill's Service 128 N Monroe
Copelan Service 109 Roosevelt Blvd
Croupe Lyle L 915 Center
Daum Fredk H 110 S McKean
Dorcy's Sunoco Service 422 W Jefferson
Dreher Ralph E 225 N Main
Dunn Jas H 301 E Brady
Ellis Walter 17 Hansen Av
English Wm B Esso 521 W Cunningham
Ferguson's Sunoco Service 335 N Main
Frank's Esso Station 204 E Brady
Gladden Richd L 340 Center
H & S Service E Jefferson at 4th
Hampton Jos E 417 S Main
Hays Amoco Service 100 1st
Hume Bros 228-30 New Castle
Independent Service Roosevelt Blvd
Johnson H C & Son 115 Roosevelt Blvd
Johnson's Pennzoil 203 Kittanning
Karnes Arnold Super Service 113 E Brady

Markham Pennzoil Service Roosevelt Blvd
McCall Al Service 425 S Monroe
McKissick Guy 1101 Center
McLaughlin Service 101 Roosevelt Blvd
McMurty Jas C 134 New Castle
Mifflin Service 505 New Castle
Murdick's Service 235 E Jefferson
Pat's Service Station 579 W Cunningham
Pennsylvania Refining Co 121 W North
Pennzoil Super Service 222 W Jefferson
Puff's Bill Cities Service E Jefferson cor 3rd and 416 W Jeff.
Red Head Oil Co 408 S Main
Reith's Russ Gulf 515 W Jefferson
Sanders Amoco Service 401 W Jefferson
Shaffer's Super Service 232 W Jefferson
Sleigher's Service Grant cor 10th E. Butler
Stein's Sunoco Service 423 S Main
Tiberi Thos Service 320 Eau Claire
Walker's Pennzoil Service 501 W Cunningham
White's Kendall 118 N Monroe

took over the new Kendall station in 1940. When Cupps went to serve his country during World War II, Arnold Karnes began to operate the station.

In 1946, after his return from military service, Cupps assumed management of the Sunoco station on South Main Street across from the present Super America. He had a two-car rack on one side and a washing bay on the other. All were outside which was not unusual at that time. Eddie Hampton had the Gulf Station just north of Cupps' Sunoco. Cupps soon left that location and found himself running the Mifflin Station across the street from the Broad St. School. In 1949 he quit service stations and went to work at Armco. (Much of the general information in this chapter came from *The Gas Station In America*, by John A. Jakle and *Pump and Circumstance*, by John Margolies.)

### A Collection Of Gasoline Station Facts And Trivia

A gasoline station in Washington D.C. has the record—fifty-two pumps.

During World War II a large number of females became gas station attendants.

Standard's famous sign with the torch was introduced in 1945.

SOCONY – Standard Oil Company of New York

Pegasus was Standard's mascot then later became the logo for Mobil.

Neon began to be used extensively in signage in the 1920's

Esso came from S.O. (Standard Oil) – changed its name to Exxon in 1972.

Gas companies began to pass out free road maps in the teens.

Before 1920, few roads were named or marked.

S & H Green Stamps were given with many gasoline purchases--the company was founded in 1896 by Sperry and Hutchinson.

The car ran over a cable which rang a bell inside to let the attendant know he had a customer.

Cities Service became Citgo.

Vincent Lopez and his Pure Oil Orchestra could be heard on the radio in the 1930's.

The early grease pit, if there was one, was outside next to the station.

Marilyn Monroe's only commercial was done for the Union Oil Co. The ad showed a service-station attendant putting oil in her pink convertible.

Pumping one's own gas was not legal everywhere—by 1982 all but two states had made self-service stations legal.

Mose Campbell ran a service station at the corner of Center Ave. and Monroe St. It was later operated by Al McCall. They both specialized in the recapping of tires. Joe Archer, as a boy, worked for Mose. Archer took over the station after Campbell quit.

Arnie Covert, for a time, operated the station across from the Burger Hut.

Mr. Covert and Harold Irvin were co-operators of a station at the corner of First and Jefferson Streets. When it closed, Irvin went to work for Arnold Karnes and stayed with him until Karnes retired in 1973.

Ray Andre started at the New Castle St. station which is now operated by Bill Steiner. Ray moved to W. Cunningham St. where he had a very good tire business, selling the General Tire.

Keagle's Trading post was across route 8 from the Holiday Inn. It was a service station and a car dealer. Keagle's sold Desotos.

Mr. Sutton had several stations; one was at the southeast corner of Chestnut and Jefferson Streets. He had managers operate the stations for him. Harold Irvin worked for Sutton before he was hired by Arnold Karnes. Mr. Karnes broke his back in 1966—the injury forced him to retire at age sixty-two.

Many states had "chain-store taxes" which influenced oil companies such as Standard Oil to lease more of their stations.

Ray Barto had the Atlantic station on Center Ave. in the building that presently has the Donut Connection.

There was certainly no shortage of stations on Butler's Southside. Beside Barto was the Penn Drake and just east of it Jack Sanders operated the Mobile station. Sanders, later ran the Cloverleaf Restaurant on Cunningham Street.

Standard Motor Company at Main and Brady Streets had a service station at their location.

There was a Pennzoil station, run by Dick Daubenspeck, on the northeast corner of Church and W. Jefferson Streets just next to the Sinclair station. Jinks Cirillo ran the Sinclair for about a year; he also, for a short time, ran the Esso station on the site of today's Medicine Shoppe.

A man named Spino ran an independent gas station on E. Jefferson Street where Cavalero's market was later. During a gas war they sold seven gallons of gas for a dollar. The regular price was six gallons for a dollar. This is back when they pumped it into the globe.

Maco's had a service station on Bessemer Ave. where it joins Hansen Avenue. Then they moved up the street across from the present car lot.

Russ Lawton had a gas station on the corner where Allied Auto is today.

## JINKS CIRILLO

Mr. Jinks Cirillo had started his service station career at 235 E. Jefferson Street with Merle Sarver in 1942. The business was called Merle J. Sarver's Sinclair Super Service Station, and was located directly across Jefferson Street from the First United Presbyterian Church. Sarver, during the early part of World War II, moved to the Brady Street station, which was later operated by Arnold Karnes.

After his military service Jinks rejoined Merle Sarver in the Mifflin service station on East New Castle Street near the Broad Street School. From there they moved to a station across from the Cabana out on New Castle Road where the Peking Chinese Restaurant is presently located. Mr. Sarver bought the station from a man named Groover who had had built and operated it. Sarver and Cirillo then moved to the point, then back to Mifflin, then to the Sinclair Station across from the Moose on Jefferson Street. After that he moved to the Gulf, then down to Hansen Avenue where Jimmy Ellis' business is located. Cirillo related that if things were not going well, Sarver did not hesitate to leave for another station.

Mr. Cirillo is presently seventy-one years of age. He fondly remembers the days when the pumps were right at the curb. There were two on Jefferson Street right across the street from each other. One was run by Joe Scialabba and directly across the street was Mr. Smith's pump. They were near the corner of Franklin

Seven different brands were available at this Harrisville station

Street. He vaguely remembers a pump up around the Nixon Hotel and some of my old photographs show curbside pumps outside what is now the Butler News and along Saxonburg's Main Street.

Mr. Cirillo ran the Sinclair station on West Jefferson Street, across from the Moose, for about a year. Then he became the proprietor of the Gulf station at the corner of Cunningham and Jefferson Streets in the early 1960's and remained there until his retirement. In addition to selling gasoline, oil, tires and such he specialized in brakes and state inspections. He counted among his steady customers, Steighner's Crane Service, Butler Floor, Schenck Construction Company, Jack Barber the blacktopper, in addition to his regular trade.

Most of the earliest gasoline stations had a single pump and offered no service, just gasoline. The business evolved to the point where gasoline was just one of the many services and products offered. The station was a place for camaraderie, much like a barber shop. Now the situation has changed again. The motorist pumps the gas himself at a convenience store where absolutely no services are available. If the car needs brakes, a new muffler or tail pipes there are other businesses which specialize in those services. This is the era of the specialist.

**Mobilegas station on North Main at the site of the present city parking lot**

## Famous Visitors

It must have been 1959 or 1960. I had been practicing the guitar for a few years and was quite flattered when I was asked by a couple of musicians to sit-in during an engagement (gig) at the Central Hotel in Chicora. I don't remember how our music sounded but I know we weren't thrown out of the place so it must have been bearable. As it tuned out the evening was somewhat memorable even if the music wasn't. During a break, the manager asked me if I would like to see something interesting that had to do with history. "Of course," I answered not having the slightest inkling of what I was in for. The bartender opened a safe and pulled out a musty, old book. It was a hotel-guest book from many years ago. He began flipping through the compendium until he found the page he wanted. He then held the book in front of my face and directed my eyes to the name signed there—William F. Cody. "Buffalo Bill!" I said. "Are you telling me that he was a guest here?" The manager responded, "He sure was and I have his signature right here to prove it."

I often wondered if the manager was having some fun at my expense or if Buffalo Bill really had spent the night in Chicora's Central Hotel. I eventually came to the conclusion that the signature was probably bogus because Buffalo Bill was a westerner; he rode the plains and would be uncomfortable in Butler County's hilly terrain.

But Buffalo Bill did visit Butler. The evidence was in the library all along—I just didn't know it.

### COLONEL CODY TO MAKE HIS FAREWELL VISIT TO BUTLER

Col. W. F. Cody, Buffalo Bill, announces his intention to retire personally from the public arena. He will bid adieu from the saddle to his patrons in every city visited. The commencement of the farewell tone was inaugurated at Madison Square Garden (the temple of amusement so long a point of interest to the New York public and visitors that is soon to pass away) with a most sensational success. Col. Cody's farewell tour of the continent will be as complete as his farewell tour of Europe. Each and every prominent city and town will be visited.

The experience of Buffalo Bill on the plains covers the era when the Louisiana Purchase was almost unsettled and the state of Texas and the western possessions acquired from Mexico were passing from a state of savagery to their grandly developed prosperity. In middle manhood he was a conspicuous figure in the thrilling history. For thirty summers and several winters in the larger capitals, with the exception of a few intermittent Indian campaigns, he has been actively engaged in an instructive depiction of that once strenuous and picturesque epoch. This work has been recognized in the shape of realistic entertainment. Its travels have been so extensive in Europe and America that it has become as familiar as it is popular. Recognizing the changing conditions and the approach of father time, the old scout has decided to retire from the onerous duties and anxieties coupled with his personal appearance and supervision. To do so while still active and energetic he believes wiser so that he may devote more time to his interests in the west. These embrace promising agricultural, oil, coal mining and gold claim lands. The inroads that time has made on his associates, both red and white, naturally assist in his coming to this conclusion.

Col. Cody will bid farewell to Butler County folk on Friday, June 7, with two performances.
(copied from the *Butler Citizen* dated June 6, 1912 by Dave and Audrey Craig)

### BUFFALO BILL'S FAREWELL VISIT TO BUTLER TOMORROW

When the roads meet at a parting and the time comes to say goodbye, memory runs back to the early days when we were young and strong, and full of hope and endeavor. Now our old friend, "Buffalo Bill," says he is on his last tour of America, preparatory to his retirement from the arena.

This announcement comes suddenly and sharply and the American people will bid farewell to Col. Wm. F. Cody with regret. He has been a historian in giving living moving pictures, such as were never before projected; in a realistic manner, creating in that line a new entertainment.

For thirty years this dauntless American pony-express rider, army scout, Indian fighter, guide to the Grand Duke Alexia, chosen comrade of Sheridan, Sherman, Custer, Merritt, Crook, Miles, Carr and other United States generals of the army, has gone over the world carrying with him his congress of Indians, cowboys, vaqueros, and cavalry of all nations teaching history in a way never before attempted.

Impressive object lessons are invaluable. When made through the eye they are more lasting than in any other manner, and inspire the other senses to a full grasp of the subject. Scenes thus witnessed render their review in books, reproduction in painting or revival in discussion of continuous value, they have sent the merit of permanency attached to the original negative, and, like the camera, "cannot lie" or exaggerate, as might a simple description; for seeing is believing."

Buffalo Bill will appear in Butler tomorrow.
(copied from the *Butler Citizen* dated June 6, 1912 by Dave and Audrey Craig)

# EVERYTHING READY FOR APPEARANCE WILD WEST TODAY

Around five o'clock this morning, the three railroad trains of Buffalo Bill's Wild West and Pawnee Bill's Far East will be on the side tracks of the Pennsylvania Railroad in Butler and the work of unloading the mammoth exhibition well under way. The attraction will undoubtedly draw one of the largest crowds from out of town seen here in a long time. The " two Bill's " do not give a street parade. Reserved seats will be on sale all day at the City Drug store.

Thirty years ago, W. F. Cody, affectionately known throughout the entire world as Buffalo Bill made his bid for fame and fortune. His work is done, all the honors mankind can bestow on fellow man have been heaped upon him and now in the wellness of his glory Col. Cody announces his positive retirement from active life. He seeks a rest well requited, and the good will and heartiest well wishes come to him from his million friends.

Buffalo Bill is still a sturdy specimen of the great far west; he has not measured his full length of time, he seeks the recompense so justly so nobly earned - peaceful days away from the glamour, the noise, the thrill and excitement consequent upon his unusual life of activity; he will outlive history; his fame will go to future generations as one of the greatest American characters: There isn't a man, child of yesterday or a child, man of tomorrow that will not express sincere regret at his leave taking. He has decided the step will be final.

Col. Cody will positively announce at such performance. He wants to bid you goodbye in person, to acknowledge his debt of gratitude for the continuous loyalty of a great nation for so many years. Every feature of the Wild West and Far East this season has been improved, new acts added, sensations of every kind joined to the refining influence of oriental and occidental splendor.

It seems strange in these days of the flying machine, the telegraph, the iron battle ships, and the printed newspaper, to review the western wilderness that stretches through thousands of years now reaching the end of its path, conquered by countless pioneers, many of whom sacrificed their lives in laying the foundations of the empire of the new great west and of whom Mark Twain said: "They are no simpering-dainty-kidgloved weaklings, but stalwart-dauntless braves brimful of push and energy and loyalty endowed with every attribute that goes to make up a peerless and magnificent manhood, the very pick of the world's glorious ones and he spoke the truth."

The remarkable scene disclosing undulating prairies, plateau, desert washes and snow capped mountains, built with every accessory of artistic design and veracity splendidly shown as a background for "pioneer ever in frontier days," which acts as an influence to pull out of the pigeon holes of memory the one time current action of the danger days of American history.

As a necessary sedative to the excitements of the "Wild West" is the visualizing of the "Far East" with its suave orientals from Turkey, Persia, Arabia, and India and their elusive personalities, strange tongues. The strange garments seem to keep them in an isolated atmosphere of intrigue and fascination over the entire "Far East" continent.

The rough riding with military detachments of various nationalities and "pastime of the pioneer" are more significantly emphasized than ever. There is the most wonderful collection of trained horses ever seen under one management. Then for those who crave excitement, a thrill and many of them will be given in the bronco busting acts, the Zouave drills, the cavalry dashes, the marvelous death daring Cossacks, the attack of the caravan, the train robbery, life in the wild west as it was years ago, and many more features of vital interest.

These alone would constitute the ordinary entertainment and that's just where the distinction of the Buffalo Bill and Pawnee Bill exhibition exists. This is not an ordinary show, add to the heart quivering deeds of dare devil heroism and the Wild West, the pageantry, tinsel, flash and silken rustle of the gem studded and swarthy skinned actors, from the far east. Feats of running, events mysterious magic from the burning desert sands, and you have out a slight mental picture of what you will see when bidding an affectionate farewell to the greatest of them all, the world famous Buffalo Bill.

Today's performance will commence at 2 and 8 p. m. Doors open one hour earlier.
(copied from the *Butler Citizen* dated June 7, 1912 by Dave and Audrey Craig)

## Man On The Street

What are you kicking about? The Buffalo Bill show has had 28 days of bad weather out of the 32 it has been out this season. That's enough to discourage anyone. Buffalo Bill is getting old, and it is a wise move on the part of the old scout to farewell while the farewelling is good. Last night the hero of the plains looked much older than he did on his previous visit to Butler. He didn't have the dash which characterized him on other visits and his shooting was far from what it was.

The first time Buffalo Bill visited Butler was more than 30 years ago--and he didn't come that time with a two section wild west show by any means, but with a modest theatrical company appearing in the old opera house in the second story of the present Niggel and Martincourt building on East Jefferson Street, which for a time in those early days of the town was devoted to the drama. Buffalo Bill appeared as the star in "May Cody's Revenge," and the boys of that day all envied "Jim" Mechling because he had the distinction of playing the part of the "bear" in the show.
(*The Butler Times*, June 8, 1912)

**The Cowboy Band With Buffalo Bill's Show**

William Sweeney's Cowboy Band with the Buffalo Bill Wild West and Pawnee Bill Far East is not only entertaining, but is interesting from a spectacular standpoint. In addition to being a finished artist, each member of the organization is a skilled horseman. Schooled by Mr. Sweeney, an old frontiersman, formerly bandmaster of the Nineteenth United States Infantry, when the Wild West was everything that the term implies, they execute their various maneuvers with the same apparent ease as though they were in a band stand.

The Indian battles, the oriental spectacle, old fashioned fox hunt, attacking the wagon train and numerous other features participated in by people of all nations, forms one of the most original and entertaining spectacular exhibitions conceivable. In addition to the many historical features, there are many novelties which are conducted under the personal supervision and direction of Messrs. Cody and Lillie.

(*The Butler Times*, June 8, 1912)

**George Washington**

After reading these articles concerning Buffalo Bill, I wondered how many other famous visitors had stepped foot in Butler County. Most of the old county histories agree that George Washington was one of the first "white" men to pass through Butler County. In 1753 Governor Dinwiddie of Virginia sent a young George Washington and a guide, Christopher Gist, to deliver a message to the French contingent at Fort LeBoeuf in what is now Venango County. Dinwiddie was demanding that the French withdraw from the area which Virginia claimed.

On the return journey, the weakened horses caused such a delay that Washington and Gist continued on foot. As they trekked through the woods near present-day Evans City, an Indian fired a shot at Washington. Fortunately the Indian missed. Can you imagine how the course of history would have changed had the Indian been a more accurate marksman?

**Joseph Boneparte**

Joseph Boneparte (1768-1844), older brother of Napoleon served in the Italian campaign. The following year he became a diplomat of the First Republic of France, first at the court of Parma and later at Rome. During the Napoleonic Wars, Joseph acted as an envoy for his brother, signing treaties with the United States, Austria, Great Britain and the Vatican. In 1806 Napoleon made Joseph King of Naples and two years later, King of Spain.

After the final defeat of Napoleon, Joseph immigrated to the United States remaining here until 1832. It was during that visit, in 1820 to be exact, that his travels brought him to Butler County where he spent a night at the White Horse Tavern near Prospect. He eventually returned to Europe, lived briefly in England, then settled in Italy.

**The Marquis de Lafayette**

Another famous Frenchman passed through Butler County on June 1, 1825 and his visit was well-documented in the *Butler County Sentinel*. The Marquis de Lafayette was a French nobleman, political leader, and general of the late eighteenth and early nineteenth centuries who served as a general in the American army during the Revolutionary War, fighting alongside his friend George Washington at the Battle of Yorktown and elsewhere. He became a hero in the United States for his help in winning the war. James A. McKee reports in the *Butler Eagle* of 1925, "It is just a hundred years this summer since General Lafayette paid a visit to Butler. At that time the city had a population of about 450 and the county less than 10,000. Efforts are being made to base some formal observance of the event in Pittsburgh and Erie, Mercer and Meadville are likely to fall in line.

The *Butler County Sentinel* of June 4, 1825 gives an account of General Lafayette's passing through Butler on Wednesday June 1, en route from Pittsburgh to Erie and his entertainment by the people of the community.

"The night previous to the famous general's arrival a committee met at the courthouse and planned for the reception. A committee of two was appointed to meet General Lafayette and his party on the road and escort them into town. Another committee of two was appointed to prepare refreshments and another committee of two to escort the general as far as Mercer.

In the morning there must have been some stir and excitement in the village. Two triumphal arches were erected, one at each end of the town. Banners bearing the words, "Welcome Lafayette," wreathed in spring flowers and roses were hung on the arches. The citizens of the borough assembled at the south end

John F. Kennedy on Butler Courthouse steps

of Main Street and formed in single file in two lines.

When General Lafayette had passed between the lines the people fell in at the rear of the escort and marched to the square in front of the courthouse. A banquet was served in the Mechling Hotel on the south side of West Diamond Street opposite the courthouse. [The hotel stood on ground now occupied by the west half of the Lafayette Building.]

The report states that after the banquet, General Lafayette walked out among the people assembled to see him, shook hands with many and talked with men whom he identified as soldiers of the War of the Revolution. He arrived in the town at 12 o'clock and left at 4. As he was taking his departure he stood up in his carriage, waved his hand to the people and exclaimed, 'Farewell my friends. This is the last time you will see me.' He arrived at Mercer at 1 o'clock the next morning where he was again entertained. He then proceeded on his way to Erie...."

## Famous Political Figures

I could find no record of any U.S. president ever visiting Butler County during his term in office. However, a couple of presidential hopefuls came to Butler during their campaigns. There is a monument to President John F. Kennedy near the Lyndora Post Office in recognition of his visit to Butler which occurred on October 15, 1960. Early in his campaign, Kennedy spoke to a large crowd on the Diamond. Accompanying the presidential aspirant on that visit were David L. Lawrence, governor of Pennsylvania; Senator Joseph S. Clark; and Kennedy's sister, Mrs. Peter Lawford. His wife Jacqueline, then expecting a child, did not make the trip to Butler.

The presidential entourage had lunch at Butler's Williard Hotel that day. The Nixon Hotel was nearby and might have been chosen had it not been for some local politics. You see, Butler County was heavily Republican at that time and Mr. C. Stewart Shoemaker, owner of the Nixon had changed the name of his hotel to the "Nixon Lodge." It was a play on the names of the Republican candidates, Richard Nixon and Henry Cabot Lodge. The banner was hung from the facade of the hotel and was directly in front of Mr. Kennedy as he spoke.

Stories handed down by word-of-mouth have it that President Taft once stayed at the Phillip's mansion in Penn Township.

When George Bush was Richard Nixon's running mate, the vice-presidential candidate was campaigning in the area and stayed at the Rath farm in Penn Township.

Others of a political bent who visited Butler were Estes Kefauver (1955) and those

213

who wrote about politics, Drew Pearson (1937). I heard Eleanor Roosevelt speak in Miller Auditorium circa 1960. She also made an earlier visit to Butler in 1947.

Another Democratic candidate, William Jennings Bryan, visited Butler on two different occasions. He spoke at the Opera House on the Diamond in 1898 then a spoke before a capacity crowd at the Park Theater in 1902. Bryan, who called himself "the candidate of the ordinary American," lost three presidential elections as the nominee of the Democratic Party, although he gathered substantial votes in the south and west. At the 1896 Democratic national convention, just two years before his Butler visit, he delivered the much remembered "Cross of Gold" speech in favor of unlimited coinage of silver and against the gold standard. Mr. Bryan was a fundamentalist in religion, and opposed the teaching of the theory of evolution in schools and assisted the prosecution in the Scopes Trial.

## Pennsylvania's Portage Railway and Canal

Before the mighty railroads traversed Pennsylvania's hills and valleys, many people were making the trip west. There wasn't much choice as to method of transportation—horseback, horsedrawn wagon, watercraft, or feet. The Kittanning trail led right to Butler County and was used by the very earliest travelers. Who knows what persons may have walked through Butler County at that time?

The Erie Canal, which made an all-water trip across New York State possible, was completed in 1825. Within a few years the canal's positive effect upon New York's economy was evident. So much so that Pennsylvania lawmakers thought, "If it's working in New York State we should build one in Pennsylvania."

Construction began and by 1835 the Portage Railroad and Canal system was completed from Philadelphia to Pittsburgh. Pennsylvania's terrain, unlike New York's, necessitated the building of tracks up the sides of intervening mountains forming inclined railways of great slope. It nearly bankrupted our state. However, for a few years the new railroad and canal system was used by those heading west. Charles Dickens, writing in 1842, described a trip he took over the canal and railway in his *American Notes*. The route traversed Pennsylvania and when it reached the Allegheny River just above Freeport, the canal actually crossed the river. John Roebling, of Saxonburg built the world's first suspended aqueduct as was related in the prologue of this work. The point is this—thousands of folks made the trip across Pennsylvania on this system; they crossed the Allegheny above Freeport which put them in or right on Butler County's doorstep. Most however, continued south to Pittsburgh on the West Side of the Allegheny River. A few well-known characters probably traveled across Butler County to the Franklin Trail and points north.

During the 1860's and 70's the oil excitement in Venango County was quite an attraction. Not only were the hopeful, working classes hurrying to those oil boom towns, but dignitaries such as Presidents Grant and Hayes, Henry Ward Beecher, Horace Greely, Artemus Ward and Mark Twain made the trip to oil country to satisfy their curiosity. The first oil well was drilled in 1859; the first railroad which traversed Butler County to the oil country, the Karns City and Parker Railroad, was opened in 1876. The shortest and most convenient route from the large urban areas on the East Coast to the oil country led through Butler County. It is likely, but evidence is difficult to come by, that at least a few famous personages passed through Butler on their trips to Venango County.

While were speculating, let us consider John Wilkes Booth. This man, who assassinated President Lincoln, traveled from Franklin to Washington D. C. just a day or two before his terrible deed. His trip very likely took him through Butler County but there is, of course, no record of it.

We do know that when the oil excitement was occurring in Butler County, John D. Rockefeller visited the area and his company, Standard Oil, secured many leases all over the county.

We may speculate that famous personalities such as those just mentioned traveled through our county but in many cases they didn't stop here and their presence went unobserved. According to Paul Giddens, Don Pedro, the Emperor of Brazil, visited Venango County to observe the oil activity. The emperor must have spent more than a day in Butler because the local newspaper, the *Citizen*, had to make an appeal to Butler's residents to back off and give the emperor some breathing room—so many well-meaning Butlerites were accosting him.

## Speakers Entertainers and Athletes

Butler had a number of famous visitors speak or appear at the old opera house, the armory or one of the early theaters. The Park Theater which was on the south side of the Diamond opened in 1891. In 1903 a major fire destroyed and/or severely damaged the Armory, Park Theater, Central Hotel, Younkins, and Leighner and Thompson buildings. The fire was discovered at 10:00 p.m. during a show featuring Minnie Seward.

Alameda Park, which opened on July 4, 1901, had its share of famous visitors such as Louis Armstrong, Paul Whiteman and his orchestra, Carrie Nation (1908) and Lillian Russell (1917). (There is more information on Miss Russell in *Butler County, the Second Hundred Years,* pg. 46-48)

The New York Yankees played their Butler farm club annually but 1938 stands out as a memorable year. The New York team's lineup that year read like a hall of fame list. The famous Yankees who played in that exhibition game at Pullman Park were Joe Dimaggio, Lou Gehrig, George Selkirk, Bill Knickerbocker, Jobe Powell, Red Rolfe, Frank Verdi and Mickey Gordon. Whitey Ford played for the Butler team in 1947. The Yankee story is also covered *in Butler County, the Second Hundred Years,* Chapter 14.

Edgar Guest was an English born American poet who wrote about such subjects as friendship, family affection and the home. He came to America as a boy. One of his famous lines is "It takes a heap o' livin' to make a house a home." He made a personal appearance in Butler in 1921.

Evangeline Booth was the first woman to serve as a general in the Salvation Army. She was elected to the position in 1934 and served for five years. Her father, William Booth, founded the Salvation Army. She began preaching at age 17 and was sent by the Salvation Army to Canada to supervise activities there. She spoke in Butler in 1930. Billy Sunday preached in Butler in 1913.

Amelia Earhart came to the Pittsburgh-Butler airport for instrument instruction. Her teacher was Burt Bluchen. Ms. Earhart trained here for three months in preparation for her solo Atlantic crossing.

This, by all means, is not a complete list and even these references are certainly not "chiseled in stone." It is easy to guess or assume about others who probably passed through Butler County, but until documentation is found one should abstain.

Butler County has its share of famous people who were born and/or grew up here—sports figures, beauty contest winners, a secretary of defense and a U.S. senator. For those who are interested in pursuing this topic, Denise Throm's book, *Reflections of Butler County, Pennsylvania* includes most of those famous Butlerites.

Friedman's Jefferson Street Store

## Contractors, Builders and Developers
### Phillip Tack

The Phillip Tack family migrated from Germany to the United States in 1881. Mr. Tack was hopeful of finding work in the coalfields of Orangeville, Ohio, just across the state line from Greenville, Pa. This objective did not work out prompting other moves to Greenville, Pa. then Coaltown, Butler County. One more move in 1885 proved to be the right one. The family purchased a house at the bottom of Morton Avenue and there raised a total of ten children, five girls and five boys.

Mr. Tack opened and operated a stone yard and a construction business in a shop behind his Morton Avenue home. He purchased rough stone which was shipped to his yard on the adjacent B & O Railroad track. Mr. Tack and his sons cut, shaped and placed the stone for walls and building foundations. With five sons he had a resident work force. Stories handed down through the family indicate that Phillip Tack was a hard worker and even harder to work for. A family member reports that he paid his sons on Saturday evenings by emptying his pockets of change and throwing it down to the bottom of the stairs. This is one reason the sons left early and started their own businesses.

Several of the boys started their own construction companies; it was something they knew.

Tack moving bank vault down E. Cunningham St.

John, who had been born in Coaltown in 1883, took a job hauling oil well supplies with the Keystone Pipe and Supply Company. He was very good at working with the teams of horses. He and his wife Maggie did not move very far from their parents. They built a house on Patterson Avenue and raised seven children there.

John's team of horses, "Bill and Doc," were stabled behind the Patterson Avenue house. Eventually trucks replaced the horses and what were stables became garages and storage areas. As his hauling business grew John found it necessary to move to another house on Fairview Avenue--it had more garage space. Even the new quarters proved to be insufficient so John purchased the old Billingsley barn on Spring Street just off Center Avenue. This served as his headquarters until he retired.

When John's three sons, Frederick, Kenneth and John Jr., returned from military service after World War II, they persuaded their father to expand his business to include ready-mixed concrete and building materials. He acquiesced and the family opened a builder's supply business on Bantam Avenue. Ironically, the night of the dinner celebrating this new partnership and business saw a disastrous fire, which virtually destroyed the Tack's Spring Street property. They salvaged much of the equipment and moved it to the Bantam Avenue location.

John, like his father was a very stern taskmaster—a difficult man to work for. Although his expectations often seemed to be in the realm of impossibility, he succeeded at most every job he set out to do, and must be given credit for some remarkable accomplishments. John Tack approached nearly any job with enthusiasm and the more difficult the task seemed the more he seemed to enjoy it. He especially liked moving heavy and cumbersome objects—the challenges seemed to give him a great deal of satisfaction.

Tack's gasoline-powered shovel

The photograph on the previous page shows John and his crew moving a twenty-ton vault from a Main Street bank to the Southside Bank on Center Avenue. The Wayne Street Viaduct, built in 1915, had a weight limit of fifteen tons and the vault weighed twenty. The seemingly impossible part of the task was getting the heavy vault across the Connoquenessing Creek. None of the bridges were built to handle that much weight. No other heavy haulers even wanted the job. But John figured out a way to make the delivery without crashing any bridges. The Bessemer Railroad ran through Butler along the north side of the creek. There was a switchover just north of town, so John took the vault down East Cunningham Street using one Packard truck to pull and another to keep the load from running away. There the vault was loaded onto a railroad flatcar and taken to North Butler where it was switched over to the B & O track which followed the south side of the Connoquenessing Creek. It was then hauled back to Center Avenue on the B & O track where it was unloaded and pulled the rest of the way to the Center Avenue bank. The entire project was a good example of the man's ingenuity.

John had the first gasoline-powered shovel in Butler. He borrowed $5000 to buy the machine. The truck in the photo above belonged to Sam Mahan, one of John's competitors. Mr. Mahan's business was in the old Walter's mill building which was originally the site of the Cunningham brothers' gristmill.

John's son Homer operated his own excavating and hauling business. He was an excellent gasoline-powered, shovel operator and enjoyed working in front of crowds where he could show off his abilities. He put on a memorable show during the excavating for the Penn Theater in Butler. Another son, John Jr. quit the Bantam Avenue business and developed and built the Garden Grove plan of lots along Old Plank Road south of Butler. Kenneth sold the John Tack & Sons business in 1967 and founded the Sugar Creek Rest nursing home near Worthington.

The Tack Shelter in Butler Memorial Park was built to honor John Tack Sr. Butler's Memorial Park was a place he had worked hard to develop and promote.

A large number of building foundations, retaining walls and flagstone sidewalks built by the Tacks, will continue to survive in Butler for many generations.

### Harry Wimer

Harry Wimer, who is considered by many to be the premier builder of Butler County, constructed some of Butler County's most impressive buildings. Mr. Wimer was born in Butler County on August 5, 1874, the son of Philip S. and Rebecca J. (Love) Wimer. Philip had been a soldier in the Union Army during the Civil War. When the hostilities ended, he returned to Butler County and took up farming in Penn Township. Philip Wimer died in 1909 at a relatively young age.

At the death of his father, Harry Wimer, who was in eighth grade, was forced to quit school in order to support his mother. He walked from East Butler, where they lived with the Gilliand family, back and forth to work in Butler. Many people made that three-mile walk but it was certainly an effort. (*Butler County, the Second Hundred Years*, pg. 93) Wimer furthered his education by taking a special course in architecture through the International Correspondence School. He also took a business course at the Butler Business College. Before opening his own contracting business, Mr. Wimer increased his knowledge of the building trade by working for other firms. At one of his jobs in Pittsburgh he was put in charge of millwork for the Bentz Brothers, and soon became their superintendent. When he believed he was ready he returned to Butler and went

Elm Court

into the contracting business with J.S. Hobaugh. After three years, he separated from Hobaugh, incorporated, and started his own business—the Harry Wimer Construction Company Inc.

In 1893 Wimer built his first house; it was on "Lick Hill" along Route 68 north of Butler. After just a few jobs people were beginning to notice the quality of his work; his reputation was soon established. Over the ensuing years he constructed a very large number of public buildings as well as beautiful residences not only in Butler but also in Beaver County. Wimer built both Phillips' mansions, Elm Court and Phillips' Hall, in addition to the Phillips Gas Company office on Main Street. This was probably one of the most expensive buildings ever built in Butler, costing $34,000 in 1929 dollars. The architect on the Gas Company building was Benno Jensen, one of Pittsburgh's most renowned architects. Mr. Wimer also built the Hill United Presbyterian Church, the Butler Eagle Office Building, the Butler Theater, the Millerstown Deposit Bank in Chicora, the Butler Savings and Trust Company, which is yet Butler's tallest building, Butler Senior High School [red brick building], Montgomery Ward which is presently known as the Holly Pointe building, the Telephone Company building on Washington Street, the Buick Building which was located at the northeast corner of Brady and Main Streets, the hangars at the Pittsburgh-Butler Airport, Castle Rubber Company's office building, and a number of impressive homes in the area, especially on Belmont Road. Wimer also made all the wooden parts for the Austin automobile, which was built in Butler in the 1930's. The wooden parts were inside the car on the door and head panels. Wimer's planing mill and scrap yard were on Negley Avenue where Hutchison's Cleaners was later located.

In 1897 Harry Wimer married Lenore C. Infield, of Sandy Lake, Pennsylvania. To Mr. and Mrs. Wimer four children were born: Betty R., who married Arthur Moore; Donald C., a member of the Wimer Contracting Company, and a graduate of Carnegie Institute of Technology; Walter L., a student of the same institute; and Evan A., Donald's son. Mr. Wimer's grandson, "Bim" Wimer, who continues to operate the Harry Wimer Construction Company and provided me with much of this information, said his grandfather's "hey-day" was in the 1920's. He contracted to build the seven-span Wurtenburg Bridge over the Slippery Rock Creek on Route 488, near Ellwood City. Our nation was entering the Great Depression and hindsight points out that the acceptance of the contract for the bridge turned out to be a mistake. Even though the bridge was successful, the fact that building bridges was out of his milieu, along with the general economic situation, turned out to be the downfall of the company.

During the Depression Harry Wimer opened a business on south Main Street and sold refrigerators and other appliances. Mr. Wimer died in 1950 and left a legacy of buildings in this area which will never be duplicated.

### The Phillips' Mansion
Harry Wimer was obviously the Phillips family's choice when it came to builders. He finished Phillips Hall, the mansion on Route 8 south in 1927. Thomas Phillips was 53 years of age when he and his family moved from their

Butler Savings and Trust Company

substantial home on Second Street in Butler into their new Penn Township home.

Mr. Phillips owned three of the four corners at the intersection of Route 8 and Airport Road. He did not own the corner where the Stepp Inn is located. From the high windows of the newly constructed mansion it was possible to see sections of Butler. Today the trees are larger and more luxuriant and block the view, but the water tower on North Main Street Hill is easily visible from mansion.

When Harry Wimer built the magnificent building it sat on 200 acres and consisted of just the large home and a water tower. In 1942 another building, which is currently the Ray Lassinger residence, was built for one of Mr. Phillips' daughters. She lived there only a short time before it became the servants' quarters.

The mansion is without a doubt, one of Butler County's most impressive buildings. It comprises 30,750 square feet and the servants' quarters, behind the main building, is half again as large as the main building. The original plan for the home did not include the ballroom; that was added in 1926 when Mr. Phillips ran for governor of Pennsylvania.

The second floor of the mansion housed the sleeping quarters. The west end was for the family and it consisted of three bedrooms, three bathrooms, and a morning sitting room. The east end was for any guests who might spend the night, and the guests quarters matched the Phillips' facilities in lavishness. On the second floor is a built-in closet where the family kept its luggage. When the bottom trunk was pulled out the one above it fell into the empty space.

Before the servants' quarters were constructed, one butler and four maids each had a separate room on the second floor. In 1942 when the help moved into the newly constructed building the former servants' space was converted into a bar. A brass elevator was installed which opened into the bar.

In the corner, where it was easily accessible, was a metal box which held the switches for much of the mansion's lighting. Mr. Phillips had a system of buttons in every bathroom as well as in his office that contolled the lights in this box. The lights were signals to family members and servants. The box was removed some years ago.

Mr. Lassinger, the present owner of the estate, worked for the Phillips family in the 1960's and remembers a very large ironing board. When the maids were not performing their daily duties, they often helped Mrs. Phillips make dresses in the sewing room, which was located in the east end of the main building. In 1935 when the Lindburgh kidnapping occurred, a fearful Mr. Phillips bought an iron gate and had it placed outside the west end of the house. Today the gate is yet in the house but has been moved to the entryway of the morning-sitting room. There is a chandelier in every room; the one in the dining room is the oldest, dating to the time when candles rather than electric light bulbs were used. When the chandeliers were converted to electricity the wires had to be placed on the outside. Mrs. Succop, a sister of Thomas Phillips Jr., who sold the mansion to Ernie Pandelous had removed all of the chandeliers; Mr. Pandelous however asked that the chandeliers be put back and Mrs. Succop obliged. Mr. Pandelous operated a restaurant and inn at the mansion; it was called Ernie's Esquire Supper Club.

Mr. Lassinger purchased the mansion in 1987 at a sheriff's sale. He was the second highest bidder of eight. Mr. and Mrs. Lassinger presently live in what was the servants' house while they are gradually restoring the estate.

Outside the present sunroom, is a small lawn. It was designed by Mr. Phillips and evinces the shape of four clovers. In the center of this shrubbery are five statues, which were chosen and placed by

Mrs. Phillips. This lawn area was originally a rose garden. At one time there was a mirror on the inside wall which reflected the goldfish pond just outside the window. The pond had very luxuriant water lilies with large floating leaves. The Phillips children added goldfish in the pond many of which have grown to more than twelve inches in size.

The Phillips children took music lessons on the mansion pipe organ. The pipes are still in the basement but the organ has been stored in the garage.

The backside of the house is the side Mr. Phillips wanted to display to guests and/or passers-by. Therefore the two lanes, which access the mansion, meet and give visitors a view of the back. The driveway to the right, or south, was used for deliveries.

The main house which is a splendid example of Georgian architecture, originally sported shutters but they were removed in Mr. Phillips' attempts to achieve a maintenance free home. He became frustrated when the wooden shutters needed painted or replaced so he removed them permanently. The windows are original and continue to work well because they were part of the super steel structure, which makes up the skeleton of the mansion. This skeleton was constructed of concrete and steel and has been so firm that there has been no shifting to distort the windows and doorframes. All the floors and walls are concrete because Mr. Phillips was deathly afraid of fire. Evidence of that fear is a water hose which reached from one end to the other of his home [it is yet in the mansion]. Stories have it that Mr. Phillips lost a very dear sister in a fire when he was young. The house is insulated with a very expensive cork, which will char but never burn. Mr. Phillips had another fire-insurance policy, so to speak. It was the water tower mentioned earlier which held 21,000 gallons of water. It was fitted with a surge pump to assure that it was always filled.

In spite of the fact that Mr. Phillips' business was oil and gas, the mansion was heated with wood because Mrs. Phillips did not like the smell of burning oil. The heating system in the house consisted of a wood-fired boiler with radiators in every room. The cement walls were

Lavish interior of the Butler Theater

naturally cold which necessitated that large pipes, eight inches in diameter, be used in the heating system. Each room is also adorned with a marble fireplace. The basement was filled with firewood, which was burned each winter.

In the 1920's when Henry Ford began to produce Model T's, Mr. Phillips built a garage in which his chauffeur lived. The chauffeur's quarters consisted of two bedrooms, two bathrooms, and a livingroom. The ground floor was used to store the vehicles. The building is now used to store Mr. Lassinger's antique and classic automobiles.

Vern Wise Belmont Road Home Built by Harry Wimer

### George Schenck & Company

No discussion of Butler builders and contractors would be complete without the inclusion of the George Schenck Company. Several generations of Schencks have been in the building and contracting business and many of Butler's finest buildings are a testament to the creativity and skill of this family. Their involvement in building goes back more than one hundred years.

An 1892 *Butler Citizen* newspaper article was devoted to architect Peter Schenck. "Much of the architectural beauty discernable in Butler emanated from the master mind of Peter Schenck, who is the only man engaged in this pursuit in the town. He was born in Butler in 1854. His ancestors came from Germany and located here over sixty years ago. Their children received a common school education, but by industrious habits, they are all in good circumstances today.

St. Paul's Church built by George Schenck

Peter Schenck, the architect, learned the carpentry and stair-builders trade, also attended night school and studied drawing. He worked five years in Allegheny and seven in Butler and was a contractor from 1885 until 1891. He launched into a profession which has been highly congenial to his taste and has given to Butler such places as the Armory building and many other handsome structures. He is married and has two children. His office is located near his home at 301 West Jefferson Street."

Polk's City Directory for 1930 lists under contractors, Elmer W. Schenck, 230 West Cunningham Street; George Schenck & Company, 413 W. Jefferson Street; and Theodore L. Schenck, 406 North McKean Street. When George Schenck passed away on May 31, 1936 his obituary recognized him as "a contractor who erected many of the older buildings in the city in which he was born and spent his entire life."

The George Schenck & Company contracting firm is responsible for many of Butler's impressive buildings, for example: St. Andrew's

Church on North Main Street; Trinity Lutheran Church on Sunset Drive; the West Penn Power Company building on Hansen Avenue; St. Paul's Convent and School; King David Apartments; dozens of private homes including the Jaffe home on Duffy Road; the Butler Armory; the Butler Courthouse reconstruction after the fire in 1883; Citizen's Bank on South Main Street; St. Fidelis School in Herman; and what many consider to be the most magnificent building in Butler, St. Paul's Roman Catholic Church on McKean Street.

## St. Paul's Church

The first Catholic Church to be built in Butler was St. Peter's and it was located at the top of Jefferson Street hill just west of First Street. The remains of an old stone quarry, which belonged to the church, may yet be seen near the office of Dr. DiCuccio. St. Peter's congregation later moved to a new place of worship on Franklin Street where they are today. Their old church is gone but the stone quarry played an important part in the building of St. Paul's massive and beautiful edifice.

"St. Paul's Church, Butler, Pennsylvania, represents the aurora of a new and freshened artistic growth, and a bright ray of hope on the horizon of contemporary Catholic art in the United States...beautiful and faultless before the eyes of men; in solemn architecture and fretted towers and delicate pinnacles; in rugged walls and massive buttresses and lofty branching arches; in pointed vaults and glimmering ceilings and a wealth of carved foliage.

St. Paul's is perhaps one of the most harmonious and most complete Catholic structures erected in the United States in the last hundred years...we become amazed that such a beautiful structure seating one thousand persons, furnished and decorated to the last degree, and complete in every detail, should represent the comparatively modest total outlay of but $140,000...A number of churches erected...in various parts of the United States, whose total cost has been two or three times that of St. Paul's, Butler and this colossal expenditure has purchased nothing that can compare to its quality of architecture and art.

The work was entrusted to Mr. John T. Comes, an architect of Pittsburgh, whose native ability and previous training and experience made him eminently qualified for the task. [George Schenck & Company was the general contractor.] He threw himself into the work with energy and enthusiasm, supervised every detail of the building and with one or two exceptions nothing that went into it was without his approval...St. Paul's is an adaptation of late English Gothic...The exterior is constructed entirely, from footings to top of spire, of beautiful colored local sandstone. The trimming stone is of the same material dressed smooth, to give an agreeable contrast to the rougher texture employed in the general wall surface. [John Hobaugh of Butler, did all the stonework.]

The choice of the Gothic style for this particular church was most happy. Not only for its intrinsic beauty, but also for special local conditions, it was the most logical, and shows its conformity to ancient methods of church building. The congregation owned a stone quarry, hence the use of its own material was at once most economical, and besides it gave more local character and individuality to the structure. The stones are laid up in a random manner and in cement mortar, just as the builders of the Middle Ages were wont to construct...There are no sham supports, no galvanized iron sanded over to imitate stone.

One of the most charming effects of the entire church is the approach from the side street, where there is a series of gradual and successive elevations from the basement entrance to the top of the cross on the spire. Up, up, to aisle wall, to transept, to clerestory roof, tower, all climbing higher and higher, with increasing delicacy until the very

Arlington Hotel razed for the construction of Montgomery Ward's

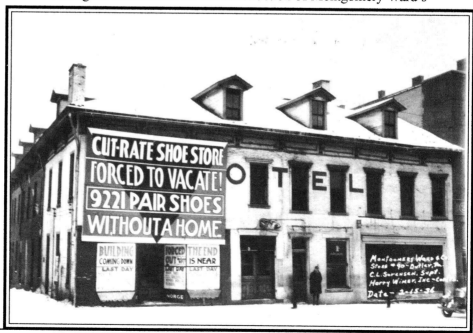

summit of the cross is reached.

The tower built entirely of stone, is an exceedingly graceful part of the structure, with a strong, sturdy base, rising and developing smoothly into an octagon. This is usually very difficult but the architect has handled it well by means of the heavy corner buttresses, which are not only ornamental but have a vital structural function in sustaining the load of the stone spire...the cross surmounting the tower is small, and the slender lines give at once the optical illusion of great height...The massive and noble proportions of the tower are produced by leaving its wall surfaces comparatively plain, the windows being inserted only where absolutely needed.

The artistic effect of St. Paul's has been achieved by its great dignity of fine, and the use of simple wall surfaces. Ornament has been used very sparingly, the only exception being the sculptured statue of St. Paul over the tower entrance."
(Excerpts quoted from *St. Paul's Church - Butler, Pennsylvania* "Our Church, Our Standard," Eightieth Anniversary, Feb. 17, 1947)

## William A. Morgan Jr.

Mr. William A. Morgan, Jr. is, among many other things, a developer. He has renovated more old, Butler buildings than anyone I can think of--buildings that would be gone today, had he not spent his time and money to make them new again.

Bill Morgan has had his business and corporate offices in the City of Butler since 1953 when he bought Dight's Diner at the corner of Washington and Jefferson Streets. This was the beginning of a restaurant chain, which eventually served western Pennsylvania, Eastern Ohio and northern West Virginia. After purchasing the Diner, Mr. Morgan built the Wonder Boy Drive-in at the top of North Main Street Hill in Bon Aire. It had the first Teletray, curb service in Pa. In 1955, Mr. Morgan became the fifth Kentucky Fried Chicken franchise holder in the U.S.A. He opened a Kentucky Fried Chicken carryout adjacent to the Washington Street diner. From those humble beginnings his restaurant chain grew to 52 locations. In the Butler area he had not only the diner but the KFC carry-out, the Garden Gate restaurant and the large Wonder Boy restaurant on North Main Street Extension. Each of his restaurants had a coffee shop and dining room, six of which featured curb service with car hops. In 1970, the entire restaurant chain was sold. But his retirement lasted less than two years; Mr. Morgan was too young at the age of forty. It was at this time that he was commissioned a Kentucky Colonel.

In 1972 Mr. Morgan bought the Spaide Shirt Factory which had been built in 1918. He converted it into the beautiful professional office complex that it is today. The Brugh Avenue building--known as the Morgan Management Building--received the highest award in the U.S. shortly after the renovation, the Honor Award for Excellence in Design.

In 1976 the Nixon Hotel site was purchased and Morgan Center opened its doors "on the Diamond" January 1, 1978. Twenty years later, the entire building was remodeled with a whole new facade and all five floors were upgraded. This was part of the agreement wherein Citizen Bank moved its headquarters into Morgan Center in 1998, occupying the entire first floor.

1973 also saw the addition of 10,000 square feet of office space at the street level of the Tier Parking Garage. This property was completely upgraded in 1999; a new corner entrance was added and the complex was renamed Morgan's Washington Centre.

1973 was also the year in which Morgan interests purchased eight and one-half acres at the junction of Routes 38, 68, and 422. This property now houses an office building, a facility which is occupied by UPS and three warehouse outlets. Morgan's Diner opened in 1976 and is known for old -fashioned, home cooking.

Mr. Morgan developed the first modern automatic car wash in Butler in 1969 on Route 8 north of Butler and seven years later a second automatic car wash on the New Castle Road. It was built with the addition of five self-service bays. Eastland Plaza also had five self-service bays for autos and trucks.

Mr. Morgan also owns a tractor-trailer fleet which transports mushrooms from the Butler County Mushroom Farm. He also had a Shasta Travel trailer sales and was the dealer for Stylex Homes in the Butler area.

Old Spaide Shirt Factory is now the Morgan Management Building

Through his various business enterprises, Mr. Morgan has provided jobs for a large number of local people. The wages paid to his employees and the rents on his various offices and retail outlets help to generate the local economy. He has taken buildings which had become eyesores, renovated them and made them jewels.

Phillip's Hall in Penn Township built by Harry Wimer

# Celebrate
# 2000
## With A
# Geraldine
# Freehling

## Watercolor

# DISTILLING AND BREWING
## Distilleries

In 1802 Harm Jan Huidekoper traveled through western Pennsylvania, north of Pittsburgh, for his employer, the Holland Land Company. The observations noted in his report were not very flattering to the pioneers of this area. "The log cabins are shabbier, the clearings smaller and more slovenly, the fields more carelessly tilled than in almost any other frontier area." Huidekoper also commented on the pioneers' excessive use of distilled spirits. "When the neighbors get together for a house raising, a harvesting, or some other work, a jug of whiskey is usually secluded in a cool nook and all those helping with the work, take periodic breaks for a swallow or more of the spirits."

Drinking of alcoholic beverages was not a moral issue on the frontier until about 1830. In fact, whiskey was the choice of most Butler County settlers. Spirits were served even at church functions and such formal confabs as Presbytery meetings. The official stance of most churches toward drinking spirits was temperance. When the minister of the local church made visits to his parishioners, it was customary and proper that he be served a drink upon his arrival, then perhaps, "one for the road." If he visited several such obliging families he would soon be feeling the effects of the libations. Huidekoper reported that it was not unusual to see a farmer lying drunk in his field or for that matter, a minister meandering his way back to the church or manse.

A story from Brown's 1895 history, which was related by J. E. Muder of Saxonburg, reflects an attitude toward liquor which was typical in the early 1800's. "The Rev. Schweitzerbarth sent Mr. Sarver a message, saying he would be on hand the next Sabbath to preach. Sarver knew that there was little in the house with which to entertain his old friend, and announced to his wife, Betsy, that he would go out and kill a deer. He went forth, shot a deer and returned jubilant. Next, he told his wife that he would go to Jacob Staley's for a quart of whiskey, which he did; and returning, exclaimed in jubilant tones, 'Now, Schweitzerbarth, you can come; Betsy has got the meat and I have got the whiskey.' Wild honey, corn-whiskey and venison made very good fare, which no one enjoyed better than some of the visiting evangelists of early days."

When the baby cried, mother soaked a crust of bread in whiskey and gave it to the infant—it was an effective, pioneer pacifier. If that surprises you, consider the fact that parents sometimes gave their overactive children opium, which of course could be purchased at that time without a prescription. Years of observing alcohol's abuse however, led many of the pioneers to a realization of the negative consequences involved with alcohol and discouraged many of them from imbibing. But generally speaking, many people weren't aware or didn't care about the health risks of alcohol, opium and other drugs.

An interesting story involving a Butler County church is found in the Pittsburgh Press, April 4, 1976, pg. 5. The Middlesex United Presbyterian Church organized in 1799 and the congregation met in a series of log structures until 1842 when the present edifice was built. The story concerns a log chapel built in 1817 on land given by a man named Lyon. The church never procured a formal title to the land, and in 1826, when the surrounding Lyon farm was sold, the new owner wanted the ten acres which had been given to the church. He coveted a spring on the church property because he wanted to use the spring water in the distillation of whiskey.

Church trustees reacted firmly and even went to court over the matter. While the pros and cons were being hashed out, the spring took a definite stand on the issue and simply dried up. "First time it had ever been known to go dry," said Mrs. Caroljo Lee, Middlesex historian. This was so dramatic, that the court awarded five acres to each party, with the church getting the spring. "As soon as the decision was announced the spring burst forth again," Mrs. Lee said.

Alcohol played a large part in pioneer history even before Abraham Boyd founded the Middlesex church. According to an English map maker named Lewis Evans,

"The English manner of carrying on the Indian trade is this: The regular traders undertake twice or oftener each year journeys to the Indian villages, their pack-horses laden with shrouds, match-coats, hats, looking-glasses, beads and bracelets of glass, knives, and all manner of gaudy toys and knacks for children, as well as guns, flints, powder and lead, and kegs of potent rum to be watered when they arrive in the Indian country. When there, these traders live with the Indians, selling them goods in prospect of the season's fur catch and often keeping one or more squaws as wives and are trusted by their neighbors for they are content with a mere trifle of two or three hundred per cent profit above the cost of the trade goods and transport which it is said are neigh equal.

Other traders there are who frequently creep into the woods with spirituous liquor and cheating trifles, after the Indian hunting camps, in the winter season, and putting down several kegs before them, make them drunk selling their liquor at ten times its value to the great injury of the fair trader who supplies them with all the conveniences for hunting; for as they will sell even their wearing shirt for inebriating liquors, they must be supplied anew in the fall of the year by a trader. These traders are the most vicious and abandoned wretches of our nation and the Indians hold them in great contempt as a set of mean-dishonest-mercenary fellows and complain that they debauch their young women, and even their wives, when the husbands are from home or drunk. When your Indian has once got a smack of rum he is never sober for ten days or until there is no more left. Days and nights are passed in jovial, amorous topers and in convivial songs, dances, and sacrifices to Venus; for in these frolics both sexes take such liberties with each other, and act without constraint or shame such scenes as they would abhor when sober or in their senses. But at last, the liquor running low, and being most of them sick through intoxication, they become more sober; and now the dejected, lifeless sots would pawn everything they own for a mouthful of spirits to settle their stomachs." (*The Allegheny*, Way, Frederick Jr., pp. 38-40)

Imported rum was the most common intoxicant during the era when traders were about the only white men who traveled the frontier. As settlement increased, distilleries were opened and whiskey gradually replaced rum.

Many pioneer families were involved in the distilling of whiskey. Brown's history estimates that in western Pennsylvania there may have been one distillery for every ten families. Most pioneer stills had a capacity of less than one hundred gallons and they were operated sporadically to transform surplus grain into a commodity for which there was some market—it was a matter of economics. Whiskey rather than grain, was much more easily transported over the mountains by packhorses and brought the pioneer farmer a nice profit. In 1792 a gallon of whiskey could be purchased for approximately twenty-eight cents. It may seem like a trifling sum today but it added up; the early county histories make it clear that distillery owners became affluent and often invested in land, grist mills, tanneries, saw mills, and other businesses.

A cursory look at the earlier Butler County histories shows that distilling was one of the largest local industries of the early 1800's. A large distillery was built on the site of the bottle works [presently Oesterling's feed store]. At the time it was one of the largest distilleries in western Pennsylvania. John Cratty ran a distillery in Butler Township, a short distance northwest of Butler borough. Samuel Duncan had a small operation in Cranberry which obtained a wide reputation for the fine quality of whiskey he turned out. Thomas Fleming's distillery of 1799 in Buffalo Township was very small compared with the large Guckenheimer & Co. distillery nearby in the southeast corner of the township. The large distillery was turning out fifty barrels a day! The business consisted of three large brick buildings, two of which were warehouses and the property was assessed at $27,000. A fire wiped-out the business in 1889.

In 1803 James Hemphill opened a distillery in Millerstown [Chicora]. It was the first manufacturing industry in the community. Business must have been good because In 1838, James Hemphill's son established a distillery on the brow of a hill hear the Hoch home and planing mill, also in Millerstown. Whiskey was produced there until 1846. In 1849 Martin Hoch and Martin Reiber established a distillery in Donegal Township. According to Brown's history Martin Reiber, along with his brothers, George and Jacob, also owned a distillery on Sullivan Run a short distance northwest of Butler. Not too far away from Millerstown, in Oakland Township, James Douglas was operating a distillery, also in 1803. David McJunkin established a distillery early in Centre Township. Muddy Creek Township had no distilleries because of its proximity to Slippery Rock, which was very well endowed with manufacturers of spirits. "Hugh Henderson was the leading distiller of Worth Township and old settlers who loved good whiskey, looked upon the product of Henderson's still as very fine indeed." The reputation and success of Henderson's whiskey however, did not deter Jonathan Dean and William Vogan from opening their own distilleries nearby. All three businesses flourished until the 1830's when the temperance movement halted or at least, severely curtailed their profits. A man named McMurry established a distillery on McMurray's Run in 1810, and Thomas Kelly opened his distilling business in Parker Township in 1844. William McCandless and Robert Hays each engaged in the whiskey making business in Franklin Township. Their particular business was opened in 1857 and continued to manufacture whiskey for a number of years. Hugh Murrin owned 400 acres in Venango Township and there built one of the Butler County's first gristmills then later a distillery.

Numerous distilleries which produced thousands of gallons of whiskey flourished in the Jackson Township area in the early days. George Rapp, founder of Harmony, in 1806 built a distillery on the Little Connoquenessing. Beginning in 1805 the Harmonists had three feasts each year. The bountiful meals immediately became a yearly tradition. Rapp's group prepared and consumed the products of their farms, with native wine, whiskey, beer, sauerkraut, rice, ginger cakes and other foods. The site of the feasts was a large barn.

By 1814 the village of Harmony boasted 130 buildings including a tavern with twelve rooms. The list of village businesses included a brewery, and two distilleries--one built of brick and the other of stone. In 1837, David Zeigler and Aaron Schontz converted the great barn of the Harmonists into a steam, flouring mill and later Jacob Zeigler built a distillery near the big mill above Harmony. Nearby Zelienople had a distillery as early as 1804. It was operated by Daniel Fiedler. Lewis Blakeley, about that same time, established and operated a distillery in Forward Township. The distilling industry was of considerable importance in Forestville, in northern Butler County, between 1830 and 1847, there being ten distilleries in operation within a radius of three miles.

Prior to 1850 there were at least three distilleries in Butler borough. One was located on what was later the site of the Klinger's mill and warehouse at 117-125 South Monroe Street; another was located at the old Reiber mill, just above the Bessemer and Lake Erie freight station on the Connoquenessing Creek, and a third was located in Reiber hollow on the road out to the present Alameda Park. The number of area distilleries began to decline after 1850 but a distillery named Zimmerman & Co. operated as late as 1874 on Butler's Jefferson Street. Historian James McKee credits the railroad with bringing about the demise of local distilleries. "Larger establishments crowed out the small ones...."

<br>

### The Borough of Butler

"The following statement will, perhaps, prove interesting to some of your readers. It is not presumed that a statement, embracing so many particulars, is entirely accurate in all its details; but it is thought to be nearly correct. It shows, when compared with the situation of this place about five years since, an advance in prosperity equaled by but few villages in the western part of this state. This will appear evident when we recollect, that at the period referred to, there was not a brick building in the place except the courthouse, nor was the number of tradesmen more than half what it is at present. In the enumeration of trades, the master workmen only are mentioned.

Tradesmen—Blacksmiths, 3; Shoemakers, 4; Tailors, 3; Tanners, 2; Saddlers, 2; Potters, 2; Plasterers, 2; Bricklayers, 2; Cabinetmakers, 3; Carpenters, 4; Farmers, 2; hatters, 2; Wagonmakers, 1; Painters, 1; Coopers, 1; Chairmakers, 1.

Professions—Lawyers, 7; Physicians, 2; Clergymen, 2; Schoolteachers, 4.

Various—Stores, 14; Taverns, 7; Printing Presses, 2; unitedly circulating 1200 papers per week.

Public Buildings—Courthouse with offices; Academy with a public library, jail, and four churches, i.e.—Associate Reformed, Methodist, Presbyterian and Roman Catholic. The two former of which are brick—the two latter of stone. (The Episcopalians also have started preaching, and have it in contemplation to erect an elegant chapel.)

In the vicinity of the town are several mills, three brickyards in full operation, and some invaluable mines of coal. In the village the number of dwelling houses is about 70, of which 21 are brick. A large fine toned bell in the courthouse cupola serves to collect the citizens when necessary—and a good engine bids defiance to the influence of fire. The population of our village is probably between 600 and 800, and is rapidly increasing. A general spirit of intelligence is believed to be characteristic of the citizens of Butler." *Butler Sentinel*, May 16, 1829

## Breweries And Taverns

Butler had six taverns in 1804 and the number gradually increased as the town grew. Butler's taverns, being on the busy route between Pittsburgh and places north, counted among their customers many travelers as well as local trade. That story is covered in chapter 4 of *Butler County, the Second Hundred Years*.

As we have seen, whiskey was the most popular drink in Butler County during the first several decades of the nineteenth century. Orchards and vineyards were yet rare so wine was not readily available. And it seemed that only the German settlers knew the fundamentals of brewing. But as time passed the popularity of whiskey experienced a gradual decline. Factors causing the demise of distilled spirits were certainly the temperance movement, which gained strength in the 1830's, and a growing awareness that the abuse of whiskey carried with it, negative health effects. As whiskey consumption declined, cider, wine and beer became more often the choice of thirsty pioneers. S. W. Fletcher reports in *Pennsylvania Agriculture and Country Life 1640-1840*, that the typical western Pennsylvania farmer "put up" forty barrels of cider each year.

Whiskey wasn't the only "manufactured" thirst quencher in early Butler. Just after the Civil War the borough had several small breweries within its limits. Jordan Eyth immigrated to America in 1839. He was part of a large family with four brothers and five sisters. Over the course of his lifetime Jordan was a butcher, ran a hotel, and during the 1870's and 80's, operated a brewery on the banks of the Connoquenessing Creek at Water Street [now Liberty].

There was also an early brewery located on the McClymond's lot between South Main Street and Lyons Avenue but details on that operation are sketchy.

Andrew Miller however, is given credit for the establishment of the first brewery in Butler about 1845. His son John continued the business until 1880. Miller moved his brewery business at least twice. The original location was a log building just to the east of South Cemetery on Morton Avenue. The operation was small; it used a nearby natural spring—perhaps the Federal Spring, as its water source. According to James McKee, sometime later Miller opened another brewery on the northeast corner of Main and Cunningham Streets. Then in the 1870's, Miller opened his third brewery on Race Street, between Diamond and Chestnut Streets, approximately where the Farmers' Market is today. "Neither the brewery nor another small competing brewery owned by George Knight, could generate enough business and they closed in the 1880's." *(Butler Eagle*, April 29, 1991)  At that time there was much competition from those who made their own home brew, especially those of German ancestry.

The Butler Brewing Company was founded in 1874 by H. W. Kline, David Smith, Frank Peffer, George McLean and L.A. Thompson. Their new plant was erected at a cost of $50,000. It stood on Negley Avenue near the Bessemer Railroad close to the site of the original Cunningham Mill. The plant prospered until the Volstead act put it out of business.

A contributing factor to the demise of Butler County's small breweries was the formation of the Independent Brewing Company in 1902. This brewery took over the old Butler Brewing Company and became the largest and longest, continuously-operated brewery in Butler. John Negley bought the brewing company and increased its business enough to employ more than fifty men. An article in the *Butler Times*, March 6, 1907 announced the appointment of William McCafferty, as the new manager of the brewery and further reported, "The plant commenced several days ago to brew beer and at present is brewing to its capacity, but as it requires three months to prepare the beer for consumption it will be some time in May before the local company will be in shape to deliver beer to the patrons in this city, and no deliveries will be made to private consumers until the brew of the Butler plant is ready for use. In the meantime Butlerites who desire their beer by the case or keg will have to continue sending away for it the same as in the past."

---

## ANCIENT LANDMARK WILL GIVE WAY TO

## A MODERN BUILDING

### Rookery Known to Police as "White Line Roost" is Being Razed

### WAS ONCE FAMOUS OLD TIME TAVERN

The razing of the old log and frame building on East Diamond street next to the community building, known in recent times as "White Line Roost" removes one of the ancient landmarks of the town. The original building was erected about 1804 or 1805. For many years it was occupied as an old time tavern, the last proprietor being Jordan Eyth who conducted a tavern and a bar over 50 years ago. For 30 years the building was occupied as offices and small shops and the past year and a half it had been vacant.

The "White Line" gang had been using it during the fall and winter as a convenient place to gather at night and sleep off their jags, where they would not be bothered by the police. Fear that the gang would set the building on fire some night caused the owner to shut it up tight and eventually to tear it down.

No intimation has been given of the use to be made of the ground. It has been intimated that plans are under consideration for the erection of an automobile and service garage that will occupy the lot from Diamond street to the Vogeley alley.
(copied from the *Butler Citizen* dated Dec. 27, 1917 by Dave and Audrey Craig)

Hand-blown bottles made at the nearby Butler Bottle Works were used when the brewery was first opened. When the bottle works burned down, the Hamilton Bottle Works on Monroe Street became the supplier. The Butler brew was being distributed and enjoyed throughout the county area. Beer was sold in bottles and one-gallon, wooden kegs. The late Max Baptiste worked at the Hamilton Bottle Works and remembers the Independent brewery very well. The dark beer had a kick—"four or five guys could get drunk on a one gallon keg."

"Baptiste recalled a Belgian man with a horse and carriage who would deliver a keg of beer to his house each week. Baptiste said he would pour beer from the keg into quart canning jars and seal them so his father could drink them later." Max was too young to drink then but his father would pour the kids a bit from time to time."

A *Butler Eagle* article on December 1, 1918 announced that "the manufacture of beer stopped at the Independent Brewing Company plant at midnight, Nov. 30, in compliance with Federal regulations. In January 1919, the president signed a bill that allowed breweries to make a low alcohol brew. The Butler plant brewed this for awhile, but the product did not sell. The brewing industry went underground. By the time prohibition was repealed in 1933, the former brewery had become a storage building and the Butler breweries had passed into history.

### Francis Laube, Saxonburg Brewer

Francis Laube came from a family of brewers. His father learned to brew beer in Prague in the early 1800's and was soon operating the town brewery in Zwickau, Germany. Francis was put to work in the brewery while his brother Karl rented a brewery in a town five hours away. Many of Laube's friends, at the time, were migrating to America and the young brewer decided to join them—he had heard of opportunities in the new world. The first time he saw his father cry was when Francis told him that he was going to America.

In 1837, Francis Laube along with some friends, set sail. They landed in Baltimore and immediately headed for Pittsburgh. Some of their acquaintances and even some of Laube's relatives had preceded him to western Pennsylva-

## EXPLOSION AT BREWERY

One of the most distressing accidents in the history of Butler occurred at the new brewery about five o'clock last Thursday evening. Three men, Emil Yost, aged 25 years, boss painter, of New York City, George Freil, aged 40 years, cooper at the Brewery and Julius Finn, a young Jew of Buffalo, N.Y. were engaged at painting the interior of one of the big vats in the stock cellar into which the beer, after brewing, is run to cool.

The material used in painting was a shellac or varnish, commonly used to paint the interior of beer vats. One of the principal ingredients is wood alcohol, which is highly volatile and combustible. On this account the vat was full of the vapors of the paint and the men could not use an open light at their work, but an electric light on a loose wire was carried into the vat to enable them to see.

In some way the glass bulb of the electric light was broken, a terrible explosion occurred and the men found themselves at the bottom of a furnace of seething flames. Finn climbed out first and was least burned. As fast as they could, the others followed. Outside John Zeigler, William Neidell and others who were about, cut and tore the burning clothes from the unfortunate men. Ambulances and doctors were summoned and the men taken to the Hospital. Strips of flesh peeled from their bodies with their clothes.

At 8 a.m. Friday morning Friel died being smothered to death by dropsy of the larynx caused by inhaling the fumes. Two hours later Yost died. He also had breathed the flames into his lungs.

Friel and his wife and daughter lived in one of the Zahradneck houses on the Three Degree Road. He moved from Pittsburg to Butler but a few months ago and his remains were taken to Pittsburg by his brother for burial.

Yost was to have finished his work and left Butler Friday evening for New York City where he expected to meet his family on their arrival home from Germany where they have been visiting. His body was shipped to New York, Saturday.

Julius Finn, the last of the three men burned, died in the hospital, Saturday night. A stronger vitality enabled him to fight off death longer than the other men.

The tank in which the horror occurred is one of the worst death traps imaginable. It and ten others similar occupy the stock cellar. They are simply big wooden barrels of tanks, about 20 feet in length, 12 or 15 in diameter and lying on their sides. In the end and near the floor is an oval hole 12 by 18 inches, about as large in relation to the tank as a bunghole is to a barrel. Into this hole the men had to crawl and drag their materials, ladders and lights after them and through it they had to crawl after the explosion. The light was absolutely necessary to enable the men to see what they were doing as the interior of the tanks is as dark as Egypt.
*Butler Citizen*, July 10, 1903

nia. Several had put down roots in a German village about thirty miles north of Pittsburgh but Laube believed he would make his home in Pittsburgh. Just about the time Laube arrived, there had been a brewer in Pittsburgh by the name of Vetter who had recently passed away. Laube's brother-in-law, Mr. Hammer bought Vetter's small operation and hired Laube to run it. He was in a new country and doing what he knew best—brewing beer. The entire Vetter business consisted of a copper kettle, one barrel, a dozen one-fourth barrels and a little hogs-head for molasses. He got his hops and had his malt made in the Franklin brewery in Pittsburgh. Laube sold his beer in various amounts; the price was three cents a glass.

Business was brisk enabling them to enlarge the brewery that first autumn. However, the barley harvest was so poor that year that Laube substituted wheat and oats. This was not as successful as barley based beer. Business was slow and the following spring Hammer sold the brewery. Laube was able to acquire a job at Straub's brewery.

In 1884, newly married to Friedericka Hoffmann, the young couple rented an old building in Pittsburgh and started a guest and boarding house. They applied for a liquor license but were unsuccessful. They sold their beer anyway because the "constable of the third ward would close his eyes occasionally for five dollars." Beer was three cents a glass; whiskey was the same. A room was $1.50 to $2.00 a week.

Laube's father-in-law, Mr. Hoffmann, talked him into buying a house in Saxonburg on Water Street. He had desired to own his own brewery for years, so Laube immediately added a brew house to his new, Saxonburg residence, dug a well, and bought everything necessary to open his brewery. He brewed thirty-five times during the second part of 1847 and while he didn't consider business to be very good Laube's beer was slowly becoming known and loved in the region. During the time his brewery was operating Laube was a professional musician. He traveled all over the eastern part of the United States playing the flute and violin. He planned his musical engagements so they would not conflict with brewing times. However there were occasions when Mrs. Laube or some hired man ran the brewery.

Laube realized that he needed to make lager beer to compete with the big city brewers. [Lager beer contains a relatively small amount of hops and is aged for up to six months to allow sedimentation. It was very popular at that time.] He needed some new equipment and his well was drying up; he was forced to haul water. 1861 was a banner year for Laube's business. He sold a great deal of beer to a soda works in the Natrona area. Through that summer Laube delivered two, wagon-loads of beer every week. He bought himself a new, beer kettle and at the end of the year tallied $332 which was not bad for those days. In 1863 he put his son Karl and Henry Hammer to work to learn the brewing trade. They had to purchase one dollar stamps for the beer kegs but the operation made a profit of $582 and Laube had the pleasure of working with his family.

In 1865 Laube rented the Union House on Saxonburg's Main Street for four years for $215 a year. He now had a retail outlet for his beer. The War Between the States was just recently over, the economy was good, and Saxonburg's festivals were well attended. Laube made $627 for the year.

In 1867 Butler County Laube was not able to get a beer license from the county. While the shooting festival was taking place Laube sold beer openly, without the proper license, and went to jail for it. While he was locked up, his wife brewed the beer. The family made $865 that year.

Laube's spirits were understandably low as a result of his run-in with the law. He purchased a house with a barn

231

on River Street in Natrona. It had a good cellar and he made plans to move there. He was brewing more lager beer and business was better than ever. He bought brand new barrels in Pittsburgh and stored them in his newly acquired barn. Unfortunately when he was off on a delivery his barn burned and all the new barrels were destroyed. The house was saved and a new, block barn was erected to replace the one which had burned but needless to say, the incident was a major set back to the Laube business.

1869 found Laube living in Natrona while he continued to operate his hotel in Saxonburg. He purchased a new, copper kettle at a cost of $110. He also enlarged his business so that he could make his own malt. He had a strong, cool boat, three mending vats, one match vat, a new malt den, a fermenting cellar, new pumps and hose. Everything was updated and he still made a profit of $402 that year.

Laube brewed beer and stored it in his fermenting cellar. As soon as the lager, beer barrels were full he brewed ordinary beer. He walled up the inner door of the cellar, all but a little opening in the top just large enough to put quarter barrels through. There he let his beer age. Laube was finding it diffucult to purchase malting barley and hops. farmers were dropping the two grains for other more profitable crops. Laube quit making his own malt in 1872. He purchased it "already made" in Pittsburgh which of course saved him a great deal of work.

Around 1875 Laube saw that things were changing at an accelerated pace in the brewing business. Many brands of beer were being shipped in from different places—the competition was becoming formidable. Larger breweries could afford to automate; they could afford to advertise, and most of all they purchased raw materials by the railroad car and therefore received a much better price per unit. They could undersell the small local breweries. A man asked Laube one day if he would like to trade his house for the man's saloon in Natrona. Laube accepted. He continued to operate his hotel in Saxonburg but he was now purchasing all of his beer in Pittsburgh. There you have the life and hardships of an early Butler County brewer.

[This material was taken from a diary Mr. Laube wrote for his family.]

# Crime and Punishment

In *Butler County the Second Hundred Years*, the authors discussed the "end of the century effect." As the last century was coming to a close, a large number of inventions and discoveries appeared. Ironically, a century later, as the millennium draws to a close, the opposite is happening. Many Butler County residents are storing food, water, firewood and medical supplies; some are even purchasing generators and kerosene heaters in anticipation of Y2K. We may be forced to live for a time as the pioneers lived. We hope that the ominous forebodings turn out to be "much ado about nothing" and that none of the feared "shut downs" come to pass. We do not know at this point whether or not computer glitches will put a damper on the Butler County bicentennial or our quality of life in general. By the time you read this you will know—it will be history.

During the spring of 1999, history of a different sort was being made in the nation's capital. President William Jefferson Clinton's impeachment will no doubt go down as the "trial of the century." It had many of the characteristics of an intriguing trial. "People are fascinated by trials because they're like mystery stories—you don't know what the ending is, and they're full of twists," says Lawrence Friedman, a law professor at Stanford University. "A trial is a good story. As novelists know, it's the specificity of detail that makes a story compelling, and in a trial we become familiar with people's lives in the kind of detail we rarely get in any other way. And then it all comes to a climax when the jury makes the decision," says Douglas Linder, who teaches a course on famous trials at the University of Missouri law school. Many of the famous trials of the twentieth century are memorable because they dealt with sex, murder, debaucheries and celebrities in high places.

A *Pittsburgh Press* article dated January 11, 1999 includes a very thorough litany of famous twentieth century trials from the Scopes "monkey trial," and the kidnap/murder of the Lindbergh baby, to the O.J. Simpson trial. According to Peter Carlson of the *Washington Post*, the first memorable trial of the century came in 1907, when Harry K. Thaw was tried for the murder of Stanford White, America's most famous architect. This trial was followed closely by Butlerites because Thaw, a rich playboy, was born and raised in nearby Pittsburgh. Thaw "married Evelyn Nesbit, a show girl who was the Marilyn Monroe of her day. Nesbit told her husband, Thaw, that White had once lured her to his secret love nest and raped her. Out of his mind with rage, Thaw strolled up to White during a musical performance at Madison Square Garden and shot him dead as the crowd watched in horror...For weeks, witnesses provided steamy testimony about the kinky sex lives of White and his rich friends and their show biz sweethearts. After a deadlocked jury necessitated a second trial Thaw was found not guilty by reason of insanity.

Irvin S. Cobb, one of the great reporters of the day, explained why he thought the Thaw trial transfixed the nation: "You see, it had in it wealth, degeneracy, rich old wasters, delectable young chorus girls and adolescent artists' models; the behind-the-scenes of Theatredom and the Underworld, and the Great White Way...the abnormal pastimes and weird orgies of overly aesthetic artists and jaded debauchees. In the cast of the motley show were Bowery toughs, Harlem gangsters, Tenderloin panderers, Broadway leading men, Fifth Avenue clubmen, Wall Street manipulators, uptown voluptuaries and downtown thugs." [I don't think we've changed a great deal—this would make for an exciting trial today.]

When Audrey Fetters and I wrote *Butler County, the Second Hundred Years,* we took great pains to avoid negative information which would cast aspersions on long dead ancestors and therefore embarrass present-day Butlerites. To our surprise we found that many people were highly interested, excited and in some cases, even proud of the bad behavior of their ancestors. They badgered us for more details. I believe that the popularity of Jim Clements' English classes' books, *Builders Dreamers Scandals Schemers* and *Favorite Sons & Sons of Guns,* is further proof that this attitude prevails. I asked Jim if he had gotten any deleterious reaction from people whose ancestors were the villains in both of his well-done books. He responded, "In a couple of cases we were asked by the families [descendents] to please desist and not publish the stories. But in some of the other cases, especially those which are yet unsolved, the families welcomed the fresh attention brought to the incidents."

The development of our county has indeed generated many fascinating topics and events—many of these are of course negative. As we already discussed, a large number of our early residents flocked to Butler County to work in the oil fields and coal mines, or later to make a life for themselves in our burgeoning factories such as the Standard Steel Car Company, Armco and the Standard Plate Glass Company. People who relocate whether it be to an oil boomtown, or as a result of a gold rush, are generally the more adventurous types. That's putting it nicely. There were always the worst toughs among the camp followers. Some were veterans of the Civil War in those oil-boom years. Some never intended to make money from the oil--there was enough easy money floating around that it wasn't necessary to dirty the hands. Many were hungry for luxury--aren't we all? There was always a great deal of excitement, crime, good food, alcohol, pretty faces and other amenities to be found in the boom towns. Some ministers of the day likened the boom towns to Sodom and Gomorrah. The point is that men and women of that kind cannot be expected to always behave in a desirable manner, and they didn't; they did whatever they felt was necessary to make money.

If you think that I am laying the foundation for the last part of this book, you are correct. I have researched a goodly number of Butler County's crimes and found many of them to be related to the draw of the oil, the industries and the railroads--and also to alcohol. I believe they are fascinating, and would like to present here a smattering of such events.

### Mills Murder Case

Before 1900 the small village of Petersville was located just east of Connoquenessing along what is now Route 68. During the oil excitement of the 1880's and 90's the borough became quite a busy and thriving community. Peter Dugan, who was twenty-eight years of age and unmarried, was at the time working as a pumper on the Welsh farm. Dugan was a native of Oakland Township, the son of Michael Dugan and grandson of Matthew Dugan who had been one of the earliest settlers in the Chicora area. In those days, oil well workers generally put in twelve-hour shifts and worked six days a week. It wasn't practical to travel back and forth to work even if it were only a few miles. So Dugan, who took care of four wells, generally slept in the boiler house and ate at Dilliman's or another Petersville area boarding house. If one got to know some of the locals well enough there was an occasional dinner invitation.

On December 23, 1891, Peter Ripper, Dugan's foreman, went to the boiler house and found Dugan lying on the mattress dead; the body was still warm and blood was flowing from two holes in Dugan's head. James F. Mills, who was an oil worker on the same farm, was arrested and charged with the crime.

Witnesses who knew both Mills and Dugan told of an on-going quarrel, which had resulted in several fistfights, many threats, and even some knife wielding. Acquaintances thought that the continuing argument was over a woman, but the eventual trial brought out the fact that the disagreement was simply over the question of who was the better man.

A *Butler Citizen* report sheds some light on the animosity which existed between the two men. According to that newspaper article, Francis Norris of Petersville rented a team of horses and a buggy to the two men; he also loaned Mills his rubber coat as it had been raining a great deal. "They came to my [Norris'] shop at 2:30 a.m. and kicked at the door. Dugan came in and fell on his back laughing. Norris' coat was ripped up the back.

### Unpunished Crimes

In the very early days of our county, the wheels of justice sometimes turned at a very slow pace. Many criminals were caught and punished but many escaped. It was not unusual for criminals to escape punishment, as it was an easy matter to flee to one of the western states and lose one's identity by assuming a new name. James A. McKee relates the following stories which shed some light upon local law enforcement in the early 1800's.

"Not long after the county courts were organized in Butler, an Indian was seen by two hunters walking along the Franklin Road also known as the Old Venango Trail in the western part of the county in the present limits of Connoquenessing Township. The hunters discussed the presence of the Indian in the community. He was peaceful and attending to his own business. The hunters discussed the question of killing the Indian. One wanted to shoot him from ambush and the other objected. The Indian passed on and soon after the hunters separated and went to their homes.

Several weeks later the dead body of the Indian was discovered hidden in a hollow log not far from where he had last been seen alive. He had been murdered. Although the name of the man who murdered the Indian was known in the community, he was never brought to justice, due largely to the prevailing prejudice against Indians by the settlers, many of whom had suffered from Indian atrocities during the war of the Revolution and the Indian wars.

*Butler Eagle*, July 3, 1925, James A. McKee

Mills tried to pull Dugan's overcoat off and bumped the pumper's head against the floor. Dugan got up and struck Mills in the face knocking him into the corner. Mills pulled out a knife and Dugan responded by taking out his own knife; they dared each other. Both said "Come on you son of a b----." However, no blows were struck with the knives. Mills said to Dugan, "If you think you can lick me, blaze away." Mills said he was not afraid of anybody and Dugan responded 'Don't put any cowboy bluffs on me." Dugan stuck his knife into the side of the building and asked Mills to do the same. Mills would not so Dugan put his knife into his pocket. They agreed to fight at half-past ten then changed the time to half-past eleven and shook hands on the fight plans. Norris went out as the place was too small for the three people especially when two of them were fighting and brandishing knives. "I never did recover my overcoat," said Norris.

Preliminary investigation found that the day before his death, Dugan had engaged two boys to take care of his wells because he and Mills were going "out on the town." Mills and Dugan rented the team and buggy and traveled to Renfrew to a dance. The three-mile trip to Renfrew began with an argument then a wrestling match, which found the two men rolling in the mud. Knives were flashed and threats were again made but in spite of these problems the pair purchased a quart of whiskey and started on their way—together. Later they were seen drinking at a Renfrew bar where they each purchased a pint "for the road" before the bar closed. On the way back to Petersville, the intoxicated pair became lost and inquired of several people as to directions. Eyewitnesses report that the two men upset the wagon on the road and Dugan was dragged a piece. In all the confusion, they lost two blankets. They arrived back at the Welsh farm about four o'clock in the morning where they talked briefly with Hugh Blair who was in charge of another boiler house there. Blair said they both seemed to be in a good humor and neither was very drunk although they were quite disheveled and covered with mud. Blair went back to his boiler house and had just fallen asleep when Mills aroused him stating that he was afraid to go to bed for fear that Dugan would kill him. Mills sat and talked to Blair for some time complaining of Dugan and occasionally tapping the floor with a hammer he had in his hand. Mills finally said, "Hugh, I'm going down and kill that son of a b----." Blair had no idea that Mills meant what he said and nonchalantly rolled over and went back to sleep.

Dugan was sleeping in his boiler house on a mattress on the floor between the two Dilliman boys he had left in charge of the operation—Willie 13 and Albert 7. The older of the two boys was awakened when he heard a pounding sound and saw a man leaving the boiler house. The boy jumped up and went to the door where he saw Mills by the light of the burning gas jet. Willie could plainly see that Mills was carrying a hammer. The boy closed the door and just a short time after he had lain down, felt blood running on him. It was then that he noticed Dugan's head--it was dripping with blood.

The news of the murder spread rapidly and someone immediately sent for Sheriff Brown. The sheriff arrived to find Mills quietly sleeping in his boiler house and based upon preliminary evidence immediately apprehended him. As the sheriff and Mills were walking to the buggy, Mills whispered to Willie Dilliman, "Get that hammer and hide it." Dilliman didn't know what hammer he meant. The authorities found the hammer lying on a bench outside Mills' boiler house.

Mills expressed surprise at his arrest

and at the news of Dugan's murder, saying he had parted with Dugan at the edge of the woods. He admitted they had fought but claimed they had "shaken hands after the scuffle."

Peter Ripper took charge of Dugan's body after the coroner's inquest, washed it and took it to Evans City. At the trial, Ripper described what he found: "Dugan's head was covered with blood. There were two large round holes about and inch and a half each in his head which matched the size of Mills' hammer. There was a large pool of blood on the mattress and some splashes of blood on the wall and window."

On January 4, 1917, the coroner was called to Bredinville on the Three Degree to investigate the death of a young woman named Mary Abdella, aged about 25. The woman was found dead in bed in her home. Investigation revealed that the woman had been strangled with a silk handkerchief which had been forced down her throat. The coroner's jury called it a case of murder by persons unknown. The murderer escaped and has never been apprehended.

## The Escape

John W. Higginss who was in jail for wife beating rattled his cell door until he attracted the sheriff's wife's attention. He then told her of the escape. Shortly after eight o'clock Friday evening, March 4th, a boy ran down the street near the jail shouting, "The prisoners are escaping! The prisoners are on the roof." In a few minutes several hundred men and boys of the town surrounded the jail. A rope was found hanging from the north side of the building and it was thought at first that some of the prisoners were yet on the roof, but that proved to be a mistake. Six men had escaped. The names of those who escaped were James F. Mills, T.J. Black, Jesse Smith, Charles Miller, Joseph Gibson, and James Britin.

At noon the next day, George Limberg came to town and told of two men, one of whom looked like Mills, having slept in his barn over night. A sizable party was quickly organized and started in pursuit through the woods northeast of town, searching barns and other buildings as they went. The searchers paired up. They came to an old vacant house near Oneida Station on the Shenango Railroad. Two members of the search party, Detective Allen, and Colonel Redic approached the house just as escapee Jesse Smith came out. Allen covered Smith with his pistol and ordered him to surrender. Just then Allen looked toward the window and saw Mills inside with his gun aimed at the detective. Allen dropped off his horse and ran back to Redic, allowing Mills and Smith to temporarily elude the search party. It wasn't long until Smith was apprehended hiding in a treetop. Smith said that Mills arranged the escape, that Black and the others sawed a hole in the ceiling of Mills' cell and that when everything was ready last Friday evening the piece of iron was broken out. Mills let a rope down from the back window of the jail and the entire group escaped. Smith said that somebody on the outside furnished the rope. Smith also said that he was glad to be rid of Mills, and warned that the suspected murderer had a pistol and said he would not be taken alive.

November 29, 1915, a coal miner living near Claytonia was slashed to death with a razor by Joe Delliapo, while on his way home after attending a party in the village. The coroner's inquest revealed that there had been a quarrel over a card game. The slayer escaped and has never been heard of in this part of the country.

Britin was arrested Saturday at Callery Junction. He wouldn't divulge anything. Black was caught in a feed box in Renfrew. Mills eluded the authorities for a week but was captured at Marienville, Forest County. Hundreds of people were on the street to welcome him back to Butler and his reception was as enthusiastic as that ever received by any man in Butler, according to the *Butler Citizen*. The newspaper article does not give the reason for Mills' popularity.

He was taken from the train at the junction and driven to the jail where he was stripped of his old clothing, given a new prison uniform and placed in a lower cell, which was more secure than the upper ones. His pistol was taken from him and the discovery was made that it was a side or rim fire while the cartridges in it were center fire and that accounts for its failure to discharge when it was aimed at Detective Allen. Mills told authorities that after he had escaped from the officers near Oneida, he made his way toward Millerstown, passing through that village on Sunday evening. He crossed the bridge at Foxburg Tuesday night and by traveling at night and hiding by day he managed to elude the officers until Friday afternoon.

He made a mistake at a coal station in Clarion County when he asked the conductor of a freight train for a ride to Kane. The conductor was agreeable and told him to get into a freight car, and then growing suspicious of the man, locked the car and wired ahead of his capture. At Marienville Deputy Sheriff Kuhn of that county met the train. Mills was taken, held and identified, then brought back to Butler. A $500 reward was divided between Conductor Thurston and Deputy Sheriff Kuhn of Forest County.

**The Mills Trial**

Court convened at one o'clock Monday March 24, 1892 with Judge Hazen residing for the trial of the case of the Commonwealth vs. James F. Mills, accused of the murder of Peter Dugan. The *Citizen* reported that "We have not had an exciting murder trial since that of W.H. White for the murder of Patrick Eagan in March of 1881...this one attracted a large number of spectators—more than the courtroom could accommodate. Mills came in to the courtroom hand-cuffed to the deputy sheriff. He had been furnished with a suit of good clothes and "is not an unattractive looking man" reported the *Butler Citizen*.

Colonel Thompson, for the defense, after a preliminary speech, moved the court for a continuance of the case stating that the regular term of the March quarter sessions had ended the previous Sunday and that no special term had been ordered and published for this week, or panel of jurors drawn and that therefore it was beyond the jurisdiction of the court to try the defendant. Thompson read an opinion of the Supreme Court on a case taken up from Dauphin County to sustain his motion.

Messrs. Bowser and Reiber for the prosecution countered this by citing the general law of 1834, the special laws for Butler County of 1863 and 1864, and the general law of 1875 under which the rule of court fixing the terms was made. Judge Hazen stated that if Thompson's position were correct "there are now

## The Ann Girty Tragedy

Among the first settlers to locate in the northern part of Connoquenessing Township, near Whitestown, were Thomas Girty, his wife, Ann Girty, and their son Thomas Jr., who took up 400 acres of land about 1795 or 1796. The elder Girty died about 1803 and was probably buried at Girty's Run in Allegheny County, where the family came from. The records in the county commissioners' office show that in 1803, Thomas Girty, a single man, was assessed with 400 acres of land.

The members of the Girty family were inoffensive persons, attending strictly to their own affairs, but because of the belief that they were relatives of the notorious Simon Girty, the white renegade of the war of the Revolution and the subsequent Indian wars, the family was avoided. Ann Girty was accused of witchery and other false accusations were spread about other family members.

During the absence of Thomas Girty, Jr., who was in Ohio in 1803, Davy Kerr, a squatter on the 400-acre tract held by the Girtys, went to the cabin where Ann Girty lived, determined to drive her off the premises or scare her so that she would leave him in possession. Before going to the cabin he had armed himself with a horse pistol. Mrs. Girty refused to leave the cabin. Kerr threatened violence. Mrs. Girty seized a flaming firebrand from the fire and struck the intruder in the face. Kerr retaliated by shooting the woman in the breast, inflicting a wound from which she died six weeks later.

Although the Allegheny County courts had jurisdiction in Butler County territory at the time, Kerr was never prosecuted, although he was guilty of an atrocious murder. Shortly after the crime was committed, Kerr gave up his claim and left the community.

So bitter was the feeling against Ann Girty at the time that the trustees of the Mt. Nebo Presbyterian Church, near Whitestown, refused to allow her to be buried in the church cemetery. She was interred on the farm where she lived. For more than a century the grave was marked by a fence made of chestnut rails and for many years children avoided the lonely spot in the woods because they believed that Ann Girty was a witch and capable of working great mischief in the neighborhood. Thomas Girty, the son of Ann Girty, never returned to Butler County after the death of his mother. He lived and died in Adams County, Ohio.

The suspicion that this Girty family was related to the notorious Simon Girty was correct, although they could never be charged with anything more serious than attending to their own business. A sister of Thomas Girty, Sr., married Israel Gibson and located in Butler County previous to 1800. She died in 1801 and was the third person buried in Mt. Nebo Cemetery, where two years later her sister-in-law, Ann Girty was refused burial. After the death of Ann Girty, Israel Gibson lived on the tract of land for a number of years. Then it became the property of Abdiel McClure, and it is now known as the Coats farm. The site of the original Girty cabin is about a mile and a half south of Whitestown on the west side of the Franklin highway and in sight of the present Coats residence.

*Butler Eagle*, July 6, 1925, James A. McKee

several illegally convicted men in the Western Penitentiary." He sent for and read the order of court fixing the quarter session terms, which were made in September of 1878 and which fixed the terms for two weeks or so long as necessary, and therefore overruled the motion and sealed exceptions." Mr. McQuistion for the defense then asked for a change of venue on the grounds of the apparent ill will of the public here towards the prisoner, and this was also overruled.

Forty-three of the jurors called were present so the impaneling began. Most of the jurors, after questioning, were stood aside. Several did not believe in capital punishment, some had already formed an opinion regarding the case. One was excused for deafness, another for poor health and one because he had taken part in the hunt for Mills. After three and one-half hours of work, twenty-two jurors had been examined; only one had been accepted. As the day had reached the hour of five o'clock, Mills was sent back to jail, the lone juror was put in the charge of a tipstaff and the sheriff was directed to provide for the rest of the jurors at a hotel. Court adjourned until nine o'clock the next morning.

The impaneling resumed the following day and when the court adjourned for dinner, eleven jury members had been chosen. Only after the commonwealth had exhausted its peremptorily challenges was the twelfth juror selected and accepted.

The defense had thirteen different men, who were either social acquaintances of Mills' or who worked with him, testify as to his peaceful nature and good reputation. Their testimony spoke highly of Mills. "He was honest in his dealings; he was not a drunk. He was a sociable, obliging and clever fellow, and a superior workman, well thought of, respected by all who knew him."

James F. Mills was age 32 at the time of his trial. He had been born and raised in Orange County, New York, and had lived in Butler County for only thirteen months. His mother's maiden name was Fullerton, sister of Judge Fullerton of New York.

During the cross-examination, Mills claimed he didn't remember the events of the fatal evening. He didn't remember talking to Mr. Blair; he didn't remember the trip back from Renfrew; he didn't remember when he got to his own boiler house. He only remembered being awakened by the whistle in the morning. He got up, put on his coat, took a drink, shut off the fire in the boiler and went to Buco's boarding house. Mills remembered being covered with mud. A Mr. McCaffety told Mills of Dugan's death. Mills remembered nothing of the hammer and did not believe that he had struck Dugan on the head with the hammer.

Dr. Hoover was then called and questioned as to the effects of alcohol on the human system and brain. He stated that alcohol sometimes causes acute mania and that any person suffering from it would be unaccountable for deeds committed while the mania lasted. Upon recovering the person would have no recollection of anything done during the mania. Dr. Hoover was followed, by Drs. Graham, Zimmerman, and Bell who agreed with and reinforced his testimony.

When the jury went out they first took a vote as to whether or not Mills did the killing and all agreed that he had. The second ballot was on the degree of murder, and they found that they were evenly divided, half for a first-degree verdict and half for a second. The second-degree jurors did not believe that Mills was entirely responsible for his actions and gradually won the others to their way of thinking. At half-past ten o'clock on Saturday night, the jury, after being out seven hours, returned a verdict of "Guilty of murder in the second degree." Mills received the maximum sentence for second-degree murder, which was twelve years in the penitentiary. He received an additional two years for breaking jail. The *Butler Citizen* reported that every one seemed satisfied with the verdict.

Interestingly, in 1912, just ten years after James F. Mills was sent to the penitentiary for the murder of

---

**Business Building Has Been Completed**

A handsome addition to the business blocks of Center Avenue has just been completed by J. C. Mills at the intersection of the avenue and Connoquenessing Creek. the building is a substantial brick and stone structure, five stories high and equipped with elevators and other modern conveniences.

the building was erected by Mr. Mills to accommodate his shoe and leather business, which he began a few years ago in a small way in a little frame building on Center Avenue. Besides manufacturing shoes, Mr. Mills will deal in leather, groceries, meats, etc.

The new building reflects much credit on the enterprise and business ability of the owner and is an example for other businessmen in the district to follow.
*Butler Citizen*, Feb. 16, 1912

Patrick Dugan, a "J. C. Mills," arrived in Butler, secured some investment money and built the three story building on Center Avenue, between the Bessemer railroad tracks and the bridge, and opened a shoe manufacturing business. Rumor had it that J. C. Mills had learned the shoemaking trade in prison. Many prisoners were taught the shoemaking trade while they were incarcerated; it was considered to be part of their rehabilitation and it was believed that the skill was likely to help ex-cons become useful members of society. When he came to Butler, Mills said that he had a wife and daughter living in New York City. He told some of his friends that he learned the shoe making trade while employed as a sailor on the coast trade. In August 1912 Mills mysteriously disappeared and left several creditors "holding the bag" including a Southside church from which he had borrowed $700. He was never heard from again in Butler.

According to John Autenreith, after Mills absconded with the money, his building became the property of two brothers who opened a candy company on the premises. They hired a small number of girls and most of the building was used in the candy making process. Perhaps business wasn't so good or the owners needed more money than the company was generating. In an effort to turn a profit, the brothers decided to torch the building. They placed in the building, some kind of slow acting fuses which were scheduled to ignite at a later time and start a fire which was meant to consume the building. In the meantime the two, would-be arsonists jumped on one of the many trains passing through Butler and were on their way to Florida—they wouldn't be anywhere near Butler when the building went up in smoke.

Unfortunately for the brothers, a man from Larkin & Company, finishing up his shift around midnight, saw flames inside the candy-company building--the fuses had worked. The Larkin employee ran to the Southside fire station, reported the fire and the firemen were quick to knock down the door and extinguish the fire. Evidence of arson was obvious and plentiful. The brothers were tried for the arson, found guilty and sent to prison.

### Creditors are Over Anxious
### Mills Store on Center Avenue Has Been Closed on Execution
### Location of Mills Unknown at Present

Something of a sensation in business circles was sprung yesterday morning when Deputy Sheriff Dodds closed the doors of the J. C. Mills grocery store and shoe factory on Center Avenue on executions issued by the Leedom and Worrall wholesale grocer's house of Butler. Investigations conducted by other creditors during the day developed the information that J. C. Mills, the proprietor of the store and the factory, had not been seen about the place for about two weeks and that his present whereabouts are unknown. The property owned by Mills is heavily encumbered, it is said and it is also said that there are a large number of creditors outside of the holders of the mortgages on the real estate. The creditors in Butler yesterday evening discussed bankruptcy proceedings as a means of protecting their claims.

Mills came here about six years ago and started a shoe repairing shop on Center Avenue between the Bessemer railroad tracks and the bridge. He purchased the lot on which the shop stood in a year or two and last year he erected a three-story, brick building with a two-story basement.

On the first floor of the building he conducted a grocery store and shoe store; he had a real estate and insurance office on the second floor and had an apparently flourishing business.

Information was given out yesterday by persons associated with Mills in business that he has left Butler in company with his wife two weeks ago to go to Cleveland with

the intentions of buying machinery for his shoe factory. It is said that he had a sum of money with him variously estimated at from $1,000 to $4,000. It is also said that inquiry at the Cleveland house where Mills dealt brought the information that he had not been there.

Mills has not been located as of last night and the creditors are much up in the air pending some definite information about him and the amount of his liabilities.

(copied from the *Butler Citizen* dated Aug. 12, 1912 by Dave and Audrey Craig)

## Motion in Bankruptcy was Begun

### Legal Proceedings Taken to Conserve Interests of Creditors in Mills Property

### Present location of defendant is not discovered

The affairs of J. C. Mills, trading as J. C. Mills and Co., will be wound up in bankruptcy court. Yesterday attorney James E. Marshall, representing a number of the creditors, filed a petition for bankruptcy in the United States court and the case was referred to the referee in bankruptcy for this district, James W. Hutchison, for the appointment of a receiver.

At the same time, Attorney Marshall made a motion in court for an injunction restraining the Leedom-Worall Company, one of the creditors that issued an execution Monday from selling the property levied on, pending the proceedings in bankruptcy. The motion was granted and August 24 set as the time for hearing the matter set forth in the petition.

Not a trace of Mills has been found by those in Butler, who would like to know where he went after leaving the city and the reasons for his mysterious departure. The fact that Mills has not done anything in Butler that would lead to criminal proceedings being instituted against him adds to the mystery, as none of his creditors were inclined to make him trouble. That the man intended making a long stay when he left Butler is evident from the condition in which the sheriff found his living rooms when the levy was made Monday morning.

All the clothing had been taken out of the rooms and the beds had been stripped to the mattresses. It is said that Mills borrowed all the money he could get from his personal friends a day or two before leaving. It is also said that a Southside church is a creditor to the amount of $700 borrowed from a fund the church had on hand.

One of the employees of the store says that about four weeks ago a strange man came to the store and had a conference with Mills. The stranger took Mills to one side, showing him a letter and engaged him in conversation. It is said that Mills showed his embarrassment at the time but did not explain the presence of the stranger. Since the financial trouble started, the stranger returned to Butler and inquired for Mills and seemed disappointed that he could not find him.

Mills appeared to be a man of many accomplishments and had a wide range of practical knowledge covering subjects from business accounting to civil and construction engineering.

He told some of his business friends that he learned the shoe making trade while employed as a sailor on the coast trade. Before coming to Butler he said he was employed as an engineer on a steamboat on the Ohio river.

When he came to Butler, he had a wife and a daughter living in New York City. The wife died and Mills subsequently married a Butler woman, His daughter was killed in an automobile accident in New York a few years ago.

(copied from the *Butler Citizen* Dated Aug. 13, 1912 by Dave and Audrey Craig)

## Moonshiners

In 1884 the Grandmother well was drilled just a mile west of Saxonburg. The well, a gusher, was struck by one Patrick Golden, a well-known Butler County oil contractor and producer. This well was the impetus for the rapid growth of the oil boomtown, Golden City. Saxonburg also experienced a great deal of peripheral growth as a result of the well. As the news spread, all sorts of people flocked to the newest Eldorado. Oil producers, drillers, tool-dressers, pumpers and speculators arrived in an unending stream. In retrospect it may certainly be said that such boomtowns usually harbored a quota of crooks, gamblers, vagrants and cardsharps—and Golden City was no exception. Before the town was two weeks old there were several gambling places which were operating twenty-four hours a day.

The prevailing form of gambling in this area in the 1880's was playing cards—poker. So fascinating were the card games that even the school children as young as ten could be found playing penny ante. To promote and organize their gambling activities, some of the young men of nearby Saxonburg organized a club, which they called the "Lone Star Club." The membership fee was $25, which was quite a sum of money at that time. The members of this club rented a vacant house on the south edge of the community and spent countless hours there gambling and whiling away the time.

Possibly the most negative aspect of the entire scenario was the enormous amount of liquor which was sold illegally—meaning that the state and federal taxes were not paid on these alcoholic beverages. The liquor was not sold in the bars of established businesses, but rather it flowed freely in the gambling joints and was to be had by just about anybody who had such a desire. All attempts on the part of local law enforcement agencies to find an illicit still or some other source of the spirits proved unsuccessful until a well-planned investigation finally collared the culprits.

Of all the eccentric personages who drifted into Saxonburg during the oil excitement one of the most memorable was certainly a Mr. Gib Morgan. He soon became the town character playing his role quite well. Morgan didn't work much except for an occasional odd job at a hotel or livery stable yet he never seemed to lack money. Although he was generally accepted, even liked, by the town's people, he was frequently the butt of jokes. His main fault was his desire for whiskey, but he rarely drank enough to do him any harm. He was especially known for his story telling in which he was usually the main character or hero. Most thought the stories were "whoppers" and they told him so, but this only seemed to pique his creativity.

One evening after exchanging some ghost stories with the boys, someone suggested a visit to the haunted house—the old Wagner place about half a mile north of Saxonburg near the present Green Acres.

**Birch Affair**

"Strange as it may seem, the perpetrators of several of the most atrocious murders in the county have escaped detection and punishment even in recent years."

The Birch affair at Zelienople, May 12, 1923, is still fresh in the minds of many persons. Henry Birch, manager of a tea store, closed his place of business Saturday night and walked to his home on the edge of town along the main highway. An unknown assassin shot him down in his own yard and then made his escape. Birch's wife was walking near her husband when the shot was fired. All she ever told about the affair was that as she and her husband were walking around the corner of the house, they were approached by a stranger who fired a shot and fled.

The coroner, the district attorney's office and the state police have worked on the case and all possible clues were investigated, but all trails came to a dead end. It is common belief that there were persons close to the Birch family who knew the facts, but they would not talk."

*Butler Eagle*, July 8, 1925, James A. McKee

The Wagner house was a dilapidated, old building, two stories high, which had been abandoned some years before. Frightening stories had been circulated through the area of lights being seen in the windows, of the sounds of chains clanking, and of eerie groans and shrieks coming from the farmhouse—it was believed to be haunted. No murder, suicide, or crime had ever taken place in the house; thus people could not understand why it would be haunted. Yet because of the stories, no one ever ventured near enough to investigate.

Gib and the others were in the mood for some ghosts so they set out for the old Wagner place. The moon was not out, the night was rather dark, but the stars gave enough light to make certain objects vaguely visible. It didn't take very long to complete the walk to the old farm. Gib, for some unknown reason, was behind the group and as he neared the house his companions had already started a hasty retreat. He heard footsteps approaching at a run. "Don't go down there! Didn't you see it? That house is really haunted! We not only heard cries and groans—we saw a ghost! Just as we approached the house the door opened and a tall figure in white was floating toward us!" Gib said that he was about to get to the bottom of this and asked if any of his companions were courageous enough to stay with him. His calmness and the fact that he was packing a revolver gave four of the young men enough courage to join him and they cautiously headed back toward the old house. They walked through the open door pointing the rays of a lantern ahead of them.

When they went into the kitchen, it seemed to be bare but for a large cupboard which Gib examined

241

carefully. "Boys, this cupboard is nothing more than a cleverly concealed door; where it leads I don't know but since we're here to find out let's do just that." He inserted the end of a pickax into the back of the cupboard and began to pry. Soon a snap was heard and the entire unit moved, revealing a four-foot wide opening which seemed to lead through the kitchen wall and into the hillside.

They had to stoop and proceed single file. They continued this way until they suddenly entered into a cavern-like chamber about twenty feet wide and thirty feet long, with a high roof. It seemed to be a natural cave but later it was learned that it was an abandoned mine, and the tunnel, which led from the old Wagner house, was the entrance. As they stood quietly in the underground chamber they heard the muffled sounds of voices coming from somewhere ahead of them. They strode silently across the floor in the direction of the voices and discovered another door concealed behind some boards.

When they opened the door they encountered two men busily at work tending a whiskey still. The men who were unarmed and out numbered offered no resistance and were quickly subdued by Gib and his friends. As he shackled the moonshiners, Gib said to his "deputies," "I owe you all an explanation. In the first place, my name is not Gib Morgan. I am a detective with the United States Revenue Service—My name is George Meredith and these men are under arrest!" One of the moonshiners replied, "We're only hired to make this whiskey. We do the work and get paid fifteen dollars a week but have no interest in the business whatsoever." Meredith replied, "I'll tell you right now that by working for this outfit you are in this thing as deep as they are and you are liable for a heavy sentence unless you turn in your bosses."

It worked; the two men were soon telling all. "The only person we ever see is Job Sweeny who comes by every other week to check on things and pay us our wages. We don't know who the big boss is. We created the ghosts by holding a lantern under a sheet, rattling chains and moaning. We wanted to keep people away from our operation."

This story or some facsimile of it was in *The Oil and Gas Man's Magazine* in 1909. As a young teacher in the 1960's, I was relating the above story to a class I had at Knoch High School, when a student, David Glitsch, excitedly told me that the "cave" was in his back yard. I stopped at his house on the way home. He lived in the right area, just north of Green Acres along the "Butler" road where the old Wagner farmhouse had been. Dave showed me a hole in the ground approximately two feet in diameter. The entrance to the hole was somewhat concealed by bushes. The opening went straight down about four feet and then made a ninety-degree turn. I did not want to explore the hole, coal mine, cave or whatever it was. I wish now that I had investigated a bit further. A short time later the hole was filled with rocks and dirt, and grass was then planted over the area. I don't think it could be found today but it always offered me some small testimony that the Gib Morgan story was authentic.

## Celebrated Baby Case

"The celebrated Harbison-Monks baby case got into the county courts in 1887, and was not closed until May, 1888. Robert Harbison and his wife were residents of the southeastern part of the county. After the birth of their baby boy, trouble arose between the two and they separated. The case reached the courts in August 1887. On the order of Judge Aaron L. Hazen, then president judge, the child, a few months old, was placed in custody of the father. This order was carried out. A few days later the mother abducted the baby and fled with him to Kansas. Her brothers, Martin and John Monks, and Wendel Hickey assisted her in the abduction.

The abduction was followed by the arrest of the Monks brothers and Hickey for contempt of court, and they were committed to jail. One of the brothers was stricken with typhoid fever while in prison and, after some delay, all were released on bail on condition that they produce the child in court. On May 12, 1888, they produced both the child and the mother. The legal battle that followed was the most exciting witnessed in the county courts in more than half a century. The Hon. Charles McCandless and Col. John M. Thompson represented the father, while former Judge E. McJunkin, James M. Galbreath and S. F. Bowser represented the mother. After a hearing, Judge Hazen discharged the writ of habeas corpus and remanded the defendants to the custody of the sheriff except the child, which was ordered to be placed in the custody of the father.

At this point the scene in the courtroom verged on riot. The mother declared she would never surrender the child, whom she was holding in her arms at the time, and Judge Hazen ordered Sheriff O. C. Redic to enforce the court order. The sheriff went to the woman and demanded the baby. The frantic mother refused to surrender it and the officer didn't try to take it. A dramatic scene was enacted when the judge ordered Sheriff Redic to deputize men to take the child. Sheriff Redic, a Civil War veteran and a man of striking appearance, openly defied the court, when he arose to his feet and said, "By the Great Eternal [a pet swear word at that time], I refuse to execute the order." The court then deputized the father to take the child, but the mother clung to her baby until the father gave up.

Public sympathy was with the mother and the baby and sentiment was growing among the crowd in the courtroom that boded no good to the court and the officials who attempted to carry out an unreasonable order. Another writ was issued ordering the mother to surrender the child, but she defied the court, and she and her baby and her two brothers went to jail.

The case was taken up again on Saturday morning, May 14. The courtroom was crowded with partisans on both sides of the controversy. The incarceration of the mother and the baby in the jail for two days had been the talk of the community, and an angry crowd had assembled about the courthouse. The mother had secured a light chain which she had fastened about the body of her baby and then to herself with a padlock and that she had made the declaration that if the child was taken it would be over her dead body. It was known to some of the officers that the frantic woman had a revolver concealed in a handbag in her lap and that she was desperate enough to use the weapon.

The proceedings in the Harbison-Monks baby case Saturday morning May 14, 1888 were punctuated with thrilling incidents. No decision had been reached at noon when court took a recess and it was believed that the mother and baby would be sent back to jail to spend Sunday unless the case was settled in some way. A crowd of men thronged the streets about the courthouse at the noon hour and discussed the situation. Open threats of violence were made if the court refused to discharge the mother and her baby at the afternoon session.

Luckily cooler heads intervened, and during the noon recess friends of Harbison, who had been holding out under advice of his attorneys, prevailed on him to discharge his counsel and employ new attorneys, which he did. The leaders in the movement to compromise the case and save the community from the disgrace of a riot were the late Judge John M. Greer, and the late Simeon Nixon.

Attorney Greer was called into the case as counsel for Harbison. A hasty conference was held during the noon hour with the attorneys for Mrs. Harbison, with the result that terms of settlement were agreed upon, whereby the mother would retain posession of the child and the father would be given certain privileges to see him at suitable times.

The ugliest crowd a judge ever faced in the county had assembled in the courtroom at 1:30. Every seat was filled and a line of men stood with their backs against the wall around three sides of the room, grim looking and silent. Harbison had been told that if he did not change his attitude and the woman and child went to jail that night, he would not get out of town alive, and that if recommitted the mother and baby would never remain in jail over Sunday.

Court did not call until 2 o'clock. The mother and baby, the father and attorneys for both sides were present when Judge Hazen took his seat. The attorneys had been busy during the recess, but no one knew the result of the conference. The court officials themselves were in the dark. A pin dropping on the floor could have been heard as Attorney John M. Greer arose and asked that his client's original petition and all of the rulings under it be set aside and that the mother, the baby, and the two Monks boys and Hickey be discharged from jail. It was a welcome denouement for Judge Hazen, who made the order forthwith and did not neglect to express his gratification over the happy turn of affairs. The court took a recess of about ten minutes while members of the bar and friends of the couple crowded about the plucky mother and expressed their pleasure over the turn of affairs. The baby, who was the cause of all the fuss, came in for much admiration, and the father was allowed to hold the sturdy boy in his arms for a few minutes.

The courthouse was clear of the crowd in ten minutes. That evening the janitor picked up a bushel basket full of stones and brickbats about the building and in the courtroom, and later a number of rifles and shotguns were found under the abutment of the South Main Street bridge, where they had been put by their owners.

The near approach to a mob outbreak that would have disgraced the community is indicated by a story told by Sheriff O. C. Redic a few years before his death. After the case had been settled an old soldier and prominent citizen of the county was discussing the matter with the sheriff. He said, "Sheriff, if the woman and her baby had been sent to jail over Sunday and some of your friends had come to you and asked for their release, what would you have done? The sheriff replied, I would have resigned my position and joined the crowd in working for her release."
*Butler Eagle*, June 29 and 30, James A. McKee

### A Story Related to the Wigton Family Massacre

In *Butler County, the Second Hundred Years,* Audrey Fetters and I expressed our feelings that certain historical events which took place here had been hashed and rehashed so many times that further mention of such would be redundant. The Wigton family massacre is certainly a prime example. However, a local history buff has given me an obscure copy of the confession and salvation of Sam Mohawk, taken from an issue of the *Democratic Herald*, which was published in Butler on April 10, 1844, less than one year after the crime. Never before have I seen or heard the information included in this account.

Reverend Gottlieb Bassler, pastor of the First English Lutheran Church of Butler, was the principal spiritual advisor for Mohawk as he awaited his trial and ultimately, his execution, and it was Bassler who prepared the following narrative. The account becomes tedious at times, certainly not due to Reverend Bassler's literary style, but rather as a result of the content itself. I pray that the good Reverend will forgive my editing of his lengthy report.

"He maintained to the last that he was 'crazy,' that he labored under some unusual and strange excitement of mind during the whole of that eventful period which intervened between his leaving Butler in the stage and returning a prisoner. Of the truth of the narrative as far as Samuel Mohawk's recollection served him, the writer has no doubt. Being frequently with him, he had a good opportunity to become acquainted with his exercises of mind after his imprisonment. Only after his trial did he manifest much contrition for sin. For sometime he seemed bowed down on account of his transgressions; felt as he expressed it 'very bad.' In reading the Gospel of Luke which had been procured for him in the Seneca tongue, he met with the incident of the young man coming to Christ and asking what he must do to be saved. He saw that he had broken God's law, and deserved death, eternal death or, as he expressed it, 'to go to bad place.' He was pointed to the Lamb of God, and as we humbly trust, looked up in faith. He gave many pleasing proofs of being renewed by God's Holy Spirit.

He earnestly desired to profess Christ, and a short time before his execution he was baptized in the prison in the presence of a few witnesses. On the day previous to his execution and on the morning of the day itself, he conversed as usual, though there was more solemnity in his appearance and conduct than there had been previously. He engaged with much earnestness in the religious exercises that were held with him in his cell, especially those that were held with him immediately before he was led out to the scaffold. When he led in prayer himself, which he did at the close of the exercises in the cell, he seemed to pour out his whole soul before God. As the awful hour arrived he manifested no unwillingness, no hesitation, and made no delays. He was very particular in having everything properly adjusted. On the scaffold he seemed to engage earnestly in the religious exercises.

Of singing he was fond, often engaging in it in his cell. When the hymn was sung on the scaffold, he sang also, the hymn having been explained to him previously. When the hymn had been sung he was asked whether he had anything more to say. He answered, 'guess not,' which was a common phrase with him. He then added, 'me ready.' He bade adieu to the sheriff, the attendants, and his spiritual advisor with much affection. When he shook hands with the writer [Bassler] he smiled, as he usually did on meeting him in his cell, and said, 'Me see you,' casting his glance upwards. When he rose from his seat when the rope was adjusted, when the cap was drawn, and during the eventful moment which intervened before the drop fell, he was calm and evinced not the slightest trepidation as far as the writer was able to observe."

Bassler interjects at this point, "We might ask here what was the immediate cause of all this crime, suffering, excitement, expense, and of the final dreadful catastrophe? The answer comes to us in a solemn warning voice, 'alcohol.' This is what made of Sam Mohawk, first a vagabond; this caused him to wander from his home; this stirred up the devil in him, and excited the devils without him, to urge him on to the dreadful deed for which he forfeited his life. The vendor of the 'firewater' made a few shillings or dollars at most; the state received something for the license; but what a price! Seven lives! Leaving all expense and waste of time out of our calculation. Where is the guilt?

The rest of the article is Mohawk Sam's recollection and confession of the murders. He was angry; he was drunk; he had been chased out of two or three drinking establishments by the proprietors. He reported that he continually heard the Indian voice of his mother, aunt, son and other Indian acquaintances. It was all in his mind because investigations found no substance to the voices. (A copy of the *Democratic Herald* article appeared in the *Butler Citizen*, Wednesday, April 18, 1883)

When Mohawk Sam was incarcerated in the Butler County Prison for his confessed murder of the Wigton family, two young men were given the job of guarding the Indian. Although Mohawk was in chains, the two young men each took twelve-hour shifts watching the prisoner. One of the young men was John Henry Negley, an apprentice lawyer; the other was Charles Gillespie. The latter was a naturally gifted artist who had done portraits for some of Butler's prominent personages and families. [The Wigton murders took place in 1843 and the camera wasn't invented until Civil War days.] As Gillespie guarded

Mohawk, perhaps out of boredom or perhaps because he was so talented, he took a wooden shingle approximately 8 1/2 by 11 inches and sketched the Indian's portrait. All who saw it agreed that it was a very good likeness. Charles Gillespie then gave the portrait to the other guard, John Negley, who liked it so much that he took it home, framed it, and hung it on the wall. Over one hundred years passed by and in 1950 local historian, John Autenreith, happened to see the drawing displayed on the wall of the Edgar Negley home.

Negley would not sell the portrait to Autenreith but would allow it to be photographed. Autenreith, knowing the value of the drawing, offered to leave $100 as collateral while he took the drawing to the studio of Doug DeCoux, *Butler Eagle* photographer at the time. DeCoux used the best cameras available in Butler but in spite of the modern, photographic equipment, the photographs did not come out well. Disappointed but not yet ready to give up, Autenreith decided to look for a local artist to draw a picture of the portrait. If he could not have the original drawing or a photograph of it he would settle for an artist's rendition of an artist's rendition. Jane Schmoker, a friend of Autenreith's, was a very good artist and she agreed to make a drawing of the portrait. Upon completion of the job a very satisfied Autenreith paid Ms. Schmoker $35. Unfortunately the drawing of the portrait was stolen and will probably never be tracked down.

In the meantime Edgar Negley died and all of his furniture and belongings were auctioned off. Autenreith arrived too late to purchase the old Gillespie drawing of Mohawk Sam. It was purchased by June Peppers, a Cherokee Indian and local antique dealer. She had a store in Butler. Not long after the purchase however she closed her Butler operation and moved back to Oklahoma. Chances are very slim that the original portrait will ever be returned to Butler.

There is a happy ending of sorts to this story. Between the time that Doug DeCoux made his unsuccessful attempt at photographing the drawing and the death of Edgar Negley, a good photograph of the drawing was taken in the studio of Harry O. Price. A German camera salesman, Dieter Schmidt, was calling on Price with some state-of-the-art cameras. Hearing of this, Autenreith quickly borrowed the drawing again and took it to Price's shop were it was successfully photographed. Autenreith presently is the owner of the photograph.

(This story was related to the author by John Autenreith)

### Nancy Ann McCandless
Late on an October evening in 1868, on Swamp Road near Unionville, Nancy Ann McCandless was killed instantly as she ate at the supper table. The table was full with family, friends, and neighbors who had been helping with the harvest; dinner was later than usual that evening. The bullet, which had come in through the open window, passed clear through Ms. McCandless' head and into a corner cupboard where it shattered a milk pitcher. There was so much talking and noise at the table that no one had heard the gunshot. Most thought that Nancy had merely fainted and slumped over her plate. But the growing pool of blood indicated something much more serious. It may have been a stray bullet from a nighttime raccoon hunter; other than that it was difficult to fathom why anyone would purposely kill Nancy. A search party was formed and a large group of men immediately began to search the area. Someone rode into Butler for the sheriff.

The search was uneventful but the sheriff began to question many of the people who had known Nancy and a story started to form. A few months earlier, Nancy had been courted by a young man named Zachary Taylor Hockenberry, from out around Prospect. Others spoke up adding that Hockenberry went into Butler on Saturday nights and loafed in front of the bank at the corner of Main and Jefferson Streets as was the tradition. The men would converse, observe and stand on the curb spitting tobacco juice into the gutter while their women shopped. Some of the men had been teasing Hockenberry about losing his girlfriend Nancy, as apparently the romance had been curtailed. Hockenberry had been heard by several of the men as saying something to the effect, "don't worry about me losing the girlfriend. I'm going to fix it so nobody will want her and then she'll be mine and only mine." But he would not elaborate on his plan. Some of the people being questioned by the sheriff had remembered Hockenberry's comments and he quickly became the prime suspect.

An analysis of the bullet indicated it had been shot from a gun of a type used during the Civil War—the kind that fired a lead ball, which was put in place with a ramrod. The paper wads, which had been used for packing, had been torn from a newspaper [some stories say the pages were from the Bible]. The sheriff and his party arrived at Zachary Taylor Hockenberry's house during the wee small hours of the morning. A search of the house found matching newspapers Hockenberry had torn and used as wadding. He had apparently loaded the gun right in his house. Hockenberry was immediately arrested and locked up in the Butler County jail where he confessed to the crime. He explained however, that he wasn't trying to kill Nancy Ann McCandless, but rather he was trying to shoot her nose off. Without a nose she would not be attractive to any other man therefore Hockenberry could have her all to himself. Perhaps Nancy moved just as the shot was fired; perhaps Hockenberry was not a good shot. Whatever, he killed her but it was not pre-meditated murder; the killing was in fact, an accident. Some of the McCandless family actually liked Zachary Taylor Hockenberry and spoke in his defense during the trial, but to no avail.

The trial was held in December. The jury was unanimous in its verdict. They believed that Hockenberry had tried to kill Ms. McCandless and found him guilty! It was not a public hanging as were many in those days, rather on December 7, 1869, the sheriff and a couple of assistants hung Hockenberry right in the jail cell. [Any violent prisoner who would not cooperate was thrown down and strapped on to a "body board." The prisoners hands were cuffed and his feet were tied to the board and if he were of small stature sandbags were tied to his legs to add weight. Next, the noose was secured around the criminal's neck and a trap door opened, dropping him eight feet to break his neck. Good hanging was an art; if it were done incorrectly the victim would strangle to death, sometimes slowly, usually over a period of twenty minutes. If the neck was broken, as was Hockenberry's, death was instantaneous.]

After the execution Hockenberry's body was taken by some of the McCandless's to Stanley McCandless' farm where he was buried. Some of the history books record that Hockenberry was buried in the Prospect cemetery but there is no proof of that. Stanley McCandless was born in 1899 and has lived on his 1000 acre farm all of his life. He knows where the grave is located.

In the fall of 1998, I made an appointment to visit Mr. Stanley McCandless. Tim Shaffer and Bill Bryant both know Stanly well and said that in spite of his age, he is "as sharp as a tack." I knocked on Mr. McCandless' door and when there was no answer I walked right in as I had been instructed to do by Bill Bryant. Mr. McCandless' house had very little furniture and reminded me of an eighteenth century setting, a few antiques, no curtains, and the kitchen offered the smell of harvest time. Stanley was lying on a couch; he was covered with a thin blanket and the television set was blaring. I introduced myself and told him how much I appreciated his offer to talk to me. I asked about his health since he seemed to be "laid-up" on the couch. He told me that he had been run over by his own truck the day before. As he was getting out of the truck, the brakes failed, it drifted and ran over his leg. I asked the 100 year old McCandless if he had been driving, and he replied, "Well up until then I had been."

We had a nice discussion. I didn't want to tire him under the circumstances, but I did ask about Zachary Taylor Hockenberry. Stanley remembered the story and told me that they didn't bury murderers in church cemeteries. "Hockenberry was buried near Unionville, along Swamp Road up near a fence row. They mustn't have buried him very deep because when I was a boy the old timers remembered a time when the dogs dug him up. He had to be re-buried."

Hangings occurred in Butler during the 1800's. We know for certain of the hangings of Mohawk Sam, and Zachery Taylor Hockenberry. Our investigations of the old Butler County newspapers do not render any other reports of hangings. However, I recall discussions of many years ago with the late Mrs. Nellie Isanogle, nee Hughes, who lived at 130 Morton Avenue. She was born before 1900 and claimed that as a young girl, she observed many hangings in front of Butler's courthouse. The gallows was right in front of the courthouse. "Sometimes it took twenty minutes before the victim died. They shook and twitched all over and their knees would come up to touch their chins." [I can find no official records of any hangings in Butler other than those of Sam Mohawk and Zachary Taylor Hockenberry.]

### The McKeever Robbery
The Eagle went to press last week before a full account of the McKeever robbery could be obtained, it having been committed between midnight and Thursday morning. The facts, as since developed, are about as follows: The McKeever residence, which fronts on the Butler and Millerstown road, about four miles from the former place, is a two-

story building, and since Hugh McKeever's death, which occurred a year ago, the household has consisted of Jane and Margaret McKeever, and a simple-male pauper named Bess. The McKeevers have been industrious and frugal, and have acquired considerable money. Just before Hugh died he told his sisters that after he was gone they would find something in the barn that would be of use to them. It was not until about a month ago that they discovered what he referred to. It proved to be a tin bucket containing gold and silver coin and paper money, estimated to be worth about $900. This was found in a grain barrel, and was taken to the house and put in a trunk, under the girls' bed on the second floor, the money still remaining in the bucket.

Between midnight and daybreak, last Thursday morning, three men came to the McKeever farmhouse. The first thing they did was to fasten the rear door so that it could not be opened from the inside. This was done by tying one end of a rope or cord to the doorknob and the other end to a post. This done, they went to the front door and broke it open with a rafter, which they took into the house and used as a brace against the door leading upstairs. Their object in doing this was to keep the inmates of the house prisoners on the second floor until they could ransack the rooms on the first floor. The noise had aroused Bess, however, and he had come down stairs and was standing in a chimney corner yelling when the robbers entered. A pistol shot was fired at him, but it missed its mark, the bullet being afterwards found imbedded in the chimney-jamb. They evidently soon discovered that Bess was harmless, for they paid no further attention to him but turned everything in the lower part of the house upside down and "inside out" in their search for money. Bureau drawers, clothes, etc., were ransacked and then thrown into the middle of the floor. Failing to secure any valuable plunder here, they next turned their attention to the apartments upstairs. On opening the stair door they saw the girls at the top of the stairs, and as they showed a disposition to fight, discharged a revolver and by this means drove them back from their vantage point. They went up, but the two sisters with commendable bravery attempted to overpower the invaders, but of course, were unsuccessful. Margaret was knocked down with a club, receiving a sore bruise on her head, and Jane, who attempted to protect her sister, was taken in hand by robber number two, who struck her on the head and face with a club, discoloring one of her eyes, and choked her considerably.

Margaret, in the meantime, had broken loose from her assailant's grasp, and went to Jane's assistance. The women by this time were nearly overcome by exhaustion, so the burglars let them go, and began their search for treasure anew. They soon came on to the trunk, under the bed, lifted the bucket of coin out, and after taking an additional $300 in coin and bills, which the women had themselves earned and saved, they departed, having

### Jail Attack

In all of the 121 years since the county courts were organized there has never been a jail delivery by a mob. Only once in that time has the jail been attacked. The Bennet affair is familiar to most of the present generation, and forms an incident in the history of the county because of the serious consequences that followed a rash act.

The night of September 13, 1902, Jerry Bennett, who was intoxicated at the time, was arrested by the city police for attempting to assault the eight-year-old daughter of J. H. Wagner. Fearing trouble, the police hurried Bennet to the county jail and locked him up. The arrest was made about 8 o'clock, and the streets were crowded with people who did not know at the time, the nature of the charge made against the prisoner.

Threats of lynching were made and about 9 o'clock, when the saloons closed and turned a drunken mob loose on the streets, trouble started. Sheriff Thomas R. Hoon prepared to resist the mob and protect the prisoner. By 10 o'clock the mob was beyond control of the city police and an assault was made on the residence part of the jail, while threats were made to secure dynamite and blow up the prison. Within half an hour the front door of the jail residence had been battered down, and every window in the residence had been shattered with stones. Mrs. Sarah J. Hoon, wife of the sheriff, who was lying on a sick bed, was injured by a stone, which struck her.

Sheriff Hoon, a man of 60, and a physical giant, stood in the doorway and faced the mob as it battered at the wooden door with a 10x12 piece of building timber sixteen feet long, and pushed the leaders back. Someone fired a revolver shot. The ball struck the side of the courthouse, caromed onto the ground, and hit a drunken rioter in the leg. The shrieks of the wounded man appeared to throw the rioters into a panic and in a few minutes the streets about the jail were vacant except for a few stragglers. The mob did not get inside the door of the jail residence. Sheriff Hoon was roughly handled, but was not seriously hurt. Fearing the mob would return to renew the attack, an armed guard was thrown around the jail for the remainder of the night.

Two days later Bennet went into court and entered a plea of guilty to the charge made against him. Judge Samuel Miller of Mercer, who was presiding, sentenced him to fifteen years in the Western Penitentiary. As a result of the riot several arrests were made, but identification of the gang of men who manned the battering ram that broke down the jail door was next to impossible and little came of the prosecutions."
*Butler Eagle*, June 25, 1925

secured about $1200 in all.

Thursday morning the women came to town and made information, and from the description of the two men they had seen upstairs, it was believed the names of the men wanted were Louch and Simpson. Warrants were issued and placed in the hands of officers, and in the afternoon of the same day, Sheriff Kramer, County Detective Dobson and Constable McCandless arrested these two men in Butler. Simpson, who conducts a fish market on a small scale near the West Penn Depot, was plying his business when taken in to custody. Louch has been employed as a section hand on the S. & A. R.R. Both men are comparative strangers here and are known to but few of our citizens. They claim to have come from Erie about three weeks ago. The two suspects were taken to Justice Walker's office, and Margaret McKeever was sent for. She was not able to identify Louch and Simpson in a line up as being the men who had committed the robbery so the two were set free and the case remained unsolved.
(*Butler Eagle*, November 26, 1886)

### Pioneer Woman Died Tuesday
#### Sensational Robbery In This County Has Been Recalled
#### Miss McKeever Last Survivor Of Family

Miss Margaret McKeever, aged, 95, the oldest resident of Oakland Township died at 7:30 Tuesday morning at the house of her niece, Mrs. W. B. Davis, from complications incident to old age. The deceased was the last survivor of the family of James McKeever, who settled in Oakland Township in 1819. She was born in Ireland and was brought to this country by her parents when two years of age. She was related to William Beatty who in early days ran the Eagle Hotel on South Main Street, Butler at the corner of Cunningham, and was one of Butler's most distinguished citizens. Descendants of the family are still living in Detroit and Chicago. Miss McKeever was a member of the Presbyterian church. Funeral services will be held at the residence of her niece, Mrs. W. B. Davis, Thursday at 1:00 o'clock and the burial will be in the North Cemetery, this city.

Miss McKeever and her sister, Jane, who died about two years ago, were the victims of a sensational robbery about 25 years ago, when masked men entered their home in Oakland Township, tortured the old ladies into revealing the hiding place where they kept their money.

The amount of money taken was never known as the old people did not know how much money they had in the house. The money was secreted in tin cans, coffee pots and other receptacles in various parts of the house. The robbers did not get all of the money but it was later known that one man concerned in the affair got $300 as his share of the "swag."

The robbery caused the greatest sensation for the time. The ladies were unable to identify the men who committed the crime and it looked as though they would never be discovered. After Louch and Simpson were exonerated, suspicion pointed to three notorious crooks that were then in Butler--Tom Haggerty, Sheldon E. Wilson and J. Brown, who suddenly disappeared. It was supposed that the gang had an accomplice. The disappearance of a well known resident of the McKeever neighborhood strengthened that suspicion for a time, but no evidence was obtained against the man.

A few months later, Haggerty, Wilson and Brown attempted to rob a German farmer in Clarion County, near Knox. The farmer and his two sons were armed with Winchester rifles, Brown was shot dead in his tracks in the door yard and Haggerty and Wilson ran for their lives. In attempting to rescue their fallen companion Haggerty and Wilson were both arrested. They were tried in the Clarion county courts and sent to the penitentiary for 17 years each.

While in the penitentiary, Haggerty made a confession of the McKeever robbery in Butler County implicating Wilson and Brown, and named the accomplice. The accomplice who was enjoying his freedom and ill-gotten gains was James L. Conn, a man well known in the McKeever neighborhood and a friend of the family.

Haggerty said that Conn got $300 for his part in the affair and that the money had been sent to him by post office order to the Karns City Post Office. The order was issued in Pittsburgh. Anthony Allen who was county detective at the time investigated the story and found it to be correct. Haggerty had purchased a money order in the Pittsburgh office for $300 payable to Conn at Karns City.

Conn, Haggerty and Wilson were indicted at the December term of court, 1887, but were never tried. Five or six years later Conn was arrested in Ohio and brought to Butler for trial. He was released from jail on bail pending the outcome of the investigation. Later he disappeared, his bail was forfeited and he has never been seen since. It is said that he is living somewhere on the Pacific coast.

Haggerty completed his term in the penitentiary for the Clarion County job and after his release, it is said that he was killed in an attempt at robbery near McDonald. Wilson died shortly after his release.

Haggerty, Wilson and Brown were the slickest trio of crooks that ever made Butler their headquarters. They were blamed for numerous robberies but never caught. Haggerty lived on Monroe Street with a widow woman who kept a few boarders. Wilson was a polished gentleman, well-dressed and fine looking. He boarded at the Lowry House most of the time and associated with oil men and operators about the town. Brown was also very much of a gentleman and usually lived at some boarding house.

(copied from the *Butler Citizen* dated Jan. 3, 1912 by Dave and Audrey Craig)

### Desperadoes

"On Thursday of last week Mr. John Larrimer of Oakland Twp., came to town and made information against James and William Barnhart, Jr., of Fairview Twp., for breaking into his store and stealing some shoes. Esq. Walker made out a warrant for them, but none of our constables here coveted the job of attempting the arrest, as these particular Barnharts are noted desperadoes and when together and drinking are liable to use their knives and pistols very freely. They are charged with exciting a riot in Millerstown last March, and with cutting a man named Andrew, and although Esq. Gaisford made out warrants for the old man, Wm. Barnhart, and his three sons Wm., Charles and James, no attempt has ever been made to arrest them. Mr. Peter Kramer was in town Thursday evening, and the case was stated to him, and he was induced to undertake the job of arresting the men. He took Constable Croup of Butler Twp. and Constable McCandless of Butler with him, Friday morning, and drove up to that vicinity. Leaving McCandless at Troutman to watch James' house he and Croup proceeded towards the Barnhart place and found the old man, Wm. Jr., and Charles on the public road near Haysville, and after some little conversation told them that they were his prisoners. They offered no resistance, although Charles had a pistol in his pocket. Kramer and Croup went with them to their house to change clothes. At the house the old lady gave the officers quite a lecture, and said that she prayed for her dear boys every night. Kramer sent for McCandless to bring the wagon up and when it came they drove to Troutman. James happened to be there and Kramer arrested him and brought the whole party to Butler. The prisoners were taken before the justice and committed to jail.

On Saturday evening Al McDonald, a son-in-law of Barnhart, against whom Larrimer had also made information, was brought in by deputy constables, Hutchinson and Craig, who chased him all around Fairview before capturing him.
The *Butler Citizen*, October 15, 1884

## Railroad Payroll Robbery

In the early days of the railroad when it was being built through Butler the workers were paid in cash; no bank drafts were used. The paymaster and paywagon traveled to Butler from Pittsburgh. It was purposely made to look like any other wagon and the paymaster and his clerks dressed in ordinary clothes so as to avoid being noticed by any criminals. It took all of a day, sometimes two, to make the trip from Pittsburgh. One day in the 1880's as the wagon lumbered north along the dirt road to Butler it was ambushed about ten miles south of Butler in what is now Penn Township.

The group of robbers stood in the woods at the roadside and ordered everyone off the wagon and had them stand at the side of the road with their hands raised. The criminals then searched the pay crew, took their guns, and smashed their shotguns and rifles across a tree. Then the masked bandits loaded their leather saddle bags with the heavy metal coins while one of the thieves kept the pay crew covered with a shotgun. After all the saddle bags were filled and loaded on the horses, the bandits clubbed and broke all four wheels with rails from a nearby fence. With all four wheels collapsed, the wagon was out of commission. The culprits then unhitched the team, took the horses in tow, and headed north toward Butler. The pay crew was stranded on the lonely road and it was some time before anyone came along. The stolen horses were found later grazing in a farmer's field along with a herd of cattle.

After word of the robbery spread, some people in the area of what is now Lyndora reported seeing a group of strangers on horseback riding north. Others in the area of the West End near what is now Broad Street, reported seeing the same group. The next reports had the group at the top of Mercer Road hill where Rose Hill Cemetery is now located. They were reported to have left the road there and took to the woods.

A little while later they were seen emerging from the woods about a quarter of a mile farther north. The horses seemed to be exhausted and observers noticed that on leaving the woods, the saddle bags were nowhere to be seen. Later that day when a farmer was in the thicket he noticed that several trees had been slashed with an axe or hatchet--it was probably done so they could find the hidden loot later.

There is no record of the stolen money ever being found or of the robbers return to retrieve it. It's possible that they approached the cache from the Alameda Park area and made their exit the same way. It's possible that the cache is yet stashed there.

The old Mercer Road which was called the Mercer Pike, is just west of the present Mercer Road up on the west side of the high bank. It runs to the cemetery and then goes down the hill for about a thousand feet. (As related to the author by John Autenreith)

## The Braun-Steelsmith Case

"The most sensational trial of any sort ever held in Butler County was that of Mrs. Sadie Braun, by her father and next friend, Amos Steelsmith vs Wm Braun libel to divorce. The case was taken up in our court before Judge Barker, last Friday morning, and the jury was selected...The history of the trial can best be told by giving a brief history of the joint lives of W. F. and Sadie Braun as it was made public on the witness stand. In 1894 Sadie Steelsmith, then 19 years old, attended W. P. Braun's dancing academy on Highland Ave. Pittsburg. The two became engaged against her parents' wishes, eloped to Michigan and were married there. Later Mr. Steelsmith took Mr.Braun into the oil business with him and a nice home on West Jefferson Street was built for his son-in-law. In 1896 a daughter...was born to the Brauns.

During Mr. Braun's absence in 1897 his wife became too intimate with Elmer C. Blue, ball player, wrestler and all-around, sporting man. About Feb. 9, 1898 she and Blue disappeared and a day or two later her father found his daughter with Nettie Rickman, a sister of Blue, in a house in Chicago. Shortly after this Braun had Blue arrested at Braeburn, Pa. on a charge of desertion, preferred by Blue's Chicago wife. On trial of this charge he was acquitted.

About the first of March, 1898, a reconciliation was effected between the Brauns and in the presence of his attorneys, Murphy and Forquer, Mr. Braun signed and was sworn to a paper drawn up by Mr. Galbreath, in effect exonerating his wife of any misconduct with Blue.

The Brauns then went to Pittsburg and on April 10, 1898 took a furnished house at 5441 Penn Ave. On June 25, 1898 Mr. Braun started a fine drug store at Sixth St. and Duquesne Way, Pittsburg. Mrs. Braun helped in the store. On Oct. 20, 1898 Mrs. Braun came home with her child, and shortly afterwards filed her libel in divorce.

She charged Braun with habitually using obscene, profane and insulting language to her, with tearing a waist off her to get a letter, with choking her, with forcing her to take medicines to produce an abortion, and with criminally associating with Lillian Hostetter, who live above the pharmacy. About fifty Pittsburg witnesses attended the trial and all these things were sworn to as being true or untrue by the respective sides.

On January 11, 1899, Mrs. Braun gave birth to twins, and Mr. Braun disclaimed the paternity of these children. He charged his wife with unfaithfulness while living in Pittsburg.

On Monday afternoon a number of witnesses testified that they would not believe Braun, while others said that his reputation for truth and veracity was good. Tuesday morning J. M. Galbreath presented the law points for the plaintiff and Levi McQuistion for the defendant. Attorneys Watson and Forquer argued to the jury for the defendant and Thompson for the plaintiff. Judge Barker's charge occupied about an hour and the jury retired shortly after noon. After being out two hours the courthouse bell called for court again, the jury came in, and their verdict was recorded for the plaintiff, granting a divorce.

Judge Barker has won the respect and admiration of all the Butler Bar by his professional conduct of this trial. Judge Barker left town this afternoon on the 2:35 train without making the usual decree granting the divorce on payment of costs and the Brauns are still married until the decree is filed.
(*Butler Citizen*, June 1, 1899)

### The Gibson Gang

They were called one of the most ruthless, terror inspiring, murderous gangs ever spawned and while they committed most of their crimes in the Midwest, the gang actually had its beginnings in Butler County.

Ira and Clair Gibson, brothers, were born and raised near Mt. Nebo, in Conoquenessing Township. Their home, which was on Double Road, is no longer standing. One of their friends and neighbors throughout their early and teen years was Boyd Double. I interviewed Mr. Double in July 1995 when he was 97 years of age. He had a very interesting story to tell. The following information was gleaned from the Troy Double interview, a lengthy article in *True* magazine, a chapter by Joe Self in *Builders Dreamers Scandals Schemers*, and an article in the *Butler Eagle*, the particular copy given to me by Boyd Double has no date.

The 1920's was the era of Al Capone, John Dillinger, Pretty Boy Floyd, and a host of other gangsters. Len Bash, born and raised in Middlefield, Ohio, while not so well known, gradually became one of the most desperate criminals in the Midwest.

Bash says he was crooked even during his early years. "Even while I was going to grammar school, I was picking up side money robbing trap lines which had been set by local farmers. When trapping was poor I stole chickens. I had no real need to do these things as my parents were well above average financially. When I stole a hundred dollars from the cash register in my father's place of business and was caught by his partner, my father moved the family to Quincy, Illinois so I would be protected from disgrace. Not, however, until after he had nearly knocked my head off."

Bash became a bootlegger during prohibition. He and some of his cohorts set up a huge still on an island in the middle of the Mississippi River. He was making lots of money. He invested some of the money he had accumulated in an Akron, Ohio roadhouse. It was there that he met Ira and Clair Gibson. The three men had the same objectives—they wanted lots of money and did not mind how they acquired it. They soon forged a business association of sorts.

They knew of a fur dealer in St. Louis who would buy any pelts—no matter how hot they may be. The trio devised the following plan: Bash would visit fur farms, pretending he was interested in buying stock in them. The managers would talk freely regarding the systems of protection that they had against thieves. As soon as Bash figured out all the security related details, and after a short waiting period, they would return at night, knock the foxes in the head with a club, throw them into the car and flee. Pelts at the time were worth, on the average, $250 each.

In the months that followed the gang's formation, raids were made on numerous fox farms throughout eastern Ohio and western Pennsylvania. Since the foxes, even penned-up, were difficult to club, Clair and Ira prepared a supply of small, strychnine-filled meatballs. Upon reaching a particular farm, they would walk up to the pens, tossing meatballs, which were gobbled up by the always-hungry foxes.

One night the criminals raided a farm near Kent, Ohio, where they made the mistake of feeding the poison to a bunch of sick and mangy foxes which had been isolated in a hospital pen. They didn't discover their mistake until they had loaded seventeen almost worthless animals into the roadhouse basement. They visited C. O. Emory, a Butler fur dealer. Emory, seeing the inferior condition of the pelts, paid much less than the market rate. Due to the numerous losses sustained by local fox farmers, the police had been investigating the burglaries and knew that some mangy foxes had been stolen and had tipped-off area fur dealers to be on the lookout. When Mr. Emory notified the authorities of the mangy fox pelts, Len Bash was apprehended and arrested. His attorneys negotiated with the prosecutors and arrived at a plea bargain. Bash was sentenced to the Ohio Penitentiary for no less than one or no more than seven years. On August 15, 1930 he entered the penitentiary. He took the rap alone and the code among criminals dictated that Ira and Clair really owed him for that.

The Gibson brothers, less Len Bash, but with a couple of new cronies, decided to rob banks—after all that's where the big money was. Their bank robberies generally followed a similar plan. They would steal a fast car, usually a Buick or Studebaker, and have a driver drop them off just before the bank opened. As a clerk, janitor, or sometimes the bank manager approached the front door around 8:30 in the morning, the desperadoes would often wait until all the bank personnel arrived, then take what they could—usually less than ten thousand dollars along with securities. Sometimes they got lucky and the heist netted as much as forty or fifty thousand dollars.

Their tactics were quite clever. Prior to the robbery they would pose as painters and actually set up the ladders and other equipment and even begin painting a house or some such building. At the planned time, they would quickly, doff their paint clothes, drive to a bank, rob it and twenty minutes later they would be back at the residence diligently painting away with the easy nonchalance that marks veteran workmen.

Clair Gibson conceived another bright idea. "There is a firm in Chicago that handles tear gas, burglar alarms and various gadgets for bank protection. They're always hiring salesmen. I'll get hired and bankers will be glad to show me their protection setup when I call on them. It's kind of similar to what we did with the fox farm robberies." Bash had rejoined the gang after serving his time in the penitentiary. Since he was so glib and convincing, they decided to have him become the phony salesman. They gave him a stack of fake recommendations and sent him to Chicago. The tear gas company was very cordial and in less than two days Bash was armed with authentic credentials under the name of Lee Derickson, and a signed and sealed "roving commission" to sell their products in any locality he may care to visit. The Chicago sales manager also gave Bash a letter of introduction to a friend who had a firm in Springfield, Illinois, which carried a line of machine guns, pistols, and guns of various types designed for bank protection. So in a very short time Bash had become a salesman for two business establishments handling the very items his mob needed to commit robberies. And since he had the proper credentials, he had nothing to fear in the event police stopped him and searched his car. He carried a sufficient supply of "samples" to arm his entire gang to the teeth.

The gang was always changing cars, usually stolen, and was always switching license plates. They would bury plates, then dig them up as needed. They usually wore thin silk gloves when they were in the cars and before they abandoned a vehicle they rubbed the car both inside and out with oiled rags to obliterate any and all fingerprints. They would also smash the glass in the speedometer and turn the mileage back, sometimes thousands of miles. Naturally this added to the confusion for the police. Immediately after the

---

**Umbrella Man**

John T. Howard, the itinerant umbrella mender, caused something of a sensation two weeks ago by drawing a revolver on conductor Underwood of the B.R.&P. It happened as the conductor was ejecting Howard from the train. The umbrella man later fired several shots at a railroad detective who tried to capture him. Howard said he pulled the gun to protect himself as the conductor was attempting to put him off the trail when it was in motion. The umbrella man was found guilty and sentenced to six months in the workhouse. *Butler Citizen*, May 11, 1911

bank hold-ups, the Gibson gang often took temporary hostages who were forced to stand on the running boards and hang onto the doors. This would discourage the police from shooting at the get-away car. As soon as they were sure they had eluded the police they would release the hostages. As they sped away from the bank they shot out the windows of the houses and shops along the way. This discouraged gunfire from any of the resident gun owners who may have been aware of what was happening and may have been tempted to help the police. And finally—they scattered handfuls of large-headed, roofing nails along the street behind the getaway car. These nails punctured many tires of pursuing police vehicles and allowed the gang to escape more than once.

Ira was the oldest of the brothers and while Clair liked to play boss, it was Ira who made most of the decisions. After several of the early bank robberies Clair stated that he'd like to "bump off" one of the bankers to teach them all a little respect and it didn't matter which one. The other gang members tried to explain that there was no use killing anyone when it wasn't necessary. They were all very aware of which states had the death penalty and which did not and they planned their crimes accordingly. Ohio, unlike the Dakotas and Minnesota, used the electric chair on its murderers. The prospect of the chair terrified Clair, but with his attitude it was only a matter of time until the younger Gibson brother killed some innocent person; he had already killed gang member Whitey Johnson in an argument.

Their trail of crime and bloodshed took them all the way to Kaylor, South Dakota where they robbed the First National Bank. Their modus operandi again proved successful and as Clair was backing out the door and about to jump in the car, young Fred Voll, assistant cashier of the bank, ran from the bank shouting the alarm. Without a moment's hesitation, Clair jerked a sawed-off shotgun from the floor of the car and aimed it at Voll. Young Voll's father, seeing his son's danger through the bank window, shouted hoarsely but at that instant, Clair pulled the trigger and killed the assistant cashier. Clair Gibson had carried out his threat.

Ira and Clair, as early as 1932, had contemplated robbing the Butler County National Bank, which was at the corner of Main and Diamond Streets and is presently known as the Lafayette Building. But after talking to cousin Homer Gibson who lived in Prospect and had worked at the Standard Steel Car Company as a guard, the gang changed their objective. They instead, made plans to rob the Armco and the Standard Steel Car Company's payroll.

The gang planned this payroll robbery for more than a year to avoid any possibility of a slip-up. Bash temporarily holed-up in New Castle and drove back and forth daily between that city and Butler, studying the bank's location, the route to the post office, and the streets used by the mail trucks. Bash also worked out the escape route using back roads which led into Ohio. Unfortunately for Bash, his days were numbered; he would not be a part of the anticipated Butler robbery. His crime spree was rapidly coming to an end. Here is how it happened.

The planning for the Butler robbery was complete but after robbing five banks in five days in four different states, the gang decided to lay low for a while. The Butler job could wait. They rented a cottage on the lake at Lebanon, Missouri and actually did some fishing and relaxing.

One of the recent additions to the gang, Milton Chestnut, wrecked his car near Springfield. As usual, the police investigated and found tear gas, rifles, shotguns and extra license plates. They were able to trace the first four numbers of one of the plates to an earlier bank robbery. This was the beginning of the end for the ruthless gang. When Chestnut was questioned he cracked; he told everything he knew. With the information he provided, the police were able to apprehend several of the gang members including Len Bash. Ultimately, when the trial was held, the jury was out only ten minutes. Chestnut was sentence to 25 years and Bash received life in the Ohio State Penitentiary.

The much-diminished gang now consisted only of Clair and Ira Gibson and their cousin Homer. Nevertheless they decided to pull the Butler job. The robbery had been so well planned it would be a shame not to carry it out—the payroll was like a ripe plum ready for the picking.

The trio arrived in Butler on the morning of August 24, 1934 in two cars, both stolen. The bandits watched as the mail truck left the Butler post office. The lone, unarmed driver, Maxwell C. Lackey, proceeded down West Jefferson Street in an open, unguarded mail truck. Lackey was filling in for the regular driver, Troy Double, who had called in sick. [Mr. Double was the same person I interviewed and mentioned at the beginning of this story.] The bandits followed the truck to a point on Pillow Street where a Plymouth sedan swung in front of the mail truck blocking its way. A Terraplane moved alongside the truck and two goggled men wearing gloves leaped from the car to the running boards of the truck and covered Lackey with automatic pistols. "Get down," one demanded. Another entered the back of the truck and tossed three mail pouches into the black, Hudson Terraplane. One pouch held the payroll shipment. The third bandit, at the wheel of the Plymouth, abandoned that car and jumped into the driver's seat of the Terraplane. The car sped away heading toward Lyndora and then to Ohio along the preplanned escape route. By the time the authorities were notified and the police arrived the bandits had made their escape.

The Plymouth sedan, which was abandoned on Pillow Street, was eventually traced to its East Palestine, Ohio owner. The Terraplane was found in Ohio. The bandits had carefully chiseled all registration numbers from the stolen cars. The robbery had netted the gang $50,000 in cash.

The Gibson brothers were still at large, but Ira had become gravely ill. He was hiding in Minnesota where he was confined to bed and was suffering excruciating pain in his kidneys. It was in a Rochester, Minnesota hospital on September 7, 1934 that Ira Gibson died in agony of severe peritonitis. He was only thirty-two years of age. The obituary in the Butler Eagle 9/20/1934 tells us that he was married and had a son. Ira's body was brought back to Butler County and was buried in the Mt. Nebo cemetery. Ironically this is the same cemetery where church officials refused to bury Ann Girty.

The loss of Ira Gibson and Len Bash still did not stop the gang. On November 1, 1935, Clair Gibson and a couple of newly acquired accomplices held up the Farmer's National Bank of Conneautville, Pennsylvania and escaped with $4,700. According to their custom they had kidnapped three bank employees and forced them to ride several miles out of town on the running boards of the getaway car. Near Belmond, the stolen car ran out of gas. The criminals, now without a getaway car, took a position in the middle of the road in order to apprehend an oncoming vehicle. The first car to approach was not the police but was rather a vehicle driven by James Zrostlik. He, his wife of three years, and their baby were on their way to early morning mass at St. Wenceslaus' Church near Britt. At the first shot from Clair's pistol, James Zrostlik slumped over the wheel of his car—dead. The gang commandeered the Zrostlik car and was able to complete their escape.

It was another automobile accident seven months later that was the downfall of the remaining gang members. One morning in May, near St. Louis, one of the new members of the gang, Robert Markwell, crashed into a telephone pole. Although he and his common-law wife, Betty, were not severely injured, they knew the police investigation would find the guns, extra license plates and other incriminating evidence which was in the car. Hastily, Markwell and Betty hid everything suspicious in the nearby weeds. A witness, however, observed the entire incident and tipped off the police. Enough evidence was found hidden in the weeds to link Markwell to the Zrostlik murder, to the Gibson gang, and thus the gang to several bank robberies. Markwell and Betty though, seemed to vanish into thin air. They had made their way, in another stolen car, to Rochester, Minnesota where Clair Gibson was hiding. It turned out to be Markwell's last trip—after an argument Gibson shot and killed him. Gibson was now for the most part—alone. The terrible gang had been decimated.

At Loon Lake, near Roseburg, Oregon, the panic stricken Gibson and his girlfriend waitress, Violet, rented a cottage under the alias of Mr. and Mrs. Carl Vines. Gibson was becoming paranoid—he was living in mortal fear. He refused to have anything to do with the other residents at the lake. He had become highly suspicious and had developed a great fear of all strangers. On several occasions he vented his rage by beating and choking his girlfriend. Naturally, such strange actions and activities were noticed and aroused the curiosity of the people around them. And when Clair paid the rent on their cabin for a year in advance with bills of large denominations, the suspicious proprietor of the resort notified the sheriff. From pictures on file at the sheriff's office Clair Gibson was identified and immediately arrested.

He was taken to the police station where he talked. He readily confessed to more than twenty bank robberies—naming his accomplices on each job. This of course, led to several other arrests. On August 11, 1937, Clair Gibson pleaded guilty in Ramsey County Criminal Court in Minnesota to bank robbery, and was promptly sentenced to forty years in the Minnesota state prison at Stillwater. Nevertheless, Clair Gibson breathed a sigh of relief as Minnesota did not have the death penalty. Due to an objection by the federal

254

prosecutor however, the judge rescinded the original sentence and designated an Iowa prison as the place of incarceration. Gibson was trapped! He knew that the moment he crossed the Iowa State line, he would be forced to stand trial for the slaying of James Zrostlik and Iowa had the death penalty.

On August 14th, Gibson's attorney arrived at the jail for a talk with his client. He requested that Clair be moved to another cell for the sake of privacy during the interview. As the turnkey unlocked Clair's cell, Gibson charged out the door and raced madly up two flights of stairs to the third floor. Climbing onto the railing, he paused for a moment. "You'll never take me back to Iowa to hang!" He screamed and dove headfirst to the concrete floor forty feet below. The fall of the Gibson gang was at that moment completed, closing the books on one of the most terrible, blood-thirsty gangs which ever existed in this nation.

In the meantime, the famous Butler payroll robbery was coming to a conclusion. After five years of investigation, running down clues in half-a-dozen, mid-west states, Federal investigators positively identified the three bandits who staged the sensational robbery in Butler on the morning of August 24, 1934. The Gibson gang was named as the perpetrators.

By the time the case was cracked and the news appeared in the *Butler Eagle*, both Ira and Clair Gibson were dead. Their accomplice, cousin Homer Gibson, who supplied information on the payroll movements, was serving ten years in the Ohio State penitentiary for previous crimes. Homer Gibson confessed to the Butler crime, implicating the dead Gibson brothers, also admitting that years earlier they had robbed the Harmony interurban streetcar station at Petersville.

Interestingly, Police disclosed that on the day of the robbery in Butler, a local resident identified the Gibson brothers at the scene of the holdup. Fearing reprisal, the resident failed to tell police what he had seen until 1939—five years later.

## Millerstown Murder

The oil boom began in Millerstown [name was later changed to Chicora] in 1873 with the Shreve and Kingsley well. Almost overnight it was another bustling community. Millerstown was characterized as being on the rough edge of society. Twelve-hour workdays, six days a week were commonplace and money flowed like water.

The time was the spring of 1881. A hard worker could easily get a job in the growing petroleum business or one of the related service industries. Many had aspirations of striking it rich. More than a few achieved their goals and their descendants are yet living in luxury—most however, did not.

Charles Eagan was one of the hopeful. He moved to Millerstown and was soon working for the Western Union Telegraph Company as a repairman. Another man who chose Millerstown to be his new home was William White. Mr. White was a boilermaker by trade.

Eagan was a large muscular man who weighed over two hundred pounds; White, on the other hand, was a rather small man. Both men were married and had families; both chose Millerstown as their home. It is unfortunate that Egan and White's paths ever crossed.

Details are sketchy but it was reported that White and Eagan had been conducting a continuing feud. They had quarreled and even come to blows more than once. It was not reported in the *Butler Citizen* as to just what the ongoing disagreement between the two men was all about. However, the seriousness of the matter is indicated by the fact that Eagan had paid a third man two hundred dollars to shoot White. Why the hit man failed is not known.

On Tuesday night of March 1, 1881 the feud reached its culmination. White and James Crowley, who worked for White, had been drinking in Millerstown's Central Hotel where White heard talk that Eagan and a man named Hill were going to "beat him up." Others warned White of the coming trouble and advised him to stay away from Eagan as it was not a fair match. Nevertheless, White and his friend Crowley left the Central Hotel and went to another Millerstown drinking establishment known as the Ocean Saloon. White was armed with a knife that when opened, measured about six inches in length.

A Mr. Delamater operated the Ocean Saloon. White looked in the window of the establishment and saw Eagan so he and Crowley decided to go to the Schreiber House instead where they had five more drinks. About 11:30 p.m. the two men left the Schreiber House and went back to the Ocean Saloon. White entered in the back door and Crowley went in the front door.

Crowley testified later that he entered the Ocean Saloon about thirty seconds behind White but that White and Eagan were already standing at the bar and that the conversation between the two men was quickly becoming heated. According to Crowley, White tried to avoid a confrontation by walking away and leaning against a far wall. Eagan went after him, grabbed him by the shoulders with both hands and shoved him against the wall. During the fray, Eagan slapped White twice in the face and head. It was then that White took his left hand out of his pocket and struck at Eagan with the knife. Eagan was cut several times in the right arm and side before others in the room separated the two men. But very soon Eagan resumed the attack to his own demise because White in turn cut Eagan again, this time in the left groin, severing a large artery and causing his death in minutes.

During the excitement and with the attention being focused on Eagan, White made his escape. There was no hint as to his whereabouts for five days until Sunday morning when an unsigned note was given to the East Brady police. The note told that White could be found hiding in an oil-well shanty on the Barnhart farm a mile west of Millerstown. Two policemen drove a wagon to Millerstown where they searched most of the shanties and outbuildings on the farm but to no avail. They were about to leave when they found another small building. Upon investigation of that building they accosted White; he was nonchalantly heating some coffee. A chase ensued and White was apprehended, taken to Butler, charged with the murder of Charles Eagan, and lodged in the Butler jail.

During the five days during which time White was a fugitive, the county commissioners had offered a reward of two hundred dollars for the arrest of the boilermaker. At the suggestion of Judge Bredin, the reward was increased to five hundred dollars. Some private individuals later raised the total to about eight hundred dollars. The two East Brady policemen who arrested White worked for the Pinkerton Agency and for their work, collected the reward.

The White homicide case went to trial on June 22, 1881. The defendant pleaded not guilty and put his fate upon God and his country. With so many witnesses to the murder it is surprising that the jury took twenty-four hours to reach a verdict. They retired at 5 o'clock Saturday and agreed upon a verdict at 5 o'clock Sunday. The court reassembled and the courthouse was filled with men women and children all anxious to know the verdict.

The jury soon came in as everyone waited breathlessly. On being asked by Clerk Wright as to their verdict they announced it as "guilty of murder in the second degree." After the trial it came out that when the jury first retired they stood nine for the second and three for murder in the first degree. Not one of the jury members was for acquittal. White was sentenced to twelve years in Western Penitentiary which was the maximum punishment for second degree murder.

## A Very Neat Swindle

Several farmers living along the Butler plank road between Allegheny City and Glade Mills have been neatly victimized during the past week by a set of swindlers to the extent of at least $150. William McDonald, one of the victims, was seen in Allegheny last night and says the swindlers operated in this way: A barouche containing four well-dressed men stopped at Plankerton's Hotel on the Perrysville road last Wednesday and one of the men announced that the party was prospecting for oil territory in that neighborhood and that they would likely call and examine the farms of residents along the Butler road. The next day the alleged prospective tour commenced and the first person called on was John Shafer. His land was examined by an alleged expert who accompanied the party and pronounced it excellent oil territory. The territory was then leased and the lease made out and the farmer given a check for $50 as a bonus. The prospectors stopped at Shafer's house all night and in payment for their lodging and stabling of the team presented a check on a Butler bank for $20, purporting to be signed by Mr. Stoughton of Butler. The bill for the lodging and stabling amounted to $4.50 and the farmer gave them $15.50 in change.

Several other grangers were visited and the same racket worked successfully in most cases. Some of the farmers became suspicious, and while they leased their lands, refused to be taken in by the change scheme. One of the latter communicated his suspicions to Shafer on Friday last and he went to Butler on Saturday and found the check given him was bogus. This exposure spread like wildfire and the four men were eagerly sought all over the county, but they had disappeared.
*Butler Citizen*, May 6, 1887

## Stolen Goods Recovered

A curious and pleasant story is told of a prisoner in the county jail going out with a detective, unearthing a lot of silverware in the woods near Butler and returning the same day.

Some two months ago a man named Hedricks broke into the house of Mr. C. T. Birney, a grocer at Tarentum, and carried off considerable silverware which was treasured as the wedding presents of Mrs. Birney. They were worth some five or six hundred dollars, but to her they were much more valuable on account of the associations connected with them. Her husband offered a handsome reward, and officer J. J. Finney, of Hite Station, A.V.R.R., set about the work of recovery.

After several weeks of patient work, he became satisfied that Hedricks, a black visaged, broad shouldered shambler, who had hovered around that country for some time must surely be the man. Officer Finney located him at Saltsburg, arrested and relocated him in our new jail. Hedricks acknowledged the theft, but would not disclose the manner in which he disposed of the stolen silverware. Yesterday he changed his mind, and in company with a police officer left for Phillips City in Butler County. There they took a buggy and drove out among the oil wells and into the woods. Hedricks was not handcuffed, but he knew that the officer with him had his hand on a thumping revolver all the time, and that he was a dead shot. They came to a big rock half hidden by some trees, and here Hedricks gave the signal to stop. Hedricks lost no time in pulling out the stolen silverware, piece by piece, until it was all in sight. For weeks it had been hidden in a crevice under the rock. loading it into the buggy, the return journey was begun. It was accomplished without incident, and Hedricks was back in his cell before sunset that evening.
*Butler Citizen*, April, 27, 1887

## Miller Murder Case

John and Catherine Miller lived in the southwest corner of Center Township, four miles north of Butler, near the Mercer Road. She was 68, just a few years younger than her husband, John. The couple had been married for fifteen years. Mr. Miller was her second husband. As of late, things were not going well for the Millers. Catherine's health had been failing; some of the neighbors thought she was insane. The medical profession did not understand as much about memory loss and the related problems of aging and dementia as it does today. Dr. Bell had been treating her for a good six years and believed that her intellect was of low order and that she was often irrational. Mr. Miller had more than his share of aches and pains and had been getting feeble over the past few years. Old age was certainly taking its toll on both the Millers.

It was the month of March; daylight hours were getting longer, the sun was warmer than it had been since last autumn. Robins were singing and spring was definitely in the air. The seed catalog had arrived in the mail and it was time to start thinking about the garden, although John couldn't do much of the heavy work himself anymore. It was nevertheless fulfilling to plan. Seeing the flowers, green grass and budding leaves is always invigorating and gives one a new outlook on life.

A young man named Neff arrived at the Miller house on Wednesday, March 30, 1898. He was delivering some manure which Mr. Miller had ordered for his garden. The young Neff knocked on the door but was unable to get a response. He tried the knobs on both doors but they were locked. Rather than leave the manure and have to return for his money, Neff thought he would try once more, this time pounding for all he was worth. He was soon rewarded by the appearance of Mrs. Miller but he noted that her face evinced a look of distress. He soon learned the reason for her demeanor. She breathlessly told him that her husband had fallen down the cellar steps and was dead! Neff bolted into the house and down the narrow steps where he found Mr. Miller lying in a pool of blood. Surprisingly the old man was yet breathing and moaning. Amidst the moans he seemed to be trying to tell Neff something so the young man put his head down near Mr. Miller's face in an effort to hear. The message was garbled but clear—it was Mrs. Miller who pushed her husband down the steps—she had tried to kill him!

Neff went outside for help and flagged down Alex Brewster, a neighbor who happened to be passing by. The two men rushed back to Mr. Miller's aid but it was two late, Miller was dead. Coroner Jones arrived that afternoon and his on-site analysis determined that Mr. Miller had died of a fractured skull which was caused by a blow to the back of the head. Miller's jaw was also fractured and there were several additional deep wounds in his skull. All together the coroner counted sixteen wounds in Miller's head and neck area. It was obvious that Mr. Miller had encountered more than just a fall down the cellar steps. Coroner Jones also noted two large bloody stones lying near the body. Mrs. Miller was arrested for the murder of her husband!

The trial began on June 16, 1898. It was the first murder case to be tried in Butler County since the famous Mills case of 1892. Attorneys J.M. Thompson and J.D. Marshall represented the defendant. District Attorney Christley was assisted by W.A. Forquer. At two o'clock the defendant was brought into court and her counsel made a motion declaring her insane and asked the court to impanel the jury as to whether she was insane or not before she was asked to plead. The court permitted the order.

As part of the investigation as to her sanity or lack thereof, a son-in-law of Mrs. Miller, who had visited her in Mercer where she was being incarcerated was called to testify. He reported that during the visit, Mrs. Miller talked, laughed, sang, walked the floor and did not recognize him. A brother of the defendant, also visited her in Mercer and gave a similar testimony to that of her son-in-law. Mrs. Miller's stepson had visited her in jail and tried to interest her in things about the children but was unsuccessful. The three men were unanimous in their beliefs that the old lady was insane.

Four medical doctors who had visited, and/or talked with Mrs. Miller since the murder, were called to testify. Dr. Bell, Mrs. Miller's doctor, stated that although the old lady showed symptoms of insanity, she could be "shaming." "It is either insanity or feign." Another medical man, Dr. Bippus, testified that he thought Mrs. Miller's mental condition had been normal but he noticed a change since she had been in jail. "Under the circumstances she is about what would be expected." But in conclusion, Dr. Bippus agreed with Dr. Bell that Mrs. Miller's acts could have been feigned. The third physician, Dr. McCandless noticed a "reduction in flesh" which he believed could have resulted from confinement and worry. His opinion too, was that her acts were not insanity but for effect. The fourth doctor, Doctor Hope, was the jail physician. He had seen Mrs. Miller about a dozen times and formed the opinion that her intellect was rather dull. Dr. Hope added that she would not talk to him but she did whatever he asked her to do. Sheriff Riddle, of Mercer County, testified that her actions were hard to describe. According to the sheriff, Mrs. Miller had the liberty of the entire ladies department of the jail, but acted so strangely that she was placed in a cell by herself. Sheriff Riddle further testified that it was soon after a visit to Mrs. Miller by her brothers that she began to act in this unusual manner. A brother of Mrs. Miller, swore that he and his brothers did not suggest to her to act insane and added that he did consider his sister to be insane.

Even Reverend Cronenwett, Mrs. Miller's minister, testified that he believed her actions were feigned. Cronenwett, pastor of St. Mark's Lutheran Church, was a very influential and widely respected man of the cloth at that time. He visited with Mrs. Miller three times after the death of her husband and testified that on all three occasions she seemed rational. They talked seriously; he wanted her to make her peace with God. Although she was nervous and claimed her innocence, the Reverend Cronenwett thought her actions were faked to bolster her insanity plea.

District Attorney, Christley and his assistant, Forquer, both thought she "ought to hang as high as Hainan" but considering her age and probable action of the pardon board, were willing to accept a second-degree plea which is what her attorneys were asking. The court directed Reverend Cronenwett to again engage Mrs. Miller in conversation to determine whether or not she knew who she was and what her attorneys proposed doing. She knew well enough and although she protested some, the plea was signed. The court fixed her term at twelve years and the sheriff took her to Western Penitentiary. It was reported that during her first evening in prison she was as gentle as a lamb. Her only request was for a rocking chair which was granted. The *Butler Citizen* reports in its January 5, 1899 issue that Mrs. Miller died of typhoid fever while serving time in Western Penitentiary.

---

## Have A Wonderful Bicentennial

**Ralph E. Goldinger**

# Index

260

262

264